Purnell's Encyclopedia of
ASSOCIATION
FOOTBALL

Contributors

Brian Glanville
David Prole
Jack Rollin (Statistics Consultant)
Martin Tyler

Norman S. Barrett M.A. Editor-in-Chief
Graeme Wright Executive Editor
Derek Aslett Art Editor

This book was planned and edited
for Purnell by Publicare

© 1972
Purnell & Sons Ltd.
Revised and reprinted 1973
Revised 1974, reprinted 1975
SBN 361 021111 9

Made and printed in Great Britain by
Purnell & Sons Ltd., Paulton, Bristol

Purnell's Encyclopedia of
ASSOCIATION
FOOTBALL

Norman S. Barrett M.A.

Purnell Books, Maidenhead

Contents

Foreword

by
Sir Stanley Rous, CBE
President, Fédération Internationale de Football Association, 1961–74

The publication of this volume should provide a welcome and important addition to the books on Association Football available in the English language.

It is comprehensive and detailed, and its scope is universal. I am pleased to see that a large part of the book is concerned with the game in other parts of the world because it is important that those who follow the game with keen interest should know and understand what is happening in other continents and countries.

To date FIFA, the international body responsible for world football, has 140 national Football Associations affiliated to it. There are approximately 16 million players registered with the national associations affiliated to FIFA and some 300,000 referees.

These are significant figures. They are an indication of the size and scope of the problems which confront FIFA, and testify to the increasing popularity of the sport throughout the world.

Ease and speed of travel mean that the Soccer world is shrinking. Already there are certain limited intercontinental competitions, and the growth of competition at this level will be augmented in the coming decade.

This development, along with the increasingly keen competition evidenced in the World Cup tournament and the Olympic Games football tournament, makes it imperative for all those concerned with the future of the game, whether as players, administrators, officials, or followers, to become as well informed as possible on the quality and standard of play in other parts of the world.

The job of FIFA in ensuring uniformity of interpretation of the Laws of the Game has become of key importance in this era of expansion and development. International competition is not possible without continuous and careful work in training referees and other officials to safeguard the spirit of the game and the spirit of the Laws of the Game.

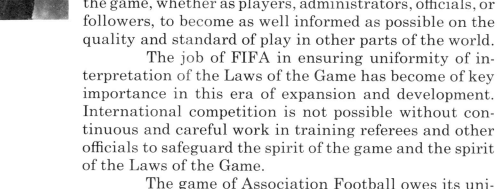

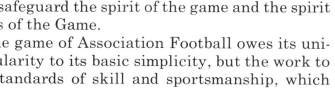

The game of Association Football owes its universal popularity to its basic simplicity, but the work to maintain standards of skill and sportsmanship, which

are the essence of the game, is becoming increasingly complex in the modern era.

Modern techniques of training, methods of coaching, and tactical thinking have become increasingly sophisticated, and it is important for all of us to gain as much insight as possible into these matters. At the same time it is vital not to lose the essential quality of the game, which, while keenly competitive, depends upon an attitude to sport requiring discipline and a sense of fair play. However keen the competition, if these essential qualities are lost the future for the game would not be good.

The modern game was established in Great Britain in the last century; it can be dated from the foundation of the Football Association late in the year 1863. FIFA was not founded until 1904.

The development since that time would have surprised the pioneers; the changes in the Laws, the methods of play, the numbers of players, clubs, and countries involved would cause them both astonishment and delight.

The history of the sport, as set out in this publication, serves to show how the game has grown from those beginnings to the present complex reality. It is a fascinating story, which is of interest well beyond the circles of those who are concerned only with the game itself.

The reference section should prove invaluable, and the various features on outstanding teams and matches should remain of perennial interest.

Readers of this comprehensive book will study with particular interest such sections as those entitled 'Riots & Tragedies' and 'Controversies & Scandals'. Reminder of the mistakes of the past can often prevent similar mistakes in the future. Also with particular care will be read the section intriguingly entitled 'Gamesmanship & Cheating'. I trust this will be read by everyone in close conjunction with the section on the Laws of the Game and all relevant references to the spirit of the game.

My last thought is simply that anything which serves to spread information and knowledge about the game is welcome. The more people are informed about the Laws, tactics, coaching, techniques of play, the development of skills, and the history and development of the game, the healthier the future of the sport would seem to be.

I therefore recommend this publication and have great pleasure in doing so.

Stanley Rous

Stanley Rous

Soccer
Round the World

History of Soccer

Soccer is, in its present organized form, a modern sport. As such, its history is well documented and its development easily traced. We know, for example, that the Football Association was founded on Monday, October 26, 1863, at the Freemason's Tavern, Great Queen Street, Lincoln's Inn Fields, London, to draw up a unified set of rules. But what had been happening before then?

The Chinese and the Japanese can claim some of the earliest references to football. In the *History of the Han Dynasty*, which covers the period in Chinese history from 206 BC to AD 25, mention is made of 'tsu chu': *tsu* meaning to 'kick with the foot', *chu* meaning 'the ball made of leather and stuffed'. The Japanese game was played on a small field with trees at each corner and would appear to be a forerunner of *kemari*. Kemari, dating from the seventh century, was played by eight men kicking a ball to one another on a ground approximately 14 metres square. In the four corners were a pine tree, a willow, a cherry tree, and a maple. Some sources think the game may have been imported from China, and it is known that there were sporting events between the two nations. A text from about 50 BC in the Munich Ethnological Museum records what may well have been the first ever football internationals.

The Ancient Greeks had a ball game called *episkyros*, which the Romans adapted, calling it *harpastum*. It was a vigorous game,

Left: Calcio, the branch of football developed in Florence, was played by teams usually sponsored by the nobility. Betting on games of Calcio was often heavy.

Left: Football in Britain was less sophisticated and was more like a battle. Not surprisingly, this 'mob football' was banned by the authorities, yet football in Britain could not be stopped by the lawmakers.

with its object being to win the ball from all your opponents. This game may well be the ancestor of modern soccer, for it is almost certain that the Roman legions would have taken their game with them when they conquered Britain.

Centuries later men were still chasing a ball, using either hands or feet. In Florence, Italy, the game of *calcio* developed, reaching its height in the 16th century. Large wagers were made on the teams, which were of 27 a side, one wearing green, the other red. In Britain, things were less organized. The fierce Shrove Tuesday games were more like battles than sport, as players chased the ball through the streets with little regard to person or property. Not surprisingly the game became known as 'mob football'.

Popular though the game may have been with a great number of people, it was not so well received by others. Merchants in London, prevented from going about their business by footballers playing in the streets, asked King Edward II to ban it. Consequently, on April 13, 1314 came the first of many acts designed to repress football. It stated that: 'For as much as there is a great noise in the city caused by hustling over large balls ... we command and forbid on behalf of the King, on pain of imprisonment, such game to be used in the city in future.'

Edward III, and later Richard II and Henry IV, found an even greater evil in the game— it interfered with archery practice. In Scotland, too, the lawmakers tried to put an end to the spread of football, but with no more success than their English counterparts. Football, for all its fury, disorganization, and danger to limb and liberty, survived to be tamed and made respectable in the 19th century.

The public schools, such as Eton, Harrow, Winchester, and Rugby, did much to organize football. Each school had its own variations. Some permitted holding and running with the ball, bodily tackling, and hacking (the unpleasant practice of kicking an opponent's shins). Others, because they played on courtyards and in cloisters, preferred a dribbling game with little bodily contact.

As students went on to the universities, they realized the need for a uniform game, and in 1846 a set of rules was drawn up at Cambridge University. In 1862, Mr J. C. Thring, one of those responsible for the Cambridge rules, drew up another set. Consisting of 10 rules, it was called *The Simplest Game*.

At this time, there were a number of clubs springing up, especially in London, and there was an even greater need for one definitive set of rules. With this object in mind, the representatives of the clubs met in October 1863 to form the Football Association. Eleven clubs were enrolled as the original members, but they soon fell out when it came to drawing up the rules. It was now that the supporters of the dribbling and the carrying games went their separate ways and football became two separate games: soccer and rugby. But the dispute was not over handling the ball. It was over hacking. The supporters of the handling game wanted hacking to remain part of the game, and when they were defeated at a meeting on December 1 they withdrew from the Football Association.

The Football Association grew slowly at first, but it also grew strongly, and today it is respected throughout the world. In 1871, it introduced the FA Cup as a competition for the clubs affiliated to it, and a year later it organized the first official international, between England and Scotland. As a result, the Scottish Football Association was founded in 1873. The Scots had a profound influence on soccer in two respects.

Above: A season ticket was just three shillings in 1883–84 at West Bromwich. But with the legalization of professionalism in 1885, prices soon went up.
Left: Blackburn Rovers attack the Notts County goal in the 1891 FA Cup final. The days of amateur finalists were past.
Below: Sir Stanley Rous, president of FIFA, presides over the third round draw of the 1970–71 Fairs Cup.

They initiated the passing game, and they gave football its first professionals. Professionalism was illegal, but in the early 1880s, especially in Lancashire, it was not uncommon for clubs to entice Scottish players south and to reward them for their skills. The effect of this was to take the stronghold away from the truly amateur clubs in the South to the Northern clubs, such as Blackburn and Preston.

The Football Association were unable to ignore the rise of professionalism, and in 1885 they wisely decided to legalize it. Three years later the Football League was founded, and the modern game was well on its way. European countries soon followed Britain's lead in establishing national associations and league and cup competitions. Internationals were played, and in 1904 the Fédération Internationale de Football Association (FIFA) was born. The years that followed saw soccer spread to all corners of the globe, becoming the world's most popular sport, in terms of both players and spectators.

FIFA

On May 21, 1904, representatives from Belgium, Denmark, France, the Netherlands, Spain, Sweden, and Switzerland met in Paris to found FIFA (Fédération Internationale de Football Association). At the beginning of 1972, the world governing body of soccer had 140 affiliated members, with six confederations—Africa, Asia, North and Central America and the Caribbean, Oceania, South America, and Europe—responsible for the game on their respective continents.

The two men mostly responsible for FIFA were Robert Guérin, a Frenchman, and C. A. W. Hirschman, a Dutch banker. They hoped the British associations would help them, but the British were indifferent, content to be insular. Nevertheless Guérin and Hirschman developed their idea, and the growth of FIFA is proof of their foresight.

Other countries soon joined the initial members, and in 1905 England also entered FIFA. They were warmly welcomed, and D. B. Woolfall of the Football Association was elected president. Scotland, Wales, and Ireland joined several years later. But in the next 22 years the British withdrew from FIFA twice—the first time after World War I to boycott their former enemies, the second time in 1928 over the question of amateurism. It was 1946 before they rejoined.

Sir Stanley Rous became president of FIFA in 1961, but his distinguished term of office ended in 1974 when he was deposed by Brazil's Joao Havelange.

World Cup

The idea of a world soccer championship is as old as FIFA itself, but it was not until 1929 that FIFA gave Uruguay the go-ahead to stage the first World Cup tournament in 1930. Now it rivals the Olympic Games as the world's most important sporting occasion. Its prize was, up to 1970, the Jules Rimet Trophy, named after the Frenchman who was president of FIFA from 1920 to 1954. In 1970, Brazil won it for the third time to keep the cup permanently. A new prize, called the FIFA World Cup, was presented by FIFA.

The choice of Uruguay for the first tournament meant that the strongest European countries did not enter. Only France, Belgium, and Yugoslavia embarked on the two-week voyage across the Atlantic to oppose the South Americans. There were 13 entries in all, and they were seeded into four groups.

As expected, Uruguay, the Olympic gold medallists in 1924 and 1928, and Argentina won through to the semi-finals. Yugoslavia and, surprisingly, the United States, with six former British professionals, joined them. Both semi-finals ended in a 6–1 victory for the South Americans, making the final a repeat of the 1928 Olympic Games. The match was fast and furious. Uruguay opened the scoring, but Argentina equalized and then went ahead. Eventually Uruguay pulled back and in the end they won the first World Cup 4–2.

Uruguay did not defend the trophy four years later in Italy. There were 32 entries for the 1934 World Cup, and preliminary matches were played to find 16 qualifiers. This time a knock-out system was used.

Spain almost caused an upset by holding Italy to a 1–1 draw in a second round match best described as a battle. For the replay they had seven players out through injury and could not hold the Italians. Italy then defeated Austria in a sea of mud to meet Czechoslovakia, who had beaten Germany in the other semi-final. The final was notable for the fact that both sides were captained by their goalkeepers. The skilful, short-passing game of the Czechs put them a goal ahead, but Italy equalized with only eight minutes remaining and they scored the winner in extra time.

They were to win again at Paris in 1938, when 36 countries entered. The British remained absent. Switzerland provided the upset of the first round by holding Germany and then beating them 4–2 in the replay. Another surprise was Cuba's defeat of

Romania. Both, however, went out in the second round, the Swiss to Hungary, the Cubans by eight goals to Sweden.

These two countries met in one semi-final, with the Hungarians proving too cultured for the Swedes, while in the other semi-final Italy beat Brazil in a bad-tempered match. The final was a good one, both sides playing their best football. Colaussi put Italy ahead, but almost from the kick-off Titkos equalized. By half time, Italy had added another two goals, and although both sides scored again in the second half, there was no denying the Italians victory.

It was another 12 years before the next World Cup competition, and this time it returned to South America, to Brazil. England took part for the first time, and, as in 1930, the group system was used. And for the only time a final pool, rather than semi-finals and a final, determined the winner.

It was expected that Brazil and England would be contenders for the trophy, but this

Right: Argentina's 'keeper Botasso dives in vain as Uruguay score their third goal in the 1930 World Cup final.

Right: Hector Castro gets Uruguay's fourth. Uruguay won 4–2 to take the first World Cup.

Right: England's Bert Williams (far left) saves in one of the rare United States attacks on his goal in the 1950 tournament. The Americans, however, scored the only goal of the match to cause one of soccer's greatest upsets ever.

was not to be. England were beaten by the United States in one of football's greatest upsets, and then lost to Spain. Sweden provided another surprise by leading their group ahead of Italy.

The final pool was made up of Brazil, Spain, Sweden, and Uruguay. Brazil started in magnificent style, beating Sweden 7–1 and Spain 6–1. All they had to do was draw with Uruguay, who had drawn with Spain, to win the cup and £10,000 per player. In the event, an iron Uruguayan defence held out until just after half-time, when Brazil scored. But then the Brazilian pressure eased, and the Uruguayans scored twice to rob Brazil of their prize.

Brazil's defeat was unexpected, but Hungary's defeat in Switzerland in 1954 was a greater shock. This was the Hungary of Grosics, Boszik, Czibor, Hidegkuti, Kocsis, and, above all, Puskas. Just three weeks before the World Cup they had defeated England 7–1. What happened was that the Hungarians were out-thought by the West German manager, Sepp Herberger. Both teams were in the same group, but, as two teams from each group qualified for the quarter-finals in this World Cup, the Germans could afford to lose to Hungary. Herberger played six reserves against a full-strength Hungary. The Hungarians won 8–3, but they did not know the full strength of the Germans. In addition, and perhaps more significant, Puskas was injured and did not play again until the final. There, Hungary and West Germany met again, but this time the Germans were at full strength. At first it was all Hungary, as Puskas and Czibor scored. But that was all, and the Germans netted three times to defeat a side thought unbeatable.

Also remembered from the 1954 World Cup is the famous 'Battle of Berne', the quarter-final between Hungary and Brazil in which three players were sent off and after which the players continued the fight in the dressing rooms.

It was a different Brazil, however, who travelled to Sweden in 1958 to win the Jules Rimet Trophy with exciting, fluent football. For the first time, Wales, England, Scotland, and Northern Ireland all qualified. Wales and Northern Ireland outdid their fellow-British by making the quarter-finals. The Irish were outplayed by France 4–0, but it took a goal by Pelé to put Brazil through against Wales. Meanwhile, West Germany and Sweden also entered the semi-finals. Pelé got a hat-trick against France, and he then picked up two more in the final as the Brazilians unleashed all their brilliance on Sweden.

Nine of the Brazilian side travelled to Chile in 1962 for what is considered the most disappointing of World Cup tournaments. The football was, on the whole, defensive, and the vicious play was seen at its worst in the Group 2 match between Chile and Italy. Players kicked and punched their opponents and the police had to enforce a sending-off.

England emerged from their group behind Hungary to go into the quarter-finals, where

Above: Stan Matthews loses out to Belgium's Constant Huysmans in a 1954 group match. England, 3–1 up at one stage, were held to a 4–4 draw.

Right: Czibor (11) wheels away after scoring Hungary's second goal of the 1954 final. But within a minute the West Germans had pulled a goal back.

Right: German centre-forward Morlock slides the ball past Grosics and West Germany are on the way to a surprise 3–2 victory over the favourites.

13

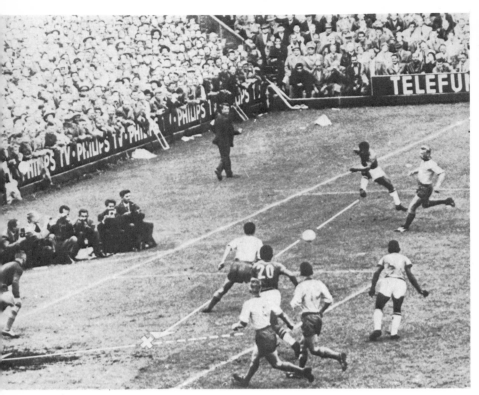

Above: Brazilian star Garrincha hits the ball across the goalmouth for Vavá (20) to score Brazil's first goal and equalizer against Sweden in the final of the 1958 World Cup.
Right, above: Pelé scores Brazil's third goal in their 5–2 triumph over the Swedes. Four years later, in 1962, Brazil retained the World Cup.
Right, below: In 1966, it was England's turn to taste World Cup success. Geoff Hurst gets his hat-trick and England's fourth goal against West Germany.

Brazil beat them 3–1. Brazil then swept Chile aside 4–2 to reach the final, where they met Czechoslovakia in Santiago. The two finalists had already played out a scoreless draw in Group 3, but this time the Czech defence let them down after they had taken a lead through Masopust. Brazil scored three times to win the cup for the second tournament running.

The great surprise of the 1966 tournament was the appearance in the quarter-finals of the little North Koreans, who drew with Chile and then beat Italy in their group. More sensational was their 3–0 lead over Portugal after only 24 minutes of their quarter-final. But then Eusebio scored four times and the Portuguese eventually won 5–3. In the quarter-finals between England and Argentina and West Germany and Uruguay, three players were sent off, and another player received his marching orders in the semi-final between West Germany and Russia. The other semi-final, between England and Portugal, was much less physical and produced fine football. Bobby Charlton scored twice, and the Portuguese could manage only a Eusebio penalty.

The final was a match of changing fortunes. First West Germany led through Haller, only for Hurst to equalize minutes later. In the 78th minute Peters scored, and the trophy seemed England's. Joy was short-lived. In injury time Weber scored after Emmerich's free kick had bounced off the defensive wall. What happened in extra time is history. Geoff Hurst's two goals, one still disputed, gave him the first hat-trick in

a World Cup final, and they gave England a 4–2 victory, the first 'home' win since 1934.

Strict refereeing saved the 1970 tournament from the violent play that was seen in 1962 and 1966. The Mexico World Cup produced much open, exciting football, with Uruguay, Russia, Italy, Mexico, Brazil, Peru, West Germany, and England making the quarter-finals. Italy, with a 4–1 win, scored three more goals against Mexico than they had totalled in their three group matches; Uruguay beat Russia; Brazil scored four against Peru; and West Germany avenged their 1966 defeat by beating England 3–2 in extra time, after recovering from a two-goal deficit.

The Germans went into extra time again in their semi-final against Italy, with the score at 1–1. They scored two more, but the Italians managed three in a see-saw struggle, and went through to meet Brazil, who beat Uruguay in a rough match.

In the final, the Italians equalized a Pelé header in the first half and held on until Gerson scored in the 65th minute. Jairzinho became the first player to score in every round of the World Cup, and just before the whistle Brazil's captain, Carlos Alberto, added a fourth from a perfect Pelé pass. It was a magnificent victory, and did much good for soccer throughout the world.

The sad thing about the 1974 tournament in Germany was the decline of the Brazilians. Without Gerson, Tostão, Clodoaldo, and above all Pelé, who could not be persuaded out of his retirement from international football, they played a defensive and physi-

cal game completely alien to their usual style. And although they reached the third-place match, they lost to Poland, the surprise team of the tournament, who had qualified at the expense of England. Scotland could claim to be the unluckiest side, for they were eliminated despite being the only team to emerge without a defeat. Draws against Brazil and Yugoslavia were not enough to make up for beating Zaïre by only 2–0.

Instead of quarter-finals, the last eight played in two further groups, with the winners meeting in the final at Munich. There, Holland were one up before a German touched the ball, Johan Neeskens scoring from a penalty given when Johan Cruyff was brought down. But in a sensational match, West Germany equalized through a Paul Breitner penalty and won it before half-time with a typical Gerd Müller goal. The Dutch, with their captain, Cruyff, outstanding, had played the best football of the tournament, and were desperately unlucky to lose.

Above: Gordon Banks saves magnificently from Pelé's header in the group match between Brazil and England in 1970. Brazil won 1–0 and went on to take the Jules Rimet Trophy for the third time.

Right: A sensational opening to the 1974 final, as Johan Neeskens hammers a penalty past Maier to put the Netherlands one up before a West German player had touched the ball.

Right: Gerd Müller (13) swivels on a half-chance and leaves the Dutch goalkeeper flat-footed to give the Germans victory.

World Club Championship

The World Club Championship is played for each year by the winners of the European Cup and the South American Cup (Copa de los Libertadores). It is also known as the Intercontinental Championship.

The competition is run on a home-and-away basis, with the winner being decided on goal aggregate. This has not always been so. From 1960 to 1968, the championship was decided on games won. Therefore, if each side won a game, there had to be a replay. As this had to be played on the same continent as the second leg, the home side in the second leg had the advantage of a sympathetic crowd. The goal aggregate system was adopted in 1969.

The World Club Championship has a history of violence. In fact, in 1971 Ajax of

Below: Auld grabs Maschio after a foul by the Argentinian, one of a number of violent scenes from the deciding match of the 1967 World Club Championship between Celtic and Racing Club.

Amsterdam refused to go to Uruguay to play Nacional. They were only too aware of the treatment other European clubs had received at the hands of South American teams.

Perhaps the worst championship was in 1967. Celtic won at home and travelled to Argentina for the second leg against Racing Club. Before the game was under way, their goalkeeper, Ronnie Simpson, was hit on the head by a stone and had to be replaced. During the game their players were repeatedly fouled. Racing Club won, and so there had to be a replay. It was a brutal match in which six players were sent off—four Celtic, two Racing Club.

The next year, Manchester United were treated just as badly. Bobby Charlton required stitches after he was kicked in the shin during the first game against Estudiantes de la Plata. This Argentinian side contested three championships in succession, and each was marked by violence. In their second match against AC Milan in

Right and far right: It was incidents such as these that led to four Celtic and two Racing Club players getting their marching orders.

Below: Little Jimmy Johnstone suffered fouling and other less pleasant indignities at the hands of the South Americans.

1969, Combin, the Milan centre-forward, had his nose broken, and Prati was kicked in the back while having treatment. The next year, Van Deale of Feyenoord played 'blind' for 20 minutes after his glasses were broken by Pachame, the player who had injured Charlton in 1968.

But not every championship has been violent. Some of the great club sides have won: the Real Madrid of Santamaria, Puskas, and Di Stefano in 1960; the Santos of Pelé, Zito, and Coutinho in 1962 and 1963; the Internazionale of Facchetti, Mazzola, and Suarez in 1964 and 1965. These clubs won with players of skill and imagination. They did not need to revert to foul tactics to become the champion club in the world.

Right: Medina bursts into tears after being sent off in the Manchester leg of the 1968 tie between Manchester United and Estudiantes de la Plata. Below: Estudiantes' 'keeper Poletti bears the brunt of the United attack.

Amateur and Olympic Soccer

If the Football Association thought it had solved the amateur/professional problem by legalizing professionalism in 1885, it was sadly mistaken. The breakaway of many amateur clubs from the Football Association in 1906 threatened to disrupt the excellent progress the FA was making in England. And it was over the principle of amateurism that the British withdrew from FIFA in 1928. Both these disputes were later resolved, but the amateur game still caused problems. The practice of players being rewarded for their skills was still a part of the amateur game almost 90 years after the FA had sought to correct matters, and they finally decided to abolish the difference between amateurs and professionals in 1974.

The international scene is no less compli-

Above: Poland's Kazimierz Deyna scores the winning goal against Hungary in the final of the 1972 Olympic soccer tournament in Munich. He also starred in their dazzling displays in the 1974 World Cup.

The Ilford goalkeeper thwarts a Bishops Stortford attack in the 1974 FA Amateur Cup final at Wembley, but Ilford lost 4–1. This was the last Amateur Cup tournament, the FA having decided to abolish the difference between amateurs and professionals at the end of that season.

cated. Players are not openly paid, but in some countries, such as the Communist-bloc countries, the approach to soccer is more professional than amateur. Because they are competing for the prestige of their country, players are given as much time for training and playing as they need. Officially they have well-paid jobs as teachers, army officers, or civil servants. Some are students. Yet they play soccer as much as a British professional does. These countries say they have no professional football, and so their players must be amateurs. As a result, those countries observing the strictest principles of amateurism have little chance of competing on equal terms with them. And it is not surprising that, between 1952 and 1972, the Olympic Games soccer title was won only by Hungary, Russia, Yugoslavia, and Poland.

In Britain, there were approximately a hundred times more amateurs than professionals in the early 1970s, all under the control of the Football Association, to which the Amateur Football Alliance was affiliated.

The FA Amateur Cup was first competed for in 1893–94. Before that the amateur clubs had competed in the FA Cup, but the growing strength of the professional clubs gave them little chance of success. In fact, it was the development of professionalism that led to the 'amateur split' of 1906. Many amateurs in the Football Association resented losing any of their authority to the professionals, and when the FA decided that the professional clubs should be affiliated to their county associations, the Middlesex and Surrey associations rebelled. They formed the Amateur Football Defence Federation, which later became the Amateur Football Association. The dispute was finally set-

tled in 1914, and the Association later changed its name to Alliance.

The FA's next major problem was the question of payment to amateur players for time lost from work ('broken-time' payments). Some members of FIFA approved such payments, and in 1923 the British associations asked FIFA to accept the FA's 1884 definition of an amateur. FIFA refused, and Britain and Denmark, Olympic finalists in 1908 and 1912, did not enter the 1924 Olympics.

The International Olympic Committee tried to resolve the problem before the 1928 Olympic Games, but without success. The matter deteriorated when FIFA insisted that the IOC accept the principle of broken-time payments or their members would not enter the 1928 Olympics. Soccer had become one of the major attractions of the Olympics, and the IOC had to accept. The British associations then resigned from FIFA.

The 1924 and 1928 Olympic Games were significant for other reasons than the absence of Britain and Denmark. As well as showing how popular soccer now was, they revealed the strength of South American football. At Paris in 1924, a quarter of a million people watched the soccer competition, including the 41,000 who saw Uruguay beat Switzerland 3–0 in the final. In 1928, there was an all South American final, Uruguay beating Argentina in a replay. Two years later the same two countries were to meet in the first World Cup final.

Yet at the time of the 1972 Munich Olympics, these were the only victories by a South American side. Nor had Great Britain, who won the first two Olympic tournaments, appeared in another final. Italy won in 1936 and Sweden in 1948. Then the 'state sponsored' teams took over. Sometimes there was little difference between their Olympic team and World Cup team.

The Olympic soccer scene has not been without incident. In 1920, Belgium were awarded the final when their Czech opponents walked off the field after the second Belgium goal. In 1960, Yugoslavia, the eventual gold medallists, won their semifinal against Italy on the drawing of lots. The score was still 1–1 after extra time. And in 1968, three Bulgarians and a Hungarian were sent off and the referee and linesmen were bombarded with cushions. Hungary's 4–1 victory over Bulgaria gave them their second successive Olympic title and their third title altogether. The tournament also confirmed the opinion that the truly amateur countries had little chance of victory against countries dedicated to success to earn international prestige.

Europe and UEFA

Whereas by 1880 the British countries had their own football associations and were soon to embark on the Home International Championship, soccer on the Continent was in its early stages. But thanks to British students and businessmen, the game soon advanced. By the end of the 19th century, though becoming organized, it was still a long way behind British soccer in skills and tactics. By the end of the first half of the 20th century, the Continentals had not only caught up but had actually gone ahead of the British.

Denmark and the Netherlands were among the first to take up football. As in Britain, it was a mixture of the different footballing games, but soccer soon became the accepted code. What are thought to be the oldest clubs outside Britain come from these two countries. In 1879, the Copenhagen Boldspil Klub took up soccer, and that same year the Haarlem FC was founded. Ten years later both the Danes and the Dutch founded national associations, although it was another 10 years before the official Danish FA was set up.

In Germany, too, the game was taking a strong hold, with more than 400 clubs in existence in 1900, when the German Football Association was founded. A German team went to England in 1901, playing two representative matches and losing both; to the 'Amateurs of England' 12–0 and to the 'Professionals of England' 10–0. These are not regarded as true internationals though.

The first international match outside Britain was played in 1902, Austria beating Hungary 5–0 in Vienna. Two years later, Belgium and France drew 3–3 to begin a regular series that is still contended today. Other international rivalries were soon established, most of them between neighbouring countries, because travel was difficult in those times. The first international between a British side and Continental opponents was on June 6, 1908, between England and Austria in Vienna. England won 6–1 and then won 11–1 two days later.

It was fitting that Austria were England's opponents, for it was the Austrian Empire that gave Continental soccer its great impetus. The Hungarians made the initial advance, helped by the English coach Jimmy Hogan. And it was Hogan, teaching players the need for ball control and short passing, who helped the Austrians overtake them. The real driving force, however, was Hugo Meisl, the Austrian team manager. The result of his efforts was the Austrian *Wunderteam* of the 1930s that lost only twice (both times to England) in their 27 matches between May 1931 and May 1934. The *Wunderteam* usually lined up as follows: Hiden; Rainer, Blum or Seszta; Braun, Smistik, Nausch; Zischek, Gschweidl, Sindelar, Schall, Vogel.

Italy ended Austria's brief era in their 1934 World Cup semi-final and went on to become world champions. This was the Italy of Vittorio Pozzo, who before World War I had lived in England and had returned to Italy to develop what he had learnt in conversation with Manchester United's Charlie Roberts and Derby County's Steve Bloomer. Under his guidance the Italians retained the World Cup in 1938. Italy had also been Olympic champions in 1936. Between 1934 and 1939, the Italian national side lost only 4 of their 39 matches.

One of those four was a 2–3 defeat by England a few months after Italy had won the 1934 World Cup. The British at this time still regarded Continental football as inferior, and, apart from playing internationals, tended to remain aloof.

By the time of the 1950 World Cup, though, it was obvious that the rest of Europe had caught up with the British. Those who refused to believe this were soon brought to their senses when Hungary beat England 6–3 at Wembley in 1953. It was the first time England had lost at home to a Continental side.

A year after Hungary's historic victory, the European Union of Football Associations (UEFA) came into being. This body operates under the auspices of FIFA and is responsible for football in Europe. As such, it is the administrative force behind such competitions as the European Football Championship, the European Cup, the Cup-Winners Cup, and the UEFA Cup (formerly the Fairs Cup).

Below: Rudi Hiden clears an England attack at Stamford Bridge in 1932. Austria's 4–3 defeat in this match was one of only two suffered by the *Wunderteam* over a three-year period.

Above: Manchester United centre-half Charlie Roberts, on whom Vittorio Pozzo based the attacking centre-halves so prominent in his Italian sides of the 1930s.
Below: The end of an era—the England defence are left bewildered by the Hungarian masters, who ended England's unbeaten home record with their dazzling 6–3 victory at Wembley in 1953.

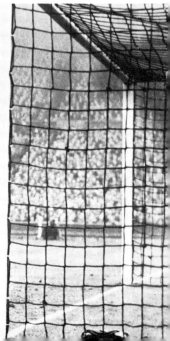

Herbert Wimmer is congratulated by jubilant team-mates after scoring West Germany's second goal against Russia in the 1972 European Championship final, which the Germans won 3–0.

European Football Championship (Nations' Cup)

A European national championship was one of UEFA's earliest ideas, but it was not until 1957 that such a competition was supported by a majority of members. At first the competition was known as the European Nations' Cup, but today it is the European Football Championship, and its prize is the Henri Delaunay Cup, named after the first secretary of UEFA.

The championship is played over a two-year period following the World Cup. Until 1966, it was played on a knock-out basis with home and away fixtures. But for the third championship, UEFA decided on a similar system to that used for the World Cup. Countries are organized into eight groups, the leaders of which go through to the quarter-finals. Up to and including this stage, all matches are home and away. The semi-finals, third-place match, and final are played in one country.

The first championship was held from 1958 to 1960. Disappointingly, only 17 countries entered. The four British teams, Italy, and West Germany were among those who did not take part. Spain, who beat Poland in the first round, withdrew from the second round for political reasons. They were drawn to play Russia.

The semi-finals and final were played in France in July 1960. The Russians beat Czechoslovakia 3–0 and Yugoslavia beat France by the odd goal of nine. The final went into extra time with the score at 1–1, Yugoslavia's point coming from an own goal by Netto. But Ponedelnik scored to make Russia the first European champions.

The second competition, from 1962 to 1964, saw 29 entries. There were several surprises. England were eliminated by France, and Yugoslavia lost to Sweden. In the quarter-finals, Spain, Hungary, Russia and Denmark won, although the amateur Danes had to play a third match against little Luxembourg.

The final stages were held in Spain in June, and the host nation emerged as champions. They were hard-pressed by the Hungarians in their semi-final but survived to face Russia, who had easily disposed of Denmark. This time there was no political withdrawal. Spain started in fine style with a goal after 5 minutes. But the Russians soon equalized and continued with a packed defence. It took a brilliant opportunist goal by centre-forward Marcelino to give Spain the title.

Their defence of the Henri Delaunay Cup found Spain up against world champions England in the quarter-finals of the 1966–68 championship. England won both matches and went through to meet Yugoslavia in the semi-finals in Italy in June. Italy and Russia were the other semi-finalists, and their match produced a most unsatisfactory result. With no score after extra time, the game was decided on the toss of a coin. The fates favoured Italy. The other semi-final, a hard, physical match in which Mullery was sent off, was won by Yugoslavia thanks to a late goal by Dzajic.

The Italians were somewhat fortunate in the final, too. They scored a late equalizer from a free-kick to force a replay two days later. Then, with five changes in their side, they proved too strong for the exhausted Yugoslavs and won 2–0.

The 1970–72 Championship saw the emergence of a marvellous footballing side in West Germany. Captained by Franz Beckenbauer in an 'attacking sweeper' role, inspired by the fluent running and brilliant passing of Gunter Netzer in midfield, and with Gerd Müller as deadly as ever in front of goal, the Germans swept through to the final, beating Russia comprehensively by 3–0.

On the way to the final, West Germany had humiliated England at Wembley in the quarter-finals and had accounted for host country Belgium in the semi-finals. Belgium had knocked out the holders, Italy, in the quarter-finals. The manner of West Germany's triumphs made them favourites for the World Cup in Munich in 1974.

Above: Francis Lee scores with a spectacular header in England's 3–0 win over Greece at Wembley in the 1970–72 European Championship.

Below: The anguish of Gordon Banks, beaten by Gunter Netzer's penalty in the quarter-final first leg. West Germany won the match 3–1 and went on to win the Championship at Brussels.

Left: Netzer, West Germany's midfield star, and Norman Hunter(11) in the quarter-final second leg. The 0–0 draw was no help to England after their earlier defeat.

Below: Breitner, Müller, Lee, Bell, and Maier at Wembley in 1972, when West Germany emerged as a new European and world footballing force.

European Cup

The highlight of the European soccer season is the final of the European Cup. It is the climax of a competition that brings together the champion clubs from the countries of Europe to determine the champion club of Europe.

The first European Cup competition was held in the 1955–56 season, but the idea of a European competition for clubs had been tossed around since the 1920s. In 1927, the Mitropa Cup was started, although not all countries (including those of Britain) participated. After World War II, attempts were made to establish competitions, but many of the matches between European clubs were friendlies. And it was one such friendly that aroused enthusiasm for an all-embracing European competition. In 1954, Wolverhampton Wanderers beat the great Hungarian side Honved, and the manner of their victory led one English newspaper to call them 'champions of the world'.

Such a claim was exaggerated, but it prompted Gabriel Hanot of the French newspaper *L'Équippe* to suggest details for a European Cup. Many countries expressed interest, but neither FIFA nor UEFA were prepared to run it. This did not trouble *L'Équippe*, however. They called to Paris the representatives of 18 leading clubs to discuss the competition and set up a committee to organize it. The clubs were: AC Milan (Italy), Anderlecht (Belgium),

Above: Real Madrid with the European Cup after the 1960 final that saw them win the trophy for the fifth successive time.

Below: Jubilant Celtic as Gemmell's shot beats Sarti to put the Scots on level terms with Inter-Milan in 1967. Celtic won with a goal by Chalmers to bring the European Cup to Britain for the first time.

Chelsea (England), Djurgarden (Sweden), Hibernian (Scotland), Holland Sport (Netherlands), KB Copenhagen (Denmark), Moscow Dynamo (Russia), Partizan Belgrade (Yugoslavia), Rapid Vienna (Austria), Real Madrid (Spain), Reims (France), Rot-Weiss Essen (West Germany), Saarbrucken (the Saar), Servette Geneva (Switzerland), Spartak Prague (Czechoslovakia), Sporting (Portugal), and Vörös Lobogo (Hungary). Fifteen of the clubs sent someone to Paris. Those who did not were Hibernian, Spartak Prague, and Moscow Dynamo.

FIFA suddenly began to take an interest in this new competition. They approved it on the conditions that the participants received the approval of their national associations; that UEFA took over the organization; and that the title 'Europe Cup' was kept back for a national cup. The competition was named the European Champion Clubs Cup, though to everyone it became the European Cup, and 16 clubs entered for 1955–56. Chelsea, England's entry, withdrew on the advice of the Football League. Not all the initial entrants were league champions, but from 1956–57 onwards, only league winners and the European Cup holders were eligible. The rounds are on a home-and-away basis, with the final being played on a predetermined ground.

The first five years of the competition were dominated by one club—Real Madrid. And the excitement this club generated by its fluent, attacking style of play ensured the European Cup of immediate success. There was no emphasis, as there was later, on

defensive tactics in away matches. Real knew only one game: the attacking game. With such players as Di Stefano, Rial, Gento, Kopa, and later Puskas up front and Santamaria, Munoz, and Zarraga behind them, they played it brilliantly.

Perhaps their greatest display came when they won their fifth successive European Cup. That season, 1959–60, they scored 31 goals in just seven matches, and seven of those were in the final against Eintracht Frankfurt at Hampden Park. Puskas scored four times to give him a record 12 goals in the competition. Di Stefano added the remainder. Real went on to win the first World Club Championship, against Penarol. The team that had reigned over Europe now ruled the world. But it was the end of an era. The next year they lost to Barcelona in the first round, and so ended the run that began in 1955–56 with a 7–0 aggregate win over Servette Geneva.

Real Madrid made the European Cup final again in 1961–62. But the old magic was going, and despite Puskas's hat-trick they lost to a Benfica side determined to keep the trophy they had won the previous year. Benfica, with their emphasis on attack and with such outstanding players as Costa Pereira, Germano, Coluna, Aguas, and Eusebio, looked capable of emulating Real Madrid.

It was not to be. For the next three years the European Cup went to Italy, despite two attempts by Benfica to add a third European title. AC Milan ended the Portuguese club's hopes of a hat-trick in 1962–63. The next two years, Internazionale kept the trophy in Milan, beating Real Madrid in 1963–64 and Benfica in 1964–65. In 1963–64, Inter became the first club to win without losing a single match, which was an indication of the defensive nature of their football. With their strong men, Facchetti and Burgnich, at the back and with a midfield well marshalled by Suarez, they could comfortably contain most opponents. The next season, however, Real broke through that defence in the semi-finals and went on to beat Partizan Belgrade for their sixth European Cup.

Inter won through to the final again in 1966–67. Their opponents were Celtic of Scotland, the first British side to reach the final stage of the competition. The Scots were famed for their attacking play, and it needed all their brilliance to crack holes in the Italian wall after Mazzola's penalty had put Inter ahead. In the second half, first Gemmell and then Chalmers scored, and for the first time the European Cup went to Britain.

It stayed there another year, though this

Above: George Best ends his magnificent solo run with Manchester United's second goal in the 1968 final against Benfica.

Left: Brian Kidd scores the third of United's four goals.

Below: Sormani lays off the pass from which Prati scored the first of AC Milan's four goals against Ajax Amsterdam in the 1969 final.

Above: A defensive error by Celtic, and Feyenoord equalize through Israel in the 1970 final. In the last minutes of extra time, Kindvall netted the winner for the Dutch club.

Above: Dick Van Dijk gets Ajax's first goal in the 1971 final against Panathinaikos at Wembley. Ajax won 2–0.

Uli Hoeness (white) slots in his first to put Bayern Munich on the way to their splendid 4–0 victory over Atlético Madrid in the replayed final of the 1974 European Cup. They had forced a replay only in the last seconds of the first game with a long drive from stopper Schwarzenbeck. It would have been a disaster had the Spaniards won the Cup, after their disgraceful display in the semi-final first-leg with Celtic in which they had three players sent off. The West German champions, however, won by playing exciting football, continuing the tradition of Ajax who had won the previous three tournaments.

time in England with Manchester United. Their victory over Benfica at Wembley in 1968 was an emotional one. United had been the first English club to enter the European Cup, disregarding the Football League in doing so. And it was after a European Cup quarter-final in 1958 that their plane crashed at Munich and eight of the famous 'Busby Babes' were killed. At Wembley, Bill Foulkes and Bobby Charlton were survivors of that fateful February day. So too was manager Matt Busby, and it was for him that a capacity crowd urged Manchester United to a 4–1 victory in extra time.

United defended the cup as far as the semi-finals in 1968–69, going out to AC Milan. The Italians won the European Cup for the second time by convincingly beating Ajax

of Amsterdam. But the appearance of the Dutch club reflected the rising standards of football in the Netherlands.

The next year, Feyenoord reached the final, where they showed their superiority over favourites Celtic. It was not until the closing minutes of extra time that Kindvall scored the winner, but Feyenoord's victory was more decisive than the score suggests. Nor was this the end of the Dutch clubs. Even though Feyenoord went out surprisingly in the first round in 1970–71, Ajax, with their attack led by the brilliant Johan Cruyff, arrived at Wembley where they won the final without too much trouble. Their opponents were the surprise team of the season—Panathinaikos of Greece. Among their victims were Everton and Red Star Belgrade, whom they beat after losing 4–1 away. Much of the Greeks' success was due to their manager, Ferenc Puskas. The 'Galloping Major' had first played in the European Cup for Honved in 1956–57, had triumphed with Real Madrid in 1960, and in 1970–71 had taken his 'unknowns' to the heights of European football.

In those 15 years, the European Cup had more than fulfilled the dreams of the men who first conceived it. It has proved an enormous money-spinner, and even if some could claim that the home-and-away system encourages defensive play, others could argue that the competition has also produced much attacking football. Perhaps more than anything, the European Cup has taken club football outside the confines of national competition and given it a more international outlook.

European Cup-Winners Cup

The European Cup-Winners Cup is the youngest of the three major European Club competitions. It is open to the winners of the national cup competitions, such as the FA Cup, although if the winner is eligible for the European Cup, the runner-up qualifies. This also applies if the cup winner is the holder of the Cup-Winners Cup. The format is the same as for the European Cup.

Knock-out cup competitions have not been as popular in all countries as in the British countries, and only six countries were interested when UEFA first suggested a competition for cup winners in 1958. Consequently the idea had to be shelved for a time. But in 1960, the Mitropa Cup, which had been revived yet again in 1955, was not contested. This increased the number of potential entrants to 10, and so it was decided to hold the first European Cup-Winners Cup over the 1960–61 season. The Mitropa Committee organized the first contest, but UEFA's Executive Committee took over from 1961–62, when there were 23 entries.

British clubs have fared better in this competition than they have in the European Cup. Between 1960–61 and 1972–73, Tottenham Hotspur, West Ham United, Manchester City, Chelsea, and Rangers won the cup, and Rangers (twice), Liverpool, and Leeds were losing finalists.

Rangers, with impressive victories over Borussia Mönchengladbach (11–0 aggregate) and Wolverhampton Wanderers, reached the first final. For the only time in the competition, the final also was played on a home-and-away basis, but this did not help the Scots, who lost both legs to Fiorentina. The Italian club won through to the final again in 1961–62, but it took almost four months for Atlético Madrid to beat them. The final in Glasgow was a 1–1 draw, and it was not until the beginning of the next season that the match was replayed in Stuttgart. This time the Spaniards won 3–0.

The next year it was Atlético Madrid's turn to be losing finalists. Their conquerors were Spurs, who two years earlier had accomplished a League and FA Cup double and in 1962 had won the Cup again. With Greaves and Dyson to the fore, they displayed all their brilliance in trouncing the Spaniards 5–1. Yet much of the limelight of the 1962–63 competition belonged to the Welsh non-league club Bangor City. They

won 2–0 at home over AC Napoli, but lost 1–3 in Naples. Had the away goals rule been in force then (it was introduced in 1966–67), the Welshmen would have won. As it was, they had to go to Highbury for a replay, which the Italians won 2–1.

Two seasons later, the Welsh were in the news again. Second Division Cardiff City eliminated 1963–64 winners Sporting Lisbon and only narrowly lost to Real Zaragoza. The Spanish side, however, met their match at Upton Park, and West Ham went on to beat Munich 1860 and become the second London club to win the Cup-Winners Cup. For Moore, Hurst, and Peters, there would also be a World Cup medal the next year.

The next two years, Liverpool and then Rangers tried to keep the cup in Britain, but both times it went to Germany. Borussia Dortmund won it in 1965–66 and Bayern Munich in 1966–67. There were possibilities of a German hat-trick in 1967–68 when SV Hamburg became the fourth German finalists in as many years. They had to fight to get there, though. Cardiff City held them to a draw in Hamburg, only to lose 2–3 in Cardiff. The Welshmen had previously beaten Moscow Torpedo in the quarter-finals. AC Milan were the other finalists, and they put paid to German hopes with a 2–0 victory.

Slovan Bratislava of Czechoslovakia made history in 1968–69 by becoming the first club from an Iron Curtain country to win either the European Cup or the Cup-Winners Cup. Then it was England's turn again when Manchester City beat Gornik Zabrze of Poland in Vienna.

Gornik and City met again the next season, this time in the quarter-finals. City won a tie that included a replay, but then found

Above: Jimmy Greaves puts Spurs on the way to a 5–1 victory over Atlético Madrid in the 1963 European Cup-Winners Cup final.

Below: Alan Sealey (right) scores his second goal for West Ham against Munich 1860 in the 1965 final.

themselves drawn against Chelsea. The London club won 2–0 on aggregate and travelled to Athens to play Real Madrid. It was the ninth European final for both Real and Gento, but success was elusive. Zoco's goal in injury time meant Chelsea had to endure anxious moments in extra time, but the tie went to a replay. Chelsea, however, were not to be denied, and their 2–1 win two days later returned the European Cup-Winners Cup to London for a third time.

Left: Real Madrid 'keeper Borja is beaten by Dempsey's shot in the replay of the 1971 final, won 2–1 by Chelsea.

Below: Neil Young (right) about to open Manchester City's account in the 1970 final against Gornik Zabrze in Vienna.

The British tenure of the trophy continued the next season when Rangers made it third time lucky with a 3–2 victory over Moscow Dynamo in Barcelona. It was the first time a Russian club had contested the final of a major European club competition. But not for the first time, Rangers' over-excitable fans let them down, rushing onto the field to celebrate each Scottish goal and then battling with the Spanish **police** after the match. As a result, Rangers **were** banned from competing in Europe for one year.

In the 1973 final, inspired goalkeeping by Milan's Vecchi and some curious decisions by the Greek referee combined to defeat Leeds United 1–0, and UEFA's subsequent suspension of the referee cast serious doubts not only on the handling of this match but also on previous important European matches in which Italian clubs had been involved. Milan reached the final again in 1974, but were surprisingly beaten by FC Magdeburg, East Germany's first representative in a European final.

UEFA Cup (Fairs Cup)

The UEFA Cup is the most recent of the three major European club trophies. Yet it is the oldest competition, for it is the successor to the Fairs Cup, which was conceived before the European Cup. Originally, it was the International Inter-City Industrial Fairs Cup. In 1969 it became the European Fairs Cup, and in 1971 Barcelona, the first winners, and Leeds United, the 1970–71 winners, played for permanent possession of the cup. For 1971–72 there was a new trophy, donated by UEFA and bearing its name.

UEFA Cup entry is open to a certain number of clubs from each member country, depending on its club strength. England's allocation, for example, is four. The holders gain automatic entry. All rounds, including the final, are home-and-away fixtures, and away goals count double.

There was a time when the Fairs Cup was thought of as the least important European competition, but this was not so in its later years. It is certainly not true of the UEFA Cup. In many instances, the clubs have finished in the top bracket of the national leagues, often ahead of the cup winners. A look at some of the entries for the first UEFA Cup shows just how strong the competition is—Leeds United, Tottenham Hotspur, Wolves, Aberdeen, Atlético Madrid, Real Madrid, Juventus, Ferencvaros, and AC Milan. From these, Spurs and Wolves emerged to contest the first European final between English clubs, with Spurs the winners 3–2 on aggregate.

When the Inter-City Fairs Cup was first thought of, it was not for clubs. It was for cities that regularly held industrial or trade fairs. Ernst B. Thommen of Switzerland, a vice-president of FIFA, put forward the idea in 1950, but he had to wait until UEFA was created in 1954 before a Fairs Cup committee could be set up. Twelve cities from 10 countries made up the first entries, and it was decided to spread the competition over two years to avoid clashes with domestic fixtures. As it was, the first Fairs Cup took three years and was virtually forgotten by the public long before the final between Barcelona and London. The London side was made up of players from the London clubs, whereas Barcelona comprised mostly players from CF Barcelona. Similarly Birmingham, England's other entry, was really Birmingham City. They reached the first semi-finals, and were finalists in the next two competitions. The second Fairs Cup ran for two seasons (1958–60), and then the competition settled down as an annual event.

A feature of the Fairs Cup was the success of Spanish and English clubs. Of the first eight finals, Spanish clubs won six and provided three runners-up. Barcelona won the cup three times and were runners-up once; Valencia won it twice and were beaten finalists when Real Zaragoza won.

Then it was England's turn. Leeds United lost to Dynamo Zagreb in 1966–67, but they won in 1967–68, when their opponents were the Hungarian club Ferencvaros, who had won the trophy in 1964–65. There was another England-Hungary final the next year, this time between Newcastle United and Ujpest Dozsa, who had accounted for Leeds in the quarter-finals. The Tynesiders' performance surprised many of their

Left: Jackie Sinclair scores to clinch the 1969 Fairs Cup semi-final for Newcastle against Rangers.

Below: John Radford heads Arsenal's second goal of the 1970 final second leg. Arsenal beat Anderlecht 4–3 on aggregate.

Above: Billy Bremner's spectacular header knocks Liverpool out of the 1970–71 Fairs Cup and puts Leeds through to the final.

Left: Derek Dougan of Wolves outjumps Spurs' Mike England in the first leg of the 1972 UEFA Cup final, which was won by Spurs.

countrymen, but there was no doubting their quality in the final legs. Taking a 3–0 lead to Budapest, they came back from a two-goal deficit to win 3–2 and take the cup with a convincing 6–2 aggregate.

Next came Arsenal. A quarter-final victory of 9–1 over Dinamo Bacau was followed by an impressive win over Ajax, European Cup finalists the previous year. In the final, they lost to Anderlecht 1–3 in Brussels, but Kennedy's goal there proved decisive. At home Arsenal scored three times while their

impregnable defence kept the Belgian forwards at bay.

Whoever won the Fairs Cup in 1970–71 won the right to play Barcelona for permanent possession of the cup. That honour went to Leeds, whose final with Juventus ended in a 3–3 draw. Leeds, with two goals in Turin, won on 'away goals'. The final was noteworthy in another way. The Turin leg had to be replayed after a torrential storm forced the first match to be abandoned.

So it was that an English and Spanish side met to decide the final destination of the Fairs Cup. And again it was a Spanish victory. Barcelona, with home advantage, beat Leeds 2–1 to keep the cup they had first won by beating London in 1958.

British clubs, however, continued to dominate the competition, and the first contest for the UEFA Cup, in 1971–72, also produced the first all-British European final. Spurs won 2–1 at Wolves and a fine Mullery header at White Hart Lane gave them a 3–2 aggregate victory. Spurs were unlucky in 1972–73 to go out to Liverpool in the semi-final on the away-goals rule. Liverpool, who won the League title that year, went on to beat Borussia Mönchengladbach in the final. Then, in 1973–74, Britain's long run came to an end. Spurs were involved again, and their ability to play far above their League form got them to the final, but Feyenoord held them to a 2–2 draw at White Hart Lane and beat them 2–0 in Rotterdam, where rioting Spurs fans shamed the club who found themselves facing UEFA sanctions.

Britain

To non-Britons, the fact that there are four national sides in one political country appears strange. Many still think of the British as English and wonder why a player like George Best does not play for England. After all, he is the same nationality as Bobby Moore. The issue becomes even more complicated when they see an Englishman like Bob Wilson playing for Scotland. (Under FIFA rules a player may represent the country of his parents if he is not required by the country of his birth.) Perhaps the simplest answer is that Great Britain is really four countries (England, Northern Ireland, Scotland, and Wales) united under one government. In football, these countries do not have any central government but have their own associations. And they are proud of their national independence.

The English organized football when they founded the Football Association in 1863. Nine years later came the first official match with Scotland, in Glasgow on November 30, 1872. As a result, the Scottish Football Association was founded in March the following year. Wales and Ireland followed. The Welsh were first, playing Scotland on March 25, 1876 and establishing the Football Association of Wales two months later. In Ireland, the Irish Football Association was formed in 1880, and Ireland played their first internationals against England and Wales in February 1882.

At this time there was no club competition as there is today. Nor were there any professional clubs. It was the era of the amateur. Fixtures were usually friendlies or cup-ties.

The FA Cup had first been contested in 1871–72, and among the first entries were Queen's Park of Glasgow. They played their first game in the semi-finals, against Wanderers in London. When the game ended in a draw and had to be replayed, the Scots were forced to withdraw. They could not afford to return to London at a later date. But they were interested in the competition and decided to start a similar one in Scotland. The Scottish Cup came into being with the Scottish FA, but several months before that Queen's Park supplied the entire Scottish team that held England to a goalless draw in the 1872 match against England.

South of the border, the FA Cup was to bring about the downfall of the amateur clubs. The Cup, instead of being a competitive outlet, became, for some clubs, a goal in itself. A number of northern clubs enticed

Above: Wembley Stadium, where numerous Britons have won a place in football history by their exploits in the FA Cup. But when it comes to internationals, Wembley is home to the English only.

Below: Scotland's Pat Crerand and England's Terry Cooper (right). If some countries had their way, there would be no England, Scotland, Wales, or Northern Ireland at World Cup and European Championship level. Britain would be the country represented.

good players, often from Scotland, with promises of well-paid jobs in the area or even money. It was something the FA could not ignore, and in 1885 professionalism was legalized, although with a number of restrictions.

With professionalism came another problem. There were not enough matches. Those clubs paying professionals needed something to attract crowds regularly. The answer was a competition run on similar lines to the baseball leagues in America, and in 1888 the Football League was set up.

Again the Scots followed the English and

started their own league in 1890. It was only a matter of time before professionalism, already being practised in underhand ways to keep players in Scotland, was accepted. In 1893, the Scottish FA finally permitted it.

In Ireland, football was to come up against a different problem—politics. The game went to Ireland in 1878, when Queen's Park and another Scottish club, Caledonian, played an exhibition match in Belfast. This match and others that followed aroused an enthusiasm that led to the foundation of the Irish Football Association. The Irish FA Cup began that same year, 1880, and 10 years later eight clubs formed the Irish League. But the political disruptions in Ireland after World War I also saw the break-up of the Irish FA and League. In 1921, the Leinster clubs broke away and formed the Football League of the Irish Free State. Other clubs joined them, and soon two new competitions emerged, the FA of Ireland League and the FA of Ireland Cup. The FA of Ireland joined FIFA in 1923, but the Belfast-based Irish FA remained the only association representing Ireland in the Home International Championship. Teams representing the FA of Ireland are termed 'Republic of Ireland' and those representing the Irish FA are termed 'Northern Ireland'.

The FA of Wales, in comparison, has had few problems, although it did almost run out of money as a result of establishing the Welsh Cup competition in 1877. The Welsh League did not come into being until 1902. It is nowhere near as strong as the leagues in the other countries, and the strongest Welsh clubs compete in the English Football League.

As a result of this, and also because the best Welsh players belong to English clubs, Wales often find it impossible to field their strongest international side. This problem is shared by Ireland and even by Scotland, many of whose leading players are with English clubs. These associations are entirely dependent on the English clubs for the release of players for internationals. Yet any suggestion that all four associations should combine and field a Great Britain international side is always strongly resisted. And although the Home International Championship has declined in importance with the proliferation of world-wide competition, the England–Scotland rivalry remains intense, and Wales and Ireland continue to look on the 'domestic' clashes as an important source of revenue.

Northern Ireland v Scotland at Windsor Park, Belfast, in 1967. Scotland's Ronnie Simpson, anticipating perfectly, saved Johnny Crossan's penalty. For the Irish and Welsh, the Home International Championship is an important source of revenue, even if the glory usually goes to the stronger England and Scotland sides.

Home International Championship

The British Home International Championship is football's oldest international series. It has been contested annually between England, Scotland, Wales, and (Northern) Ireland since 1883–84.

The associations of these four countries had come together for the first time in 1882 to draw up a uniform set of rules, and at the same time they arranged the remaining international fixture, between Scotland and Ireland. They met in the first full series of the Championship, in which the Scots won all their games. Scotland led the table again the next three seasons, without losing a match, although in 1885–86 they had to share the honours with England.

England and Scotland have dominated the series. By 1971, the English had won outright 28 times and the Scots 22 times. Wales, on the other hand, had only seven outright wins and the Irish had just one. Only once had all four countries finished level, and that was in 1955–56.

England first won the series outright in 1887–88, when Fred Dewhurst of Preston North End scored a hat-trick in the 5–0 trouncing of Scotland in Glasgow. The advent of professionalism and the skills of the Corinthian amateurs had helped improve the standard of play in England. Wales notched their first international victories in 1881 and 1882, 1–0 and 5–3 over England, but it was not until 1906–07 that they won the Championship. The Irish had to wait longer for their first international win, 4–1 over Wales in 1886–87, and in 1902–03 they shared the Championship with England and Scotland. It was not until 1913–14 that they won outright.

In 1949–50 and in 1953–54, the Home International Championship matches were used as qualifying games for the 1950 and 1954 World Cups. The top two in the table could go forward to the finals, yet in 1950 Scotland, who finished second, did not take advantage of their position and stayed at home. Again in 1966–67 and 1967–68 the series was used as a qualifying competition, this time for the European Championship. Scotland won the first season and England the second, but England qualified by having 9 points to Scotland's 8 over the two-year period.

Traditionally, the England–Scotland match was played in the spring and the other home internationals were spread throughout the season. In 1969, however, it was decided to play all the games over a week at the end of the season. Then all players would be available for their countries. But this has not necessarily improved the Championship, for many players are thoroughly exhausted after a season of League, League Cup, FA Cup, and European matches.

Below: Hughie Gallacher, centre-forward of the 'Wembley Wizards', misses narrowly in that 1928 classic in which Scotland beat England 5–1.

Scenes from the Home International Championship.
Below: Welsh despair as Scotland score.
Below left: Roger Hunt of England lets fly at Northern Ireland's Pat Jennings.
Bottom: John Hughes's header puts Scotland on level terms with England in 1968.

Football League

'Arsenal 2 Leeds United 0; Coventry City 1 Nottingham Forest 1; Crystal Palace 1 Manchester United 3 . . .' Every Saturday from August to May the football results are broadcast over radio and television. Pools coupons are checked. Changes of position in the tables are eagerly noted. Can Manchester United stay at the top? Who are possibilities for relegation and promotion. Others apart from Englishmen are interested too. All over the world people follow the results of the Football League, football's largest domestic competition.

The man responsible for first organizing league football in England was William McGregor, a Scot who was a member of Aston Villa. His idea was a league with 10 or 12 clubs playing home-and-away matches, and in 1888 he wrote to five leading clubs to discuss such a venture. He thought the organizing body might be called the Associa-

An Arsenal team photo of 1930–31, the year they won their first Championship. Arsenal dominated the League in the 1930s, with five titles.

tion Football Union. A meeting followed at which it was decided to form a league, and a month later, on April 17, the first formal meeting of the Football League, as it was to be called, was held. It was made up of 12 clubs: Accrington, Aston Villa, Blackburn Rovers, Bolton Wanderers, Burnley, Derby County, Everton, Notts County, Preston North End, Stoke, West Bromwich Albion, and Wolverhampton Wanderers. Three other clubs, Halliwell, Nottingham Forest, and Sheffield

Wednesday, also applied to join, but because of the difficulty in arranging fixtures they were turned down.

The original members must have felt confident that the new competition would prove popular, for they made provision for a second division. Three of the League's early rules are of interest. The points system adopted was that still used today (2 points for a win and 1 for a draw), as was the goal-average method for resolving tied positions in the table. The other was that full-strength teams should be fielded on all occasions, and it is one that the League have strongly enforced. In 1969–70, for example, Leeds United were fined £5,000 by the Football League for fielding a reserve side.

Leeds' trouble was that they had too many matches to play. At the time, they were strongly defending their League title and were in the running for both the European Cup and the FA Cup. Overcrowded fixture lists had become more and more common in the 1960s, and increasing the season from early August to the middle of May did not really help. Nor did the introduction of computerized fixture lists in the late 1960s. When Arsenal won the League Championship–FA Cup double in 1970–71, they played 64 games in four competitions. When Preston North End achieved the first double in 1888–89, and in so doing became the first Football League champions, they played a mere 27 games.

The first increase in membership of the League was in 1891, when Darwen and Stoke City were elected. A year later, the League became two divisions, with 16 clubs in Division I and 12 in Division II. By 1894–95 there were 16 clubs in each division. At first, test matches were used to decide who should be promoted and relegated, but the system was never successful, and in 1898 the automatic promotion of the leading two Second Division clubs and the relegation of the bottom two First Division clubs was introduced. That same year the League elected another four members, so there were now 18 clubs in each division.

The first season after World War I saw 22 clubs in each division, and a season later, 1920–21, there was a new division, the Third Division (South). Formed mainly by the amalgamation of the old Southern League with the Football League, it also had 22 clubs. In 1921, a Third Division (North) was introduced to cater for the Northern clubs. Initially it had 20 members, but two more were added the next year. One club from each of the Third Divisions was promoted to the Second Division and the bottom two in each had to seek re-election.

The Football League retained a membership of 88 until 1950, when the Third Divisions were increased to 24 clubs each. Then, at the end of the 1957–58 season, came the change that introduced the Fourth Division. The top halves of each Third Division made up the new Third Division, while the bottom halves comprised the Fourth Division. Between these two divisions a four-up four-down promotion-relegation system operates.

The Third and Fourth Division clubs, often beset by financial difficulties, do not find life in the League as rewarding as those in the two top divisions do. Attempts have been made to have more teams promoted to Division II, but to no avail. The powerful clubs in the Football League, in terms of voting power, are those in the First and Second Divisions. The clubs of the Third and Fourth Divisions are merely associate members, having only one representative for every 11 clubs. Consequently they have little say in the running of the League.

First Division status is what every club

Right: Everton (blue), Division I champions in 1969–70, play the previous season's leaders, Leeds.

Right: Brighton and Aston Villa clash in a 1971–72 Third Division fixture. Villa won the division and Brighton finished second to win promotion to the Second Division.

Below: Manchester United and Wolves, two clubs with impressive records in the Football League.

Violent outbursts on the field led to repeated calls for stricter measures, and in 1971 the Football League acted—crudely and belatedly, perhaps, but there could be no denying the urgent need for action. Unable to change the Laws of the game, the League could, however, make sure they were rigidly enforced. Referees were instructed to come down heavily on offences that the season before might not have earned even a free-kick. Hundreds of players were 'booked' in the opening weeks. But as the season progressed, it could be seen that the stricter measures were meeting with some success. The Football League, well aware that their competition was the toughest in the world, were determined that it would not become the roughest.

Left: Norwich (yellow), Second Division winners in 1971–72, put paid to a Bristol City attack.

Below: Leeds captain Billy Bremner in high-flying action during their successful 1973–74 campaign.
Bottom: Colin Todd (centre), outstanding in Derby's 1971–72 team.

in the League desires, but once this has been attained, success is almost always a struggle. By the end of the 1960s, only four clubs had gone straight to the top of the First Division in their first season after promotion: Liverpool (1905–06), Everton (1931–32), Tottenham Hotspur (1950–51), and Ipswich Town (1961–62). By 1964–65 Ipswich were again in Division II.

Arsenal's double in 1970–71 gave them their eighth Championship title, one more than Everton, Liverpool, and Manchester United and two more than Aston Villa and Sunderland, early rulers of the League. Five of Arsenal's titles came in the 1930s, the first in 1930–31, when they won with 66 points. That season the Gunners scored 127 goals, yet they were bettered by runners-up Aston Villa, who scored 128. Pongo Waring scored 49 of those, 11 short of the League-record 60 by Everton's Dixie Dean in 1927–28. Compare the goal-getting feats of Aston Villa and Arsenal with the 66 goals Leeds United scored in 1968–69 when they won the Championship with a record 67 points.

In the 25 years following World War II, the club that really dominated, not just the Football League but the imagination of the football public, was Manchester United. In that time they won the First Division five times and were second seven times. Wolverhampton Wanderers, with three titles in the 1950s, were also prominent, scoring more than 100 goals a season four times in that period.

The 1960s, however, saw a change. Football became more physical as hard-tackling defences prevailed over skilful attacks.

FA Cup

When Wanderers met Oxford University in the FA Cup final of 1873, the kick-off was before noon so that the players could go on to watch the Boat Race, then a major highlight of the English sporting year. Today the Boat Race remains an important sporting occasion, but the FA Cup has become *the* sporting event of the year. Thousands fill Wembley and millions more watch on television throughout Britain and the rest of Europe.

But there is more to the FA Cup than the final. Because it is a knock-out competition, it is packed with possibilities of upsets. Each season there is a chance of giant-killing—a non-League club accounting for a League side or a small club from a lower division toppling a First Division club. Third Division Walsall did it to League champions Arsenal in 1933; in 1971 Fourth

Right: Wembley Stadium overflows as thousands upon thousands of fans come for the 1923 FA Cup final. It has been estimated that more than 150,000 crammed inside to see Bolton beat West Ham 2–0 in the first Wembley final, although the official attendance was given as 126,047.

Below: Liverpool's colourful and vociferous supporters were not enough to help the club beat Arsenal in the 1971 final. The London club's 2–1 win in extra time gave them the League and Cup double.

Division Colchester put paid to the mighty Leeds.

The FA Cup proper consists of six rounds, the semi-finals, and the final. The surprises start coming from the third round, when the First and Second Division clubs join the competition. Before the first round, there are qualifying rounds to find which amateur and non-League clubs will enter the competition proper with the Third and Fourth Division clubs. By the third round, there are 20 clubs

in with the chance of a surprise win.

The first final was played on March 16, 1872, and the Cup was won for the first of five times by Wanderers, a team of former public school and university players. In goal for them that day was C. W. Alcock, the man who had suggested a cup competition. The trophy, which was stolen and replaced in 1895, cost £20, a pound of which was given by the Glasgow club Queen's Park. The present trophy dates from 1911, when the first replacement was presented to Lord Kinnaird, then president of the FA. In his younger days, he had appeared in nine finals, winning three times with Wanderers and twice with Old Etonians.

When Queen's Park eventually contested the final for the Cup, in 1884 and 1885, they lost each time to Blackburn Rovers. Rovers completed their hat-trick in 1886. These wins were significant, for they ended both the southern dominance of the Cup and the age of the amateur. Wanderers, Oxford University, Old Etonians, Royal Engineers, and Old Carthusians were to be replaced as finalists by West Bromwich Albion, Preston North End, Aston Villa, and Blackburn Rovers, the professionals from the Midlands and the North. The Rovers won the FA Cup twice more before the end of the century, and J. H. Forrest played in all five victories. In

1927–28, they added a sixth win. One hundred years after the first Cup final, only Aston Villa had won the Cup more times.

The first of Aston Villa's seven wins was in 1887, when their victims were West Bromwich Albion. West Bromwich turned the tables when these two met again in 1882, the last final at Kennington Oval, but Villa gained revenge in 1895 in the first final at the Crystal Palace. Aston Villa should have fond memories of that South London ground. They won there another three times. A sixth win came at Stamford Bridge in the first final after World War I and the seventh at Wembley in 1957.

The FA Cup final first went to Wembley in

Right: George of Wolves lies beaten by Dimmock's shot and Spurs win the 1921 FA Cup 1–0 at Stamford Bridge.

Below: Peter Lorimer gets in a shot despite the attentions of three Sunderland defenders in the 1973 final. But thanks largely to a remarkable performance by goalkeeper Jim Montgomery, Second Division Sunderland beat mighty Leeds 1–0 in one of the biggest cup final upsets ever.

1923, but for a time it looked as if the match would never be played. Thousands upon thousands invaded the ground, through the gates or over the walls. Thanks to the police, and especially PC Scorey on his white horse Billy, the touchline was cleared and Bolton proceeded to beat West Ham 2–0. David Jack scored the first Wembley cup-final goal.

Bolton won the Cup twice more in the 1920s, but the final they will probably be best remembered for was the one they lost to Blackpool in 1953. Stanley Matthews was in that Blackpool side, and it was his third final in six years. Twice he had been on the losing side. This time Wembley wanted him to be a winner. How Matthews turned the Bolton defence inside out and helped Blackpool win 4–3 after being two goals down is part of FA Cup lore. Stan Mortensen's hat-trick in that game was the first in a 20th Century Cup final. Often forgotten, though, are the injuries to Bolton's left-half Eric Bell and left-back Ralph Brooks. Substitutes were not allowed until 1967, and before that the injured player remained as a passenger or his side played on with 10 men.

The 1950s, and to some extent the early 1960s, were notorious for cup-final injuries. Some changed the fortune of the game; others made a seemingly impossible task all that much harder. Arsenal were the first to experience the Wembley 'jinx' of the 1950s, losing Welsh international full-back Walley Barnes and going down 0–1 to Newcastle. Then it was Bolton's turn, and in 1955 Newcastle, in their 10th final, again found themselves playing 10 men. With just 20 minutes gone, Manchester City's Jimmy Meadows went down with a knee injury that ended a promising international career and Newcastle went on to their third Cup victory in five years.

The Wembley jinx remained with Manchester sides for another two years, each time concentrating on a goalkeeper. But in 1956 Manchester City's Bert Trautmann stayed on with a broken neck to see his team to victory. Manchester United's Ray Wood was not so fortunate in 1957. He suffered a fractured cheekbone, and although he later returned it was too late. Aston Villa had already put two past his deputy, Jackie Blanchflower, and United had failed in their double attempt.

The 1958 final was free of serious injury, but a United side, already depleted after the Munich disaster, suffered when 'keeper Gregg was illegally bundled, ball and all, into his goal by Bolton's Nat Lofthouse—and the goal allowed. The next two finals saw players carried off with broken legs: Nottingham Forest's Roy Dwight in 1959 (after opening the scoring) and Blackburn's David Whelan in 1960. And in 1961 Leicester's Len Chalmers was a passenger for most of the game against Spurs.

The substitution rule, when it was introduced, was more than welcome. But 92 years earlier, in the amateur days, another solution was found. When C. J. Ottaway of Old Etonians was injured in the 1875 final, Major Marindin of Royal Engineers left the field so that his side would hold no advantage. His code of honour would be out of place in the professional game the FA Cup did so much to foster.

Above: Bertie Mee (left) and Don Revie lead Arsenal and Leeds out for the 1972 FA Cup final. Leeds won 1–0 with a header by Allan Clarke.

Football League Cup

When the Football League Cup began in 1960, it did not receive a particularly warm welcome from either the leading clubs or the fans. Some First Division clubs snubbed it for years, and it was not until 1969–70 that all 92 clubs in the League entered for the first time. By then, the competition had become a good money-spinner, even if many did argue that it was an unnecessary addition to an already overcrowded season.

The League Cup was the idea of Alan Hardaker, secretary of the Football League, and in its early, less successful, days it was sometimes referred to as 'Hardaker's Horror'. At first the semi-finals and the final were two-legged affairs, but for 1967 it was decided to hold the final at Wembley.

Not even the most optimistic officials could have foreseen the publicity the first Wembley final would give their competition. Third Division Queen's Park Rangers beat First Division West Bromwich Albion. And when, two years later, Swindon Town, also in the Third, beat Arsenal, the League Cup was a guaranteed success. It was just unfortunate that these two giant-killers could not take up the passport to the Fairs Cup (UEFA Cup) that goes to the winners provided they are a First Division club.

Below: George Eastham slots home the goal that gave Stoke City a 2–1 win over Chelsea in the final of the 1971–72 League Cup.

Scottish League

The presence of the rich and powerful Football League south of the border has always affected Scottish football. By attracting many of the country's players away, it has weakened the overall strength of Scotland's domestic competition, the Scottish League. At the top of Division I, the competition is both fierce and rich with talent. Celtic's success in the European Cup is proof of that. But in the Second Division it is a different story. Gates are small, clubs are struggling for survival, and players often have to find work outside football.

When a Scottish league similar to the Football League was first suggested, the Scottish FA and leading clubs like Queen's Park were against it. They feared it would encourage professionalism. But many clubs were already making illegal payments to players to stop them going south to England, and they needed regular matches to attract spectators. These clubs won the battle and the Scottish League came into being in 1890 with 11 clubs as founder members. They were Abercorn, Cambuslang, Celtic, Cowlairs, Dumbarton, Hearts, Rangers, Renton, St Mirren, Third Lanark, and Vale of Leven. Within seasons other clubs were requesting membership.

Renton did not even complete the first League programme. After only five games, they were suspended by the Scottish FA for playing St Bernards, a club found guilty of breaking the amateur code. The team Renton played called themselves Edinburgh Saints, but they were, in effect, St Bernards, and so Renton were barred from the competition they had so strongly advocated. Renton were back for the second season, though.

The first League Championship was shared by Dumbarton and Rangers after they had drawn in a play-off. In 1891–92, Dumbarton won outright with Celtic second. Celtic won the first of their many League titles in 1892–93, but even more important was the legalizing of professionalism in May 1893. Football in Scotland openly became a business.

A Second Division of 10 clubs was introduced for the 1893–94 season. The First Division also had 10 clubs, but since then the size of the divisions has increased and decreased frequently. At one time there were 22 clubs in the First Division, but since 1955 the Scottish League has settled down to 18 clubs in the First Division and 19 in the Second.

Automatic promotion and relegation has been used since 1921–22, but the gap between the divisions is much wider than that between the English First and Second Divisions. The promoted clubs have a struggle to hold their place, while at least one of the relegated clubs regularly returns to Division I after a season. The bottom two clubs in Division II apply for re-election, but this has become a formality. For the lowly clubs there is a greater fear of leaving the League for financial reasons than for failure to win re-election.

Since the acceptance of professionalism, Glasgow rivals Celtic and Rangers have dominated the Scottish League Championship. Rangers won their first outright title in 1898–99, and by 1971 had won the title 34 times. Celtic, by then, had won the League 26 times. An even greater indication of these clubs' supremacy is the fact that it was not until 1964–65 that neither club finished in the first three. That year Kilmarnock won for the first time, and until then only seven other clubs had been successful: Dumbarton, Hearts, Hibernian, Third Lanark, Motherwell, Aberdeen, and Dundee. Of those, only the first three had won more than once. To Rangers, however, goes the honour of being the only club to win all its League matches in a season. In 1898–99 they took 36 points from 18 games.

Rangers' great period was in the 1920s and 1930s. Managed by Willie Struth and with

such great players as David Meiklejohn, Alan Morton, and Bob McPhail, they won the Championship 15 times in 20 years. Celtic and Motherwell were the only clubs to break the Rangers monopoly, and Motherwell did it in fine style. In 1931–32 they scored a record 119 goals in their 38 matches, with centre-forward Bill McFadyen getting 52 of them. Celtic's Jimmy McGrory, with 50 in 1935–36, is the only other player to reach the half-century in a season.

Celtic enjoyed a long run at the top before Rangers' great days. In the 15 years from 1904–05, Bill Maley guided sides with such players as Jimmy McMenemy, Jim Quinn, Bobby Templeton, and Patsy Gallagher to 11 titles. From 1945 until the mid-1960s, Celtic found League success elusive. Only once did they win, in 1953–54, when their captain was Jock Stein. Twelve years later he was to manage Celtic to the Championship that would lead them to European honours and start another great run of success for the green and whites.

Scotland's old rivals, Celtic and Rangers, fight it out again, this time in the 1971 Scottish Cup, which ended in a 1–1 draw. But Celtic won the replay 2–1 to emphasize their superiority with yet another League and Cup double.

Scottish Cup

Celtic go one up in the first two minutes of the 1969 Scottish Cup final from a header by Billy McNeill (5).

The monopoly that Rangers and Celtic have on the Scottish League Championship tends to take some of the interest from that competition. The Scottish Football Association Cup, on the other hand, gives other clubs a greater chance of success. There is none of the inevitability usually associated with the League, for there is always the possibility that the Glasgow clubs will be knocked out along the way. The door is always open for the giant-killers.

The desire to have a cup competition brought eight clubs together in March 1873, and from this meeting came the Scottish FA. The club that originally proposed a Scottish Cup was Queen's Park, and it was they who won the first three finals. These were played at Hampden Park, Queen's Park's home ground. Vale of Leven won the Scottish Cup for the next three years, and then it was Queen's Park's turn to complete another hat-trick.

The early days were not without incident. Vale of Leven's third victory, in 1879, came when Rangers refused to replay the final after a 1–1 draw. Vale of Leven themselves refused to appear in 1884, and so Queen's Park won for the seventh time. The next year was notable for some high scoring, with Aberdeen clubs on the losing end. On September 5, 1885, Arbroath beat Bon Accord by a record 36–0 and Dundee Harp beat Aberdeen Rovers 35–0, the two highest scores ever in British first-class competitions.

But, as in England, times were changing. Professionalism, though still illegal, was making its effects felt. New clubs emerged as powerful challengers, among them Celtic. They reached their first final in 1889 and won the Scottish Cup for the first time in 1892. Two years later, Rangers and Celtic played out their first final. Rangers, with nine internationals in their side, won 3–1. Surprisingly, perhaps, the 1971 final between these two clubs was only their ninth together, but between them they had recorded 63 appearances in the 86 finals to then. Celtic had won 21 times and Rangers 19.

One of these totals should have been increased by one. Both sides were finalists in 1909, but after a replay there was still no decision. Extra time was not played, as some spectators expected, and when the teams left the field rioting broke out. Fans pulled down the goal-posts and used wooden railings as firewood. The Scottish FA suggested a third match outside Glasgow, but Celtic and Rangers stood by a previous decision to abandon the final altogether.

By the beginning of the 1970s, only one Second Division club had won the Scottish Cup. East Fife achieved this in 1938, and their victory over Kilmarnock was even more remarkable because it came after a replay that went into extra time. Not only that: they had had to sign another player after their only outside-left was injured in the semi-final.

Back in 1921 Partick Thistle had a player problem too. They had so many injured that half-an-hour before kick-off they did not know what their team would be. In the end their coach, 40-year-old Jimmy McMenemy, played, and won his seventh winners badge as Thistle downed Rangers 1–0. McMenemy had played in six winning finals with Celtic, and only Bob McPhail emulated his feat. He won with Airdrieonians in 1924 and six times with Rangers between 1928 and 1936.

Rangers' defeat by Partick was a complete upset, for that season they had headed the League with the loss of only one game in 42. They featured in an equally sensational result in 1967, being knocked out in the first round by Second Division Berwick Rangers. The Scottish Cup, like its English counterpart, could still remind the big clubs that they were not invincible.

Scottish League Cup

The Scottish League Cup is exactly what its name implies. Unlike the Football League Cup, which is basically just another knockout competition, the Scottish League Cup is played in leagues before the knockout system is used for the quarter-finals. In this way it fulfils its original purpose—to provide the League clubs with extra games.

The Scottish League Cup is contested in the early part of the season, the opening matches being played before the League competition begins. The clubs are divided into eight groups of four clubs and one of five, the 16 clubs of the previous season's

First Division remaining separate. They compete in these sections on a league basis, playing home-and-away games (except for the five-club group). After a supplementary play-off, eight of the nine winners go into the quarter-finals, which are also on a home-and-away basis. The semi-finals and the final are played on neutral grounds, the final at Hampden Park.

The smaller clubs have often fared well in the Scottish League Cup. East Fife won it in 1947–48 as a Second Division club and later won it twice more while in the First Division. But the greatest surprise came from Partick Thistle in 1971. Just promoted from Division II, they hit four goals in the first half to beat League and Cup winners Celtic in the final.

Above: Partick Thistle winger John Gibson moves away from Celtic's Tom Callaghan. Partick's 4–1 defeat of Celtic in the 1971 Scottish League Cup was one of football's major upsets.

Right: John Radford rises above Tom McConville to score the winning goal for the English League against the League of Ireland. The Irish league sides have always been weakened by the loss of the best Irish talent to English and Scottish clubs.

Below: A winter setting for an Irish League match between Derry City (stripes) and Glentoran.

Irish Cup and Irish League

Football in Ireland has followed a somewhat rocky road since the Scottish clubs Queen's Park and Caledonian introduced the game to Belfast in 1878. Just as the island has been split into two different countries, so too has Irish football been split into two different associations: the Irish FA in Belfast and the FA of Ireland in Dublin.

Originally there was unity under the Irish FA, established in November 1880 by John McAlery, the man responsible for the Queen's Park-Caledonian game. That same season, 1880–81, the first Irish Cup was contested, seven clubs taking part. Moyola Park emerged the winners by beating Cliftonville in the final, but their journey was not without incident. A first-round protest from Avoniel that a Moyola Park player had long nails in his boots was overruled, and there was a rough semi-final against Alexander, who lost a player through a broken leg. It should have been an omen of things to come.

The worst incident was in the 1920 semi-final between Belfast Celtic and Glentoran. In many ways it reflected the political problems Ireland itself was facing. There was rioting and a shot fired into the crowd after a Celtic player was sent off. Earlier a Glentoran man had gone off injured. The match was deleted from the records and the Irish Cup was awarded to the winner of the other semi-final, the Dublin club Shelbourne.

But that is jumping too far ahead, for there had been other developments in the Irish game before then. In 1890, the Irish League was set up with Clarence, Cliftonville, Distillery, Glentoran, Linfield, Milford, Old Park, and Ulster as founder members. The first winners were Linfield, who also won the Cup and repeated their double for the next two seasons. They have enjoyed considerable success in both competitions since then, and their rivalry with Belfast Celtic and Glentoran has produced many spirited clashes.

The 1911–12 season saw a serious split in the Irish FA, with six Belfast clubs and Bohemians of Dublin withdrawing their reserve teams from the Irish Junior League and establishing a Second Division of the Irish League. Because of the dispute, there was no Irish Cup final that year and the trophy was awarded to Linfield. The rebel group went so far as to purchase a new gold cup for their own competition, but fortunately the dispute was settled before the 1912–13 season. The next major dispute was never settled.

The problem was Ireland's problem. With violence flaring up and down the country, the Irish FA considered it too dangerous to replay the 1921 semi-final between Shelbourne and Glenavon in Dublin. They decided on Belfast, which would have cost Shelbourne their home advantage. The Dublin club refused, and the Irish FA awarded the game to Glenavon, who lost to Glentoran in the final. The semi-finals were the last time a club from outside Ulster competed in the Irish Cup, for at the end of the 1920–21 season the clubs in the south set up their own league and cup competitions.

Since then the Irish Cup and Irish League have moved along in comparative peace, although football is affected by the changing moods in Northern Ireland. What troubles clubs more is that they are unable to keep their best players and so raise the standard of the domestic competitions. Former stars from England and Scotland are no consolation for the precocious talents of a George Best or a Derek Dougan. And without such players, there seems little likelihood of the Irish Cup or the Irish League ever bearing comparison with their counterparts across the Irish Sea.

Welsh Cup

The Welsh Football Association Challenge Cup is the country's foremost domestic competition, attracting clubs in the Welsh League, the Welsh clubs in the Football League, and some English clubs from just across the border. It has gained in importance since 1961 because its prize, as well as a handsome trophy, is a place in the European Cup-Winners Cup. Also since 1961, the final has been a two-legged affair. But the tie is decided on match results, not on aggregate scores. Therefore if each side wins a leg, there has to be a replay.

The Welsh Cup was first contested on October 30, 1877 between Wrexham and Druids, although there was no actual trophy at the time to present to winners Wrexham. Two seasons later, Druids began a hat-trick of Cup victories, a performance Wrexham emulated from 1908–09. Cardiff City surpassed these feats, however, in the late 1960s. Their 1971 victory over Wrexham was their fifth running, and it took them within two of Wrexham's 18 victories in the competition. Cardiff's other great claim to fame is the only FA Cup-Welsh Cup double, which they achieved in 1927, the only year the FA Cup left England in its first hundred years.

Above: Tired but happy Wrexham players after their success in the 1972 Welsh Cup.

Below: The Wrexham goalie saves cleanly in the second leg of the final against Cardiff. Wrexham won 3–2 on aggregate. Below left: Linfield and Glentoran (dark shorts), leading clubs in the Irish League, contest a 1969–70 fixture. That season saw Glentoran win their 14th League title.

Non-League Football

Apart from the major football leagues in Britain, there are dozens of other professional and semi-professional league competitions up and down the country. In England, teams from the Southern League in particular achieve nationwide fame for their exploits in the FA Cup. Yeovil Town, Bedford Town, and Worcester City have all beaten First Division sides at one time or another. In Scotland, the Highland League generally has better crowds than the Scottish Second Division, and its clubs frequently knock League sides out of the Scottish Cup.

The important non-League competitions are stepping-stones to League status, although election is difficult. In the Football League the bottom four clubs in the Fourth Division each season apply for re-election, and occasionally one might lose its place to a non-League side. In Scotland, however, the re-election of the bottom two clubs in Division II has become virtually automatic, mainly because clubs from the Highlands would find the travelling excessive.

When non-League clubs do gain election to the Football League, they are not necessarily top of their league, although it was appropriate that Cambridge United, champions of the Southern League in 1969–70, should be elected to the Fourth Division for 1970–71, taking the place of Bradford. Most newly elected clubs have done well in the League, and Scunthorpe (elected to Div. III N, 1950) and Oxford United (Div. IV, 1962) both reached the Second Division within a few years. Peterborough, however, made the most successful debut, topping Division IV in their first season (1960–61) with 134 goals, a Football League record, and an average home gate of 15,000.

Attempts have been made to establish a 'pyramid' of competitions on a regional basis, with a promotion and relegation chain providing successful clubs with a direct route from the minor leagues to the major regional leagues and perhaps eventually to the Football Leagues. A step in the right direction was the formation of a strong northern league, the Northern Premier League, in 1968, but in the early 1970s the Midlands were still without a 'premier' league.

A cup competition, the FA Challenge Trophy, for non-league professional sides, was first held in 1969–70, with an entry of 192 clubs and a final at Wembley.

Schools and Youth Football

One reason for the strength of British football is the attention paid to young players, either at school or just out of school. By nurturing the great wealth of young talent, those concerned are ensuring the healthy future of the game.

At school level in England, for example, there are about 500 local and county associations affiliated to the English Schools' Football Association (ESFA) and catering for more than 14,000 schools. They organize league and county competitions for boys in most age groups. At a national level, there are two competitions: a knock-out tournament for district teams (for players under the statutory school-leaving age) for the ESFA Trophy, the world's oldest schools football trophy; and one for individual schools, for boys over 15 and under 19, with,

Left: A startled England defence concedes a goal to Scotland in a 1965 schoolboys international for the Victory Shield.

from 1972, the winners entering the European Individual Schools' Tournament. At international level, the Schools' Football International Board arranges internationals for the Under-15s and Under-18s of England, Scotland, Wales, and Northern Ireland.

Youth football, controlled by the FA through its member county associations, provides for the needs of school-leavers who are below the age of 18 on September 1. Many youth players belong to the youth sides of professional and amateur clubs. There are youth leagues, and in England, for example, there are the FA County Youth Challenge Cup and the FA Youth Challenge Cup. At international level there is an International Youth Championship between the four Home Countries, and an International Youth Tournament for European countries, held every year and run in a similar manner to the World Cup.

South (and Central) America

Uruguay's victory at the 1924 Olympic Games in Paris took a number of Europeans by surprise. Nor was it just their victory; it was the way it was achieved. Ball control, short, precise passing, and intelligent running were combined with a high degree of fitness. Added to these qualities were a willingness to attack and an inborn brilliance that have become trademarks of the best in South American football. But there was more to this victory than sheer playing ability. It had been carefully planned. There were warm-up matches in Spain; the team had its own doctor, who was as important as the coach and physical training instructor. The campaign reflected the organization as well as the playing strength of South American soccer.

The game in South America is as old as soccer on the Continent of Europe, and, as on the Continent, the British were the missionaries. Their influence is seen, not just in the establishing of national associations, but in the names of club sides. Uruguay has its Liverpool, Chile its Everton and Wanderers. In Rosario, Argentina, there are Newell's Old Boys, and Brazil's São Paulo League has its Corinthians, a reminder of a South American tour undertaken by the famous English amateurs.

The English, however, were not the only

Above: Alberto Spencer beats Ronnie Simpson in a 1967 friendly between Penarol of Uruguay and Celtic. The Uruguayan national side was the first South American one to venture into Europe.

Below: Brazil's Tostão in action against Venezuela.

influence. The Italians, too, played an important part in the development of Latin American football. Vittorio Pozzo's Torino, on tour in Argentina at the outbreak of World War I, remained there some time, playing a number of matches during their extended visit. And the immigration of Italians to Argentina also played its part. The marriage of the ball skill of the Latin peoples to the brilliant improvisation of the coloured races produced a style of football unequalled elsewhere.

As in Britain, the earliest games of football in South America were played under a variety of rules. In 1867, a group of Englishmen founded the Buenos Aires FC in Argentina, and in 1884 Alexander Watson Hutton established a school in Buenos Aires at which soccer was played. His pupils set up their own club, and as other clubs were formed a need was seen for a controlling body. In 1893 an Argentina Football Association was founded, with Hutton as president.

This organization did not continue to govern the country's soccer for long though. Divided opinions among members led to several breakaways, and in the early 1920s some of the major clubs, including Penarol and Central of Uruguay, formed the Amateur Football Association. But by the end of the decade professionalism had found its place in South America, and in 1934 the Argentina FA again took over the running of the country's football.

The Uruguayan clubs' participation in

Above: Spectacular but dangerous. Penarol's Joria Aendro fouls Aranguiz of Universidad de Chile in a 1970 South American Cup semi-final match. The winners of the South American Cup meet the winners of the European Cup to decide the World Club Championship.

Argentina's midfield star Carlos Babington (right) challenges Italy's Facchetti in a 1974 World Cup 1st Round group match. The result was a 1–1 draw and Argentina qualified for the 2nd Round at the expense of Italy. Their good conduct on the field in this tournament did much to help them live down their shameful reputation in international football and, more significantly, mollified those who considered that Argentina should not be entrusted to stage the 1978 World Cup.

the Amateur Football Association came about because Uruguayan football was virtually run by the Argentina FA, even though a separate Uruguayan FA was established in 1900. Gradually, however, the Uruguayan game became self-governing. As in Argentina, the first club was started by an Englishman, and the famous Penarol was once a club founded by Britons building the Uruguayan railways. The absence of any colour bar proved invaluable in the rapid rise of soccer in Uruguay, and the side that won two Olympic titles and the first World Cup contained players of all races.

The same was not so in Brazil, but once the coloured player was given equal rights the Brazilians quickly made up the leeway between them and their neighbours. The game there is almost as old as in Argentina. British sailors introduced the game to Rio de Janeiro in the 1880s, and there was a league competition in Rio in the early 1900s.

These three countries have dominated South American football, but not to the extent of completely overshadowing the other countries. Colombia made football headlines for a time in the 1950s when a rebel league attracted leading players from all over the world. But this collapsed after initial success, and Colombian soccer again came under the control of the country's FA. Paraguay, Peru, and Bolivia have won the South American Championship, and all three, along with Chile, whose FA was founded as early as 1900, have qualified for the World Cup. Chile, moreover, hosted the 1962 World Cup.

The South American Championship was first held in 1916 between Uruguay, Argentina, Brazil, and Chile, who finished in that order. The other countries have participated at some time or another, but in the 1960s, with interest waning in favour of club competitions such as the Copa de los Libertadores, the competition came to a halt. Also in 1916, in July, the South American Confederation of Football Associations was founded. It was almost another 40 years before the Europeans followed their example and set up UEFA.

The Central American soccer scene is dominated by Mexico, although Cuba did reach the quarter-finals of the 1938 World Cup. In 1970, El Salvador became the third Central American country to reach the World Cup finals. In doing so, however, they sparked off a war with neighbouring Honduras after beating them in a qualifying match. The Central Americans may not find the success the South Americans do, but they do not take their football lightly.

North America

Considering how readily soccer caught the imagination in Europe and Latin America, it is perhaps difficult to understand why the game failed in North America. It was not because of competition. Football of sorts was being played in the United States quite early in the 19th century, and in Canada soccer was introduced by Scottish immigrants around 1880. But instead of developing soccer as other countries did, the North Americans combined it with rugby to produce their own games (American and Canadian football).

Originally, soccer in the United States confined itself to the universities (colleges), but in time non-scholastic clubs were founded. The first national association was the American Football Association, founded in 1884, but it was eventually disbanded and its successor is the United States Soccer Football Association, set up in 1913. A year earlier the FA of Canada had been formed.

The first three decades of the 20th century saw efforts to encourage professional soccer in the United States, but it was never a financial success and it came to an end with the Depression. Yet it was not that the American public did not like soccer. They were quite prepared to watch leading teams from Europe. It was the American teams they found uninteresting.

Nevertheless the game continued, at an amateur and sometimes semi-professional level. In Canada there was a National Soccer League, and in the United States challenge cup competitions provided players and clubs with incentives. In many parts the game owed its survival to immigrants, and it was a United States team comprising a number of immigrants that caused one of the greatest upsets in football history. In the 1950 World Cup they beat England 1–0 at Belo Horizonte, Brazil. But the soccer boom that should have followed failed to materialize.

With the 1960s came the introduction of professional soccer in Canada. But its Eastern Professional League, set up in 1961, collapsed when some of its members joined the new professional leagues in the United States. The resurgence of professional soccer there was encouraged by television coverage of the 1966 World Cup, and within a year two leagues were set up: the National Professional Soccer League and the North American Soccer League (later the United Soccer Association). In 1968 they combined to form the 17-team North American Soccer League; by the next season 12 teams had dropped out. The great American soccer experiment was deemed a failure.

In some ways, though, it was not. It helped the growth of the game, especially in the schools and the colleges, and the day may well come when the public, able to associate with home-grown players, will accept soccer. It remains to be seen whether television, to which so much American sport is geared, will. Soccer's non-stop play allows little break for commercials.

Below: The captains exchange pennants before West Ham play Dukla Prague in New York in 1963. But though matches such as these, featuring European teams, drew large crowds, there was little public enthusiasm for local teams.

Above: Phil Woosnam (17), a former Welsh forward, played for the Atlanta Chiefs before taking over as Executive Director of the National Professional Soccer League and doing much to improve the status and standard of soccer in the United States.

Left: The New York Giants play the Philadelphia Spartans in 1967.

47

Australasia

Australian and New Zealand soccer is going through a long, difficult struggle to get to the fore in these two great sporting countries. The great problem is the almost fanatical attention given to rugby league and Australian rules in Australia and to rugby union in New Zealand. But with a policy of encouraging the game at junior level, the authorities in both countries entered the 1970s with much more optimism than they had felt at the start of previous decades.

In Australia, in fact, the beginning of the 1960s had seen the game there at a crucial stage. Banned for three years by FIFA in 1960 for the poaching of players from Austria, the Australian Soccer Football Association was opposed and finally overthrown by a rival faction that is now the official Australian Soccer Federation. Australia had already enjoyed a soccer boom with the influx of European immigrants following World War II, and it enjoyed increased growth under the new federation. The highlight of the 1960s was the near success in the qualifying rounds of the 1970 World Cup. Only a 2–1 aggregate defeat by Israel kept the Australians from Mexico City, but nevertheless the publicity soccer in Australia received was invaluable. And when they qualified for the 1974 finals and performed creditably in Germany, Australia's soccer earned worldwide respect.

On the domestic scene, there were, in 1970,

an estimated quarter of a million people involved in the game throughout Australia. The states, which are affiliated to the ASF, run their own league and cup competitions, and the leading players are, in many cases, part-time professionals. The European influence is reflected in the names of clubs—Azzuri, Juventus, Croatia—but it is hoped that with great participation from native Australians the game will become Australia's leading winter sport.

In New Zealand, whose NZFA was founded in 1891, the real development began in the 1950s and 1960s with concentration on younger players. Coaching schemes and the appointment of a national coach have raised the standard of play, while at the same time sponsorship provided the national association with funds to back its ideas. The 1970 season saw the birth of a National League, with eight clubs. The following season this was increased to 10, with the bottom club playing the winners of the Northern, Central, and Southern leagues in a series of test matches to determine promotion and relegation. The 1970 season also saw a change in the format of the Chatham Cup knock-out competition, which was first held in 1923 and is open to all clubs in New Zealand. The game was making progress, and with many schools actually preferring soccer to rugby union, New Zealand soccer just needed to taste international success to make it a strong rival of rugby union.

Below: It is on their young players that Australia and New Zealand hold much hope for their future, and both countries boast sound youth schemes.
Bottom: New Zealand (black shirts) meet an England XI at Wellington. Visits by English club and representative sides have done much to arouse interest in soccer in rugby-dominated New Zealand.

Below: New South Wales goalkeeper Ron Lord is too late to stop Alex Scott's equalizer for Everton. A record crowd of 51,566 saw Everton defeat the home side 4–1 at the Sydney Cricket Ground.

Africa

The emergence of African nations in the athletics world during the 1960s confirmed what a number of people already knew — that the African athlete is a potential champion once he has harnessed his natural skills to a competitive outlet. In soccer, Benfica's Eusebio and Salif Keita, who went from Mali to French club St Etienne in 1968, have shown this ability. And at the beginning of the 1970s, it remained to be seen whether the decade would provide the African footballer with sufficient opportunities to find success on his own continent.

As elsewhere, the British played an important part in the early development of soccer in Africa. In South Africa, soccer had to take second place to rugby, the more physical game appealing to the pioneers. But in the north, the Arab countries found soccer more to their liking. Egypt competed in the 1934 World Cup, having already finished fourth in the 1928 Olympic Games, and Morocco qualified for the 1970 World Cup finals.

The first phase of development was in South Africa in the 1880s. In 1893 the FA of South Africa was founded, and tours by the Corinthians around the turn of the century helped create interest in the game.

A considerable increase in popularity occurred in the 1940s, thanks mainly to the presence of many leading English players during World War II. The adoption of professionalism in 1959 and the formation of a National League was another boost. With a number of English professionals going to South Africa now, the domestic scene looks promising.

Internationally, the prospect is not hopeful. Opposition to South Africa's racial policies led to FIFA's suspension of the FA of South Africa in 1964. Rhodesia also suffered suspension in 1970, for similar reasons, just at a time when the country's soccer was on an upward trend. In addition to the FA of South Africa, there is a Non-European South African Soccer Federation. But it has not been admitted to FIFA because the world body recognizes only one FA per country, even if it has been suspended.

The split between white and black Africa is a tragedy for soccer. With co-operation between all African countries, the continent could emerge as a powerful challenger to Europe and South America. Nevertheless, the untapped talent is there, especially in the emerging African countries. And with the development of competitions along the lines of the European Championship and the European Cup, soccer's future in Africa appears bright.

Zaire defenders converge on Scotland's Joe Jordan in the 1974 World Cup. This was Zaïre's first ever match in the World Cup finals, and the 'Leopards' were by no means disgraced in their 2–0 defeat. And although Yugoslavia put a record nine past them in their next match, they made the holders Brazil struggle to score the three they needed to qualify for the next round.

Asia

As the history of the game shows, certain types of football games were played in China and Japan more than 2,000 years ago. Today, the Chinese and Japanese, as well as their fellow Asians, still play and enjoy a form of football. Now, however, the game is universal—soccer.

Because much of Asia is so removed from the footballing centres of the world, and because Asian club and national sides are rarely seen in Europe, people tend to ignore the game there. Consequently, it came as a surprise when North Korea reached the quarter-finals of the 1966 World Cup ahead of Italy and Chile. It was even more astounding when, with little over a quarter of the game gone, they were three goals up on Portugal in the quarter-final, before succumbing to the genius of Eusebio. Yet the North Koreans had been preparing for this tournament for eight years. It was obvious that the game in Asia was more than just a developing one.

The British took soccer to Asia. Soldiers, sailors, and traders introduced the game in different parts of the vast continent, which stretches east from the Suez Canal to Japan. India was one of the first countries in which the game was played, but hockey has since proved much more popular there and in Pakistan. Elsewhere the game soon caught on, and quite early in the 20th century national associations were being founded. The Football Association of Japan, for example, was set up in 1921; the Iranian Football Federation in 1922; and the Israel Football Association in 1928, when the state was still the British mandate of Palestine.

In 1954, the Asian Confederation of Football Associations was formed to promote the game in Asia. This it has done successfully, establishing coaching schemes and inaugurating competitions such as the Asian Cup, which is held every four years. With the Asian Games and Malaysia's Mederka Tournament as well, the Asian countries have their share of international competitions.

One powerful Asian nation not a member of the Confederation, and therefore of FIFA, at the time of the 1970 World Cup was mainland China. (Nationalist China became a member in 1954.) But a year later China was accepted into the United Nations, a move that gave promise of greater participation in world sport as well as world politics. Should that promise be realized and China joins FIFA, the Asian bid for world honours will be much stronger. The Chinese have a great interest in soccer, and if they use the game for international prestige as the Eastern European countries do, they will have the facilities and the administrative machinery to support their challenge. Size would be no great handicap. The North Koreans showed that there is no substitute for speed, tactics, and ball skills.

Above: The Japanese defence crumbles against a visiting English side. Given time, however, the Japanese, along with other Asian nations, could emerge as a threat to European and South American supremacy.

Below: Israel's Itzhak Shum bursts past Australia's 'keeper Roger Romanawicz and Jim Rooney. The Israelis qualified for the 1970 World Cup at Australia's expense.

Laws of the Game

The Laws of football may be altered only at the annual meeting of the International Football Association Board. This body meets every June, and is made up of representatives of the four British Football Associations and of FIFA. The British associations each have one vote and FIFA has four, and an alteration of the Laws requires a three-quarters majority.

The Laws of the game are supplemented by 'Decisions of the International Board', which serve to clarify, emphasize, reinforce, or merely restate the Laws. There are also a series of 'Questions and Answers', which have been approved by the Board and clarify some of the finer points of the game or deal with unusual circumstances.

Nevertheless, many Laws are insufficiently clear, and are open to a wide range of interpretation. Others make for a somewhat erratic system of punishments for offences.

The 17 Laws of the game are headed as follows:

I—The Field of Play
II—The Ball
III—Number of Players
IV—Players' Equipment
V—Referees
VI—Linesmen
VII—Duration of the Game
VIII—The Start of Play
IX—Ball in and out of Play
X—Method of Scoring
XI—Offside
XII—Fouls and Misconduct
XIII—Free-Kick
XIV—Penalty-Kick
XV—Throw-In
XVI—Goal-Kick
XVII—Corner-Kick

The *field of play* is marked out as in the diagram. It must be rectangular, and for international matches the range of dimensions is 110–120 yards by 70–80 yards. The *ball*, made of leather or any other material approved by the International Board, has a circumference of 27 to 28 inches and must weigh 14 to 16 ounces at the beginning of the game.

Soccer is played between two teams of 11 *players*. This used to be a simple fact, but the advent of substitutes has complicated matters slightly. However, the governing bodies have been careful to restrict substitution so that the nature of the game has not altered. And although substitutes are used tactically, their primary purpose remains

that of reducing the disadvantage experienced by teams with injured players. The maximum number of substitutes allowed in any competition is two, selected from five nominated players. In most British competitions only one is permitted, and he must be nominated before the match. The 11 players on a team consist of 10 outfield players and a goalkeeper, who is the only one allowed to handle the ball (but only within his own penalty area). A goalkeeper may be substituted by one of the outfield players at any time, with the permission of the referee.

The law relating to *players' equipment* is framed to prevent serious injury and provides for the inspection of players' boots before the game. Strict standards determine the type of studs used. Goalkeepers must wear distinguishing colours.

A game of football is controlled by a *referee*, whose decisions are final. He is helped by two *linesmen*. The referee enforces the Laws, keeps a record of the game, and acts as timekeeper. He can stop the game for any infringement of the Laws, and can

Below: The field of play.

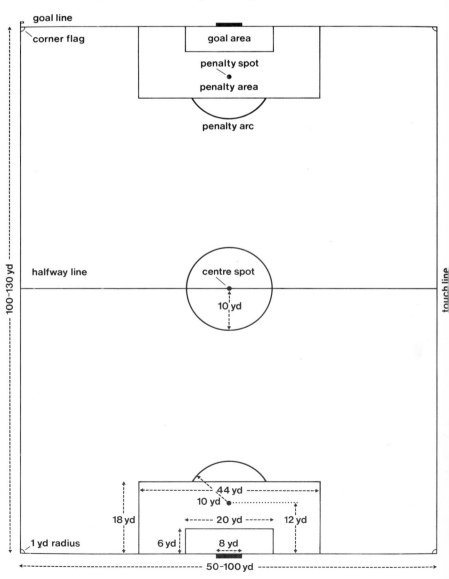

goal line
corner flag
goal area
penalty spot
penalty area
penalty arc
100–130 yd
halfway line
centre spot
10 yd
touch line
44 yd
10 yd
18 yd
20 yd
12 yd
1 yd radius
6 yd
8 yd
50–100 yd

suspend or terminate the game for such reasons as bad weather or interference by spectators. He can caution players guilty of misconduct or 'ungentlemanly behaviour', and can send off persistent or serious offenders.

The referee uses a whistle to start or stop the game. The linesmen signal to the referee by means of a flag. Their duties are to indicate when the ball goes out of play, and which side is entitled to the resultant kick or throw, and generally to assist the referee to control the game in accordance with the Laws. The referee is, however, the sole judge of any decision. He may reverse a decision after consulting a linesman, but he cannot reverse a decision once he has restarted play.

A referee should refrain from stopping play for an offence if he judges that to do so would give an advantage to the offending side. This is known as the 'advantage clause', but once applied, it cannot be revoked. The referee can still deal with the offending player, however.

The Laws of the Game do not authorize referees to accompany their decisions with signals. Nevertheless, some orchestrate play with their own improvisations.

The *duration of the game* is 90 minutes, divided into two periods of 45 minutes with a half-time interval of up to 5 minutes. The referee should make allowance at the end of each period for time lost through stoppages for injury or any other cause. Time is also added for the taking of a penalty kick after the expiry of normal time.

Before the *start of play*, opposing captains toss a coin, the winner choosing either to kick off or which end to start from. The teams change ends at half-time. At the start of the game, the ball is placed on the centre-spot and all the players must be in their own half of the field. No player from the side not kicking-off may be nearer than 10 yards from the ball. A player from the side kicking-off plays the ball, which must travel at least its own circumference into the opposing half of the field. The kicker may not play the ball again until it has been touched by another player. The game is restarted in the same way after a goal has been scored (by the team conceding the goal) and after the half-time interval (by the team who did not kick-off).

The game is restarted after any other temporary suspension (not covered by the various kicks or the throw-in) by means of a 'dropped ball'. The referee drops the ball at the place where it was when play was suspended, and no player is allowed to play the ball until it has touched the ground.

The ball is deemed *out of play* when it has *wholly* crossed the goal-line or touch-line or when the referee has stopped the game. For a goal to be scored, the ball must pass over the goal-line, between the posts and under the cross-bar, provided it does so in accordance with the Laws. This is the only *method of scoring*. A goal cannot be allowed, for example, if it is prevented by some 'outside agent', such as a spectator or a dog, from passing over the line.

The team scoring the greater number of goals is the winner; if an equal number of goals are scored, the game is a 'draw'. In certain circumstances, such as cup replays, 'extra time' (usually 15 minutes each way) is added in an attempt to get a result. In certain two-legged ties, as in European international club competitions, the result may be determined by an 'away goals' rule. In this, goals scored away from home are counted double when the aggregate scores are equal. Ties in these competitions have been decided on the toss of a coin (or coloured disc), but the taking of penalties has been introduced to avoid this. Five players from each side take penalties to determine the winner, and if the scores are still level players continue to take penalties, one from each side, until the

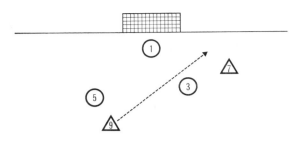

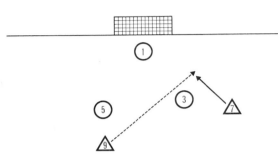

tie is resolved.

Law XI—*Offside*—is one of the most controversial in soccer. It states that a player is offside if he is nearer his opponents' goal-line than the ball *at the moment the ball is played*, unless there are two of his opponents nearer to their own goal-line than he is or the ball last touched an opponent. In addition, a player cannot be offside in his own half or direct from a goal-kick, corner-kick, throw-in, or dropped ball. A linesman should be in a position to indicate when a player is offside, and the penalty is an indirect free-kick to the other side.

The controversy surrounding this Law arises because a player does not have to touch the ball to be offside, and a referee need not penalize a player in an offside position if in his opinion the player is not interfering with play or seeking to gain advantage. The phrasing of the Law allows a wide range of interpretation.

The Law dealing with *fouls and misconduct* is perhaps the most complicated. Offenders may be punished by the award of a direct or an indirect free-kick or a penalty-kick to the opposition; they can also be cautioned or sent off.

There are nine offences punishable by the award of a *direct free-kick*: kicking or attempting to kick an opponent; tripping; jumping at an opponent; violently charging an opponent (a fair charge is made shoulder to shoulder); charging from behind (unless being obstructed); holding; pushing; striking or attempting to strike an opponent; or handling the ball. If any of these fouls are com-

Above: Climbing on an opponent to gain height is a foul punishable by a direct free-kick.

mitted in the penalty area, a penalty-kick is awarded, whether or not the ball was in the area at the time of the offence. There is no provision in the Law to punish any of these offences unless they are intentional. In practice, however, an offence such as tripping is often penalized even when unintentional.

An *indirect free-kick* is awarded against the player committing any of the following four offences: dangerous play; charging a player when the ball is not within playing distance; intentional obstruction (running or standing between an opponent and the ball without attempting to play the ball); charging the goalkeeper, except when he is holding the ball, is obstructing an opponent, or is outside his goal-area. In addition, an indirect free-kick is awarded against a goalkeeper if he takes more than four steps while holding, bouncing, or throwing the ball in the air and catching it again without its being played by another player. He may receive a similar penalty for time-wasting. Indirect free-kicks are also awarded for certain offences that earn a caution or a sending-off.

A player may be *cautioned* for entering or leaving the field without the referee's permission; for persistent infringement of the Laws; for dissent from the referee's decision; and for ungentlemanly conduct (which covers a multitude of unspecified sins). A player may be *sent off* for violent or serious offences (including spitting at a player or official), for using 'foul or abusive language', or for persistent misconduct after receiving a caution.

The last five Laws deal with the so-called 'set pieces' of football, the various kicks and the throw-in. For all of these kicks, the ball must be stationary and on the ground, and the player taking the kick may not play the ball again until it is touched by another player.

When a free-kick is being taken, opposing players must stand at least 10 yards from the ball (except when, in the case of an indirect free-kick, they are standing on their own goal-line, between the goal-posts). Failure to do so warrants a caution.

A goal can be scored from a *direct free-kick*. But another player (of either side) must touch the ball before a goal can be scored after an *indirect free-kick*. The referee signals the award of an indirect free-kick by raising his arm.

For a *penalty-kick*, all players except the taker and the opposing goalkeeper must be outside the penalty area (but within the field of play) and at least 10 yards from the ball. The goalkeeper must stand on his goal-line until the ball is kicked. The kick is taken from the penalty-spot, and the kicker must play the ball forward and may not touch it again until it has been touched by another player (he may not, for example, take a direct rebound from the posts or cross-bar).

When the ball leaves the field of play (except when a goal is scored), a throw-in, goal-kick, or corner-kick results.

If the ball passes over a touch-line, a *throw-in* is awarded at the place it went out to the side opposing the player who last touched the ball. The thrower must use both hands to deliver the ball from behind and over his head; he must face the field of play and have part of each foot grounded on or behind the touch-line, but not in front of it. He cannot play the ball again until it has been touched by another player. A goal cannot be scored direct from a throw-in. The penalty for an improper throw is the award of a throw-in to the other side.

If the ball passes over the goal-line (except when a goal is scored), a goal-kick is awarded to the defending team if the ball was last played by a member of the opposing side, or a corner-kick is awarded to the attacking team if the ball was last played by a defender. The kicks are taken from the side the ball went out.

A *goal-kick* is taken from within the goal-area, and all opposing players must be outside the penalty-area. If the ball is not kicked out of the penalty-area, or is touched by any player (even the taker of the kick) before it leaves the penalty-area, it has to be retaken. This is an anomaly in the Laws, for it gives defenders the opportunity to rectify a mistake illegally, but without punishment. A goal cannot be scored direct from a goal-kick.

For a *corner-kick*, the ball must be placed wholly within the quarter-circle at the corner-flag. Opposing players must be at least 10 yards from the ball. A goal can be scored direct from a corner-kick.

Above: The problem that many referees face. Who is the offender? Is Jackie Charlton holding Martin Chivers back, or is Chivers pushing Charlton away?

Above: Jersey pulling is a frequent fault at all levels of football, yet often goes undetected by the referee. It is this niggling type of foul that leads to flare-ups, with the player retaliating ending up in the referee's book . . . not the first offender.

Right: Bobby Charlton, and not the ball, is the object of this tackler's boot. Kicking an opponent is penalized by a direct free-kick. Such fouls were frequent when the 'tackle from behind' was part and parcel of English football.

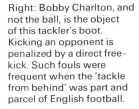

Referees and Refereeing

The football referee is one of the most maligned figures in sport. Poorly paid, part-time, but completely dedicated to the game, he has to suffer strong criticism from players, spectators, and press. And often his decisions—made on the spur of the moment and in the cauldron of a stadium bursting with screaming fans—are put under the microscope of the slow-motion television replay. A referee's good decisions go largely unnoticed, his bad ones stand out for all to see. It is, indeed, a thankless task.

Most referees employ the 'diagonal system' of controlling a match, operating from corner to corner of the pitch, with the two linesmen patrolling, respectively, the opposite halves of the touchline. The linesmen are merely assistants, however, and it is the referee's decisions that are final. Among other things, he has to enforce the laws, maintain discipline on the pitch, act as timekeeper, keep the score, and decide whether the pitch is fit for play.

In his black 'blouse' with white detachable collar and black shorts, white topped black stockings, and lightweight football boots, the referee is armed with two watches (one of which has 'stop' action), two whistles, two pencils, note-pad, score-card, pocket-knife, coin, and a copy of the rules of the competition.

The prospective referee has to pass written and oral tests before qualifying to serve in lower-grade competitions. Reports are made by assessors on referees' performances, and

Below: Peter Osgood leaves an FA Disciplinary Committee hearing, which gives the player the opportunity of appealing against cautions by referees. There is some strength in the argument by referees that the hearings do not give them sufficient support in their attempts to keep football clean.
Below right: Bobby Charlton hammers the ball home, but referee Homewood, right on the spot, disallowed the goal. He ruled that Charlton had infringed the Laws by shouting 'Leave it', without using his team-mate's name.

Below: When a goalkeeper grabs a player's foot and prevents him scoring what would have been a certain goal, the referee is empowered only to award a penalty and a caution (or a sending off). Would it place too much onus on the referee to allow him the discretion to award a goal in such circumstances?

referees are promoted to higher grades on ability. They gain experience by running the line at higher-grade matches. Only Grade I referees are appointed to matches in the major competitions, and they must have a high standard of fitness. Referees for international matches must be from a neutral country and are selected from the official list of international referees.

Suggestions have been made from time to time that refereeing standards would improve if referees were paid more, or if there were more than one referee controlling a match. These are only partial answers to the problem, however. It cannot be denied that a referee paid to devote all his time to the game might be better prepared to make decisions and be able to recognize situations in the play more readily. It is also true that a referee, while perhaps not needing someone to share the responsibility, could do with extra help. For example, for the most important aspect of the game, the scoring of

Left: An interesting incident from the 1971 England–Scotland match illustrates the decision referees must make on the spur of the moment. If the man on the line handles and the ball crosses the line, the referee can give a goal, provided he has not blown for hands. If he allows play to go on and the ball does not cross the line, strictly there should be no penalty. In this case, the defender handled the ball onto the crossbar and the referee gave a goal, though it was doubtful whether the ball crossed the line. However, justice was done.

goals, there is no guarantee that someone is going to be on the goal-line to decide whether the ball has crossed the line or not. Yet the fact remains that the basic tools of the referee's trade—the Laws of the game—are inadequate and vague, and it can be argued that the bodies responsible for maintaining a consistent interpretation of the Laws are more concerned with discipline on the field. Instructions are liable to be given to 'clamp down' on certain offences, and as a result all sorts of injustices are perpetrated. And inevitably, it is the poor referee who gets the blame.

Below left: The referee administers a warning.
Below: The referee applies the advantage rule and waves play on.
Bottom: Bobby Moore makes a nigh-perfect side-of-the-foot pass. He is well balanced, has kept his knee over the ball at the moment of impact, and follows through after kicking. Note, too, how his eyes are on the ball.

Soccer Skills and Techniques

The primary skills of association football all involve the ability to play with a ball. In simple terms, the outfield players have to be able to control the ball and direct passes and shots at goal effectively; the goalkeeper has to cultivate a similar feel for it with his hands, as well as having to kick accurately in his clearances. Only freak players will succeed in football without mastering the basic *kicking* technique.

This technique falls broadly into two parts, one to keep the ball along the ground, the other for lofting it in the air. The former involves contact with the ball either with the instep of the foot or the side of the foot. The principles are the same. Contact should be made through an imaginary mark on the middle of the ball; if the kick is aimed below this point, the ball will be lifted off the ground. The non-kicking foot should be

Left: A beautifully balanced Alan Hudson gets all his power into this instep kick. The follow through ensures that the ball got exactly where he intended.

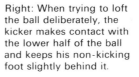

Right: When trying to loft the ball deliberately, the kicker makes contact with the lower half of the ball and keeps his non-kicking foot slightly behind it.

Right: Colin Bell, by keeping his non-kicking foot alongside the ball and his kicking leg over it, is in a perfect position to make a crisp, low pass.

Above: By keeping the ball close to him, Francis Lee has full control of it. He can either run with it or pass. Note the position of his head. His eyes are on the ball, his head is not so low down as to prevent his glancing around the field.

placed alongside the ball, and at the moment of impact the knee on the kicking leg should be directly over the ball. The eyes should be focused firmly on it throughout the movement.

Many young players make the mistake of not striking the ball firmly enough. If it is hit firmly with the leg following through, like a cricket bat in a classic off-drive, the ball will travel crisply to its intended target. The common fault that destroys accuracy is the failure of the player to swing his leg on a line through the ball. Often the line is across it instead, and the pass or shot is hooked or sliced.

The deliberately lofted pass requires some of the very factors that are faults in the on-the-ground technique. Contact should be made with the lower half of the ball, and the non-kicking foot should be placed slightly behind the ball. Again the ball should be struck firmly, but this time with the body leaning slightly back away from the ball. The leg swing should be as long as possible, again on a line through the ball and again following through, and the knee should be straightened powerfully just before contact.

Football is very much a game that rewards the effort a player is willing to give to developing his skills. Practice of the kicking techniques will cultivate the priceless ability to be able to play the ball in any direction that the player requires during a match. The instep and sidefoot methods are the core of the techniques. Once mastered, they can be embroidered with the sophisticated skills of using the outside of the foot, deliberately swerving the ball, backheeling, etc.

On a par with kicking or passing in terms of primary importance is *trapping* ability—the ability to stop the ball when it is passed to you before passing it on to a team-mate or having a shot at goal. Trapping or 'killing' the ball relies on a technique of cushioning or taking the pace off the ball's movement as it arrives. Whether a player is trying to trap it with his feet, chest, thigh, or head, the object is to make it fall at his feet and not bounce away out of playing distance. If the player presents a firm surface to the ball, it will bounce away just like a shot rebounds off a goalpost. But if the surface is relaxed and is slightly withdrawn as the contact is made, the sting is taken out of the ball and it falls to the feet.

Positioning as the ball is on its way to the player is crucial. First, he should decide which part of the body he is going to use, and then he should move the selected part into line with the flight of the ball. As with the kicking technique, his eyes should be focused all the time on the ball, with perhaps one quick glance permitted so that he knows what is going on around him. In this way, he can have some idea what he is going to do with the ball when he has controlled it.

Heading is another of football's fundamental skills, and young players should be introduced to the technique as early as possible. In heading, confidence is the most important factor. A ball, often heavy with mud, that strikes the head will hurt. But if the head strikes the ball, there is no pain. The ball should be struck with the forehead, which is a strong, bony surface and is relatively flat—the ball can be directed accurately from it. Strong neck muscles give added power, but, especially if the header is made from a standing position, power can be imparted from the whole body. A twist of the neck will send the ball off at an angle.

The type of heading a player uses depends on what position he is playing. Defenders concentrate on leaping high to send powerful headers preferably to a team-mate, but often in any direction as long as it is away from danger. Forwards, on the other hand, concentrate on accuracy to send their headers into goal or to glance the ball delicately down to a better-placed colleague. The most effective header at goal is often the downward header, where the striker climbs above the flight of the ball and directs his header down into the bottom of the net.

With a working knowledge of trapping, the kicking and passing techniques, and heading, the outfield player needs but one more attribute to have a grasp of the game's rudiments—*ball control*, the ability to run with the ball. Dribbling, or the ability to weave with the ball past a succession of opponents, is a skill given to few players, although any player can develop the skill to beat another. But dribbling is not always successful against sophisticated defences. Rather, what is required is simply to be able to carry the ball twenty yards or so without its moving out of playing reach. This is best done by using the outside of the foot, which leaves the player in the best position to move off to either side if challenged. Although the player should concentrate on the ball, he should look up quickly from time to time so that he can judge what is happening around him, and see when he is being put under pressure by an opponent. Not concentrating on the ball is a fault common to young children when they first start to play, but over-concentration becomes a fault when older players will not look up to assess situations around them.

The basic attributes of a *goalkeeper* are less easy to define. He must have the ability to catch the ball, and quick reflexes to stop shots. He must have the courage to do these two things under the mental pressure of knowing that a mistake is very likely to cost his team a goal and under the physical pressure of the challenge of strong forwards. The most common catch he will have to make will be from crosses and corner-kicks. This should be accomplished two-handed overhead with the fingers, slightly relaxed and

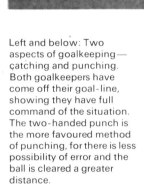

Above: Chesting the ball is a trapping technique requiring much practice. Note how Frank McLintock relaxes his body to take the sting out of the ball, which then falls to his feet. If the body is too taut, the ball will bounce away.

Left and below: Two aspects of goalkeeping—catching and punching. Both goalkeepers have come off their goal-line, showing they have full command of the situation. The two-handed punch is the more favoured method of punching, for there is less possibility of error and the ball is cleared a greater distance.

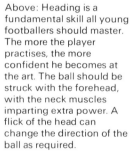

Above: Heading is a fundamental skill all young footballers should master. The more the player practises, the more confident he becomes at the art. The ball should be struck with the forehead, with the neck muscles imparting extra power. A flick of the head can change the direction of the ball as required.

pointing upwards, forming a cradle to collect the ball. Generally in dealing with shots, the 'keeper should try whenever possible to get his whole body behind the ball, so that if it slips through his hands there is a second line of defence. His eyes should be fully focused on the path of the ball all the time.

But what a goalkeeper needs most of all is the indefinable quality of judgement. Not only is his own positional play important, but he is in a position to control the movements of the defenders in front of him by telling them when he wants the ball or what they can best do in any situation. He must be in command of his own penalty-area and inspire confidence in those in front of him. His own positional play revolves very much around his decisions about when to come off his goal-line. He must come out either to narrow the angle or hurl himself at the feet of an opponent who has broken through. He must come off his line to collect crosses, either to catch or punch them away—but it is always a matter of judgement and anticipation. And if a 'keeper errs, the scoresheet usually tells the tale.

For the outfield players, the secondary techniques they require are dependent on which positions they are playing. *Defenders* need to use their basic kicking techniques to play strong, lengthy clearances up the field. Often these will be deep, lofted passes up to their front men, sometimes short, sidefoot balls to midfield players who are free. The power to head the ball clear is crucial. Sometimes full-backs are free to carry the ball up the touchline before starting a counter-attack. All the basics will be tested.

But defenders have to tackle and they have to mark opponents. Like heading, *tackling* can be painful, but the risk of injury is minimized if the tackler goes in wholeheartedly wanting to win the ball. The block tackle in which two players meet front on is the basic method. The attempt to win the ball should be made at the same time as the opponent is about to play the ball. The non-tackling foot is placed to the side of the ball and all of the tackler's weight goes onto it as contact is made with the ball The tackle is made with the inside of the foot and aimed at the centre of the ball. The patient defender will wait for exactly the right moment to make his challenge, and then will go in with every possible ounce of effort.

The other most common method of taking the ball from opponents is the slide tackle. This is often employed when a forward has broken through and a defender is chasing from behind. The non-tackling foot, the one nearer the opponent, should be level with the ball, and the other foot is thrown in at the ball. Again the timing of the movement is important.

Marking falls into two categories, marking players and marking space. The former requires one defender to watch closely an immediate opponent so that he can prevent this opponent from making an effective contribution to the game, either by tackling him quickly or by intercepting passes aimed at him. Naturally the opponent will not stand still to allow himself to be marked, so it is important that the defender follows him when he moves about. The effective marker is the man who does not become distracted from his task. He must not watch the ball to the exclusion of watching his man. He may allow himself to be drawn away from his man only when he is sure he is going to win the ball for his side or when he is forced to help a colleague who is in difficulties.

Marking space is more complicated and a product of team defensive systems. Defenders are responsible for particular areas

Opposite page: George Best, an outstanding exponent of the art of dribbling, keeps the ball as close to his foot as possible. And by controlling it with the outside of the foot he can change direction away from the challenger.

Below left: The block tackle, two players meeting front on, is the basic tackling method. Alan Gilzean, the better balanced of the two with his weight on his non-tackling foot, wins the ball by pushing it through Bobby Charlton's legs. The sliding tackle (bottom), best made with the outside foot, calls for split-second timing, for if unsuccessful it leaves the tackler on the ground, temporarily out of the game.
Below: No. 5 moves over to mark the space left vacant by his beaten team-mate. Defenders mark either space or players, or both.

of the pitch, and must mark whichever opponent enters their zone. In principle, when this attacker leaves the defender's zone he immediately enters another area, and the defender responsible for this area marks him. Most teams play a flexible system which requires defenders to mark both space and men, dependent on differing situations.

Demands on the basic skills of *midfield players* are equally great. They always have to work in areas where there are many players, so their control must be quick and their passes hit with precision. They may be able to move forward for long-range shots at goal, so their kicking technique must be highly developed. They, too, will be required to win the ball for their side with strong tackling. But a critical quality in the middle of the field is the need to support the man in possession. One of the game's greatest sayings is that it is the man off the ball who plays the football. Ideally the man in possession should have three alternatives to pass to; certainly he should have two. The midfield men should always be looking to run unselfishly to help colleagues.

Forwards, perhaps, have the hardest task of all in modern football. All their basic skills will be tested under severe pressure, and they are expected to score goals as well. Shooting from any angle and from any distance must be developed to a fine degree. It is a skill that must be performed quickly when opportunities arise, or they will be lost. At the first sight of goal, a striker should be prepared to try a shot. There is no written rule for shooting. The good ones are those that go in, whether off the full instep or the back of the knee.

A forward is expected to act as a 'target' for his defenders' clearances. Long balls will find him, often unsupported, upfield. There he must control the ball until help arrives. This can be done by shielding the ball from an opponent, keeping his body in between the ball and the opponent who is trying to make the tackle. It is perfectly within the laws provided that the ball is kept within playing distance all the time. The only way an opponent can win the ball is by tackling from behind, which is extremely difficult to do without committing a foul.

Below: Free-kicks give teams a chance to put into practice their well rehearsed ploys. The player taking the kick has a number of options, but it is essential that his team-mates are aware of his intentions. The defence have to be prepared for all possibilities, with the 'wall' the accepted method of blocking a direct shot. It must, however, be at least 10 yards from the ball.

Forwards particularly must also work unselfishly in the team cause by making decoy runs off the ball. When a forward moves about the field, almost certainly one, if not two, defenders are drawn with him. This makes space for other players to build attacks at goal. But, above all, a forward must be brave; to score goals he frequently has to put himself into frantic goalmouth situations in which he may get hurt. He has to accept physical tackling from defenders, and he must be resilient to survive and still keep looking for opportunities to score.

All the players have their own particular roles to fulfil, and these are extended to include play at football's *set-pieces*—when the ball goes out of play or when a free-kick is awarded.

Perhaps the most common of these situations is the *throw-in*, a simple move but one that often results in the team taking the throw forfeiting possession when they really should not. A basic error is that too many team-mates run close to the thrower. Each player is marked so that the area becomes congested and the man who receives the ball cannot open up the play. The most common method is to throw the ball to a team-mate's feet. He plays the ball back to the thrower who is facing the way he wants to play the ball and can see what is happening around him. Another method is to throw the ball into the path of a team-mate making a sharp, unexpected run to throw off an opponent. And many clubs have a long-throw expert, usually a strongly built player, who can send slow, hanging balls into the opponents' goalmouth from positions up to 20 yards from the corner-flag.

A *goal-kick* is in a sense a set-piece, and it is important that a goalkeeper can kick the ball to around the half-way line. With the basic kicking technique he should achieve this, but, if he cannot, a bad kick puts his team under immediate pressure. And if a defender has to take the kicks, it puts an additional, unnecessary pressure on him.

Corners and *free-kicks* have become crucial routes to goalscoring chances since intelligent defensive tactics have made it harder to find ways to goal in free play. There are many routines for both situations, but any

Below: When taking on the defence, the selfless forward will try to draw defenders towards him before passing to an unmarked team-mate with space to move in.

team should plan their moves around what players they have at their disposal. For example, if a team has two big defenders who are outstanding in the air, plans for exploiting their skills should govern the thinking at corner-kicks. Yet it is no good their both standing at the far post waiting for the corner if there is no one in the team who can hit a corner that far. At free-kicks a player who has a strong shot may be looking to try directly for goal, but it is useless if he chips the ball over a defensive 'wall' for another player if his team-mates are not expecting the move. The secret, therefore, is to work out ideas in training, to plan for every situation that could arise, and even work a form of code, either by calling out numbers or making gestures, so that every player involved knows what to expect. A team that can exploit set-pieces starts with an enormous advantage.

But whatever any player attempts to accomplish at any stage of any game, he will be calling on his own basic skills and techniques. No player, however well versed in the theory of the game's tactics, can exist without them.

Below: For a long time, coaching was alien to British football. But with its acceptance, and with the emergence of outstanding young coaches, like Malcolm Allison (left), the British game took on a new dimension.

Coaching

If Britain taught the world about football, the world certainly taught Britain about football coaching. Both in Europe and in South America, those connected with the game realized the importance of having someone to instruct players of all ages in both techniques and tactics. Developments had begun abroad before World War I, but the message was finally brought home to Britain only in the late fifties, by which time English football had fallen far behind her international opponents in thinking and tactics.

For decades, professional clubs had been administered by a manager and a trainer. The manager ran the club, picked the team, and sometimes saw the players only on match days. The trainer kept the players physically in trim and tended to their injuries. Indeed, perceptive coaches such as Jesse Carver and George Raynor, men ahead of their time, were forced to leave Britain to have their philosophies accepted. Raynor managed the 1958 Swedish World Cup side who reached the final of the competition.

Gradually, through the influence of Sir Stanley Rous, who founded the FA Coaching Scheme, and Walter Winterbottom, England's team manager in the fifties, coaches became the rule rather than the eccentric exception. Managers were recruited from ex-professionals with coaching qualifications, and wore track suits rather than those of the grey-flannel variety. Clubs who had managers who were essentially administrators, such as Eric Taylor of Sheffield Wednesday, brought in coaches to control playing matters.

The coach holds a simple brief: he has to get the best out of the players he has at his disposal. He works on the weaknesses of individuals, trying to improve the left foot of one player, increasing the speed of another, and developing the heading power of a third. He controls the education of young players, ensuring that they retain their good habits and rid themselves of the bad ones while they are still young enough to do so.

But, above all, the coach is responsible for devising the best team tactics to suit his squad of players. It is up to him to decide the basic team plan, 4–3–3, 4–2–4, or whatever, to decide which player is to occupy which position, and to drill his team into his chosen method of organizing them on the field. He organizes plans for taking corners, free-kicks, and throw-ins; he has to ensure that the players are fully capable of putting his ideas into practice on the field. At the same time he has to ensure that his players are not over-coached, that they can think for themselves on the field and exploit situations that at times might be contrary to an overall plan. Teams that are not flexible in this way can be predictable and easy to play against.

To be successful, the coach must be able to communicate to his players. They must respect him and he must be able to inspire them. He must know when to be firm, when to be kind, which players respond to being yelled at, and which react better to encouragement. Much of the time he has to combine a deep knowledge of football with an equally deep grasp of human psychology.

British football took its time to appreciate coaching, but by 1970 it had done so with a vengeance. In all of the game's spheres, the coach is the man who matters.

Above: Don Howe (second from left) coached Arsenal to a League and Cup double before becoming manager of West Bromwich Albion in 1971. Left: Former England and Wolves 'keeper Bert Williams takes a coaching class for young goalkeepers.

Below: The dribbling game of organized soccer's early days.

Evolution of Tactics

The professional footballer has evolved into an extremely well organized being. Coaches have tuned his skills to high levels so that he can deal with any situation a particular game produces. His fitness has been built up to cope with a game that continually increases the physical demands that it puts on those who play it. But, above all, he has become disciplined by team tactics—this means that throughout a game he has deliberately to plot his movements in relation to those of his team-mates.

This is a far cry from the days, a mere 120 years or so ago, when football, which had no legal professionalism, was still sorting out the basic problem of how many players a team should be allowed. Many games were played with more than 15 players a side, and tactics had developed no further than an instinctive desire to chase after the ball.

Gradually administrators began to bring some sort of organization into the game. The first clubs were formed in the late 1850s, and in 1863 the Football Association was constituted. Soccer was still a game to be played by a varying number of players, but English clubs built their sides around a basic system of a goalkeeper, one full-back, two half-backs, and seven or eight forwards. The emphasis was entirely on attack, and often the half-backs would be upfield supporting their forwards.

AF–F

And this quality of support was the basic tactic, as indeed it was to remain for as long as football was played. But dribbling in an entirely individual way was the essence of the game: once a player gained possession he would carry the ball on his own until he was dispossessed or the ball ran free. It was then that the support mattered, as team-mates would be at hand ready to challenge for the ball as it broke loose.

It was in Scotland in the 1870s that the first real tactical innovation came about. In 1872 the first of the annual England versus Scotland encounters was played in Glasgow. It was a 0–0 draw, and the following year England won 4–2 at Kennington Oval. But from then on, for about a dozen years, the Scots dominated these matches. They did so because tactically they were one step—an important one—ahead of their rivals. Where-

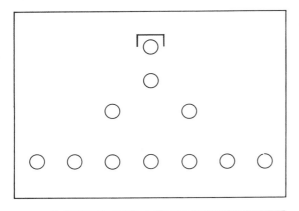

Left: A line-up for the dribbling game, in which the emphasis was on carrying the ball, with team-mates up in support.

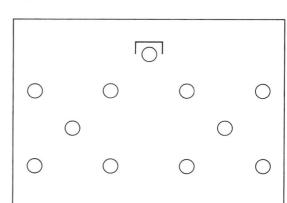

Right: The 4-2-4 formation used by Brazil in the 1958 World Cup.

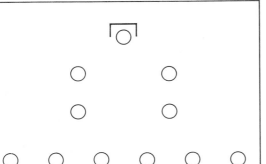

Left: The Scottish line-up of the 1870s was more balanced, with two full-backs and two half-backs supporting the goalkeeper.

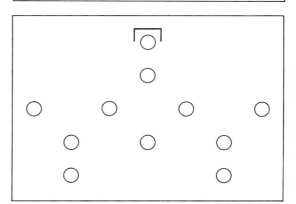

Right: *Catenaccio*, with the sweeper patrolling behind the back four.

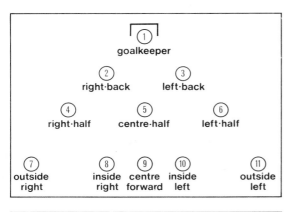

circled numbers with labels:
① goalkeeper
② right-back ③ left-back
④ right-half ⑤ centre-half ⑥ left-half
⑦ outside right ⑧ inside right ⑨ centre forward ⑩ inside left ⑪ outside left

Left: The 2-3-5 system introduced in the 1880s.

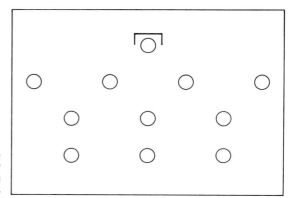

Right: 4-3-3, basically the formation used by England in winning the 1966 World Cup.

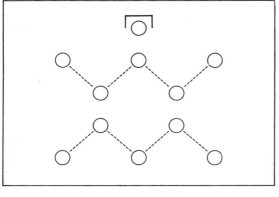

Left: The W–M formation of the 'third-back' game

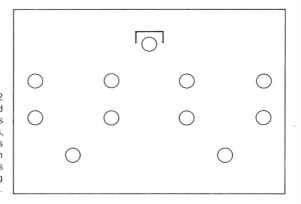

Right: The 4-4-2 formation reflected the defensive trends of the late 1960s, when the emphasis seemed to be on preventing goals rather than scoring them.

as England continued to rely on the dribbling game, with almost all of their forces committed to attack, Scotland began to deploy their team in a more balanced formation and to pass the ball amongst their players instead of waiting until one player lost it at the end of a dribble. The Scots still played with six forwards, but with two full-backs and two half-backs they gave far greater protection to their goalkeeper. And the innovation of passing meant that they were able for the first time to use the full space of the pitch. The individualism that had led to vast numbers of players chasing the ball like two rival packs of hounds was giving way to a spirit of co-operation. The realization that football was a team game was slowly dawning.

In 1885, professional football was legalized, and at about the same time England began to counteract Scotland's superiority with a 2–3–5 system. (In describing tactical systems in this way, the goalkeeper is ignored.) The 2–3–5 system was made up as follows: two full-backs—one on either side of the field; three half-backs—a right-half, a centre-half, and a left-half; and five forwards —two wingers who would operate on the touchlines, two inside-forwards to support a winger each, and a centre-forward. Positionally the system was a rigid one. Rarely, for example, would a winger leave his touch-line, even if he was not receiving the ball for long periods of a game. The most important player in the system was often the centre-half. His was an attacking role, and often the team's most talented all-round player would be chosen for this position.

With marking a relatively undeveloped skill, the centre-half could move forward into the area that later became known as the midfield, and spray long passes to the wingers or through the middle to the centre-forward. But despite this particular attacking ploy, the character of football was slowly drifting away from its early, bright attacking philosophy. 'Stop them scoring, and we can't lose,' was becoming an unwritten law— one that still dominated football more than 80 years later and showed no signs of being ousted.

From the 1880s the game consolidated around this basic system, and it was not until after World War I that the next major tactical change arose—because of a rule that had been in existence for nearly 60 years, the offside law. This stated that a player was offside if there were fewer than three opponents between him and his opponents' goal when the ball was last played by a team-mate. The credit for exposing and exploiting this rule is usually given to a full-back who played for Newcastle United, Billy

McCracken. McCracken and his full-back partner would advance to as near the half-way line as possible (a player cannot be offside in his own half), moving up quickly and timing their runs, so that they would often catch two or three forwards offside. Opponents could find no way to master this trap, and though it was an unpopular ploy with spectators and the press, Newcastle were very successful with it and other teams began to imitate.

In 1925, the law was changed to read two opponents instead of three. Not only did it condemn the offside trap as being extremely risky, it also altered the whole nature of the centre-half's play. No longer could he make expansive surges upfield, prompting and supporting his forwards. The risk of exposing his defence to forwards now with a considerably better chance of remaining onside was too great. Instead, the centre-half became a third or centre-back, with virtually no scope to attack, and his job now was to police the opposing centre-forward.

Full-backs began to play much wider and were responsible for marking the wingers. Whereas the wing-halves, who had played closer to the touchlines when the centre-half was patrolling the centre of the field, now had to cover these crucial central areas and mark opposing inside-forwards. Attack, which had stemmed from the old centre-half, was switched to the wings, and wing-halves and inside-forwards were briefed to get the ball to the touchlines. The winger's job was then straightforward enough—he had to beat his full-back and cross the ball to the centre-forward in the goalmouth.

It was at Arsenal that the tactic took firm root—thanks largely to the thinking of veteran inside-forward Charlie Buchan. And at that time what manager Herbert Chapman did the rest of football followed. Herbie Roberts was Arsenal's third-back, and Chapman compensated for the loss of the attacking centre-half by signing such superbly skilled wing-halves and inside-forwards as Alex James and David Jack.

Arsenal's switch and its resulting popularity exposed perhaps for the first time the basic problem of football tactics. Tactics work only when the talents that the team has at its disposal are welded into an overall plan. In a sense, the talents come first. The best tactic for the skills available is secondary. Thus Arsenal, with full-backs such as Male and Hapgood and wingers such as Bastin and Hulme, had all that was required to make Chapman's system a success. Too many imitators followed the system blindly, paying no heed to the players on their books and what skills they possessed. Square pegs

Below: The two men who gave soccer the 'third-back' game: the Arsenal manager Herbert Chapman and veteran inside-forward Charlie Buchan.

Below: Arsenal's Herbie Roberts (centre) became the first stopper centre-half, forsaking the traditional attacking role to police centre-forwards such as Dixie Dean (right), who were taking advantage of the new offside law.

Above: Hungary score again against England at Wembley in 1953. For centre-half Harry Johnston (5), the match was exceptionally frustrating. Used to marking the opposing centre-forward, he was left all at sea by the deep-lying Hidegkuti. Below: Alf Ramsey sees Merrick beaten yet again.

were continually forced into round holes. As a result, Arsenal, even after Chapman's death in 1934, maintained a superiority until World War II.

A few months before Chapman's death, the 1933 Cup final saw players being numbered for the first time. Everton wore numbers 1 to 11 from their goalkeeper to their outside-left; Manchester City wore 12 to 22, from outside-left to goalkeeper. The numbers were merely an aid to the large crowd in identifying who was who. But it was the start of one of soccer's misconceptions, that the number a player wore was an indication of what position he was going to play. It was a misconception that, many believe, was to cost England their unbeaten home record against foreign opposition 20 years later.

What had evolved from Herbert Chapman was the breakdown of the theory that football teams had two types of players: attackers, who attacked, and defenders, who defended. Arsenal had wing-halves and inside-forwards who did both, sprinting forward in support of an attack one moment and back alongside the centre-half the next. The system was called the W-M, because the line-up took the shape of these letters, one above the other. The link came in the middle of the field where the two wing-halves and the two inside-forwards were constantly switching positions.

In defence, the full-backs had a secondary role, that of providing cover when the opposition was building up attacks on the opposite side of the field. For example, if the opponents' outside-left had the ball, the right-back would challenge him; at the same

time the left-back would leave his charge, the right-winger, and come around almost behind the centre-half. Thus a well-hit, long crossfield pass from one winger to the other could sometimes expose the limitations of the system. The Wolverhampton Wanderers team of the early fifties, with wingers Jimmy Mullen and Johnny Hancocks, exploited this ploy with some success.

But the beginning of the end for the W-M system, which had spanned World War II and beyond, and the beginning of the serious tactical heartsearching in British football occurred on November 25, 1953. The result is history, a 6-3 thrashing for England by Hungary, the first defeat on English soil at the hands of a Continental side. But the Hungarians did it by exposing the W-M system and England's general tactical short-sightedness. For example, the misconception about numbers blew up in England's faces. Nandor Hidegkuti wore Hungary's number 9, the traditional shirt of the centre-forward. Harry Johnston was England's centre-half and set out to mark the number 9 as usual. But Hidegkuti played deep, like a wing-half or a modern midfield player, and Johnston did not know where to go. Nor did his colleagues, including right-back Alf Ramsey, offer much help. England were ripped to pieces.

Basically, Hungary played a 4-2-4 system, with Hidegkuti operating as one of the middle two. By drawing Johnston out of position, he set up acres of space for two attacking inside-forwards, Kocsis and Puskas, to move into. The system of the covering full-back did no more than keep these two strikers onside. Instead of the conventional defensive systems, the Hungarians stretched a line of four defenders across the pitch using two full-backs with two centre-backs between them.

In this system a great onus fell on the two players in the middle of the field, who were to support both attack and defence. Thus in theory a team playing 4-2-4 would have six attackers and six defenders. Manchester City learned a quick lesson from the Hungarians, and, using Don Revie in Hidegkuti's role, won the FA Cup in 1956. The Brazilians, with Didi steering the ship from midfield, won the 1958 World Cup in a similar way. But in the 1958 final, Brazil mothered another invention out of necessity. In the early minutes of the match Sweden put Brazil under a lot of pressure, and the two midfield players were unable to instigate attacks. Mario Zagalo, the left-winger, forsook his touchline and moved into midfield. For 20 minutes Brazil, almost by instinct, played 4-3-3. For Alf Ramsey it may have

Left: With the advent of 4-3-3 and 4-4-2, more and more was required of the target man, the forward whose job it was to win and hold the ball until support came. Geoff Hurst, hard-working and selfless, had all the qualities for that demanding role.

Above: The 1970 World Cup saw the return of that almost forgotten man of soccer, the winger. Brazil's Jairzinho and others thrilled millions with their willingness to go past a defence and cross to their strikers.
Right: England, however, still relied on the full-back to attack down the flanks. Terry Cooper (white shirt) was a fine example of the overlapping full-back.

Right: Don Revie (left) played the Hidegkuti deep-lying centre-forward role for Manchester City when they won the FA Cup in 1956.

been the first clue to a functional system of football that won England the 1966 World Cup.

When Ramsey took charge of the England team, they were playing a 4-2-4 system. But Ramsey found over a period of two or three years that he could not find certain types of players to make the system work. He experimented with several wingers, but could not find the men to do the job. Similarly, to carry the entire midfield load he had not two players sufficiently dominating. In December 1965 in Madrid, England played without wingers and with Bobby Charlton, 'brilliantly inconsistent' as an outside-left, playing in midfield. England not only won 2-0 but played with industry and organization.

The absence of wingers changed the role of the full-backs; they had to attack down the flanks. Full-backs had overlapped before —occasional sorties down the wing by the more adventurous of the breed—but never had they so much space to move into. Ramsey

Above: Using a large wall at a free-kick can be a dubious tactic, for it leaves more attacking players unmarked.

Below: Jackie Charlton roars in to score against Portugal in 1969. Bringing up the big men from the defence is an effective move for set pieces.

wanted attack to stem from the midfield and full-backs, and the front three players had to run unselfishly to make space for the other players. Football had entered an age in which the all-purpose player replaced the specialist. Every defender had to possess the skills of an attacker, and no forward could spare himself defensive duties at some time during a game.

The 1966 World Cup had a distinct defensive bias, but Ramsey's functionalism won it. The Italians had committed themselves to even greater defensive efforts, using a 'catenaccio' system designed to stifle attacks by weight of numbers. Basically they used a fifth defender, a 'sweeper' who operated behind the back four. He was not responsible for a particular attacker, but had to pick off any threats that penetrated beyond the back four. Whereas England's four defenders marked particular zones or areas of the pitch, the Italian back four would each mark a particular attacker—a man-to-man system —certain in the knowledge that the sweeper

would tidy up when any attacker wriggled free. Ramsey's idea of adding a fourth midfield player to the system—now 4–4–2— failed to win the 1970 World Cup, but it was indicative of the defensive philosophy that prevailed, particularly when the stakes were at their highest.

Brazil won the competition with a form of 4–3–3 that emphasized the purpose of team tactics. It was designed to fit the capabilities of their players. Tactical understanding involves both planning and restricting. The planning is to make the most of each individual's abilities; the restricting takes into account the elements of chance and, of course, the skills of known opponents. From the Scots of the early 1870s to Billy McCracken, from the 1953 Hungarians to the 1970 Brazilians, and from Herbert Chapman to Sir Alf Ramsey, the men who have planned tactics with a combination of innovation and imagination are those who have combined these two principles to the best effect.

Equipment

One of football's great advantages is that it can be enjoyed without the proper equipment. Many of the finest footballers have learnt their skills with a tennis ball in the street. But when the game is played properly, with a marked-out pitch and a referee, equipment is as essential as all the other Laws. Out there in the middle, wearing his team strip and playing with a proper ball and proper goalposts, even the youngest player knows the game is for real.

For the player in any club, the moment he first dons the club's colours is a proud one, especially if that club is one with a long and successful history. Famous players will have worn those colours in the past, perhaps in the days when knickerbockers were the fashion in shorts, and shirts were made of heavy woollen material. Those days are long gone, and today finds the leading clubs wearing strips to suit the weather: light, short-sleeved shirts for the warmer days of the season, thicker, long-sleeved shirts for mid-winter. Shorts, too, are lightweight, and a lot briefer. Even goalkeepers, who of course wear a different coloured jersey, have moved with the fashions. Their crew-necked and collared sweaters are a considerable change from the days of heavy polo-necked jerseys.

Stockings, less subject to fashionable changes, are another essential. A well fitting pair of stockings provide a comfortable cushion for the feet, especially on the hard grounds encountered early in the season. They should be held up by tape, not tied too tight as to restrict the circulation. And inside the stockings fit the shin-guards. Modern shin-guards are extremely light, and there is no excuse for not wearing this extremely important piece of equipment. The shins are particularly vulnerable, and kicks can cause serious injuries.

The final item in the player's personal equipment is his boots, at one time heavy with high sides and hard toes, but now lightweight and cutaway in the so-called Continental style. There are some who do not think the modern boot gives enough protection around the ankle, and the increased number of ankle injuries may support this. But there is no definite proof, and few players would deny their preference for the light, 'glove-fitting' boot.

With bars virtually a thing of the past, studs are now the Laws' principal concern as regards equipment. A player with dangerous studs is a menace, and referees and linesmen should always make sure boots comply with the regulations. Studs must be made of leather, rubber, aluminium, plastic, or some similar material, and they must be round and solid, not less than half an inch in diameter. They must not project more than three-quarters of an inch. The base must not protrude more than a quarter of an inch from the sole, or, if the studs are the screw-in type, the metal seating must be embedded in the sole of the boot. Apart from this seating, no other form of metal plate, covered or not, is allowed.

For his own sake, too, a player should make sure his studs are in first-class condition, for uneven studs will affect his balance, especially on slippery grounds. Most professionals use more than one pair of boots: boots with short studs for hard grounds, boots with long studs for heavily grassed or wet grounds.

The ball also comes in for special attention in the Laws. It must be round, between 27 and 28 inches in circumference, and must weigh between 14 and 16 ounces at the start of the game. The pressure must be equal to atmospheric pressure (15 lb per sq. in. at sea level). The outer casing is almost invariably made of leather, which may be silicone treated to make the casing watertight and to provide the white, lemon, orange, or black and white colouring. Coloured balls, as opposed to the natural tan ones, have to be used under floodlighting.

So, kitted out and with a regulation ball, the player now needs a pitch to play on: not any old piece of ground but a properly marked pitch of approved size, complete with goals, nets, and corner-flags. The goal-posts and cross-bar can be made of wood, metal, or some other approved material and can be square, rectangular, round, half-round, or elliptical. But their width and depth must not exceed 5 inches. Should the cross-bar break during a match played under the rules of competition, the game must be stopped until it is repaired or replaced. If this cannot be done, the game must be abandoned.

Rope and other materials are not acceptable substitutes. The net, which can be made from hemp, jute, or nylon, is held up by supports coming down from the top of the uprights. Care must be taken to ensure that there is room for the goalkeeper to move about in his goal.

Finally, so that the pitch complies with the Laws, there must be four corner-posts, not less than 5 feet high, with a flag on top. These must not be moved by players taking corner-kicks. Though not compulsory, there can also be flag-posts at the halfway line, and if used they must be no less than a yard outside the touchline.

How fashions have changed from the 1930s to the 1970s—although Alex James did wear baggier shorts than most of his contemporaries.

Below: The lightweight boot of the modern footballer.
Bottom: Special shin-guards and Achilles tendon protectors.

Fitness Training

By the 1970s, football was being played at such a pace that physical fitness had become a prerequisite at all levels of the game. Every team had to concern itself with the problem of getting its players match fit, and no team could afford to carry players who could not last the pace.

Good health in a general sense is, of course, a basis for fitness, but the way the game is played dictates the specific physical capacities footballers must have. Because a match lasts for 90 minutes, stamina is very important. The goalkeeper apart, each player is on the move for almost all the playing time, and consequently he must be strong enough to stay the course.

At the same time, when any player is playing the ball or is immediately involved close to the ball, either by running to support a team-mate in possession, making a decoy run, chasing an opponent to make a tackle, or marking him closely, movements require speed and sharpness. Quickness off the mark and the ability to sprint over distances from 5 to 20 yards are a vital part of a good footballer's basic equipment.

Stamina training is often done before the start of a new season, to give the players a solid foundation on which to build their speed. Long-distance running, varying from simple lapping of the pitch to exhausting cross-country climbs over hilly grounds, will mould durability. For many years, lapping formed the core of the regular

Above: Some hurdling for Jackie Charlton during a training session.

Below left: Sand dunes are an ideal venue for pre-season stamina training. Below: Weights feature regularly in a footballer's training routines. They are rarely of the heavy variety, however.

professional training session. But once the season is under way, stamina can be maintained simply by playing matches, especially in a programme of two games a week.

Sharpness in the sprints, however, requires constant practice if a player is to maintain his speed. There are many routines for doing this, with players running either with a ball or without one, but most of them are based on the principle of the 'doggie' or 'shuttle run'. Marks are made at intervals from a starting line. The intervals can vary, depending on the distance the players are concentrating on, but usually they are from 5 to 20 yards apart and there are four or five of them. The players sprint to the first mark, turn and sprint back to the start, then sprint to the second mark and back to the start, then to the third, and so on. After a short rest, the exercise is repeated. Over the weeks precious seconds can be knocked off the time taken to complete the course, and naturally this sharpens the players for match days.

General body strength can be increased by weight-training and circuit-training—a series of exercises performed in the gymnasium—and both should be performed only under qualified supervision. But the real secrets of keeping fit for football are training hard and training often. Whatever talent he possesses, no player will serve his side well unless he regularly attends his club's keep-fit sessions, putting one hundred per cent effort and enthusiasm into what is a chore, but what makes the game itself so much more enjoyable.

Treatment of Injuries

Injuries are all too commonplace in football. A hard tackle or an accidental clash often leaves a player writhing on the ground, another patient for the healing hands of the trainer waiting on the sideline for the referee's permission to énter the field. To those on the terraces, the trainer is just the man with the sponge—the 'magic sponge' as it is sometimes called, for the ability of a squeeze of ice-cold water down the neck to work wonders. But this man is a specialist, able to tell in a moment how badly a player is injured. And in that moment he must decide whether to take him off or let him play on, with perhaps a spurt of the anaesthetic spray to kill the pain. The player may want to stay on, but the trainer knows from experience that aggravation of the injury might increase the recovery time.

There was a time when the player would have continued as long as he could limp. But that was before substitutes. And times, as well as attitudes, have changed since the days when the trainer was often little more than the man with the sponge. Now he is usually a physiotherapist and a fully qualified graduate of the FA's coaching and training scheme. And he has at his disposal treatment rooms and gymnasiums that would make physiotherapists at some hospitals quite jealous. Gone are the days when the treatment room was often just the dressing room, consisting of first-aid cabinet and a rubbing-table. The equipment at some famous clubs includes the latest infra-red and ultra-short-wave apparatus, and even portable X-ray machines to determine the severity of an injury.

The attitude to the treatment of injuries has changed, too. In the vast majority of cases, the theory that rest is the best cure for an injury finds little support in football's medical world. For one thing, clubs want a

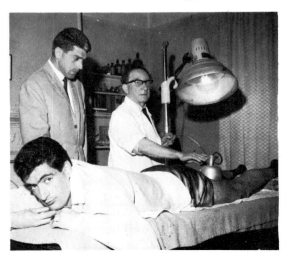

Above: Weights play an important role in bringing a player back to fitness after injury.

Left: A player undergoes heat treatment for a muscular injury.

Above: A quick burst of the anaesthetic spray to kill the pain and it's on with the game again.

player back in action as soon as possible. Getting him fit in the shortest possible time can make an enormous difference in today's highly competitive football, and perhaps save thousands of pounds on the transfer market. But there is another factor, the psychological factor. The fully fit player is mentally fit as well as physically. And it is the trainer's job to build the player's confidence and his mental attitude along with his body. Therefore the practice pitch plays as important a part in a player's treatment as the gymnasium. The player finds the road to recovery no holiday: he has to work much harder than if he was fully fit. But when the day comes that he takes his place in the team again, he and his team-mates know that both mind and body are attuned to produce 100 per cent effort—thanks to the man with the 'magic sponge'.

The Manager

It is not an easy life, the life of a soccer manager. Success can bring rewards, but failure too often ends in dismissal. And in football the difference between success and failure is slight. Fans have short memories. They have nothing but praise for the manager when their team wins promotion. But when it is relegated or sits perilously near the bottom of the table, they soon chant for his dismissal. The manager is the obvious scapegoat for the club's directors, too. To them the club is a business. And if the manager cannot show a profit on the league table, his position is in jeopardy.

The knowledge that his position is only as safe as his team's performance hangs over the head of every manager. But it is not something he can afford to worry about. His days are far too short. Managers live football for 24 hours a day, seven days a week, no matter what their division, what

their league. There are meetings with directors to be attended, coaching sessions and team talks to be participated in, letters to be answered, press interviews to be conducted, reports from scouts to be read. Teams have to be selected. Players have to be supported at Disciplinary Commission hearings. And when the players have gone home and the club closes down for the night, the manager could well drive some distance to watch a match involving forthcoming opponents or a player he is interested in. Some well-known managers have been known to go to bed with a pad and pencil at hand so they can write down any thoughts that come into their head while they are supposedly resting.

The majority of managers tend to have been players, some of them very successful. But a great playing career is by no means a passport to managerial success. Great players have been known to fail as managers. And Herbert Chapman, manager of Huddersfield and then Arsenal in the 1920s and 1930s, spent much of his playing career in Spurs' reserves. But he knew how to get the best out of his players, to adopt tactics that suited the talents of his players. That was his strength.

Times have changed since Chapman's day. Today, the manager is often indistinguishable from his players as he leads them in coaching sessions. The track-suited Sir Alf Ramsey provides a fine example, making a striking contrast to some of his predecessors, who could be seen at England training sessions in suit, collar, and tie. Ramsey, establishing a club atmosphere, found World Cup success in 1966. Yet within years he was being severely criticized. Managers at all levels of the game could easily sympathize with him.

Sir Alf Ramsey (left, above, and Don Revie (left, with Billy Bremner) epitomize the track-suited manager of modern football. In 1974 Revie superseded Ramsey as England team manager.

Above: Joe Mercer (left) and Malcolm Allison worked well together as manager and coach to take Manchester City to footballing heights. Other clubs, too, have profited from such manager-coach partnerships.

The Ground and Groundstaff

Old Trafford, Highbury, Molineux, Ibrox—British grounds as famous as the clubs that play there. Every home game sees them packed with fans, no matter what the weather, and no matter what the weather, the game almost always goes on. The fact that it does is a tribute to those members of the club who rarely get a mention: the groundstaff.

With the major clubs now playing more games in a season than ever before, the need for efficient repair and maintenance of a ground is of paramount importance. Many league clubs have a large groundstaff working all year round, and their job is not made any easier by the ever-decreasing off-season. During those few months between May and August, the ground has to be dressed with fertilizer and the bare patches either re-turfed or resown with a strong, quick-growing grass. The ground under the surface needs careful treatment as well, especially in the goal-areas and down the centre of the pitch. Constant wear in those parts causes packed layers of soil, called 'pans', to form, and unless they are broken up surface water will not drain properly. Proper drainage is an important consideration at every ground, and most pitches have an elaborate drainage system running under them.

After a match, the groundstaff's job often starts before the last fan has left the ground. Divots of turf have to be replaced, skid marks raked out, and the odd holes filled in. The pitch then has to be lightly rolled and spiked, the latter to assist aeration and drainage.

Probably the groundstaff's greatest enemies are frost and snow, for a referee is well within his rights to call off a match if he considers the pitch dangerous, and the club loses considerably. The use of braziers and the laying of straw are old-fashioned, but inexpensive, ways of combating frost and snow, but now other more expensive methods are being tried out. Arsenal, in the 1960s, experimented with a system using underground electric wires to heat the soil, but the Gunners' groundstaff found they could not spike the surface to drain the ground properly and flooding occurred. So they tried another plan: underground pipes through which hot air was blown.

Another aspect of the modern football ground requiring constant attention is the floodlighting. There are two main systems—the corner-tower system (with perhaps two additional centre towers) and the side-lighting system, which is less expensive to install and run but causes greater glare. The tower system gives off a much greater illumination without increasing the glare, and consequently it has been preferred by the majority of bigger clubs.

Floodlighting comes to Hampden Park in 1961. At the time of installation, the Glasgow stadium's extensive lighting system incorporated 240 spotlights at a cost of £60,000.

The Transfer System

Rumours of transfers, transfers at undisclosed fees, rush journeys by managers to register newly acquired players—all an integral part of the soccer scene. So too are the disputes between clubs and players over transfers and contract renewals. They all help to make the transfer system one of the most controversial aspects of the game.

Yet the system, as it is today, is better than the retain-and-transfer system operated by Football League clubs until 1963. Prior to that date, a club could keep a player until they wanted to transfer him. But in 1960, George Eastham refused to renew his contract with Newcastle United and, with assistance from the Professional Footballers' Association, he challenged the club's legal right to hold him. The Eastham Case was virtually a test case between the PFA and the League. It ended in 1963 with Mr Justice Wilberforce's ruling that the retain-and-transfer system was in restraint of the footballer's trade and was therefore unlawful.

This does not mean, however, that a player can change clubs as the mood takes him. He signs a contract for a certain period, and at the end of that period the club has the option of offering the player a new contract or releasing him. If they no longer want him, he is placed on the *open to transfer* list or is given a *free transfer*. But if the player does not want to sign a new contract, and the club are not prepared to release him, he is said to be 'in dispute' with the club. Either party can then appeal to the League Management Committee, and later to an independent tribunal if the League cannot settle the dispute. The player may appeal also if he considers his transfer fee is too high.

Unless a player is granted a free transfer, he cannot be approached by other clubs, whether he is transfer-listed or not. Approaches must always be to the player's club. In such a transfer, the player receives 5 per cent of his transfer fee (minimum £250). In the case of a free transfer, the player is entitled to at least £250 over the period of his new contract. But if a player requests a transfer, he loses his right to a share of the transfer fee. No player can be transferred against his will.

Once transferred, the player must be registered with the Football Association and the Football League before he can play for his new club. Players transferred after March 16 cannot play for their new club that season without special League permission. Nor can a player who has already played in a round of a cup competition play for his new club in a later round of that competition. He is said to be 'cup-tied'.

Opposite page: Jimmy Greaves featured in an Anglo-Italian transfer in 1961 when he went to AC Milan. But within months he was back in England, at a cost of £99,999 to Spurs.

Left: Alan Ball, who cost Arsenal £220,000 in 1972, a fee that soon became almost commonplace. Below: Dutch star Johan Cruyff in airborne action for Ajax against Juventus in the 1973 European Cup final—after which he went to Barcelona for a world record fee of £922,300.

Pay

With the abolition of the maximum wage in 1961, a new era began for the English professional footballer. Fulham and England international Johnny Haynes became England's first £100-a-week footballer, and others soon followed. Today, many First Division players earn that much; the Bobby Moores and the George Bests considerably more. On top of the basic wage, there are bonuses, advertising contracts, and numerous perks. But even England's best-paid footballer would have to go a long way to catch up on the highly rewarded stars of European and South American soccer, especially with Pelé, reputedly a dollar millionaire.

Prior to 1961, the English footballer's wages were controlled by the Football League. The maximum wage originated in 1901, to prevent clubs luring players with promises of better wages. Then the maximum was £4 a week during the season. It was increased to £5 in 1910 and £9 in 1920, but two years later it was reduced to £8 (£6 in the summer months). There it remained until 1947, when it was raised to £12 for players who had been five years with their club. From 1958, a player could earn £20 a week, and then in 1961, with the Professional Footballers' Association threatening strike action, the maximum wage was abolished.

Above: George Best, reputedly one of Britain's highest paid footballers. Below: Best's £30,000 house and expensive car are visible signs of the soccer star's affluence since the abolition of the maximum wage. In Best's case they also contributed to the pressures that precipitated his premature retirement from the game.

Scouting

In all the publicity surrounding the latest star on the football scene, one man may not be mentioned—the man who discovered him, the scout. More often than not, though, that is what he wants, for the more anonymous the scout is the better. It gives him the opportunity to go to all sorts of matches without too much attention being paid to him.

The practice of scouting is almost as old as organized soccer. But never has it been as intense as it is today. The major clubs run a network of scouts to recruit promising young players, and even the small clubs have one or two scouts looking around. Sometimes they are former players. They may even be just ardent fans. But they must not be coaches on the FA panel or registered referees.

Because of the intensity of the scouting network, few promising youngsters are not signed on associate forms long before they can leave school. Some, like Chelsea's Alan Hudson, become stars. Others never make the grade. Ray Kennedy may have been one of the latter. Rejected by Port Vale, he returned to his home near Newcastle. There he was spotted by Arsenal scout Don Emerson and sent to London for a trial. Three seasons later, and just 19, he was helping the Gunners win the 'double', and Arsenal's efficient scouting system had possibly saved them thousands of pounds on the transfer market.

Right: Liverpool manager Bill Shankly and the player his efficient scouting system found for him—the explosive Kevin Keegan (7). Keegan was playing for Fourth Division Scunthorpe when a Shankly scout spotted him, and he cost Liverpool a mere £35,000 in 1971. By 1972 he had been capped for England.

Five-a-side Soccer

As training exercise or as a game in its own right, five-a-side soccer is usually played indoors, though originally it was an outdoor game. Its non-stop formula brings out the best in its exponents, encouraging quick running, precise passing, and individual ball skills.

As part of a team's training, five-a-side helps players develop the control they require on the bigger pitch. Because the ball is not allowed to go above shoulder height and because the goals are reduced in size, passing and shooting should ideally be along the ground. And because the game is played on a small pitch, surrounded by walls, the passing must be accurate or possession can easily be lost.

Right: Sir Stanley Matthews playing in a five-a-side match for football's older generation. Below: An encounter between Queen's Park Rangers and Southampton. Only the goalkeeper is allowed in the semi-circular goal area.

Basically, the rules are similar to those of the parent game, but there is no offside and there are no goal-kicks, throw-ins, or corners. At each goal is a semi-circular goal area in which only the goalkeeper is allowed. If the ball goes over the side walls, play recommences with a bounce-up; if it goes over the back walls, the goalkeeper rolls the ball back into play. Players are allowed to use the walls to beat an opponent with a 'wall pass' or to play the ball through to a team-mate. Games usually last seven minutes each way.

Goal Average

Goal average is a method used to determine league placings between teams with the same number of points. It is used in some national leagues, including the Football League. Other methods employed by some leagues, such as the Scottish League, include goal difference (goals 'for' minus goals 'against') and most wins. Other leagues use a play-off or take the results of the matches between the teams concerned.

To work out a team's goal average, you divide the number of goals scored by the number conceded. For example, a team that scores 70 goals against 40 has a goal average of 1·75. This figure, however, has no real meaning. It is just a convenient 'tiebreaker', which has been used by the Football League since its inception in 1888. It is particularly useless in small leagues, and is no longer used in World Cup final groups.

It is not difficult to demonstrate the unfairness of goal average. Imagine the top two teams on the last day of the season with the same number of points and exactly the same goal record, 80–20. One side wins 7–1, the other 3–0. The side winning 3–0 finishes with the best goal average. However, had their original goal records been 60–20, the side winning 7–1 would have finished top.

The first time the Football League championship was decided on goal average was 1923–24, when Huddersfield (60–33) beat Cardiff City (61–34) by 0·024. They had the same goal difference (27) but Huddersfield scored *fewer* goals. At the other end of the table, the second relegated team was also determined on goal average. Nottingham Forest (42–64) stayed up at the expense of Chelsea (31–53). Again the goal difference was the same (22), but this time the lucky club scored *more* goals. The Football League should have learnt its lesson.

Glossary of Terms

Right: Sunderland's Charlie Hurley executes a well judged sliding tackle.

Banana kick (shot) Term used for a ball swerved in flight. The kicker 'bends' the ball by using the inside or outside of his foot.

Blind side The side of one or more players away from the ball or the play.

Booking See *Caution*.

Catenaccio A tactical system, basically defensive, with a sweeper operating behind four backs, three midfield players, and two strikers.

Caution A formal warning by the referee to a player for persistent infringement of the Laws, dissension by word or action, ungentlemanly conduct, or leaving or rejoining the game without the referee's permission. The player is said to be 'booked' because the Referee enters the caution in his notebook.

Centre A pass from near the touchline into the goalmouth.

Centre-back(s) The player(s) positioned between the left and right full-backs.

Chip A short, stabbed kick, usually over the top of the defence.

Corner-kick Method of restarting play when the ball crosses the goal-line, having last touched a player of the defending side. It is taken from the quarter-circle at the applicable corner, and defenders must be 10 yards from the ball. The kicker can score direct from a corner.

Cross See *Centre*.

Dribbling The art of running with the ball at the feet, particularly as a means of beating opponents.

Dropped ball Method of restarting play after stoppage not caused by a contravention of the Laws. The referee drops the ball between two opposing players who may play it only after it has touched the ground.

Foul An offence against an opposing player.

Goal-kick Method of restarting play when the ball crosses the goal-line, having last touched a player of the attacking side. The kick must leave the penalty area.

Hand-ball An infringement when a player, apart from the goalkeeper, intentionally touches the ball with his hand or arm.

Jockeying When a defender positions himself between the ball-carrier and the goal, often forcing him wide, to make it difficult for him to make good use of the ball.

Kick-off Method of starting play at the beginning of each half and of restarting after a goal.

Linkman See *Midfield player*.

Marking Covering a player so that his teammates cannot pass to him effectively. There are two main methods of marking: *man-to-man*, in which a defender concentrates on a particular opponent, and *zonal*, in which a defender covers the player or players in a certain section of the field.

Midfield player The player who links the defence with the attack. Basically he operates in the centre of the field, but should move up or back as play dictates.

Obstruction When a player, not playing the ball himself, puts himself between an opponent and the ball to block that opponent.

Offside Basically a player is offside if he is in front of the ball and there are fewer than two defenders between him and the goal-line at the moment that the ball *is played to him* (not when he receives the ball). A player cannot be offside from a goal-kick, corner-kick, throw-in, or dropped ball, or if he is in his own half, or if the ball was last touched or played by an opponent. He may be in an offside position, but not be offside, provided that he does not interfere with play or gain any advantage for his side.

Over the top/ball A term used when a player, going in to make a tackle, kicks over the top of the ball and fouls an opponent.

Overlapping When a player goes up outside the ball-carrier, often the winger, to receive the ball, or when he takes over the role of the winger.

Penalty-kick Offences by the defending side in the penalty-area incur a penalty-kick if they are of the type punishable by a direct free-kick.

Running off the ball Players not in possession moving into a good position to receive the ball, or to divert the attentions of defenders from other players.

Screening Keeping the ball away from an opponent by shielding it while playing it.

Selling a dummy Indicating to move or pass one way and then going another way.

Sending-off The referee can send off a player who is guilty of violent conduct or serious foul play, who uses foul or abusive language, or who continues to abuse the Laws after being cautioned.

Set-piece Any dead-ball situation at which practised moves can be attempted.

Shoulder-charge A lawful charge, shoulder to shoulder, on an opponent. The ball must be within playing distance.

Sliding tackle When the tackler slides in to rob his opponent of the ball.

Square ball/pass A cross-field pass.

Stopper Originally the centre-half in the third-back game. Now more usually one of two centre-backs.

Striker A player who operates mostly upfield to score goals.

Substitute A player who stands by to replace a team-mate because of injury or for tactical reasons. In English and Scottish competitions, one substitute is permitted; in international matches and European competitions two substitutes can be used. The substitute(s) must be named before the match.

Sweeper The player behind the defensive four in a *catenaccio* line-up.

Tackle from behind A tackle made from behind the ball-carrier. A fair tackle from behind is rarely possible because the tackler usually kicks his opponent before playing the ball.

Tactical foul Any foul committed so that the opposing side loses its advantage. Handling a through ball and tripping are common examples.

Target man Usually a striker who collects the clearances from defence and holds the ball until support arrives.

Third-back game The tactical system in which the centre-half moved back from midfield to play as a centre-back. Resulted from the change in the offside law in 1925.

Through ball A pass through or over a defence for a team-mate to run on to.

Throw-in Method of restarting play when the ball crosses the touch-line.

Trapping The art of controlling the ball with foot, chest, stomach, thigh, and sometimes head before making use of it.

Ungentlemanly conduct Conduct by players that is considered against the spirit of the game; punishable by an indirect free-kick and a caution.

W formation The formation of the forwards in the third-back game. The inside forwards moved back to fill the area left vacant by the centre-half, leaving the wingers and centre-forward ahead of them, and so forming a W.

Wall The line-up of defending players between the ball and the goal at a free-kick. The wall must be at least 10 yards from the ball.

Wall pass A pass immediately deflected on by the receiver for the original passer to run on to. Sometimes referred to as a 'quick one-two'.

Work rate Term used to describe a player's participation in a game; i.e. his running off the ball, chasing, tackling, passing, etc.

Facts and Figures

International Who's Who

Ademir, Marques (Brazil), was the leading goalscorer in the 1950 World Cup, four of his seven goals coming in the final pool match against Sweden. A slim centre-forward blessed with speed, skill, and intelligence, he formed a brilliant inside trio with Zizinho and Jair. His clubs were Fluminense and Vasco da Gama, but a series of injuries after the World Cup shortened his career.

Albert, Florian (Hungary), European Footballer of the Year in 1967, won his first international cap in 1958 while still only 17. The ability to shoot well with either foot, plus his positional and tactical skills, brought this exciting, but temperamental, centre-forward many goals. He was a member of the Ferencvaros side the won the Fairs Cup in 1964–65.

Allchurch, Ivor (Wales), the 'golden boy' of Welsh soccer, won a record 68 caps and was awarded the MBE for his services to football. This artistic inside-forward's career spanned 19 seasons and embraced stays at Swansea, Newcastle, Cardiff, and then Swansea again. He played an important part in Wales' reaching the quarter-finals of the 1958 World Cup.

Ivor Allchurch (right)

Allison, Malcolm, became manager of Manchester City in 1971, having been Joe Mercer's lieutenant since 1965. One of the best coaches in soccer, this explosive Londoner, whose playing days were spent at West Ham, is recognized as the driving force that swept Manchester City to domestic and European success. He took over at Crystal Palace in 1973 but failed to halt their slide from Division I to Division III.

Altafini, José (Brazil and Italy), nicknamed 'Mazzola' because of his resemblance to that great Italian forward, moved to AC Milan after being replaced in the 1958 Brazilian side by Vavá. In Italy, the blond, strongly built centre-forward, excellent in the air, enjoyed great success. He played for Italy in the 1962 World Cup and scored both Milan's goals in the 1963 European Cup final.

Amancio, Amaro (Spain), displayed brilliance and opportunism for Real Madrid and Spain in the 1960s, either at inside- or outside-right. A star of Spain's success in the 1964 European Nations Cup, he also played a key role in Real's 1964 and 1966 European Cup campaigns, scoring the equalizer against Partizan Belgrade in the 1966 final.

Anastasi, Pietro (Italy), has the dubious privilege of being the world's most expensive footballer. Juventus paid Varese an estimated £440,000 for this young striker in 1968—and he had not yet played for Italy. Soon after, however, he became the first Sicilian to be capped, scoring Italy's second goal in the replayed final of the 1968 European Football Championship.

Andrade, Rodriguez (Uruguay), was left-half in the Uruguayan side that won the 1950 World Cup, following in the footsteps of his uncle, José, who helped Uruguay to victory in 1930. This fine coloured player, from the Penarol club, also featured prominently in the 1954 World Cup as an old-fashioned attacking centre-half.

Armfield, Jimmy (England), first played for Blackpool in 1954 and went on to captain club and country in a career that ran until 1970–71. A stylish right-back, he was at his peak in the 1962 World Cup. He played 43 times for England and made a record 573 appearances for Blackpool.

Babington, Carlos (Argentina), fair-haired midfield star in the 1974 World Cup, could have been a Stoke City player in 1972, but despite having an English father he could not get a work permit. Typical of his creative flair was the delicate chip into the path of Huracán clubmate Rene Houseman that enabled the young left-winger to volley his tremendous goal against Italy.

Ball, Alan (England), who played such an influential role in England's World Cup triumph of 1966, became Britain's most expensive player in 1972 when Arsenal paid Everton a reputed £220,000. Everton had purchased him from Blackpool after the World Cup, and at Goodison this tireless little runner developed into an astute, constructive midfield player, guiding the club to League and Cup successes.

Bambrick, Joe (Ireland), gained a place in the record books with his double hat-trick against Wales in Belfast in 1930. Two years later, on Christmas Eve, the Irish centre-forward moved from Linfield to Chelsea and in 1939 was transferred to Walsall.

Banks, Gordon (England), rightly won acclaim as the world's premier goalkeeper following the 1966 World Cup, and consolidated his position in the 1970 tournament. Strongly built and particularly courageous, he inspires confidence in team-mates and demoralizes opponents with his brilliance.

Banks began with Chesterfield in 1958–59, but the next season saw him at Leicester, and in 1963 he won his first cap against Brazil at Wembley. He went to Stoke for £52,500 in 1967. Elected Footballer of the Year in 1972, he later sustained a serious eye injury in a car crash.

Gordon Banks

Barnes, Walley (Wales), a full-back of intelligence and versatility, played a leading part in the Arsenal resurgence after World War II, as well as captaining his country. Arsenal made him a left-back in 1943 and with Laurie Scott he formed a formidable back line to a powerful defence, winning a Championship medal in 1948 and a Cup winners medal in 1950.

Bassett, Billy (England), was only 5 ft 5½ in tall, but his speed and ball control made him the outstanding outside-right of the 19th century. He played in three Cup finals with West Bromwich between 1886 and 1895 and made 16 England appearances. He later became chairman of West Bromwich.

Bastin, Cliff (England), had won every honour in English soccer by the time he was 21. Arsenal took him from Exeter as a 17-year-old and put him on the left wing, where he struck up a fine understanding with Alex James. A remarkable left-foot shot and his penchant for dashing into scoring positions brought 157 League goals for Arsenal, 33 of them in 1932–33.

Baxter, Jim (Scotland), was one of the best attacking midfield players of the early 1960s. But a broken leg in 1964 virtually ended a brilliant career for Rangers and Scotland and began a period of high fees and lethargy in England. Both Sunderland and Nottingham Forest paid £100,000 for him, yet Forest released him for nothing after 48 games. He returned to Rangers, but the genius was gone.

Franz Beckenbauer

Beckenbauer, Franz (West Germany), Bayern Munich's poised and elegant half-back, crowned a wonderful 1973–74 season by leading his country to victory in the World Cup at Munich, playing his now customary free role at the back. He had already led his club to League and European Cup triumphs that season. He was prominent in the 1966 and 1970 World Cups, when Germany were 2nd and 3rd, won a European Cup-Winners Cup medal in 1967, and was European Footballer of the Year in 1972 after Germany's European Championship success.

Bell, Colin (England), finally managed in 1974 to reproduce consistently for England the form that had contributed so much to Manchester City's success. An ideal midfield player with the ability to score and make goals, he revels in hard work.

Bene, Ferenc (Hungary), was 18 when he won his first cap, at outside-right. But it was as a centre-forward in the 1964 Olympics that the Ujpest star displayed all his glorious gifts—control, acceleration, shooting power, and intelligent running off the ball. He scored a memorable solo goal against Czechoslovakia in the Olympic final and another against Brazil in the 1966 World Cup.

Best, George (Northern Ireland), brought to British football a magical quality that made

George Best

Ron Burgess

him the idol of thousands. But the pressures of fame are demanding, and eventually culminated in 1972 in his premature retirement. At his peak he can be unplayable, his balance and ball control taking him swerving through packed defences. His courage and coolness in front of goal have resulted in numerous goals, some quite exceptional. He was European and English Footballer of the Year in 1968, when he played a vital part in Manchester United's European success.

Bingham, Billy (Northern Ireland), an ebullient right-winger, won 56 caps for Northern Ireland, equalling Danny Blanchflower's record. He starred in the Luton side that went to Wembley in the 1959 FA Cup, having already played for Glentoran and Sunderland, and won a Championship medal with Everton in 1962–63. After a short spell with Port Vale, he ventured into management, taking over the Northern Ireland side in 1968.

Blanchflower, Danny (Northern Ireland), captained Spurs to the 'double' in 1961, the FA Cup in 1962, and the Cup-Winners Cup in 1963. An intelligent and skilful right-half, he was the ideal general of a fluent, talented side, his long, accurate passes setting his forwards into action time and again. He moved to Barnsley from Glentoran in 1948–49 and was at Aston Villa from 1951 to 1954, when he went to Tottenham. England's Footballer of the Year in 1958 and again in 1961, he won a record 56 international caps.

Blenkinsop, Ernie (England), was a stylish left-back who relied on a highly developed positional sense rather than physical strength. He won two Championship medals with Sheffield Wednesday in 1928–29 and 1929–30 before going to Liverpool in 1934. He began his career with Hull City and ended it at Cardiff.

Bloomer, Steve (England), slight and pale-faced, did not look like a footballer. But between 1892 and 1914 he scored 352 League goals for Derby County and Middlesbrough. His 28 goals in 23 internationals was an England record lasting 50 years. He could pass with pin-point accuracy, and his sudden shots were hit with exceptional power.

Boniperti, Giampiero (Italy), remembered in England for his two goals against England for FIFA XI in 1953, began with Juventus as a centre-forward but later became a constructive inside-right, linking well with John Charles in the late 1950s.

Bowen, Dave (Wales), Arsenal's fine left-half and captain of the 1950s, became manager of his previous club, Northampton Town, taking them from the Fourth Division to the First in five seasons, 1960–61 to 1964–65. He was appointed manager of Wales in 1964.

Bozsik, Josef (Hungary), the attacking wing-half of the magnificent Hungarians who won the 1952 Olympic title and twice annihilated England, without peer in his position. With Honved, like most of the Magyar magicians, he was an intelligent distributor who could score goals as well as create them. He was sent off during the 'Battle of Berne' in the 1954 World Cup, and in the 1958 tournament appeared as an inside- or centre-forward. He made his 100th appearance for Hungary in 1962.

Breitner, Paul (West Germany), wide-ranging left-back of West Germany's World Cup winning side in 1974, scored two all-important goals for them on the way to the final—with long-range right-foot shots against Chile and Yugoslavia—and then coolly slotted home the equalizer from the penalty spot against Holland. He also featured in Germany's European Championship win in 1972 and helped his club Bayern Munich to their European Cup success of 1974, before going to Real Madrid.

Billy Bremner

Bremner, Billy (Scotland), put his volatile temperament behind him to put Leeds United among the greats. With the dynamic little redhead organizing the defence, firing the attacks, Leeds consistently dominated the late 1960s and early 1970s—though often missing the prizes. An outside-right who eventually became a right-half, he formed a midfield pairing with Johnny Giles that was the envy of most clubs. First capped by Scotland in 1965, he was later given the captaincy. England's Footballer of the Year in 1970, he has won League, FA Cup, League Cup, and Fairs Cup medals.

Britton, Cliff (England), enjoyed a distinguished career as both player and manager. An elegant, constructive right-half, he won a Cup winners medal with Everton in 1933. The

next year he won his first England cap. As manager of Burnley, he took them to Division I and Wembley in 1947.

Brook, Eric (England), possessed one of the fiercest shots in football between the wars. Though an outside-left, he often popped up in the middle to score match-winning goals. He moved from Barnsley to Manchester City in 1929 and played in the 1933 and 1934 Cup finals.

Buchan, Charlie (England), tall, willowy, and an exceptional header of the ball, began with Arsenal as an amateur and returned to them from Sunderland in 1925 for £2,000 plus £100 a goal in his first season. He scored 21. A mere five England caps belied the fact that he was the outstanding inside-forward of his day, but the selectors may have felt that his clever, original play was too difficult for others to understand. At Highbury, he helped found the 'third-back' game and led Arsenal in the 1927 FA Cup final.

Frank Buckley

Buckley, Frank (England), will be remembered most for his discovery, development, and profitable transfer of young talent while manager of Wolves. A former centre-half with Derby County, he built up a fine side that just missed the League title in 1938 and 1939 and lost the 1939 FA Cup final.

Burgess, Ronnie (Wales), learnt his football on the slag-heaps of South Wales and worked as a miner before joining Tottenham, where he became a dynamic, aggressive half-back. An inspiring captain of club and country, he led Spurs to the top of Division II in 1949–50 and Division I the very next season. He later managed Swansea and Watford.

Burgnich, Tarcisio (Italy), a veteran of the great Inter-Milan of the mid-1960s, ideally complemented Giacinto Facchetti at the back of Inter and Italian sides. Later in his career, he moved from right-back to become an equally effective, and uncompromising, sweeper. A member of Italy's Olympic team when with Juventus, he played in the 1966, 1970, and 1974 World Cups.

Busby, Sir Matt (Scotland), won a permanent place in soccer history for his rebuilding of Manchester United after World War II, when they did not even have a home ground, and again after the famous 'Busby Babes' had perished at Munich. As a player, he was a skilful half-back with Manchester City, playing in the 1933 and 1934 Cup finals, and Liverpool. He captained Scotland during the war. But he will be best remembered for his days at Old Trafford. He believed in letting players make full use of their natural talents, and his formidable scouting system ensured he found the best. The climax of his career was United's European Cup victory in 1968.

Byshovets, Anatoli (USSR), nominally a winger but more accurately a striker, came to the fore with Kiev Dynamo in 1967. Courageous, strong, and well balanced, he scored four of Russia's six goals in the 1970 World Cup.

Byrne, Roger (England), left-back and captain of the 'Busby Babes', died in the Munich disaster at the height of his career. A regular member of the England team, he was a scientific player with a tactical foresight that enabled him to dictate the course of play.

Caldow, Eric (Scotland), a fast left-back, strong in the tackle and positionally sound, gained numerous honours in the 1950s and 1960s as captain of Scotland and Rangers. A triple fracture of the left leg in the 1963 England match ended his international career.

Camsell, George (England), was unlucky to be a contemporary of Dixie Dean's, for his international appearances were thus limited. Strongly built, he was hard to shake off the ball and was a prolific scorer. In 1926–27 he scored a League-record 59 goals (Dean got 60 the next season), helping Middlesbrough run away with the Second Division title.

Carbajal, Antonio (Mexico), set a record by playing in five successive World Cup finals— the first in 1950, the last in 1966. A courageous, acrobatic goalkeeper, he also played in the 1948 Olympics.

Carey, Johnny (Republic of Ireland), though usually at right-back in the post-war Manchester United side, played in every position but outside-right for the club and in seven positions for Ireland. He captained United to victory in the 1948 Cup final, instructing his team to 'keep playing football' when they were a goal down. The previous year he had led the Rest of Europe against Great Britain. He was Footballer of the Year in 1949, and later turned successfully to management.

Carlos Alberto (Brazil) captained the Brazilians to World Cup victory in 1970. An adventurous right-back, he is nonetheless cool under pressure and commanding. It was fitting he should score Brazil's fourth goal of the final, accepting a perfect pass from Santos team-mate Pelé.

Raich Carter

Carter, Raich (England), was the complete inside-forward, constructive, a good reader of the game, and able to strike or scheme for goals. He captained Sunderland when they won the Cup in 1937, and in 1946 won another winners medal with Derby County, where he formed a devastating partnership with Peter Doherty. Prematurely silver-haired, he inspired Hull City to the Third Division (North) title in 1948–49.

Chapman, Herbert, soccer's first major innovator, was the guiding force behind the great Huddersfield side of the 1920s and the Arsenal of the 1930s. At Huddersfield he turned an ordinary side into League champions, and at Highbury he created a side rich with talent. With Charlie Buchan he devised the

John Charles

'third-back game', and he converted Alex James into the player to make his W-formation tick. If somewhat negative, his thinking was also highly functional—as his teams proved.

Charles, John (Wales), physically strong, skilful and dominant in the air, was a world-class player at both centre-half and centre-forward. In 1950, and just 18, he became the youngest Welsh international, and in 1958 he helped Wales reach the World Cup quarter-finals.

Leeds converted Charles into a centre-forward, and 42 League goals in 1953–54 and 38 in 1956–57 proved his ability. But Leeds could not hold him, and later in 1957 he went to Juventus for an unprecedented £65,000 fee. He won three league and two cup medals in Italy before returning to Leeds in 1962. But several months later he was back in Italy, with Roma. Sadly, his greatness had passed, and the next three seasons saw him in Wales, with Cardiff City, before becoming player-manager of non-League Hereford.

Charlton, Bobby (England), survived the Munich disaster to become the most-capped and most-loved footballer in English soccer. Few honours eluded him. He was European and English Footballer of the Year in 1966 and won World Cup, European Cup, Football League, and FA Cup medals. His 106 caps and 49 goals were both England records.

Manchester United took him as a youngster, and even then the powerful left-foot shot, the defence-splitting passes, the astute little flicks, and the ability to beat his man were apparent. United employed him as an inside-forward, but Alf Ramsey saw him as England's deep-lying centre-forward for the 1966 World Cup. His 106th cap came against West Germany in the 1970 World Cup.

Charlton, Jack (England), may well have suffered from younger brother Bobby's fame. That he became a first-class centre-half with England and Leeds is proof of both his skills and determination. Honours came late for him, but from 1966 there were winners medals in the World Cup, Fairs Cup, League Championship, FA Cup, and League Cup. He was England's Footballer of the Year in 1967, and in 1972 he played, and scored in, his 600th League game for Leeds.

Chivers, Martin (England), recovered from a serious knee injury that kept him out of the 1968–69 season to lead the Spurs and England attacks. Big and strong, with a touch belying his size, he has, however, been unable to reproduce his best form consistently. Spurs bought him from Southampton in 1967–68 for a reputed £80,000 plus a player valued at £45,000, then a record fee.

Martin Chivers

Clodoaldo (Brazil), midfield pivot with Santos, proved one of the finds of the 1970 World Cup. Just 20, he provided strength in the Brazilian midfield with his non-stop running and creative passing. His shot from Tostãos' return pass after a 30-yard run from midfield put Brazil level in the semi-final against Uruguay.

Clough, Brian (England), a high-scoring centre-forward with Middlesbrough and Sunderland in the 1950s and early 1960s, emerged from the 1960s as England's most controversial and outspoken manager. But he was undeniably successful, taking Derby County to Division I in 1969 and to the League Championship in 1972. He left Derby in October 1973, took his right-hand man Peter Taylor with him to Third Division Brighton, and in July 1974 landed the vacant Leeds managership, but was sensationally sacked six weeks later.

Cohen, George (England), and Ray Wilson, England's 1966 World Cup full-backs, are considered by many as the best pairing England have ever fielded. Cohen, the right-back, was strong in the tackle, quick in the recovery, and always prepared to overlap and provide telling crosses. His early retirement with a knee injury was a loss neither England nor Fulham could fill.

Bobby Charlton   Jack Charlton

Bobby Collins

Collins, Bobby (Scotland), Footballer of the Year in 1965, captained Leeds back to Division I in 1964. Tough and tireless in the midfield, he had won League and Cup honours with Celtic in the early 1950s before going to Everton and then Leeds. A badly fractured leg in 1965 should have ended his career, yet he recovered to lead Bury to Division II in 1968.

Coluna, Mario (Portugal), won a record 73 caps for his country between 1954 and 1966. Mozambique born, he started out as a centre-forward, but it was from the midfield that he drove Benfica to three successive European Cup finals in the early 1960s, and another in 1968. His left-foot volley scored the decisive goal in the 1961 final. Under his captaincy, Portugal reached the quarter-finals of the 1966 World Cup.

Cooper, Terry (England), shows in his willingness and ability to overlap and beat his man that he began as a winger. His goal won the League Cup for Leeds in 1968. But his attacking skills should not hide the fact that he rates among the foremost left-backs of modern football. First capped in 1969, he appeared in England's four matches in the 1970 World Cup.

Cooper, Tom (England), enjoyed a long career between the wars with Port Vale, Derby County, and Liverpool. A right-back, he was renowned for his excellent positional sense, sure tackling, and calm clearances under pressure.

Copping, Wilf (England), a strong, aggressive, and at times ruthless left-half, gained a place in England's football history with his memorable display in the 'Battle of Highbury'. His first club was Leeds, but it was with Arsenal that he won League Championship medals in 1935 and 1938 and a Cup winners medal in 1936. He was England's trainer when they beat Portugal 10-0 in 1947.

Corso, Mario (Italy), was transformed into a player of international class when Helenio Herrera made him a deep-lying tactical winger. His immaculate distribution and his mid-field linking with Suarez were essential to the Inter-Milan machine that won the European Cup and World Club Championship in 1964 and 1965. But a violent temper and uncontrollable moods did not enhance his international career.

Costa Pereira, Alberto da (Portugal), kept goal for Benfica in their first four European Cup finals of the 1960s. A late developer who won most of his caps in his 30s, he was a safe, reassuring player who scorned the spectacular acrobatics of some other Latin goalkeepers. Portugal could have done with him for the 1966 World Cup.

Cowan, Jimmy (Scotland), turned in such a brilliant display for Scotland at Wembley in 1949 that the game is remembered as 'Cowan's match'. Scotland, thanks to the Morton 'keeper, won 3-1 to take the Home International Championship. His practice of scraping a line from the penalty spot to aid his judgement of crosses was eventually banned when others copied him.

Cox, Sammy (Scotland), left Glasgow Rangers in 1955 with four Championship medals, three Scottish Cup winners medals, and a winners and losers medal from the Scottish League Cup. At one time with Queen's Park, he was slightly built but nevertheless strong in the tackle and courageous. A fine attacking half-back, he later moved to left-back for club and country.

Crerand, Pat (Scotland), formed with Bobby Charlton and Nobby Stiles the midfield trio that drove Manchester United to victory in the European Cup. He had gone to Old Trafford from Celtic in 1963. A thoughtful player with a firm belief in attacking, constructive football, he initiated numerous attacks with long, shrewd passes.

Cresswell, Warney (England), used a wonderful positional sense to seemingly stroll through a game because he anticipated the flow of play so well. Composed and elegant, he had few peers as a full-back, though England capped him only 10 times between 1921 and 1930, during which time he played for South Shields. He was Everton's left-back in the 1933 Cup final.

Crompton, Bob (England), Blackburn's captain and right-back when they won the League in 1912 and 1914, won an official 41 caps at a time when England rarely played foreign competition. Though solidly built, he was not typical of the bruising defender of the time and was even criticized for not using his weight enough.

Johan Cruyff

Cruyff, Johan (Netherlands), became the world's most expensive footballer in 1973 when he went from Ajax to Barcelona for £922,300. And he repaid the Spanish club immediately by inspiring them to their first League title for 14 years. The mainspring of Ajax's triple success in the European Cup from 1971 to 1973, he possesses all the qualities essential for a striker in an era of massed defences. But Cruyff is more than a mere striker. In the manner of Di Stefano, he is an orchestrator, setting up attacks and finishing them with deadly accuracy. He captained the exciting Dutch side that reached the final of the 1974 World Cup.

Cubillas, Teofilo (Peru), though 20, performed with the maturity and finesse of older men in the 1970 World Cup. His five goals in four matches made him the tournament's third-highest scorer, but he will be remembered for his ball-playing skills and intelligent distribution as much as for his goals.

Ron Davies

Cullis, Stan (England), led the talented Wolves of the late 1930s and in 1939 became, at 22, England's youngest captain. He was principally a third-back stopper. As an authoritarian manager, he devised the long pass to hard-running wingers that Wolves used so effectively in the 1950s. Wolves surprisingly dismissed him in 1964 and he later went to Birmingham City.

Czibor, Zoltan (Hungary), played on the left-wing for those magnificent Hungarians of the early 1950s. He had outstanding ball control and could go past most full-backs before either crossing or loosing a shot at goal. On tour with Honved at the time of the 1956 Hungarian uprising, he decided not to return home and joined Barcelona. He scored twice in the second leg of their 1960 Fairs Cup final.

Davies, Ron (Wales), strong and formidable in the air, headed the First Division goal-scorers in 1966–67 and 1967–68, many of his goals coming from powerfully placed headers. Chester, Luton Town, and Norwich City all benefited from the big centre-forward's scoring talents before Southampton secured him in 1966. In 1969 he hit four against Manchester United. He went to Portsmouth in 1973.

Dean, Dixie (England), put himself in the record books, perhaps for all time, when he scored 60 goals for Everton when they won the 1927–28 First Division Championship. His tally for his matches that season was an astonishing 82.

Bill Dean, as he preferred to be known, was powerfully built and his heading was superb. He specialized in coming in to meet crosses from the wing. But he was by no means just a goal-scoring centre-forward, and he made many openings for team-mates with his precise deflections. With Dean leading their attack, Everton won the League Championship twice and the FA Cup once. He scored a record 379 goals in the Football League in a career that began with Tranmere Rovers in 1923–24 and ended with Notts County in 1938–39. Capped 16 times, he scored 18 goals for England.

Delaney, Jimmy (Scotland), a dashing and fearless outside-right, was suspected of being brittle-boned because of his numerous injuries. He was a member of the fine Celtic side of the 1930s and after the war was an inspired purchase by Matt Busby as he rebuilt Manchester

United. He had a unique collection of winners medals—Scottish Cup, FA Cup, and Irish Cup (with Derry City).

Deyna, Kazimierz (Poland), scored both his country's goals when Poland beat Hungary 2–1 in the final of the 1972 Olympics. A cultured midfield player, with a powerful, accurate shot, he captained Poland to third place in the 1974 World Cup, in which they scored most goals and played some of the most exciting football. Deyna himself scored three.

Dickinson, Jimmy (England), remained loyal to Portsmouth throughout his career, making a Football League-record 764 appearances between 1946 and 1965. A sturdily built, reliable wing-half, he gained League Championship medals in 1948–49 and 1949–50, and among his 48 internationals were appearances in two World Cups.

Didi (Brazil), of Fluminense and Botafogo, was the midfield key to Brazil's World Cup victories in 1958 and 1962. He had also played in the 1954 tournament. He was a skilful distributor, and when he lost some of his speed he compensated with thoughtful positioning. Altogether he played 72 times for Brazil, scoring 24 goals. As a manager committed to attacking football, he took Peru to the quarter-finals of the 1970 World Cup.

Dimmock, Jimmy (England), filled the left-wing berth in Charlie Buchan's 'best ever team for modern times', yet England picked him only three times. Perhaps he was too much of an individualist. Certainly he was clever to the point of being cheeky, but he was fast, penetrative, and a good finisher. He made 400 League appearances for Spurs and scored a great individual goal to win them the 1921 FA Cup.

Di Stefano, Alfredo (Argentina and Spain), voted European Footballer of the Year in 1957 and again in 1959, will always be a contender for the title of the most complete centre-forward of all time. Tall and well built, he possessed excellent control and acceleration, passed astutely—often seemingly intuitively—was a fine header, and finished with power and accuracy. To these qualities he added exceptional stamina that allowed him to dictate play from any point of the field when well into his 30s.

He first played for River Plate in 1944, and won 7 caps for his native Argentina before joining the rebel Colombian League. In 1953 he went to Spain, for whom he played 31 times. But it was for Real Madrid he performed his magic, scoring more than 500 goals for them, a record 49 in his 58 European Cup matches.

Leaving Real in 1964 he played for Español, before turning to management—with almost immediate success. He was Argentina's Manager of the Year in 1970 for his feats with Boca Juniors, and the following season he took Valencia to the Spanish League Championship.

Docherty, Tommy (Scotland), in his playing days a forceful international wing-half with Preston and Arsenal, became a controversial, outspoken, and much travelled manager. His charges included the talented young Chelsea side that won the 1965 League Cup and reached the 1967 FA Cup final, Rotherham United, Queen's Park Rangers, Aston Villa, and Porto (Portugal). Appointed Scotland's team manager in 1971, he gave them an immediate boost before taking over an ailing Manchester United in 1972.

Doherty, Peter (Northern Ireland), a tall, gifted ball player with an elusive swerve and a powerful left-foot shot, is universally recognized as Northern Ireland's finest inside-forward. He won wide acclaim also as the manager who took the national side to the quarter-finals of the 1958 World Cup. A player in the Di Stefano mould, he had a great influence on all his teams,

although his playing career was somewhat tempestuous and chequered. His clubs numbered Glentoran, Blackpool, Manchester City, where he won a Championship medal in 1937, Derby County, for whom he scored in the 1946 FA Cup triumph, Huddersfield, and finally Doncaster Rovers.

Dooley, Derek, enjoyed two short seasons of fame with Sheffield Wednesday before a leg amputation ended his career in 1953. Cumbersome and with little or no style, he was nonetheless a prolific goal-scoring centre-forward who hit 46 goals in 30 Second Division games in 1951–52. He was appointed manager of his old club in 1970.

Derek Dougan

Dougan, Derek (Northern Ireland), the stormy petrel who became chairman of the Professional Footballers' Association in 1970, is one of football's most thoughtful and articulate players. He is also one of its most enigmatic. Since beginning his League career with Portsmouth in 1957, the big Irish centre-forward journeyed to Blackburn, Aston Villa, Peterborough, and Leicester before seemingly settling at Wolverhampton.

Douglas, Bryan (England), successor to Stanley Matthews on England's right-wing, had the ball control and ability to swerve past opponents that characterized the maestro. He was also a fine, selfless inside-forward, appearing there for Blackburn, his only club, in the 1960 FA Cup final. His 36 caps included matches in the 1958 and 1962 World Cups.

Drake, Ted (England), a dashing, physical centre-forward, began his League career with a hat-trick for Southampton in 1931–32 and ended it with four goals for Arsenal in 1939. From 1934 he was a prolific goal-getter for Arsenal, scoring 42 League goals in 1934–35, including a record seven in the game at Villa Park. He was Chelsea's manager when they won the League Championship in 1954–55.

Ducat, Andy (England), wore England colours at both soccer and cricket. Arsenal brought him from Southend as a centre-forward and converted him into a constructive right-half. But they had to sell him to Aston Villa in 1911 to remain solvent. He collected a Cup winners medal with Villa in 1920 before being transferred to Fulham.

Duncan, Dally (Scotland), outside-left in the Derby County side that won the 1946 FA Cup, was a raiding winger of the W-formation school. Hull City discovered him and sold him

to Derby, where he remained from 1932 to 1946. As a manager, he took Luton to the First Division in 1955 and Blackburn to Wembley in 1960.

Dunne, Jimmy (Republic of Ireland and Northern Ireland), brilliant in the air and quick at shooting near goal, scored nearly 150 goals for Sheffield United before Arsenal signed him one Saturday morning in 1933. The same afternoon he took part in their 6-0 victory over Middlesbrough. But the move was not entirely satisfactory and Dunne was later transferred to Southampton.

Dunne, Tony (Republic of Ireland), a full-back whose speed, finesse, and anticipation made up for what he lacked in size, was an integral part of Manchester United's successful sides of the 1960s. A calm, determined defender, he showed a willingness to move up into attack, putting over crosses like a first-class winger.

Dzajic, Dragan (Yugoslavia), first capped when only 17, scored the goal that beat England in the semi-finals of the 1968 European Football Championships. A winger with a willingness to strike for goal, he has been called the best Yugoslav footballer of all time. His club is Red Star, and he played for the Rest of the World against Brazil in 1968.

Eastham, George (England), the man whose High Court action against Newcastle in the early 1960s ended the retain-and-transfer system, made headlines again in 1972 as a 35-year-old when his goal won the League Cup for Stoke—their first ever major trophy. An inside-forward of the most subtle skills, he was capped 19 times while with Arsenal—he went to Highbury from Newcastle in 1960—and went to Stoke in 1966.

Edwards, Duncan (England), made his league debut for Manchester United at 16 in April 1953, and two years later, at 18 years 183 days, became the youngest player capped for England. His talent was enormous. Physically powerful, a superb shot with either foot, he may well have emerged as the finest wing-half ever to play for England. Sadly fate intervened. On February 21, 1958, aged 21 and winner of 18 caps and two League Championship medals, Duncan Edwards died, a victim of the Munich air disaster.

Edwards, Willis (England), joined Leeds United from Chesterfield in 1925 and became one of the most cultured wing-halves of the next decade. His positioning, ball control, and passing made him ideally suited for an attacking role in complement to the robust defence of Wilf Copping. A particular skill of his was bringing down a high ball and distributing it in one movement.

England, Mike (Wales), moved from Blackburn to Tottenham in 1966 and collected a Cup winners medal the following year. A tall centre-half who can also fill the centre-forward berth

Ted Drake scores against Brentford.

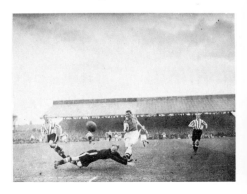

Neil Franklin

Peter Doherty

Duncan Edwards

effectively, he is dominant in the air and strong on the ground. Many consider him without a British rival in his position.

Eusebio (Portugal), European Footballer of the Year in 1965, came to prominence with Benfica in the early 1960s. Mozambique born and nicknamed the 'Black Panther', he is a natural footballer, easy moving and graceful. He scored two goals in Benfica's 5-3 defeat of Real Madrid in the 1962 European Cup final and his explosive right-foot shooting helped them to the 1963, 1965, and 1968 finals. Portugal first capped him at 19, and it was virtually his performance that took Portugal through their quarter-final against North Korea in the 1966 World Cup. He scored four goals in that match, and his nine in the tournament made him its top scorer.

Evans, Bobby (Scotland), won numerous honours with Celtic in the 1950s, when he was capped 48 times. A sturdily built half-back who

Giacinto Facchetti

Mike England

began as a right-half but later moved to the centre, he was strong in defence yet retained an attacking flair. After leaving Celtic in 1960, he went to Chelsea, Newport County, Morton, Third Lanark, and Raith Rovers in about six seasons.

Facchetti, Giacinto (Italy), Inter-Milan's goal-scoring left-back, captained Italy to the final of the 1968 European Football Championship and the 1970 World Cup. Tall and strong, he dominates aerial clashes, and his speed and power make him a difficult man to stop when he goes forward. He was an integral part of Inter's *catenaccio* system when they won the European Cup and World Club Championship in 1964 and 1965.

Fenyvesi, Mate (Hungary), replaced Czibor and Hungary's outside-right in 1954 and went on to win 70 caps. A fine left-foot shot, he won the Fairs Cup for Ferencvaros in 1965 with the only goal of the final. He successfully combined his footballing career with that of a veterinary surgeon.

Finney, Tom (England), is often compared with Stanley Matthews, yet he was the more complete player. He was brilliant on either wing, an incisive inside-forward if necessary, or a creative deep-lying centre-forward. England capped him 76 times in four different positions, and he scored a then record 30 goals in those matches. He remained faithful to Preston, collecting a Cup runners-up medal in 1954. That year, and in 1957, he was voted Footballer of the Year. Like Matthews he could twist and turn to the byline and cross pin-point centres, but he could also cut in and shoot powerfully with either foot.

Flowers, Ron (England), a driving, authoritative half-back typical of the type used by Wolves in the 1950s and early 1960s, won Championship medals in 1954, 1958, and 1959, and a winners medal in the 1960 FA Cup. His two penalties in the 1962 World Cup made him England's top scorer in the tournament.

Fontaine, Just (France), scored a record 13 goals in the 1958 World Cup finals, four of them against West Germany in the third-place match. As a striking inside-forward, he combined effectively with the deep-lying centre-forward Kopa. In 1959 he moved from Nice to Reims and scored 10 goals for them *en route* to the final of that year's European Cup.

Ford, Trevor (Wales), a fiery, provocative centre-forward, cost £69,000 in transfer fees for his moves from Swansea to Aston Villa to Sunderland, who in 1950 paid the first ever £30,000 fee. A dashing opportunist, he was a physical player, as goalkeepers would testify. He was at his best for Wales, for whom he scored 23 times in 38 matches.

Foulke, Billy (England), a giant of a man and one of football's greatest characters, kept goal for Sheffield United when they won the Cup in 1899 and 1902. It seems scarcely credible that he weighed 22 stone when playing for his last club, Chelsea. Several of his clashes with referees have become soccer folk lore.

Franklin, Neil (England), went to Colombia in 1950 in search of riches in the rebel League and so ended an England and Stoke career that had seen him established as the country's foremost centre-half. Within weeks he returned, to a suspension and transfer. He went to Hull, but was unable to re-establish himself, and later played for Crewe and Stockport.

Gallacher, Hughie (Scotland), one of the 'Wembley Wizards', was the complete centre-forward. Quick witted and superbly balanced, he had near perfect ball control, speed, and a baffling swerve. He was remarkable in the air, despite being only 5 ft 6 in tall. He netted 22 goals in 19 internationals. But for all his brilliance and the adulation of thousands, his career was tempestuous and he died in 1957 a lonely man.

Having helped Airdrieonians win the 1924 Scottish Cup, he went south to Newcastle, and in 1927 captained them to the First Division Championship. Chelsea purchased him in 1930,

Hughie Gallacher

but he was never happy there and later moved to Derby, Notts County, Grimsby Town, and Gateshead.

Gallagher, Patsy (Ireland), may have been slight, but his stamina, courage, and skill more than compensated. His determination and ball control were such that he rarely lost the ball, and his centre-forward always benefited from his distribution. He won six League medals and four Scottish Cup winners medals with Celtic between 1911–12 and 1926, when he went to Falkirk.

Garrincha (Brazil), the 'Little Bird', made one of the most positive contributions to Brazil's World Cup successes of 1958 and 1962. With elusive swerves and sudden acceleration he could burst past defences to lay on scoring chances. Or he could score himself with formidable long-range shots or soaring headers. A controversial domestic career saw him with Botafogo, Corinthians, and Flamengo.

Gento, Franciso (Spain), nicknamed 'Paco', appeared in all Real Madrid's European finals from 1956 to 1971, captaining them to a sixth European Cup victory in 1966. A small, compact left-winger, with a fine turn of speed and instant acceleration, he had the most remarkable ball control. He combined almost intuitively with Di Stefano. As well as setting up numerous goals, he scored some vital ones, especially his extra-time winner in the 1958 European Cup final.

Germano (Portugal) spent several seasons as Europe's leading centre-half before injury finished his career prematurely. He was a commanding centre-half for Benfica in their 1961 and 1962 European Cup triumphs, his speed of recovery and ball control being specially admired. But cartilage trouble kept him out of

Johnny Giles

the 1963 final, and though he came back strongly in the 1964–65 competition it was only temporarily.

Gerson (Brazil) commanded Brazil's midfield in the campaign to the 1970 World Cup victory. An outstanding strategist with a clever positional sense, he always seemed to have space in which to move, and his subtle passes rarely went astray. His left-foot drives from outside the area could be vicious, and one such produced the goal that opened the Brazilian floodgates in the final. His club was Botafogo, where he went after a dispute with Flamengo.

Giles, Johnny (Republic of Ireland), took over Bobby Collins's midfield role at Leeds and with Billy Bremner formed the motor of the side after 1965. Manchester United must have regretted selling him in 1963, when he was an outside-right. As a taker of free-kicks, he is without peer, finding the right head in the opposition area or unerringly slotting home penalties. It is no exaggeration that Leeds are rarely the same without him.

Gillespie, Billy (Ireland), played 24 times for Leeds before embarking on a long career with Sheffield United. He joined them in 1911–12, captained them to a Cup win in 1925, and played his last game in 1931. Usually remembered for his baldness, he ranks alongside Doherty and McIlroy among Ireland's inside-forwards, a master strategist and goal-maker.

Gillespie, Bob (Scotland), was the last amateur to captain Scotland, being called in at centre-half against England at Hampden in 1933. Scotland won 2–1. The 1932–33 season was the last of his 14 with Queen's Park, whom he had joined as a centre-forward. When he moved into defence, he helped pioneer the third-back game in Scotland.

Gilzean, Alan (Scotland), a tall, elegant striker, can either score goals or set them up with deft flicks of the ball by head or foot to fellow forwards. His goal-scoring skills won Dundee the Scottish Championship in 1961–62

Billy Gillespie

and took them to the semi-finals of the European Cup the next season. With Spurs from 1964 he was a constant provider for Jimmy Greaves and later Martin Chivers.

Goodall, John (England), one of the pioneers of scientific football in England, earned lasting fame as one of the Preston North End 'Invincibles' who in 1889 did the first League and Cup double. A prolific goal-scorer at either inside-right or centre-forward, he went to Derby County in 1890, joining his brother Archie (an Irish international), and played on the losing side in the 1898 Cup final.

Greaves, Jimmy (England), played his first League game in 1957 and retired in 1971 having scored 491 goals. Of these, 357 were in League matches for Chelsea, Spurs, and West Ham, and 44 came in 57 England appearances. Nine others were for AC Milan during a brief, unhappy spell there in 1961, when Chelsea sold him for £80,000. Spurs brought him back to England for £99,999, and in 1970 they traded him to West Ham as part of a record deal for Martin Peters.

A marksman with a powerful left-foot shot and wonderful reflexes, he led the First Division goalscorers five times and he boasted the remarkable record of scoring in his first match for all his teams. With his premature retirement at 31, football lost a true artist.

Greig, John (Scotland), a tall, powerfully built defender, won many honours with Rangers prior to 1966, when he was Scotland's Footballer of the Year. But later, as Rangers' captain, he had to watch rivals Celtic pass through a golden period, although he himself remained an automatic choice for the national side.

Gren, Gunnar (Sweden), won a gold medal in the 1948 Olympics and 10 years later guided Sweden to the finals of the World Cup. After the Olympics, he went to Italy, playing inside-right in AC Milan's *Grenoli* inside-forward trio of Gren, Nordahl, and Liedholm—all Swedes. He later played for Fiorentina and Genoa.

Grimsdell, Arthur (England), captained Spurs to promotion in 1919–20 with a Second Division record 70 points and the next season led them to victory in the FA Cup. A powerfully built left-half, he was a strong, clean tackler, excellent in attack or defence, and a tough, but respected, captain.

Grosics, Gyula (Hungary), goalkeeper of the Magnificent Magyars who routed England in 1953 and 1954, played in three World Cups and won 89 caps, despite being suspended a year in 1954 after a conviction for smuggling. Often spectacular, he was an inspiration to those in front with his sure handling and coolness under pressure.

Gylmar (Brazil) ended his international career by winning his 100th cap, against England in 1969. He had played in three World Cups, the first two—1958 and 1962—resulting in winners medals. Sure in handling and positional play, he displayed an extraordinary brilliance as a stopper of penalties, including two against England at Wembley in 1956. With Santos he enjoyed all their successes of the early 1960s.

Hagan, Jimmy (England), played a number of times as England's inside-left in war-time internationals but won only one official cap, in 1948. Against Scotland at Wembley in 1942 he scored 50 seconds after the kick-off. He began with Derby in 1935–36 and went to Sheffield United in 1938, immediately helping them to Division I. In 1970 he was appointed manager of Benfica.

Hall, Willie (England), was sadly stricken with thrombosis during World War II and eventually lost both legs. It was a tragic end to a career that had seen him equal the England scoring record of five goals, all in succession against

Alan Gilzean

Jimmy Greaves

David Hay

Ireland in 1938. Solid, fair-haired, and cheerful, he was signed by Spurs from Notts County in 1932 as an inside-left, but it was on the right, in combination with Stanley Matthews, that he demolished the Irish.

Haller, Helmut (West Germany), one of the outstanding players of the 1966 World Cup—he scored Germany's first goal in the final—was first capped at 18. After the 1962 World Cup, he went to Bologna, helping them win the Italian Championship in 1963–64, but after contractual disputes moved to Juventus in 1968. He is equally at home as striker or schemer.

Hamrin, Kurre (Sweden), an outside-right with the ability to cut in through the defence and shoot hard, scored an outstanding individual goal in the 1958 World Cup semi-final against West Germany, dribbling past several defenders before netting Sweden's third goal. Apart from a spell with AIK Stockholm, he spent his playing days in Italy with Juventus, Padova, Fiorentina, AC Milan, and Napoli. He won winners medals in the European Cup with AC Milan in 1969 and in the Cup-Winners Cup in 1961 with Fiorentina and 1968 with Milan.

Hanappi, Gerhardt (Austria), a versatile half-back who also played centre-forward for Austria and right-back for the Rest of the World side that drew with England in 1953, was capped 96 times and was eight times Austrian Footballer of the Year. He played in all Austria's matches in the 1954 World Cup, in which they finished third.

Hapgood, Eddie (England), captain in the notorious 'Battle of Highbury' and England's football ambassador during the troubled 1930s, was a vital factor in Arsenal's League and Cup success in that decade. Slight for a full-back, he relied successfully on skills, interceptions, and anticipation. He was a firm believer in fair play and true sportsmanship, refusing to be provoked even when an Italian broke his nose in that 1934 international at Highbury.

Hardwick, George (England), first played for England during World War II, and after the Victory Internationals made 13 consecutive appearances at left-back in partnership with Laurie Scott. In 1947 he was at right-back for Great Britain. A well-built elegant footballer, he played for Middlesbrough until 1950, when he became player-manager of Oldham Athletic.

Hardy, Sam (England), rates as one of the greatest England goalkeepers. His judgement was so good that he rarely needed to make spectacular saves for he was invariably in position when the shot was made. Liverpool bought him from Chesterfield in 1905 and he won a

Championship medal in his first season. With Aston Villa from 1912 to 1921 he collected two Cup winners medals, and he finished his long career of 550 League games with Nottingham Forest in 1924–25.

Hay, David (Scotland), right-back for Celtic when they reached the final of the European Cup in 1970, developed as a powerful midfield star for club and country. First capped in 1970, he was a dominating force in Scotland's fine 1974 World Cup campaign, after which he signed for Chelsea for £250,000, a Scottish record.

Haynes, Johnny (England), the first English £100-a-week footballer, could have found greater fortune with numerous clubs, yet he remained faithful to Fulham, even when it meant seasons of Second Division football. Not that this affected England selection: the last 22 of his 56 internationals, which included the 1962 World Cup, were as captain. An inside-forward of masterly technique, he will always be remembered for his superb passing to the wings or through the centre.

Herberger, Sepp (West Germany), managed West Germany to victory in the 1954 World Cup, his shrewd tactics ensuring his team went into the final knowing more about the Hungarians than they knew about the Germans. He had control of the national side from 1936 to 1963, during which time the West Germans

also made the World Cup semi-finals in 1958 and the quarter-finals in 1962.

Herrera, Helenio (France), twice capped as a naturalized Frenchman, brought *catenaccio* to the fore with his all-conquering Inter-Milan of the 1960s. Flamboyant and controversial, he managed several Spanish clubs with astonishing success before going to Barcelona in 1958 to help break Real Madrid's supremacy. Though League Champions, his team lost to Real in their 1960 European Cup semi-final, and Herrera, sacked, made his way to Italy.

Hibbs, Harry (England), was, like Sam Hardy, a 'keeper capable of making the most difficult shots look easy. His positional sense and his handling were of the highest standard, and his lack of inches was rarely a handicap. Birmingham were his only club, and he collected a Cup runners-up medal with them in 1931. As manager of Walsall, he coached the young Bert Williams.

Hidegkuti, Nandor (Hungary), on the right-wing for the side that won the 1952 Olympic title, later emerged as the deep-lying centre-forward whose long, defence-splitting passes led to countless goals by inside-forwards Puskas and Kocsis. In England, he will always be remembered for his hat-trick on that November day at Wembley in 1953 when the Hungarians humbled the English. His club was MTK Budapest.

Hill, Jimmy, as chairman of the PFA, was a major figure in the struggle to abolish the maximum wage. At the time, he was a striking inside-forward with Fulham. In late 1961, he was appointed manager of Coventry City, taking them from the Third Division to the First in five seasons. But before their first-ever Division I game, he left to become a knowledgeable, analytical soccer commentator on TV.

Hoeness, Uli (West Germany), equally at home in midfield or as a striker, emerged as an international star in West Germany's European Championship winning team of 1972, scoring a fine goal at Wembley in the quarter-final against England. In 1974 he scored two goals for Bayern Munich in their 4–1 win over Atlético Madrid in the replayed European Cup final and figured prominently in Germany's World Cup win.

Hogan, Jimmy, may be remembered in Birmingham for taking Aston Villa back to Division I in 1938, but he will be best remembered in Austria and Hungary as the coach who stressed ball control and positional skills. He played an essential part in the success of the Austrian *Wunderteam*, and the Hungarians of the 1950s reflected the value of his teachings.

Howe, Don (England), coach of the Arsenal 'double' side of 1970–71, made 23 consecutive appearances for England, including 4 in the 1958 World Cup. A tall right-back with a sound positional sense, he spent most of his playing

Harry Hibbs

days at West Bromwich. He ended his playing career at Highbury, and in 1967 became Arsenal's chief coach, returning to West Bromwich in 1971 as manager.

Hulme, Joe (England), winner of three League Championship medals, became the only player to have appeared in five Wembley FA Cup finals. Apart from his last Cup final, with Huddersfield in 1938, he won all his honours with Arsenal. A flying right-winger, he thrived on Alex James's long crossfield passes, making full use of his great speed to out-distance defences. Of his 114 League goals, 108 were scored for Arsenal.

Hunt, Roger (England), played a vital role in England's World Cup success of 1966. Strong, durable, courageous, and a hard-shooting marksman, he was the ideal inside-forward for Ramsey's team. At club level, he enjoyed all Liverpool's triumphs of the 1960s, and when he left Anfield for Bolton in 1969 he had scored a club record 245 goals.

Hurley, Charlie (Republic of Ireland), a fine, dominating centre-half, made a record 356 League appearances for Sunderland between 1957 and 1969 and provided necessary strength to the Eire defence, in later years as player-manager. In 1969 he moved to Bolton as player-manager and in 1972 became manager of Reading.

Hurst, Geoff (England), scored the first-ever hat-trick in a World Cup final, in 1966. His goal against Argentina had put England through to the semi-finals, yet he had started the tournament as a reserve. With his ball control and ability to run tirelessly into space, he established himself as England's target man into the 1970s. With West Ham, he enjoyed the FA Cup and Cup-Winners Cup success of the mid-1960s, before going to Stoke in 1972.

Pat Jennings

Ivanov, Valentin (USSR), came to notice with the Russian sides that reached the quarter-finals of the 1958 and 1962 World Cups and the final of the 1960 and 1964 European Nations Cups. Developed by Moscow Torpedo into a goal-making, goal-scoring inside-forward, he was Russia's Footballer of the Year in 1957 and captain of the national side from 1962 to 1966.

Jack, David (England), a tall, skilful inside-right able to weave through the strongest defences, scored the first Wembley Cup final goal—for Bolton against West Ham in 1923. In 1926 he scored the goal that beat Man-

chester City, and in 1930, with Arsenal, he won his third Cup winners medal. Arsenal paid the first-ever five-figure fee to purchase him in 1928, and he helped them to the Championship title in 1930–31 and 1932–33.

Jackson, Alec (Scotland), put a hat-trick past England's 'keeper when the 'Wembley Wizards' beat England 5-1. With his great acceleration, dribbling skills, and opportunism, he approached genius as a right-winger. Herbert Chapman took him from Aberdeen to Huddersfield in 1925 and he helped them accomplish their League hat-trick and reach two Cup finals. After two seasons at Chelsea (1930 to 1932) he went into non-League football.

Jair Rosa Pinto (Brazil) was perhaps the key man in the Zizinho-Ademir-Jair forward trio that took Brazil so close to victory in the 1950 World Cup. A shrewd tactician, a tormentor of defences, he won 39 caps altogether. He found fame with Vasco da Gama and then moved to Palmeiras, Santos, and São Paulo.

Charlie Hurley

Jairzinho (Brazil) became, in 1970, the first player to score in every match of a World Cup tournament when he scrambled in Pelé's header to put Brazil 3-1 up on Italy in the final. As Garrincha's successor on the right wing, he showed with his deceptive ball control and immaculately placed crosses that a class winger could still open defences, no matter how packed or brutal.

James, Alex (Scotland), a popular figure immediately recognizable in his baggy pants, was the linkman between defence and attack during Arsenal's great days of the 1930s, an inside-left of genius. Arsenal bought him in 1929 from Preston, where he had a reputation as a goal-scorer, but Herbert Chapman made him a goal-maker whose long, raking passes to raiding wingers were perhaps the main reasons for Arsenal's four Championships and three Cup finals in seven seasons. However, it was a minor mystery that he won no more than eight Scottish caps—one as a member of the 'Wembley Wizards', for whom he scored twice.

Jennings, Pat (Northern Ireland), reputed to possess the largest pair of hands in English football, established himself as one of Britain's foremost 'keepers in the late 1960s. Spurs paid Watford £27,000 for him in 1964, and he won honours with them in the 1967 FA Cup and 1971 League Cup. In the 1972–73 season, he won another League Cup medal and was voted Footballer of the Year.

John, Bob (Wales), played a club-record 421 League games for Arsenal, as well as 50 Cup ties, including the finals of 1927, 1930, and 1932. His best position was left-half, where he performed his tasks quietly and efficiently, but he also appeared at inside-left and was outside-left in the 1932 Cup final, scoring Arsenal's only goal.

Johnston, Harry (England), Footballer of the Year in 1951 and a Blackpool man all his

playing days, captained his side to three FA Cup finals—1948, 1951, and 1953, when he led the winners. A consistent half-back, he provided Matthews and Mortensen with impeccable passes to thrust home attacks.

Johnstone, Bobby (Scotland), an alert, graceful inside-forward with a fine shot, won Championship medals with Hibs in the early 1950s and later found FA Cup success with Manchester City. He scored their third goal in 1956, having scored their only goal the previous year when they lost to Newcastle. Also in 1955 he scored for Great Britain against the Rest of Europe.

Johnstone, Jimmy (Scotland), contributed much to Celtic's run of success in the 1960s, often making or scoring the goals that brought so many honours. With his ability to beat a defence with either footwork or speed and to cap a move with a glorious shot, this tiny, red-haired right-winger was a welcome performer in a defence-orientated game. On the debit side were a tendency to hold the ball too long and a short temper that led to trouble with authority.

Jones, Bryn (Wales), went from Wolves to Arsenal in 1938 as England's most expensive footballer. The Gunners paid £14,000 for the intelligent, ball-playing inside-left in the hope he would prove the successor to Alex James, but war interfered with their plans. From 1946 he played only 41 League games before going to Norwich in 1949.

Jones, Cliff (Wales), was a natural on either wing, possessing beautiful ball control and the ability and willingness to attack defences. He was a vital cog in the smooth-flowing Spurs machine that did the 'double' in 1961, retained the Cup in 1962, and won the Cup-Winners Cup in 1963. In 1968–69, Spurs, who paid Swansea £35,000 for him in 1958, allowed him to go to Fulham on a free transfer.

Jonquet, Robert (France), captained Reims to their two European Cup finals against Real Madrid in 1956 and 1959. A centre-back commanding in the air and on the ground, he was also a skilful ball player able to work the ball out of defence and initiate attacking moves. He was captain of France in the 1954 World Cup and again in 1958 when they took third place.

Jurion, Josef (Belgium), was one of the few world-class footballers to play in spectacles. He began his international career in 1955 as an outside-right, but when Anderlecht moved him

Jimmy Johnstone

Fred Keenor

Denis Law (left)

inside he developed as a commanding midfield schemer, capable of delicately touched passes or powerful shots at goal. Belgium's Footballer of the Year in 1957 and 1962, he won 64 caps, a number of the later ones as captain.

Keenor, Fred (Wales), took the FA Cup out of England for the first time as captain of Cardiff City when they beat Arsenal in 1927. A sturdy centre-half who would never admit defeat, he joined Cardiff in 1913 and helped them climb from the Southern League to Division I. He was a key member of the successful Welsh side of the 1920s.

Kelly, Bob (England), with his sinuous dribbling and flashing shot, was one of England's leading forwards of the 1920s, appearing in all forward positions. He was with Burnley during their unbeaten League run of 30 games in 1920–21. In 1925 he went to Sunderland and two years later, in his 30s, moved to Huddersfield, playing in the 1928 and 1930 Cup finals.

Jack Kelsey

Kelsey, Jack (Wales), played many outstanding games for Arsenal between 1951 and 1962, but probably gave of his best when Wales reached the quarter-finals of the 1958 World Cup. Powerfully built, with the safest of hands, he produced breathtaking saves, often courageous ones. But his fearlessness ended his career. In a 1962 Brazil–Wales international, Vavá crashed into him, seriously injuring his back.

Kindvall, Ove (Sweden), was a prolific goalscorer with IFK Norrköping before becoming an 'exile' in the Netherlands with Feyenoord. In 1968–69 he helped them win the Dutch Championship and the following season his extra-time goal against Celtic won them the European Cup. His speed, opportunism, antici-

pation, and powerful shooting make him a most lethal striker.

Kinnaird, Lord Arthur, took part in nine Cup finals, for the Wanderers and Old Etonians, and was on the winning side five times: 1873, 1877, 1878, 1879, 1882. In the days when hacking was permitted, the red-bearded Kinnaird was prominent where the fray was thickest. In 1911, he was presented with the FA Cup to mark his 21 years as president of the FA.

Kocsis, Sandor (Hungary), the 'Golden Head', had few peers as a header of the ball. Though not a tall player, he could leap higher than most and had a powerful technique. Inside-right of those magnificent Hungarians of the 1950s, he was leading goalscorer, with 11, in the 1954 World Cup, and altogether scored 75 goals in his 68 internationals. Like Puskas, he did not return with Honved after the 1956 Hungarian Uprising and eventually went to Spain, winning further honours with Barcelona.

Kolev, Ivan (Bulgaria), won a record 76 Bulgarian caps, and played more than 600 games for CSKA Sofia before retiring in 1968. Originally an outside-left, he developed into a midfield general, master-minding CSKA's enormous domestic success. He played in three Olympic Games and three World Cup tournaments.

Kopa, Raymond (France), was at outside-right for Real Madrid in the 1957, 1958, and 1959 European Cups. He was more happy, though, as a deep-lying centre-forward and shone there for Reims in the 1956 European Cup and for France, in tandem with Fontaine, in the 1958 World Cup. His superb footwork deceived many an opponent, and his distribution was always sure.

Kubala, Ladislav (Czechoslovakia, Hungary, and Spain), enjoyed a much travelled career. Budapest born, he played for Czechoslovakia and Hungary before signing for Barcelona, despite Hungarian opposition, in 1951. When naturalized, he added 15 Spanish caps to his 11 Czech and 3 Hungarian ones. A superb ball-playing inside- or centre-forward with a powerful shot and renowned ability to beat a

man with a double-shuffle feint, he helped Barcelona to European success before 1961. As a manager, he worked in Spain, Switzerland, the United States, and Canada before being appointed Spain's manager in 1969.

Labruna, Angel (Argentina), a hard-working inside-forward affectionately known as 'El Viejo'—the old one—was recalled to the national side in the 1958 World Cup at the age of 40. Thus his 36 caps were won over two decades. To River Plate, he gave 26 years of service, playing in 1,150 games and scoring 457 goals.

Lato, Grzegorz (Poland), one of the shooting stars of Poland's 1974 World Cup side, finished as leading scorer in the tournament with seven, including the winner in the third-place match against Brazil with a typical break up the right flank.

Law, Denis (Scotland), with his lightning reflexes, superb heading, and ability to convert the half-chance into a goal, was one of Europe's most exciting footballers of the 1960s. In 1964 he was European Footballer of the Year. If somewhat temperamental, the Scottish striker has always been highly valued. Manchester City paid Huddersfield a record £55,000 for him in 1960 and sold him to Torino in 1961 for £100,000. A year later Manchester United brought him back to England for £115,000. He went back to Manchester City on a free transfer in 1973, and enjoyed an Indian summer for Scotland, taking his haul of caps to a record 55, the last against Zaïre in the 1974 World Cup finals.

Lawton, Tommy (England), rivals Dixie Dean as Britain's best ever centre-forward. He had the same menace in the air and was formidable on the ground, strong on the ball and a fierce shot. Everton paid Burnley £6,500 in 1936 when he was only 17, and in 1938–39 he scored 34 goals when they won the Championship. That season he won the first of 23 caps. In 1945 he went to Chelsea, and then in 1947 came his amazing move to Third Division Notts County for the first £20,000 fee. After helping them to promotion he went to Brentford and Arsenal, but later returned to Notts as manager.

Tommy Lawton

Lee, Francis (England), began with Bolton as a goalscoring right-winger, but Manchester City found his courageous running, control, and strong shooting more useful in the middle and made him a striker. As such he thrived, helping City to a hat-trick of honours from 1967–68 and playing for England. A cool taker of penalties he hit 13 from the spot in the 1971–72 League season.

Leonidas da Silva (Brazil), a short, coloured, gymnastic centre-forward, popularized the bicycle kick—the overhead shot at goal. He used both feet, controlling the ball with one and making the shot with the other. He was the star of the 1938 World Cup, leading the tournament goalscorers with eight, four of them coming in Brazil's match against Poland.

Liddell, Billy (Scotland), fast and fearless, gave Liverpool long and faithful service in a career embracing a club-record 492 League games. Able to shoot with either foot and a powerful header of the ball, he could fill any position in the forward line and was a formidable opponent advancing with the ball at foot. In 1947 and 1955 he played for Great Britain against the Rest of Europe.

Billy Liddell

Liedholm, Nils (Sweden), went to AC Milan from IFK Norrköping after Sweden's success at the 1948 Olympics. Unlike team-mates Gren and Nordahl, he remained there throughout the 1950s, helping the re-emergence of Milan as an Italian force, and playing in the 1958 European Cup final. Later that year, he captained Sweden to the final of the World Cup.

Lofthouse, Nat (England), a powerfully built centre-forward, made his debut for Bolton at 15 and went on to play more than 500 games for them, including two Cup finals. He collected a winners medal in 1958 and a runners-up medal in 1953, when he was Footballer of the Year. In his 33 England appearances, he scored 30 goals.

Lubanski, Wlodzimierz (Poland), capped 20 times before he was 21, is one of Eastern Europe's most prolific goalscorers, A centre- or inside-forward, he is strongly built but well balanced. He helped Gornik Zabrze reach the final of the European Cup-Winners Cup in 1969–70.

McColl, Ian (Scotland), filled the right-half berth in the famous post-war Rangers defence known as the 'Iron Curtain'. A good covering defender with a long, accurate pass, he played almost 600 games for Rangers, featuring in their 'treble' of 1948–49. For a brief spell in the 1960s he was Scotland's manager.

McCracken, Bill (Ireland), is said to be responsible for the 1925 change in the off-side law, even though he had retired in 1923. An Irish international with Distillery when he joined Newcastle in 1904, the forceful, intelligent full-back featured in the famous pre-war Magpies sides. So successfully had he sprung the offside trap that the law was changed so that only two players, instead of three, had to be nearer the goal-line when the ball was played.

McGrory, Jimmy (Scotland), Celtic's prolific goalscoring centre-forward between the wars, put away 550 goals in his first-class career. In British league football, he is the only leading scorer to have averaged more than a goal a match. In 1928 he scored eight against Dunfermline, and in 1936 notched four against Motherwell in five minutes. He was manager of Kilmarnock and then, from 1945 to 1965, of Celtic.

McIlroy, Jimmy (Northern Ireland), with Danny Blanchflower, did so much to get Northern Ireland to the 1958 World Cup quarter-finals. At Burnley he guided the club to the 1959–60 Championship and to Wembley in 1962. He was an outstanding strategist, a skilful inside-forward. In 1963 he moved to Stoke, helping them back to Division I.

Mackay, Dave (Scotland), became a legend in his own time, the man who kept coming back. As an all-purpose left-half with Hearts and then Spurs, he won almost every honour going. He was a dynamic, driving member of the Spurs 'double' side of 1960–61 and an astute captain to Wembley in 1967, having twice come back after breaking a leg. In 1968 he embarked on a new career as a stopper at Derby County, immediately captaining them back to Division I. He was joint Footballer of the Year in 1969. In 1971 he went to Swindon as player-manager and became Derby's manager in 1973 after a spell with Nottingham Forest.

McLintock, Frank (Scotland), after four frustrating Wembleys, suddenly discovered success at the beginning of the 1970s when he captained Arsenal to victory in the 1969–70 Fairs Cup and to their 'double' the next season. He was also Footballer of the Year in 1971. At first an imaginative midfield player with Leicester and then Arsenal, whom he joined in 1964, he later became a commanding figure in the back four. He was transferred to Queen's Park Rangers in 1973.

McMullan, Jimmy (Scotland), a constructive left-half with a pass of pin-point accuracy, enjoyed a distinguished career with Partick Thistle and Manchester City. But he is best remembered as the captain of the 'Wembley Wizards', to whom he said the night before the match: 'Go to bed and pray for rain.' It rained, and England were beaten 5–1.

McNeill, Billy (Scotland), boasts a collection of honours few could surpass. The first of a succession of winners medals came in 1965, when he was the first Scottish Footballer of the Year and his header won the Scottish Cup for Celtic. Two seasons later the powerful centre-half was the on-field general of the campaign that saw Celtic champions of Europe and treble winners in Scotland.

McParland, Peter (Northern Ireland), will be less remembered for his two goals for Aston Villa in the 1957 Cup final than for his charge on Ray Wood that cost Manchester United their 'keeper. A strong-running fierce-shooting winger, he scored many valuable goals, especially his five in the 1958 World Cup. He later played for Wolves and Plymouth and in North America.

McPhail, Bob (Scotland), won a record seven Scottish Cup winners medals, the first with Airdrieonians in 1924, the others with the mighty Rangers of the 1920s and 1930s. In addition, he collected nine Championship medals. A powerful inside-forward, he scored 281 goals in 466 matches for Rangers and struck up a fine left-wing partnership with Alan Morton.

McWilliam, Peter (Scotland), was the original member of that select band to have played in and later managed FA Cup winners. As an artistic left-half with Newcastle, he collected a winners medal in 1910, as well as three Championship medals, and as a manager he drove Spurs to promotion in 1920 and the Cup the following season.

Male, George (England), Arsenal's right-back during the illustrious days of the 1930s, was the ideal complement to Eddie Hapgood. Strong tackling and fine positional play made him one of the finest defenders of his day. He played 19 times for England following his debut in the notorious 'Battle of Highbury' of 1934.

Mannion, Wilf (England), with his elusive body swerve, bewildering ability with the ball, and speed to use an opening, was one of England's most exciting inside-forwards after World War II. But his career was not trouble-free. Middlesbrough suspended him when he refused to re-sign his contract, and in 1955, when with Hull, he was banned by the League for refusing to testify on illegal payments.

Marché, Roger (France), a strongly built, robust left-back, became France's most capped player in 1959 when he played in his 63rd international. He began his career with FC Mohon, but moved to Reims after the war, helping them to Championship and Cup honours before going to Racing Club de Paris in 1953.

Martin, Con (Republic of Ireland and Northern Ireland), opened his international career as Eire's substitute goalkeeper against Spain in 1946, later played against England at centre-half, and was right-half in his debut for Northern Ireland. He began with Glentoran and then had a short spell with Leeds before giving eight seasons' service to Aston Villa.

Masopust, Josef (Czechoslovakia), with Svatopluk Pluskal and Jan Popluhar, made one of Europe's finest half-back lines. The trio did much to get Czechoslovakia to the 1962 World Cup final, in which Masopust, a skilful left-half, opened the scoring. Later that year he was named European Footballer of the Year. In the late 1960s, he left Dukla Prague to play in Belgium.

Stanley Matthews (left)

Matthews, Sir Stanley (England), was the first footballer to be knighted, an honour received a month before his 50th birthday. That day he played in his star-studded testimonial, climaxing a career that began with Stoke in 1932 at 17 and encompassed 701 League games and 54 full internationals. He had been a schoolboy international centre-half, but it was on the right-wing that he won world renown for his skills and his longevity. His tantalizing body swerve, devastating acceleration, superb ball control, and pin-point passing made him the nightmare of opposing backs.

Stoke sold him to Blackpool in 1947 for a mere £11,500, and he played in three Cup finals, collecting his winners medal in the drama-packed 'Matthews final' of 1953. In 1962 he returned to Stoke for £2,500, and his presence alone doubled the gates. It also helped Stoke back to Division I in 1963, when he was Footballer of the Year. He had previously won the award in 1948 and had been European Footballer of the Year in 1956.

Mazurkiewicz, Ladislao (Uruguay), did not develop as a goalkeeper until 1963, yet in 1966 he was giving an immaculate performance against England in the opening match of the

World Cup. Though a little short, he makes up for any handicap with surprising agility and courage. He enjoyed Penarol's success in the South American Cup and World Club Championship, and played in his third World Cup in 1974.

Mazzola, Sandrino (Italy), having led Inter-Milan's attack when they won the European Cup and World Club Championship in successive years, emerged in the 1968 European Championship as a constructive inside-forward, and it was in this midfield role that he guided Italy to the final of the 1970 World Cup. His father was the Torino star Valentino Mazzola.

Sandro Mazzola

Mazzola, Valentino (Italy), moved from Venice to Torino in 1942 to become the tactical genius of that great side, superbly linking defence and attack. A slight, elusive inside-left, he won 12 caps and was the country's leading goal-scorer in 1946–47 with 29. He died along with his team-mates in the Superga air disaster of 1949.

Meazza, Giuseppe (Italy), and Giovanni Ferrari were the only two to play in both Italy's World Cup sides of 1934 and 1938, Meazza captaining the latter. Each time he was at inside-right, though he was often at centre-forward for Ambrosiana Inter. Incisive and perceptive, he scored 33 goals in 53 internationals, and in domestic football netted 218 league goals, three times topping the goal-scoring lists.

Meiklejohn, David (Scotland), a powerfully built, authoritative half-back, played 635 games for Rangers, captaining the side over a long period and winning 11 Championship and 4 Cup winners medals. It was his penalty in 1928 that helped break Rangers' quarter-century drought in the Scottish Cup.

Meisl, Hugo, was the man most responsible for the Austrian *Wunderteam* of the 1930s, instilling in his players faith in Jimmy Hogan's coaching. It was Meisl who in 1912 first took Hogan to Vienna. As a slight, clever inside-forward, he helped found the club now known as FK Austria, and later he was a leading proponent of FIFA.

Mercer, Joe (England), ranks among the foremost British footballing personalities. As an attacking wing-half with Everton he won Championship honours in 1939; in a more defensive role he captained Arsenal to the Championship in 1948 and 1953 and to Wembley in 1950 and 1952. In 1950 he was Footballer of the Year. Management at Sheffield United and Aston Villa ended in a breakdown, but Manchester City coaxed him back, and with Malcolm Allison's help he took them back to Division I in 1966. Then, from 1968 to 1970

he saw them win the Championship, the Cup, the League Cup, and the Cup-Winners Cup. In 1972, he became manager of Coventry.

Meredith, Billy (Wales), linked with Stanley Matthews as the greatest outside-right of all time, was a winger of the classic mould, dribbling the ball to the corner flag before crossing immaculately. But he was not averse to popping up in goalscoring situations, as in the 1904 Cup final for Manchester City. He had joined City in 1894, but in 1906 went to Manchester United, winning League and Cup honours before returning to City in 1921.

Milburn, Jackie (England), 'Wor Jackie' to Newcastle fans, scored two memorable goals in the 1951 Cup final for the first of three Cup winners medals. Originally an outside-right, he became a dangerous centre-forward with outstanding acceleration and a powerful shot with either foot. He scored 10 times in his 13 internationals. Later, as player-coach of Linfield, he won Irish League and Cup honours.

Monti, Luisito (Argentina and Italy), secured by Juventus from Boca Juniors after playing for Argentina in the 1928 Olympics and 1930 World Cup, aided them to four successive Championships (1932–35). Vittorio Pozzo saw a role for the ruthless, strong tackling centre-half in the national side, and his 18 Italian caps included the 1934 World Cup success.

Moore, Bobby (England), received the World Cup in 1966, climaxing a hat-trick of winning

Billy Meredith

Bobby Moore

Wembley finals. He captained West Ham when they won the FA Cup in 1964 and the Cup-Winners Cup in 1965. In 1964 he was Footballer of the Year, and he was the 1966 World Cup Player of the Tournament. A tall, cultured defender, he played in the 1962 World Cup and was England's captain again in 1970. Happiest as a second stopper in a No. 6 shirt, he stamps his authority on play immediately, tackling, covering, and distributing faultlessly. He went to Fulham in 1974 after 16 years with West Ham.

Mortensen, Stan (England), scored over 200 goals for Blackpool, but none as vital as his three in the 1953 FA Cup final—the first hat-trick in a Wembley final. He overcame a serious war-time injury to become one of England's finest striking inside-forwards. He scored four against Portugal in his full England debut in 1947.

Morton, Alan (Scotland), truly earned his nickname the 'Wee Blue Devil'. Though only 5 ft 4 in tall, this elusive winger possessed dribbling ability, ball control, and passing skills that put him in a class of his own. He joined Rangers from Queen's Park in 1920 and won numerous honours until his retirement in 1932–33, including 31 Scottish Caps.

Mullen, Jimmy (England), a Frank Buckley discovery, was only 16 when he made his League debut for Wolves in 1939. As a raiding winger, he was essential to the Championship-winning Wolves of the 1950s, having already won a Cup winners medal in 1949. After war-time internationals, he was capped 12 times.

Müller, Gerd (West Germany), European Footballer of the Year in 1970, led the 1970 World Cup goalscorers with 10, 6 from hat-tricks against Bulgaria and Peru. A strong shot with either foot, a powerful header of the ball, he converts the slightest chance, often the seemingly impossible ones. With Müller as their marksman, Bayern Munich enjoyed League, Cup, and Cup-Winners Cup success after 1966, culminating in their European Cup triumph of 1974, Müller scoring twice in the replayed final. He went on to score the winner in the World Cup final against Holland in Munich that year.

Gérd Müller

Pelé (right)

Neeskens, Johan (Netherlands), dynamic, versatile midfield star of the 1974 World Cup, was a major force in Ajax's European Cup treble from 1971 to 1973. He scored five World Cup goals, including three net-bursting penalties, before joining team-mate Cruyff at Barcelona for some £500,000.

Netto, Igor (USSR), captained his country to victory in the 1956 Olympics and the 1960 European Nations Cup, and to the quarter-finals of the 1962 World Cup. A most astute wing-half, he was strong in defence, and towards the end of his international career of 56 caps he moved to centre-back.

Netzer, Günter (West Germany), was the dominant midfield figure in the fine German side that won the European Championship in 1972 and in the title-winning Borussia Mönchengladbach team of the early 1970s. An elegant mover and a superb passer of the ball, Netzer had won only 14 caps in five years before taking over Overath's role soon after the 1970 World Cup.

Nicholson, Bill (England), joined Spurs in 1936, was right-half in the 'push-and-run' side that won promotion in 1950 and the Championship in 1951, and managed the 'double' and cup-winning sides of the 1960s. As a manager he showed the same confidence and tactical shrewdness he displayed as a player, as unafraid to spend heavily as to tackle strongly.

Nordahl, Gunnar (Sweden), led Sweden's attack in the 1948 Olympics and AC Milan's when they won the Italian League in 1951 and 1955. With Gren and Liedholm he made up Milan's *Grenoli* trio. A strongly built centre-forward, he topped the Italian goalscoring list five times and twice represented Europe—against Britain in 1947 and England in 1953.

Ocwirk, Ernst (Austria), remained the attacking centre-half at a time when the third-back game was favoured. His mid-field mastery, achieved through the neatest ball control and long, accurate passes out of defence, made Austria a European power in the early 1950s. In 1956 he left FK Austria for Sampdoria in Italy, playing mostly as a deep-lying inside-forward, but returned to manage FK in the 1960s.

Odermatt, Karl (Switzerland), emerged as a midfield player of undeniable class during the qualifying rounds of the 1970–72 European Championship. A smooth, non-stop runner with glorious ball-playing skills, the Basle schemer creates panic in defences, laying on passes to his strikers or letting loose long-range, curving shots, such as the one that forced a draw with England at Wembley in 1971.

Orsi, Raimondo (Argentina and Italy), starred for Argentina in the 1928 Olympics before moving to Juventus, where he played in their five Championship teams (1931–35). A strong, fast left-winger, he was capped 35 times for Italy and scored their equalizer in the 1934 World Cup final.

Overath, Wolfgang (West Germany), impressed tremendously in the 1966 and 1970 World Cups as a skilful, hard-working midfield player with formidable shooting power. He played for the World XI against Brazil in 1968 and has won League and Cup medals with 1FC Cologne. He won back his place in the West German side from Netzer for the 1974 World Cup, and played a leading part in their triumph.

Paul, Roy (Wales), moved from Swansea to Manchester City in 1950 and captained them to victory in the FA Cup six years later. Versatile enough to play forward or back, he was best as a wing-half, able to win the ball in the tackle and distribute it intelligently. A number of his 33 internationals were played as captain.

Peacock, Bertie (Northern Ireland), played an important part in Celtic's 'double' in 1953–54, making up a most competent half-back line with Bobby Evans and Jock Stein. Firm and persistent in defence, he was thoughtful and creative in possession. In 1958 he saw Northern Ireland to the quarter-finals of the World Cup but did not play in the 4–0 defeat by France.

Pelé (Brazil) is the best known of all foot-ballers, and probably the finest. His talents are legendary: the intuitive ability to produce the unexpected, the selfless touches that set up goals for team-mates, the ball control that allows him to outwit the closest marking, and the soaring header and shooting power that have brought more than 1,000 goals. He was a world star at 17 when Brazil first won the World Cup. In 1970, when his presence dominated that World Cup, he was indisputably the king, heading the first goal of the final and making two others.

Born into an impoverished, coloured family, he has become one of the world's richest sportsmen. Santos, who made him their first-choice inside-left when he was 16, have benefited greatly from their star, triumphing in competitions from the Sao Paulo League to the World Club Championship.

Pennington, Jesse (England), played 25 times for his country, being recognized as the finest left-back of the pre-World War I era. His tackling was always sure, his positioning admirable. In 1919–20 he captained West Bromwich, his only club, to the League Championship. He was scrupulously fair, preferring to lose a match than condescend to poor sportsmanship.

Peters, Martin (England), came out of the 1966 World Cup as one of England's new stars, an all-purpose midfield player able to defend strongly or suddenly ghost through into a striking position to head or shoot forcefully. His passing, crisp and intelligent, is a special feature of his game. In 1970 he left West Ham, whom he helped win the Cup-Winners Cup in 1965, to go to Spurs in Britain's first ever £200,000 transfer.

Picchi, Armando (Italy), more than any other player, epitomized *catenaccio*. With Picchi as sweeper and defensive general, Inter-Milan dominated European and world football in the mid-1960s. As a player he was negative and uncompromising, but as manager of Juventus for a short spell before his death in 1971 he showed talent and vision in building a young, exciting team.

Piola, Silvio (Italy), a tall, powerful centre-forward, was a central figure in the Italian team that retained the World Cup in 1938. He made his international debut in 1935 and won the last of his 33 caps in 1952. As a goalscorer in domestic competitions he was prolific, netting over 300 for Pro Vercelli, Lazio, Torino, Juventus, and Novara.

Planicka, Frantisek (Czechoslovakia), capped 74 times as his country's goalkeeper between the wars, captained the Czechs to the final of the 1934 World Cup, making several glorious saves *en route*. But his failure to stop Orsi's dipping shot probably cost his side victory. Short and sturdy, he was exceptionally courageous and possessed lightning reflexes. Under his leadership, Slavia Prague dominated the 1920s and 1930s in Czechoslovakia.

Popluhar, Jan (Czechoslovakia), had few rivals in Europe as a stopper centre-half at the time of the 1962 World Cup, in which he played magnificently to help Czechoslovakia into the finals. With Slovan Bratislava he was a tower of strength. His performances were rewarded in 1963 when he was chosen to play for the Rest of the World against England.

Pozzo, Vittorio, Italy's manager when they won the World Cup in 1934 and 1938, did an inestimable amount for that country's football. After playing a major role in the founding of Torino, he spent some time in England where he was greatly influenced by the Manchester United of Charlie Roberts, and he moulded his tactics around an attacking centre-half. Though demanding and ruthless, he was respected by all his players.

Puddefoot, Syd (England), enjoyed a lengthy career, first as a prolific centre-forward and later as a scheming inside-forward. At West Ham, where he began and ended, he was the fans' idol—'Our Syd'. But in 1922 he went to Falkirk in the first £5,000 transfer, only to return south to Blackburn in 1925 and create their Cup victory in 1928.

Puskas, Ferenc (Hungary and Spain), the 'Galloping Major' of the magnificent Hungarians of the 1950s, possessed one of the fiercest left-foot shots in football history. England felt its power when they fell 6–3 at Wembley in 1953; Eintracht Frankfurt were four times on the receiving end in the 1960 European Cup final; and Benfica had to allow a hat-trick before beating Real Madrid 5–3 in the 1962 final.

Though captain of Hungary for many of his 84 internationals—in which he scored 83 goals—Puskas preferred exile to returning to Hungary in 1956 with the touring Honved, and two years later Real Madrid signed him. Europe was again to be awed by the brilliant ball control and fulminating shot of the stocky inside-left. He played four times for Spain, three in the 1962 World Cup. In 1971 he made his fourth European Cup final as manager of Greek club Panathinaikos.

Rahn, Helmut (West Germany), a powerful outside-right with a thundering shot, scored two of the goals that won West Germany the World Cup in 1954. Four years later, when the Germans were semi-finalists, he scored seven in the tournament, and in his 40 internationals his goal tally was 19. He won League and Cup honours with Rot-Weiss Essen before joining 1FC Cologne.

Ramallets, Antonio (Spain), ranks alongside Ricardo Zamora as his country's finest goalkeeper. Spectacular, courageous, and confident, he won 35 caps in the decade following the 1950 World Cup. With Barcelona he enjoyed the domestic and Fairs Cup triumphs of the 1950s, but his errors were partly responsible for the club's defeat in the 1961 European Cup final.

Ramsey, Sir Alf (England), enigmatic manager of England when they won the World Cup in 1966 and lost it in 1970, made his name in the managerial field with Ipswich, guiding them from the Third Division to the League Championship in five seasons. In doing so he emulated his performance as a Spurs player of winning the Second and First Division titles in successive seasons. Spurs bought him from Southampton in 1949, and he won the nickname 'The General' for his steady, constructive play at right-back for club and country. The resolute qualities displayed in the player were later evident in the manager, with his preference for players with a high workrate rather than the spectacular individualist.

Rattin, Antonio (Argentina), deserves to be remembered for more than his dismissal from the 1966 World Cup quarter-final against England. A giant centre-half and captain of

Jesse Pennington

club, Boca Juniors, and country, he was, despite his ruthless approach, a player of immense talents. Too often, though, he had to forsake his attacking role for a negative defensive one.

Reilly, Laurie (Scotland), though on the small side for a centre-forward at 5 ft 7 in, was one of the most dangerous of his day. In 1952–53 he scored 50 goals for Hibernian, who had taken the League title the previous two seasons. Quick, tenacious, and always willing to improvise, he frequently turned a match with a goal in the last minutes.

Revie, Don (England), the man who made the great Leeds side of the 1960s and 1970s, came to the fore as a scheming inside-forward with Leicester and then, after a short stay at Hull, became the deep-lying centre-forward of Manchester City's 'Revie plan'. In 1955, when City lost at Wembley, he was Footballer of the Year, and the next season he collected his Cup winners medal. Transfers followed to Sunderland and Leeds, and it was at Leeds that, as manager, he was able to give full expression to his ideas. Buying shrewdly and encouraging youth, he built, from a mediocre Second Division side, one of Europe's foremost teams. It was a great loss to the club when Revie became England team manager in 1974.

Richardson, W. G. (England), scored both West Bromwich's goals when they won the Cup in 1931 as a Second Division side. Later in the year the fierce-shooting centre-forward put four past West Ham in five minutes in a Division I match at Upton Park. Apart from 19 for Hartlepools in 1928–29, all 'Ginger' Richardson's 217 League goals were for West Bromwich.

Riva, Luigi (Italy), a former left-winger, emerged from the defensiveness of Italian

Don Revie

'Gigi' Riva

football as a courageous and formidable striker. He scored 7 of Italy's 10 goals to take them to Mexico for the 1970 World Cup, and his deadly left foot was largely instrumental in Cagliari's winning their first ever Championship, in 1969–70. He is held in high veneration in Sardinia, and it is estimated that he has earned over £100,000 in a year.

Rivelino (Brazil), with his explosive left-foot shots and swerving free-kicks, was one of the delights of the 1970 World Cup. Essentially a midfield player with Corinthians, he was nominally Brazil's outside-left at Mexico, but enjoyed a more roving commission, often coming through from a deep-lying position to unleash a powerful drive.

Rivera, Gianni (Italy), captained AC Milan to the European Cup and World Club Championship in 1969, when he was European Footballer of the Year. Few of the game's honours have eluded him. One of football's most elegant players, he is an adroit midfield schemer with an abundance of talent. He was first capped in 1962 at 18, and the 1974 World Cup was his fourth tournament.

Roberts, Herbie (England), moved from wing-half to centre-half for Arsenal with instructions from Herbert Chapman to concentrate on defence, police the middle, and refuse to go upfield. So was created the stopper centre-half of the 'third-back game', and so successfully did the tall, phlegmatic Roberts fill the role that Arsenal won the Championship four times and the Cup twice from 1930 to 1936.

Robson, Bobby (England), as a midfield provider, spurred England's forwards to remarkable feats in 1960–61, and later in the 1960s, as a manager, took Ipswich back to Division I. His 20 internationals, which included the 1958 World Cup, came during a six-year stay at West Bromwich that was sandwiched between spells at Fulham.

Rocco, Nereo (Italy), who gained one Italian cap in 1934 as a robust inside-left with Triestina, made his name as a manager with Padova before becoming the driving force of the AC Milan of the 1960s. In 1963 he went to Torino for a short spell, then returned to Milan, taking them to the European Cup and World Club Championship in 1969.

Rocha, Pedro (Uruguay), had much to do with Penarol's success in 1966 when they won the South American Cup and the World Club Championship. That same year, the tall, elegant inside-forward helped Uruguay reach the quarter-finals of the World Cup. His fluent control and orchestration were missed in Mexico in 1970, when he was injured in the first match. Later he moved to São Paulo in Brazil.

Rous, Sir Stanley, secretary of the FA from 1934, when he refereed the FA Cup final, to 1962, when he became president of FIFA, is well suited to the administration of soccer. He has shown a breadth of vision and grasp of problems that have benefited the game in England and throughout the world, especially in developing countries. When he was deposed as president of FIFA in 1974 at the age of 79, he left behind him a fine record of achievement.

Rowe, Arthur (England), has a special place in Spurs' history as the manager who developed the 'push-and-run' style that took the club to the Second and First Division titles in successive seasons (1949–51). In his playing days he had been Tottenham's captain and England's centre-half against France in 1934.

Rowley, Arthur, tall and heavily built with a fierce left-foot shot he used often and accurately, retired in 1965 with a Football League record of 434 goals. Of these, 183 came in seven seasons with Shrewsbury Town, the

rest with West Bromwich, Fulham, whom he helped to Division I in 1948–49, and Leicester City.

Rowley, Jack (England), was a Frank Buckley discovery but never played for Wolves, who sold him to Bournemouth. Manchester United bought him in 1937, and as a free-scoring centre-forward he helped them win the FA Cup in 1948, scoring twice in the final, and the League in 1952, when his 30 goals included three hat-tricks. In 1954 he went to Plymouth Argyle as player-manager.

Sagar, Ted (England), who kept goal for Everton from March 1929 to May 1953, created a Football League long-service record for one club. During this time—24 years and 1 month—Sagar played in 465 League matches, not counting wartime games. He won Championship honours in 1932 and 1939, a Cup

Ted Sagar   Djalma Santos

Rivelino

winners medal in 1933, and four England caps in 1936.

Sandor, Karoly (Hungary), occupied the right-wing berth for Hungary at the 1962 World Cup, having played twice in Sweden four years earlier. In full flight, he was a most exciting performer with his close ball control and pace. He won 75 caps altogether, and in 1964 scored twice for MTK Budapest in the final of the European Cup-Winners Cup.

Santamaría, José (Uruguay and Spain), moved from Nacional to Real Madrid and from 1958 was centre-half in their successful European Cup sides. He had been Uruguay's stopper in the 1954 World Cup and was to play for Spain in Chile in 1962. His tackling was always sure, if sometimes bordering on the ferocious, and his heading confident.

Santos, Djalma (Brazil), numbered four World Cups (1954–1966) among his 101 caps, which were a South American record. A strong tackler with a sound positional sense, he gave strength to the Brazilian defence at right-back, but still retained the desire to overlap when the occasion arose. In 1970, now 41 and playing for Atlético Paranaense, he was voted Brazilian defender of the year.

Santos, Nilton (Brazil), partnered Djalma Santos (no relation) at left-back in the 1958 and 1962 World Cup finals. Of the Botafogo club, tall, powerful, and elegant, he was in the Brazilian side as early as 1949. He was sent off during the notorious 'Battle of Berne' of 1954.

Sarosi, Gyorgy (Hungary), captained his country to the final of the 1938 World Cup. An excellent centre-forward with fine ball control and strong finishing, he was also a most capable attacking centre-half, and played for both Ferencvaros and Hungary in either position. In 1937 he scored five against Czechoslovakia, and a year later he formed a formidable World Cup striking force with Szengeller.

Scarone, Hector (Uruguay), short, slight, but not lacking in skill or courage, wove victory in the 1924 and 1928 Olympics and the 1930 World Cup with his tricky runs and swerving shots. Usually at inside-right, he won 64 caps. Nacional were his primary club, but Barcelona and Ambrosiana-Inter benefited from his prolific goal-scoring during spells in Spain and Italy.

Schiaffino, Juan (Uruguay and Italy), Uruguay's outstanding forward when they won the 1950 World Cup, went to AC Milan in 1954 for a world record £72,000 and won four caps for Italy. He had played 22 times for Uruguay, including another World Cup in 1954 when he was an inspiring midfield general. In 1950 his equalizer turned the 'final' away from Brazil.

Schnellinger, Karl-Heinz (West Germany), found a new role in the 1970 World Cup as a sweeper. Prior to that he had been one of Europe's most formidable left-backs, strong in the tackle and dominating, though his first World Cup, in 1958, had seen him at right-half. In 1963 he was transferred from 1FC Cologne to AS Roma, but later went to AC Milan, helping them to European and World Club Championship honours.

Schoen, Helmut (Germany), turned to coaching after a knee injury ended a playing career in which he won 16 international caps between 1937 and 1941 as an inside-forward. In the 1960s he took over the West German side from Sepp Herberger and was responsible for guiding it to the final of the 1966 World Cup, winning the European Championship in 1972, and finally the World Cup in 1974.

Karl-Heinz Schnellinger

Scott, Elisha (Northern Ireland), made his debut as Liverpool's goalkeeper on January 1, 1913, and went on to make a club record 428 appearances before moving to Belfast Celtic in 1934. His keen sense of anticipation and wonderful reflex saves were major factors in Liverpool's Championships of 1921–22 and 1922–23. At a time when the Irish played only the Home Countries, he won 31 caps.

Scott, Laurie (England), George Hardwick's full-back partner for England from 1946, would have won more than 17 caps but for a severe knee injury in 1948. Solidly built and fast in the recovery, he joined Arsenal from Bradford City in 1937 and enjoyed their post-war League and Cup successes before moving to Crystal Palace in 1951.

Jimmy Scoular

Scoular, Jimmy (Scotland), with Jimmy Dickinson and Reg Flewin, made up the fine half-back line that helped Portsmouth win successive Championships (1948–50). In 1953, the flamboyant, hard-tackling right-half

went to Newcastle, and two years later captained them to a Wembley victory. He finished his playing days with Bradford and emerged in the 1960s as a shrewd, inspiring manager of Cardiff.

Seed, Jimmy (England), enjoyed FA Cup success as both player and manager. In 1921 his pass to Jimmy Dimmock brought Spurs the winning goal, and in 1947 he managed Charlton to their first Cup win, having watched them lose the previous year. Spurs released their talented inside-right in 1927, when he was 32, only to see him win League honours with Sheffield Wednesday in 1929 and 1930.

Seeler, Uwe (West Germany), winner of a record 72 caps, scored in four World Cups, captaining the Germans to the final and semi-finals respectively in 1966 and 1970. By 1970 he had reverted to midfield, but with his acrobatic headers and deadly finishing he was not far removed from the striker who had led the West German League scorers on five occasions. In 1968 he captained SV Hamburg to the European Cup-Winners Cup final.

Sewell, Jackie (England), moved from Notts County to Sheffield Wednesday in 1951 for a record £34,000, only to go down to Division II almost immediately. But his 22 goals contributed to promotion the next season, when he

Len Shackleton

Uwe Seeler

won three of his six England caps. In 1953 he scored a fine solo goal against the Hungarians, and in 1957 collected a Cup winners medal with Aston Villa.

Shackleton, Len (England), won only five caps. Had this gifted, elusive inside-forward not been such an individual, had he bowed to authority, he must surely have won more. Rejected by Arsenal, he spent a brief spell at Bradford before Newcastle paid £13,000 for him in 1946. Six goals against Newport County on his debut showed his brilliance but, unsettled, he soon took his rebellious talents to Sunderland.

Shankly, Bill (Scotland), having enjoyed a distinguished career that saw him as Preston's right-half in the 1937 and 1938 Cup finals, managed Carlisle, Grimsby, Workington, and Huddersfield before going to Liverpool in 1959. Since then he has become a legend—shrewd, gruff but kind, witty, often quoted—and he developed the formidable and successful Liverpool side of the 1960s. He retired in 1974.

Shesternev, Albert (USSR), whether as centre-half or sweeper, was the most consistent Russian defender of the 1960s, and by the 1970 World Cup was his country's captain. He had played in the 1966 tournament, when the Russians were semi-finalists, and was first capped in 1963. In 1970 he took the Russian Army team to the national championship.

Simpson, Ronnie (Scotland), won an envious list of honours, including his five Scottish caps, as Celtic's goalkeeper from 1965–66 to 1969–70. In 1967 he was Scotland's Footballer of the Year. Yet he was in his mid-30s when Celtic signed him from Hibs, and had earlier won FA Cup honours with Newcastle United in 1952 and 1955. As a teenager with amateur Queen's Park he had been Britain's 'keeper at the 1948 Olympics.

Sindelar, Matthias (Austria), the 'Man of Paper', illustrated fully the class and technique that made the *Wunderteam* of the 1930s so memorable. His footwork, ball control, and body swerve were impeccable, making him Europe's outstanding centre-forward. His tactical awareness made him the ideal player for Hugo Meisl to mould his attacking side around. He won 44 caps and his club was FK Austria.

Sipos, Ferenc (Hungary), stylish and determined on the ground, dominating in the air, gave strength to the Hungarian defence in three World Cups. In 1958 he was at centre-half, but the next two tournaments saw him one of the two centre-backs. He began as an inside-forward with MTK Budapest (he later played for Honved) and retained his ball-playing skills in defence.

Sivori, Enrique (Argentina and Italy), cost Juventus a world record £91,000 to River Plate in 1957 and, with John Charles, helped them win three League titles in four seasons. A small, dynamic inside-left, he had superb ball control, an exciting ability to push the ball between an opponent's legs, and a powerful left-foot shot that brought most of his 135 League goals before he went to Napoli in 1965.

Slater, Bill (England), having been a Cup finalist with Blackpool in 1951 and an Olympic representative in 1952, embraced professionalism with Wolves and made a major contribution to their success after 1953. A muscular half-back, he captained them to Cup victory and was Footballer of the Year in 1960, when Wolves narrowly missed a League hat-trick and the 'double'.

Smith, Bobby (England), after a disappointing career with Chelsea, became the robust but skilful centre-forward of Spurs' 'double' side. That 1960–61 season was a lucrative one for him. In addition to 28 League goals, he scored the opener in the Cup final and bagged eight

Joe Smith (right)

Smith, Joe (England), captained Bolton to victory in the 1923 and 1926 Cup finals, but in 1953 it was Bolton that his Blackpool side beat in the 'Matthews final'. A strong inside-left who formed a formidable left-flank attack with Ted Vizard, he made 450 League appearances for Bolton before joining Stockport in 1927. As a manager he bought soundly and guided Blackpool to three Wembley finals.

Spencer, Alberto (Ecuador and Uruguay), caused some controversy after leading Uruguay's attack against England at Wembley in 1964. For though with Penarol, the coloured centre-forward was still an Ecuador national. He won his first cap for that country at 16. A prolific scorer, fast, powerful, and incisive, he scored five goals altogether in Penarol's 1961 and 1966 World Club Championship victories.

Steel, Billy (Scotland), a stocky inside-left lightning quick at making or taking goals, played so brilliantly in his first international, in April 1947, that a month later he was playing for Great Britain against the Rest of Europe, and soon Derby were paying Morton a record £15,000 for him. In 1950 he returned to Dundee, and in 1954, having won 30 caps, went to America.

inside-forward was an outstanding midfield leader when Spain won the Nations Cup in 1964 and Inter won the European Cup and World Club Championship in 1964 and 1965.

Swift, Frank (England), huge of hand and frame, was England's first-choice goalkeeper after World War II, twice as captain. With Manchester City he had won Cup and League honours in the 1930s, gaining a place in FA Cup history when, just 19, he fainted from nervous strain at the end of the 1934 final. He died in the 1958 Munich air disaster when travelling as a journalist.

Frank Swift

in his six internationals. He scored again in the 1962 Cup final and gained a Cup-Winners Cup winners medal the next year.

Smith, G. O. (England), was said to be England's greatest centre-forward in the period before World War I. Always an amateur, he played for Old Carthusians and the Corinthians, winning 19 caps between 1893 and 1901 when, at 29, he retired. If somewhat reluctant to head the ball, he finished strongly with his feet, and his dribbling was both penetrative and a pleasure to watch.

Smith, Gordon (Scotland), earned the nickname of 'Scotland's Stanley Matthews' for his dazzling displays on the wing. But the form shown at club level rarely appeared in internationals. His 18 caps were won between 1946 and 1957. He is best remembered for European Cup displays, helping Hibs and Dundee to the semi-finals in 1955 and 1962 respectively. He wore Hearts' colours in the 1961 European Cup.

Jock Stein

Stein, Jock, went to Celtic in 1951 from the obscurity of non-League football in Wales. Three years later the sturdy centre-half was captaining Celtic to a Scottish League and Cup double. That in itself was a Cinderella story, but Stein was to reach greater heights as a manager. In 1960 he saved Dunfermline from relegation and led them to a Scottish Cup triumph the next year. A short spell with Hibs in 1964 and then he was back at Celtic. With his arrival came an era of glory, with a perpetual list of League, Cup, and League Cup honours climaxed by the European Cup victory of 1967.

Stephenson, Clem (England), having helped Aston Villa win the FA Cup in 1913 and 1920, was signed by Huddersfield manager Herbert Chapman in 1921 when it seemed he had seen his best days. It was an inspired buy. The clever, scheming inside-left led Huddersfield to a Cup victory in 1922 and a hat-trick of League titles from 1923–24.

Stiles, Nobby (England), emerged from the 1966 World Cup as a major character of international football, loved in England, detested and victimized elsewhere. A short but totally combative wing-half, he was often in conflict with authority, but his defensive qualities were essential to both England and Manchester United, with whom he won League honours in 1965 and 1967 and a European Cup winners medal in 1968. In 1971 he moved to Middlesbrough.

Suarez, Luis (Spain), European Footballer of the Year in 1960, cost Inter-Milan £210,000 to secure from Barcelona in 1961. With superb ball control and a powerful shot, the immaculate

Ernie Taylor

Taylor, Ernie (England), a skilful and entertaining inside-forward, played in three FA Cup finals for three clubs, winning with Newcastle in 1951 and Blackpool, partnering Stanley Matthews, in 1953. In 1958 he was given special permission to join Manchester United after the Munich disaster, and his experience did much to help a young and inexperienced side reach Wembley, only to lose to Bolton.

Taylor, Tommy (England), had played 19 times and scored 16 goals, including two hat-tricks, for England at the time of his death in the Munich disaster. A Barnsley product, he won League honours with Manchester United in 1956 and 1957 and scored their goal in the 1957 Cup final. He was the ideal centre-forward, strong and sure both in the air and on the ground.

Templeton, Bobby (Scotland), a supremely gifted but wayward outside-left, never fully realized the tremendous potential of his superb ball control and tactical genius. Some of his

Clem Stephenson

John Thomson

best performances were for Scotland, for whom he played 11 times, first while with Aston Villa in 1901–02 and again during stays with Newcastle, Woolwich Arsenal, and Kilmarnock.

Thomson, John (Scotland), a strong, brave goalkeeper with lightning reflexes and cat-like leaps, died tragically in 1931 during a Rangers–Celtic match. His mother had once dreamt that he would be badly injured while keeping goal. Only 22, he had helped Celtic win the Scottish Cup twice and had just begun his international career, and with his death he became a legend in Scottish football.

Tostão (Brazil) recovered from a major eye operation to play a vital role in Brazil's 1970 World Cup victory. A splendid ball artist with goalscoring genius, he selflessly played the role of 'target man', holding the ball before giving passes for others to score from. At 19 he had won a place in the 1966 World Cup party after outstanding performances as Cruzeiro's centre-forward. He was transferred to Vasco da Gama for a record £220,000 in 1972, but an eye injury curtailed his career.

Van Hanegem, Wim (Netherlands), joined Feyenoord in 1969, and it was no coincidence that they won the European Cup that season. Possessing great vision and a powerful and accurate left foot, he won a UEFA Cup medal in 1974 and played an important part in his country's reaching the final of the 1974 World Cup.

Van Himst, Paul (Belgium), made his international debut in 1960 at 17, when he was Belgium's Footballer of the Year—an award he won again in 1962 and 1965. Strong on the ball yet possessing delicate skills, he began at centre-forward but became a striking inside-forward able to work from midfield, Always with Anderlecht, he is usually one of Belgium's leading goalscorers.

Vavá (Brazil), a bustling centre-forward in the English style, scored nine goals as leader of the Brazilian attack in the successful World Cup campaigns of 1958 and 1962. He first came to notice as a teenager with Vasco da Gama. After the 1958 World Cup he played for Atlético Madrid until returning to Brazil and Palmeiras in time to win selection for the 1962 tournament.

Veitch, Colin (England), captained and did so much to mould the great Newcastle side that won the League three times and played in five FA Cup finals from 1904 to 1911. Versatile—he was inside-left, centre-forward, centre-half, and right-half in those finals—and

an astute reader of a game, he is one of the all-time 'greats' among wing-halves.

Vizard, Ted (Wales), occupied the left-wing position for Bolton for 21 years, appearing at Wembley in the Cup-winning sides of 1923 and 1926. His control and technique allowed him a long career, and Wales have had few finer wingers than 'Vizard the Wizard'. His partnership with inside-left Joe Smith gave Bolton a formidable and penetrative left flank.

Vogts, Berti (West Germany), small, fair-haired terrier of a right-back, played a prominent part in his country's 1974 World Cup triumph, especially in the final, where he did a fine job of marking Johan Cruyff. He also played in the 1970 World Cup, and in the 1973 UEFA Cup final for his club, Borussia Mönchengladbach.

Voronin, Valeri (USSR), played a major part in Russia's success in the 1960s, winning over 50 caps, yet his career was virtually destroyed by a public humiliation for his life style following a car crash. He began as an attacking right-half with Moscow Torpedo in the late 1950s, and by the time of the 1964 Nations Cup he was one of Europe's most forceful midfield men.

Waddell, Willie (Scotland), a fast, fearless right-winger, helped Rangers win the League four times and the Scottish Cup twice between 1938 and 1955. In 1957 he took over Kilmarnock and by 1965 they had been League champions once, runners-up four times, and Scottish Cup finalists four times. It was understandable Rangers should call on him in 1969 to restore their former glory.

Walker, Billy (England), enjoyed distinguished careers as player and manager. A superb goal-scoring inside-left and splendid strategist, he made more than 500 appearances for Aston Villa, whom he captained to victory in the 1920 FA Cup. He collected a runners-up medal in 1924. As a manager, he had two Wembley successes, with Sheffield Wednesday in 1935 and with Nottingham Forest in 1959.

Walker, Tommy (Scotland), spent most of his football career with Hearts, winning 20 caps during the 1930s as a strong-shooting inside-forward giving immaculate distribution. As manager he guided the club to the League Championship in 1958 and 1960, the Cup in 1956, and the League Cup four times, producing such stars as Dave Mackay and Alex Young. In 1966, however, Hearts dismissed him.

Billy Walker

Tostão (right)

Ray Wilson

Walter, Fritz (Germany and West Germany), with his superb control and imaginative use of the ball, guided West Germany to their 1954 World Cup win as captain and midfield tactician. His brother Otmar led the attack. Four years later, and then 37, Fritz was equally effective in Sweden. An inside-forward who was first a striker but later a schemer, he won 61 caps between 1940 and 1958.

Waring, Pongo (England), scored 49 goals when Aston Villa totalled a First Division record 128 goals in 1930–31, yet were only runners-up to Arsenal. Big and strong, he was one of the most dangerous centre-forwards between the wars, amassing 245 League goals for Tranmere, Aston Villa (from 1928 to 1935), Barnsley, Wolves, and Accrington Stanley.

Weaver, Sam (England), is best remembered for his early use of the long throw into the opposition goalmouth. Yet he deserves better, for he was among the finest left-halves of the 1930s, strong and skilful. Hull City transferred him in 1929 to Newcastle, with whom he won a winners medal in the 1932 Cup final, and he spent three seasons with Chelsea before the war.

Wedlock, Billy (England), though only 5 ft 4½ in tall, was highly esteemed as an attacking centre-half before World War I. With a non-stop approach to the game, he constantly supported his forwards, and his recovery was such that he rarely lost control of the midfield. Usually known as 'Fatty' or 'Smiler', he helped Bristol City to Division I in 1906 and to the 1909 FA Cup final.

White, John (Scotland), was the essence of the brilliant Spurs of the early 1960s. With his nigh faultless positioning and anticipation, his immaculate ball control, and his intelligent passing, especially the pin-point centres to Bobby Smith, he fired the attack that won the League, the FA Cup (twice) and the Cup-Winners Cup in three seasons. He began in virtual obscurity with Alloa Athletic before going to Falkirk. Spurs signed him in 1959, using him as a right-winger before returning him to his inside-right position. When he died in July 1964, struck by lightning on a London golf course, football lost one of its finest talents.

Whittaker, Tom, trainer of the great Arsenal of the 1930s, won world fame for his healing powers and many, other than his team, benefited from his ministrations. He was a strong left-back for Arsenal until a knee injury in 1925 put paid to his career, and he turned to training. In 1947 he became Arsenal's manager, leading them to two Championship titles and two Cup finals.

Williams, Bert (England), succeeded Frank Swift as England's goalkeeper in 1949 and went on to win 24 caps. With Wolves he collected a Cup winners medal in 1949 and a Championship medal in 1954. Strongly built and extremely brave in the face of oncoming for-

wards, he was capable of the most amazing acrobatic saves. England has had few better 'keepers.

Wilson, Ray (England), developed late but played for his country 63 times from 1960 to 1968, establishing himself as one of the game's outstanding left-backs. Fast, strong, and an excellent passer, he was well suited to the Ramsey role of overlapping full-back, and in the 1966 World Cup only one error marred an otherwise impeccable performance. He began with Huddersfield in 1955–56 as a wing-half and in 1964 moved to Everton, playing for them in the 1966 and 1968 FA Cup finals.

Winterbottom, Walter, England manager and FA chief coach from 1946 to 1963, had a strong influence on English football in that period. The former Manchester United centre-half stressed the importance of practical coaching on the field and the incorporation of personal skills into team tactics. He initiated England's under-23 and Youth teams. But at a senior level he was hampered by having to work with a selection committee.

Woodburn, Willie (Scotland), won 24 caps, five Scottish Championship medals, and four Scottish Cup and two League Cup winners medals as a strong, dominating centre-half for Rangers after 1938. But he will be remembered, too, as the player who, in 1954, was barred from soccer indefinitely after a history of disciplinary offences had been taken into account. The ban was lifted in 1957, when he was 36.

Woodley, Vic (England), was not a showy goalkeeper, but he was safe and authoritative. Chelsea's 'keeper of the 1930s, he won 19 caps in the three seasons prior to World War II, and in 1946–47 he helped Derby to win the FA Cup for the first time.

Woodward, Vivian (England), played more than 60 times for England in amateur and full internationals, winning Olympic gold medals in 1908 and 1912. From 1908 to 1915 he played, always as an amateur, for Spurs and then Chelsea. A centre-forward who relied on accuracy and artistry rather than speed and power, he could create as well as score goals and held his attack together skilfully.

Wright, Billy (England), when he led England against Scotland in April 1959, became the first footballer to win 100 caps. When he retired in August that year he had 105. He had captained England since 1948. Originally an inside-forward, he soon staked his claim to the right-half berth, but in the 1954 World Cup he moved to centre-half, where his courage, determination, and remarkable leap were ideally suited.

Wright played more than 500 games for Wolves, captaining them to victory in the Cup

Ricardo Zamora, with Dixie Dean threatening.

in 1949 and in the Championship in 1954, 1958, and 1959. He was Footballer of the Year in 1952. Yet when he had joined Wolves, Frank Buckley almost sent him home because he was too small. In 1962 he became manager of Arsenal, but, though doing much that was good, he did not produce immediate results and was replaced in 1966.

Yachin, Lev (USSR), well over 6 ft tall and given to courageous and spectacular saves, ranks high on any list of all-time great goalkeepers. Winner of a record 74 caps, he starred in the 1958 World Cup (the first of three), and in the 1960 and 1964 Nations Cups, in which Russia were winners and runners-up respectively. All his domestic football was played for Moscow Dynamo, but one of his most brilliant performances was for the Rest of the World against England in 1963.

Young, George (Scotland), his country's most capped player when he retired in 1957, dominated the defence in one of Rangers' great periods. Tall and strongly built, yet surprisingly mobile, he was equally commanding at centre-half or right-back. He captained his country in 50 of his 75 representative appearances (53 peace-time internationals) and won six League and four Cup winners medals.

Mario Zagalo

Zagalo, Mario (Brazil), participated in the three victories that gave Brazil permanent possession of the Jules Rimet Trophy. With Flamenco and in Brazil's 1958 and 1962 sides, he was the tireless midfield runner, virtually creating a new role. In 1970, given charge of the World Cup squad at short notice after success with Botafogo, he gambled on Tostão and produced a side that showed attacking football was winning football—a doctrine he sadly forgot in the 1974 World Cup.

Zamora, Ricardo (Spain), despite a dreadful day against England in 1931 when he let in seven goals, was one of Spain's outstanding goalkeepers. Spectacular and safe, acrobatic and assured in handling, he was outstanding in the Olympics of 1924 and 1928 and the 1934 World Cup. Capped 47 times, he began with Español and Barcelona before going to Real Madrid in 1930 for a record £6,000.

Zito, José (Brazil), was, at right-half, the midfield link in Brazil's 4-2-4 in the 1958 World Cup, strong in attack or defence. In 1962 his role was just as important, and it was his header that gave Brazil the lead in the final. With Santos, he was a major factor in their South American Cup/World Club Championship doubles of 1962 and 1963.

Zizinho (Brazil), with Ademir and Jair, formed the famed Brazilian inside-forward trio of the 1950 World Cup. A superb ball player, imaginative and intuitive, he filled the popular conception of the Brazilian footballer, and he belied a seemingly frail physique by still going strong in the national side in 1956 at 35. With Flamengo, he won numerous domestic honours before going to Bangú.

World Competitions

WORLD CUP

1930: URUGUAY

Group 1

France	(3) **4**	Mexico	(0) **1**
Laurent, Langiller, Maschinot (2)		Carreno	
Argentina	(0) **1**	**France**	(0) **0**
Monti			
Chile	(1) **3**	**Mexico**	(0) **0**
Vidal, Subiabre (2)			
Chile	(0) **1**	**France**	(0) **0**
Subiabre			
Argentina	(3) **6**	**Mexico**	(0) **3**
Stabile (3), Varallo (2), Zumelzu		Lopez, Rosas (F), Rosas (M)	
Argentina	(2) **3**	**Chile**	(1) **1**
Stabile (2), Evaristo (M)		Subiabre	

	P	W	D	L	F	A	Pts
Argentina	3	3	0	0	10	4	6
Chile	3	2	0	1	5	3	4
France	3	1	0	2	4	3	2
Mexico	3	0	0	3	4	13	0

Group 2

Yugoslavia	(2) **2**	Brazil	(0) **1**
Tirnanic, Beck		Neto	
Yugoslavia	(0) **4**	**Bolivia**	(0) **0**
Beck (2), Marianovic, Vujadinovic			
Brazil	(1) **4**	**Bolivia**	(0) **0**
Visintainer (2), Neto (2)			

	P	W	D	L	F	A	Pts
Yugoslavia	2	2	0	0	6	1	4
Brazil	2	1	0	1	5	2	2
Bolivia	2	0	0	2	0	8	0

Group 3

Romania	(1) **3**	Peru	(0) **1**
Staucin (2), Barbu		Souza	
Uruguay	(0) **1**	**Peru**	(0) **0**
Castro			
Uruguay	(4) **4**	**Romania**	(0) **0**
Dorado, Scarone, Anselmo, Cea			

	P	W	D	L	F	A	Pts
Uruguay	2	2	0	0	5	0	4
Romania	2	1	0	1	3	5	2
Peru	2	0	0	2	1	4	0

Group 4

USA	(2) **3**	Belgium	(0) **0**
McGhee (2), Patenaude			
USA	(2) **3**	**Paraguay**	(0) **0**
Patenaude (2), Florie			
Paraguay	(1) **1**	**Belgium**	(0) **0**
Pena			

	P	W	D	L	F	A	Pts
USA	2	2	0	0	6	0	4
Paraguay	2	1	0	1	1	3	2
Belgium	2	0	0	2	0	4	0

Semi-Finals

Argentina	(1) **6**	USA	(0) **1**
Monti, Scopelli, Stabile (2), Peucelle (2)		Brown	
Uruguay	(3) **6**	**Yugoslavia**	(1) **1**
Cea (3), Anselmo (2), Iriarte		Seculic	

For Alf Ramsey, a prophecy fulfilled. He holds the Jules Rimet Trophy won by England in 1966. In 1970, however, the trophy became the permanent possession of the Brazilians after their third World Cup success.

Final

Uruguay	(1) **4**	Argentina	(2) **2**
Dorado, Cea, Iriarte, Castro		Peucelle, Stabile	

Uruguay: Ballesteros; Nasazzi, Mascheroni; Andrade, Fernandez, Gestido; Dorado, Scarone, Castro, Cea, Iriarte
Argentina: Botasso; Della Torre, Paternoster; Evaristo (J), Monti, Suarez; Peucelle, Varallo, Stabile, Ferriera, Evaristo (M)

1934: ITALY

1st Round

Italy	(3) **7**	USA	(0) **1**
Schiavio (3), Orsi (2), Meazza, Ferrari		Donelli	
Czechoslovakia	(0) **2**	**Romania**	(1) **1**
Puc, Nejedly		Dobai	
Germany	(1) **5**	**Belgium**	(2) **2**
Conen (3), Kobierski (2)		Voorhoof (2)	
Austria	(1) (1) **3**	**France**	(1) (1) **2**
Sindelar, Schall, Bican		Nicolas, Verriest (pen.)	
Spain	(3) **3**	**Brazil**	(1) **1**
Iraragorri (pen.), Langara (2)		Silva	
Switzerland	(2) **3**	**Netherlands**	(1) **2**
Kielholz (2), Abegglen		Smit, Vente	
Sweden	(1) **3**	**Argentina**	(1) **2**
Jonasson (2), Kroon		Belis, Galateo	

SUMMARY OF FINALS

Year	Venue	Attendance	Winners		Runners-up	
1930	Montevideo, Uruguay	100,000	Uruguay	4	Argentina	2
1934	Rome, Italy	55,000	Italy	2	Czechoslovakia	1
1938	Paris, France	65,000	Italy	4	Hungary	2
1950	Rio de Janeiro, Brazil	199,854	Uruguay	4	Brazil	1
1954	Berne, Switzerland	55,000	West Germany	3	Hungary	2
1958	Stockholm, Sweden	49,737	Brazil	5	Sweden	2
1962	Santiago, Chile	69,068	Brazil	3	Czechoslovakia	1
1966	Wembley, England	93,000	England	4	West Germany	2
1970	Mexico City, Mexico	110,000	Brazil	4	Italy	1
1974	Munich, West Germany	75,000	West Germany	2	Netherlands	1

Hungary	(2) **4**	Egypt	(1) **2**
Teleky, Toldi (2), Vincze		Fawzi (2)	

2nd Round

Germany	(1) **2**	Sweden	(0) **1**
Hohmann (2)		Dunker	
Austria	(1) **2**	**Hungary**	(0) **1**
Horwath, Zischek		Sarosi (pen.)	
Italy	(0) (1) **1**	**Spain**	(1) (1) **1**
Ferrari		Regueiro	
Replay			
Italy	(1) **1**	**Spain**	(0) **0**
Meazza			
Czechoslovakia	(1) **3**	**Switzerland**	(1) **2**
Svoboda, Sobotka, Nejedly		Kielholz, Abegglen	

Semi-Finals

Czechoslovakia	(1) **3**	Germany	(0) **1**
Nejedly (2), Krcil		Noack	
Italy	(1) **1**	**Austria**	(0) **0**
Guaita			

Third Place Match

Germany	(3) **3**	Austria	(1) **2**
Lehner (2), Conen		Horwath, Seszta	

Final

Italy	(0) (1) **2**	Czechoslovakia	(0) (1) **1**
Orsi, Schiavio		Puc	

Italy: Combi; Monzeglio, Allemandi; Ferraris, Monti, Bertolini; Guaita, Meazza, Schiavio, Ferrari, Orsi
Czechoslovakia: Planicka; Zenisek, Ctyroky; Kostalek, Cambal, Krcil; Junek, Svoboda, Sobotka, Nejedly, Puc

1938: FRANCE

1st Round

Switzerland	(1) (1) **1**	Germany	(1) (1) **1**
Abegglen		Gauchel	
Replay			
Switzerland	(0) **4**	**Germany**	(2) **2**
Wallaschek, Bickel, Abegglen (2)		Hahnemann, Loertscher (o.g.)	
Cuba	(0) (2) **3**	**Romania**	(1) (2) **3**
Tunas, Maquina, Sosa		Covaci, Baratki, Dobai	
Replay			
Cuba	(0) **2**	**Romania**	(1) **1**
Socorro, Maquina		Dobai	
Hungary	(4) **6**	**Dutch East Indies**	(0) **0**
Kohut, Toldi, Sarosi (2), Szengeller (2)			
France	(2) **3**	**Belgium**	(1) **1**
Veinante, Nicolas (2)		Isemborghs	
Czechoslovakia	(0) (0) **3**	**Netherlands**	(0) (0) **0**
Kostalek, Boucek, Nejedly			
Brazil	(3) (4) **6**	**Poland**	(1) (4) **5**
Leonidas (4), Peracio, Romeo		Wilimowski (4), Piontek	
Italy	(1) (1) **2**	**Norway**	(0) (1) **1**
Ferrari, Piola		Brustad	

102

2nd Round

Sweden (4) **8** **Cuba** (0) **0**
Andersson, Jonasson,
Wetterstroem (4),
Nyberg, Keller

Hungary (1) **2** **Switzerland** (0) **0**
Szengeller (2)

Italy (1) **3** **France** (1) **1**
Colaussi, Piola (2) Heisserer

Brazil (1) (1) **1** **Czechoslovakia** (1) (1) **1**
Leonidas
 Nejedly (pen.)

Replay
Brazil (0) **2** **Czechoslovakia** (1) **1**
Leonidas, Roberto Kopecky

Semi-Finals

Italy (2) **2** **Brazil** (0) **1**
Colaussi, Romeo
Meazza (pen.)

Hungary (3) **5** **Sweden** (1) **1**
Szengeller (3), Nyberg
Titkos, Sarosi

Third Place Match

Brazil (1) **4** **Sweden** (2) **2**
Romeo, Leonidas (2), Jonasson, Nyberg
Peracio

Final

Italy (3) **4** **Hungary** (1) **2**
Colaussi (2), Piola (2) Titkos, Sarosi
Italy: Olivieri; Foni, Rava; Serantoni, Andreolo,
Locatelli; Biavati, Meazza, Piola, Ferrari,
Colaussi
Hungary: Szabo; Polgar, Biro; Szalay, Szucs,
Lazar; Sas, Vincze, Sarosi, Szengeller, Titkos

1950: BRAZIL

Group 1

Brazil (1) **4** **Mexico** (0) **0**
Ademir (2), Jair,
Baltazar

Yugoslavia (3) **3** **Switzerland** (0) **0**
Tomasevic (2),
Ognanov

Yugoslavia (2) **4** **Mexico** (0) **1**
Bobek, Cajkowski (2), Casarin
Tomasevic

Brazil (2) **2** **Switzerland** (1) **2**
Alfredo, Baltazar Fatton, Tamini

Brazil (1) **2** **Yugoslavia** (0) **0**
Ademir, Zizinho

Switzerland (2) **2** **Mexico** (0) **1**
Bader, Fatton Velasquez

	P	W	D	L	F	A	Pts
Brazil	3	2	1	0	8	2	5
Yugoslavia	3	2	0	1	7	3	4
Switzerland	3	1	1	1	4	6	3
Mexico	3	0	0	3	2	10	0

Group 2

Spain (0) **3** **USA** (1) **1**
Basora (2), Zarra Souza (J)

England (1) **2** **Chile** (0) **0**
Mortensen, Mannion

USA (1) **1** **England** (0) **0**
Gaetjens

Spain (2) **2** **Chile** (0) **0**
Basora, Zarra

Spain (0) **1** **England** (0) **0**
Zarra

Chile (2) **5** **USA** (0) **2**
Robledo, Pariani, Souza (J)
Cremaschi (3), Prieto

	P	W	D	L	F	A	Pts
Spain	3	3	0	0	6	1	6
England	3	1	0	2	2	2	2
Chile	3	1	0	2	5	6	2
USA	3	1	0	2	4	8	2

Group 3

Sweden (2) **3** **Italy** (1) **2**
Jeppson (2), Carapellese,
Andersson Muccinelli

Sweden (2) **2** **Paraguay** (1) **2**
Sundqvist, Palmer Lopez (A), Lopez (F)

Italy (1) **2** **Paraguay** (0) **0**
Carapellese,
Pandolfini

	P	W	D	L	F	A	Pts
Sweden	2	1	1	0	5	4	3
Italy	2	1	0	1	4	3	2
Paraguay	2	0	1	1	2	4	1

Group 4

Uruguay (4) **8** **Bolivia** (0) **0**
Schiaffino (4),
Miguez (2), Vidal,
Ghiggia

	P	W	D	L	F	A	Pts
Uruguay	1	1	0	0	8	0	2
Bolivia	1	0	0	1	0	8	0

Final Pool

Uruguay (1) **2** **Spain** (2) **2**
Ghiggia, Varela Basora (2)

Brazil (3) **7** **Sweden** (0) **1**
Ademir (4), Chico (2), Andersson (pen.)
Maneca

Uruguay (1) **3** **Sweden** (2) **2**
Ghiggia, Miguez (2) Palmer, Sundqvist

Brazil (3) **6** **Spain** (0) **1**
Jair (2), Chico (2), Igoa
Zizinho, Parra (o.g.)

Sweden (2) **3** **Spain** (0) **1**
Johnsson, Mellberg, Zarra
Palmer

Uruguay (0) **2** **Brazil** (0) **1**
Schiaffino, Ghiggia Friaça

	P	W	D	L	F	A	Pts
Uruguay	3	2	1	0	7	5	5
Brazil	3	2	0	1	14	4	4
Sweden	3	1	0	2	6	11	2
Spain	3	0	1	2	4	11	1

1954: SWITZERLAND

Group 1

Yugoslavia (1) **1** **France** (0) **0**
Milutinovic

Brazil (4) **5** **Mexico** (0) **0**
Baltazar, Didi,
Pinga (2), Julinho

France (1) **3** **Mexico** (0) **2**
Vincent, Naranjo, Balcazar
Cardenas (o.g.),
Kopa (pen.)

Brazil (0) (1) **1** **Yugoslavia** (0) (1) **1**
Didi Zebec

	P	W	D	L	F	A	Pts
Brazil	2	1	1	0	6	1	3
Yugoslavia	2	1	1	0	2	1	3
France	2	1	0	1	3	3	2
Mexico	2	0	0	2	2	8	0

Group 2

Hungary (4) **9** **South Korea** (0) **0**
Czibor, Kocsis (3),
Puskas (2), Lantos,
Palotas (2)

West Germany (1) **4** **Turkey** (1) **1**
Klodt, Morlock, Suat
Schaefer, Walter (O)

Hungary (3) **8** **West Germany** (1) **3**
Hidegkuti (2), Pfaff, Herrmann,
Kocsis (4), Puskas, Rahn
Toth

Turkey (4) **7** **South Korea** (0) **0**
Burhan (3), Erol,
Lefter, Suat (2)

	P	W	D	L	F	A	Pts
Hungary	2	2	0	0	17	3	4
W.Germany	2	1	0	1	7	9	2
Turkey	2	1	0	1	8	4	2
S. Korea	2	0	0	2	0	16	0

Play-off
West Germany (3) **7** **Turkey** (1) **2**
Morlock (3), Mustafa, Lefter
Walter (O), Walter (F),
Schaefer (2)

Group 3

Austria (1) **1** **Scotland** (0) **0**
Probst

Uruguay (0) **2** **Czechoslovakia** (0) **0**
Miguez, Schiaffino

Austria (4) **5** **Czechoslovakia** (0) **0**
Stojaspal (2),
Probst (3)

Uruguay (2) **7** **Scotland** (0) **0**
Borges (3), Miguez (2),
Abbadie (2)

	P	W	D	L	F	A	Pts
Uruguay	2	2	0	0	9	0	4
Austria	2	2	0	0	6	0	4
Czechoslovakia	2	0	0	2	0	7	0
Scotland	2	0	0	2	0	8	0

Group 4

England (2) (3) **4** **Belgium** (1) (3) **4**
Broadis (2), Anoul, (2), Coppens,
Lofthouse (2) Dickinson (o.g.)

Switzerland (1) **2** **Italy** (1) **1**
Ballaman, Hugi Boniperti

England (1) **2** **Switzerland** (0) **0**
Mullen, Wilshaw

Italy (1) **4** **Belgium** (0) **1**
Pandolfini (pen.), Anoul
Galli, Frignani,
Lorenzi

	P	W	D	L	F	A	Pts
England	2	1	1	0	6	4	3
Italy	2	1	0	1	5	3	2
Switzerland	2	1	0	1	2	3	2
Belgium	2	0	1	1	5	8	1

Play-off
Switzerland (1) **4** **Italy** (0) **1**
Hugi (2), Ballaman, Nesti
Fatton

Hungarian 'keeper Grosics dives but Rahn's shot beats him to give West Germany the 1954 World Cup by three goals to two. Buzanski (2), Zakarias (6), and Schaefer (20) watch anxiously

Quarter-Finals
West Germany (1) **2** **Yugoslavia** (0) **0**
Horvat (o.g.), Rahn
Hungary (2) **4** **Brazil** (1) **2**
Hidegkuti, Kocsis (2), Santos (D) (pen.),
Lantos (pen.) Julinho
Austria (5) **7** **Switzerland** (4) **5**
Koerner (A) (2), Ballaman (2),
Ocwirk, Wagner (3), Hugi (2),
Probst Hanappi (o.g.)
Uruguay (2) **4** **England** (1) **2**
Borges, Varela, Lofthouse, Finney
Schiaffino, Ambrois

Semi-Finals
West Germany (1) **6** **Austria** (0) **1**
Schaefer, Morlock, Probst
Walter (F) (2 pens.),
Walter (O) 2
Hungary (1) (2) **4** **Uruguay** (0) (2) **2**
Czibor, Hidegkuti, Hohberg (2)
Kocsis (2)

Third Place Match
Austria (1) **3** **Uruguay** (1) **1**
Stojaspal (pen.), Hohberg
Cruz (o.g.), Ocwirk

Final
West Germany (2) **3** **Hungary** (2) **2**
Morlock, Rahn (2) Puskas, Czibor
West Germany: Turek; Posipal, Kohlmeyer;
Eckel, Liebrich, Mai; Rahn, Morlock, Walter (O),
Walter (F), Schaefer
Hungary: Grosics; Buzansky, Lantos; Bozsik,
Lorant, Zakarias; Czibor, Kocsis, Hidegkuti,
Puskas, Toth

1958: SWEDEN

Group 1
West Germany (2) **3** **Argentina** (1) **1**
Rahn (2), Schmidt Corbatta
N. Ireland (1) **1** **Czechoslovakia** (0) **0**
Cush
West Germany (1) **2** **Czechoslovakia** (0) **2**
Schaefer, Rahn Dvorak (pen.), Zikan
Argentina (1) **3** **N. Ireland** (1) **1**
Corbatta (2: 1 pen.), McParland
Menendez
West Germany (1) **2** **N. Ireland** (1) **2**
Rahn, Seeler McParland (2)
Czechoslovakia (3) **6** **Argentina** (1) **1**
Dvorak, Zikan (2), Corbatta
Feureisl, Hovorka (2)

	P	W	D	L	F	A	Pts
West Germany	3	1	2	0	7	5	4
Czechoslovakia	3	1	1	1	8	4	3
N. Ireland	3	1	1	1	4	5	3
Argentina	3	1	0	2	5	10	2

Play-off
N. Ireland (1) (1) **2** **Czechoslovakia** (1) (1) **1**
McParland (2) Zikan

Group 2
France (2) **7** **Paraguay** (2) **3**
Fontaine (3), Amarilla (2: 1 pen.)
Piantoni, Kopa, Romero
Wisnieski, Vincent
Yugoslavia (1) **1** **Scotland** (0) **1**
Petakovic Murray
Yugoslavia (1) **3** **France** (1) **2**
Petakovic, Fontaine (2)
Veselinovic (2)
Paraguay (2) **3** **Scotland** (1) **2**
Aguero, Re, Parodi Mudie, Collins
France (2) **2** **Scotland** (0) **1**
Kopa, Fontaine Baird
Yugoslavia (2) **3** **Paraguay** (1) **3**
Ognjanovic, Rajkov, Parodi, Aguero,
Veselinovic Romero

Tom Finney scores from the penalty spot to give England a 2–2 draw in their group match against Russia in 1958. But the Russians won their play-off for a quarter-final place.

	P	W	D	L	F	A	Pts
France	3	2	0	1	11	7	4
Yugoslavia	3	1	2	0	7	6	4
Paraguay	3	1	1	1	9	12	3
Scotland	3	0	1	2	4	6	1

Group 3
Sweden (1) **3** **Mexico** (0) **0**
Simonsson (2), Liedholm (pen.)
Hungary (1) **1** **Wales** (1) **1**
Bozsik Charles (J)
Wales (1) **1** **Mexico** (1) **1**
Allchurch Belmonte
Sweden (1) **2** **Hungary** (0) **1**
Hamrin (2) Tichy
Hungary (1) **4** **Mexico** (0) **0**
Tichy (2), Sandor, Bencsics
Sweden (0) **0** **Wales** (0) **0**

	P	W	D	L	F	A	Pts
Sweden	3	2	1	0	5	1	5
Hungary	3	1	1	1	6	3	3
Wales	3	0	3	0	2	2	3
Mexico	3	0	1	2	1	8	1

Play-off
Wales (0) **2** **Hungary** (1) **1**
Allchurch, Medwin Tichy

Group 4
England (0) **2** **USSR** (0) **2**
Kevan, Finney (pen.) Simonian, Ivanov (A)
Brazil (1) **3** **Austria** (0) **0**
Mazzola (2), Santos (N)
England (0) **0** **Brazil** (0) **0**
USSR (1) **2** **Austria** (0) **0**
Ilyin, Ivanov (V)
Brazil (1) **2** **USSR** (0) **0**
Vavá (2)
England (0) **2** **Austria** (1) **2**
Haynes, Kevan Koller, Koerner

Below: Zagalo gets the fourth of Brazil's five against Sweden in the 1958 final.
Below right: The 1958 Brazilians, having shown a new brand of football magic, do a lap of honour round the Rasunda Stadium.

	P	W	D	L	F	A	Pts
Brazil	3	2	1	0	5	0	5
England	3	0	3	0	4	4	3
USSR	3	1	1	1	4	3	3
Austria	3	0	1	2	2	7	1

Play-off

USSR (0) **1** **England** (0) **0**
Ilyin

Quarter-Finals
France (1) **4** **N. Ireland** (0) **0**
Wisnieski,
Fontaine (2),
Piantoni
West Germany (1) **1** **Yugoslavia** (0) **0**
Rahn
Sweden (0) **2** **USSR** (0) **0**
Hamrin, Simonsson
Brazil (0) **1** **Wales** (0) **0**
Pelé

Semi-Finals
Brazil (2) **5** **France** (1) **2**
Vavá, Didi, Pelé (3)   Fontaine, Piantoni
Sweden (1) **3** **West Germany** (0) **1**
Skoglund, Gren,   Schaefer
Hamrin

Third Place Match
France (0) **6** **West Germany** (0) **3**
Fontaine (4),   Cieslarczyk, Rahn,
Kopa (pen.), Douis   Schaefer

Final
Brazil (2) **5** **Sweden** (1) **2**
Vavá (2), Pelé (2),   Liedholm,
Zagalo   Simonsson
Brazil: Gylmar; Santos (D), Santos (N); Zito,
Bellini, Orlando; Garrincha, Didi, Vavá, Pelé,
Zagalo
Sweden: Svensson; Bergmark, Axbom; Boer-
jesson, Gustavsson, Parling; Hamrin, Gren,
Simonsson, Liedholm, Skoglund

1962: CHILE

Group 1
Uruguay (0) **2** **Colombia** (1) **1**
Cubilla, Sasia   Zaluaga
USSR (0) **2** **Yugoslavia** (0) **0**
Ivanov, Ponedelnik
Yugoslavia (2) **3** **Uruguay** (1) **1**
Skoblar, Galic,   Cabrera
Jerkovic

USSR (3) **4** **Colombia** (1) **4**
Ivanov (2), Chislenko,   Aceros, Coll, Rada,
Ponedelnik   Klinger
USSR (1) **2** **Uruguay** (0) **1**
Mamikin, Ivanov   Sasia
Yugoslavia (2) **5** **Colombia** (0) **0**
Galic, Jerkovic (3)
Melic

	P	W	D	L	F	A	Pts
USSR	3	2	1	0	8	5	5
Yugoslavia	3	2	0	1	8	3	4
Uruguay	3	1	0	2	4	6	2
Colombia	3	0	1	2	5	11	1

Group 2
Chile (1) **3** **Switzerland** (1) **1**
Sanchez (L) (2),   Wuthrich
Ramirez
West Germany (0) **0** **Italy** (0) **0**
Chile (0) **2** **Italy** (0) **0**
Ramirez, Toro
West Germany (1) **2** **Switzerland** (0) **1**
Brulls, Seeler   Schneiter
West Germany (1) **2** **Chile** (0) **0**
Szymaniak (pen.),
Seeler
Italy (1) **3** **Switzerland** (0) **0**
Mora, Bulgarelli (2)

	P	W	D	L	F	A	Pts
West Germany	3	2	1	0	4	1	5
Chile	3	2	0	1	5	3	4
Italy	3	1	1	1	3	2	3
Switzerland	3	0	0	3	2	8	0

Group 3
Brazil (0) **2** **Mexico** (0) **0**
Zagalo, Pelé
Czechoslovakia (0) **1** **Spain** (0) **0**
Stibranyi
Brazil (0) **0** **Czechoslovakia** (0) **0**
Spain (0) **1** **Mexico** (0) **0**
Peiro
Brazil (0) **2** **Spain** (1) **1**
Amarildo (2)   Adelardo
Mexico (2) **3** **Czechoslovakia** (1) **1**
Diaz, Del Aguila,   Masek
Hernandez (H) (pen.)

	P	W	D	L	F	A	Pts
Brazil	3	2	1	0	4	1	5
Czechoslovakia	3	1	1	1	2	3	3
Mexico	3	1	0	2	3	4	2
Spain	3	1	0	2	2	3	2

Group 4
Argentina (1) **1** **Bulgaria** (0) **0**
Facundo
Hungary (1) **2** **England** (0) **1**
Tichy, Albert   Flowers (pen.)
England (2) **3** **Argentina** (0) **1**
Flowers (pen.),   Sanfilippo
Charlton, Greaves
Hungary (4) **6** **Bulgaria** (0) **1**
Albert (3), Tichy (2),   Sokolov
Solymosi
Argentina (0) **0** **Hungary** (0) **0**
England (0) **0** **Bulgaria** (0) **0**

	P	W	D	L	F	A	Pts
Hungary	3	2	1	0	8	2	5
England	3	1	1	1	4	3	3
Argentina	3	1	1	1	2	3	3
Bulgaria	3	0	1	2	1	7	1

Bobby Charlton was considered England's best
forward in the 1962 World Cup in Chile. Four
years later he was a World Cup hero.

Quarter-Finals
Yugoslavia (0) **1** **West Germany** (0) **0**
Radakovic
Brazil (1) **3** **England** (1) **1**
Garrincha (2), Vavá   Hitchens
Chile (2) **2** **USSR** (1) **1**
Sanchez (L), Rojas   Chislenko
Czechoslovakia (1) **1** **Hungary** (0) **0**
Scherer

Semi-Finals
Brazil (2) **4** **Chile** (1) **2**
Garrincha (2),   Toro,
Vavá (2)   Sanchez (L) (pen.)
Czechoslovakia (0) **3** **Yugoslavia** (0) **1**
Kadraba,   Jerkovic
Scherer (2: 1 pen.)

Third Place Match
Chile (0) **1** **Yugoslavia** (0) **0**
Rojas

Final
Brazil (1) **3** **Czechoslovakia** (1) **1**
Amarildo, Zito, Vavá   Masopust
Brazil: Gylmar; Santos (D), Santos (N); Zito,
Mauro, Zozimo; Garrincha, Didi, Vavá, Ama-
rildo, Zagalo
Czechoslovakia: Schroiff; Tichy, Novak; Pluskal,
Popluhar, Masopust; Pospichal, Scherer,
Kvasnak, Kadraba, Jelinek

1966: ENGLAND

Group 1

England	(0) 0	**Uruguay**		(0) 0
France	(0) 1	**Mexico**		(0) 1
Hausser		Borja		
Uruguay	(2) 2	**France**		(1) 1
Rocha, Cortes		De Bourgoing (pen.)		
England	(1) 2	**Mexico**		(0) 0
Charlton, Hunt				
Uruguay	(0) 0	**Mexico**		(0) 0
England	(1) 2	**France**		(0) 0
Hunt (2)				

	P	W	D	L	F	A	Pts
England	3	2	1	0	4	0	5
Uruguay	3	1	2	0	2	1	4
Mexico	3	0	2	1	1	3	2
France	3	0	1	2	2	5	1

Group 2

West Germany	(3) 5	**Switzerland**		(0) 0
Held, Haller (2: 1 pen.)				
Beckenbauer (2)				
Argentina	(0) 2	**Spain**		(0) 1
Artime (2)		Pirri		
Spain	(0) 2	**Switzerland**		(1) 1
Sanchis, Amancio		Quentin		
Argentina	(0) 0	**West Germany**		(0) 0
Argentina	(0) 2	**Switzerland**		(0) 0
Artime, Onega				
West Germany	(1) 2	**Spain**		(1) 1
Emmerich, Seeler		Fuste		

	P	W	D	L	F	A	Pts
West Germany	3	2	1	0	7	1	5
Argentina	3	2	1	0	4	1	5
Spain	3	1	0	2	4	5	2
Switzerland	3	0	0	3	1	9	0

Group 3

Brazil	(1) 2	**Bulgaria**		(0) 0
Pelé, Garrincha				
Portugal	(1) 3	**Hungary**		(0) 1
Augusto (2), Torres		Bene		
Hungary	(1) 3	**Brazil**		(1) 1
Bene, Farkas,		Tostao		
Meszoly (pen.)				
Portugal	(2) 3	**Bulgaria**		(0) 0
Vutzov (o.g.),				
Eusebio, Torres				
Portugal	(2) 3	**Brazil**		(0) 1
Simoes, Eusebio (2)		Rildo		
Hungary	(2) 3	**Bulgaria**		(1) 1
Davidov (o.g.),		Asparoukhov		
Meszoly, Bene				

	P	W	D	L	F	A	Pts
Portugal	3	3	0	0	9	2	6
Hungary	3	2	0	1	7	5	4
Brazil	3	1	0	2	4	6	2
Bulgaria	3	0	0	3	1	8	0

Group 4

USSR	(2) 3	**North Korea**		(0) 0
Malafeev (2),				
Banischevski				
Italy	(1) 2	**Chile**		(0) 0
Mazzola, Barison				
Chile	(1) 1	**North Korea**		(0) 1
Marcos (pen.)		Pak Seung Jin		
USSR	(0) 1	**Italy**		(0) 0
Chislenko				
North Korea	(1) 1	**Italy**		(0) 0
Pak Doo Ik				
USSR	(1) 2	**Chile**		(1) 1
Porkujan (2)		Marcos		

	P	W	D	L	F	A	Pts
USSR	3	3	0	0	6	1	6
North Korea	3	1	1	1	2	4	3
Italy	3	1	0	2	2	2	2
Chile	3	0	1	2	2	5	1

Quarter-Finals

England	(0) 1	**Argentina**		(0) 0
Hurst				
West Germany	(1) 4	**Uruguay**		(0) 0
Held, Beckenbauer,				
Seeler, Haller				
Portugal	(2) 5	**North Korea**		(3) 3
Eusebio (4: 2 pens.)		Pak Seung Jin,		
Augusto		Yang Sung Kook,		
		Li Dong Woon		
USSR	(1) 2	**Hungary**		(0) 1
Chislenko, Porkujan		Bene		

Semi-Finals

West Germany	(1) 2	**USSR**		(0) 1
Haller, Beckenbauer		Porkujan		

England	(1) 2	**Portugal**		(0) 1
Charlton (R) (2)		Eusebio (pen.)		

Third Place Match

Portugal	(1) 2	**USSR**		(1) 1
Eusebio (pen.), Torres		Malafeev		

Final

			West	
England	(1) (2) 4		**Germany**	(1) (2) 2
Hurst (3), Peters			Haller, Weber	

England: Banks; Cohen, Wilson; Stiles, Charlton (J), Moore; Ball, Hurst, Hunt, Charlton (R), Peters

West Germany: Tilkowski; Hottges, Schnellinger; Beckenbauer, Schulz, Weber; Held, Haller, Seeler, Overath, Emmerich

North Korean goalkeeper Li Chan Myung takes the ball from the Italian Fogli's head.

1970: MEXICO

Group 1

Mexico	(0) 0	**USSR**		(0) 0
Belgium	(1) 3	**El Salvador**		(0) 0
Van Moer (2),				
Lambert (pen.)				
USSR	(1) 4	**Belgium**		(0) 1
Byshovets (2),		Lambert		
Asatiani,				
Khmelnitsky				
Mexico	(1) 4	**El Salvador**		(0) 0
Valdivia (2),				
Fragoso, Basaguren				
USSR	(0) 2	**El Salvador**		(0) 0
Byshovets (2)				
Mexico	(1) 1	**Belgium**		(0) 0
Pena (pen.)				

	P	W	D	L	F	A	Pts
USSR	3	2	1	0	6	1	5
Mexico	3	2	1	0	5	0	5
Belgium	3	1	0	2	4	5	2
El Salvador	3	0	0	3	0	9	0

Group 2

Uruguay	(1) 2	**Israel**		(0) 0
Maneiro, Mujica				
Italy	(1) 1	**Sweden**		(0) 0
Domenghini				
Uruguay	(0) 0	**Italy**		(0) 0
Sweden	(0) 1	**Israel**		(0) 1
Turesson		Spiegler		
Sweden	(0) 1	**Uruguay**		(0) 0
Grahn				
Italy	(0) 0	**Israel**		(0) 0

	P	W	D	L	F	A	Pts
Italy	3	1	2	0	1	0	4
Uruguay	3	1	1	1	2	1	3
Sweden	3	1	1	1	2	2	3
Israel	3	0	2	1	1	3	2

With the score 2–2 after 90 minutes of the 1966 final, England manager Ramsey exhorts his exhausted players to overcome their fatigue and bring England victory in extra time.

Above: Teofilo Cubillas, one of the stars of the 1970 World Cup, scores his and Peru's first goal against the Moroccans.

Below: Pelé, in his fourth World Cup, in action against Czechoslovakia. In this match, Brazil, full of flair and brilliance, gave immediate notice of their intention to win the Jules Rimet Trophy a third time.

Bottom: The World Cup is Brazil's, and Pelé and Brito are surrounded by jubilant fans.

Group 3

England	(0) **1**	**Romania**	(0) **0**
Hurst			
Brazil	(1) **4**	**Czechoslovakia**	(1) **1**
Rivelino, Pelé		Petras	
Jairzinho (2)			
Romania	(0) **2**	**Czechoslovakia**	(1) **1**
Neagu, Dumitrache (pen.)		Petras	
Brazil	(0) **1**	**England**	(0) **0**
Jairzinho			
Brazil	(2) **3**	**Romania**	(0) **2**
Pelé (2), Jairzinho		Dumitrache, Dembrovski	
England	(0) **1**	**Czechoslovakia**	(0) **0**
Clarke (pen.)			

	P	W	D	L	F	A	Pts
Brazil	3	3	0	0	8	3	6
England	3	2	0	1	2	1	4
Romania	3	1	0	2	4	5	2
Czechoslovakia	3	0	0	3	2	7	0

Group 4

Peru	(0) **3**	**Bulgaria**	(1) **2**
Gallardo, Chumpitaz, Cubillas		Dermendjiev, Bonev	
West Germany	(0) **2**	**Morocco**	(1) **1**
Seeler, Müller		Houmane	
Peru	(0) **3**	**Morocco**	(0) **0**
Cubillas (2), Challe			
West Germany	(2) **5**	**Bulgaria**	(1) **2**
Libuda, Müller (3: 1 pen.), Seeler		Nikodimov, Kolev	
West Germany	(3) **3**	**Peru**	(1) **1**
Müller (3)		Cubillas	
Bulgaria	(1) **1**	**Morocco**	(0) **1**
Jetchev		Ghazouani	

	P	W	D	L	F	A	Pts
West Germany	3	3	0	0	10	4	6
Peru	3	2	0	1	7	5	4
Bulgaria	3	0	1	2	5	9	1
Morocco	3	0	1	2	2	6	1

Quarter-Finals

Uruguay	(0) (0) **1**	**USSR**	(0) (0) **0**
Esparrago			
Italy	(1) **4**	**Mexico**	(1) **1**
Domenghini, Riva (2), Rivera		Gonzales	
Brazil	(2) **4**	**Peru**	(1) **2**
Rivelino, Tostao (2), Jairzinho		Gallardo, Cubillas	
West Germany	(0) (2) **3**	**England**	(1) (2) **2**
Beckenbauer, Seeler, Müller		Mullery, Peters	

Semi-Finals

Italy	(1) (1) **4**	**West Germany**	(0) (1) **3**
Boninsegna, Burgnich, Riva, Rivera		Schnellinger, Müller (2)	
Brazil	(1) **3**	**Uruguay**	(1) **1**
Clodoaldo, Jairzinho, Rivelino		Cubilla	

Third Place Match

West Germany	(1) **1**	**Uruguay**	(0) **0**
Overath			

Final

Brazil	(1) **4**	**Italy**	(1) **1**
Pelé, Gerson, Jairzinho, Carlos Alberto		Boninsegna	

Brazil: Felix; Carlos Alberto, Brito, Wilson Piazza, Everaldo; Clodoaldo, Gerson; Jairzinho, Tostao, Pelé, Rivelino
Italy: Albertosi; Burgnich, Cera, Rosato, Facchetti; Bertini (Juliano), Mazzola, De Sisti; Domenghini, Borinsegna (Rivera), Riva

1974: WEST GERMANY

First Round

Group 1

West Germany	(1) **1**	**Chile**		(0) **0**	
Breitner					
East Germany	(0) **2**	**Australia**		(0) **0**	
Sparwasser, Streich					
West Germany	(2) **3**	**Australia**		(0) **0**	
Overath, Cullmann,					
Müller					
Chile	(0) **1**	**East Germany**	(0) **1**		
Ahumada		Hoffmann			
Australia	(0) **0**	**Chile**		(0) **0**	
East Germany	(0) **1**	**West Germany**	(0) **0**		
Sparwasser					

	P	W	D	L	F	A	Pts
East Germany	3	2	1	0	4	1	5
West Germany	3	2	0	1	4	1	4
Chile	3	0	2	1	1	2	2
Australia	3	0	1	2	0	5	1

Group 2

Brazil	(0) **0**	**Yugoslavia**	(0) **0**
Scotland	(2) **2**	**Zaïre**	(0) **0**
Lorimer, Jordan			
Yugoslavia	(6) **9**	**Zaïre**	(0) **0**
Bajevic 3, Dzajic,			
Surjak, Katalinski,			
Bogicevic, Oblak,			
Petkovic			
Scotland	(0) **0**	**Brazil**	(0) **0**
Brazil	(1) **3**	**Zaïre**	(0) **0**
Jairzinho, Rivelino,			
Valdomiro			
Scotland	(0) **1**	**Yugoslavia**	(0) **1**
Jordan		Karasi	

	P	W	D	L	F	A	Pts
Yugoslavia	3	1	2	0	10	1	4
Brazil	3	1	2	0	3	0	4
Scotland	3	1	2	0	3	1	4
Zaïre	3	0	0	3	0	14	0

Group 3

Netherlands	(1) **2**	**Uruguay**	(0) **0**
Rep 2			
Sweden	(0) **0**	**Bulgaria**	(0) **0**
Netherlands	(0) **0**	**Sweden**	(0) **0**
Bulgaria	(0) **1**	**Uruguay**	(0) **1**
Bonev		Pavoni	
Netherlands	(2) **4**	**Bulgaria**	(0) **1**
Neeskens 2 (2 pens.),		Krol (o.g.)	
Rep, De Jong			
Sweden	(0) **3**	**Uruguay**	(0) **0**
Edström 2, Sandberg			

	P	W	D	L	F	A	Pts
Netherlands	3	2	1	0	6	1	5
Sweden	3	1	2	0	3	0	4
Bulgaria	3	0	2	1	2	5	2
Uruguay	3	0	1	2	1	6	1

Group 4

Italy	(0) **3**	**Haiti**	(0) **1**
Rivera, Benetti,		Sanon	
Anastasi			
Poland	(2) **3**	**Argentina**	(0) **2**
Lato 2, Szarmach		Heredia, Babington	
Italy	(1) **1**	**Argentina**	(1) **1**
Perfumo (o.g.)		Houseman	
Poland	(5) **7**	**Haiti**	(0) **0**
Lato 2, Deyna,			
Szarmach 3, Gorgon			
Argentina	(2) **4**	**Haiti**	(0) **1**
Yazalde 2,		Sanon	
Houseman, Ayala			
Poland	(2) **2**	**Italy**	(0) **1**
Szarmach, Deyna		Capello	

	P	W	D	L	F	A	Pts
Poland	3	3	0	0	12	3	6
Argentina	3	1	1	1	7	5	3
Italy	3	1	1	1	5	4	3
Haiti	3	0	0	3	2	14	0

Above: Anguish for Scotland's captain, Billy Bremner (4), against Brazil in Group 2. Quick to pounce on a goalkeeping fumble, he could only watch as the ball slid the wrong side of the post. It was the nearest the Scots got to breaking down the uncharacteristically solid Brazilian defence.

Right: Brazil's Luis Pereira, perhaps the outstanding centre-back of the 1974 tournament, sadly forgot his skills and was sent off for a blatant foul on Johan Neeskens in the deciding second round match against the Netherlands.

Below: A confrontation between Yugoslavia's midfield star Branko Oblak (left) and Willie Morgan of Scotland. A 1–1 draw meant that Yugoslavia, who had scored nine goals against Zaïre, and Brazil qualified for the second round at the expense of Scotland.

Above: Jan Domarski (left) splashes in to challenge as West German captain Franz Beckenbauer forces the ball clear of the waterlogged pitch in the deciding match of Group B. The Poles, who needed to win, could consider themselves unlucky, as the conditions did not suit their fast-raiding style and they went down 1–0.

Left: Poland's Grzegorz Lato, who led the 1974 World Cup goalscorers with seven.

Below: Only referee Jack Taylor keeps his feet as West Germany's Paul Breitner heads a misplaced punch by his own goalkeeper off the line in the final to prevent a Dutch equalizer early in the second half.

Second Round

Group A

Brazil	(0) **1**	**East Germany**	(0) **0**		
Rivelino					
Netherlands	(2) **4**	**Argentina**	(0) **0**		
Cruyff 2,					
Krol, Rep					
Brazil	(1) **2**	**Argentina**	(1) **1**		
Rivelino, Jairzinho		Brindisi			
Netherlands	(1) **2**	**East Germany**	(0) **0**		
Neeskens,					
Rensenbrink					
Netherlands	(0) **2**	**Brazil**	(0) **0**		
Neeskens, Cruyff					
Argentina	(1) **1**	**East Germany**	(1) **1**		
Houseman		Streich			

	P	W	D	L	F	A	Pts
Netherlands	3	3	0	0	8	0	6
Brazil	3	2	0	1	3	3	4
East Germany	3	0	1	2	1	4	1
Argentina	3	0	1	2	2	7	1

Group B

West Germany	(1) **2**	**Yugoslavia**	(0) **0**
Breitner, Müller			
Poland	(1) **1**	**Sweden**	(0) **0**
Lato			
Poland	(1) **2**	**Yugoslavia**	(1) **1**
Deyna (pen.), Lato		Karasi	
West Germany	(0) **4**	**Sweden**	(1) **2**
Overath, Bonhof,		Edström,	
Grabowski,		Sandberg	
Hoeness (pen.)			
West Germany	(0) **1**	**Poland**	(0) **0**
Müller			
Sweden	(1) **2**	**Yugoslavia**	(1) **1**
Edström,		Surjak	
Torstensson			

	P	W	D	L	F	A	Pts
West Germany	3	3	0	0	7	2	6
Poland	3	2	0	1	3	2	4
Sweden	3	1	0	2	4	6	2
Yugoslavia	3	0	0	3	2	6	0

Third Place Match

Poland	(0) **1**	**Brazil**	(0) **0**
Lato			

Final

West Germany	(2) **2**	**Netherlands**	(1) **1**
Breitner (pen.),		Neeskens (pen.)	
Müller			

West Germany: Maier; Vogts, Schwarzenbeck, Beckenbauer, Breitner; Bonhof, Hoeness, Overath; Grabowski, Müller, Holzenbein

Netherlands: Jongbloed; Suurbier, Haan, Rijsbergen (De Jong), Krol; Jansen, Van Hanegem, Neeskens; Rep, Cruyff, Rensenbrink (Van der Kerkhof)

OLYMPIC GAMES SOCCER FINALS

1908	Great Britain	2	Denmark	0
1912	Great Britain	4	Denmark	2
1920*	Belgium	2	Czechoslovakia	0
1924	Uruguay	3	Switzerland	0
1928	Uruguay	1	Argentina	1
	replay	2		1
1936†	Italy	2	Austria	1
1948	Sweden	3	Yugoslavia	1
1952	Hungary	2	Yugoslavia	0
1956	USSR	1	Yugoslavia	0
1960	Yugoslavia	3	Denmark	1
1964	Hungary	2	Czechoslovakia	1
1968	Hungary	4	Bulgaria	1
1972	Poland	2	Hungary	1

*Czechoslovakia disqualified after second Belgium goal.
†After extra time.

WORLD CLUB CHAMPIONSHIP

Decided on matches won

1960	Real Madrid (Spain)	0:5	*Penarol (Uruguay)		0:1
1961	Penarol (Uruguay)	0:5:2	*Benfica (Portugal)		1:0:1
	(play-off in Montevideo)				
1962	*Santos (Brazil)	3:5	Benfica (Portugal)		2:2
1963	Santos (Brazil)	2:4:1	*AC Milan (Italy)		4:2:0
	(play-off in Rio de Janeiro)				
1964	Internazionale (Italy)	0:2:1	*Independiente		1:0:0
	(play-off in Madrid)		(Argentina)		
1965	*Internazionale (Italy)	3:0	Independiente		0:0
			(Argentina)		
1966	*Penarol (Uruguay)	2:2	Real Madrid (Spain)		0:0
1967	Racing Club (Argentina)	0:2:1	*Celtic (Scotland)		1:1:0
	(play-off in Montevideo)				
1968	*Estudiantes de la Plata	1:1	Manchester United		0:1
	(Argentina)		(England)		

Decided on aggregate

1969	*AC Milan (Italy)	3:1	Estudiantes de la Plata		0:2
			(Argentina)		
1970	Feyenoord Rotterdam	2:1	*Estudiantes de la Plata		2:0
	(Netherlands)		(Argentina)		
1971	Nacional (Uruguay)	1:2	*†Panathinaikos (Greece)		1:1
1972	Ajax Amsterdam	1:3	*Independiente		1:0
	(Netherlands)		(Argentina)		
1973	Independiente (Argentina)	1	‡Juventus (Italy)		0

* Home team in 1st leg.   † Panathinaikos replaced Ajax Amsterdam, who withdrew.
‡Juventus replaced Ajax, who withdrew; championship decided on one game, in Rome.

INTERNATIONAL YOUTH TOURNAMENT

1948	London	England	3	Netherlands	2
1949	Rotterdam	France	4	Netherlands	1
1950	Vienna	Austria	3	France	2
1951	Cannes	Yugoslavia	3	Austria	2
1952	Barcelona	*Spain	0	Belgium	0
1953	Brussels	Hungary	2	Yugoslavia	0
1954	Cologne	*Spain	2	West Germany	0
1955–56	*Group system only*				
1957	Madrid	Austria	3	Spain	2
1958	Luxembourg	Italy	1	England	0
1959	Sofia	Bulgaria	1	Italy	0
1960	Vienna	Hungary	2	Romania	1
1961	Lisbon	Portugal	4	Poland	0
1962	Bucharest	Romania	4	Yugoslavia	1
1963	London	England	4	Northern Ireland	0
1964	Amsterdam	England	4	Spain	0
1965	Essen	East Germany	3	England	2
1966	Belgrade	†Italy	0	†USSR	0
1967	Istanbul	USSR	1	England	0
1968	Cannes	Czechoslovakia	2	France	1
1969	Leipzig	*Bulgaria	1	East Germany	1
1970	Glasgow	*East Germany	1	Netherlands	1
1971	Prague	England	3	Portugal	0
1972	Barcelona	England	2	West Germany	0
1973	Florence	England	3	East Germany	2
1974	Malmö	Bulgaria	1	Yugoslavia	0

* Won by the drawing of lots.   † Joint winners.

Above: Pachame, aware of George Best waiting to pounce, heads clear during the second match of the 1968 World Club Championship. Estudiantes won the title, but their methods in doing so did nothing to improve the image of Argentinian football in Britain.

Right: A delighted John Sissons turns away after scoring England's fourth goal against Northern Ireland in the final of the 1963 International Youth Tournament.

European Competitions

EUROPEAN FOOTBALL CHAMPIONSHIP (NATIONS' CUP)

1958–60 (final rounds in France)

Preliminary Round

Czechoslovakia	0:4	*Republic of Ireland	2:0

1st Round

*France	7:1	Greece	1:1
*USSR	3:1	Hungary	1:0
*Romania	3:0	Turkey	0:2
Austria	1:5	*Norway	0:2
*Yugoslavia	2:1	Bulgaria	0:1
*Portugal	2:3	East Germany	0:2
Czechoslovakia	2:5	*Denmark	2:1
Spain	4:3	*Poland	2:0

Quarter-Finals

Yugoslavia	1:5	*Portugal	2:1
*France	5:4	Austria	2:2
Czechoslovakia	2:3	*Romania	0:0

USSR won outright: Spain withdrew

Semi-Finals

Yugoslavia	5	France	4
USSR	3	Czechoslovakia	0

Final

USSR	2	Yugoslavia	1

(after extra time)

USSR: Yachin; Tchekeli, Kroutikov; Voinov, Maslenkin, Netto; Metreveli, Ivanov, Ponedelnik, Bubukin, Meshki
Scorers: Metreveli, Ponedelnik
Yugoslavia: Vidinic; Durkovic, Jusufi; Zanetic, Miladinovic, Perusic; Sekularac, Jerkovic, Galic, Matus, Kostic
Scorer: Netto (o.g.)

* Home team in 1st leg.

1962–64 (final rounds in Spain)

1st Round

*Spain	6:1	Romania	0:3

Goussarov (left) hammers the ball past Italian 'keeper Sarti in the second leg of Russia's second round match of the 1962–64 Nations' Cup.

Northern Ireland	2:2	*Poland	0:0
*Denmark	6:3	Malta	1:1
*East Germany	2:1	Czechoslovakia	1:1
*Hungary	3:1	Wales	1:1
*Italy	6:1	Turkey	0:0
*Netherlands	3:1	Switzerland	1:1
Sweden	2:1	*Norway	0:1
*Republic of Ireland	4:1	Iceland	2:1
*Yugoslavia	3:1	Belgium	2:0
*Bulgaria	3:1:1	Portugal	1:3:0
(play-off in Bulgaria)			
France	1:5	*England	1:2

Albania won outright: Greece withdrew

Luxembourg	*bye*
USSR	*bye*
Austria	*bye*

2nd Round

*Spain	1:1	Northern Ireland	1:0
*Denmark	4:0	Albania	0:1
Republic of Ireland	0:3	*Austria	0:2
Hungary	2:3	*East Germany	1:3
*USSR	2:1	Italy	0:1
Luxembourg	1:2	*Netherlands	1:1
Sweden	0:3	*Yugoslavia	0:2
France	0:3	*Bulgaria	1:1

Quarter-Finals

Denmark	3:2:1	*Luxembourg	3:2:0
(play-off in Denmark)			
*Spain	5:2	Republic of Ireland	1:0
Hungary	3:2	*France	1:1
USSR	1:3	*Sweden	1:1

Semi-Finals

USSR	3	Denmark	0
Spain	2	Hungary	1

Third Place Match

Hungary	3	Denmark	1
(after extra time)			

Final

Spain	2	USSR	0

Spain: Iribar; Rivilla, Calleja; Fuste, Olivella, Zoco; Amancio, Pereda, Marcelino, Suarez, Lapetra
Scorers: Pereda, Marcelino
USSR: Yachin; Chustikov, Mudrik; Voronin, Shesternjev, Anitchkin; Chislenko, Ivanov, Ponedelnik, Kornaev, Khusainov

*Home team in 1st leg.

1966–68 (final rounds in Italy)

Group 1

Spain	0:2	*Republic of Ireland	0:0
*Republic of Ireland	2:1	Turkey	1:2
Spain	0:2	*Turkey	0:0
Czechoslovakia	2:1	*Republic of Ireland	0:2
*Czechoslovakia	3:0	Turkey	0:0
Spain	0:2	*Czechoslovakia	1:1

	P	W	D	L	F	A	Pts
Spain	6	3	2	1	6	2	8
Czechoslovakia	6	3	1	2	8	4	7
Republic of Ireland	6	2	1	3	5	8	5
Turkey	6	1	2	3	3	8	4

Group 2

*Bulgaria	4:0	Norway	2:0
*Portugal	1:1	Sweden	2:1
Portugal	2:2	*Norway	1:1
Bulgaria	2:3	*Sweden	0:0
Sweden	1:5	*Norway	3:2
*Bulgaria	1:0	Portugal	0:0

	P	W	D	L	F	A	Pts
Bulgaria	6	4	2	0	10	2	10
Portugal	6	2	2	2	6	6	6
Sweden	6	2	1	3	9	12	5
Norway	6	1	1	4	9	14	3

Group 3

Austria	0:2	*Finland	0:1
*Greece	2:1	Finland	1:1
*USSR	4:0	Austria	3:1
*USSR	4:1	Greece	0:0
*USSR	2:5	Finland	0:2
*Greece	4:1	Austria	1:1

(second match abandoned after 84 minutes)

	P	W	D	L	F	A	Pts
USSR	6	5	0	1	16	6	10
Greece	6	2	2	2	8	9	6
Austria	6	2	2	2	8	10	6
Finland	6	0	2	4	5	12	2

Group 4

*West Germany	6:0	Albania	0:0
*Yugoslavia	1:1	West Germany	0:3
Yugoslavia	2:4	*Albania	0:0

	P	W	D	L	F	A	Pts
Yugoslavia	4	3	0	1	8	3	6
West Germany	4	2	1	1	9	2	5
Albania	4	0	1	3	0	12	1

Group 5

Hungary	2:2	*Netherlands	2:1
*Hungary	6:2	Denmark	0:0
*Netherlands	2:2	Denmark	0:3
*East Germany	4:0	Netherlands	3:1
East Germany	1:3	*Denmark	1:2
*Hungary	3:0	East Germany	1:1

	P	W	D	L	F	A	Pts
Hungary	6	4	1	1	15	5	9
East Germany	6	3	1	2	10	10	7
Netherlands	6	2	1	3	11	11	5
Denmark	6	1	1	4	6	16	3

Group 6

*Romania	4:1	Switzerland	2:7
*Italy	3:1	Romania	1:0
Romania	5:7	*Cyprus	1:0
Italy	2:5	*Cyprus	0:0
*Switzerland	5:1	Cyprus	0:2
Italy	2:4	*Switzerland	2:0

	P	W	D	L	F	A	Pts
Italy	6	5	1	0	17	3	11
Romania	6	3	0	3	18	14	6
Switzerland	6	2	1	3	17	13	5
Cyprus	6	1	0	5	3	25	2

Group 7

*Poland	4:0	Luxembourg	0:0
*France	2:4	Poland	1:1
France	1:1	*Belgium	2:1

111

France	3:3	*Luxembourg	0:1
Belgium	5:3	*Luxembourg	0:0
Belgium	1:2	*Poland	3:4

	P	W	D	L	F	A	Pts
France	6	4	1	1	14	6	9
Belgium	6	3	1	2	14	9	7
Poland	6	3	1	2	13	9	7
Luxembourg	6	0	1	5	1	18	1

Paul Madeley and Sigi Held dispute possession in the quarter-final first leg of the 1972 European Championship. West Germany's shock 3–1 win at Wembley put paid to England's aspirations to the European title and set the Germans on a road that ended with a superb, cultured victory over Russia in Belgium.

Group 8

Scotland	1:3	*Wales	1:2
England	2:2	*Northern Ireland	0:0
*Scotland	2:0	Northern Ireland	1:1
*England	5:3	Wales	1:0
Wales	0:2	*Northern Ireland	0:0
*England	2:1	Scotland	3:1

	P	W	D	L	F	A	Pts
England	6	4	1	1	15	5	9
Scotland	6	3	2	1	10	8	8
Wales	6	1	2	3	6	12	4
Northern Ireland	6	1	1	4	2	8	3

Quarter-Finals

*England	1:2	Spain	0:1
Yugoslavia	1:5	*France	1:1
Italy	2:2	*Bulgaria	3:0
USSR	0:3	*Hungary	2:0

Semi-Finals

Yugoslavia	1	England	0
Italy	0	USSR	0

(Italy won on toss after extra time)

Third Place Match

England	2	USSR	0

Final

Italy	1	Yugoslavia	1
	2		0

Italy: Zoff; Burgnich, Facchetti; Ferrini (Rosato), Guarneri, Castano (Salvadore); Domenghini, Juliano (Mazzola), Anastasi, Lodetti (De Sisti), Prati (Riva)
Scorers: (1st match) Domenghini
(2nd match) Riva, Anastasi

Yugoslavia: Pantelic; Fazlagic, Damjanovic; Pavlovic, Paunovic, Holcer; Petkovic (Hosic), Acimovic, Musemic, Trivic, Dzajic
Scorer: Dzajic
(names in brackets played in replay)

*Home team in 1st leg

1970–72 (final rounds in Belgium)

Group 1

*Czechoslovakia	1:4	Finland	1:0
*Romania	3:4	Finland	0:0
Romania	0:2	*Wales	1:0
Czechoslovakia	3:1	*Wales	1:0
Romania	0:2	*Czechoslovakia	1:1
Wales	1:3	*Finland	0:0

	P	W	D	L	F	A	Pts
Romania	6	4	1	1	11	2	9
Czechoslovakia	6	4	1	1	11	4	9
Wales	6	2	1	3	5	6	5
Finland	6	0	1	5	1	16	1

Group 2

Hungary	3:4	*Norway	1:0
*France	3:3	Norway	1:1
*Bulgaria	1:4	Norway	1:1
*Hungary	1:2	France	1:0
Hungary	0:2	*Bulgaria	3:0
Bulgaria	1:2	*France	2:1

	P	W	D	L	F	A	Pts
Hungary	6	4	1	1	12	5	9
Bulgaria	6	3	1	2	11	7	7
France	6	3	1	2	10	8	7
Norway	6	0	1	5	5	18	1

Group 3

Greece	1:2	*Malta	1:0
Switzerland	1:1	*Greece	0:0
Switzerland	2:5	*Malta	1:0
England	1:5	*Malta	0:0
*England	3:2	Greece	0:0
England	3:1	*Switzerland	2:1

	P	W	D	L	F	A	Pts
England	6	5	1	0	15	3	11
Switzerland	6	4	1	1	12	5	9
Greece	6	1	1	4	3	8	3
Malta	6	0	1	5	2	16	1

Group 4

*Spain	3:1	Northern Ireland	0:1
USSR	3:6	*Cyprus	1:1
Northern Ireland	3:5	*Cyprus	0:0
Spain	2:7	*Cyprus	0:0
*USSR	2:0	Spain	1:0
*USSR	1:1	Northern Ireland	0:1

	P	W	D	L	F	A	Pts
USSR	6	4	2	0	13	4	10
Spain	6	3	2	1	14	3	8
Northern Ireland	6	2	2	2	10	6	6
Cyprus	6	0	0	6	2	26	0

Group 5

Portugal	1:5	*Denmark	0:0
*Scotland	1:0	Denmark	0:1
*Belgium	2:2	Denmark	0:1
*Belgium	3:0	Scotland	0:1
*Belgium	3:1	Portugal	0:1
*Portugal	2:1	Scotland	0:2

	P	W	D	L	F	A	Pts
Belgium	6	4	1	1	11	3	9
Portugal	6	3	1	2	10	6	7
Scotland	6	3	0	3	4	7	6
Denmark	6	1	0	5	2	11	2

Group 6

Sweden	1:1	*Republic of Ireland	1:0
Italy	2:2	*Austria	1:2
*Italy	3:2	Republic of Ireland	0:1
Austria	0:1	*Sweden	1:0
Austria	4:6	*Republic of Ireland	1:0
Italy	0:3	*Sweden	0:0

Left: George Best complains to referee Taylor about the ruthlessness of the Spanish tackling during Northern Ireland's group match in 1972. Because of disturbances in Belfast, the Irish home match was played at Hull.

	P	W	D	L	F	A	Pts
Italy	6	4	2	0	12	4	10
Austria	6	3	1	2	14	6	7
Sweden	6	2	2	2	3	5	6
Republic of Ireland	6	0	1	5	3	17	1

Group 7

Yugoslavia	1:2	*Netherlands	1:0
Yugoslavia	2:0	*Luxembourg	0:0
Netherlands	0:3	*East Germany	1:2
East Germany	5:2	*Luxembourg	0:1
*Netherlands	6:8	Luxembourg	0:0
Yugoslavia	2:0	*East Germany	1:0

	P	W	D	L	F	A	Pts
Yugoslavia	6	3	3	0	7	2	9
Netherlands	6	3	1	2	18	6	7
East Germany	6	3	1	2	11	6	7
Luxembourg	6	0	1	5	1	23	1

Group 8

*Poland	3:1	Albania	0:1
*West Germany	1:3	Turkey	1:0
*Turkey	2:0	Albania	1:3
West Germany	1:2	*Albania	0:0
*Poland	5:0	Turkey	1:1
West Germany	3:0	*Poland	1:0

	P	W	D	L	F	A	Pts
West Germany	6	4	2	0	10	2	10
Poland	6	2	2	2	10	6	6
Turkey	6	2	1	3	5	13	5
Albania	6	1	1	4	5	9	3

Quarter-Finals

West Germany	3:0	*England	1:0
Belgium	0:2	*Italy	0:1
USSR	0:3	*Yugoslavia	0:0
*Hungary	1:2:2	Romania	1:2:1
(play-off at Belgrade)			

Semi-Finals

USSR	1	Hungary	0
West Germany	2	Belgium	1

Third Place Match

Belgium	2	Hungary	1

Final

West Germany	3	USSR	0

West Germany: Maier, Hoettges, Breitner, Schwarzenbeck, Beckenbauer, Wimmer, Heynckes, Hoeness, Müller, Netzer, Kremers
Scorers: Müller (2), Wimmer
USSR. Rudakov; Dzodzuashvili, Khurtsilava, Kaplichnyi, Istomine, Konkov (Dolmatov), Troshkine, Kolotov, Baidazhnyi, Banishevsky (Kozinkevich), Onishenko

* Home team in 1st match.

EUROPEAN CUP

1955–56

1st Round

Real Madrid	2:5	*Servette Geneva	0:0
Partizan Belgrade	3:5	*Sporting Lisbon	3:2
*AC Milan	3:4	1FC Saarbrucken	4:1
*Rapid Vienna	6:0	PSV Eindhoven	1:1
Hibernian	4:1	*Rot-Weiss Essen	0:1
*Djurgaarden Stockholm	0:4	Gwardia Warsaw	0:1
*Vörös Lobogo	6:4	RSC Anderlecht	3:1
*Stade de Reims	2:2	AGF Aarhus	0:2

2nd Round

*Real Madrid	4:0	Partizan Belgrade	0:3
AC Milan	1:7	*Rapid Vienna	1:2
*Hibernian	3:1	Djurgaarden Stockholm	1:0
*Stade de Reims	4:4	Vörös Lobogo	2:4

Semi-Finals

*Real Madrid	4:1	AC Milan	2:2
*Stade de Reims	2:1	Hibernian	0:0

Final (Paris)

Real Madrid	4	Stade de Reims	3

Real Madrid: Alonso; Atienza, Lesmes; Munoz, Marquitos, Zarraga; Joseito, Marchal, Di Stefano, Rial, Gento
Scorers: Di Stefano, Rial (2), Marquitos
Stade de Reims: Jacquet; Zimny, Giraudo; Leblond, Jonquet, Siatka; Hidalgo, Glovacki, Kopa, Bliard, Templin
Scorers: Leblond, Templin, Hidalgo

* Home team in 1st leg.

1956–57

Preliminary Round

OGC Nice	1:5	*AGF Aarhus	1:1
Atlético Bilbao	2:3	*FC Porto	1:2
*Borussia Dortmund	4:1:7	Spora Luxembourg	3:2:0
(play-off at Dortmund)			
Manchester United	2:10	*RSC Anderlecht	0:0
*Dynamo Bucharest	3:1	Galatasaray	1:2
*Slovan Bratislava	4:0	Legia Warsaw	0:2

1st Round

*Real Madrid	4:1:2	Rapid Vienna	2:3:0
(play-off at Madrid)			
OGC Nice	1:2:3	*Rangers	2:1:1
(play-off at Paris)			
*Atlético Bilbao	3:3	Honved	2:3
(2nd leg at Brussels)			
*Manchester United	3:0	Borussia Dortmund	2:0
Red Star Belgrade	4:2	*Rapid Heerlen	3:0
*CDNA Sofia	8:2	Dynamo Bucharest	1:3
Grasshoppers Zurich	0:2	*Slovan Bratislava	1:0
*Fiorentina	1:1	IFK Norrköping	1:0
(2nd leg at Rome)			

Right: European Champions Real Madrid in early 1957.

113

2nd Round

*Real Madrid	3:3	OGC Nice	0:2
Manchester United	3:3	*Atlético Bilbao	5:0
*Red Star Belgrade	3:1	CDNA Sofia	1:2
*Fiorentina	3:2	Grasshoppers Zurich	1:2

Semi-Finals

*Real Madrid	3:2	Manchester United	1:2
Fiorentina	1:0	*Red Star Belgrade	0:0

Final (Madrid)

Real Madrid	2	Fiorentina	0

Real Madrid: Alonso; Torres, Lesmes; Munoz, Marquitos, Zarraga; Kopa, Mateos, Di Stefano, Rial, Gento
Scorers: Di Stefano (pen.), Gento
Fiorentina: Sarti; Magnini, Cervato, Scaramucci, Orzan, Segato; Julinho, Gratton, Virgili, Montuori, Bizzarri

---

* Home team in 1st leg.

1957–58

Preliminary Round

*Seville	3:0	Benfica	1:0
*AGF Aarhus	0:3	Glenavon	0:0
Wismut Karl-Marx-Stadt	1:3:1	*Gwardia Warsaw	3:1:1
(play-off at Berlin won on toss after extra time)			
Vasas Budapest	1:6	*CDNA Sofia	2:1
Manchester United	6:3	*Shamrock Rovers	0:2
Red Star Belgrade	5:9	*Stade Dudelange	0:1
*Rangers	3:1	St Etienne	1:2
*AC Milan	4:2:4	Rapid Vienna	1:5:2
(play-off at Zurich)			

1st Round

*Seville	4:0	AGF Aarhus	0:2
Ajax Amsterdam	3:1	*Wismut Karl-Marx-Stadt	1:0
Vasas Budapest	1:2	*Young Boys Berne	1:1
*Manchester United	3:0	Dukla Prague	0:1
Red Star Belgrade	2:2	*IFK Norrköping	2:1
*Borussia Dortmund	4:1:3	CCA Bucharest	2:3:1
(play-off at Bologna)			
AC Milan	4:2	*Rangers	1:0
Real Madrid	2:6	*Antwerp	1:0

2nd Round

*Real Madrid	8:2	Seville	0:2
Vasas Budapest	2:4	*Ajax Amsterdam	2:0
*Manchester United	2:3	Red Star Belgrade	1:3
AC Milan	1:4	*Borussia Dortmund	1:1

Semi-Finals

*Real Madrid	4:0	Vasas Budapest	0:2
AC Milan	1:4	*Manchester United	2:0

Final (Brussels)

Real Madrid	3	AC Milan	2

(after extra time: 2–2 at full time)
Real Madrid: Alonso; Atienza, Lesmes; Santisteban, Santamaria, Zarraga; Kopa, Joseito, Di Stefano, Rial, Gento
Scorers: Di Stefano, Rial, Gento
AC Milan: Soldan; Fontana, Beraldo; Bergamaschi, Maldini, Radice, Danova; Liedholm, Schiaffino, Grillo, Cucchiaroni
Scorers: Schiaffino, Grillo

---

* Home team in 1st leg.

1958–59

Preliminary Round

Wiener SK	1:7	*Juventus	3:0
Dukla Prague	2:2	*Dynamo Zagreb	2:1
Schalke 04	0:5:3	*KB Copenhagen	3:2:1
(play-off at Enschede)			
*Atlético Madrid	8:5	Drumcondra	0:1
MTK Budapest	3:3	*Polonia Bytom	0:0
*Wismut Karl-Marx-Stadt	4:0:5	Petrolul Ploesti	2:2:0
(play-off at Kiev)			

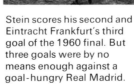

Stein scores his second and Eintracht Frankfurt's third goal of the 1960 final. But three goals were by no means enough against a goal-hungry Real Madrid.

*I.F.K. Gothenburg	2:0:5	Jeunesse Esch	1:1:1
(play-off at Gothenburg)			
Sporting Lisbon	4:2	*DOS Utrecht	3:1
*Standard Liège	5:1	Heart of Midlothian	1:2
Stade de Reims	4:6	*Ards	1:2

Besiktas Istanbul won outright: Olympiakos Piraeus withdrew
Young Boys Berne won outright: Manchester United withdrew

1st Round

*Real Madrid	2:1	Besiktas Istanbul	0:1
*Wiener SK	3:0	Dukla Prague	1:1
Schalke 04	2:2	*Wolverhampton Wanderers	2:1
*Atlético Madrid	2:0:3	CDNA Sofia	1:1:1
(play-off at Geneva after extra time)			
Young Boys Berne	2:4	*MTK Budapest	1:1
*Wismut Karl-Marx-Stadt	3:2	IFK Gothenburg	0:2
Standard Liège	3:3	*Sporting Lisbon	2:0
*Stade de Reims	4:3	Helsinki Palloseura	0:0

2nd Round

Real Madrid	0:7	*Wiener SK	0:1
*Atlético Madrid	3:1	Schalke 04	0:1
*Young Boys Berne	2:0:2	Wismut Karl-Marx-Stadt	2:0:1
(play-off at Amsterdam)			
Stade de Reims	0:3	*Standard Liège	2:0

Semi-Finals

*Real Madrid	2:0:2	Atlético Madrid	1:1:1
(play-off at Zaragoza)			
Stade de Reims	0:3	*Young Boys Berne	1:0

Final (Stuttgart)

Real Madrid	2	Stade de Reims	0

Real Madrid: Dominguez; Marquitos, Zarraga; Santisteban, Santamaria, Ruiz; Kopa, Mateos, Di Stefano, Rial, Gento
Scorers: Mateos, Di Stefano
Stade de Reims: Colonna; Rodzik, Giraudo; Penverne, Jonquet, Leblond; Lamartine, Bliard, Fontaine, Piantoni, Vincent

---

* Home team in 1st leg.

1959–60

Preliminary Round

*Jeunesse Esch	6:1	LKS Lodz	0:2
*OGC Nice	3:1	Shamrock Rovers	2:1
*Fenerbahce	1:3	Vasas Csepeli	1:2
Barcelona	2:6	*CDNA Sofia	2:2
*AC Milan	2:3	Olympiakos Piraeus	2:1
Wolverhampton Wanderers	1:2	*ASK Vorwaerts Berlin	2:0
IFK Gothenburg	1:6	*Linfield	2:1
*Red Star Bratislava	2:2	FC Porto	1:0
*Rangers	5:2	RSC Anderlecht	2:0
Wiener SK	0:2	*Petrolul Ploesti	0:1

Eintracht Frankfurt won outright: Kuopion Palloseura withdrew

1st Round

*Real Madrid	7:5	Jeunesse Esch	0:2
OGC Nice	1:2:5	*Fenerbahce	2:1:1
(play-off at Geneva)			
Barcelona	2:5	*AC Milan	0:1
Wolverhampton Wanderers	1:3	*Red Star Belgrade	1:0
*Sparta Rotterdam	3:1:3	IFK Gothenburg	1:3:1
(play-off at Bremen)			
*Rangers	4:1	Red Star Bratislava	3:1
Wiener SK	3:2	*Odense BK 09	0:2
Eintracht Frankfurt	4:1	*Young Boys Berne	1:1

2nd Round

Real Madrid	2:4	*OGC Nice	3:0
*Barcelona	4:5	Wolverhampton Wanderers	0:2

Rangers	3:0:3	*Sparta Rotterdam	2:1:2
(play-off at Highbury)			
*Eintracht Frankfurt	2:1	Wiener SK	1:1

Semi-Finals

| *Real Madrid | 3:3 | Barcelona | 1:1 |
| *Eintracht Frankfurt | 6:6 | Rangers | 1:3 |

Final (Hampden Park, Glasgow)

| Real Madrid | 7 | Eintracht Frankfurt | 3 |

Real Madrid: Dominguez; Marquitos, Pachin; Vidal, Santamaria, Zarraga; Canario, Del Sol, Di Stefano, Puskas, Gento
Scorers: Di Stefano (3), Puskas (4)
Eintracht Frankfurt: Loy; Lutz, Hoefer; Weilbacher, Eigenbrodt, Stinka; Kress, Lindner, Stein, Pfaff, Meier
Scorers: Kress, Stein (2)

* Home team in 1st leg.

1960-61

Preliminary Round

Benfica	2:3	*Heart of Midlothian	1:0
Ujpest Dozsa	2:3	*Red Star Belgrade	1:0
*AGF Aarhus	3:0	Legia Warsaw	0:1
*Fredrikstad	4:0	Ajax Amsterdam	3:0
*Rapid Vienna	4:0	Besiktas Istanbul	0:1
IFK Malmö	3:2	HIFK Helsinki	1:1
CDNA Sofia	0:4	*Juventus	2:1
*Stade de Reims	6:5	Jeunesse Esch	1:0
Young Boys Berne	5:4	*Limerick	0:2
Spartak Kralove	3:—	*CCA Bucharest	0:—
(CCA withdrew after 1st leg)			
*Barcelona	2:3	Lierse SK	0:0

Wismut Karl-Marx-Stadt won outright: Glenavon withdrew

1st Round

*Benfica	6:1	Ujpest Dozsa	2:2
*AGF Aarhus	3:1	Fredrikstad	0:0
*Rapid Vienna	3:0:1	Wismut Karl-Marx-Stadt	1:2:0
(play-off at Basle)			
*IFK Malmö	1:1	CDNA Sofia	0:1
*Burnley	2:2	Stade de Reims	0:3
SV Hamburg	5:3	*Young Boys Berne	0:3
*Spartak Kralove	1:0	Panathinaikos	0:0
Barcelona	2:2	*Real Madrid	2:1

2nd Round

*Benfica	3:4	AGF Aarhus	1:1
*Rapid Vienna	2:2	IFK Malmö	0:0
SV Hamburg	1:4	*Burnley	3:1
*Barcelona	4:1	Spartak Kralove	0:1

Semi-Finals

| *Benfica | 3:1 | Rapid Vienna | 0:1 |

The goal by Aguas that put Spurs out of the 1961–62 European Cup. In the first leg of their semi-final, Benfica had won 3–1, and the single goal at White Hart Lane was enough to give them an aggregate win of 4–3.

| *Barcelona | 1:1:1 | SV Hamburg | 0:2:0 |
| (play-off at Brussels) | | | |

Final (Berne)

| Benfica | 3 | Barcelona | 2 |

Benfica: Costa Pereira; Joao, Angelo; Neto, Germano, Cruz; Augusto, Santana, Aguas, Coluna, Cavem
Scorers: Aguas, Ramallets (o.g.), Coluna
Barcelona: Ramallets; Foncho, Gracia; Verges, Gensana, Garay; Kubala, Kocsis, Evaristo, Suarez, Czibor
Scorers: Kocsis, Czibor

* Home team in 1st leg.

1961-62

Preliminary Round

FK Austria	0:2	*CCA Bucharest	0:0
*1FC Nuremberg	5:4	Drumcondra	0:1
Servette Geneva	5:2	*Hibernians Valletta	0:1
Dukla Prague	4:2	*CDNA Sofia	4:1
Feyenoord	3:8	*IFK Gothenburg	0:2
Tottenham Hotspur	2:8	*Gornik Zabrze	4:1
Standard Liège	2:2	*Fredrikstad	1:0
*ASK Vorwaerts Berlin	3:—	Linfield	0:—
(Linfield withdrew after 1st leg)			
Rangers	3:3	*AS Monaco	2:2
Partizan Belgrade	1:2	*Sporting Lisbon	1:0
Juventus	2:1	*Panathinaikos	1:1
Odense BK 1913	6:9	*Spora Luxembourg	0:2
Real Madrid	2:3	*Vasas Budapest	0:1

1st Round

Benfica	1:5	*FK Austria	1:1
1FC Nuremberg	2:1	*Fenerbahce	1:0
Dukla Prague	3:2	*Servette Geneva	4:0
Tottenham Hotspur	3:1	*Feyenoord	1:1
*Standard Liège	5:2	Valkeakosken Haka	1:0
Rangers	2:4	*ASK Vorwaerts Berlin	1:1
Juventus	2:5	*Partizan Belgrade	1:0
Real Madrid	3:9	*Odense BK 1913	0:0

2nd Round

Benfica	1:6	*1FC Nuremberg	3:0
Tottenham Hotspur	0:4	*Dukla Prague	1:1
*Standard Liège	4:0	Rangers	1:2
Real Madrid	1:0:3	*Juventus	0:1:1
(play-off at Paris)			

Semi-Finals

| *Benfica | 3:1 | Tottenham Hotspur | 1:2 |
| *Real Madrid | 4:2 | Standard Liège | 0:0 |

Final (Amsterdam)

| Benfica | 5 | Real Madrid | 3 |

Benfica: Costa Pereira; Joao, Angelo; Cavem, Germano, Cruz; Augusto, Eusebio, Aguas, Coluna, Simoes
Scorers: Aguas, Cavem, Coluna, Eusebio (2; 1 pen.)
Real Madrid: Araquistain; Casado, Miera; Felo, Santamaria, Pachin; Tejada, Del Sol, Di Stefano, Puskas, Gento
Scorer: Puskas (3)

* Home team in 1st leg.

1962-63

Preliminary Round

*AC Milan	8:6	US Luxembourg	0:0
Ipswich Town	4:10	*Floriana Valletta	1:0
Galatasaray	1:3	*Dynamo Bucharest	1:0
*Polonia Bytom	2:4	Panathinaikos	1:1
*Dundee	8:0	1FC Cologne	1:4
Sporting Lisbon	2:5	*Shelbourne	0:1
RSC Anderlecht	3:1	*Real Madrid	3:0
*CDNA Sofia	2:4	Partizan Belgrade	1:1
Feyenoord	3:1:3	*Servette Geneva	1:3:1
(play-off at Dusseldorf)			
Vasas Budapest	4:7	*Fredrikstad	1:0
*FK Austria	5:2	HIFK Helsinki	3:0
Esbjerg BK	2:0	*Linfield	1:0
Dukla Prague	3:1	*ASK Vorwaerts Berlin	0:0
*IFK Norrköping	2:1	Partizan Tirana	0:1

Milan fans rob Dino Sani of his shirt as they celebrate AC Milan's 2–1 victory over Benfica in the 1963 final.

1st Round

*AC Milan	3:1	Ipswich Town	0:2
*Galatasaray	4:0	Polonia Bytom	1:1
Dundee	0:4	*Sporting Lisbon	1:1
RSC Anderlecht	2:2	*CDNA Sofia	2:0
*Feyenoord	1:2:1	Vasas Budapest	1:2:0
(play-off at Anvers)			
Stade de Reims	2:5	*FK Austria	3:0
Dukla Prague	0:5	*Esbjerg BK	0:0
Benfica	1:5	*IFK Norrköping	1:1

2nd Round

AC Milan	3:5	*Galatasaray	1:0
Dundee	4:2	*RSC Anderlecht	1:1
Feyenoord	1:1	*Stade de Reims	0:1
*Benfica	2:0	Dukla Prague	1:0

Semi-Finals

*AC Milan	5:0	Dundee	1:1
Benfica	0:3	*Feyenoord	0:1

Final (Wembley)

AC Milan   2   Benfica   1

AC Milan: Ghezzi; David, Trebbi; Benitez, Maldini, Trapattoni; Pivatelli, Dino Sani, Altafini, Rivera, Mora
Scorer: Altafini (2)
Benfica: Costa Pereira; Cavem, Cruz; Humberto, Raul, Coluna; Augusto, Santana, Torres, Eusebio, Simoes
Scorer: Eusebio

1963–64

Preliminary Round

Internazionale Milan	0:1	*Everton	0:0
*AS Monaco	7:1	AEK Athens	2:1
Jeunesse Esch	1:4	*Valkeakosken Haka	4:0
*Partizan Belgrade	3:3	Anorthosis Nicosia	0:1
Benfica	3:5	*Distillery	3:0
Borussia Dortmund	4:3	*Lyn Oslo	2:1
*Gornik Zabrze	1:0:2	FK Austria	0:1:1
(play-off at Vienna)			
*Dukla Prague	6:2	FC Valletta	0:0
*FC Zurich	3:1	Dundalk	0:2
*Galatasaray	4:0	Ferencvaros	0:2
Spartak Plovdiv	0:3	*Partizan Tirana	1:1
PSV Eindhoven	4:7	*Esbjerg BK	3:1
IFK Norrköping	0:2	*Standard Liège	1:0
*Dynamo Bucharest	2:1	Motor Jena	0:0
Real Madrid	1:6	*Rangers	0:0

1st Round

*Inter-Milan	1:3	AS Monaco	0:1
Partizan Belgrade	1:6	*Jeunesse Esch	2:2

Borussia Dortmund	1:5	*Benfica	2:0
Dukla Prague	0:4	*Gornik Zabrze	2:1
*FC Zurich	2:0:2	Galatasaray	0:2:2
(play-off at Rome won on toss after extra time)			
PSV Eindhoven	1:0	*Spartak Plovdiv	0:0
AC Milan	1:5	*IFK Norrköping	1:2
Real Madrid	3:5	*Dynamo Bucharest	1:3

2nd Round

Inter-Milan	2:2	*Partizan Belgrade	0:1
Borussia Dortmund	4:1	*Dukla Prague	0:3
FC Zurich	0:3	*PSV Eindhoven	1:1
*Real Madrid	4:0	AC Milan	1:2

Semi-Finals

Inter-Milan	2:2	*Borussia Dortmund	2:0
Real Madrid	2:6	*FC Zurich	1:0

Final (Vienna)

Inter-Milan   3   Real Madrid   1

Inter-Milan: Sarti; Burgnich, Facchetti; Tagnin, Guarneri, Picchi; Jair, Mazzola, Milani, Suarez, Corso
Scorers: Mazzola (2), Milani
Real Madrid: Vicente; Isidro, Pachin; Zoco, Santamaria, Muller; Amancio, Felo, Di Stefano, Puskas, Gento
Scorer: Felo

1964–65

Preliminary Round

Dynamo Bucharest	2:5	*Sliema Wanderers	0:0
*Rangers	3:2:3	Red Star Belgrade	1:4:1
(play-off at Highbury, London)			
*Rapid Vienna	3:2	Shamrock Rovers	0:0
Liverpool	5:6	*KR Reykjavik	0:1
*RSC Anderlecht	1:1:0	Bologna	0:2:0
(play-off at Barcelona won on toss after extra time)			
Panathinaikos	2:3	*Glentoran	2:2
1FC Cologne	0:2	*Partizan Tirana	0:0
*DWS Amsterdam	3:1	Fenerbahce	1:0
Lyn Oslo	1:3	*Lahden Reipas	2:0
Vasas Györ	2:4	*Chemie Leipzig	0:2
*Lokomotiv Sofia	8:0	Malmö FF	3:2
*Real Madrid	4:5	Odense BK 09	0:2
*Dukla Prague	4:0:0	Gornik Zabrze	1:3:0
(play-off at Duisburg won on toss after extra time)			
La Chaux de Fonds	2:2	*St Etienne	2:1
Benfica	5:5	*Aris Bonnevoie	1:1

1st Round

*Inter-Milan	6:1	Dynamo Bucharest	0:0
*Rangers	1:2	Rapid Vienna	0:0
*Liverpool	3:1	RSC Anderlecht	0:0
1FC Cologne	1:2	*Panathinaikos	1:1
*DWS Amsterdam	5:3	Lyn Oslo	0:1
*Vasas Györ	5:3	Lokomotiv Sofia	3:4
*Real Madrid	4:2	Dukla Prague	0:2
Benfica	1:5	*La Chaux de Fonds	1:0

2nd Round

*Inter-Milan	3:0	Rangers	1:1
Liverpool	0:0:2	*1FC Cologne	0:0:2
(play-off at Rotterdam won on toss after extra time)			
Vasas Györ	1:1	*DWS Amsterdam	1:0
*Benfica	5:1	Real Madrid	1:2

Semi-Finals

Inter-Milan	1:3	*Liverpool	3:0
Benfica	1:4	*Vasas Györ	0:0

Final (Milan)

*Inter-Milan   1   Benfica   0

Inter-Milan: Sarti; Burgnich, Facchetti; Bedin, Guarneri, Picchi; Jair, Mazzola, Peiró, Suarez, Corso
Scorer: Jair
Benfica: Costa Pereira; Cavem, Cruz; Neto, Germano, Raul; Augusto, Eusebio, Torres, Coluna, Simoes

1965–66

Preliminary Round

Real Madrid	1:5	*Feyenoord	2:0
Kilmarnock	0:1	*Nendori Tirana	0:0
RSC Anderlecht	0:5	*Fenerbahce	0:1
Derry City	3:5	*Lyn Oslo	5:1
*Dynamo Bucharest	4:3	Odense BK 09	0:2
Ferencvaros	4:9	*Keflavik Reykjavik	1:1
*Panathinaikos	4:0	Sliema Wanderers	1:1
Manchester United	3:6	*HJK Helsinki	2:0
ASK Vorwaerts Berlin	0:3	*Drumcondra	1:0
Benfica	8:10	*Stade Dudelange	0:0
Levski Sofia	1:6	*Djurgaarden Stockholm	2:0
Sparta Prague	0:4	*Lausanne	0:0
Gornik Zabrze	3:2	*Linz ASK	1:1
Werder Bremen	5:5	*Apoel Nicosia	0:0
*Partizan Belgrade	2:2	FC Nantes	0:2

1st Round

Real Madrid	2:5	*Kilmarnock	2:1
*RSC Anderlecht	9:–	Derry City	0:–
(Derry conceded 2nd leg; ground ruled unfit)			
Inter-Milan	1:2	*Dynamo Bucharest	2:0
*Ferencvaros	0:3	Panathinaikos	0:1
Manchester United	2:3	*ASK Vorwaerts Berlin	0:1
Benfica	2:3	*Levski Sofia	2:2
*Sparta Prague	3:2	Gornik Zabrze	0:1
*Partizan Belgrade	3:0	Werder Bremen	0:1

2nd Round

Real Madrid	0:4	*RSC Anderlecht	1:2
*Inter-Milan	4:1	Ferencvaros	0:1
*Manchester United	3:5	Benfica	2:1
Partizan Belgrade	1:5	*Sparta Prague	4:0

Semi-Finals

*Real Madrid	1:1	Inter-Milan	0:1
*Partizan Belgrade	2:0	Manchester United	0:1

Final (Brussels)

Real Madrid	2	Partizan Belgrade	1

Real Madrid: Araquistain; Pachin, Sanchis; Pirri, De Felipe, Zoco; Serena, Amancio, Grosso, Velasquez, Gento
Scorers: Amancio, Serena
Partizan Belgrade: Soskic; Jusufi, Milhailovic; Becejac, Rasovic, Vasovic; Bajic, Kovacevic, Hasanagic, Galic, Pirmajer
Scorer: Vasovic

* Home team in 1st leg.

1966–67

Extra Preliminary Round

CSKA Sofia	2:4	*Sliema Wanderers	1:0
*ASK Vorwaerts Berlin	6:6	Waterford	0:1

Preliminary Round

*Celtic	2:3	FC Zurich	0:0
FC Nantes	3:5	*Reykjavik FC	2:2
Vojvodina Novi Sad	1:0	*Admira Vienna	0:0
Atlético Madrid	2:3	*Malmö FF	0:1
*Ajax Amsterdam	2:2	Besiktas Istanbul	0:1
*Liverpool	2:1:2	Petrolul Ploesti	0:3:0
(play-off at Brussels)			
RSC Anderlecht	10:2	*Valkeakosken Haka	1:0
*Gornik Zabrze	2:1:3	ASK Vorwaerts Berlin	1:2:1
(play-off at Budapest)			
*CSKA Sofia	3:0	Olympiakos Piraeus	1:1
Dukla Prague	2:4	*Esbjerg FK	0:0
Linfield	3:6	*Aris Bonnevoie	3:1
*Munich 1860	8:2	Omonia Nicosia	0:1
*Vasas Budapest	5:2	Sporting Lisbon	0:0
*Internazionale Milan	1:0	Moscow Torpedo	0:0

Valerengen won outright: Nendori Tirana withdrew

1st Round

Celtic	3:3	*FC Nantes	1:1
*Vojvodina Novi Sad	3:0:3	Atlético Madrid	1:2:2
(play-off at Madrid)			
*Ajax Amsterdam	5:2	Liverpool	1:2
*Dukla Prague	4:2	RSC Anderlecht	1:1
*CSKA Sofia	4:0	Gornik Zabrze	0:3
Linfield	4:1	*Valerengen	1:1
Real Madrid	0:3	*Munich 1860	1:1
*Inter-Milan	2:2	Vasas Budapest	1:0

2nd Round

Celtic	0:2	*Vojvodina Novi Sad	1:0
Dukla Prague	1:2	*Ajax Amsterdam	1:1
CSKA Sofia	2:1	*Linfield	2:0
*Inter-Milan	1:2	Real Madrid	0:0

Semi-Finals

*Celtic	3:0	Dukla Prague	1:0
*Inter-Milan	1:1:1	CSKA Sofia	1:1:0
(play-off at Bologna)			

Final (Lisbon)

Celtic	2	Inter-Milan	1

Celtic: Simpson; Craig, Gemmell; Murdoch, McNeill, Clark; Johnstone, Wallace, Chalmers, Auld, Lennox
Scorers: Gemmell, Chalmers
Inter-Milan: Sarti; Burgnich, Facchetti; Bedin, Guarneri, Picchi; Domenghini, Mazzola, Cappellini, Bicicli, Corso
Scorer: Mazzola (pen.)

1967–68

1st Round

Benfica	1:0	*Glentoran	1:0
(won on away-goals rule)			
Rapid Vienna	1:3	*Besiktas Istanbul	0:0
Kiev Dynamo	2:1	*Celtic	1:1
Juventus	0:2	*Olympiakos Piraeus	0:0
Vasas Budapest	1:8	*Dundalk	0:1
*Manchester United	4:0	Hibernians Valletta	0:0
*St Etienne	2:3	Kuopion Palloseura	0:0
RSC Anderlecht	3:2	*Wismut Karl-Marx-Stadt	1:1
Hvidovre Copenhagen	2:3	*FC Basle	1:3
Sparta Prague	1:1	*Skeid Oslo	0:1
Sarajevo	2:3	*Olympiakos Nicosia	2:1
Real Madrid	1:2	*Ajax Amsterdam	1:1
*Valur Reykjavik	1:3	Jeunesse Esch	1:3
(won on away-goals rule)			
*Gornik Zabrze	3:1	Djurgaarden Stockholm	0:0
Rapid Bucharest	0:3	*Trakia Plovdiv	2:0

Eintracht Brunswick won outright: Dynamo Tirana withdrew

Above: Celtic bring the European Cup home to an ecstatic Parkhead after the 2–1 defeat of Inter-Milan at Lisbon in 1967.

Below: Bobby Charlton hits his second goal to take Manchester United's tally to four against Benfica in the 1968 final.

Above: Billy Bremner (left) and Billy McNeill before the second leg of the 1970 semi-final between Celtic and Leeds. Having already won 1–0 at Elland Road, Celtic clinched a place in the final with an impressive 2–1 win at Hampden Park.

2nd Round

Manchester United	0:2	*Sarajevo	0:1
Real Madrid	2:4	*Hvidovre Copenhagen	2:1
Eintracht Brunswick	0:2	*Rapid Vienna	1:0
*Benfica	2:0	St Etienne	0:1
*Vasas Budapest	6:5	Valur Reykjavik	0:1
Gornik Zabrze	2:1	*Kiev Dynamo	1:1
*Juventus	1:0	Rapid Bucharest	0:0
*Sparta Prague	3:3	RSC Anderlecht	2:3

Quarter-Finals

Juventus (play-off at Berne)	2:1:1	*Eintracht Brunswick	3:0:0
*Manchester United	2:0	Gornik Zabrze	0:1
*Real Madrid	3:1	Sparta Prague	0:2
Benfica	0:3	*Vasas Budapest	0:0

Semi-Finals

*Manchester United	1:3	Real Madrid	0:3
*Benfica	2:1	Juventus	0:0

Final (Wembley)

Manchester United	4	Benfica	1

(after extra time: 1:1 at full time)

Manchester United: Stepney; Brennan, Dunne; Crerand, Foulkes, Stiles; Best, Kidd, Charlton, Sadler, Aston
Scorers: Charlton (2), Best, Kidd
Benfica: Henrique; Adolfo, Humberto, Jacinto, Cruz; Graça, Coluna; Augusto, Eusebio, Torres, Simoes
Scorer: Graça

---

* Home team in 1st leg.

1968–69

1st Round

Celtic	0:4	*St Etienne	2:0
Manchester United	3:7	*Waterford	1:1
Fenerbahce	0:2	*Manchester City	0:1
*RSC Anderlecht	3:2	Glentoran	0:2
*AEK Athens	3:2	Jeunesse Esch	0:3
Ajax Amsterdam	1:4	*1FC Nuremberg	1:0
AC Milan	1:4	*Malmö FF	2:1
Spartak Trnava	1:4	*Steaua Bucharest	3:0
AB Copenhagen	3:1	*FC Zurich	1:2
Rapid Vienna	3:3	*Rosenborg Trondheim	1:3
Lahden Reipas	1:2	*Floriana Valletta	1:0
*Real Madrid	6:6	Union Limassol	0:0
Benfica	0:8	*Valur Reykjavik	0:1

Red Star Belgrade won outright: Carl Zeiss Jena withdrew

Below: Van Duivenbode of Ajax Amsterdam leaps over a prostrate Kurt Hamrin during the 1969 final. Ajax, in their first European Cup final, were overwhelmed 4–1 by the experienced Inter-Milan. Three years later, it was a different story.

2nd Round

*Manchester United	3:1	RSC Anderlecht	0:3
*Celtic	5:1	Red Star Belgrade	1:1
*Rapid Vienna	1:1	Real Madrid	0:2
(won on away-goals rule)			
Spartak Trnava	9:7	*Lahden Reipas	1:1
*AEK Athens	0:2	AB Copenhagen	0:0
*Ajax Amsterdam	2:2	Fenerbahce	0:0
AC Milan	bye		
Benfica	bye		

Quarter-Finals

*Ajax Amsterdam (play-off at Paris)	1:3:3	Benfica	3:1:0
*AC Milan	0:1	Celtic	0:0
*Manchester United	3:0	Rapid Vienna	0:0
*Spartak Trnava	2:1	AEK Athens	1:1

Semi-Finals

*AC Milan	2:0	Manchester United	1:0
*Ajax Amsterdam	3:0	Spartak Trnava	0:2

Final (Madrid)

AC Milan	4	Ajax Amsterdam	1

AC Milan: Cudicini; Anquilletti, Schnellinger; Maldera, Rosato, Trapattoni; Hamrin, Lodetti, Sormani, Rivera, Prati
Scorers: Prati (3), Sormani
Ajax Amsterdam: Bals; Suurbier (Muller), Van Duivenbode; Pronk, Hulshoff, Vasovic; Swart, Cruyff, Danielsson, Groot (Nuninga), Keizer
Scorer: Vasovic (pen.)

---

* Home team in 1st leg.

1969–70

Preliminary Round

KB Copenhagen	1:4	*Turun Palloseura	0:0

1st Round

*AC Milan	5:3	*Avenir Beggen	0:0
*Leeds United	10:6	Lyn Oslo	0:0
*Red Star Belgrade	8:4	Linfield	0:2
Celtic	0:2	*FC Basle	0:0
Spartak Trnava	2:4	*Hibernians Valletta	2:0
*Galatasaray	2:3	Waterford	0:2
Ferencvaros	1:4	*CSKA Sofia	2:1
Legia Warsaw	2:8	*UT Arad	1:0
*ASK Vorwaerts Berlin	2:1	Panathinaikos	0:1
St Etienne	0:3	*Bayern Munich	2:0
*Standard Liège	3:1	Nendori Tirana	0:1
*Feyenoord	12:4	KR Reykjavik	0:0
(2nd leg in Rotterdam)			
Kiev Dynamo	2:3	*FK Austria	1:1
*Fiorentina	1:2	Oester Vaexjoe	0:1
*Benfica	2:3	KB Copenhagen	0:2
*Real Madrid	8:6	Olympiakos Nicosia	0:1
(2nd leg in Madrid)			

2nd Round

*Leeds United	3:3	Ferencvaros	0:0
*Celtic	3:0	Benfica	0:3
(won on toss)			
Fiorentina	2:0	*Kiev Dynamo	1:0
Feyenoord	0:2	*AC Milan	1:0
Galatasaray	0:1	*Spartak Trnava	1:0
(won on toss)			
*Legia Warsaw	2:1	St Etienne	1:0
*ASK Vorwaerts Berlin	2:2	Red Star Belgrade	1:3
(won on away-goals rule)			
*Standard Liège	1:3	Real Madrid	0:2

Quarter-Finals

Leeds United	1:1	*Standard Liège	0:0
*Celtic	3:0	Fiorentina	0:1
Legia Warsaw	1:2	*Galatasaray	0:0
Feyenoord	0:2	*ASK Vorwaerts Berlin	1:0

Semi-Finals

Celtic	1:2	*Leeds United	0:1
Feyenoord	0:2	*Legia Warsaw	0:0

Final (Milan)

Feyenoord	2	Celtic	1

(after extra time: 1–1 at full time)

Feyenoord: Pieters Graafland; Romeyn (Haak), Israel, Laseroms, Jansen, Van Duivenbode; Hasil, Van Hanegem; Wery, Kindvall, Moulijn
Scorers: Israel, Kindvall
Celtic: Williams; Hay, Gemmell; Murdoch, McNeill, Brogan; Johnstone, Wallace, Hughes, Auld (Connelly), Lennox
Scorer: Gemmell

---

* Home team in 1st leg.

1970–71

Preliminary Round

FK Austria	1:3	*Levski Spartak	3:0

1st Round

*Everton	6:3	Keflavik Reykjavic	2:0
*Celtic	9:5	KPV Kokkola	0:0
Waterford	3:1	*Glentoran	1:0
*Cagliari	3:0	St Etienne	0:1
*Slovan Bratislava	2:2	BK 1903 Copenhagen	1:2
Ajax Amsterdam	2:2	*Nendori Tirana	2:0
Legia Warsaw	4:2	*IFK Gothenburg	0:1
Red Star Belgrade	0:4	*Ujpest Dozsa	2:0
Standard Liège	2:5	*Rosenborg Trondheim	0:0
*Borussia Mönchengladbach	6:10	EPA Larnaca	0:0
FC Basle (won on away-goals rule)	2:2	*Moscow Spartak	3:1
UT Arad (won on away-goals rule)	1:0	*Feyenoord	1:0
*Atlético Madrid	2:2	FK Austria	0:1
Panathinaikos	2:5	*Jeunesse Esch	1:0
Carl Zeiss Jena	4:1	*Fenerbahce	0:0
*Sporting Lisbon	5:4	Floriana Valletta	0:0

Pieters Graafland watches Gemmell's thunderbolt put Celtic a goal up in the 1970 final. But minutes later Israel equalized for Feyenoord, and in extra time Kindvall clinched the trophy for the Dutch club.

2nd Round

Everton (won on penalty kicks after extra time)	1:1	*Borussia Mönchengladbach	1:1
Celtic	7:3	*Waterford	0:2
*Red Star Belgrade	3:3	UT Arad	0:1
*Carl Zeiss Jena	2:2	Sporting Lisbon	1:1
*Panathinaikos	3:1	Slovan Bratislava	0:2
Legia Warsaw	0:2	*Standard Liège	1:0
Atlético Madrid	1:3	*Cagliari	2:0
*Ajax Amsterdam	3:2	FC Basle	0:1

Quarter-Finals

Panathinaikos (won on away-goals rule)	1:0	*Everton	1:0
*Ajax Amsterdam	3:0	Celtic	0:1
*Atlético Madrid (won on away-goals rule)	1:1	Legia Warsaw	0:2
Red Star Belgrade	2:4	*Carl Zeiss Jena	3:0

Semi-Finals

Panathinaikos (won on away-goals rule)	1:3	*Red Star Belgrade	4:0
Ajax Amsterdam	0:3	*Atlético Madrid	1:0

Final (Wembley)

Ajax Amsterdam	2	Panathinaikos	0

Ajax Amsterdam: Stuy; Neeskens, Vasovic, Hulshoff, Suurbier; Rijnders (Blankenburg), Muhren; Swart (Haan), Cruyff, Van Dijk, Keizer
Scorers: Van Dijk, Haan
Panathinaikos: Economopoulos; Tomaras, Vlahos, Elefterakis, Kamaras, Sourpis, Grammos, Filakouris, Antoniadis, Domazos, Kapsis

---

* Home team in 1st leg.

1971–72

Preliminary Round

*Valencia	3:1	US Luxembourg	1:0

1st Round

*Internazionale Milan	4:2	AEK Athens	1:3
Arsenal	3:4	*Stromsgodset Drammen	1:0
Benfica	4:3	*Wacker Innsbruck	0:1
Celtic	1:3	*BK 1903 Copenhagen	2:0
CSKA Moscow	1:3	*Galatasaray	1:0
*Ajax Amsterdam	2:0	Dynamo Dresden	0:0
*Olympique Marseille	2:1	Gornik Zabrze	1:1
Grasshoppers Zurich	1:8	*Lahden Reipas	1:0
*Valencia (won on away-goals rule)	0:1	Hajduk Split	0:1
*Standard Liège	2:3	Linfield	0:2
*Ujpest Dozsa	4:0	Malmö FF	0:1
Borussia Mönchengladbach	5:2	*Cork Hibernians	0:1
*Feyenoord	8:9	Olympiakos Nicosia	0:0
*CSKA Sofia	3:1	Partizan Tirana	0:0
Sliema Wanderers	4:0	*Akranes	0:0
*Dynamo Bucharest (won on away-goals rule)	0:2	Spartak Trnava	0:2

2nd Round

Ajax Amsterdam	2:4	*Olympique Marseille	1:1
Arsenal	2:3	*Grasshoppers Zurich	0:0
*Benfica	2:0	CSKA Sofia	1:0
Feyenoord	3:2	*Dynamo Bucharest	0:0
Inter-Milan	1:4:0	*Borussia Mönchengladbach	7:2:0

(match ordered to be replayed, following crowd misconduct; 2nd leg played before re-arranged 1st leg)

*Celtic	5:2	Sliema Wanderers	0:1
Standard Liège	0:2	*CSKA Moscow	1:0
Ujpest Dozsa	1:2	*Valencia	0:1

Quarter-Finals

*Ajax Amsterdam	2:1	Arsenal	1:0
Benfica	0:5	*Feyenoord	1:1
*Inter-Milan (won on away-goals rule)	1:1	Standard Liège	0:2
Celtic	2:1	*Ujpest Dozsa	1:1

Semi-Finals

*Ajax Amsterdam	1:0	Benfica	0:0
*Inter-Milan (won on penalties)	0:0	Celtic	0:0

Final (Rotterdam)

Ajax Amsterdam	2	Inter-Milan	0

Ajax Amsterdam: Stuy; Suurbier, Hulshoff, Blankenburg, Krol, Haan, Neeskens, Muhren, Swart, Cruyff, Keizer
Scorer: Cruyff (2)
Inter-Milan: Bordon; Bellugi, Burgnich, Giubertoni (Bertini), Facchetti, Oriali, Mazzola, Bedin, Jair (Pelizzaro), Boninsegna, Frustalupi

---

* Home team in 1st leg.

1st Round

Ajax Amsterdam	*bye*		
*CSKA Sofia	2:2	Panathinaikos	1:0
Bayern Munich	1:6	*Galatasaray	1:0
Omonia Nicosia	1:2	*Waterford	2:0
Kiev Dynamo	1:2	*TS Innsbruck	0:0
Gornik Zabrze	5:5	*Sliema Wanderers	0:0
*Real Madrid	3:1	Keflavik Reykjavic	0:0
Arges Pitesti	2:4	*Aris Bonnevoie	0:0
*Anderlecht	4:3	Vejle	2:0
Spartak Trnava	*bye*		
Benfica	0:4	*Malmö FF	1:1
*Derby County	2:2	Zeljeznicar	0:1
*Celtic	2:3	Rosenborg	1:1
*Ujpest Dozsa	2:2	Basle	0:3
*FC Magdeburg	6:3	Turun Palloseura	0:1
Juventus	0:3	*Marseille	1:0

2nd Round

Ajax Amsterdam	3:3	*CSKA Sofia	1:0
Bayern Munich	9:4	*Omonia Nicosia	0:0
(1st leg in Augsburg)			
*Kiev Dynamo	2:1	Gornik Zabrze	0:2
Real Madrid	1:3	*Arges Pitesti	2:1
*Spartak Trnava	1:1	Anderlecht	0:0
*Derby County	3:0	Benfica	0:0
Ujpest Dozsa	1:3	*Celtic	2:0
*Juventus	1:1	FC Magdeburg	0:0

Quarter-Finals

*Ajax Amsterdam	4:1	Bayern Munich	0:2
Real Madrid	0:3	*Kiev Dynamo	0:0
Derby County	0:2	*Spartak Trnava	1:0
*Juventus	0:2	Ujpest Dozsa	0:2
(won on away-goals rule)			

Semi-Finals

*Ajax Amsterdam	2:1	Real Madrid	1:0
*Juventus	3:0	Derby County	1:0

Final (Belgrade)

Ajax Amsterdam	1	Juventus	0

Ajax Amsterdam: Stuy; Suurbier, Hulshoff, Blankenburg, Krol; Haan, Neeskens, Muhren; Rep, Cruyff, Keizer
Scorer: Rep
Juventus: Zoff; Marchetti, Salvadore, Morini, Longobucco; Furino, Causio (Cuccureddu), Capello; Altafini, Anastasi, Bettega (Haller)

*Home team in 1st leg.

Above: Kevin Hector after scoring his second goal in the 1972-73 quarter-final second-leg game between Derby and Spartak Trnava at the Baseball Ground. It turned out to be the winning goal for Derby. Below: Agonizing moments for Roger Davies and three Spartak defenders as Hector's shot crosses the line.

Right: Johnny Rep of Ajax in action against Juventus in the 1973 final. At 20 the youngest player on the field, he scored the only goal of the game with a fifth-minute header.

1973-74

1st Round

*Bayern Munich	3:1	Atvidaberg	1:3
(won on penalties)			
*Dynamo Dresden	2:2	Juventus	0:3
*CSKA Sofia	3:1	SW Innsbruck	0:0
Ajax Amsterdam	bye		
Ujpest Dozsa	3:3	*Waterford	2:0
*Benfica	1:1	Olympiakos Piraeus	0:0
Spartak Trnava	2:1	*Viking Stavanger	1:0
*Saria Voroshilovgrad	2:1	Apoel Nicosia	0:0
*FC Bruges	8:2	Floriana Valletta	0:0
*FC Basle	5:6	Fram Reykjavik	0:2
(2nd leg in Olten, Switzerland)			
*Vejle	2:2	Nantes	1:0
Celtic	6:3	*TPS Turku	1:0
Liverpool	1:2	*Jeunesse Esch	1:0
*Red Star Belgrade	2:1	Stal Mielec	1:0
Dynamo Bucharest	1:11	*Crusaders	0:0
*Atlético Madrid	0:1	Galatasaray	0:0

2nd Round

*Bayern Munich	4:3	Dynamo Dresden	3:3
CSKA Sofia	0:2	*Ajax Amsterdam	1:0
Ujpest Dozsa	1:2	*Benfica	1:0
*Spartak Trnava	0:1	Saria Voroshilovgrad	0:0
FC Basle	1:6	*FC Bruges	2:4
*Celtic	0:1	Vejle	0:0
*Red Star Belgrade	2:2	Liverpool	1:1
Atlético Madrid	2:2	*Dynamo Bucharest	0:2

Quarter-Finals

*Bayern Munich	4:1	CSKA Sofia	1:2
Ujpest Dozsa	1:1	*Spartak Trnava	1:1
(won on penalties)			
Celtic	2:4	*FC Basle	3:2
Atlético Madrid	2:0	*Red Star Belgrade	0:0

Semi-Finals

Bayern Munich	1:3	*Ujpest Dozsa	1:0
Atlético Madrid	0:2	*Celtic	0:0

Final (Brussels)

Bayern Munich	1	Atlético Madrid	1
(replay)	4		0

Bayern Munich: (first game) Maier; Hansen, Breitner, Schwarzenbeck, Beckenbauer, Roth, Torstensson (Dürnberger), Zobel, Müller, Hoeness, Kappelmann.
Scorer: Schwarzenbeck
Atlético Madrid: (first game) Reina; Melo, Capon, Adelardo, Heredia, Eusebio, Ufarte (Becerra), Luis, Garate, Irureta, Salcedo (Alberto)
Scorer: Luis
Bayern Munich: (replay) As for first game (no subs)
Scorers: Hoeness 2, Müller 2
Atlético Madrid: (replay) Reina; Melo, Capon, Adelardo (Benegas), Heredia, Eusebio, Salcedo, Luis, Garate, Alberto (Ufarte), Becerra

*Home team in 1st leg.

The 1974 European Cup final was the first to go to a replay. Georg Schwarzenbeck had scored a dramatic equalizer for Bayern Munich in the last minute of extra time, but the Germans convincingly demolished Atlético Madrid in the second match 4-0. Top left: Gerd Müller (leaping high), scorer of two of the goals, finds time to help out his defence at a corner-kick. Centre left: Uli Hoeness sweeps past the Spanish 'keeper after a run from the halfway line to score his second and his team's fourth. Left: The triumphant Bayern Munich side hold the trophy aloft after an orgy of shirt swopping.

121

EUROPEAN CUP-WINNERS CUP

1960–61

Qualifying Round
Red Star Brno	1:2	*ASK Vorwaerts Berlin	2:0	
*Rangers	4:1	Ferencvaros	2:2	

Quarter-Finals
Fiorentina	3:6	*Lucerne	0:2	
Dynamo Zagreb	0:2	*Red Star Brno	0:0	
Wolverhampton Wanderers	0:5	*FK Austria	2:0	
Rangers	3:8	*Borussia Mönchengladbach	0:0	

Semi-Finals
*Fiorentina	3:1	Dynamo Zagreb	0:2	
*Rangers	2:1	Wolverhampton Wanderers	0:1	

Final
Fiorentina	2:2	*Rangers	0:1

Fiorentina: Albertosi; Robotti, Castelletti; Gonfiantani, Orzan, Rimbaldo; Hamrin, Micheli, Da Costa, Milan, Petris
Scorers: (1st leg) Milan (2); (2nd leg) Milan, Hamrin
Rangers: Ritchie; Shearer, Caldow; Davis, Paterson, Baxter; Wilson, McMillan, Scott, Brand, Hume (2nd leg, Millar)
Scorer: (2nd leg) Scott

1961–62

Preliminary Round
Atlético Madrid	3:4	*Sedan-Torcy	2:1
Leicester City	4:3	*Glenavon	1:1
Motor Jena (1st leg at Linz)	2:5	*Swansea Town	2:1
Leixoes Porto	2:5	*La Chaux de Fonds	6:0
Ujpest Dozsa	5:10	*Floriana Valletta	2:2
*Dunfermline Athletic	4:4	St Patrick's Athletic	1:0
*Rapid Vienna	0:5	Spartak Varna	0:2

1st Round
Atlético Madrid	1:2	*Leicester City	1:0
*Werder Bremen	2:3	AGF Aarhus	0:2
*Motor Jena (2nd leg at Erfurt)	7:2	Alliance Dudelange	0:2
*Leixoes Porto	1:1	SK Progressul	1:0
Ujpest Dozsa	1:3	*Ajax Amsterdam	2:1
*Dunfermline Athletic	5:0	Vardar Skoplje	0:2
Dynamo Zilina	3:1	*Olympiakos Piraeus	2:0
*Fiorentina	3:6	Rapid Vienna	1:2

Quarter-Finals
Atlético Madrid	1:3	*Werder Bremen	1:1
*Motor Jena (2nd leg at Gera)	1:3	Leixoes Porto	1:1
*Ujpest Dozsa	4:1	Dunfermline Athletic	3:0
Fiorentina	2:2	*Dynamo Zilina	3:0

Semi-Finals
Atlético Madrid (2nd leg at Malmö)	1:4	*Motor Jena	0:0
*Fiorentina	2:1	*Ujpest Dozsa	0:0

Final (Hampden Park, Glasgow)
Atlético Madrid	1	Fiorentina	1
(replay at Stuttgart)	3		0

Atlético Madrid: Madinabeytia; Rivilla, Calleja; Ramirez, Chuzo (replay Griffa), Glaria; Jones, Adelardo, Mendonça, Peiró, Collar
Scorers: (final) Peiró; (replay) Jones, Mendonça, Peiró
Fiorentina: (final) Sarti; Orzan, Castelletti; Ferretti, Gonfiantani, Rimbaldo; Hamrin, Bartu, Milani, Dell-Angelo, Petris
Scorer: Hamrin

Fiorentina: (replay) Albertosi; Robotti, Castelletti; Malatrasi, Orzan, Marchesi; Hamrin, Ferretti, Milani, Dell-Angelo, Petris

1962–63

Preliminary Rounds
*Rangers	4:0	Seville	0:2
*Lausanne	3:2	Sparta Rotterdam	0:4
*OFK Belgrade	2:3	Chemie Halle	0:3
*Ujpest Dozsa	0:5	Zaglebie Sosnowiec	0:0
Napoli	0:3:2	*Bangor City	2:1:1
(play-off at Highbury, London)			
*St Etienne	1:3	Vitoria Setubal	1:1
Odense BK 09	1:8	*Alliance Dudelange	1:1
Botev Plovdiv	2:5	*Steaua Bucharest	3:1

1st Round
*Tottenham Hotspur	5:3	Rangers	2:2
Slovan Bratislava	1:1	*Lausanne	1:0
*OFK Belgrade	5:2	Portadown	1:3
Napoli	1:1:3	*Ujpest Dozsa	1:1:1
(play-off at Lausanne)			
1FC Nuremberg	0:3	*St Etienne	0:0
Odense BK 09	1:5	*Sturm Graz	1:3
Botev Plovdiv	4:1	*Shamrock Rovers	0:0
*Atlético Madrid	4:1	Hibernians Valletta	0:0

Quarter-Finals
Tottenham Hotspur	0:6	*Slovan Bratislava	2:0
*OFK Belgrade	2:1:3	Napoli	0:3:1
(play-off at Marseille)			
1FC Nuremberg	1:6	*Odense BK 09	0:0
Atlético Madrid	1:4	*Botev Plovdiv	1:0

Semi-Finals
Tottenham Hotspur	2:3	*OFK Belgrade	1:1
Atlético Madrid	1:2	*1FC Nuremberg	2:0

Final (Rotterdam)
Tottenham Hotspur	5	Atlético Madrid	1

Tottenham Hotspur: Brown; Baker, Henry; Blanchflower, Norman, Marchi; Jones, White, Smith, Greaves, Dyson
Scorers: Greaves (2), White, Dyson (2)
Atlético Madrid: Madinabeytia; Rivilla, Rodrigues; Ramiro, Griffa, Glaria; Jones, Adelardo, Chuzo, Mendonça, Collar
Scorer: Collar (pen.)

1963–64

Preliminary Round
Sporting Lisbon	0:3:3	*Atalanta	2:1:1
(after extra time in play-off at Madrid)			
*Apoel Nicosia	6:0	Gjoevik Lyn	0:1
Manchester United	1:6	*Willem II Tilburg	1:1
*Olympique Lyonnaise	3:3	Odense BK 09	1:1
*Olympiakos Piraeus	2:0:2	Zaglebie Sosnowiec	1:1:0
(play-off at Vienna)			
*SV Hamburg	4:3	US Luxembourg	0:2
Barcelona	2:3	*Shelborne	0:1
Celtic	5:5	*FC Basle	1:0
Dynamo Zagreb	0:1:1	*Linz ASK	1:0:1
(play-off at Linz won on toss after extra time)			
Slovan Bratislava	4:8	*Helsinki Palloseura	1:1
Borough United	0:2	*Sliema Wanderers	0:0
*Fenerbahce	4:0	Petrolul Ploesti	1:1
*MTK Budapest	1:1	Slavia Sofia	0:1

1st Round
*Sporting Lisbon (2nd leg at Lisbon)	16:2	Apoel Nicosia	1:0
Manchester United	0:4	*Tottenham Hotspur	2:1
*Olympique Lyonnaise	4:1	Olympiakos Piraeus	1:2
SV Hamburg (play-off at Lausanne)	4:0:3	*Barcelona	4:0:2
*Celtic	3:1	Dynamo Zagreb	0:2

Rangers fans at Barcelona in 1972. Their team had contested the first European Cup-Winners Cup final in 1961 but had lost 4–1 over two legs to Italian club Fiorentina.

Slovan Bratislava	1:3	*Borough United	0:0
*Fenerbahce	4:0	Linfield	1:2
MTK Budapest	0:2	*Motor Zwickau	1:0

Quarter-Finals

Sporting Lisbon	1:5	*Manchester United	4:0
Olympique Lyonnaise	1:2	*SV Hamburg	1:0
*Celtic	1:1	Slovan Bratislava	0:0
*MTK Budapest	2:1:1	Fenerbahce	0:3:0
(play-off at Rome)			

Semi-Finals

Sporting Lisbon	0:1:1	*Olympique Lyonnaise	0:1:0
(play-off at Madrid)			
MTK Budapest	0:4	*Celtic	3:0

Final (Brussels)

Sporting Lisbon	3	MTK Budapest	3
(replay at Antwerp)	1		0

Sporting Lisbon: Carvalho; Gomez, Peridis (replay Pendes); Baptista, Carlos, Geo; Mendes, Oswaldo, Mascarenhas, Figueiredo, Morais
Scorers: (final) Figueiredo (2), Dansky (o.g.) (replay) Morais
MTK Budapest: Kovalik; Keszei, Dansky; Jenei, Nagy, Kovacs; Sandor, Vasas, Kuti, Bodor, Halapi
Scorers: (final) Sandor (2), Kuti

* Home team in 1st leg.

1964-65

Preliminary Round

West Ham United	1:1	*La Gantoise	0:1
*Sparta Prague	10:6	Anorthosis Famagusta	0:0
(2nd leg at Pilzno)			
*Slavia Sofia	2:1	Cork Celtic	0:1
*Lausanne	2:0	Honved	0:1
Real Zaragoza	3:3	*FC Valletta	0:1
Cardiff City	0:1	*Esbjerg BK	0:0
Valkeakosken Haka	0:2	*Skeid Oslo	1:0
Torino	3:2	Fortuna Geleen	1:2
*Steaua Bucharest	3:2	Derry City	0:0
Dynamo Zagreb	0:3	*AEK Athens	2:0
Legia Warsaw	3:1	*Admira Vienna	1:0

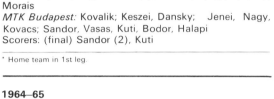

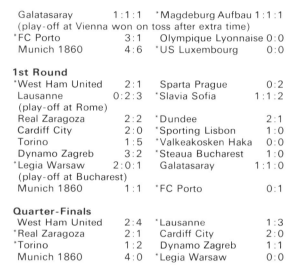

Alan Sealey (left), Bobby Moore, and Martin Peters parade their prize after West Ham's 2–0 win over Munich 1860 at Wembley in 1965. Two years earlier another London club, Spurs, had won the Cup-Winners Cup.

Galatasaray	1:1:1	*Magdeburg Aufbau	1:1:1
(play-off at Vienna won on toss after extra time)			
*FC Porto	3:1	Olympique Lyonnaise	0:0
Munich 1860	4:6	*US Luxembourg	0:0

1st Round

*West Ham United	2:1	Sparta Prague	0:2
Lausanne	0:2:3	*Slavia Sofia	1:1:2
(play-off at Rome)			
Real Zaragoza	2:2	*Dundee	2:1
Cardiff City	2:0	*Sporting Lisbon	1:0
Torino	1:5	*Valkeakosken Haka	0:0
Dynamo Zagreb	3:2	*Steaua Bucharest	1:0
*Legia Warsaw	2:0:1	Galatasaray	1:1:0
(play-off at Bucharest)			
Munich 1860	1:1	*FC Porto	0:1

Quarter-Finals

West Ham United	2:4	*Lausanne	1:3
*Real Zaragoza	2:1	Cardiff City	2:0
*Torino	1:2	Dynamo Zagreb	1:1
Munich 1860	4:0	*Legia Warsaw	0:0

Below: West Ham hero Alan Sealey and Martin Peters in jubilant mood after one of Sealey's two goals, both of which came within two minutes. The 1965 final is considered by many critics as one of the finest games ever played at Wembley.

Semi-Finals

*West Ham United	2:1	Real Zaragoza	1:1
Munich 1860	0:3:2	*Torino	2:1:0
(play-off at Zurich)			

Final (Wembley Stadium)

West Ham United	2	Munich 1860	0

West Ham United: Standen; Kirkup, Burkett; Peters, Brown, Moore; Sealey, Boyce, Hurst, Dear, Sissons
Scorer: Sealey (2)
Munich 1860: Radenkovic; Wagner, Kohlars; Bena, Reich, Luttrop; Heiss, Kuppers, Brunnenmeier, Grosser, Rebele

* Home team in 1st leg.

1965-66

1st Round

Borussia Dortmund	5:8	*Floriana Valletta	1:0
CSKA Sofia	2:2	*Limerick	1:0
Stiinta Cluj	1:2	*Wiener Neustadt	0:0
*Atlético Madrid	4:1	Dynamo Zagreb	0:0
Olympiakos Piraeus	1:1	*Omonia Nicosia	0:1
*Magdeburg Aufbau	1:2	Spora Luxembourg	1:2
*Sion	5:1	Galatasaray	1:2
Celtic	6:1	*Go Ahead Deventer	0:0
*AGF Aarhus	2:2	Vitoria Setubal	1:1
Kiev Dynamo	6:4	*Coleraine	1:0
Rosenborg Trondheim	3:3	*KR Reykjavik	1:1
Honved	10:6	*Lahden Reipas	2:0
*Dukla Prague	2:0	Stade Rennes	0:0
Standard Liège	2:1	*Cardiff City	1:0
Liverpool	0:2	*Juventus	1:0

2nd Round

*Borussia Dortmund	3:2	CSKA Sofia	0:4
Atlético Madrid	2:4	*Stiinta Cluj	0:0
*West Ham United	4:2	Olympiakos Piraeus	0:2
*Magdeburg Aufbau	8:2	Sion	1:2
Celtic	1:2	*AGF Aarhus	0:0
Kiev Dynamo	4:2	*Rosenborg Trondheim	1:0
Honved	3:1	*Dukla Prague	2:2
(won on away-goals rule)			
*Liverpool	3:2	Standard Liège	1:1

Quarter-Finals

Borussia Dortmund	1:1	*Atlético Madrid	1:0
*West Ham United	1:1	Magdeburg Aufbau	0:1
*Celtic	3:1	Kiev Dynamo	0:1
Liverpool	0:2	*Honved	0:0

Semi-Finals

Borussia Dortmund	2:3	*West Ham United	1:1
Liverpool	0:2	*Celtic	1:0

Final (Hampden Park, Glasgow)

Borussia Dortmund	2	Liverpool	1
(after extra time: 1-1 at full time)			

Borussia Dortmund: Tilkowski; Cyliax, Redder; Kurrat, Paul, Assauer; Libuda, Schmidt, Held, Sturm, Emmerich
Scorers: Held, Yeats (o.g.)
Liverpool: Lawrence; Lawler, Byrne; Milne, Yeats, Stevenson; Callaghan, Hunt, St John, Smith, Thompson
Scorer: Hunt

* Home team in 1st leg.

1966-67

Preliminary Round

Standard Liège	1:8	*Valur Reykjavik	1:1

1st Round

Bayern Munich	1:3	*Tatran Presov	1:2
*Shamrock Rovers	4:4	Spora Luxembourg	1:1
Spartak Moscow	3:3	*OFK Belgrade	1:0
*Rapid Vienna	4:5	Galatasaray	0:3
*Standard Liège	5:1	Apollon Limassol	1:0
(2nd leg at Namur)			
*Chemie Leipzig	3:2	Legia Warsaw	0:2
Vasas Györ	0:4	*Fiorentina	1:2
Sporting Braga	1:3	*AEK Athens	0:2
*Racing Club Strasbourg	1:1	Steaua Bucharest	0:1

Slavia Sofia	1:4	*Swansea Town	1:0
*Servette Geneva	1:2	IF Finströms Kamraterna	1:1
Sparta Rotterdam	1:6	*Floriana Valletta	1:0
Real Zaragoza	2:3	*Skeid Oslo	3:1
Everton	0:2	*Aalborg BK 85	0:1
Rangers	1:4	*Glentoran	1:0

2nd Round

Bayern Munich	1:3	*Shamrock Rovers	1:2
Rapid Vienna	1:1	*Spartak Moscow	1:0
Standard Liège	1:1	*Chemie Leipzig	2:0
(won on away-goals rule)			
*Vasas Györ	3:0	Sporting Braga	0:2
Slavia Sofia	0:2	*Racing Club Strasbourg	1:0
*Servette Geneva	2:0	Sparta Rotterdam	0:1
*Real Zaragoza	2:0	Everton	0:1
*Rangers	2:0	Borussia Dortmund	1:0

Quarter-Finals

Bayern Munich	0:2	*Rapid Vienna	1:0
(after extra time)			
Standard Liège	1:2	*Vasas Györ	2:0
Slavia Sofia	0:3	*Servette Geneva	1:0
*Rangers	2:0	Real Zaragoza	0:2
(won on toss after extra time)			

Semi-Finals

*Bayern Munich	2:3	Standard Liège	0:1
Rangers	1:1	*Slavia Sofia	0:0

Final (Nuremberg)

Bayern Munich	1	Rangers	0
(after extra time)			

Bayern Munich: Maier; Nowak, Kupferschmidt; Roth, Beckenbauer, Olk; Nafziger, Ohlhauser, Müller, Koulmann, Brenniger
Scorer: Roth
Rangers: Martin; Johansen, Provan; Jardine, McKinnon, Greig; Henderson, Smith A., Hynd, Smith D., Johnston

* Home team in 1st leg.

1967-68

1st Round

Steaua Bucharest	2:2	*FK Austria	0:1
*SV Hamburg	5:2	Randers Freja	3:0
*AC Milan	5:1	Levski Sofia	1:1
Tottenham Hotspur	2:4	*Hajduk Split	0:3
Cardiff City	1:2	*Shamrock Rovers	1:0
Spartak Trnava	2:2	*Lausanne	3:0
*Aberdeen	10:4	KR Reykjavik	0:1
*Valencia	4:4	Crusaders	0:2
*Moscow Torpedo	0:1	Motor Zwickau	0:0
Standard Liège	3:0	*Altay Izmir	2:0
Olympique Lyonnaise	3:2	*Aris Bonnevoie	0:1

Rangers 'keeper Norrie Martin moves to save as a Bayern Munich attack is stifled by the defence. It was not until extra time that the Germans put the ball in the net to take the 1967 Cup-Winners Cup.

Neil Young turns away after scoring the first of Manchester City's two goals against Gornik Zabrze in the 1970 final at Vienna. Francis Lee, with penalty, got the other to give the English club a 2–1 victory.

Vitoria Setubal	5:2	*Fredrikstad	1:1	
*Vasas Györ	5:4	Apollon Limassol	0:0	
*Bayern Munich	5:2	Panathinaikos	0:1	
Wislaw Cracow	4:4	*HJK Helsinki	1:0	
NAC Breda	2:1	*Floriana Valletta	1:0	

2nd Round

*Bayern Munich	6:1	Vitoria Setubal	2:1
SV Hamburg	1:4	*Wislaw Cracow	0:0
Cardiff City	1:4	*NAC Breda	1:1
AC Milan	2:1	*Vasas Györ	2:1
(won on away-goals rule)			
*Olympique Lyonnaise	1:3	Tottenham Hotspur	0:4
(won on away-goals rule)			
*Standard Liège	3:0	Aberdeen	0:2
*Moscow Torpedo	3:3	Spartak Trnava	1:1
*Valencia	3:0	Steaua Bucharest	0:1

Quarter-Finals

*SV Hamburg	2:0:2	Olympique Lyonnaise	0:2:0
(play-off at Hamburg)			
AC Milan	1:1:2	*Standard Liège	1:1:0
(play-off at Milan)			
*Cardiff City	1:0:1	Moscow Torpedo	0:1:0
(play-off at Augsburg)			
Bayern Munich	1:1	*Valencia	1:0

Semi-Finals

*SV Hamburg	1:3	Cardiff City	1:2
*AC Milan	2:0	Bayern Munich	0:0

Final (Rotterdam)

AC Milan	2	SV Hamburg	0

AC Milan: Cudicini; Anquilletti, Schnellinger; Trapattoni, Rosato, Scala; Hamrin, Lodetti, Sormani, Rivera, Prati
Scorer: Hamrin (2)
SV Hamburg: Ozcan; Sondemann, Kurbjohn; Dieckemann, Horst, Schulz H.; Dorfel B., Kramer, Seeler, Hornig, Dorfel G.

* Home team in 1st leg.

1968–69

1st Round

West Bromwich Albion	1:2	*FC Bruges	3:0
(won on away-goals rule)			
*Dunfermline Athletic	10:2	Apoel Nicosia	1:0
IFK Norrköping	2:4	*Crusaders	2:1
FC Porto	2:2	*Cardiff City	2:1
1FC Cologne	1:3	*Girondins Bordeaux	2:0
*Slovan Bratislava	3:0	Bor	0:2
Torino	0:3	*Partizan Tirana	1:1
Sliema Wanderers	1:1	*US Rumelange	2:0
(won on away-goals rule)			
Lyn Oslo	1:4	*Altay Izmir	3:1
*Randers Freja	1:2	Shamrock Rovers	0:1
Barcelona	1:3	*FC Lugano	0:0
*Olympiakos Piraeus	2:2	Fram Reykjavik	0:0
ADO The Hague	4:2	*AK Grazer	1:0
Dynamo Bucharest won outright: Vasas Györ withdrew			

2nd Round

West Bromwich Albion	1:4	*Dynamo Bucharest	1:0
*Dunfermline Athletic	4:0	Olympiakos Piraeus	0:3
*Lyn Oslo	2:2	IFK Norrköping	0:3
Slovan Bratislava	0:4	*FC Porto	1:0
*Randers Freja	6:2	Sliema Wanderers	0:0
1FC Cologne	1:3	*ADO The Hague	0:0
Torino	*bye*		
Barcelona	*bye*		

Quarter-Finals

*Barcelona	3:2	Lyn Oslo	2:2
*1FC Cologne	2:3	Randers Freja	1:0
Slovan Bratislava	1:2	*Torino	0:1
*Dunfermline Athletic	0:1	West Bromwich Albion	0:0

Semi-Finals

Slovan Bratislava	1:1	*Dunfermline Athletic	1:0
Barcelona	2:4	*1FC Cologne	2:1

Final (Basle)

Slovan Bratislava   3   Barcelona   2

Slovan Bratislava: Vencel; Filo, Hrivnak, Jan Zlocha, Horvath, Hrdlicka; Cvetler, Moder (Bizon), Josef Capkovic, Jokl, Jan Capkovic

Scorers: Cvetler, Hrivnak, Jan Capkovic

Barcelona: Sadurni; Franch (Pereda), Eladio; Rife, Olivella, Zabalza; Pellicer, Castro (Mendoza), Zaldua, Fuste, Rexach

Scorers: Zaldua, Rexach

* Home team in 1st leg.

1969–70

Preliminary Round

*Rapid Vienna	0:1	Moscow Torpedo	0:1
(won on away-goals rule)			

1st Round

Manchester City	3:3	*Atlético Bilbao	3:0
AS Roma	0:3	*Ards	0:1
*Rangers	2:0	Steaua Bucharest	0:0
Cardiff City	7:5	*Mjoendalen	1:1
Schalke 04	1:3	*Shamrock Rovers	2:0
*Magdeburg Aufbau	1:1	MTK Budapest	0:1
Olympique Marseille	0:2	*Dukla Prague	1:0
PSV Eindhoven	2:4	*Rapid Vienna	1:2
St Gallen	1:1	*Frem Copenhagen	2:0
*IFK Norrköping	5:0	Sliema Wanderers	1:1
*Dynamo Zagreb	3:0	Slovan Bratislava	0:0
*Lierse SK	10:1	Apoel Nicosia	0:0
Gornik Zabrze	2:5	*Olympiakos Piraeus	2:0
*Goeztepe Izmir	3:3	US Luxembourg	0:2
Levski Sofia	4:4	*IBV Reykjavik	0:0
*Academica Coimbra	0:1	Kuopion Palloseura	0:0

2nd Round

Manchester City	3:5	*Lierse SK	0:0
*Gornik Zabrze	3:3	Rangers	1:1
*Goeztepe Izmir	3:0	Cardiff City	0:1
*AS Roma	1:0	PSV Eindhoven	0:1
(won on toss after extra time)			
Schalke 04	0:1	*IFK Norrköping	0:0
*Levski Sofia	4:0	St Gallen	0:0
Academica Coimbra	0:2	*Magdeburg Aufbau	1:0
Dynamo Zagreb	1:2	*Olympique Marseille	1:0

Quarter-Finals

Manchester City	0:1	*Academica Coimbra	0:0
*AS Roma	2:0	Goeztepe Izmir	0:0
Gornik Zabrze	2:2	*Levski Sofia	3:1
(won on away-goals rule)			
Schalke 04	3:1	*Dynamo Zagreb	1:0

Semi-Finals

Manchester City	0:5	*Schalke 04	1:1
Gornik Zabrze	1:2:1	*AS Roma	1:2:1
(replay at Strasbourg won on toss)			

Final (Vienna)

Manchester City   2   Gornik Zabrze   1

Manchester City: Corrigan; Book, Booth, Heslop, Pardoe; Doyle (Bowyer), Oakes, Towers; Bell, Lee, Young

Scorers: Young, Lee (pen.)

Gornik Zabrze: Kostka; Gorgon, Oslizlo, Latocha, Florenski (Deja), Olek, Szoltysik, Wilczek (Skowronck), Banas, Lubanski, Szarzynski

Scorer: Oslizlo

* Home team in 1st leg.

1970–71

Preliminary Round

TJ Gottwaldov	2:2	*Bohemians	1:2
Partizan Tirana	1:2	*Atvidaberg	1:0

1st Round

Honved	1:3	*Aberdeen	3:1
(won on penalties after extra time)			

Moscow Dynamo's Dolmatov (3) thwarts Rangers' Colin Stein, who opened the scoring for the Glasgow club in the 1972 final at Barcelona. A great display by Rangers was marred by their fans, who invaded the pitch to celebrate every Rangers goal and at the end of the match did battle with the Spanish police.

Willie Johnstone receives the adulation of delirious fans after his second, and Rangers' third, goal against Moscow Dynamo.

*Cardiff City	8:0	Larnaca	0:0
Chelsea	1:5	*Aris Salonika	1:1
*Manchester City	1:1	Linfield	0:2
(won on away-goals rule)			
Real Madrid	0:5	*Hibernians Valletta	0:0
PSV Eindhoven	1:1	*TJ Gottwaldov	2:0
(won on away-goals rule)			
Benfica	1:8	*Olympija Ljubljana	1:1
FC Nantes	5:2	*Stromsgodset Drammen	0:3
*Wacker Innsbruck	3:2	Partizan Tirana	2:1
*CSKA Sofia	9:2	Valkeakosken Haka	0:1
*ASK Vorwaerts Berlin	0:1	Bologna	0:1
(won on away-goals rule)			
FC Bruges	1:2	*Offenbach Kickers	2:0
*Goeztepe Izmir	5:0	US Luxembourg	0:1
Gornik Zabrze	1:8	*Aalborg BK	0:1
FC Zurich	7:7	*Akureyi	1:0
*Steaua Bucharest	1:1	Karpaty Lvov	0:0

2nd Round

Chelsea	1:1	*CSKA Sofia	0:0
Manchester City	1:2	*Honved	0:0
Gornik Zabrze	1:3	*Goeztepe Izmir	0:0
*PSV Eindhoven	4:3	Steaua Bucharest	0:0
ASK Vorwaerts Berlin	0:2	*Benfica	2:0
(won on penalties after extra time)			
*FC Bruges	2:2	FC Zurich	0:3
*Cardiff City	5:2	FC Nantes	1:1
*Real Madrid	0:2	Wacker Innsbruck	1:0

Quarter-Finals

Real Madrid	0:2	*Cardiff City	1:0
Chelsea	0:4	*FC Bruges	2:0
*Manchester City	0:2:3	Gornik Zabrze	2:0:1
(play-off at Copenhagen)			
*PSV Eindhoven	2:0	ASK Vorwaerts Berlin	0:1

Semi-Finals

*Chelsea	1:1	Manchester City	0:0
Real Madrid	0:2	*PSV Eindhoven	0:1

Final (Athens)

Chelsea	1	Real Madrid	1
(replay at Athens)	2		1

Chelsea: (final) Bonetti; Boyle, Harris; Hollins (Mulligan), Dempsey, Webb; Weller, Hudson, Osgood (Baldwin), Cooke, Houseman

Scorer: Osgood

Real Madrid: (final) Borja; José Luis, Benito, Zoco, Zunzunegui; Pirri, Grosso, Velazquez; Perez (Fleitas), Amancio, Gento (Grande)

Scorer: Zoco

Chelsea: (replay) Bonetti; Boyle, Harris; Cooke, Dempsey, Webb; Weller, Hudson, Osgood (Smethurst), Baldwin, Houseman

Scorers: Dempsey, Osgood

Real Madrid: (replay) Borja; José Luis, Zunzunegui; Pirri, Benito, Zoco; Fleitas, Amancio, Grosso, Velazquez (Gento), Bueno (Grande)

Scorer: Fleitas

* Home team in 1st leg.

1971–72

Preliminary Round

FK Austria	2:2	*Odense BK 09	4:0
(won on away-goals rule)			
*Hibernians Valletta	3:0	Fram Reykjavik	0:2

1st Round

Atvidaberg	4:1	*Zaglebie Sosnowiec	3:1
FK Austria	1:1	*Dynamo Tirana	1:0
Barcelona	3:3	*Distillery	1:0
Bayern Munich	1:6	*Skoda Pilzen	0:1
*Dynamo East Berlin	1:1	Cardiff City	1:1
(won on penalties)			
Chelsea	8:13	*Jeunesse Hautcharage	0:0
Moscow Dynamo	2:1	*Olympiakos Piraeus	0:2
Eskisehirspor	0:4	*Mikkelin Palloilijat	0:0

*Beerschot	7:1	Famagusta	0:0
Liverpool	1:2	*Servette Geneva	2:0
*Sporting Lisbon	4:3	Lyn Oslo	0:0
Rangers	1:1	*Stade Rennes	1:0
Red Star Belgrade	7:1	*Komlo Banyasi	2:2
Sparta Rotterdam	1:2	*Levski Spartak	1:0
Steaua Bucharest	0:1	*Hibernians Valletta	0:0
Torino	1:4	*Limerick	0:0

2nd Round

*Torino	1:0	FK Austria	0:0
Bayern Munich	0:3	*Liverpool	0:1
*Atvidaberg	0:1	Chelsea	0:1
(won on away-goals rule)			
Moscow Dynamo	1:1	*Eskisehirspor	0:0
Red Star Belgrade	1:2	*Sparta Rotterdam	1:1
*Rangers	3:3	Sporting Lisbon	2:4
(won on away-goals rule)			
Dynamo East Berlin	3:3	*Beerschot	1:1
Steaua Bucharest	1:2	*Barcelona	0:1

Quarter-Finals

Bayern Munich	1:0	*Steaua Bucharest	1:0
(won on away-goals rule)			
Dynamo East Berlin	2:2	*Atvidaberg	0:2
Moscow Dynamo	2:1	*Red Star Belgrade	1:1
Rangers	1:1	*Torino	1:0

Semi-Finals

Moscow Dynamo	1:1	*Dynamo East Berlin	1:1
(won on penalties)			
Rangers	1:2	*Bayern Munich	1:0

Final (Barcelona)

Rangers	3	Moscow Dynamo	2

Rangers: McCloy; Jardine, Mathieson, Greig, Johnstone, Smith, McLean, Conn, Stein, Macdonald, Johnston
Scorers: Stein, Johnston (2)
Moscow Dynamo: Pilgul; Basalacev, Dolmatov, Zikov, Dolbonosov, Zukov, Baidazhnyi, Jakobik (Eshtrekhov), Sabo, Mahovikov, Evrizhin
Scorers: Eshtrekhov, Mahovikov

*Home team in 1st leg.

1972-73

1st Round

AC Milan	4:3	*Red Boys Differdange	1:0
Legia Warsaw	2:9	*Vikingur Reykjavik	0:0
*Moscow Spartak	1:0	FC Den Haag	0:0
Atlético Madrid	0:2	*Bastia	0:1
Sparta Prague	0:4	*Standard Liège	1:2
Ferencvaros	0:6	*Floriana Valletta	1:0
*Schalke 04	2:3	Slavia Sofia	1:1
Cork Hibernians	2:4	*Pesoporikos Larnaca	1:1
Besa	1:0	*Fremad Amager	1:0
(won on away-goals rule)			
Hibernian	1:6	*Sporting Lisbon	2:1
Wrexham	1:2	*FC Zurich	1:1
*Hajduk Split	1:1	Fredrikstad	0:0
*Rapid Vienna	0:2	PAOK Salonika	0:2
(won on away-goals rule)			
*Rapid Bucharest	3:0	Landskrona	0:1
*Carl Zeiss Jena	6:2	Mikkelin Palloilijat	1:3
Leeds United	1:1	*Ankaragücü	1:0

2nd Round

AC Milan	1:2	*Legia Warsaw	1:1
Moscow Spartak	4:1	*Atlético Madrid	3:2
(won on away-goals rule)			
Sparta Prague	0:4	*Ferencvaros	2:1
Schalke 04	0:3	*Cork Hibernians	0:0
*Hibernian	7:1	Besa	1:1
Hajduk Split	1:2	*Wrexham	3:0
(won on away-goals rule)			
Rapid Bucharest	1:3	*Rapid Vienna	1:1
Leeds United	0:2	*Carl Zeiss Jena	0:0

AC Milan's Chiarugi hammers an ill-gotten free-kick past the Leeds wall to score the only goal of the 1973 final. The Greek referee favoured the Italians to such an extent that even the Greek crowd booed him off at the end of the match.

Referee Christos Michas before the game. He was later suspended by UEFA.

Quarter-Finals

AC Milan	1:1	*Moscow Spartak	0:1
Sparta Prague	1:3	*Schalke 04	2:0
Hajduk Split	2:3	*Hibernian	4:0
*Leeds United	5:3	Rapid Bucharest	0:1

Semi-Finals

*AC Milan	1:1	Sparta Prague	0:0
*Leeds United	1:0	Hajduk Split	0:0

Final (Salonika)

AC Milan	1	Leeds United	0

AC Milan: Vecchi; Sabadini, Zignoli, Anquilletti, Turone, Rosato (Dolci), Sogliano, Benetti, Bigon, Rivera, Chiarugi
Scorer: Chiarugi
Leeds United: Harvey; Reaney, Cherry, Bates, Madeley, Hunter, Lorimer, Jordan, Jones, Gray F. (McQueen), Yorath

*Home team in 1st leg.

1973-74

1st Round

FC Magdeburg	0:2	*NAC Breda	0:0
*Banik Ostrava	1:2	Cork Hibernians	0:1
Beroe Stara Zagora	7:4	Fola Esch	0:1
(both games played in Stara Zagora)			
Atlético Bilbao	0:2	*Moscow Torpedo	0:0
Sporting Lisbon	0:2	*Cardiff City	0:1
Sunderland	2:1	*Vasas Budapest	0:0
Malmö FF	0:11	*Pesoporikos Larnaca	0:0
FC Zurich	2:1	*Anderlecht	3:0
(won on away-goals rule)			
Brann Bergen	2:7	*Gzira United (Malta)	0:0
Glentoran	2:2	*Chimia Vilcea	2:0
Rangers	2:4	*Ankaragücü	0:0
Borussia Mönchengladbach	7:9	*IBV Reykjavik	0:1
Olympique Lyon	0:2	*Lahden Reipas	0:0
PAOK Salonika	1:1	*Legia Warsaw	1:0
Rapid Vienna	0:2	*Randers Freja	0:1
*AC Milan	3:1	Dynamo Zagreb	1:0

2nd Round

FC Magdeburg	0:3	*Banik Ostrava	2:0
*Beroe Stara Zagora	3:0	Atlético Bilbao	0:1
Sporting Lisbon	1:2	*Sunderland	2:0
*FC Zurich	2:1	Malmö FF	0:1
(won on away-goals rule)			
Glentoran	1:3	*Brann Bergen	1:1
*B. Mönchengladbach	3:2	Rangers	0:3
PAOK Salonika	3:4	*Olympique Lyon	3:0
*AC Milan	0:2	Rapid Vienna	0:0

Quarter-Finals

*FC Magdeburg	2:1	Beroe Stara Zagora	0:1
*Sporting Lisbon	3:1	FC Zurich	0:1
B. Mönchengladbach	2:5	*Glentoran	0:0
*AC Milan	3:2	PAOK Salonika	0:2

Semi-Finals

FC Magdeburg	1:2	*Sporting Lisbon	1:1
*AC Milan	2:0	B. Mönchengladbach	0:1

Final

FC Magdeburg	2	AC Milan	0

FC Magdeburg: Schulze; Enge, Zapf, Gaube, Abraham, Pommerenke, Seguin, Tyll, Raugust, Sparwasser, Hoffmann
Scorers: Lanzi (o.g.), Seguin
AC Milan: Pizzabella; Anquilletti, Sabadini, Lanzi, Schnellinger, Maldera, Tresoldi, Benetti, Bigon, Rivera, Bergamaschi (Turini)

*Home team in 1st leg.

1955-58

Group 1
*Barcelona	6:1	Copenhagen	2:1

	P	W	D	L	F	A	Pts
Barcelona	2	1	1	0	7	3	3
Copenhagen	2	0	1	1	3	7	1
Vienna				*Withdrew*			

Group 2
Birmingham City	0:2	*Internazionale Milan	0:1
Birmingham City	1:3	*Zagreb	0:0
Internazionale Milan	1:4	*Zagreb	0:0

	P	W	D	L	F	A	Pts
Birmingham City	4	3	1	0	6	1	7
Inter-Milan	4	2	1	1	6	2	5
Zagreb	4	0	0	4	0	9	0

Group 3
Lausanne	3:7	*Leipzig	6:3

	P	W	D	L	F	A	Pts
Lausanne	2	1	0	1	10	9	2
Leipzig	2	1	0	1	9	10	2
Cologne				*Withdrew*			

Group 4
London	5:1	*Basle	0:0
*London	3:0	Frankfurt	2:1
*Frankfurt	5:2	Basle	1:6

	P	W	D	L	F	A	Pts
London	4	3	0	1	9	3	6
Frankfurt	4	2	0	2	10	10	4
Basle	4	1	0	3	7	13	2

Semi-Finals
Barcelona	3:1:2	*Birmingham City	4:0:1
(play-off at Basle)			
London	1:2	*Lausanne	2:0

Final
Barcelona	2:6	*London	2:0

Barcelona: (1st leg) Estrems; Olivella, Segarra; Gracia, Gensana, Ribelles; Vasora, Evaristo, Martínez, Villaverde, Tejada
Scorers: Tejada, Martínez
Barcelona: (2nd leg) Ramallets; Olivella, Segarra; Verges, Bruges, Gensana; Tejada, Evaristo, Martínez, Suarez, Vasora
Scorers: Suarez (2), Martínez, Evaristo (2), Verges
London: (1st leg) Kelsey (Arsenal); Sillett P. (Chelsea), Langley (Fulham); Blanchflower (Spurs), Norman (Spurs), Coote (Brentford); Groves (Arsenal), Greaves (Chelsea), Smith (Spurs), Haynes (Fulham), Robb (Spurs)
Scorers: Greaves, Langley (pen.)
London: (2nd leg) Kelsey (Arsenal); Wright (West Ham), Cantwell (West Ham); Blanchflower (Spurs), Brown (West Ham), Bowen (Arsenal); Medwin (Spurs), Groves (Arsenal), Smith (Spurs), Bloomfield (Arsenal), Lewis (Chelsea)

1958-60

1st Round
Barcelona	2:5	*Basle	1:2
*Internazionale Milan	7:1	Olympique Lyonnaise	0:1
*Belgrade	6:5	Lausanne	1:3
Chelsea	3:4	*Frem Copenhagen	1:1
*Union St Gilloise	6:0	Leipzig	0:1
AS Roma	3:1	*Hanover 96	1:1
*Zagreb	4:0	Ujpest Dozsa	2:1
Birmingham City	2:2	*1FC Cologne	2:0

Quarter-Finals
*Barcelona	4:4	Inter-Milan	0:2

Belgrade	0:4	*Chelsea	1:1
*Union St Gilloise	2:1	AS Roma	0:1
*Birmingham City	1:3	Zagreb	0:3

Semi-Finals
Barcelona	1:3	*Belgrade	1:1
Birmingham City	4:4	*Union St Gilloise	2:2

Final
Barcelona	0:4	*Birmingham City	0:1

Barcelona: (1st leg) Ramallets; Olivella, Rodri; Gracia, Segarra, Gensana; Coll, Kocsis, Martínez, Ribelles, Villaverde
Barcelona: (2nd leg) Ramallets; Olivella, Gracia; Verges, Rodri, Segarra; Coll, Ribelles, Martínez, Kubala, Czibor
Scorers: Martínez, Czibor (2), Coll
Birmingham City: Schofield; Farmer, Allen; Watts, Smith, Neal; Astall, Gordon, Weston, Orritt (2nd leg, Murphy), Hooper
Scorer: (2nd leg) Hooper

* Home team in 1st leg.

1960—61

1st Round
AS Roma	0:4	*Union St Gilloise	0:1
1FC Cologne	3:1	*Olympique Lyonnaise	1:2
Hibernian	2:—	*Lausanne	0:—
(Lausanne withdrew)			
Barcelona	1:4	*Zagreb	1:3
Belgrade	2:4:2	*Leipzig	5:1:0
(play-off at Budapest)			
*Internazionale Milan	8:6	Hanover	2:1
*KB Copenhagen	8:3	FC Basle	1:3
*Birmingham City	3:2	Ujpest Dozsa	2:1

Quarter-Finals
AS Roma	2:0:4	*1FC Cologne	0:2:1
(play-off at Rome)			
Hibernian	4:3	*Barcelona	4:2
*Inter-Milan	5:0	Belgrade	0:1
Birmingham City	4:5	*KB Copenhagen	4:0

Semi-Finals
AS Roma	2:3:6	*Hibernian	2:3:0
(play-off at Rome)			
Birmingham City	2:2	*Inter-Milan	1:1

Final
AS Roma	2:2	*Birmingham City	2:0

AS Roma: Cudicini; Fontana, Corsini; Giuliana (2nd leg, Pestrin), Losi, Carpanesi; Orlando, Da Costa (2nd leg, Lojacono), Manfredini, Angelillo, Menichelli
Scorers: (1st leg) Manfredini (2); (2nd leg) Farmer (o.g.), Pestrin
Birmingham City: Schofield; Farmer, Sissons; Hennessey, Foster (2nd leg, Smith), Beard; Hellawell, Bloomfield, Harris, Orritt, Auld (2nd leg, Singer)
Scorers: (1st leg) Hellawell, Orritt

* Home team in 1st leg.

1961—62

1st Round
*Valencia	2:5	Nottingham Forest	0:1
Internazionale Milan	2:2:5	*1FC Cologne	4:0:3
(play-off at Milan)			
Heart of Midlothian	3:2	*Union St Gilloise	1:0
Leipzig	2:4	*Spartak Brno	2:1
MTK Budapest	3:10	*Racing Club Strasbourg	1:2
Novi Sad	0:2	*AC Milan	0:0
Red Star Belgrade	1:4	*FC Basle	1:1
*Hibernian	3:3	Belenenses	3:1
Espanol	1:2	*Hanover 96	0:0
Sheffield Wednesday	2:5	*Olympique Lyonnaise	4:2
Dynamo Zagreb	7:2	*Copenhagen	2:2
Barcelona	0:3	*West Berlin	1:0

Jim Langley of Fulham, London's left-back against Barcelona in the first leg of the 1958 final, scored from a penalty.

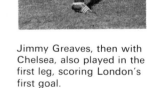

Jimmy Greaves, then with Chelsea, also played in the first leg, scoring London's first goal.

Winger Harry Hooper scored Birmingham's only goal in their 1960 final tie against Barcelona, who won the Fairs Cup for the second time running.

Bertie Auld was on Birmingham's left wing in the first leg of the 1961 final, which they lost to Roma. Auld, however, went on to win European Cup honours six years later with Celtic.

2nd Round

Valencia	4 : —	*Lausanne	3 : —
(2nd leg not played)			
Inter-Milan	1 : 4	*Heart of Midlothian	0 : 0
*MTK Budapest	3 : 0 : 2	Leipzig	0 : 3 : 0
(play-off at Bratislava)			
Novi Sad	1 : 9	*Iraklis Salonika	2 : 1
*Red Star Belgrade	4 : 1	Hibernian	0 : 0
*Espanol	5 : 0	Birmingham City	2 : 1
*Sheffield Wednesday	4 : 0	AS Roma	0 : 1
*Barcelona	5 : 2	Dynamo Zagreb	1 : 2

Quarter-Finals

*Valencia	2 : 3	Inter-Milan	0 : 3
MTK Budapest	4 : 2	*Novi Sad	1 : 1
Red Star Belgrade	1 : 5	*Espanol	2 : 0
Barcelona	2 : 2	*Sheffield Wednesday	3 : 0

Semi-Finals

*Valencia	3 : 7	MTK Budapest	0 : 3
Barcelona	2 : 4	*Red Star Belgrade	0 : 1

Final

*Valencia	6 : 1	Barcelona	2 : 1

Valencia: Zamora; Verdu, Chicao; Piquer, Mestre, Sastre; Ficha, Ribebe (2nd leg, Urtiaga), Waldo, Guillot, Coll
Scorers: (1st leg)
(2nd leg) Guillot
Barcelona: Pesudo; Benitez, Rodri (2nd leg, Garay), Olivella (2nd leg, Fuste), Verges, Gracia, Cubilla, Kocsis, Re (2nd leg, Goyvaerts), Villaverde, Camps
Scorer: (1st leg) Kocsis (2); (2nd leg) Kocsis

* Home team in 1st leg.

1962–63

1st Round

*Valencia	4 : 2	Celtic	2 : 2
Dunfermline Athletic	0 : 2	*Everton	1 : 0
*Hibernian	4 : 3	Copenhagen	0 : 2
*DOS Utrecht	3 : 2	Tasmania Berlin	2 : 1
AS Roma	3 : 10	*Altay Izmir	2 : 1
(2nd leg at Istanbul)			
Real Zaragoza	2 : 6	*Glentoran	0 : 2
Red Star Belgrade	1 : 1	*Rapid Vienna	1 : 0
Barcelona	1 : 1 : 3	Belenenses	1 : 1 : 2
(all legs at Barcelona)			
Ferencvaros	3 : 4	*Viktoria Cologne	4 : 1
*Sampdoria	1 : 2	Aris Luxembourg	0 : 0
*Petrolul Ploesti	4 : 0	Spartak Brno	2 : 1
Leipzig	0 : 2	*Vojvodina Novi Sad	1 : 0
Bayern Munich	3 : —	*FC Basle	0 : —
(2nd leg not played)			
*Drumcondra	4 : 2	Odense BK 09	1 : 4
Union St Gilloise	0 : 4	*Olympique Marseille	1 : 2
Dynamo Zagreb	2 : 0	*FC Porto	1 : 0

2nd Round

*Valencia	4 : 2 : 1	Dunfermline Athletic	0 : 6 : 0
(play-off at Lisbon)			
Hibernian	1 : 2	*DOS Utrecht	0 : 1
AS Roma	4 : 2	*Real Zaragoza	2 : 1
*Red Star Belgrade	3 : 0 : 1	Barcelona	2 : 1 : 0
(play-off at Nice)			
Ferencvaros	0 : 6	*Sampdoria	1 : 0
*Petrolul Ploesti	1 : 0 : 1	Leipzig	0 : 1 : 0
(play-off at Budapest)			
*Bayern Munich	6 : 0	Drumcondra	0 : 1
*Dynamo Zagreb	2 : 0 : 3	Union St Gilloise	1 : 1 : 2
(play-off at Linz)			

Quarter-Finals

*Valencia	5 : 1	Hibernian	0 : 2
*AS Roma	3 : 0	Red Star Belgrade	0 : 2
*Ferencvaros	2 : 0	Petrolul Ploesti	0 : 1
Dynamo Zagreb	4 : 0	*Bayern Munich	1 : 0

Semi-Finals

*Valencia	3 : 0	AS Roma	0 : 1
Dynamo Zagreb	1 : 2	*Ferencvaros	0 : 1

Final

Valencia	2 : 2	*Dynamo Zagreb	1 : 0

Valencia: Zamora; Piquer, Chicao; Paquito, Quincoces, Sastre; Mañó, Sanchez Lage, Waldo, Ribelles, Urtiaga (Núñez)
Scorers: (1st leg) Waldo, Urtiaga; (2nd leg) Mañó, Núñez
Dynamo Zagreb: Skoric; Belin, Braun, Biscam (Raus), Markovic, Perusic, Kobsnac, Zambata, Knez, Matus, Lamza
Scorer: (1st leg) Zambata

* Home team in 1st leg.

1963–64

1st Round

*Real Zaragoza	6 : 3	Iraklis Salonika	1 : 0
*Lausanne	2 : 2 : 3	Heart of Midlothian	2 : 2 : 2
(play-off at Lausanne)			
*Atlético Madrid	2 : 0	FC Porto	1 : 0
*Juventus	2 : 1 : 1	OFK Belgrade	1 : 2 : 0
(play-off at Trieste)			
FC Liège	2 : 0	*Aris Luxembourg	0 : 0
Arsenal	7 : 2	*Staevnet Copenhagen	1 : 3
Partick Thistle	4 : 3	*Glentoran	1 : 0
*Spartak Brno	5 : 2	Servette Geneva	0 : 1
*1FC Cologne	3 : 1	La Gantoise	1 : 1
Sheffield Wednesday	4 : 4	*DOS Utrecht	1 : 1
AS Roma	3 : 2	*Hertha Berlin	1 : 0
Belenenses	2 : 2	*Tresnjevka Zagreb	0 : 1
*Ujpest Dozsa	0 : 3	Lokomotiv Leipzig	0 : 2
Lokomotiv Plovdiv	3 : 2	*Red Flag Brasov	1 : 1
*Rapid Vienna	1 : 3	Racing Club Paris	0 : 2
Valencia	1 : 2	*Shamrock Rovers	0 : 2

2nd Round

Real Zaragoza	2 : 3	*Lausanne	1 : 0
*Juventus	1 : 2	Atlético Madrid	0 : 1
FC Liège	1 : 3	*Arsenal	1 : 1
Spartak Brno	2 : 4	*Partick Thistle	3 : 0
*1FC Cologne	3 : 2	Sheffield Wednesday	2 : 1
*AS Roma	2 : 1	Belenenses	1 : 0
*Ujpest Dozsa	0 : 3	Lokomotiv Plovdiv	0 : 1
Valencia	0 : 3	*Rapid Vienna	0 : 2

Quarter-Finals

*Real Zaragoza	3 : 0	Juventus	2 : 0
*FC Liège	2 : 0 : 1	Spartak Brno	0 : 2 : 0
(play-off at Liège)			
1FC Cologne	1 : 4	*AS Roma	3 : 0
*Valencia	5 : 1	Ujpest Dozsa	2 : 3

Semi-Finals

Real Zaragoza	0 : 2 : 2	*FC Liège	1 : 1 : 0
(play-off at Zaragoza)			
*Valencia	4 : 0	1FC Cologne	1 : 2

Final (at Barcelona)

Real Zaragoza	2	Valencia	1

Real Zaragoza: Yarza; Cortizo, Reija; Isasi, Santamaria, Pepin; Canario, Duca, Marcelino, Villa, Lapetra
Scorers: Villa, Marcelino
Valencia: Zamora; Arnal, Villegany; Paquito, Quincoces, Roberto; Suco, Guillot, Waldo, Urtiaga, Ficha
Scorer: Urtiaga

* Home team in 1st leg.

1964–65

1st Round

Juventus	1 : 1	*Union St Gilloise	0 : 0
Stade Français	1 : 2	*Betis Seville	1 : 0
Petrolul Ploesti	2 : 1	*Goeztepe Izmir	1 : 0
Lokomotiv Plovdiv	1 : 1 : 2	*Vojvodina Novi Sad	1 : 1 : 0
(play-off at Sofia)			
DOS Utrecht	4 : 2	*KB Copenhagen	3 : 1
FC Liège	1 : 3	*Valencia	1 : 1
Shelbourne	1 : 0 : 2	*Belenenses	1 : 0 : 1
(play-off at Dublin)			
Atlético Madrid	2 : 6	*Servette Geneva	2 : 1
*FC Basle	2 : 0	Spora Luxembourg	0 : 1
*Racing Club Strasbourg	2 : 0	AC Milan	0 : 1

*Barcelona	0:2	Fiorentina	1:0
Celtic	1:3	*Leixoes Oporto	1:0
*Borussia Dortmund	4:0	Girondins Bordeaux	1:2
*Manchester United	1:6	Djurgaarden Stockholm	1:1
Kilmarnock	0:5	*Eintracht Frankfurt	3:1
Everton	5:4	*Valerengen	2:2
*Atlético Bilbao	2:2	OFK Belgrade	2:0
Antwerp	1:2	*Hertha Berlin	2:0
VfB Stuttgart	3:1	*Odense BK 1913	1:0
*Dunfermline Athletic	4:0	Oergryte Gothenburg	2:0
*Dynamo Zagreb	3:6	Grazer AK	2:0
AS Roma	0:3	*Aris Salonika	0:0
*Wiener SK	2:1	Lokomotiv Leipzig	1:0
*Ferencvaros	2:0	Spartak Brno	0:1

2nd Round

Juventus	0:1	*Stade Français	0:0
Lokomotiv Plovdiv	0:2	*Petrolul Ploesti	1:0
FC Liège	2:2	*DOS Utrecht	0:0
Atlético Madrid	1:1	*Shelbourne	0:0
Racing Club Strasbourg	1:5	*FC Basle	0:2
*Barcelona	3:0	Celtic	1:0
Manchester United	6:4	*Borussia Dortmund	1:0
Everton	2:4	*Kilmarnock	0:1
*Atlético Bilbao	2:1	Antwerp	0:0
*Dunfermline Athletic	1:0	VfB Stuttgart	0:0
AS Roma	1:1	*Dynamo Zagreb	1:0
*Ferencvaros	0:2:2	Wiener SK	1:1:0
(play-off at Budapest)			

3rd Round

*Juventus	1:1:2	Lokomotiv Plovdiv	1:1:1
(play-off at Turin)			
Atlético Madrid	0:2	*FC Liège	1:0
*Racing Club Strasbourg	0:2:0	Barcelona	0:2:0
(play-off at Barcelona won on toss after extra time)			
*Manchester United	1:2	Everton	1:1
*Atlético Bilbao	1:0:2	Dunfermline Athletic	0:1:1
(play-off at Bilbao)			
Ferencvaros	2:1	*AS Roma	1:0

Quarter-Finals

Manchester United	5:0	*Racing Club Strasbourg	0:0
*Ferencvaros	1:0:3	Atlético Bilbao	0:1:0
(play-off at Budapest)			
Juventus	bye		
Atlético Madrid	bye		

Semi-Finals

Juventus	1:3:3	*Atlético Madrid	3:1:1
(play-off at Turin)			
Ferencvaros	2:1:2	*Manchester United	3:0:1
(play-off at Budapest)			

Final (Turin)

Ferencvaros	1	*Juventus	0

Ferencvaros: Geczi; Novak, Horvath; Juhasz, Matrai, Orosz; Karaba, Varga, Albert, Rakosi, Fenyvesi
Scorer: Fenyvesi
Juventus: Anzolin; Gori, Sarti; Bercellini, Castano, Leoncini; Estacchini, Del Sol, Combin, Mazzia, Menichelli

* Home team in 1st leg.

1965–66

1st Round

Barcelona	0:7	*DOS Utrecht	0:1
*Antwerp	1:3	Glentoran	0:3
FC Porto	0:1	*Stade Français	0:0
Sporting Lisbon	4:6	*Girondins Bordeaux	0:1
Dynamo Zagreb	0:2	*FC Liège	1:0
*Munich 1860	4:3	Malmö FF	0:0
*AIK Stockholm	3:0	Daring Brussels	1:0
*AC Milan	1:1:1	Racing Club Strasbourg	0:2:1
(play-off at Milan won on toss after extra time)			

*Wiener SK	6:1	PAOK Salonika	0:2
*Chelsea	4:0	AS Roma	1:0
*Leeds United	2:0	Torino	1:0
Valencia	0:2:3	*Hibernian	2:0:0
(play-off at Valencia)			
1FC Cologne	4:13	*US Luxembourg	0:0
Everton	1:1	*1FC Nuremberg	1:0
Fiorentina	4:3	*Red Star Belgrade	0:1
*Spartak Brno	2:0	Lokomotiv Plovdiv	0:1

2nd Round

Barcelona	1:2	*Antwerp	2:0
*Hanover 96	5:1	*FC Porto	0:2
Espanol	1:4:2	*Sporting Lisbon	2:3:1
(play-off at Barcelona)			
Red Flag Brasov	2:1	*Dynamo Zagreb	2:0
Munich 1860	1:9	*Goeztepe Izmir	2:1
Servette Geneva	1:4	*AIK Stockholm	2:1
AC Milan	0:2:1	*CUF Setubal	2:0:0
(play-off at Milan)			
Chelsea	0:2	*Wiener SK	1:0
Leeds United	2:0	*Lokomotiv Leipzig	1:0
Valencia	3:5	*FC Basle	1:1
1FC Cologne	1:2	*Aris Salonika	2:0
*Ujpest Dozsa	3:1	Everton	0:2
*Dunfermline Athletic	5:4	KB Copenhagen	0:2
Spartak Brno	0:4	*Fiorentina	2:0
*Heart of Midlothian	1:3	Valerengen	0:1
Real Zaragoza	1:2	*Shamrock Rovers	1:1

3rd Round

Barcelona	1:1:1	*Hanover 96	2:0:1
(replay at Hanover won on toss)			
*Espanol	3:2:1	Red Flag Brasov	1:4:0
(play-off at Barcelona)			
Munich 1860	1:4	*Servette Geneva	1:1
Chelsea	1:2:1	*AC Milan	2:1:1
(replay at Milan won on toss)			
*Leeds United	1:1	Valencia	1:0
Ujpest Dozsa	2:4	*1FC Cologne	3:0
*Dunfermline Athletic	2:0	Spartak Brno	0:0
Real Zaragoza	3:2:1	*Heart of Midlothian	3:2:0
(replay at Zaragoza			

Quarter-Finals

*Barcelona	1:1	Espanol	0:0
Chelsea	2:1	*Munich 1860	2:0
*Leeds United	4:1	Ujpest Dozsa	1:1
Real Zaragoza	0:4	*Dunfermline Athletic	1:2

Semi-Finals

*Barcelona	2:0:5	Chelsea	0:2:0
(replay at Barcelona)			
*Real Zaragoza	1:1:3	Leeds United	0:2:1
(replay at Leeds)			

Final

*Barcelona	0:4	Real Zaragoza	1:2
(after extra time in 2nd leg: 3–2 at full time)			

Fans are removed from the pitch during the second leg of the 1969 Fairs Cup semi-final between Newcastle United and Rangers. In the early days of the Fairs Cup, violent scenes involving players, officials, and spectators were disturbingly frequent occurrences. In 1960–61, for example, Barcelona officials rushed onto the pitch and attacked the referee after he had awarded a decisive penalty to Hibernian. And later players and fans gave Scottish police anxious moments as they tried to break into the referee's dressing room.

Barcelona: Sadurni; Benitez (2nd leg, Foncho), Eladio; Montesinos, Gallego, Torres; Zaballa, Muller (2nd leg, Mas), Zaldua, Fuste, Vidal (2nd leg, Pujol)
Scorers: (2nd leg) Pujol (3), Zaballa
Real Zaragoza: Yarza; Irusquieta, Reija; Pais, Santamaria, Violeta; Canario, Santos, Marcelino, Villa, Lapetra
Scorers: (1st leg) Canario; (2nd leg) Marcelino (2)

1966–67

1st Round

Valencia	2:2	*1FC Nuremberg	1:0
*Red Star Belgrade	5:2	Atlético Bilbao	0:0
*DOS Utrecht	2:2	FC Basle	1:2
*Bologna	3:2	Goeztepe Izmir	3:1
Lokomotiv Leipzig	3:2	*Djurgaarden Stockholm	1:1
Antwerp	1:1	*US Luxembourg	0:0
Girondins Bordeaux	1:2	*FC Porto	2:1
(won on toss after extra time)			
Eintracht Frankfurt	2:5	*Drumcondra	0:1
Oergryte Gothenburg	2:2	*OGC Nice	2:1
Ferencvaros	3:3	*Olympija Ljubljana	3:0
Burnley	1:2	*VfB Stuttgart	1:0
Napoli	2:3	*Wiener SK	1:1
*Juventus	5:2	Aris Salonika	0:0
*Dynamo Pitesti	2:2	Seville	0:2
Dunfermline Athletic	3:3	*Frigg Oslo	1:1
Dynamo Zagreb	0:2	*Spartak Brno	2:0
(won on toss after extra time)			

2nd Round

Leeds United	3:5	*DWS Amsterdam	1:1
*Valencia	1:2	Red Star Belgrade	0:1
*West Bromwich Albion	5:1	DOS Utrecht	2:1
Bologna	2:2	*Sparta Prague	2:1
Lokomotiv Leipzig	0:2	*FC Liège	0:1
Benfica	1:3	*Spartak Plovdiv	1:0
Kilmarnock	1:7	*Antwerp	0:2
*La Gantoise	1:0	Girondins Bordeaux	0:0
*Eintracht Frankfurt	5:2	Hvidovre Copenhagen	1:2
Ferencvaros	0:7	*Oergryte Gothenburg	0:1
Burnley	3:5	*Lausanne	1:0
Napoli	4:2	*Odense BK 09	1:1
*Juventus	3:2	Vitoria Setubal	1:0
Dundee United	2:2	*Barcelona	1:0
Dynamo Pitesti	0:5	*Toulouse	3:1
Dynamo Zagreb	2:2	*Dunfermline Athletic	4:0
(won on away-goals rule)			

3rd Round

*Leeds United	1:2	Valencia	1:0
*Bologna	3:3	West Bromwich Albion	0:1
*Lokomotiv Leipzig	3:1	Benfica	1:2
*Kilmarnock	1:2	La Gantoise	0:1
*Eintracht Frankfurt	4:1	Ferencvaros	1:2
*Burnley	3:0	Napoli	0:0
*Juventus	3:0	Dundee United	0:1
Dynamo Zagreb	1:0	*Dynamo Pitesti	0:0

Quarter-Finals

Leeds United	0:1	*Bologna	1:0
(won on toss)			
Kilmarnock	0:2	*Lokomotiv Leipzig	1:0
*Eintracht Frankfurt	1:2	Burnley	1:1
Dynamo Zagreb	2:3	*Juventus	2:0

Semi-Finals

*Leeds United	4:0	Kilmarnock	2:0
Dynamo Zagreb	0:4	*Eintracht Frankfurt	3:0

Final

*Dynamo Zagreb	2:0	Leeds United	0:0

Dynamo Zagreb: Skoric; Gracanin, Brncic; Belin, Ramljak, Blaskovic; Cercek, Piric, Zambata, Gucmirtl, Rora
Scorer: (1st leg) Cercek (2)
Leeds United: (1st leg) Sprake; Reaney, Cooper; Bremner, Charlton, Hunter; Lorimer, Bates, Belfitt, Gray, O'Grady

Leeds United: (2nd leg) Sprake; Bell, Cooper; Bremner, Charlton, Hunter; Reaney, Belfitt, Greenhoff, Giles, O'Grady

1967–68

1st Round

Leeds United	9:7	*Spora Luxembourg	0:0
FC Liège	2:3	*PAOK Salonika	0:2
Atlético Madrid	5:2	*Wiener SK	0:1
Girondins Bordeaux	3:6	*St Patrick's Athletic	1:3
Real Zaragoza	2:3	*DOS Utrecht	3:1
*Napoli	4:1	Hanover 96	0:1
*Bologna	2:0	Lyn Oslo	0:0
Fiorentina	1:4	*Olympique Nice	0:0
Rangers	1:2	*Dynamo Dresden	1:1
Munich 1860	2:4	*Servette Geneva	2:0
Ferencvaros	1:4	*Argesul Pitesti	3:0
Liverpool	2:2	*Malmö FF	0:1
*Hibernian	3:1	FC Porto	0:3
Nottingham Forest	1:4	*Eintracht Frankfurt	0:0
*Dynamo Zagreb	5:0	Petrolul Ploesti	0:2
Sporting Lisbon	0:2	*FC Bruges	0:1
Atlético Bilbao	1:3	*Frem Copenhagen	0:2
*FC Zurich	3:0	Barcelona	1:1
*Lokomotiv Leipzig	5:0	Linfield	1:1
Dundee	1:3	*DWS Amsterdam	2:0
*Partizan Belgrade	5:1	Lokomotiv Plovdiv	1:1
*Vojvodina Novi Sad	1:3	CUF Setubal	0:1
*1FC Cologne	2:2	Slavia Prague	0:2
Goeztepe Izmir	2:0	*Antwerp	1:0

2nd Round

FC Zurich	1:1	*Nottingham Forest	2:0
(won on away-goals rule)			
Atlético Bilbao	3:1	*Girondins Bordeaux	1:0
*Dundee	3:4	FC Liège	1:1
*Vojvodina Novi Sad	0:2	Lokomotiv Leipzig	0:0
Ferencvaros	1:3	*Real Zaragoza	2:0
*Liverpool	8:1	Munich 1860	0:2
*Rangers	3:1	1FC Cologne	0:3
*Bologna	0:2	Dynamo Zagreb	0:1
Hibernian	1:5	*Napoli	4:0
Leeds United	2:1	*Partizan Belgrade	1:1
Sporting Lisbon	1:2	*Fiorentina	1:1
Goeztepe Izmir	0:3	*Atlético Madrid	2:0

3rd Round

*Ferencvaros	1:1	Liverpool	0:0
*Leeds United	1:1	Hibernian	0:1
*Vojvodina Novi Sad	1:1	Goeztepe Izmir	0:0
*FC Zurich	3:0	Sporting Lisbon	0:1
Atlético Bilbao	*bye*		
Bologna	*bye*		
Dundee	*bye*		
Rangers	*bye*		

A heart-stopping moment for Newcastle fans as Penman takes the penalty that should have put Rangers into the lead in the first leg of their 1969 semi-final. But Iam McFaul rose to the occasion brilliantly, tipping the shot around the post. Newcastle went on to win the tie 2–0 on aggregate and then beat Ujpest Dozsa in the final.

Quarter Finals

*Ferencvaros	2:2	Atlético Bilbao	1:1
Leeds United	0:2	*Rangers	0:0
*Dundee	1:1	FC Zurich	0:0
*Bologna	0:2	Vojvodina Novi Sad	0:0

Semi-Finals

Leeds United	1:1	*Dundee	1:0
*Ferencvaros	3:2	Bologna	2:2

Final

*Leeds United	1:0	Ferencvaros	0:0

Leeds United: Sprake; Reaney, Cooper; Bremner, Charlton, Hunter; Lorimer, Madeley, Jones, Giles (2nd leg, Hibbitt), Gray (2nd leg, O'Grady)
Subs: (1st leg) Belfitt for Jones; Greenhoff for Giles; (2nd leg) Bates for Hibbitt
Scorer: Jones

Ferencvaros: Geczi; Novak, Pancsics; Havasi, Juhasz, Szucs; Szoke, Varga, Albert, Rakosi, Fenyvesi (2nd leg, Katona)
Subs: (1st leg) Balint for Fenyvesi; (2nd leg) Karaba for Szoke

*Home team in 1st leg.

1968–69

1st Round

*Chelsea	5:4	Morton	0:3
*Newcastle United	4:0	Feyenoord	0:2
Aberdeen	0:2	*Slavia Sofia	0:0
*Atlético Bilbao	2:1	Liverpool	1:2
(won on toss)			
*Rangers	2:0	Vojvodina Novi Sad	0:1
Hibernian	3:2	*Ljubljana	0:1
OFK Belgrade	1:6	*Rapid Bucharest	3:1
Slavia Prague	0:5	*Wiener SK	1:0
AIK Stockholm	1:2	*Skeid Oslo	1:1
Real Zaragoza	1:2	*Trakia Plovdiv	3:0
(won on away-goals rule)			
Fiorentina	1:2	*Dynamo Zagreb	1:1
*Legia Warsaw	6:3	Munich 1860	0:2
Panathinaikos	1:2	*Daring Brussels	2:0
Eintracht Frankfurt	2:3	*Wacker Innsbruck	2:0
*Sporting Lisbon	4:1	Valencia	0:4
*Bologna	4:2	FC Basle	1:0
*Aris Salonika	1:6	Hibernians Valletta	0:0
Dundalk	1:2	*DOS Utrecht	1:1
Waregem	1:1	*Atlético Madrid	2:0
(won on toss)			
*Hansa Rostock	3:1	OGC Nice	0:2
*Goeztepe Izmir	2:0	Olympique Marseille	0:2
(won on toss)			
SV Hamburg	4:3	*Metz	1:2
*Olympique Lyonnaise	1:0	Coimbra Academica	0:1
(won on toss)			
Juventus	2:2	*Lausanne	0:0
DWS Amsterdam	1:2	*Beerschot	1:1
*Hannover 96	3:1	Odense BK 09	2:0
*Vitoria Setubal	3:3	Linfield	0:1
Leeds United	0:3	*Standard Liège	0:2
*Napoli	3:0	Grasshoppers Zurich	1:1

2nd Round

*Hibernian	3:1	Lokomotiv Leipzig	1:0
*Leeds United	2:0	Napoli	0:2
(won on toss)			
*Rangers	6:3	Dundalk	1:0
Real Zaragoza	1:3	*Aberdeen	2:0
DWS Amsterdam	0:0	*Chelsea	0:0
(won on toss)			
Newcastle United	1:1	*Sporting Lisbon	1:0
*Vitoria Setubal	5:2	Olympique Lyonnaise	0:1
*Goeztepe Izmir	3:0	Argesul Pitesti	0:2
Fiorentina	2:2	*Hansa Rostock	3:1
(won on away-goals rule)			
*SV Hamburg	4:1	Slavia Prague	1:3
Atlético Bilbao	0:1	*Panathinaikos	0:0
Legia Warsaw	0:2	*Waragem	1:0
Eintracht Frankfurt	0:1	*Juventus	0:0
*OFK Belgrade	1:1	Bologna	0:1
Ujpest Dozsa	2:9	*Aris Salonika	1:1
Hannover 96	2:5	*AIK Stockholm	4:2

3rd Round

*Leeds United	5:2	Hannover 96	1:1
*SV Hamburg	1:1	Hibernian	0:2
(won on away-goals rule)			
Ujpest Dozsa	1:2	*Legia Warsaw	0:2
Newcastle United	2:2	*Real Zaragoza	3:1
(won on away-goals rule)			
Goeztepe Izmir	1:2	*OFK Belgrade	3:0
(won on away-goals rule)			
*Atlético Bilbao	1:1	Eintracht Frankfurt	0:1
Rangers	2:2	*DWS Amsterdam	0:1
*Vitoria Setubal	3:1	Fiorentina	0:2

Quarter-Finals

*Newcastle United	5:1	Vitoria Setubal	1:3
*Rangers	4:0	Atlético Bilbao	1:2
Ujpest Dozsa	1:2	*Leeds United	0:0
Goeztepe Izmir won outright: SV Hamburg withdrew			

Semi-Finals

Ujpest Dozsa	4:4	*Goeztepe Izmir	1:0
Newcastle United	0:2	*Rangers	0:0

Final

*Newcastle United	3:3	Ujpest Dozsa	0:2

Newcastle United: McFaul; Craig, Clark; Gibb, Burton, Moncur; Scott, Robson, Davies, Arentoft, Sinclair
Subs: (1st leg) Foggon for Sinclair; (2nd leg) Foggon for Scott
Scorers: (1st leg) Moncur (2), Scott; (2nd leg) Moncur, Arentoft, Foggon
Ujpest Dozsa: Szentimihalyi; Kaposzta, Solymosi; Bankuti, Nosko, Dunai E.; Fazekas, Gorocs, Bene, Dunai A., Zambo
Scorers: (2nd leg) Bene, Gorocs

*Home team in 1st leg.

1969–70

1st Round

*Arsenal	3:0	Glentoran	0:1
Newcastle United	2:1	*Dundee United	1:0
*Liverpool	10:4	Dundalk	0:0
Ujpest Dozsa	1:2	*Partizan Belgrade	2:0
FC Bruges	0:5	*Sabadel	2:1
Hertha Berlin	0:1	*Las Palmas	0:0
Ruch Chorzow	2:4	*Wiener SK	4:1
*Rouen	2:0	Twente Enschede	0:1
*Vitoria Guimaraes	1:1	Banik Ostrava	0:1
*Sporting Lisbon	4:2	ASK Linz	0:2
*Carl Zeiss Jena	1:0	Altay Izmir	0:0
Vasas Györ	2:2	*Lausanne	1:1
Southampton	0:2	*Rosenborg Trondheim	1:0
*Hansa Rostock	3:0	Panionios Athens	0:2
*Dynamo Bacau	6:1	Floriana Valletta	0:0
*Slavia Sofia	2:1	Valencia	0:1
*Internazionale Milan	3:1	Sparta Prague	0:0
*Juventus	3:2	Lokomotiv Plovdiv	1:1
*VfB Stuttgart	3:1	Malmö FF	0:1
Ajax Amsterdam	1:3	*Hanover 96	2:0
Cagliari	1:3	*Aris Salonika	1:0
Napoli	1:2	*Metz	1:1
*Barcelona	4:2	Odense BK 09	0:0
*Gwardia Warsaw	1:1	Vojvodina Novi Sad	0:1
*Dunfermline Athletic	4:0	Girondins Bordeaux	0:2
Kilmarnock	2:3	*FC Zurich	3:1
Skeid Oslo	2:2	*Munich 1860	2:1
RSC Anderlecht	6:2	*Valur Reykjavik	0:0
*SC Charleroi	2:3	FNK Zagreb	1:1
FC Porto	2:2	*Hvidovre Copenhagen	1:0
Coleraine	2:4	*Jeunesse Esch	3:0
*Vitoria Setubal	3:4	Rapid Bucharest	1:1

2nd Round

Arsenal	0:3	*Sporting Lisbon	0:0
*RSC Anderlecht	6:7	Coleraine	1:3
*Vitoria Setubal	1:2	Liverpool	0:3
(won on away-goals rule)			
Newcastle United	0:1	*FC Porto	0:0

Bobby Moncur proved himself not only an inspiring captain and a solid centre-back for Newcastle, but also a matchwinner. Having failed to find the net in 10 years with the club, he proceeded to score three of their six goals in the 1969 two-legged final.

*Ajax Amsterdam	7:2	Ruch Chorzow	0:1
Inter-Milan	1:3	*Hansa Rostock	2:0
*Carl Zeiss Jena	2:1	Cagliari	0:0
*Hertha Berlin	3:0	Juventus	1:0
Barcelona	3:2	*Vasas Györ	2:0
Napoli	0:1	*VfB Stuttgart	0:0
*Kilmarnock	4:0	Slavia Sofia	1:2
Ujpest Dozsa	2:3	*FC Bruges	5:0
(won on away-goals rule)			
Dynamo Bacau	0:2	*Skeid Oslo	0:0
Rouen	1:2	*SC Charleroi	3:0
(won on away-goals rule)			
Southampton	3:5	*Vitoria Guimaraes	3:1
*Dunfermline Athletic	2:1	Gwardia Warsaw	1:0

3rd Round
*Newcastle United	0:1	Southampton	0:1
(won on away-goals rule)			
*RSC Anderlecht	1:2	Dunfermline Athletic	0:3
(won on away-goals rule)			
Arsenal	0:1	*Rouen	0:0
Dynamo Bacau	1:2	*Kilmarnock	1:0
*Carl Zeiss Jena	1:3	Ujpest Dozsa	0:0
Inter-Milan	2:1	*Barcelona	1:1
Hertha Berlin	1:1	*Vitoria Setubal	1:0
Ajax Amsterdam	0:4	*Napoli	1:0

Quarter-Finals
Ajax Amsterdam	1:5	*Carl Zeiss Jena	3:1
Inter-Milan	0:2	*Hertha Berlin	1:0
*RSC Anderlecht	2:1	Newcastle United	0:3
(won on away-goals rule)			
Arsenal	2:7	*Dynamo Bacau	0:1

Semi-Finals
*Anderlecht	0:2	Inter-Milan	1:0
*Arsenal	3:0	Ajax Amsterdam	0:1

Final
Arsenal	1:3	*Anderlecht	3:0

Arsenal: (1st leg) Wilson; Storey, McNab; Kelly, McLintock, Simpson; Armstrong, Sammels, Radford, George (Kennedy), Graham
Scorer: Kennedy
Arsenal: (2nd leg) Wilson; Storey, McNab; Kelly, McLintock, Simpson; Armstrong, Sammels, Radford, George, Graham
Scorers: Kelly, Radford, Sammels
Anderlecht: (1st Leg) Trappeniers; Heylens, Velkeneers, Kialunda, Cornelis (Peeters); Desanghere, Nordahl; Devrindt, Mulder, Van Himst, Puis
Scorers: Devrindt, Mulder (2)
Anderlecht: (2nd leg) Trappeniers; Heylens, Velkeneers, Kialunda, Maartens; Nordahl, Desanghere; Devrindt, Mulder, Van Himst, Puis

* Home team in 1st leg.

1970–71

1st Round
Twente Enschede	1:3	*AEK Athens	0:0
RSC Anderlecht	4:5	*Zeleznicar	3:4
SV Hamburg	1:7	*La Gantoise	0:1
*Liverpool	1:1	Ferencvaros	0:1
Leeds United	1:5	*Sarpsborg	0:0
*Coleraine	1:3	Kilmarnock	1:2
*Dundee United	3:0	Grasshoppers Zurich	2:0
Arsenal	2:2	*Lazio	2:0
Barcelona	1:3	*Katowice	0:2
Beveren-Waas	2:3	*Wiener SK	0:0
Sturm Graz	2:3	*Ilves-Kissat	4:0
*Juventus	7:4	US Rumelange	0:0
Eskisehir	0:3	*Seville	1:1
*Vitoria Guimaraes	3:1	Angouleme	0:3
*Hajduk Split	3:0	Slavia Sofia	0:1
Hertha Berlin	4:4	*Nyköping	2:1
Dynamo Dresden	0:6	*Partizan Belgrade	0:0
Dynamo Zagreb	0:6	*Barreirense	2:1
Fiorentina	1:2	*Ruch Chorzow	1:0
*Sparta Prague	2:1	Atlético Bilbao	0:1
*AB Copenhagen	7:3	Sliema Wanderers	0:2
*Dynamo Bucharest	5:0	PAOK Salonika	0:1

Mick Bates (left) gets Leeds' second goal in the first leg of the 1971 final. It was to prove a vital goal, for the second leg ended in a 1–1 draw and the tie had to be decided, in Leeds' favour, on away goals. It was the first time a final had been decided in this way.

Coming on as a substitute in the first leg of the 1970 final, Ray Kennedy played only seven minutes. But the goal he scored was vital to Arsenal's eventual victory.

Vitoria Setubal	2:2	*Lausanne	0:1
*1FC Cologne	5:0	Sedan-Torcy	1:1
Newcastle United	1:2	*Internazionale Milan	1:0
*Spartak Trnava	2:0	Olympique Marseille	0:2
(won on penalty kicks after extra time)			
*Bayern Munich	1:1	Rangers	0:1
Valencia	3:3	*Cork Hibernian	0:1
*Hibernian	6:3	Malmö FF	0:2
Pecsi Dosza	1:3	*Universitatea Craiova	2:0
Coventry City	4:2	*Trakia Plovdiv	1:0
*Sparta Rotterdam	6:9	*IA Akranes	0:0

2nd Round
Arsenal	0:2	*Sturm Graz	1:0
*Sparta Rotterdam	2:2	Coleraine	0:1
*Leeds United	1:1	Dynamo Dresden	0:2
(won on away-goals rule)			
*Liverpool	3:1	Dynamo Bucharest	0:1
Pecsi Dosza	0:2	*Newcastle United	2:0
(won on penalty kicks after extra time)			
*Bayern Munich	6:1	Coventry City	1:2
*Sparta Prague	3:0	Dundee United	1:1
*Hibernian	2:1	Vitoria Guimaraes	0:2
Twente Enschede	2:6	*Eskisehir	3:1
RSC Anderlecht	3:4	*AB Copenhagen	1:0
Beveren-Waas	1:1	*Valencia	0:1
Spartak Trnava	0:3	*Hertha Berlin	1:1
Juventus	2:2	*Barcelona	1:1
*Dynamo Zagreb	4:0	SV Hamburg	0:1
*Vitoria Setubal	2:1	Hajduk Split	0:2
1FC Cologne	2:1	*Fiorentina	1:0

3rd Round
*Arsenal	4:0	Beveren-Waas	0:0
*Leeds United	6:3	Sparta Prague	0:2
1FC Cologne	1:3	*Spartak Trnava	0:0
*Bayern Munich	2:3	Sparta Rotterdam	1:1
Twente Enschede	2:1	*Dynamo Zagreb	2:0
Liverpool	1:2	*Hibernian	0:0
Vitoria Setubal	1:3	*RSC Anderlecht	2:1
Juventus	1:2	*Pecsi Dosza	0:0

Quarter-Finals
*Juventus	2:2	Twente Enschede	0:2
1FC Cologne	1:1	*Arsenal	2:0
(won on away-goals rule)			
*Liverpool	3:1	Bayern Munich	0:1
*Leeds United	2:1	Vitoria Setubal	1:1

Semi-Finals
Leeds United	1:0	*Liverpool	0:0
Juventus	1:2	*1FC Cologne	1:0

Final
First match abandoned after 50 minutes: no score
Leeds United	2:1	*Juventus	2:1
(won on away-goals rule)			

Leeds United: (1st leg) Sprake; Reaney, Cooper; Bremner, Charlton, Hunter; Lorimer, Clarke, Jones (Bates), Giles, Madeley
Scorers: Madeley, Bates
Leeds United: (2nd leg), Sprake; Reaney, Cooper, Bremner, Charlton, Hunter; Lorimer, Clarke, Jones, Giles, Madeley (Bates)
Scorer: Clarke

Juventus: (1st leg) Piloni; Spinosi, Salvadore, Marchetti, Morini, Haller, Capello, Furino, Causio, Anastasi (Novellini), Bettega
Scorers: Bettega, Capello
Juventus: (2nd leg) Tancredi; Spinosi, Salvadore, Marchetti, Morini; Haller, Capello, Furino, Causio, Anastasi, Bettega
Scorer: Anastasi

* Home team in 1st leg.

MATCH TO DECIDE PERMANENT POSSESSION
(at Barcelona)

Barcelona	2	Leeds United	1

UEFA CUP

1971–72

1st Round

*Hertha Berlin	3:4	Elfsborg Boras	1:1
*Dundee	4:1	Akademisk Copenhagen	2:0
*Rosenborg Trondheim	3:1	IFK Helsinki	0:0
*Vasas Budapest	1:1	Shelbourne	0:1
Eintracht Braunschweig	1:6	*Glentoran	0:1
Tottenham Hotspur	6:9	*Keflavik	1:0
Aberdeen	2:1	*Celta Vigo	0:0
*FC Den Haag	5:1	Aris Luxembourg	0:1
*Wolverhampton Wanderers	3:4	Academica Coimbra	0:1
1FC Cologne	1:2	*St Etienne	1:1
Legia Warsaw	3:0	*Lugano	1:0
FC Nantes	2:1	*FC Porto	0:1
*St Johnstone	1:3	SV Hamburg	2:0
Atlético Bilbao	1:2	*Southampton	0:0
*Bologna	1:2	RSC Anderlecht	1:0
Rapid Bucharest	0:2	*Napoli	1:0
*Vitoria Setubal	1:1	Nimes	0:2
(won on away-goals rule)			
Panionios	1:1	*Atlético Madrid	2:0
(won on away-goals rule)			
*Carl Zeiss Jena	3:1	Lokomotiv Plovdiv	0:3
Real Madrid	2:2	*FC Basle	1:1
Juventus	6:5	*Marsa	0:0
*Dynamo Zagreb	6:2	Botev Vratza	1:1
*UT Arad	4:1	Austria Salzburg	1:3
Ferencvaros	1:3	*Fenerbahce	1:1
*AC Milan	4:3	Dighenis Morphou	0:0
*Moscow Spartak	2:1	VSS Kosice	0:2
*OFK Belgrade	4:2	Djurgaarden Stockholm	1:2
*Zeleznicar	3:1	FC Bruges	0:3
*Zaglebie Walbrzych	1:3	Union Teplice	0:2
*Lierse SK	0:4	Leeds United	2:0
PSV Eindhoven	0	*Chemie Halle	0
		(withdrew from 2nd leg)	

Rapid Vienna won outright: Vlanznija withdrew

2nd Round

Lierse SK	1:3	*Rosenborg Trondheim	4:0
(won on away-goals rule)			
*Rapid Bucharest	4:0	Legia Warsaw	0:2
Dundee	1:4	*1FC Cologne	2:2
Wolverhampton Wanderers	3:4	*FC Den Haag	1:0
*Zeleznicar	1:2	Bologna	1:2
(won on away-goals rule)			
Tottenham Hotspur	0:1	*FC Nantes	0:0
*Eintracht Braunschweig	2:2	Atlético Bilbao	1:2
*St Johnstone	2:0	Vasas Budapest	0:1
Vitoria Setubal	0:4	*Moscow Spartak	0:0
AC Milan	4:1	*Hertha Berlin	2:2
Carl Zeiss Jena	1:4	*OFK Belgrade	1:0
UT Arad	1:2	*Zaglebie Walbrzych	1:1
Rapid Vienna		*Dynamo Zagreb	2:0
(won on away-goals rule)			
PSV Eindhoven	1:2	*Real Madrid	3:0
(won on away-goals rule)			
*Juventus	2:1	Aberdeen	0:1
*Ferencvaros	6	Panionios (disqualified)	0

3rd Round

*AC Milan	3:0	Dundee	0:2
Wolverhampton Wanderers	1:3	*Carl Zeiss Jena	0:0
Ferencvaros	1:5	*Eintracht Braunschweig	1:2
Lierse SK	0:4	*PSV Eindhoven	1:0
Juventus	1:4	*Rapid Vienna	0:1
Zeleznicar	0:5	*St Johnstone	1:0
*Tottenham Hotspur	3:2	Rapid Bucharest	0:0
*UT Arad	3:0	Vitoria Setubal	0:1

The ability of Liverpool's John Toshack (centre) in the air caused Borussia Mönchengladbach serious trouble in the first leg of the 1973 final.

Quarter-Finals

*AC Milan	2:1	Lierse SK	0:1
Tottenham Hotspur	2:1	*UT Arad	0:1
Wolverhampton Wanderers	1:2	*Juventus	1:1
*Ferencvaros	1:2	Zeleznicar	2:1
(won on penalties)			

Semi-Finals

Wolverhampton Wanderers	2:2	*Ferencvaros	2:1
*Tottenham Hotspur	2:1	AC Milan	1:1

Final

Tottenham Hotspur	2:1	*Wolverhampton Wanderers	1:1

Tottenham Hotspur: (1st leg) Jennings; Kinnear, Knowles; Mullery, England, Beal; Gilzean, Perryman, Chivers, Peters, Coates (Pratt)
Scorer: Chivers (2)
Tottenham Hotspur: (2nd leg) Jennings; Kinnear, Knowles; Mullery, England, Beal; Gilzean, Perryman, Chivers, Peters, Coates
Scorer: Mullery
Wolverhampton Wanderers: (1st leg) Parkes; Shaw, Taylor; Hegan, Munro, McAlle, McCalliog, Hibbitt, Richards, Dougan, Wagstaffe
Wolverhampton Wanderers: (2nd leg) Parkes; Shaw, Taylor; Hegan, Munro, McAlle; McCalliog, Hibbitt (Bailey), Richards, Dougan (Curran), Wagstaffe
Scorer: Wagstaffe

---

* Home team in 1st leg.

1972–73

1st Round

*Liverpool	2:0	Eintracht Frankfurt	0:0
*AEK Athens	3:1	Salgotarjan	1:1
Dynamo Berlin	1:2	*Angers	1:1
Levski Sofia	1:5	*Universitatea Cluj	4:1
*Dynamo Dresden	2:2	Vöest Linz	0:2
*Ruch Chorzow	3:0	Fenerbahce	0:1
*FC Porto	3:1	Barcelona	1:0
FC Bruges	5:1	*Atvidaberg	3:2
Tottenham Hotspur	6:6	*Lyn Oslo	3:0
*Olympiakos Piraeus	2:1	Cagliari	1:0
*Red Star Belgrade	5:2	Lausanne	1:3
Valencia	2:2	*Manchester City	2:1
*Vitoria Setubal	6:0	Zaglebie Sosnowiec	1:1
Fiorentina	2:3	*Eskisehirspor	1:0
*Internazionale	6:1	FC Valletta	1:0
Norrköping	2:2	*UT Arad	1:0
*Honved	1:3	Partick Thistle	0:0
*Beroe Stara Zagora	7:3	FK Austria	0:1
*Feyenoord	9:12	US Rumelingen	0:0
OFK Belgrade	2:3	*Dukla Prague	2:1
*Slovan Bratislava	6:2	Vojvodina	0:1
Las Palmas	0:4	*Torino	2:0
Frem Copenhagen	3:2	*Sochaux	1:1
Twente Enschede	2:2	*Tbilisi Dynamo	3:0
*Grasshoppers Zurich	2:2	Nimes	1:1
Ararat Erevan	1:1	*EPA Larnaca	0:0
CUF Barreirense	1:2	*Racing White	0:0
Kaiserslautern	1:4	*Stoke City	3:0
*Viking Stavanger	1:0	IBV Reykjavik	0:0
*1FC Cologne	2:3	Bohemians	1:0
Hvidovre Copenhagen bye			
Borussia Mönchengladbach	3:6	*Aberdeen	2:3
(2nd leg in Nuremberg)			

2nd Round

*Liverpool	3:3	AEK Athens	0:1
*Dynamo Berlin	3:0	Levski Sofia	0:2
Dynamo Dresden	1:3	*Ruch Chorzow	0:0
*FC Porto	3:2	FC Bruges	0:3
*Tottenham Hotspur	4:0	Olympiakos Piraeus	0:1

Larry Lloyd scores Liverpool's third goal at Anfield. It was just enough, for they lost the return 2–0.

*Red Star Belgrade	3:1	Valencia	1:0
*Vitoria Setubal	1:1	Fiorentina	0:2

(won on away-goals rule)

*Internazionale	2:2	Norrköping	2:0
*Beroe Stara Zagora	3:0	Honved	0:1
OFK Belgrade	3:2	*Feyenoord	4:1

(won on away-goals rule)

*Las Palmas	2:1	Slovan Bratislava	2:0
Twente Enschede	5:4	*Frem Copenhagen	0:0
Ararat Erevan	3:4	*Grasshoppers Zurich	1:2
Kaiserslautern	3:0	*CUF Barreirense	1:1
1FC Cologne	0:9	*Viking Stavanger	1:1
*B. Mönchengladbach	3:3	Hvidovre Copenhagen	0:1

(1st leg in Nuremberg)

3rd Round

Liverpool	0:3	*Dynamo Berlin	0:1
Dynamo Dresden	2:1	*FC Porto	1:0
*Tottenham Hotspur	2:0	Red Star Belgrade	0:1
*Vitoria Setubal	2:0	Internazionale	0:1
*OFK Belgrade	0:3	Beroe Stara Zagora	0:1
*Twente Enschede	3:1	Las Palmas	0:2
Kaiserslautern	0:2	*Ararat Erevan	2:0

(won on penalties)

B. Mönchengladbach	0:5	*1FC Cologne	0:0

Quarter-Finals

*Liverpool	2:1	Dynamo Dresden	0:0
*Tottenham Hotspur	1:1	Vitoria Setubal	0:2

(won on away-goals rule)

Twente Enschede	2:2	*OFK Belgrade	3:0
B. Mönchengladbach	2:7	*Kaiserslautern	1:1

Semi-Finals

*Liverpool	1:1	Tottenham Hotspur	0:2

(won on away-goals rule)

*B. Mönchengladbach	3:2	Twente Enschede	0:1

Final

*Liverpool	3:0	B. Mönchengladbach	0:2

(1st leg originally abandoned after 27 min, 0–0)

Liverpool: (1st leg) Clemence; Lawler, Lindsay, Smith, Lloyd, Hughes, Keegan, Cormack, Toshack, Heighway (Hall), Callaghan
Scorers: Keegan 2, Lloyd
Liverpool: (2nd leg) as above except Boersma sub for Heighway
Borussia Mönchengladbach: (1st leg) Kleff; Danner, Michallik, Vogts, Bonhof, Kulik, Jensen, Wimmer, Rupp (Simonson), Netzer, Heynckes
B. Mönchengladbach: (2nd leg) Kleff; Vogts, Surau, Bonhof, Danner, Wimmer, Kulik, Jensen, Rupp, Netzer, Heynckes
Scorer: Heynckes 2

*Home team in 1st leg.

1973-74

1st Round

Feyenoord	3:2	*Oesters	1:1
Gwardia Warsaw	1:2	*Ferencvaros	0:1
Standard Liège	2:6	*Ards	3:1
Universitatea Craiova	0:1	*Fiorentina	0:0
*Ruch Chorzow	4:4	Wuppertal	1:5
*Carl Zeiss Jena	3:3	Mikkelin Palloilijat	0:0
Honved	0:5	*VSS Kosice	1:2
Lokomotiv Plovdiv	2:1	*Sliema Wanderers	0:0
*VfB Stuttgart	9:4	Olympiakos Nicosia	0:0

(2nd leg in Stuttgart)

*Tatran Presov	4:1	Velez	2:1
Kiev Dynamo	1:4	*Fredrikstad	0:0
*BK1903 Copenhagen	2:1	AIK Stockholm	1:1
*Vitoria Setubal	2:2	Beerschot	0:0
Racing White	3:1	*Espanol	0:2

Tottenham's talented Irish winger Chris McGrath (right) watches the educated left foot of Feyenoord's Wim Van Hanegem in action in the first leg of the 1974 final at White Hart Lane, which finished all square.

Rioting Spurs fans at Rotterdam during the second leg. Feyenoord won 2–0 to inflict on Spurs their first ever defeat in a major cup final. But far worse for Tottenham was the shame brought on the club by the unfortunate behaviour of a few hooligans.

Leeds United	1:6	*Strömgodset	1:1
*Hibernian	2:1	IB Keflavik	0:1
*Panachaiki	2:1	Grazer AK	1:0
Twente Enschede	3:4	*Dundee	1:2
*Lazio	3:1	Sion	0:3
*Ipswich Town	1:0	Real Madrid	0:0
*Admira-Wacker	1:1	Internazionale	0:2

(won on away-goals rule)

*Fortuna Düsseldorf	1:2	Naestved	0:2
Wolverhampton Wanderers	2:2	*Belenenses	0:1
Lokomotive Leipzig	2:2	*Torino	1:1
*Fenerbahce	5:1	Argesul Pitesti	1:1
*OGC Nice	3:0	Barcelona	0:2
Olympique Marseille	5:7	*Union Luxembourg	0:1
1FC Cologne	0:2	*Eskisehispor	0:0
OFK Belgrade	2:0	*Panathinaikos	1:1

(won on away-goals rule)

*Tblisi Dynamo	4:0	Slavia Sofia	1:2
*Aberdeen	4:3	Finn Harps	1:1
Tottenham Hotspur	5:4	*Grasshoppers Zurich	1:1

2nd Round

*Feyenoord	3:0	Gwardia Warsaw	1:1
*Standard Liège	2:1	Universitatea Craiova	0:1
*Ruch Chorzow	3:0	Carl Zeiss Jena	0:1
Honved	4:3	*Lokomotiv Plovdiv	3:2
*VfB Stuttgart	3:5	Tatran Presov	1:3
*Kiev Dynamo	1:2	BK1903 Copenhagen	0:1
*Vitoria Setubal	1:1	Racing White	0:2

(won on away-goals rule)

*Leeds United	0:0	Hibernian	0:0

(won on penalties)

Twente Enschede	1:7	*Panachaiki	1:0
*Ipswich Town	4:2	Lazio	0:4
Fortuna Düsseldorf	1:3	*Admira-Wacker	2:0
*Lokomotive Leipzig	3:1	Wolverhampton W.	0:4

(won on away-goals rule)

*OGC Nice	4:0	Fenerbahce	0:2
1FC Cologne	0:6	*Olympique Marseille	2:0
*Tblisi Dynamo	3:5	OFK Belgrade	0:1
Tottenham Hotspur	1:4	*Aberdeen	1:1

3rd Round

Feyenoord	1:2	*Standard Liège	3:0

(won on away-goals rule)

Ruch Chorzow	0:5	*Honved	2:0
VfB Stuttgart	0:3	*Kiev Dynamo	2:0
Vitoria Setubal	0:3	*Leeds United	1:1
*Ipswich Town	1:2	Twente Enschede	0:1
Lokomotive Leipzig	1:3	*Fortuna Düsseldorf	2:0
1FC Cologne	0:4	*OGC Nice	1:0
Tottenham Hotspur	1:5	*Tblisi Dynamo	1:1

Quarter-Finals

Feyenoord	1:3	*Ruch Chorzow	1:1
*VfB Stuttgart	1:2	Vitoria Setubal	0:2
Lokomotive Leipzig	0:1	*Ipswich Town	1:0

(won on penalties)

Tottenham Hotspur	2:3	*1FC Cologne	1:0

Semi-Finals

*Feyenoord	2:2	VfB Stuttgart	1:2
Tottenham Hotspur	2:2	*Lokomotive Leipzig	1:0

Final

Feyenoord	2:2	*Tottenham Hotspur	2:0

Feyenoord: (1st leg) Treytel; Rijsbergen, Van Daele, Israel, Vos; De Jong, Jansen, Van Hanegem; Ressel, Schoenmaker, Kristensen
Scorers: Van Hanegem, De Jong
Feyenoord: (2nd leg) Treytel; Ramljak, Israel, Van Daele, Vos; Rijsbergen (Boskamp), De Jong, Jansen; Ressel, Schoenmaker, Kristensen
Scorers: Rijsbergen, Ressel
Tottenham: (1st leg) Jennings; Evans, England, Beal (Dillon), Naylor; Perryman, Pratt, Peters; Coates, Chivers, McGrath
Scorers: England, Van Daele (o.g.)
Tottenham: (2nd leg) as above except Holder sub for Pratt

*Home team in 1st leg.

British Competitions

BRITISH INTERNATIONAL CHAMPIONSHIP

		Pts
1883–84	Scotland	6
1884–85	Scotland	5
1885–86	England & Scotland	5
1886–87	Scotland	6
1887–88	England	6
1888–89	Scotland	5
1889–90	England & Scotland	5
1890–91	England	6
1891–92	England	6
1892–93	England	6
1893–94	Scotland	5
1894–95	England	5
1895–96	Scotland	5
1896–97	Scotland	5
1897–98	England	6
1898–99	England	6
1899–1900	Scotland	6
1900–01	England	5
1901–02	Scotland	5
1902–03	England, Ireland & Scotland	4
1903–04	England	5
1904–05	England	5
1905–06	England & Scotland	4
1906–07	Wales	5
1907–08	England & Scotland	5
1908–09	England	6
1909–10	Scotland	4
1910–11	England	5
1911–12	England & Scotland	5
1912–13	England	4
1913–14	Ireland	5
1915–19	*Series suspended*	
1919–20	Wales	4
1920–21	Scotland	6
1921–22	Scotland	4
1922–23	Scotland	5
1923–24	Wales	6
1924–25	Scotland	6
1925–26	Scotland	6
1926–27	England & Scotland	4
1927–28	Wales	5
1928–29	Scotland	6
1929–30	England	6
1930–31	England & Scotland	4
1931–32	England	6
1932–33	Wales	5
1933–34	Wales	5
1934–35	England & Scotland	4
1935–36	Scotland	4
1936–37	Wales	6
1937–38	England	4
1938–39	England, Scotland & Wales	4
1940–46	*Series suspended*	
1946–47	England	5
1947–48	England	5
1948–49	Scotland	5
1949–50	England	6
1950–51	Scotland	6
1951–52	England & Wales	5
1952–53	England & Scotland	4
1953–54	England	6
1954–55	England	6
1955–56	England, Ireland, Scotland & Wales	3
1956–57	England	4
1957–58	England & Ireland	4
1958–59	England & Ireland	4
1959–60	England, Scotland & Wales	4
1960–61	England	6
1961–62	Scotland	6
1962–63	Scotland	6
1963–64	England, Ireland & Scotland	4
1964–65	England	4
1965–66	England	5
1966–67	Scotland	5
1967–68	England	5
1968–69	England	6
1969–70	England, Scotland & Wales	4
1970–71	England	5
1971–72	England & Scotland	4
1972–73	England	6
1973–74	England & Scotland	4

ENGLAND

Association founded: 1863
Colours: white shirts; blue shorts
Honours: World Cup, winners 1966; European Championship, 3rd 1968

v Scotland		E	S
1872	Glasgow	0	0
1873	The Oval	4	2
1874	Glasgow	1	2
1875	The Oval	2	2
1876	Glasgow	0	3
1877	The Oval	1	3
1878	Glasgow	2	7
1879	The Oval	5	4
1880	Glasgow	4	5
1881	The Oval	1	6
1882	Glasgow	1	5
1883	Sheffield	2	3
1884	Glasgow	0	1
1885	The Oval	1	1
1886	Glasgow	1	1
1887	Blackburn	2	3
1888	Glasgow	5	0
1889	The Oval	2	3
1890	Glasgow	1	1
1891	Blackburn	2	1
1892	Glasgow	4	1
1893	Richmond	5	2
1894	Glasgow	2	2
1895	Everton	3	0
1896	Glasgow	1	2
1897	Crystal Palace	1	2
1898	Glasgow	3	1
1899	Birmingham	2	1
1900	Glasgow	1	4
1901	Crystal Palace	2	2
1902	†Glasgow	1	1
1902	Birmingham	2	2
1903	Sheffield	1	2
1904	Glasgow	1	0
1905	Crystal Palace	1	0
1906	Glasgow	1	2
1907	Newcastle	1	1
1908	Glasgow	1	1
1909	Crystal Palace	2	0
1910	Glasgow	0	2
1911	Everton	1	1
1912	Glasgow	1	1
1913	Stamford Bridge	1	0
1914	Glasgow	1	3
1915–18	*Series suspended*		
1919	*Everton	2	2
1919	*Glasgow	4	3
1919–20	Sheffield	5	4
1920–21	Glasgow	0	3
1921–22	Birmingham	0	1
1922–23	Glasgow	2	2
1923–24	Wembley	1	1
1924–25	Glasgow	0	2
1925–26	Manchester	0	1
1926–27	Glasgow	2	1
1927–28	Wembley	1	5
1928–29	Glasgow	0	1
1929–30	Wembley	5	2
1930–31	Glasgow	0	2
1931–32	Wembley	3	0
1932–33	Glasgow	1	2
1933–34	Wembley	3	0
1934–35	Glasgow	0	2
1935–36	Wembley	1	1
1936–37	Glasgow	1	3
1937–38	Wembley	0	1
1938–39	Glasgow	2	1
1939–45	*Series suspended*		
1945–46	*Glasgow	0	1
1946–47	Wembley	1	1
1947–48	Glasgow	2	0
1948–49	Wembley	1	3
1949–50	Glasgow	1	0
1950–51	Wembley	2	3
1951–52	Glasgow	2	1
1952–53	Wembley	2	2
1953–54	Glasgow	4	2
1954–55	Wembley	7	2
1955–56	Glasgow	1	1
1956–57	Wembley	2	1
1957–58	Glasgow	4	0
1958–59	Wembley	1	0
1959–60	Glasgow	1	1
1960–61	Wembley	9	3
1961–62	Glasgow	0	2
1962–63	Wembley	1	2
1963–64	Glasgow	0	1
1964–65	Wembley	2	2
1965–66	Glasgow	4	3
1966–67	Wembley	2	3
1967–68	Glasgow	1	1
1968–69	Wembley	4	1
1969–70	Giasgow	0	0
1970–71	Wembley	3	1
1971–72	Glasgow	1	0
1972–73	Wembley	1	0
1973–74	Glasgow	0	2

v Wales		E	W
1879	The Oval	2	1
1880	Wrexham	3	2
1881	Blackburn	0	1
1882	Wrexham	3	5
1883	The Oval	5	0
1884	Wrexham	4	0
1885	Blackburn	1	1
1886	Wrexham	3	1
1887	The Oval	4	0
1888	Crewe	5	1
1889	Stoke-on-Trent	4	1
1890	Wrexham	3	1
1891	Sunderland	4	1
1892	Wrexham	2	0
1893	Stoke-on-Trent	6	0
1894	Wrexham	5	1
1895	Queen's Club, London	1	1
1896	Cardiff	9	1
1897	Sheffield	4	0
1898	Wrexham	3	0
1899	Bristol	4	1
1900	Cardiff	1	1
1901	Newcastle	6	0
1902	Wrexham	0	0
1903	Portsmouth	2	1
1904	Wrexham	2	2
1905	Liverpool	3	1
1906	Cardiff	1	0
1907	Fulham	1	1
1908	Wrexham	7	1
1909	Nottingham	2	0
1910	Cardiff	1	0
1911	Millwall	3	0
1912	Wrexham	2	0
1913	Bristol	4	3
1914	Cardiff	2	0
1915–18	*Series suspended*		
1919	*Cardiff	1	2
1919	*Stoke	2	0
1919–20	Highbury	1	2
1920–21	Cardiff	0	0
1921–22	Liverpool	1	0
1922–23	Cardiff	2	2
1923–24	Blackburn	1	2
1924–25	Swansea	2	1
1925–26	Selhurst Park	1	3
1926–27	Wrexham	3	3
1927–28	Burnley	1	2
1928–29	Swansea	3	2
1929–30	Stamford Bridge	6	0
1930–31	Wrexham	4	0
1931–32	Liverpool	3	1
1932–33	Wrexham	0	0
1933–34	Newcastle	1	2
1934–35	Cardiff	4	0
1935–36	Wolverhampton	1	2
1936–37	Cardiff	1	2
1937–38	Middlesbrough	2	1
1938–39	Cardiff	2	4
1939–46	*Series suspended*		
1946–47	*West Bromwich	0	1
1946–47	Manchester	3	0
1947–48	Cardiff	3	0
1948–49	Villa Park	1	0
1949–50	Cardiff	4	1
1950–51	Sunderland	4	2
1951–52	Cardiff	1	1
1952–53	Wembley	5	2
1953–54	Cardiff	4	1
1954–55	Wembley	3	2
1955–56	Cardiff	1	2
1956–57	Wembley	3	1
1957–58	Cardiff	4	0
1958–59	Villa Park	2	2
1959–60	Cardiff	1	1
1960–61	Wembley	5	1
1961–62	Cardiff	1	1
1962–63	Wembley	4	0
1963–64	Cardiff	4	0
1964–65	Wembley	2	1
1965–66	Cardiff	0	0
1966–67	Wembley	5	1
1967–68	Cardiff	3	0
1968–69	Wembley	2	1
1969–70	Cardiff	1	1
1970–71	Wembley	0	0
1971–72	Cardiff	3	0
1972–73	Wembley	3	0
1973–74	Cardiff	2	0

v Ireland		E	I
1882	Belfast	13	0
1883	Liverpool	7	0
1884	Belfast	8	1
1885	Manchester	4	0
1886	Belfast	6	1
1887	Sheffield	7	0
1888	Belfast	5	1
1889	Everton	6	1
1890	Belfast	9	1
1891	Wolverhampton	6	1
1892	Belfast	2	0
1893	Birmingham	6	1
1894	Belfast	2	2
1895	Derby	9	0
1896	Belfast	2	0
1897	Nottingham	6	0
1898	Belfast	3	2
1899	Sunderland	13	2
1900	Dublin	2	0
1901	Southampton	3	0
1902	Belfast	1	0
1903	Wolverhampton	4	0
1904	Belfast	3	1
1905	Middlesbrough	1	1
1906	Belfast	5	0
1907	Everton	1	0
1908	Belfast	3	1
1909	Bradford	4	0
1910	Belfast	1	1
1911	Derby	2	1
1912	Dublin	6	1
1913	Belfast	1	2
1914	Middlesbrough	0	3
1915–19	*Series suspended*		
1919–20	Belfast	1	1
1920–21	Sunderland	2	0
1921–22	Belfast	1	1
1922–23	West Bromwich	2	0
1923–24	Belfast	1	2
1924–25	Everton	3	1
1925–26	Belfast	0	0
1926–27	Liverpool	3	3
1927–28	Belfast	0	2
1928–29	Everton	2	1
1929–30	Belfast	3	0
1930–31	Sheffield	5	1
1931–32	Belfast	6	2
1932–33	Blackpool	1	0
1933–34	Belfast	3	0
1934–35	Everton	2	1
1935–36	Belfast	3	1
1936–37	Stoke-on-Trent	3	1
1937–38	Belfast	5	1
1938–39	Manchester	7	0
1939–45	*Series suspended*		
1945–46	*Belfast	1	0
1946–47	Belfast	7	2
1947–48	Everton	2	2
1948–49	Belfast	6	2
1949–50	Manchester	9	2
1950–51	Belfast	4	1
1951–52	Villa Park	2	0
1952–53	Belfast	2	2
1953–54	Liverpool	3	1
1954–55	Belfast	2	0
1955–56	Wembley	3	0
1956–57	Belfast	1	1
1957–58	Wembley	2	3
1958–59	Belfast	3	3
1959–60	Wembley	2	1
1960–61	Belfast	5	2
1961–62	Wembley	1	1
1962–63	Belfast	3	1
1963–64	Wembley	8	3
1964–65	Belfast	4	3
1965–66	Wembley	2	1
1966–67	Belfast	2	0
1967–68	Wembley	2	0
1968–69	Belfast	3	1
1969–70	Wembley	3	1
1970–71	Belfast	1	0
1971–72	Wembley	0	1
1972–73	Everton	2	1
1973–74	Wembley	1	0

* Unofficial Victory internationals.
† Declared unofficial following Ibrox disaster.

SCOTLAND

Association founded: 1873
Colours: blue shirts; white shorts

v England
See England v Scotland

v Wales		S	W
1876	Glasgow	4	0
1877	Wrexham	2	0
1878	Glasgow	9	0
1879	Wrexham	3	0
1880	Glasgow	5	1
1881	Wrexham	5	1
1882	Glasgow	5	0
1883	Wrexham	3	0
1884	Glasgow	4	1
1885	Wrexham	8	1
1886	Glasgow	4	1
1887	Wrexham	2	0
1888	Edinburgh	5	1
1889	Wrexham	0	0
1890	Paisley	5	0
1891	Wrexham	4	3
1892	Edinburgh	6	1
1893	Wrexham	8	0
1894	Kilmarnock	5	2
1895	Wrexham	2	2
1896	Dundee	4	0
1897	Wrexham	2	2
1898	Motherwell	5	2
1899	Wrexham	6	0
1900	Aberdeen	5	2
1901	Wrexham	1	1
1902	Greenock	5	1
1903	Cardiff	1	0
1904	Dundee	1	1
1905	Wrexham	1	3
1906	Edinburgh	0	2
1907	Wrexham	0	1
1908	Dundee	2	1
1909	Wrexham	2	3
1910	Kilmarnock	1	0
1911	Cardiff	2	2
1912	Tynecastle	1	0
1913	Wrexham	0	0
1914	Glasgow	0	0
1915–19	*Series suspended*		
1919–20	Cardiff	1	1
1920–21	Aberdeen	2	1
1921–22	Wrexham	1	2
1922–23	Paisley	2	0
1923–24	Cardiff	0	2
1924–25	Tynecastle	3	1
1925–26	Cardiff	3	0

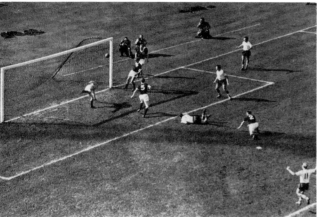

WALES
Association founded: 1876
Colours: red shirts; red shorts

v England
See England v Wales

v Scotland
See Scotland v Wales

v Ireland

Year	Venue	W	I
1882	Wrexham	7	1
1883	Belfast	1	1
1884	Wrexham	6	0
1885	Belfast	8	2
1886	Wrexham	5	0
1887	Belfast	1	4
1888	Wrexham	11	0
1889	Belfast	3	1
1890	Shrewsbury	5	2
1891	Belfast	2	7
1892	Bangor	1	1
1893	Belfast	3	4
1894	Swansea	4	1
1895	Belfast	2	2
1896	Wrexham	6	1
1897	Belfast	3	4
1898	Llandudno	0	1
1899	Belfast	0	1
1900	Llandudno	2	0
1901	Belfast	1	0
1902	Cardiff	0	3
1903	Belfast	0	2
1904	Bangor	0	1
1905	Belfast	2	2
1906	Wrexham	4	4
1907	Belfast	3	2
1908	Aberdare	0	1
1909	Belfast	3	2
1910	Wrexham	4	1
1911	Belfast	2	1
1912	Cardiff	2	3
1913	Belfast	1	0
1914	Wrexham	1	2
1915–19	*Series suspended*		
1919–20	Belfast	2	2
1920–21	Swansea	2	1
1921–22	Belfast	1	1
1922–23	Wrexham	0	3
1923–24	Belfast	1	0
1924–25	Wrexham	0	0
1925–26	Belfast	0	3
1926–27	Cardiff	2	2
1927–28	Belfast	2	1
1928–29	Wrexham	2	2
1929–30	Belfast	0	7
1930–31	Wrexham	3	2
1931–32	Belfast	0	4
1932–33	Wrexham	4	1
1933–34	Belfast	1	1
1934–35	Wrexham	3	1
1935–36	Belfast	2	3
1936–37	Wrexham	4	1
1937–38	Belfast	0	1
1938–39	Wrexham	3	1
1939–45	*Series suspended*		
1945–46	*Cardiff	0	1
1946–47	Belfast	1	2
1947–48	Wrexham	2	0
1948–49	Belfast	2	0
1949–50	Wrexham	0	0
1950–51	Belfast	2	1
1951–52	Swansea	3	0
1952–53	Belfast	3	2
1953–54	Wrexham	1	2
1954–55	Belfast	3	2
1955–56	Cardiff	1	1
1956–57	Belfast	0	0
1957–58	Cardiff	1	1
1958–59	Belfast	1	4
1959–60	Wrexham	3	2
1960–61	Belfast	5	1
1961–62	Cardiff	4	0
1962–63	Belfast	4	1
1963–64	Swansea	2	3
1964–65	Belfast	5	0
1965–66	Cardiff	1	4
1966–67	Belfast	0	0
1967–68	Wrexham	2	0
1968–69	Belfast	0	0
1969–70	Swansea	1	0
1970–71	Belfast	0	1
1971–72	Wrexham	0	0
1972–73	Everton	0	1
1973–74	Wrexham	1	0

* Unofficial Victory international.

IRELAND, NORTHERN
Association founded: 1880
Colours: green shirts; white shorts

v England
See England v Ireland

v Scotland
See Scotland v Ireland

v Wales
See Wales v Ireland

Top left: Scottish fans celebrate their country's 3-2 victory over England at Wembley in 1967. It was England's first defeat after their World Cup triumph.
Above left: Johnny Haynes (10) gets the ball in the Scottish net in the 1962 international at Hampden. The goal, however, was disallowed and the Scots beat England 2-0. That season, 1961–62, Scotland went through the Championship undefeated.
Above: Pat Jennings, hero of Northern Ireland's 1-0 defeat of England at Wembley in 1972, takes the ball high above Allan Clarke in the previous year's clash between the two countries.

Year	Venue		
1926–27	Glasgow	3	0
1927–28	Wrexham	2	2
1928–29	Ibrox	4	2
1929–30	Cardiff	4	2
1930–31	Glasgow	1	1
1931–32	Wrexham	3	2
1932–33	Edinburgh	2	5
1933–34	Cardiff	2	3
1934–35	Aberdeen	3	2
1935–36	Cardiff	1	1
1936–37	Dundee	1	2
1937–38	Cardiff	1	2
1938–39	Edinburgh	3	2
1939–45	*Series suspended*		
1945–46	*Glasgow	2	0
1946–47	Wrexham	1	3
1947–48	Glasgow	1	2
1948–49	Cardiff	3	1
1949–50	Glasgow	2	0
1950–51	Cardiff	3	1
1951–52	Glasgow	0	1
1952–53	Cardiff	2	1
1953–54	Glasgow	3	3
1954–55	Cardiff	1	0
1955–56	Glasgow	2	0
1956–57	Cardiff	2	2
1957–58	Glasgow	1	1
1958–59	Cardiff	3	0
1959–60	Glasgow	1	1
1960–61	Cardiff	0	2
1961–62	Glasgow	2	0
1962–63	Cardiff	3	2
1963–64	Glasgow	2	1
1964–65	Cardiff	2	3
1965–66	Glasgow	4	1
1966–67	Cardiff	1	1
1967–68	Glasgow	3	2
1968–69	Wrexham	5	3
1969–70	Glasgow	0	0
1970–71	Cardiff	0	0
1971–72	Glasgow	1	0
1972–73	Wrexham	2	0
1973–74	Glasgow	2	0

v Ireland

Year	Venue	S	I
1884	Belfast	5	0
1885	Glasgow	8	2
1886	Belfast	7	2
1887	Glasgow	4	1
1888	Belfast	10	2
1889	Glasgow	7	0
1890	Belfast	4	1
1891	Glasgow	2	1
1892	Belfast	3	2
1893	Glasgow	6	1
1894	Belfast	2	1
1895	Glasgow	3	1
1896	Belfast	3	3
1897	Glasgow	5	1
1898	Belfast	3	0
1899	Glasgow	9	1
1900	Belfast	3	0
1901	Glasgow	11	0
1902	Belfast	5	1
1903	Glasgow	0	2
1904	Dublin	1	1
1905	Glasgow	4	0
1906	Dublin	1	0
1907	Glasgow	3	0
1908	Dublin	5	0
1909	Glasgow	5	0
1910	Belfast	0	1
1911	Glasgow	2	0
1912	Belfast	4	1
1913	Dublin	2	1
1914	Belfast	1	1
1915–18	*Series suspended*		
1919	*Glasgow	2	1
1919	*Belfast	0	0
1919–20	Glasgow	3	0
1920–21	Belfast	2	0
1921–22	Glasgow	2	1
1922–23	Belfast	1	0
1923–24	Glasgow	2	0
1924–25	Belfast	3	0
1925–26	Glasgow	4	0
1926–27	Belfast	2	0
1927–28	Glasgow	0	1
1928–29	Belfast	7	3
1929–30	Glasgow	3	1
1930–31	Belfast	0	0
1931–32	Glasgow	3	1
1932–33	Belfast	4	0
1933–34	Glasgow	1	2
1934–35	Belfast	1	2
1935–36	Edinburgh	2	1
1936–37	Belfast	3	1
1937–38	Aberdeen	1	1
1938–39	Belfast	2	0
1939–45	*Series suspended*		
1945–46	*Belfast	3	2
1946–47	Glasgow	0	0
1947–48	Belfast	0	2
1948–49	Glasgow	3	2
1949–50	Belfast	8	2
1950–51	Glasgow	6	1
1951–52	Belfast	3	0
1952–53	Glasgow	1	1
1953–54	Belfast	3	1
1954–55	Glasgow	2	2
1955–56	Belfast	1	2
1956–57	Glasgow	1	0
1957–58	Belfast	1	1
1958–59	Glasgow	2	2
1959–60	Belfast	4	0
1960–61	Glasgow	5	2
1961–62	Belfast	6	1
1962–63	Glasgow	5	1
1963–64	Belfast	1	2
1964–65	Glasgow	3	2
1965–66	Belfast	2	3
1966–67	Glasgow	2	1
1967–68	Belfast	0	1
1968–69	Glasgow	1	1
1969–70	Belfast	1	0
1970–71	Glasgow	0	1
1971–72	Glasgow	2	0
1972–73	Glasgow	1	2
1973–74	Glasgow	0	1

* Unofficial Victory internationals.

FOOTBALL LEAGUE

	First	Pts	Second	Pts	Third	Pts
1888–89[1]	Preston N. End	40	Aston Villa	29	Wolverhampton W.	28
1889–90[1]	Preston N. End	33	Everton	31	Blackburn Rovers	27
1890–91[1]	Everton	29	Preston N. End	27	Notts County	26
1891–92[2]	Sunderland	42	Preston N. End	37	Bolton Wanderers	36

Maximum points: [1]44; [2]52

FIRST DIVISION

	First	Pts	Second	Pts	Third	Pts
1892–93[3]	Sunderland	48	Preston N. End	37	Everton	36
1893–94[3]	Aston Villa	44	Sunderland	38	Derby County	36
1894–95[3]	Sunderland	47	Everton	42	Aston Villa	39
1895–96[3]	Aston Villa	45	Derby County	41	Everton	39
1896–97[3]	Aston Villa	47	*Sheffield United	36	Derby County	36
1897–98[3]	Sheffield United	42	Sunderland	37	Wolverhampton W.	35
1898–99[4]	Aston Villa	45	Liverpool	43	Burnley	39
1899–1900[4]	Aston Villa	50	Sheffield United	48	Sunderland	41
1900–01[4]	Liverpool	45	Sunderland	43	Notts County	40
1901–02[4]	Sunderland	44	Everton	41	Newcastle U.	37
1902–03[4]	The Wednesday	42	*Aston Villa	41	Sunderland	41
1903–04[4]	The Wednesday	47	Manchester City	44	Everton	43
1904–05[4]	Newcastle U.	48	Everton	47	Manchester City	46
1905–06[5]	Liverpool	51	Preston N. End	47	The Wednesday	44
1906–07[5]	Newcastle U.	51	Bristol City	48	Everton	45
1907–08[5]	Manchester U.	52	Aston Villa	43	Manchester City	43
1908–09[5]	Newcastle U.	53	Everton	46	Sunderland	44
1909–10[5]	Aston Villa	53	Liverpool	48	Blackburn Rovers	45
1910–11[5]	Manchester U.	52	Aston Villa	51	Sunderland	45
1911–12[5]	Blackburn Rovers	49	Everton	46	Newcastle U.	44
1912–13[5]	Sunderland	54	Aston Villa	50	The Wednesday	49
1913–14[5]	Blackburn Rovers	51	Aston Villa	44	*Middlesbrough	43
1914–15[5]	Everton	46	Oldham Athletic	45	Blackburn Rovers	43
1915–19	*No competition*					
1919–20[6]	West Brom. A.	60	Burnley	51	Chelsea	49
1920–21[6]	Burnley	59	Manchester City	54	Bolton Wanderers	52
1921–22[6]	Liverpool	57	Tottenham H.	51	Burnley	49
1922–23[6]	Liverpool	60	Sunderland	54	Huddersfield T.	53
1923–24[6]	*Huddersfield T.	57	Cardiff City	57	Sunderland	53
1924–25[6]	Huddersfield T.	58	West Bromwich A.	56	Bolton Wanderers	55
1925–26[6]	Huddersfield T.	57	Arsenal	52	Sunderland	48
1926–27[6]	Newcastle U.	56	Huddersfield T.	51	Sunderland	49
1927–28[6]	Everton	53	Huddersfield T.	51	Leicester City	48
1928–29[6]	Sheffield Wed.	52	Leicester City	51	Aston Villa	50
1929–30[6]	Sheffield Wed.	60	Derby County	50	*Manchester City	47
1930–31[6]	Arsenal	66	Aston Villa	59	Sheffield Wed.	52
1931–32[6]	Everton	56	Arsenal	54	Sheffield Wed.	50
1932–33[6]	Arsenal	58	Aston Villa	54	Sheffield Wed.	51
1933–34[6]	Arsenal	59	Huddersfield T.	56	Tottenham H.	49
1934–35[6]	Arsenal	58	Sunderland	54	Sheffield Wed.	49
1935–36[6]	Sunderland	56	*Derby County	48	Huddersfield T.	48
1936–37[6]	Manchester City	57	Charlton A.	54	Arsenal	52
1937–38[6]	Arsenal	52	Wolverhampton W.	51	Preston N. End	49
1938–39[6]	Everton	59	Wolverhampton W.	55	Charlton A.	50
1939–46	*No competition*					
1946–47[6]	Liverpool	57	*Manchester U.	56	Wolverhampton W.	56
1947–48[6]	Arsenal	59	*Manchester U.	52	Burnley	52
1948–49[6]	Portsmouth	58	*Manchester U.	53	Derby County	53
1949–50[6]	*Portsmouth	53	Wolverhampton W.	53	Sunderland	52

LEADING GOALSCORERS

(Div. I from 1919–20)

Year	Player	Goals
1919–20	Fred Morris (West Bromwich)	37
1920–21	Joe Smith (Bolton)	38
1921–22	Andy Wilson (Middlesbrough)	31
1922–23	Charlie Buchan (Sunderland)	30
1923–24	W. Chadwick (Everton)	28
1924–25	F. Roberts (Manchester C.)	31
1925–26	Ted Harper (Blackburn)	43
1926–27	Jimmy Trotter (Sheffield Wed.)	37
1927–28	'Dixie' Dean (Everton)	60
1928–29	David Halliday (Sunderland)	43
1929–30	Vic Watson (West Ham)	41
1930–31	'Pongo' Waring (Aston Villa)	49
1931–32	'Dixie' Dean (Everton)	44
1932–33	Jack Bowers (Derby)	35
1933–34	Jack Bowers (Derby)	35
1934–35	Ted Drake (Arsenal)	42
1935–36	Raich Carter (Sunderland)	31
	Pat Glover (Grimsby)	31
	Bob Gurney (Sunderland)	31
1936–37	Freddie Steele (Stoke)	33
1937–38	Tommy Lawton (Everton)	28
1938–39	Tommy Lawton (Everton)	35
1939–46	*No competition*	
1946–47	Dennis Westcott (Wolverhampton)	37
1947–48	Ronnie Rooke (Arsenal)	33
1948–49	Willie Moir (Bolton)	25
1949–50	Dickie Davis (Sunderland)	25
1950–51	Stan Mortensen (Blackpool)	30
1951–52	George Robledo (Newcastle)	33
1952–53	Charlie Wayman (Preston)	24
1953–54	Jimmy Glazzard (Huddersfield)	29
1954–55	Ronnie Allen (West Bromwich)	27
1955–56	Nat Lofthouse (Bolton)	33
1956–57	John Charles (Leeds)	38
1957–58	Bobby Smith (Tottenham)	36
1958–59	Jimmy Greaves (Chelsea)	32
1959–60	Denis Viollet (Manchester U.)	32
1960–61	Jimmy Greaves (Chelsea)	41
1961–62	Ray Crawford (Ipswich Town)	33
1962–63	Jimmy Greaves (Tottenham)	37
1963–64	Jimmy Greaves (Tottenham)	35
1964–65	Andy McEvoy (Blackburn)	29
	Jimmy Greaves (Tottenham)	29
1965–66	Roger Hunt (Liverpool)	30
1966–67	Ron Davies (Southampton)	37
1967–68	George Best (Manchester U.)	28
	Ron Davies (Southampton)	28
1968–69	Jimmy Greaves (Tottenham)	27
1969–70	Jeff Astle (West Bromwich)	25
1970–71	Tony Brown (West Bromwich)	28
1971–72	Francis Lee (Manchester C.)	33
1972–73	Bryan Robson (West Ham)	28
1973–74	Mike Channon (Southampton)	21

Below: Ever so happy Liverpool. They have made sure of the 1965–66 League Championship.

NAMES OF CLUBS

Clubs are represented in the statistical tables by the names by which they were known at the time. Those names used which differ from the club's modern name are:

Birmingham, now Birmingham City
Chesterfield Town, now Chesterfield
Clapton Orient, now Orient
Leeds City, now Leeds United
Leicester Fosse, now Leicester City
Leyton Orient, now Orient
Newton Heath, now Manchester United
Rotherham County, now Rotherham United
Small Heath, now Birmingham City
Stoke, now Stoke City
The Wednesday, now Sheffield Wednesday
Walsall Town Swifts, now Walsall
Woolwich Arsenal, now Arsenal

LEADING GOALSCORERS
(Div. II from 1919-20)

1919–20	S. J. Taylor (Huddersfield)	35
1920–21	Syd Puddefoot (West Ham)	29
1921–22	Jimmy Broad (Stoke)	25
1922–23	H. Bedford (Blackpool)	32
1923–24	H. Bedford (Blackpool)	34
1924–25	Arthur Chandler (Leicester)	33
1925–26	R. Turnbull (Chelsea)	39
1926–27	George Camsell (Middlesbrough)	59
1927–28	Jimmy Cookson (West Bromwich)	38
1928–29	Jimmy Hampson (Blackpool)	40
1929–30	Jimmy Hampson (Blackpool)	45
1930–31	'Dixie' Dean (Everton)	39
1931–32	Cyril Pearce (Swansea)	35
1932–33	E. Harper (Preston)	37
1933–34	'Pat' Glover (Grimsby)	42
1934–35	J. Milsom (Bolton)	31
1935–36	Jock Dodds (Sheffield U.)	34
	Bob Finan (Blackpool)	34
1936–37	Jack Bowers (Leicester)	33
1937–38	G. Henson (Bradford)	27
1938–39	Hugh Billington (Luton)	28
1939–46	No competition	
1946–47	Charlie Wayman (Newcastle)	30
1947–48	Eddie Quigley (Sheffield Wed.)	23
1948–49	Charlie Wayman (Southampton)	32
1949–50	Tommy Briggs (Grimsby)	35
1950–51	Cecil McCormack (Barnsley)	33
1951–52	Derek Dooley (Sheffield Wed.)	46
1952–53	Arthur Rowley (Leicester)	39
1953–54	John Charles (Leeds)	42
1954–55	Tommy Briggs (Blackburn)	33
1955–56	Bill Gardiner (Leicester)	34
1956–57	Arthur Rowley (Leicester)	44
1957–58	Brian Clough (Middlesbrough)	40
1958–59	Brian Clough (Middlesbrough)	42
1959–60	Brian Clough (Middlesbrough)	39
1960–61	Ray Crawford (Ipswich)	39
1961–62	Roger Hunt (Liverpool)	41
1962–63	Bobby Tambling (Chelsea)	35
1963–64	Ron Saunders (Portsmouth)	33
1964–65	George O'Brien (Southampton)	32
1965–66	Martin Chivers (Southampton)	30
1966–67	Derek Dougan (Leicester; Wolves)	25
1967–68	John Hickton (Middlesbrough)	24
1968–69	John Toshack (Cardiff)	22
1969–70	John Hickton (Middlesbrough)	24
1970–71	Malcolm Macdonald (Luton)	24
	John Hickton (Middlesbrough)	24
1971–72	Bob Latchford (Birmingham)	23
1972–73	Don Givens (QPR)	23
1973–74	Duncan McKenzie (Nottingham Forest)	26

Below: Ipswich are foiled by the Aston Villa goalkeeper in 1962, when they won the Championship in their first season of Division I football.

1950–51[6]	Tottenham H.	60	Manchester U.	56	Blackpool 50
1951–52[6]	Manchester U.	57	*Tottenham H.	53	Arsenal 53
1952–53[6]	*Arsenal	54	Preston N. End	54	Wolverhampton W. 51
1953–54[6]	Wolverhampton W.	57	West Bromwich A.	53	Huddersfield T. 51
1954–55[6]	Chelsea	52	*Wolverhampton W.	48	*Portsmouth 48
1955–56[6]	Manchester U.	60	*Blackpool	49	Wolverhampton W. 49
1956–57[6]	Manchester U.	64	*Tottenham H.	56	Preston N. End 56
1957–58[6]	Wolverhampton W.	64	Preston N. End	59	Tottenham H. 51
1958–59[6]	Wolverhampton W.	61	Manchester U.	55	*Arsenal 50
1959–60[6]	Burnley	55	Wolverhampton W.	54	Tottenham H. 53
1960–61[6]	Tottenham H.	66	Sheffield Wed.	58	Wolverhampton W. 57
1961–62[6]	Ipswich Town	56	Burnley	53	Tottenham H. 52
1962–63[6]	Everton	61	Tottenham H.	55	Burnley 54
1963–64[6]	Liverpool	57	Manchester U.	53	Everton 52
1964–65[6]	*Manchester U.	61	Leeds United	61	Chelsea 56
1965–66[6]	Liverpool	61	*Leeds United	55	Burnley 55
1966–67[6]	Manchester U.	60	*Nottingham Forest	56	Tottenham H. 56
1967–68[6]	Manchester City	58	Manchester U.	56	Liverpool 55
1968–69[6]	Leeds United	67	Liverpool	61	Everton 57
1969–70[6]	Everton	66	Leeds United	57	Chelsea 55
1970–71[6]	Arsenal	65	Leeds United	64	*Tottenham H. 52
1971–72[6]	Derby County	58	*Leeds United	57	*Liverpool 57
1972–73	Liverpool	60	Arsenal	57	Leeds United 53
1973–74[6]	Leeds United	62	Liverpool	57	Derby County 48

* Place won on goal average.   Maximum points: [3]60; [4]68; [5]76; [6]84.

SECOND DIVISION

	First	Pts	Second	Pts	Third	Pts
1892–93[1]	Small Heath	36	†Sheffield United	35	†Darwen	30
1893–94[2]	†Liverpool	50	†Small Heath	42	Notts County	39
1894–95[3]	†Bury	48	Notts County	39	Newton Heath	38
1895–96[3]	†Liverpool	46	Manchester City	46	Grimsby Town	42
1896–97[3]	†Notts County	42	Newton Heath	39	Grimsby Town	38
1897–98[3]	†Burnley	48	†Newcastle United	45	Manchester City	39
	Automatic promotion and relegation					
1898–99[4]	Manchester City	52	Glossop N. End	46	Leicester Fosse	45
1899–1900[4]	The Wednesday	54	Bolton Wanderers	52	Small Heath	46
1900–01[4]	Grimsby Town	49	Small Heath	48	Burnley	44
1901–02[4]	West Bromwich A.	55	Middlesbrough	51	*Preston N. End	42
1902–03[4]	Manchester City	54	Small Heath	51	Woolwich Arsenal	48
1903–04[4]	Preston N. End	50	Woolwich Arsenal	49	Manchester U.	48
1904–05[4]	Liverpool	58	Bolton Wanderers	56	Manchester U.	53
1905–06[5]	Bristol City	66	Manchester U.	62	Chelsea	53
1906–07[5]	Nottingham Forest	60	Chelsea	57	Leicester Fosse	48
1907–08[5]	Bradford City	54	Leicester Fosse	52	Oldham Athletic	50
1908–09[5]	Bolton Wanderers	52	*Tottenham H.	51	West Bromwich A.	51
1909–10[5]	Manchester City	54	*Oldham Athletic	53	*Hull City	53
1910–11[5]	West Bromwich A.	53	Bolton Wanderers	51	Chelsea	49
1911–12[5]	*Derby County	54	Chelsea	54	Burnley	52
1912–13[5]	Preston N. End	53	Burnley	50	Birmingham	46
1913–14[5]	Notts County	53	*Bradford	49	Woolwich Arsenal	49
1914–15[5]	Derby County	53	Preston N. End	50	Barnsley	47
1915–19	*No competition*					
1919–20[6]	Tottenham H.	70	Huddersfield T.	64	Birmingham	56
1920–21[6]	*Birmingham	58	Cardiff City	58	Bristol City	51
1921–22[6]	Nottingham Forest	56	*Stoke	52	Barnsley	52
1922–23[6]	Notts County	53	*West Ham United	51	Leicester City	51
1923–24[6]	Leeds United	54	*Bury	51	Derby County	51
1924–25[6]	Leicester City	59	Manchester U.	57	Derby County	55
1925–26[6]	The Wednesday	60	Derby County	57	Chelsea	52
1926–27[6]	Middlesbrough	62	*Portsmouth	54	Manchester City	54
1927–28[6]	Manchester City	59	Leeds United	57	Chelsea	54
1928–29[6]	Middlesbrough	55	Grimsby Town	53	*Bradford	48
1929–30[6]	Blackpool	58	Chelsea	55	Oldham Athletic	53
1930–31[6]	Everton	61	West Bromwich A.	54	Tottenham H.	51
1931–32[6]	Wolverhampton W.	56	Leeds United	54	Stoke City	52
1932–33[6]	Stoke City	56	Tottenham H.	55	Fulham	50
1933–34[6]	Grimsby Town	59	Preston N. End	52	*Bolton Wanderers	51
1934–35[6]	Brentford	61	*Bolton Wanderers	56	West Ham United	56
1935–36[6]	Manchester U.	56	Charlton A.	55	*Sheffield United	52
1936–37[6]	Leicester City	56	Blackpool	55	Bury	52
1937–38[6]	Aston Villa	57	*Manchester U.	53	Sheffield United	53

Season	First	Pts	Second	Pts	Third	Pts
1938–39[6]	Blackburn Rovers	55	Sheffield United	54	Sheffield Wed.	53
1939–46	*No competition*					
1946–47[6]	Manchester City	62	Burnley	58	Birmingham City	55
1947–48[6]	Birmingham City	59	Newcastle United	56	Southampton	52
1948–49[6]	Fulham	57	West Bromwich A.	56	Southampton	55
1949–50[6]	Tottenham H.	61	*Sheffield Wed.	52	*Sheffield United	52
1950–51[6]	Preston N. End	57	Manchester City	52	Cardiff City	50
1951–52[6]	Sheffield Wed.	53	*Cardiff City	51	Birmingham City	51
1952–53[6]	Sheffield United	60	Huddersfield T.	58	Luton Town	52
1953–54[6]	*Leicester City	56	Everton	56	Blackburn Rovers	55
1954–55[6]	*Birmingham City	54	*Luton Town	54	Rotherham United	54
1955–56[6]	Sheffield Wed.	55	Leeds United	52	*Liverpool	48
1956–57[6]	Leicester City	61	Nottingham Forest	54	Liverpool	53
1957–58[6]	West Ham U.	57	Blackburn Rovers	56	Charlton A.	55
1958–59[6]	Sheffield Wed.	62	Fulham	60	*Sheffield United	53
1959–60[6]	Aston Villa	59	Cardiff City	58	*Liverpool	50
1960–61[6]	Ipswich Town	59	Sheffield United	58	Liverpool	52
1961–62[6]	Liverpool	62	Leyton Orient	54	Sunderland	53
1962–63[6]	Stoke City	53	*Chelsea	52	Sunderland	52
1963–64[6]	Leeds United	63	Sunderland	61	Preston N. End	56
1964–65[6]	Newcastle U.	57	Northampton Town	56	Bolton Wanderers	50
1965–66[6]	Manchester City	59	Southampton	54	Coventry City	53
1966–67[6]	Coventry City	59	Wolverhampton W.	58	Carlisle United	52
1967–68[6]	Ipswich Town	59	*Queen's Park R.	58	Blackpool	58
1968–69[6]	Derby County	63	Crystal Palace	56	Charlton A.	50
1969–70[6]	Huddersfield T.	60	Blackpool	53	Leicester City	51
1970–71[6]	Leicester City	59	Sheffield United	56	*Cardiff City	53
1971–72[6]	Norwich City	57	Birmingham City	56	Millwall	55
1972–73[6]	Burnley	62	Queen's Park R.	61	Aston Villa	50
1973–74[6]	Middlesbrough	65	Luton Town	50	Carlisle United	49

* Place won on goal average. † Promoted after test matches. Maximum points: [1]44; [2]56; [3]60; [4]68; [5]76; [6]84.

THIRD DIVISION

Season	First	Pts	Second	Pts	Third	Pts
1958–59	Plymouth Argyle	62	Hull City	61	Brentford	57
1959–60	Southampton	61	Norwich City	59	Shrewsbury Town	52
1960–61	Bury	68	Walsall	62	Queen's Park R.	60
1961–62	Portsmouth	65	Grimsby Town	62	Bournemouth & Boscombe A.	59
1962–63	Northampton T.	62	Swindon Town	58	Port Vale	54
1963–64	*Coventry City	60	Crystal Palace	60	Watford	58
1964–65	Carlisle United	60	Bristol City	59	Mansfield Town	56
1965–66	Hull City	69	Millwall	65	Queen's Park R.	57
1966–67	Queen's Park R.	67	Middlesbrough	55	Watford	54
1967–68	Oxford United	57	Bury	56	Shrewsbury Town	55
1968–69	*Watford	64	Swindon Town	64	Luton Town	61
1969–70	Orient	62	Luton Town	60	Bristol Rovers	56
1970–71	Preston N. End	61	Fulham	60	Halifax Town	56
1971–72	Aston Villa	70	Brighton & Hove A.	65	*Bournemouth & Boscombe A.	62
1972–73	Bolton Wanderers	61	Notts County	57	Blackburn Rovers	55
1973–74	Oldham Athletic	62	*Bristol Rovers	61	York City	61

* Place won on goal average. Maximum points: 92.

LEADING GOALSCORERS (Div. III)

Season	Player	Goals
1958–59	Eddie Towers (Brentford)	32
1959–60	Derek Reeves (Southampton)	39
1960–61	Tony Richards (Walsall)	36
1961–62	Cliff Holton (Watford; Northampton)	37
1962–63	G. Hudson (Coventry)	30
1963–64	Alf Biggs (Bristol Rovers)	30
1964–65	Ken Wagstaff (Mansfield; Hull)	35
1965–66	Les Allen (Queen's Park R.)	32
1966–67	Rodney Marsh (Queen's Park R.)	30
1967–68	Don Rogers (Swindon)	25
	Bobby Owen (Bury)	25
1968–69	Alex Dawson (Bury; Brighton)	24
1969–70	George Jones (Bury)	26
1970–71	Gerry Ingram (Preston)	22
1971–72	Ted MacDougall (Bournemouth)	35
	Alf Wood (Shrewsbury)	35
1972–73	Bruce Bannister (Bristol R.)	25
	Arthur Horsfield (Charlton)	25
1973–74	Billy Jennings (Watford)	26

LEADING GOALSCORERS (Div. III South)

Season	Player	Goals
1920–21	J. Connor (Crystal Palace)	28
	E. Simms (Luton)	28
	G. Whitworth (Northampton)	28
1921–22	F. Richardson (Plymouth)	31
1922–23	F. Pagnam (Watford)	30
1923–24	W. Haines (Portsmouth)	28
1924–25	J. Fowler (Swansea)	28
1925–26	J. Cock (Plymouth)	32
1926–27	D. Morris (Swindon)	47
1927–28	D. Morris (Swindon)	38
1928–29	A. Rennie (Luton)	43
1929–30	G. Goddard (Queen's Park R.)	37
1930–31	P. Simpson (Crystal Palace)	46
1931–32	C. Bourton (Coventry)	49
1932–33	C. Bourton (Coventry)	40
1933–34	C. Pearce (Charlton)	26
1934–35	R. Allen (Charlton)	32
1935–36	A. Dawes (Crystal Palace)	38
1936–37	J. Payne (Luton)	55
1937–38	H. Crawshaw (Mansfield)	25
1938–39	G. Morton (Swindon)	28
1939–46	*No competition*	
1946–47	D. Clarke (Bristol City)	36
1947–48	L. Townsend (Bristol City)	29
1948–49	D. McGibbon (Bournemouth)	30
1949–50	T. Lawton (Notts County)	31
1950–51	W. Ardron (Nottingham F.)	36
1951–52	R. Blackburn (Reading)	39
1952–53	G. Bradford (Bristol Rovers)	33
1953–54	J. English (Northampton)	28
1954–55	E. Morgan (Gillingham)	31
1955–56	R. Collins (Torquay)	40
1956–57	E. Phillips (Ipswich)	41
1957–58	S. McGrory (Southend)	31
	D. Reeves (Southampton)	31

LEADING GOALSCORERS (Div. III North)

Season	Player	Goals
1921–22	J. Carmichael (Grimsby)	37
1922–23	G. Beel (Chesterfield)	23
	J. Carmichael (Grimsby)	23
1923–24	D. Brown (Darlington)	27
1924–25	D. Brown (Darlington)	39
1925–26	J. Cookson (Chesterfield)	44
1926–27	A. Whitehurst (Rochdale)	44
1927–28	J. Smith (Stockport)	38
1928–29	J. McConnell (Carlisle)	43
1929–30	F. Newton (Stockport)	36
1930–31	J. McConnell (Carlisle)	37
1931–32	B. Hall (Lincoln)	42

Left: One of the 13 penalties Francis Lee scored for Manchester City in the 1971–72 League season.

1932–33	W. McNaughton (Hull)	39
1933–34	A. Lythgoe (Stockport)	46
1934–35	G. Alsop (Walsall)	40
1935–36	R. Bell (Tranmere)	33
1936–37	E. Harston (Mansfield)	55
1937–38	J. Roberts (Port Vale)	28
1938–39	S. Hunt (Carlisle)	32
1939–46	*No competition*	
1946–47	C. Jordan (Doncaster)	41
1947–48	J. Hutchinson (Lincoln)	32
1948–49	W. Ardron (Rotherham)	29
1949–50	{ R. Phillips (Crewe)	26
	P. Doherty (Doncaster)	26
1950–51	J. Shaw (Rotherham)	37
1951–52	A. Graver (Lincoln)	36
1952–53	J. Whitehouse (Carlisle)	29
1953–54	G. Ashman (Carlisle)	30
	{ A. Bottom (York City)	30
1954–55	{ D. Travis (Oldham)	30
	{ J. Connor (Stockport)	30
1955–56	R. Crosbie (Grimsby)	36
1956–57	R. Straw (Derby)	37
1957–58	A. Ackerman (Carlisle)	35

Derek Dooley led the Second Division goalscoring list in 1951–52 before injury put paid to a promisingly prolific career.

LEADING GOALSCORERS (Div. IV)

1958–59	Arthur Rowley (Shrewsbury)	37
1959–60	Cliff Holton (Watford)	42
1960–61	Terry Bly (Peterborough)	52
1961–62	Bobby Hunt (Colchester)	37
1962–63	Ken Wagstaff (Mansfield)	34
1963–64	Hugh McIlmoyle (Carlisle)	39
1964–65	Alick Jeffrey (Doncaster)	36
1965–66	Kevin Hector (Bradford)	44
1966–67	Ernie Phythian (Hartlepools)	23
1967–68	{ Roy Chapman (Port Vale)	25
	{ Les Massie (Halifax)	25
1968–69	Gerry Talbot (Chester)	22
1969–70	Albert Kinsey (Wrexham)	27
1970–71	Ted MacDougall (Bournemouth)	42
1971–72	Peter Price (Peterborough)	28
1972–73	Fred Binney (Exeter)	27
1973–74	Brian Yeo (Gillingham)	31

THIRD DIVISION—SOUTH

	First	Pts	Second	Pts	Third	Pts
1920–21[1]	Crystal Palace	59	Southampton	54	Queen's Park R.	53
1921–22[1]	*Southampton	61	Plymouth Argyle	61	Portsmouth	53
1922–23[1]	Bristol City	59	*Plymouth Argyle	53	Swansea Town	53
1923–24[1]	Portsmouth	59	Plymouth Argyle	55	Millwall	54
1924–25[1]	Swansea Town	57	Plymouth Argyle	56	Bristol City	53
1925–26[1]	Reading	57	Plymouth Argyle	56	Millwall	53
1926–27[1]	Bristol City	62	Plymouth Argyle	60	Millwall	56
1927–28[1]	Millwall	65	Northampton Town	55	Plymouth Argyle	53
1928–29[1]	*Charlton A.	54	Crystal Palace	54	Northampton Town	52
1929–30[1]	Plymouth Argyle	68	Brentford	61	Queen's Park R.	51
1930–31[1]	Notts County	59	Crystal Palace	51	Brentford	50
1931–32[1]	Fulham	57	Reading	55	Southend United	53
1932–33[1]	Brentford	62	Exeter City	58	Norwich City	57
1933–34[1]	Norwich City	61	*Coventry City	54	Reading	54
1934–35[1]	Charlton A.	61	Reading	53	Coventry City	51
1935–36[1]	Coventry City	57	Luton Town	56	Reading	54
1936–37[1]	Luton Town	58	Notts County	56	Brighton & Hove A.	53
1937–38[1]	Millwall	56	Bristol City	55	Queen's Park R.	53
1938–39[1]	Newport County	55	Crystal Palace	52	Brighton & Hove A.	49
1939–46	*No competition*					
1946–47[1]	Cardiff City	66	Queen's Park R.	57	Bristol City	51
1947–48[1]	Queen's Park R.	61	Bournemouth & Boscombe A.	57	Walsall	51
1948–49[1]	Swansea Town	62	Reading	55	Bournemouth & Boscombe A.	52
1949–50[1]	Notts County	58	*Northampton Town	51	Southend United	51
1950–51[2]	Nottingham F.	70	Norwich City	64	Reading	57
1951–52[2]	Plymouth Argyle	66	*Reading	61	Norwich City	61
1952–53[2]	Bristol Rovers	64	*Millwall	62	Northampton Town	62
1953–54[2]	Ipswich Town	64	Brighton & Hove A.	61	Bristol City	56
1954–55[2]	Bristol City	70	Leyton Orient	61	Southampton	59
1955–56[2]	Leyton Orient	66	Brighton & Hove A.	65	Ipswich Town	64
1956–57[2]	*Ipswich Town	59	Torquay United	59	Colchester U.	58
1957–58[2]	Brighton & Hove A.	60	*Brentford	58	Plymouth Argyle	58

* Place won on goal average.   Maximum points: [1]84; [2]92.

THIRD DIVISION—NORTH

	First	Pts	Second	Pts	Third	Pts
1921–22[1]	Stockport County	56	*Darlington	50	Grimsby Town	50
1922–23[1]	Nelson	51	Bradford	47	Walsall	46
1923–24[2]	Wolverhampton W.	63	Rochdale	62	Chesterfield	54
1924–25[2]	Darlington	58	*Nelson	53	New Brighton	53
1925–26[2]	Grimsby Town	61	Bradford	60	Rochdale	59
1926–27[2]	Stoke City	63	Rochdale	58	Bradford	55
1927–28[2]	Bradford	63	Lincoln City	55	Stockport County	54
1928–29[2]	Bradford City	63	Stockport County	62	Wrexham	52
1929–30[2]	Port Vale	67	Stockport County	63	Darlington	50
1930–31[2]	Chesterfield	58	Lincoln City	57	Wrexham	54
1931–32[3]	*Lincoln City	57	Gateshead	57	Chester	50
1932–33[2]	Hull City	59	Wrexham	57	Stockport County	54
1933–34[2]	Barnsley	62	Chesterfield	61	Stockport County	59
1934–35[2]	Doncaster Rovers	57	Halifax Town	55	Chester	54
1935–36[2]	Chesterfield	60	*Chester	55	Tranmere Rovers	55
1936–37[2]	Stockport County	60	Lincoln City	57	Chester	53
1937–38[2]	Tranmere Rovers	56	Doncaster Rovers	54	Hull City	53
1938–39[2]	Barnsley	67	Doncaster Rovers	56	Bradford City	52
1939–46	*No competition*					
1946–47[2]	Doncaster Rovers	72	Rotherham United	64	Chester	56
1947–48[2]	Lincoln City	60	Rotherham United	59	Wrexham	50
1948–49[2]	Hull City	65	Rotherham United	62	Doncaster Rovers	50
1949–50[2]	Doncaster Rovers	55	Gateshead	53	Rochdale	51
1950–51[4]	Rotherham U.	71	Mansfield Town	64	Carlisle United	62
1951–52[4]	Lincoln City	69	Grimsby Town	66	Stockport County	59
1952–53[4]	Oldham Athletic	59	Port Vale	58	Wrexham	56
1953–54[4]	Port Vale	69	Barnsley	58	Scunthorpe U.	57
1954–55[4]	Barnsley	65	Accrington S.	61	Scunthorpe U.	58
1955–56[4]	Grimsby Town	68	Derby County	63	Accrington S.	59
1956–57[4]	Derby County	63	Hartlepools U.	59	Accrington S.	58
1957–58[4]	Scunthorpe U.	66	Accrington S.	59	Bradford City	57

* Place won on goal average.   Maximum points: [1]76; [2]84; [3]80; [4]92.

FOURTH DIVISION

	First	Pts	Second	Pts	Third	Pts	Fourth	Pts
1958–59	Port Vale	64	*Coventry City	60	York City	60	Shrewsbury Town	58
1959–60	Walsall	65	*Notts County	60	Torquay United	60	Watford	57
1960–61	Peterborough U.	66	Crystal Palace	64	*Northampton Town	60	Bradford	60
1961–62	Millwall	56	Colchester U.	55	Wrexham	53	Carlisle United	51
1962–63	Brentford	62	*Oldham Athletic	59	Crewe Alexandra	59	*Mansfield Town	57
1963–64	*Gillingham	60	Carlisle United	60	Workington Town	59	Exeter City	58
1964–65	Brighton & Hove A.	63	*Millwall	62	York City	62	Oxford United	61
1965–66	*Doncaster Rovers	59	Darlington	59	Torquay United	58	*Colchester U.	56
1966–67	Stockport County	64	*Southport	59	Barrow	59	Tranmere Rovers	58
1967–68	Luton Town	66	Barnsley	61	Hartlepools U.	60	Crewe Alexandra	58
1968–69	Doncaster Rovers	59	Halifax	57	*Rochdale	56	Bradford City	56
1969–70	Chesterfield	64	Wrexham	61	Swansea City	60	Port Vale	59
1970–71	Notts County	69	Bournemouth & Boscombe A.	60	Oldham Athletic	59	York City	56
1971–72	Grimsby Town	63	Southend U.	60	Brentford	59	Scunthorpe U.	57
1972–73	Southport	62	Hereford United	58	Cambridge United	57	*Aldershot	56
1973–74	Peterborough U.	65	Gillingham	62	Colchester U.	60	Bury	59

* Place won on goal average.   Maximum points: 92 (88 in 1961–62 owing to withdrawal of Accrington Stanley).

RELEGATED CLUBS

First Division

Relegated after test matches	Pts		Pts
1892–93 Notts County	24	Accrington	23
1893–94 Darwen	19	Newton Heath	14
1894–95 Liverpool	22		
1895–96 Small Heath	20		
1896–97 Burnley	19		
1897–98 Division extended to 18 clubs			
Automatic promotion and relegation			
1898–99 Bolton Wanderers	25	The Wednesday	24
1899–1900 Burnley	27	Glossop North End	18
1900–01 Preston North End	25	West Bromwich Albion	22
1901–02 Small Heath	30	Manchester City	28
1902–03 Grimsby Town	25	Bolton Wanderers	19
1903–04 Liverpool	26	West Bromwich Albion	24
1904–05 Division extended to 29 clubs: Bury (24) and Notts County (18) re-elected			
1905–06 Nottingham Forest	31	Wolverhampton Wanderers	23
1906–07 Derby County	27	Stoke	26
1907–08 Bolton Wanderers	33	Birmingham	30
1908–09 Manchester City	34	Leicester Fosse	25
1909–10 Chelsea	29	Bolton Wanderers	24
1910–11 Bristol City	27	Nottingham Forest	25
1911–12 Preston North End	33	Bury	21
1912–13 Notts County	23	Woolwich Arsenal	18
1913–14 Preston North End	30	Derby County	27
1914–15 Division extended to 22 clubs: Chelsea (29) re-elected, Tottenham Hotspur (28) relegated			
1919–20 Notts County	36	The Wednesday	23
1920–21 Derby County	26	Bradford	24
1921–22 Bradford City	32	Manchester United	28
1922–23 Stoke	30	Oldham Athletic	30
1923–24 *Chelsea	32	Middlesbrough	22
1924–25 Preston North End	26	Nottingham Forest	24
1925–26 Manchester City	35	Notts County	33
1926–27 Leeds United	30	West Bromwich Albion	30
1927–28 Tottenham Hotspur	38	Middlesbrough	37
1928–29 Bury	31	Cardiff City	29
1929–30 *Burnley	36	Everton	35
1930–31 Leeds United	31	Manchester United	22
1931–32 Grimsby Town	32	West Ham United	31
1932–33 Bolton Wanderers	33	Blackpool	33
1933–34 Newcastle United	34	Sheffield United	31
1934–35 Leicester City	33	Tottenham Hotspur	30
1935–36 Aston Villa	35	Blackburn Rovers	33
1936–37 Manchester United	32	Sheffield Wednesday	30
1937–38 Manchester City	36	West Bromwich Albion	36
1938–39 Birmingham	32	Leicester City	29
1939–46 No competition			
1946–47 Brentford	25	Leeds United	18
1947–48 Blackburn Rovers	32	Grimsby Town	22
1948–49 Preston North End	33	Sheffield United	33
1949–50 Manchester City	29	Birmingham City	28
1950–51 *Sheffield Wednesday	32	*Everton	32
1951–52 Huddersfield Town	28	Fulham	27
1952–53 Stoke City	34	Derby County	32
1953–54 Middlesbrough	30	Liverpool	28
1954–55 Leicester City	35	Sheffield Wednesday	26
1955–56 *Huddersfield Town	35	Sheffield United	33
1956–57 Cardiff City	29	Charlton Athletic	22
1957–58 *Sunderland	32	Sheffield Wednesday	31
1958–59 Aston Villa	30	Portsmouth	21
1959–60 Leeds United	34	Luton Town	30
1960–61 Newcastle United	32	Preston North End	30
1961–62 Cardiff City	32	Chelsea	28
1962–63 Manchester City	31	Leyton Orient	21
1963–64 Bolton Wanderers	28	Ipswich Town	25
1964–65 Wolverhampton Wanderers	30	Birmingham City	27
1965–66 Northampton Town	33	Blackburn Rovers	20
1966–67 Aston Villa	29	Blackpool	21
1967–68 Sheffield United	32	Fulham	27

1968–69	Leicester City	30	Queen's Park Rangers	18
1969–70	Sunderland	26	Sheffield Wednesday	25
1970–71	Burnley	27	Blackpool	23
1971–72	Nottingham Forest	25	Huddersfield Town	25
1972–73	Crystal Palace	30	West Bromwich Albion	28
1973–74	Southampton 36, Manchester United 32, Norwich City 29.			

* Relegated on goal average

Second Division

		Pts		Pts
1920–21	Stockport County	30		
1921–22	Bradford	33	Bristol City	33
1922–23	Rotherham County	35	Wolverhampton Wanderers	27
1923–24	Nelson	33	Bristol City	29
1924–25	Crystal Palace	34	Coventry City	31
1925–26	Stoke City	32	Stockport County	25
1926–27	Darlington	30	Bradford City	23
1927–28	Fulham	33	Gateshead	23
1928–29	Port Vale	34	Leyton Orient	32
1929–30	*Hull City	35	Notts County	33
1930–31	Reading	30	Cardiff City	25
1931–32	*Barnsley	33	Bristol City	23
1932–33	Chesterfield	34	Charlton Athletic	31
1933–34	Millwall	33	Lincoln City	26
1934–35	Oldham Athletic	26	Notts County	25
1935–36	Port Vale	32	Hull City	20
1936–37	Bradford City	30	Doncaster Rovers	24
1937–38	*Barnsley	36	Stockport County	31
1938–39	*Norwich City	31	Tranmere Rovers	17
1939–46	No competition			
1946–47	Swansea Town	29	Newport County	23
1947–48	Doncaster Rovers	29	Millwall	29
1948–49	Nottingham Forest	35	Lincoln City	28
1949–50	Plymouth Argyle	32	Bradford	31
1950–51	Chesterfield	30	Grimsby Town	28
1951–52	Coventry City	34	Queen's Park Rangers	34
1952–53	Southampton	33	Barnsley	18
1953–54	Brentford	31	Oldham Athletic	25
1954–55	Ipswich Town	28	Derby County	23
1955–56	Plymouth Argyle	28	Hull City	26
1956–57	Bury	25	Port Vale	22
1957–58	Notts County	30	Doncaster Rovers	27
1958–59	Grimsby Town	28	Barnsley	27
1959–60	Hull City	30	Bristol City	27
1960–61	Portsmouth	33	Lincoln City	24
1961–62	Bristol Rovers	33	Brighton & Hove Albion	31
1962–63	*Walsall	31	Luton Town	29
1963–64	*Grimsby Town	32	Scunthorpe United	30
1964–65	Swindon Town	33	Swansea Town	32
1965–66	Middlesbrough	33	Leyton Orient	23
1966–67	Northampton Town	30	Bury	28
1967–68	Rotherham United	31	Plymouth Argyle	27
1968–69	Bury	30	Fulham	25
1969–70	Aston Villa	29	Preston North End	28
1970–71	Blackburn Rovers	27	Bolton Wanderers	24
1971–72	Charlton Athletic	33	Watford	19
1972–73	*Huddersfield Town	33	Brighton & Hove Albion	29
1973–74	Crystal Palace 34, Preston North End 31, Swindon Town 25.			

* Relegated on goal average

Third Division

		Pts		Pts		Pts		Pts
1958–59	Stockport County	36	Doncaster Rovers	33	Notts County	29	Rochdale	28
1959–60	York City	38	Mansfield Town	36	Wrexham	36	Accrington Stanley	27
1960–61	Tranmere Rovers	38	Bradford City	36	Colchester United	33	Chesterfield	32
1961–62	Torquay United	36	Lincoln City	35	Brentford	34	Newport County	22
1962–63	*Bradford	40	Brighton & Hove Albion	36	Carlisle United	35	Halifax Town	30
1963–64	Millwall	38	Crewe Alexandra	34	Wrexham	32	Notts County	27
1964–65	Luton Town	33	Port Vale	32	Colchester United	30	Barnsley	29
1965–66	Southend United	36	Exeter City	35	Brentford	32	York City	27
1966–67	Swansea Town	39	Darlington	37	Doncaster Rovers	32	Workington	31
1967–68	Grimsby Town	37	Colchester United	33	Scunthorpe United	32	†Peterborough United	
1968–69	Northampton Town	40	Hartlepools United	39	Crewe Alexandra	35	Oldham Athletic	35
1969–70	Bournemouth & Boscombe Athletic	39	Southport	38	Barrow	30	Stockport County	23
1970–71	*Reading	39	Bury	37	Doncaster Rovers	35	Gillingham	33
1971–72	*Mansfield Town	36	*Barnsley	36	Torquay United	32	Bradford	32
1972–73	*Rotherham United	41	Brentford	37	Swansea City	37	Scunthorpe United	30
1973–74	Cambridge United	35	Shrewsbury Town	31	Southport	28	Rochdale	21

* Relegated on goal average

APPLICATIONS FOR RE-ELECTION

The system of the bottom clubs retiring and then seeking re-election to the Football League is as old as the League itself. In the early days, the bottom four clubs had to apply, and from 1893 it was the bottom four in Division II. Some years there were instances of more than four clubs retiring and applying. In 1896 the number was reduced to three and in 1909 to the bottom two. With the introduction of the two-tiered Third Division in 1921, the bottom two clubs in each of the Third Divisions had to retire and apply. From 1958, it has been the last four in Division IV.

Barrow and Cambridge United (white) meet in a 1971–72 Fourth Division encounter. For Barrow, the season was their last in the Football League . . . for some time anyway. Not re-elected, they were replaced by Hereford United.

1888–89	Burnley, Derby County, Notts County, Stoke
1889–90	Bolton Wanderers, Notts County, Burnley, Stoke (replaced by Sunderland)
1890–91	Aston Villa, Accrington, Derby County, West Bromwich Albion
1891–92	Accrington, West Bromwich Albion, Stoke, Darwen (re-elected to new Division II)
1892–93	Bootle (not re-elected), Lincoln City, Walsall Town Swifts, Crewe Alexandra, Ardwick (re-elected as Manchester City), Rotherham Town, Northwich Victoria (not re-elected). *Division extended*
1893–94	Middlesbrough Ironopolis (not re-elected), Crewe Alexandra, Ardwick (re-elected as Manchester City), Rotherham Town, Northwich Victoria (not re-elected). *Division extended*
1894–95	Lincoln City, Walsall Town Swifts (replaced by Loughborough Town), Port Vale, Crewe Alexandra
1895–96	Rotherham Town, Port Vale, and Crewe Alexandra. None was re-elected and they were replaced by Blackpool, Gainsborough Trinity, and Walsall
1896–97	Burton United, Burton Wanderers (replaced by Luton Town), Lincoln City
1897–98	Lincoln City, Darwen, Loughborough Town
1898–99	Blackpool, Loughborough Town, Darwen. Blackpool and Darwen were replaced by Chesterfield and Middlesbrough
1899–1900	Barnsley, Luton Town, Loughborough Town, Luton Town and Loughborough Town were replaced by Blackpool and Stockport County
1900–01	Walsall, Stockport County, Burton United, (New Brighton resigned). Walsall and New Brighton were replaced by Doncaster Rovers and Bristol City
1901–02	Chesterfield, Stockport County, Gainsborough Trinity
1902–03	Doncaster Rovers (replaced by Bradford City), Stockport County, Burnley
1903–04	Stockport County (replaced by Doncaster Rovers), Glossop North End, Leicester Fosse
1904–05	Port Vale, Burton United, Doncaster Rovers (not re-elected). *Division extended*
1905–06	Chesterfield Town, Burton United, Clapton Orient
1906–07	Chesterfield Town, Lincoln City, Burton United, (Port Vale resigned). Burton United and Port Vale were replaced by Fulham and Oldham Athletic
1907–08	Grimsby Town, Chesterfield Town, Lincoln City, (Stoke resigned). Lincoln City and Stoke were replaced by Bradford and Tottenham Hotspur
1908–09	Chesterfield Town (replaced by Lincoln City), Blackpool
1909–10	Grimsby Town (replaced by Huddersfield Town), Birmingham
1910–11	Barnsley, Lincoln City (replaced by Grimsby Town)
1911–12	Leeds City, Gainsborough Trinity (replaced by Lincoln City)
1912–13	Stockport County, Blackpool
1913–14	Lincoln City, Nottingham Forest
1914–15	Leicester Fosse, Glossop North End (resigned after World War I)
1915–19	*No competition. Division extended in 1919*
1919–20	Lincoln City (replaced by Cardiff City), Grimsby Town (re-elected to new Division III)
1920–21	Brentford, Gillingham
1921–22	Exeter City, Southend United, Halifax Town, Rochdale
1922–23	Aberdare Athletic, Newport County, Ashington, Durham City, (Stalybridge Celtic resigned). *Division III(N) extended*
1923–24	Bournemouth & Boscombe Athletic, Queen's Park Rangers, Hartlepools United, Barrow
1924–25	Brentford, Merthyr Tydfil, Tranmere Rovers, Rotherham United
1925–26	Charlton Athletic, Queen's Park Rangers, Walsall, Barrow
1926–27	Watford, Aberdare Athletic (replaced by Torquay United), Accrington Stanley, Barrow
1927–28	Merthyr Tydfil, Torquay United, Durham City (replaced by Carlisle United), Nelson
1928–29	Exeter City, Gillingham, Hartlepools United, Ashington (replaced by York City)
1929–30	Gillingham, Merthyr Tydfil (replaced by Thames), Halifax Town, Barrow
1930–31	Newport County (replaced by Mansfield Town), Norwich City, Rochdale, Nelson (replaced by Chester)
1931–32	Gillingham, New Brighton, Rochdale, (Thames did not seek re-election: replaced by Newport County)
1932–33	Newport County, Swindon Town, New Brighton, Darlington
1933–34	Bournemouth & Boscombe Athletic, Cardiff City, Rotherham United, Rochdale
1934–35	Southend United, Newport County, Southport, Carlisle United
1935–36	Newport County, Exeter City, Southport, New Brighton
1936–37	Exeter City, Aldershot, Gateshead, Darlington
1937–38	Walsall, Gillingham (replaced by Ipswich Town), Barrow, Accrington Stanley
1938–39	Walsall, Bristol Rovers, Hartlepools United, Accrington Stanley
1939–46	*No competition*
1946–47	Norwich City, Mansfield Town, Southport, Halifax Town
1947–48	Norwich City, Brighton and Hove Albion, Halifax Town, New Brighton
1948–49	Aldershot, Crystal Palace, Southport, Bradford City
1949–50	Newport County, Millwall, Halifax Town, York City
	Division III extended
1950–51	Watford, Crystal Palace, Accrington Stanley, New Brighton (replaced by Workington Town)
1951–52	Exeter City, Walsall, Darlington, Workington Town
1952–53	Shrewsbury Town, Walsall, Workington Town, Accrington Stanley
1953–54	Colchester United, Walsall, Halifax Town, Chester
1954–55	Walsall, Colchester United, Grimsby Town, Chester
1955–56	Crystal Palace, Swindon Town, Bradford, Crewe Alexandra
1956–57	Swindon Town, Norwich City, Tranmere Rovers, Crewe Alexandra
1958–59	Oldham Athletic, Aldershot, Barrow, Southport
1959–60	Southport, Gateshead (replaced by Peterborough United), Oldham Athletic, Hartlepools United
1960–61	Exeter City, Barrow, Hartlepools United, Chester
1961–62	Doncaster Rovers, Hartlepools United, Chester, (Accrington Stanley resigned; replaced by Oxford United)
1962–63	Chester, Lincoln City, Bradford City, Hartlepools United
1963–64	Southport, York City, Hartlepools United, Barrow
1964–65	Barrow, Lincoln City, Halifax Town, Stockport County
1965–66	Rochdale, Lincoln City, Bradford City, Wrexham
1966–67	Rochdale, York City, Bradford, Lincoln City
1967–68	York City, Chester, Workington Town, Bradford. (Port Vale forced to seek re-election because of malpractices)
1967–68	York City, Chester, Workington Town, Bradford. (Port Vale forced to seek re-election because of malpractices)
1968–69	York City, Newport County, Grimsby Town, Bradford
1969–70	Newport County, Darlington, Hartlepools United, Bradford (replaced by Cambridge United)
1970–71	Lincoln City, Newport County, Hartlepool, Barrow
1971–72	Northampton Town, Barrow (replaced by Hereford United), Stockport County, Crewe Alexandra
1972–73	Crewe Alexandra, Northampton Town, Colchester United, Darlington
1973–74	Crewe Alexandra, Doncaster Rovers, Workington Town, Stockport County

Right: Johnny Dixon with the FA Cup in 1957, after Aston Villa had beaten Manchester United 2–1 and chalked up a record seven wins in the competition.

FA CUP

Year	Venue				
1872	Kennington Oval	Wanderers	1	Royal Engineers	0
1873	Lillie Bridge	Wanderers	2	Oxford University	0
1874	Kennington Oval	Oxford University	2	Royal Engineers	0
1875	Kennington Oval	Royal Engineers	1	Old Etonians	1
	Kennington Oval		2		0
1876	Kennington Oval	Wanderers	0	Old Etonians	0
	Kennington Oval		3		0
1877	Kennington Oval	*Wanderers	2	Oxford University	0
1878	Kennington Oval	Wanderers	3	Royal Engineers	1
1879	Kennington Oval	Old Etonians	1	Clapham Rovers	0
1880	Kennington Oval	Clapham Rovers	1	Oxford University	0
1881	Kennington Oval	Old Carthusians	3	Old Etonians	0
1882	Kennington Oval	Old Etonians	1	Blackburn Rovers	0
1883	Kennington Oval	*Blackburn Olympic	2	Old Etonians	1
1884	Kennington Oval	Blackburn Rovers	2	Queen's Park	1
1885	Kennington Oval	Blackburn Rovers	2	Queen's Park	0
1886	Kennington Oval	Blackburn Rovers	0	West Bromwich A.	0
	Derby		2		0
1887	Kennington Oval	Aston Villa	2	West Bromwich A.	0
1888	Kennington Oval	West Bromwich A.	2	Preston N. End	1
1889	Kennington Oval	Preston N. End	3	Wolverhampton W.	0
1890	Kennington Oval	Blackburn Rovers	6	The Wednesday	1
1891	Kennington Oval	Blackburn Rovers	3	Notts County	1
1892	Kennington Oval	West Bromwich A.	3	Aston Villa	0
1893	Fallowfield	Wolverhampton W.	1	Everton	0
1894	Goodison Park	Notts County	4	Bolton Wanderers	1
1895	Crystal Palace	Aston Villa	1	West Bromwich A.	0
1896	Crystal Palace	The Wednesday	2	Wolverhampton W.	1
1897	Crystal Palace	Aston Villa	3	Everton	2
1898	Crystal Palace	Nottingham Forest	3	Derby County	1
1899	Crystal Palace	Sheffield United	4	Derby County	1
1900	Crystal Palace	Bury	4	Southampton	0
1901	Crystal Palace	Tottenham Hotspur	2	Sheffield United	2
	Bolton		3		1
1902	Crystal Palace	Sheffield United	1	Southampton	1
	Crystal Palace		2		1
1903	Crystal Palace	Bury	6	Derby County	0
1904	Crystal Palace	Manchester City	1	Bolton Wanderers	0
1905	Crystal Palace	Aston Villa	2	Newcastle United	0
1906	Crystal Palace	Everton	1	Newcastle United	0
1907	Crystal Palace	The Wednesday	2	Everton	1
1908	Crystal Palace	Wolverhampton W.	3	Newcastle United	1
1909	Crystal Palace	Manchester United	1	Bristol City	0
1910	Crystal Palace	Newcastle United	1	Barnsley	1
	Goodison Park		2		0
1911	Crystal Palace	Bradford City	0	Newcastle United	0
	Old Trafford		1		0
1912	Crystal Palace	Barnsley	0	West Bromwich A.	0
	Bramall Lane	*	1		0
1913	Crystal Palace	Aston Villa	1	Sunderland	0
1914	Crystal Palace	Burnley	1	Liverpool	0
1915	Old Trafford	Sheffield United	3	Chelsea	0
1916–19	*No competition*				
1920	Stamford Bridge	*Aston Villa	1	Huddersfield Town	0

Top: Nat Lofthouse scores his and Bolton Wanderers' first against Manchester United in the 1958 Cup final.
Centre: Denis Law is thwarted by brave Gordon Banks in 1963, when Manchester United beat Leicester City 3–1. Leicester were losing finalists three times in the 1960s.
Above: Jackie Charlton rises above the Chelsea defence to put Leeds ahead in the 1970 final.

Below: Bury (white shirts) and Southampton meet at Crystal Palace in 1900. Bury won 4–0, and three years later beat Derby County 6–0, the largest winning margin in a final in the first 100 years of the FA Cup.

Year	Venue		Score		Score
1921	Stamford Bridge	Tottenham Hotspur	1	Wolverhampton W.	0
1922	Stamford Bridge	Huddersfield Town	1	Preston N. End	0
1923	Wembley	Bolton Wanderers	2	West Ham United	0
1924	Wembley	Newcastle United	2	Aston Villa	0
1925	Wembley	Sheffield United	1	Cardiff City	0
1926	Wembley	Bolton Wanderers	1	Manchester City	0
1927	Wembley	Cardiff City	1	Arsenal	0
1928	Wembley	Blackburn Rovers	3	Huddersfield Town	1
1929	Wembley	Bolton Wanderers	2	Portsmouth	0
1930	Wembley	Arsenal	2	Huddersfield Town	0
1931	Wembley	West Bromwich A.	2	Birmingham	1
1932	Wembley	Newcastle United	2	Arsenal	1
1933	Wembley	Everton	3	Manchester City	0
1934	Wembley	Manchester City	2	Portsmouth	1
1935	Wembley	Sheffield Wed.	4	West Bromwich A.	2
1936	Wembley	Arsenal	1	Sheffield United	0
1937	Wembley	Sunderland	3	Preston N. End	1
1938	Wembley	*Preston N. End	1	Huddersfield Town	0
1939	Wembley	Portsmouth	4	Wolverhampton W.	1
1940–45	*No competition*				
1946	Wembley	*Derby County	4	Charlton Athletic	1
1947	Wembley	*Charlton Athletic	1	Burnley	0
1948	Wembley	Manchester United	4	Blackpool	2
1949	Wembley	Wolverhampton W.	3	Leicester City	1
1950	Wembley	Arsenal	2	Liverpool	0
1951	Wembley	Newcastle United	2	Blackpool	0
1952	Wembley	Newcastle United	1	Arsenal	0
1953	Wembley	Blackpool	4	Bolton Wanderers	3
1954	Wembley	West Bromwich A.	3	Preston N. End	2
1955	Wembley	Newcastle United	3	Manchester City	1
1956	Wembley	Manchester City	3	Birmingham City	1
1957	Wembley	Aston Villa	2	Manchester United	1
1958	Wembley	Bolton Wanderers	2	Manchester United	0
1959	Wembley	Nottingham Forest	2	Luton Town	1
1960	Wembley	Wolverhampton W.	3	Blackburn Rovers	0
1961	Wembley	Tottenham Hotspur	2	Leicester City	0
1962	Wembley	Tottenham Hotspur	3	Burnley	1
1963	Wembley	Manchester United	3	Leicester City	1
1964	Wembley	West Ham United	3	Preston N. End	2
1965	Wembley	*Liverpool	2	Leeds United	1
1966	Wembley	Everton	3	Sheffield Wed.	2
1967	Wembley	Tottenham Hotspur	2	Chelsea	1
1968	Wembley	*West Bromwich A.	1	Everton	0
1969	Wembley	Manchester City	1	Leicester City	0
1970	Wembley	Chelsea	2	Leeds United	2
	Old Trafford	*	2		1
1971	Wembley	*Arsenal	2	Liverpool	1
1972	Wembley	Leeds United	1	Arsenal	0
1973	Wembley	Sunderland	1	Leeds United	0
1974	Wembley	Liverpool	3	Newcastle United	0

FA CHARITY SHIELD

Year		Score		Score
1908	*Manchester U.	1	‡Queen's Park R.	1
		4		0
1909	*Newcastle U.	2	‡Northampton Town	0
1910	‡Brighton & Hove A.	1	*Aston Villa	0
1911	*Manchester U.	8	‡Swindon Town	4
1912	*Blackburn Rovers	2	‡Queen's Park R.	1
1913	Professionals	7	Amateurs	2
1920	*West Bromwich A.	2	§Tottenham Hotspur	0
1921	†Tottenham H.	2	*Burnley	0
1922	†Huddersfield T.	1	*Liverpool	0
1923	Professionals	2	Amateurs	0
1924	Professionals	3	Amateurs	1
1925	Amateurs	6	Professionals	1
1926	Amateurs	6	Professionals	3
1927	†Cardiff City	2	Corinthians	1
1928	*Everton	2	†Blackburn Rovers	1
1929	Professionals	3	Amateurs	0
1930	†Arsenal	2	*Sheffield Wed.	1
1931	*Arsenal	1	†West Bromwich A.	0
1932	*Everton	5	†Newcastle U.	3
1933	*Arsenal	3	†Everton	0
1934	*Arsenal	4	†Manchester City	0
1935	†Sheffield Wed.	1	*Arsenal	0
1936	*Sunderland	2	†Arsenal	1
1937	*Manchester City	2	†Sunderland	0
1938	*Arsenal	2	†Preston N. End	1
1948	*Arsenal	4	†Manchester U.	3
1949	*Portsmouth	1	†Wolverhampton W.	1
1950	World Cup XI	4	FA XI	2
1951	*Tottenham H.	2	†Newcastle U.	1
1952	*Manchester U.	4	†Newcastle U.	2
1953	*Arsenal	3	†Blackpool	1
1954	*Wolverhampton W.	4	†West Bromwich A.	4
1955	*Chelsea	3	†Newcastle U.	0
1956	*Manchester U.	1	†Manchester City	0
1957	*Manchester U.	4	†Aston Villa	0
1958	†Bolton W.	4	*Wolverhampton W.	1
1959	*Wolverhampton W.	3	†Nottingham Forest	1
1960	*Burnley	2	†Wolverhampton W.	2
1961	*†Tottenham H.	3	FA XI	2
1962	†Tottenham H.	5	*Ipswich Town	1
1963	*Everton	·	†Manchester U.	0
1964	*Liverpool	2	†West Ham U.	2
1965	*Manchester U.	2	†Liverpool	2
1966	*Liverpool	1	†Everton	0
1967	*Manchester U.	3	†Tottenham H.	3
1968	*Manchester City	6	†West Bromwich A.	1
1969	*Leeds United	2	†Manchester City	1
1970	*Everton	2	†Chelsea	1
1971	§Leicester City	1	¶Liverpool	0
1972	Manchester City	1	Aston Villa	0
1973	Burnley	1	Manchester City	0
1974[1]	†Liverpool	1	*Leeds United	1

* League Champions.
† FA Cup Winners.
‡ Southern League Champions.
§ Second Division Champions.
¶ FA Cup runners-up.
[1] Won on penalties.

FOOTBALL LEAGUE CUP

Two-legged final

Season				Score
1960–61	Aston Villa	0 : 3*	†Rotherham United	2 : 0
1961–62	Norwich City	3 : 1	†Rochdale	0 : 0
1962–63	†Birmingham City	3 : 0	Aston Villa	1 : 0
1963–64	Leicester City	1 : 3	†Stoke City	1 : 2
1964–65	†Chelsea	3 : 0	Leicester City	2 : 0
1965–66	West Bromwich A.	1 : 4	†West Ham United	2 : 1

Final at Wembley

Season		Score		Score
1966–67	Queen's Park R.	3	West Bromwich A.	2
1967–68	*Leeds United	1	Arsenal	0
1968–69	Swindon Town	3*	Arsenal	1
1969–70	Manchester City	2*	West Bromwich A.	1
1970–71	Tottenham Hotspur	2	Aston Villa	0
1971–72	Stoke City	2	Chelsea	1
1972–73	Tottenham Hotspur	1	Norwich City	0
1973–74	Wolverhampton W.	2	Manchester City	1

*After extra time. †Home team in 1st leg.

Below: Billy Bremner receives the FA Charity Shield after League Champions Leeds had beaten FA Cup winners Manchester City in 1969.

F–L

SCOTTISH LEAGUE

1890–91[1]	Dumbarton	29			Celtic	21
	Rangers	29				
1891–92[2]	Dumbarton	37	Celtic	35	Hearts	34
1892–93[1]	Celtic	29	Rangers	27	St Mirren	20

Maximum points: [1]36; [2]44

FIRST DIVISION

1893–94[1]	Celtic	29	Hearts	26	St Bernard's	23
1894–95[1]	Hearts	31	Celtic	26	Rangers	22
1895–96[1]	Celtic	30	Rangers	26	Hibernian	24
1896–97[1]	Hearts	28	Hibernian	26	Rangers	25
1897–98[1]	Celtic	33	Rangers	29	Hibernian	22
1898–99[1]	Rangers	36	Hearts	26	Celtic	24
1899–1900[1]	Rangers	32	Celtic	25	Hibernian	24
1900–01[3]	Rangers	35	Celtic	29	Hibernian	25
1901–02[1]	Rangers	28	Celtic	26	Hearts	22
1902–03[2]	Hibernian	37	Dundee	31	Rangers	29
1903–04[4]	Third Lanark	43	Hearts	39	Rangers	38
1904–05[4]	Celtic	41	Rangers	41	Third Lanark	35
1905–06[5]	Celtic	49	Hearts	43	Airdrieonians	38
1906–07[6]	Celtic	55	Dundee	48	Rangers	45
1907–08[6]	Celtic	55	Falkirk	51	Rangers	50
1908–09[6]	Celtic	51	Dundee	50	Clyde	48
1909–10[6]	Celtic	54	Falkirk	52	Rangers	46
1910–11[6]	Rangers	52	Aberdeen	48	Falkirk	44
1911–12[6]	Rangers	51	Celtic	45	Clyde	42
1912–13[6]	Rangers	53	Celtic	49	*Hearts	41
1913–14[7]	Celtic	65	Rangers	59	*Hearts	54
1914–15[7]	Celtic	65	Hearts	61	Rangers	50
1915–16[7]	Celtic	67	Rangers	56	Morton	51
1916–17[7]	Celtic	64	Morton	54	Rangers	53
1917–18[6]	Rangers	56	Celtic	55	*Kilmarnock	43
1918–19[6]	Celtic	58	Rangers	57	Morton	47
1919–20[8]	Rangers	71	Celtic	68	Motherwell	57
1920–21[8]	Rangers	76	Celtic	66	Hearts	56
1921–22[8]	Celtic	67	Rangers	66	Raith Rovers	56
1922–23[7]	Rangers	55	Airdrieonians	50	Celtic	40
1923–24[7]	Rangers	59	Airdrieonians	50	Celtic	41
1924–25[7]	Rangers	60	Airdrieonians	57	Hibernian	52
1925–26[7]	Celtic	58	*Airdrieonians	50	Hearts	50
1926–27[7]	Rangers	56	Motherwell	51	Celtic	49
1927–28[7]	Rangers	60	*Celtic	55	Motherwell	55
1928–29[7]	Rangers	67	Celtic	51	Motherwell	50
1929–30[7]	Rangers	60	Motherwell	55	Aberdeen	53
1930–31[7]	Rangers	60	Celtic	58	Motherwell	56
1931–32[7]	Motherwell	66	Rangers	61	Celtic	48
1932–33[7]	Rangers	62	Motherwell	59	Hearts	50
1933–34[7]	Rangers	66	Motherwell	62	Celtic	47
1934–35[7]	Rangers	55	Celtic	52	Hearts	50
1935–36[7]	Celtic	66	*Rangers	61	Aberdeen	61
1936–37[7]	Rangers	61	Aberdeen	54	Celtic	52
1937–38[7]	Celtic	61	Hearts	58	Rangers	49
1938–39[7]	Rangers	59	Celtic	48	Aberdeen	46
1939–46	*No competition*					
1946–47[6]	Rangers	46	Hibernian	44	Aberdeen	39
1947–48[5]	Hibernian	48	Rangers	46	Partick Thistle	36
1948–49[5]	Rangers	46	Dundee	45	Hibernian	39
1949–50[5]	Rangers	50	Hibernian	49	Hearts	43
1950–51[5]	Hibernian	48	*Rangers	38	Dundee	38
1951–52[5]	Hibernian	45	Rangers	41	East Fife	37
1952–53[5]	*Rangers	43	Hibernian	43	East Fife	39
1953–54[5]	Celtic	43	Hearts	38	Partick Thistle	35
1954–55[5]	Aberdeen	49	Celtic	46	Rangers	41
1955–56[6]	Rangers	52	Aberdeen	46	Hearts	45
1956–57[6]	Rangers	55	Hearts	53	Kilmarnock	42
1957–58[6]	Hearts	62	Rangers	49	Celtic	46
1958–59[6]	Rangers	50	Hearts	48	Motherwell	44
1959–60[6]	Hearts	54	Kilmarnock	50	Rangers	42
1960–61[6]	Rangers	51	Kilmarnock	50	Third Lanark	42
1961–62[6]	Dundee	54	Rangers	51	Celtic	46
1962–63[6]	Rangers	57	Kilmarnock	48	Partick Thistle	46
1963–64[6]	Rangers	55	Kilmarnock	49	Celtic	47
1964–65[6]	*Kilmarnock	50	Hearts	50	Dunfermline Ath.	49
1965–66[6]	Celtic	57	Rangers	55	Kilmarnock	45
1966–67[6]	Celtic	58	Rangers	55	Clyde	46
1967–68[6]	Celtic	63	Rangers	61	Hibernian	45
1968–69[6]	Celtic	54	Rangers	49	Dunfermline Ath.	45
1969–70[6]	Celtic	57	Rangers	45	Hibernian	44

LEADING GOALSCORERS
(Div. I from 1919–20)

1919–20	Hugh Ferguson (Motherwell)	33
1920–21	Hugh Ferguson (Motherwell)	43
1921–22	Dunky Walker (St Mirren)	45
1922–23	John White (Hearts)	30
1923–24	David Halliday (Dundee)	38
1924–25	Willie Devlin (Cowdenbeath)	33
1925–26	Willie Devlin (Cowdenbeath)	37
1926–27	Jimmy McGrory (Celtic)	49
1927–28	Jimmy McGrory (Celtic)	47
1928–29	E. Morrison (Falkirk)	43
1929–30	Benny Yorston (Aberdeen)	38
1930–31	Barney Battles (Hearts)	44
1931–32	Bill McFadyen (Motherwell)	52
1932–33	Bill McFadyen (Motherwell)	45
1933–34	J. Smith (Rangers)	41
1934–35	D. McCulloch (Hearts)	38
1935–36	Jimmy McGrory (Celtic)	50
1936–37	David Wilson (Hamilton)	34
1937–38	Andy Black (Hearts)	40
1938–39	Alex Venters (Rangers)	34
1939–1946	*No competition*	
1946–47	R. Mitchell (Third Lanark)	22
1947–48	A. Aikman (Falkirk)	20
1948–49	A. Stott (Dundee)	30
1949–50	Willie Bauld (Hearts)	30
1950–51	Lawrie Reilly (Hibernian)	22
1951–52	Lawrie Reilly (Hibernian)	27
1952–53	Lawrie Reilly (Hibernian)	30
	Charlie Fleming (East Fife)	30
1953–54	Jimmy Wardhaugh (Hearts)	27
1954–55	Willie Bauld (Hearts)	21
1955–56	Jimmy Wardhaugh (Hearts)	30
1956–57	H. Baird (Airdrieonians)	33
1957–58	Jimmy Wardhaugh (Hearts)	28
1958–59	Joe Baker (Hibernian)	25
1959–60	Joe Baker (Hibernian)	42
1960–61	J. Harley (Third Lanark)	42
1961–62	Alan Gilzean (Dundee)	24
1962–63	Jim Millar (Rangers)	25
1963–64	Alan Gilzean (Dundee)	32
1964–65	Jimmy Forrest (Rangers)	30
1965–66	Joe McBride (Celtic)	31
1966–67	Steve Chalmers (Celtic)	23
1967–68	Bobby Lennox (Celtic)	32
1968–69	Kenny Cameron (Dundee United)	27
1969–70	Colin Stein (Rangers)	24
1970–71	Harry Hood (Celtic)	22
1971–72	Joe Harper (Aberdeen)	33
1972–73	Alan Gordon (Hibernian)	27
1973–74	Dixie Deans (Celtic)	24

Opposite page: One of the goals that helped Celtic win the Championship in 1965–66, the season they began their record run of League titles.
Top: Jimmy McGrory of Celtic, leading goalscorer in 1926–27, 1927–28, and 1935–36.
Above: Alan Gilzean, whose 24 goals in 1961–62 helped Dundee win the Championship.

RELEGATED CLUBS

1921–22	Queen's Park, Dumbarton, Clydebank
1922–23	Albion Rovers, Alloa Athletic
1923–24	Clyde, Clydebank
1924–25	Third Lanark, Ayr United
1925–26	Raith Rovers, Clydebank
1926–27	Morton, Dundee United
1927–28	Dunfermline Athletic, Bo'ness
1928–29	Third Lanark, Raith Rovers
1929–30	St Johnstone, Dundee United
1930–31	Hibernian, East Fife
1931–32	Dundee United, Leith Athletic
1932–33	Morton, East Stirlingshire
1933–34	Third Lanark, Cowdenbeath
1934–35	St Mirren, Falkirk
1935–36	Airdrieonians, Ayr United
1936–37	Dunfermline Athletic, Albion Rovers
1937–38	Dundee, Morton
1938–39	Queen's Park, Raith Rovers
1939–46	League suspended
1946–47	Kilmarnock, Hamilton Academicals
1947–48	Airdrieonians, Queen's Park
1948–49	Morton, Albion Rovers
1949–50	Queen of the South, Stirling Albion
1950–51	Clyde, Falkirk
1951–52	Morton, Stirling Albion
1952–53	Motherwell, Third Lanark
1953–54	Airdrieonians, Hamilton Academicals
1954–55	No clubs relegated
1955–56	Stirling Albion, Clyde
1956–57	Dunfermline Athletic, Ayr United
1957–58	East Fife, Queen's Park
1958–59	Queen of the South, Falkirk
1959–60	Arbroath, Stirling Albion
1960–61	Ayr United, Clyde
1961–62	St Johnstone, Stirling Albion
1962–63	Clyde, Raith Rovers
1963–64	Queen of the South, East Stirlingshire
1964–65	Airdrieonians, Third Lanark
1965–66	Morton, Hamilton Academicals
1966–67	St Mirren, Ayr United
1967–68	Motherwell, Stirling Albion
1968–69	Falkirk, Arbroath
1969–70	Partick Thistle, Raith Rovers
1970–71	St Mirren, Cowdenbeath
1971–72	Clyde, Dunfermline Athletic
1972–73	Kilmarnock, Airdrieonians
1973–74	East Fife, Falkirk

1970–71[6]	Celtic	56	Aberdeen	54	St Johnstone	44
1971–72[6]	Celtic	60	Aberdeen	50	*Rangers	44
1972–73[6]	Celtic	57	Rangers	56	Hibernian	45
1973–74[6]	Celtic	53	Hibernian	49	Rangers	48

*Place won on goal difference.   Maximum points: [1]36; [2]44; [3]40; [4]52; [5]60; [6]68; [7]76; [8]84.

SECOND DIVISION

	First	Pts	Election to First Division			
1893–94[1]	Hibernian	29	Clyde			
1894–95[1]	Hibernian	30				
1895–96[1]	Abercorn	27				
1896–97[1]	Partick Thistle	31	Partick Thistle			
1897–98[1]	Kilmarnock	29				
1898–99[1]	Kilmarnock	32	Kilmarnock			
1899–1900[1]	Partick Thistle		Partick Thistle			
1900–01[1]	St Bernard's	26				
1901–02[2]	Port Glasgow	32	Partick Thistle			
1902–03[2]	Airdrieonians	35	Airdrieonians			
1903–04[2]	Hamilton Academicals	37				
1904–05[2]	Clyde	32	Falkirk, Aberdeen, and Hamilton Academicals			
1905–06[2]	Leith Athletic	34	Clyde			
1906–07[2]	St Bernard's	32				
1907–08[2]	Raith Rovers	30				
1908–09[2]	Abercorn	31				
1909–10[2]	Leith Athletic	33	Raith Rovers			
1910–11[2]	Dumbarton	31				
1911–12[2]	Ayr United	34				
1912–13[3]	Ayr United	34	Ayr United			
1913–14[2]	Cowdenbeath	41				
1914–15[3]	Cowdenbeath	41				
1915–21	Competition suspended					
1921–22[4]	Alloa Athletic	60	Cowdenbeath	47	Armadale	45
	Automatic promotion and relegation					
1922–23[4]	Queen's Park	57	Clydebank	52	St Johnstone	50
1923–24[4]	St Johnstone	56	Cowdenbeath	55	*Bathgate	44
1924–25[4]	Dundee United	50	Clydebank	48	Clyde	47
1925–26[4]	Dunfermline Ath.	59	Clyde	53	Ayr United	52
1926–27[4]	Bo'ness	56	Raith Rovers	49	Clydebank	45
1927–28[4]	Ayr United	54	Third Lanark	45	*King's Park	44
1928–29[5]	Dundee United	51	Morton	50	Arbroath	47
1929–30[4]	*Leith Athletic	57	East Fife	57	Albion Rovers	54
1930–31[4]	Third Lanark	61	Dundee United	50	Dunfermline Ath.	47
1931–32[4]	*East Stirling	55	St Johnstone	55	Stenhousemuir	46
1932–33[6]	Hibernian	54	Queen of South	49	Dunfermline Ath.	47
1933–34[6]	Albion Rovers	45	*Dunfermline Ath.	44	Arbroath	44
1934–35[6]	Third Lanark	52	Arbroath	50	St Bernard's	47
1935–36[6]	Falkirk	59	St Mirren	52	Morton	48
1936–37[6]	Ayr United	54	Morton	51	St Bernard's	48
1937–38[6]	Raith Rovers	59	Albion Rovers	48	Airdrieonians	47
1938–39[6]	Cowdenbeath	60	*Alloa Athletic	48	East Fife	48
1939–46	Competition suspended					
1946–47[3]	Dundee	45	Airdrieonians	42	East Fife	31
1947–48[7]	East Fife	53	Albion Rovers	42	Hamilton Acad.	40
1948–49[7]	*Raith Rovers	42	Stirling Albion	42	*Airdrieonians	41
1949–50[7]	Morton	47	Airdrieonians	44	St Johnstone	36
1950–51[7]	*Queen of South	45	Stirling Albion	45	*Ayr United	36
1951–52[7]	Clyde	44	Falkirk	43	Ayr United	39
1952–53[7]	Stirling Albion	44	Hamilton Acad.	43	Queen's Park	37
1953–54[7]	Motherwell	45	Kilmarnock	42	*Third Lanark	36
1954–55[7]	Airdrieonians	46	Dunfermline Ath.	42	Hamilton Acad.	39
1955–56[5]	Queen's Park	54	Ayr United	51	St Johnstone	49
1956–57[5]	Clyde	64	Third Lanark	51	Cowdenbeath	45
1957–58[5]	Stirling Albion	55	Dunfermline Ath.	53	Arbroath	47
1958–59[5]	Ayr United	60	Arbroath	51	Stenhousemuir	46
1959–60[5]	St Johnstone	53	Dundee United	50	Queen of South	49
1960–61[5]	Stirling Albion	55	Falkirk	54	Stenhousemuir	50
1961–62[5]	Clyde	54	Queen of South	53	Morton	44
1962–63[5]	St Johnstone	55	East Stirling	49	Morton	48
1963–64[5]	Morton	67	Clyde	53	Arbroath	46
1964–65[5]	Stirling Albion	59	Hamilton Acad.	50	Queen of South	45
1965–66[5]	Ayr United	53	Airdrieonians	50	Queen of South	47
1966–67[4]	Morton	69	Raith Rovers	58	Arbroath	57
1967–68[5]	St Mirren	62	Arbroath	53	East Fife	49
1968–69[5]	Motherwell	64	Ayr United	53	East Fife	48
1969–70[5]	Falkirk	56	Cowdenbeath	55	Queen of South	50
1970–71[5]	Partick Thistle	56	East Fife	51	Arbroath	46
1971–72[5]	*Dumbarton	52	Arbroath	52	*Stirling Albion	50
1972–73[5]	Clyde	56	Dunfermline Ath.	52	*Raith Rovers	47
1973–74[5]	Airdrieonians	60	Kilmarnock	58	Hamilton Acad.	55

*Place won on goal difference.   Maximum points: [1]36; [2]44; [3]52; [4]76; [5]72; [6]68; [7]60.

147

SCOTTISH FA CUP

Year	Venue				
1874	Hampden Park	Queen's Park	2	Clydesdale	0
1875	Hampden Park	Queen's Park	3	Renton	0
1876	Hampden Park	Queen's Park	1	Third Lanark	1
	Hampden Park		2		0
1877	Hampden Park	Vale of Leven	0	Rangers	0
	Hampden Park		1		1
	Hampden Park		3		2
1878	Hampden Park	Vale of Leven	1	Third Lanark	0
1879	Hampden Park	Vale of Leven	1	Rangers	1
	Vale of Leven won replay by default				
1880	Cathkin Park	Queen's Park	3	Thornliebank	0
1881	Kinning Park	*Queen's Park	2	Dumbarton	1
	Kinning Park		3		1
1882	Cathkin Park	Queen's Park	2	Dumbarton	2
	Cathkin Park		4		1
1883	Hampden Park	Dumbarton	2	Vale of Leven	2
	Hampden Park		2		1
1884	*Queen's Park won by default from Vale of Leven*				
1885	Hampden Park	Renton	0	Vale of Leven	0
	Hampden Park		3		1
1886	Cathkin Park	Queen's Park	3	Renton	1
1887	Hampden Park	Hibernian	2	Dumbarton	1
1888	Hampden Park	Renton	6	Cambuslang	1
1889	Hampden Park	†Third Lanark	3	Celtic	0
	Hampden Park		2		1
1890	Ibrox Park	Queen's Park	1	Vale of Leven	1
	Ibrox Park		2		1
1891	Hampden Park	Hearts	1	Dumbarton	0
1892	Ibrox Park	‡Celtic	1	Queen's Park	0
	Ibrox Park		5		1
1893	Ibrox Park	Queen's Park	2	Celtic	1
1894	Hampden Park	Rangers	3	Celtic	1
1895	Ibrox Park	St Bernard's	2	Renton	1
1896	Logie Green	Hearts	3	Hibernian	1
1897	Hampden Park	Rangers	5	Dumbarton	1
1898	Hampden Park	Rangers	2	Kilmarnock	0
1899	Hampden Park	Celtic	2	Rangers	0
1900	Ibrox Park	Celtic	4	Queen's Park	3
1901	Ibrox Park	Hearts	4	Celtic	3
1902	Celtic Park	Hibernian	1	Celtic	0
1903	Celtic Park	Rangers	1	Hearts	1
	Celtic Park		0		0
	Celtic Park		2		0
1904	Hampden Park	Celtic	3	Rangers	2
1905	Hampden Park	Third Lanark	0	Rangers	0
	Hampden Park		3		1
1906	Ibrox Park	Hearts	1	Third Lanark	0
1907	Hampden Park	Celtic	3	Hearts	0
1908	Hampden Park	Celtic	5	St Mirren	1
1909	Hampden Park	Celtic	2	Rangers	2
	Hampden Park		1		1
	Cup withheld following riots				
1910	Ibrox Park	Dundee	2	Clyde	2
	Ibrox Park		0		0
	Ibrox Park		2		1
1911	Ibrox Park	Celtic	0	Hamilton Acad.	0
	Ibrox Park		2		0
1912	Ibrox Park	Celtic	2	Clyde	0
1913	Celtic Park	Falkirk	2	Raith Rovers	0
1914	Ibrox Park	Celtic	0	Hibernian	0
	Ibrox Park		4		1
1915–19	*No competition*				
1920	Hampden Park	Kilmarnock	3	Albion Rovers	2
1921	Celtic Park	Partick Thistle	1	Rangers	0
1922	Hampden Park	Morton	1	Rangers	0
1923	Hampden Park	Celtic	1	Hibernian	0
1924	Ibrox Park	Airdrieonians	2	Hibernian	0
1925	Hampden Park	Celtic	2	Dundee	1
1926	Hampden Park	St Mirren	2	Celtic	0
1927	Hampden Park	Celtic	3	East Fife	1
1928	Hampden Park	Rangers	4	Celtic	0
1929	Hampden Park	Kilmarnock	2	Rangers	0
1930	Hampden Park	Rangers	0	Partick Thistle	0
	Hampden Park		2		1
1931	Hampden Park	Celtic	2	Motherwell	2
	Hampden Park		4		2
1932	Hampden Park	Rangers	1	Kilmarnock	1
	Hampden Park		3		0
1933	Hampden Park	Celtic	1	Motherwell	0
1934	Hampden Park	Rangers	5	St Mirren	0
1935	Hampden Park	Rangers	2	Hamilton Acad.	1
1936	Hampden Park	Rangers	1	Third Lanark	0
1937	Hampden Park	Celtic	2	Aberdeen	1
1938	Hampden Park	East Fife	1	Kilmarnock	1
	Hampden Park		4		2
	After extra time				
1939	Hampden Park	Clyde	4	Motherwell	0
1940–46	*No competition*				
1947	Hampden Park	Aberdeen	2	Hibernian	1
1948	Hampden Park	Rangers	1	Morton	1
	Hampden Park		1		0
1949	Hampden Park	Rangers	4	Clyde	1
1950	Hampden Park	Rangers	3	East Fife	0
1951	Hampden Park	Celtic	1	Motherwell	0
1952	Hampden Park	Motherwell	4	Dundee	0
1953	Hampden Park	Rangers	1	Aberdeen	1
	Hampden Park		1		0
1954	Hampden Park	Celtic	2	Aberdeen	1
1955	Hampden Park	Clyde	1	Celtic	1
	Hampden Park		1		0
1956	Hampden Park	Hearts	3	Celtic	1
1957	Hampden Park	Falkirk	1	Kilmarnock	1
	Hampden Park		2		1
	After extra time				
1958	Hampden Park	Clyde	1	Hibernian	0
1959	Hampden Park	St Mirren	3	Aberdeen	1
1960	Hampden Park	Rangers	2	Kilmarnock	0
1961	Hampden Park	Dunfermline Ath.	0	Celtic	0
	Hampden Park		2		0
1962	Hampden Park	Rangers	2	St Mirren	0
1963	Hampden Park	Rangers	1	Celtic	1
	Hampden Park		3		0
1964	Hampden Park	Rangers	3	Dundee	1
1965	Hampden Park	Celtic	3	Dunfermline Ath.	2
1966	Hampden Park	Rangers	0	Celtic	0
	Hampden Park		1		0
1967	Hampden Park	Celtic	2	Aberdeen	0
1968	Hampden Park	Dunfermline Ath.	3	Hearts	1
1969	Hampden Park	Celtic	4	Rangers	0
1970	Hampden Park	Aberdeen	3	Celtic	1
1971	Hampden Park	Celtic	1	Rangers	1
	Hampden Park		2		1
1972	Hampden Park	Celtic	6	Hibernian	1
1973	Hampden Park	Rangers	3	Celtic	2
1974	Hampden Park	Celtic	3	Dundee United	0

* Dumbarton lodged a protest and were awarded a replay.
† Final replayed because of the state of the pitch.
‡ Queen's Park lodged a protest and were awarded a replay.

A joyful Kaj Johansen leaps into the arms of Henderson and MacLean after winning the 1966 Scottish Cup replay for Rangers.

Above: John Grieg looks on disbelievingly as Norrie Martin is beaten by Sammy Reid's shot and holders Rangers tumble in the first round of the 1967 Scottish Cup to Second Division Berwick Rangers.
Below: Steve Chalmers gets Celtic's fourth in the 1969 final.

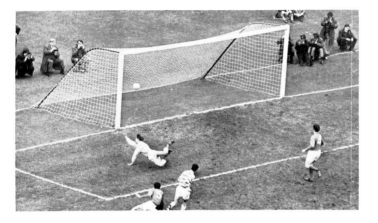

IRISH LEAGUE

1890–91	Linfield		1931–32	Linfield
1891–92	Linfield		1932–33	Belfast Celtic
1892–93	Linfield		1933–34	Linfield
1893–94	Glentoran		1934–35	Linfield
1894–95	Linfield		1935–36	Belfast Celtic
1895–96	Distillery		1936–37	Belfast Celtic
1896–97	Glentoran		1937–38	Belfast Celtic
1897–98	Linfield		1938–39	Belfast Celtic
1898–99	Distillery		1939–40	Belfast Celtic
1899–1900	Belfast Celtic		1940–47	*No competition*
1900–01	Distillery		1947–48	Belfast Celtic
1901–02	Linfield		1948–49	Linfield
1902–03	Distillery		1949–50	Linfield
1903–04	Linfield		1950–51	Glentoran
1904–05	Glentoran		1951–52	Glenavon
1905–06	{ Cliftonville / Distillery		1952–53	Glentoran
			1953–54	Linfield
1906–07	Linfield		1954–55	Linfield
1907–08	Linfield		1955–56	Linfield
1908–09	Linfield		1956–57	Glenavon
1909–10	Cliftonville		1957–58	Ards
1910–11	Linfield		1958–59	Linfield
1911–12	Glentoran		1959–60	Glenavon
1912–13	Glentoran		1960–61	Linfield
1913–14	Linfield		1961–62	Linfield
1914–15	Belfast Celtic		1962–63	Distillery
1915–19	*No competition*		1963–64	Glentoran
1919–20	Belfast Celtic		1964–65	Derry City
1920–21	Glentoran		1965–66	Linfield
1921–22	Linfield		1966–67	Glentoran
1922–23	Linfield		1967–68	Glentoran
1923–24	Queen's Island		1968–69	Linfield
1924–25	Glentoran		1969–70	Glentoran
1925–26	Belfast Celtic		1970–71	Linfield
1926–27	Belfast Celtic		1971–72	Glentoran
1927–28	Belfast Celtic		1972–73	Crusaders
1928–29	Belfast Celtic		1973–74	Coleraine
1929–30	Linfield			
1930–31	Glentoran			

SCOTTISH LEAGUE CUP

Season	Venue				
1945–46	Hampden Park	Aberdeen	3	Rangers	2
1946–47	Hampden Park	Rangers	4	Aberdeen	0
1947–48	Hampden Park	East Fife	1	Falkirk	1
	Hampden Park		4		1
1948–49	Hampden Park	Rangers	2	Raith Rovers	0
1949–50	Hampden Park	East Fife	3	Dunfermline Ath.	0
1950–51	Hampden Park	Motherwell	3	Hibernian	0
1951–52	Hampden Park	Dundee	3	Rangers	2
1952–53	Hampden Park	Dundee	2	Kilmarnock	0
1953–54	Hampden Park	East Fife	3	Partick Thistle	2
1954–55	Hampden Park	Hearts	4	Motherwell	2
1955–56	Hampden Park	Aberdeen	2	St Mirren	1
1956–57	Hampden Park	Celtic	0	Partick Thistle	0
	Hampden Park		3		0
1957–58	Hampden Park	Celtic	7	Rangers	1
1958–59	Hampden Park	Hearts	5	Partick Thistle	1
1959–60	Hampden Park	Hearts	2	Third Lanark	1
1960–61	Hampden Park	Rangers	2	Kilmarnock	0
1961–62	Hampden Park	Rangers	1	Hearts	1
	Hampden Park		3		1
1962–63	Hampden Park	Hearts	1	Kilmarnock	0
1963–64	Hampden Park	Rangers	5	Morton	0
1964–65	Hampden Park	Rangers	2	Celtic	1
1965–66	Hampden Park	Celtic	2	Rangers	1
1966–67	Hampden Park	Celtic	1	Rangers	0
1967–68	Hampden Park	Celtic	5	Dundee	3
1968–69	Hampden Park	Celtic	6	Hibernian	2
1969–70	Hampden Park	Celtic	1	St Johnstone	0
1970–71	Hampden Park	Rangers	1	Celtic	0
1971–72	Hampden Park	Partick Thistle	4	Celtic	1
1972–73	Hampden Park	Hibernian	2	Celtic	1
1973–74	Hampden Park	Dundee	1	Celtic	0

IRISH CUP

1881	Moyola Park	1	Cliftonville	0
1882	Queen's Island	2	Cliftonville	1
1883	Cliftonville	5	Ulster	0
1884	Distillery	5	Wellington Park	0
1885	Distillery	2	Limavady	0
1886	Distillery	1	Limavady	0
1887	Ulster	3	Cliftonville	0
1888	Cliftonville	2	Distillery	1
1889	Distillery	5	YMCA	4
1890	Gordon Highlanders	2	Cliftonville	2
		3		1
1891	Linfield	4	Ulster	2
1892	Linfield	7	The Black Watch	0
1893	Linfield	5	Cliftonville	1
1894	Distillery	2	Linfield	2
		3		2
1895	Linfield	10	Bohemians	1
1896	Distillery	3	Glentoran	1
1897	Cliftonville	3	Sherwood Foresters	1
1898	Linfield	2	St Columb's Hall Celtic	0
1899	Linfield	1	Glentoran	0
1900	Cliftonville	2	Bohemians	0
1901	Cliftonville	1	Freebooters	0
1902	Linfield	5	Distillery	1
1903	Distillery	3	Bohemians	1
1904	Linfield	5	Derry Celtic	0
1905	Distillery	3	Shelbourne	0
1906	Shelbourne	2	Belfast Celtic	0
1907	Cliftonville	0	Shelbourne	0
		1		0
1908	Bohemians	1	Shelbourne	1
		3		1
1909	Cliftonville	0	Bohemians	0
		2		1
1910	Distillery	1	Cliftonville	0

1911	Shelbourne	0	Bohemians	0
		2		1
1912	Linfield awarded trophy: final not played			
1913	Linfield	2	Glentoran	1
1914	Glentoran	3	Linfield	1
1915	Linfield	1	Belfast Celtic	0
1916	Linfield	1	Glentoran	0
1917	Glentoran	2	Belfast Celtic	0
1918	Belfast Celtic	0	Linfield	0
		0		0
		2		0
1919	Linfield	1	Glentoran	1
		0		0
		2		1
1920	Shelbourne awarded trophy: final not played			
1921	Glentoran	2	Glenavon	0
1922	Linfield	2	Glenavon	0
1923	Linfield	2	Glentoran	0
1924	Queen's Island	1	Willowfield	0
1925	Distillery	2	Glentoran	1
1926	Belfast Celtic	3	Linfield	2
1927	Ards	3	Cliftonville	2
1928	Willowfield	1	Larne	0
1929	Ballymena	2	Belfast Celtic	1
1930	Linfield	4	Ballymena	3
1931	Linfield	3	Ballymena	0
1932	Glentoran	2	Linfield	1
1933	Glentoran	1	Distillery	1
		1		1
		3		1
1934	Linfield	5	Cliftonville	0
1935	Glentoran	0	Larne	0
		0		0
		1		0
1936	Linfield	0	Derry City	0
		2		1
1937	Beltast Celtic	3	Linfield	0
1938	Belfast Celtic	0	Bangor	0
		2		0
1939	Linfield	2	Ballymena United	0
1940	Ballymena United	2	Glenavon	0
1941	Belfast Celtic	1	Linfield	0
1942	Linfield	3	Glentoran	1
1943	Belfast Celtic	1	Glentoran	0
1944	Belfast Celtic	3	Linfield	1
1945	Linfield	4	Glentoran	2
1946	Linfield	3	Distillery	0
1947	Belfast Celtic	1	Glentoran	0
1948	Linfield	3	Coleraine	0
1949	Derry City	3	Glentoran	1
1950	Linfield	2	Distillery	1
1951	Glentoran	3	Ballymena United	1
1952	Ards	1	Glentoran	0
1953	Linfield	5	Coleraine	0
1954	Derry City	2	Glentoran	2
		0		0
		1		0
1955	Dundela	3	Glenavon	0
1956	Distillery	2	Glentoran	2
		1		1
		1		0
1957	Glenavon	2	Derry City	0
1958	Ballymena United	2	Linfield	0
1959	Glenavon	1	Ballymena United	1
		2		0
1960	Linfield	5	Ards	1
1961	Glenavon	5	Linfield	1
1962	Linfield	4	Portadown	0
1963	Linfield	2	Distillery	1
1964	Derry City	2	Glentoran	0
1965	Coleraine	2	Glenavon	1
1966	Glentoran	2	Linfield	0
1967	Crusaders	3	Glentoran	1
1968	Crusaders	2	Linfield	0
1969	Ards	0	Distillery	0
		4		2
1970	Linfield	2	Ballymena United	1
1971	Distillery	3	Derry City	0
1972	Coleraine	2	Portadown	1
1973	Glentoran	3	Linfield	2
1974	Ards	2	Ballymena United	1

WELSH CUP

Year	Venue				
1877–78	Acton Park	Wrexham	1	Druids	0
1878–79	Wrexham	Newtown	1	Wrexham	0
1879–80	Wrexham	Druids	2	Ruthin	1
1880–81	Wrexham	Druids	2	Newtown White Stars	0
1881–82	Wrexham	Druids	2	Northwich	1
1882–83	Wrexham	Wrexham	1	Druids	0
1883–84	Wrexham	Oswestry	3	Druids	0
1884–85	Wrexham	Druids	2	Oswestry	0
1885–86	Wrexham	Druids	5	Newtown	0
1886–87	Wrexham	Chirk	4	Davenham	2
1887–88	Wrexham	Chirk	5	Newtown	0
1888–89	Wrexham	Bangor	2	Northwich	1
1889–90	Wrexham	Chirk	1	Wrexham	0
1890–91	Oswestry	Shrewsbury Town	5	Wrexham	2
1891–92	Wrexham	Chirk	2	Westminster Rovers	1
1892–93	Oswestry	Wrexham	2	Chirk	1
1893–94	Ruabon	Chirk	2	Westminster Rovers	0
1894–95	Welshpool	Newtown	3	Wrexham	2
1895–96	Llandudno	Bangor	3	Wrexham	1
1896–97	Oswestry	Wrexham	2	Newtown	0
1897–98	Oswestry	Druids	1	Wrexham	1
	Oswestry		2		1
1898–99	Chirk	Druids	2	Wrexham	2
	Chirk		1		0
1899–1900	Newtown	Aberystwyth	3	Druids	0
1900–01	Wrexham	Oswestry	1	Druids	0
1901–02	Wrexham	Wellington	1	Wrexham	0
1902–03	Wrexham	Wrexham	8	Aberaman	0
1903–04	Wrexham	Druids	3	Aberdare	2
1904–05	Wrexham	Wrexham	3	Aberdare	0
1905–06	Wrexham	Wellington	3	Whitchurch	2
1906–07	Wrexham	Oswestry	2	Whitchurch	0
1907–08	Wrexham	Chester	3	Connah's Quay	1
1908–09	Wrexham	Wrexham	1	Chester	0
1909–10	Wrexham	Wrexham	2	Chester	1
1910–11	Wrexham	Wrexham	6	Connah's Quay	1
1911–12	Cardiff	Cardiff City	0	Pontypridd	0
	Aberdare		3		0
1912–13	Cardiff	Swansea	0	Pontypridd	0
	Mid-Rhondda		1		0
1913–14	Swansea	Wrexham	1	Llanelly	1
	Oswestry		1		0
1914–15	Wrexham	Wrexham	1	Swansea	1
	Cardiff		1		0
1915–19	*No competition*				
1919–20	Wrexham	Cardiff City	2	Wrexham	1
1920–21	Cardiff	Wrexham	1	Pontypridd	1
	Shrewsbury		3		0
1921–22	Pontypridd	Cardiff City	2	Ton Pentre	0
1922–23	Swansea	Cardiff City	3	Aberdare	2
1923–24	Pontypridd	Wrexham	2	Merthyr Town	2
	Wrexham		1		0
1924–25	Wrexham	Wrexham	3	Flint	1
1925–26	Ebbw Vale	Ebbw Vale	3	Swansea	2
1926–27	Wrexham	Cardiff City	2	Rhyl	0
1927–28	Bangor	Cardiff City	2	Bangor	0
1928–29	Wrexham	Connah's Quay	3	Cardiff City	0
1929–30	Shrewsbury	Cardiff City	0	Rhyl	0
	Wrexham		4		2
1930–31	Wrexham	Wrexham	7	Shrewsbury	0
1931–32	Wrexham	Swansea	1	Wrexham	1
	Swansea		2		0
1932–33	Chester	Chester	2	Wrexham	0
1933–34	Wrexham	Bristol City	1	Tranmere Rovers	1
	Chester		3		0
1934–35	Chester	Tranmere Rovers	1	Chester	0
1935–36	Wrexham	Crewe	2	Chester	0
1936–37	Chester	Crewe	1	Rhyl	0
	Chester		3		1
1937–38	Shrewsbury	Shrewsbury	2	Swansea	1
1938–39	Wrexham	South Liverpool	2	Cardiff City	1
1939–40	Shrewsbury	Wellington Town	4	Swansea	0
1940–46	*No competition*				
1946–47	Cardiff	Chester	0	Merthyr Tydfil	0
	Wrexham		5		1
1947–48	Wrexham	Lovell's Athletic	3	Shrewsbury Town	1
1948–49	Cardiff	Merthyr Tydfil	2	Swansea Town	0
1949–50	Cardiff	Swansea Town	4	Wrexham	1
1950–51	Swansea	Merthyr Tydfil	1	Cardiff City	1
	Swansea		3		2

1951–52	Cardiff	Rhyl	4	Merthyr Tydfil	3	
1952–53	Bangor	Rhyl	2	Chester	1	
1953–54	Wrexham	Flint Town United	2	Chester	0	
1954–55	Wrexham	Barry Town	1	Chester	1	
	Cardiff		4		3	
1955–56	Cardiff	Cardiff City	3	Swansea Town	2	
1956–57	Cardiff	Wrexham	2	Swansea Town	1	
1957–58	Chester	Wrexham	1	Chester	1	
	Wrexham		2		1	
1958–59	Newport	Cardiff City	2	Lovell's Athletic	0	
1959–60	Cardiff	Wrexham	1	Cardiff City	1	
	Wrexham		1		0	
1960–61	Cardiff	Swansea Town	3	Bangor City	1	

Two-legged finals incorporated

1961–62	Bangor City	2:0:3	Wrexham	0:3:1
1962–63	Borough United	2:0	Newport County	1:0
1963–64	Cardiff City	3:0:2	Bangor City	1:2:0
1964–65	Cardiff City	5:0:3	Wrexham	1:1:0
1965–66	Swansea Town	3:0:2	Chester	0:1:1
1966–67	Cardiff City	2:2	Wrexham	1:2
1967–68	Cardiff City	4:2	Hereford United	1:0
1968–69	Cardiff City	2:3	Swansea Town	0:1
1969–70	Cardiff City	4:1	Chester	0:0
1970–71	Cardiff City	3:1	Wrexham	1:0
1971–72	Wrexham	2:1	Cardiff City	1:1
1972–73	Cardiff City	0:5	Bangor City	1:0
1973–74	Cardiff City	1:1	Stourbridge	0:0

Pedro Araya scores for Universidad de Chile in the 1970 semi-final against Penarol. Penarol won the tie but lost the final to Estudiantes de la Plata.

Competitions in Other Continents

SOUTH AMERICAN CHAMPIONSHIP

	Venue	Winners	Runners-up
1916	Buenos Aires	Uruguay	Argentina
1917	Montevideo	Uruguay	Argentina
1919	Rio de Janeiro	Brazil	Uruguay
1920	Valparaiso	Uruguay	Argentina
1921	Buenos Aires	Argentina	Brazil
1922	Rio de Janeiro	Brazil	Paraguay
1923	Montevideo	Uruguay	Argentina
1924	Montevideo	Uruguay	Argentina
1925	Buenos Aires	Argentina	Brazil
1926	Santiago	Uruguay	Argentina
1927	Lima	Argentina	Uruguay
1929	Buenos Aires	Argentina	Paraguay
1935	Lima	Uruguay	Argentina
1937	Buenos Aires	Argentina	Brazil
1939	Lima	Peru	Uruguay
1941	Santiago	Argentina	Uruguay
1942	Montevideo	Uruguay	Argentina
1945	Santiago	Argentina	Brazil
1946	Buenos Aires	Argentina	Brazil
1947	Guayaquil	Argentina	Paraguay
1949	Rio de Janeiro	Brazil	Paraguay
1953	Lima	Paraguay	Brazil
1955	Santiago	Argentina	Chile
1956	Montevideo	Uruguay	Brazil
1957	Lima	Argentina	Brazil
1959	Buenos Aires	Argentina	Brazil
1959	Guayaquil	Uruguay	Argentina
1963	La Paz	Bolivia	Paraguay
1967	Montevideo	Uruguay	Argentina

SOUTH AMERICAN CUP

(Copa de los Libertadores)

1960	*Penarol	1:1	Olimpija	0:1	
1961	*Penarol	1:1	Palmeiras	0:1	
1962	*Santos	2:2:3	Penarol	1:3:0	
	(play-off at Buenos Aires)				
1963	*Santos	3:2	Boca Juniors	2:1	
1964	*Independiente	0:1	*Nacional	0:0	

1965	*Independiente	1:1:4	Penarol	0:3:1
	(play-off at Santiago)			
1966	*Penarol	2:2:4	River Plate	0:3:2
	(play-off at Santiago)			
1967	*Racing Club	0:0:2	Nacional	0:0:1
	(play-off at Santiago)			
1968	*Estudiantes de la Plata	3:1:2	Palmeiras	1:3:0
	(play-off at Montevideo)			
1969	Estudiantes de la Plata	1:2	*Nacional	0:0
1970	*Estudiantes de la Plata	1:0	Penarol	0:0
1971	Nacional	0:1:2	*Estudiantes de la Plata	1:0:0
1972	Independiente	0:2	*Universitario	0:1
1973	*Independiente	1:0:2	Colo-Colo	1:0:1
	(play-off at Montevideo, won after extra time)			

*Home team in 1st leg

AFRICAN NATIONS CUP

1957	United Arab Republic
1959	United Arab Republic
1961	Ethiopia
1963	Ghana
1965	Ghana
1967	Congo Kinshasa
1969	Sudan
1971	Congo Brazzaville
1974	Zaïre

AFRICAN CLUB CUP

1964	Oryx Douala (Cameroons)
1965	*No competition*
1966	Stade D'Abidjan (Ivory Coast)
1967	Engelbert Lumbumbashi (Congo Kinshasa)
1968	Engelbert Lumbumbashi (Congo Kinshasa)
1969	Ismaili (United Arab Republic)
1970	Asante Kotoko (Ghana)
1971	Canon of Yaounde (Cameroons)
1972	Hafia (Guinea)
1973	Vita Club (Zaïre)

League and Cup Winners Around the World

ARGENTINA
Association founded: 1893
Colours: blue and white striped shirts; blue shorts
Honours: World Cup, runners-up 1930; South American Championship, winners 1921, 1925, 1927, 1929, 1937, 1941, 1945, 1946, 1947, 1955, 1957, 1959, runners-up 1916, 1917, 1920, 1923, 1924, 1926, 1935, 1942, 1960, 1967; Olympic Games, runners-up 1928

League Champions
1960	Independiente
1961	Racing Club
1962	Boca Juniors
1963	Independiente
1964	Boca Juniors
1965	Boca Juniors
1966	Racing Club
1967	Estudiantes de la Plata
1968	San Lorenzo
1969	Chacarita Juniors
1970	Independiente
1971	Independiente
1972	San Lorenzo
1973	Rosario Central

Above: Goalmouth action in an Argentinian league match.

AUSTRALIA
Federation founded: 1961
Colours: yellow shirts, green facings; white shorts

Cup Winners
1962	Yugal (NSW)
1963	Slavia Melbourne
1964	George Cross
1965	Hakoah-Eastern Suburbs
1966	Apia-Leichhardt
1967	Melbourne HSC
1968	Hakoah-Eastern Suburbs

AUSTRIA
Association founded: 1926
Colours: white shirts; black shorts
Honours: World Cup, 3rd 1954; Olympic Games, runners-up 1936

League Champions
1960	Rapid Vienna
1961	FK Austria
1962	FK Austria
1963	FK Austria
1964	Rapid Vienna
1965	Linz ASK
1966	Admira Energie
1967	Rapid Vienna
1968	Rapid Vienna
1969	FK Austria
1970	FK Austria
1971	Wacker Innsbruck
1972	Tirol-Svarowski-Innsbruck
1973	Tirol-Svarowski-Innsbruck
1974	Vöest Linz

Cup Winners
1960	FK Austria
1961	Rapid Vienna
1962	FK Austria
1963	FK Austria
1964	Admira Energie
1965	Linz ASK
1966	Admira Energie
1967	FK Austria
1968	Rapid Vienna
1969	Rapid Vienna
1970	Wacker Innsbruck
1971	FK Austria
1972	Rapid Vienna
1973	Tirol-Svarowski-Innsbruck
1974	Austria/WAC

BELGIUM
Association founded: 1895
Colours: white shirts; white shorts
Honours: Olympic Games, winners 1920. European Championship, third 1972

League Champions
1960	Lierse SK
1961	Standard Liège
1962	RSC Anderlecht
1963	Standard Liège
1964	RSC Anderlecht
1965	RSC Anderlecht
1966	RSC Anderlecht
1967	RSC Anderlecht
1968	RSC Anderlecht
1969	Standard Liège
1970	Standard Liège
1971	Standard Liège
1972	RSC Anderlecht
1973	FC Bruges
1974	RSC Anderlecht

Cup Winners
1964	La Gantoise
1965	RSC Anderlecht
1966	Standard Liège
1967	Standard Liège
1968	FC Bruges
1969	Lierse SK
1970	FC Bruges
1971	Beerschot
1972	RSC Anderlecht
1973	RSC Anderlecht
1974	Waregem

BRAZIL
Association founded: 1925
Colours: yellow shirts, green facings; green shorts
Honours: World Cup, winners 1958, 1962, 1970, runners-up 1950, 3rd 1938; South American Championship, winners 1919, 1922, 1949, runners-up 1921, 1925, 1937, 1945, 1946, 1953, 1957, 1959

National Champions
1971	Atlético Mineiro
1972	Palmeiras
1973	Palmeiras

League Champions (Rio de Janeiro)
1960	America
1961	Botafogo
1962	Botafogo
1963	Flamengo
1964	Fluminense
1965	Flamengo
1966	Bangu
1967	Botafogo
1968	Botafogo
1969	Fluminense
1970	Vasco da Gama
1971	Fluminense
1972	Flamengo

League Champions (São Paulo)
1960	Santos
1961	Santos
1962	Santos
1963	Palmeiras
1964	Santos
1965	Santos
1966	Palmeiras
1967	Santos
1968	Santos
1969	Santos
1970	São Paulo
1971	São Paulo
1972	Palmeiras
1973	Palmeiras

Cup Winners
1961	Bahia
1962	Santos
1963	Santos
1964	Santos
1965	Palmeiras
1966	Cruzeiro
1967	Palmeiras
1968	Santos
1969	Palmeiras
1970	Fluminense
1971	Atlético Mineiro
1972	Palmeiras

BULGARIA
Association founded: 1923
Colours: white shirts, green shorts
Honours: Olympic Games, runners-up 1968, 3rd 1956

League Champions
1960	CDNA Sofia
1961	CDNA Sofia
1962	CDNA Sofia
1963	Spartak Plovdiv
1964	Lokomotiv Sofia
1965	Levski Sofia
1966	CSKA Sofia
1967	Trakia Plovdiv
1968	Levski Sofia
1969	CSKA Sofia
1970	Levski Spartak
1971	CSKA Sofia
1972	CSKA Sofia
1973	CSKA Sofia
1974	Levski Spartak

Cup Winners
1960	CDNA Sofia
1961	CDNA Sofia
1962	Botev Plovdiv
1963	Slavia Sofia
1964	Slavia Sofia
1965	CSKA Sofia
1966	Slavia Sofia
1967	Levski Sofia
1968	Spartak Sofia
1969	CSKA Sofia
1970	Levski Spartak
1971	Levski Spartak
1972	CSKA Sofia
1973	CSKA Sofia

CZECHOSLOVAKIA
Association founded: 1922
Colours: white shirts; white shorts
Honours: World Cup, runners-up 1934, 1962; Olympic Games, disqualified finalists 1920, runners-up 1964

League Champions
1960	Spartak Hradec Kralove
1961	Dukla Prague
1962	Dukla Prague
1963	Dukla Prague
1964	Dukla Prague
1965	Sparta Prague
1966	Dukla Prague
1967	Sparta Prague
1968	Spartak Trnava
1969	Spartak Trnava
1970	Slovan Bratislava
1971	Spartak Trnava
1972	Spartak Trnava
1973	Spartak Trnava
1974	Slovan Bratislava

Cup Winners
1961	Dukla Prague
1962	Slovan Bratislava
1963	Slovan Bratislava
1964	Sparta Prague
1965	Dukla Prague
1966	Dukla Prague
1967	Spartak Trnava
1968	Slovan Bratislava
1969	Dukla Prague
1970	TJ Gottwaldov
1971	Spartak Trnava
1972	Sparta Prague
1973	Banik Ostrava
1974	Slovan Bratislava

DENMARK
Association founded: 1889
Colours: red shirts; white shorts

Honours: Olympic Games, runners-up 1908, 1912, 1960; 3rd 1948

League Champions
1960	AGF Aarhus
1961	Esbjerg BK
1962	Esbjerg BK
1963	Esbjerg BK
1964	BK 09 Odense
1965	Esbjerg BK
1966	Hvidovre Copenhagen
1967	AB Copenhagen
1968	KB Copenhagen
1969	BK 1903 Copenhagen
1970	BK 1903 Copenhagen
1971	Vejle
1972	Vejle
1973	Hvidovre Copenhagen

Cup Winners
1960	AGF Aarhus
1961	AGF Aarhus
1962	BK 09 Odense
1963	BK 09 Odense
1964	Esbjerg BK
1965	AGF Aarhus
1966	Aalborg BK
1967	Randers Freja
1968	Randers Freja
1969	KB Copenhagen
1970	Aalborg BK
1971	BK 09 Odense
1972	Vejle
1973	Randers Freja
1974	Vanlose

FINLAND
Association founded: 1907
Colours: white shirts; blue shorts

League Champions
1960	Valkeakosken Haka
1961	Idrottsföreningen Kamraterna
1962	Valkeakosken Haka
1963	Lahden Reipas
1964	Helsingin Jalkapalloklubi
1965	Valkeakosken Haka
1966	Kuopion Palloseura
1967	Lahden Reipas
1968	Turun Palloseura
1969	Kokkolan Pallo-Veikot
1970	Lahden Reipas
1971	Turun Palloseura
1972	Turun Palloseura
1973	Helsingin Jalkapalloklubi

Cup Winners
1960	Valkeakosken Haka
1961	Kotkan Työväen Palloilijat
1962	HPS
1963	Valkeakosken Haka
1964	Lahden Reipas
1965	IFK Abo
1966	Helsingin Jalkapalloklubi
1967	Kotkan Työväen Palloilijat
1968	Kuopion Palloseura
1969	Valkeakosken Haka
1970	Mikkelin Palloilijat
1971	Mikkelin Palloilijat
1972	Lahden Reipas
1973	Lahden Reipas

FRANCE
Association founded: 1919
Colours: blue shirts; white shorts

Honours: World Cup, 3rd 1958

League Champions
1960	Stade de Reims
1961	AS Monaco
1962	Stade de Reims
1963	AS Monaco
1964	Saint Etienne
1965	FC Nantes
1966	FC Nantes
1967	Saint Etienne
1968	Saint Etienne
1969	Saint Etienne
1970	Saint Etienne
1971	Olympique Marseille
1972	Olympique Marseille
1973	Nantes
1974	Saint Etienne

Cup Winners
1960	AS Monaco
1961	Sedan-Torcy
1962	Saint Etienne
1963	AS Monaco
1964	Olympique Lyonnaise
1965	Stade Rennes
1966	Racing Club Strasbourg
1967	Olympique Lyonnaise
1968	Saint Etienne
1969	Olympique Marseille
1970	Saint Etienne
1971	Stade Rennes
1972	Olympique Marseille
1973	Olympique Lyon
1974	Saint Etienne

GERMAN DEMOCRATIC REPUBLIC
Association founded: 1947
Colours: white shirts; blue shorts
Honours: Olympic Games, 3rd 1964, 1972 (equal)

League Champions
1960	ASK Vorwaerts Berlin
1961	Empor Rostock
1962	ASK Vorwaerts Berlin
1963	Motor Jena
1964	Chemie Leipzig
1965	ASK Vorwaerts Berlin
1966	ASK Vorwaerts Berlin
1967	Wismut Karl-Marx-Stadt
1968	Carl Zeiss Jena
1969	ASK Vorwaerts Berlin
1970	Carl Zeiss Jena
1971	Dynamo Dresden
1972	FC Magdeburg
1973	Dynamo Dresden
1974	FC Magdeburg

Cup Winners
1960	Motor Jena
1961	Motor Jena
1962	Halle Chemie SC
1963	Motor Zwickau
1964	Magdeburg Aufbau
1965	Magdeburg Aufbau
1966	Chemie Leipzig
1967	Motor Zwickau
1968	Union East Berlin
1969	FC Magdeburg
1970	ASK Vorwaerts Berlin
1971	Dynamo Dresden
1972	Carl Zeiss Jena
1973	FC Magdeburg
1974	Carl Zeiss Jena

GERMANY, WEST
Association founded: 1900
Colours: white shirts; black shorts
Honours: World Cup, winners 1954, 1974, runners-up 1966, 3rd 1934, 1970; European Championship, winners 1972

League Champions
1960	SV Hamburg
1961	1FC Nuremberg
1962	1FC Cologne
1963	Borussia Dortmund
1964	1FC Cologne
1965	SV Werder Bremen
1966	TSV Munich 1860
1967	Eintracht Brunswick
1968	1FC Nuremberg
1969	Bayern Munich
1970	Borussia Mönchengladbach
1971	Borussia Mönchengladbach
1972	Bayern Munich
1973	Bayern Munich
1974	Bayern Munich

Cup Winners
1960	Borussia Mönchengladbach
1961	SV Werder Bremen
1962	1FC Nuremberg
1963	SV Hamburg
1964	TSV Munich 1860
1965	Borussia Dortmund
1966	Bayern Munich
1967	Bayern Munich
1968	1FC Cologne
1969	Bayern Munich
1970	Offenbach Kickers
1971	Bayern Munich
1972	Schalke 04
1973	Borussia Mönchengladbach
1974	Eintracht Frankfurt

GREECE
Association founded: 1926
Colours: white shirts; blue shorts

League Champions
1960	Panathinaikos
1961	Panathinaikos
1962	Panathinaikos
1963	AEK Athens
1964	Panathinaikos
1965	Panathinaikos
1966	Olympiakos
1967	Olympiakos
1968	AEK Athens
1969	Panathinaikos
1970	Panathinaikos
1971	AEK Athens
1972	Panathinaikos
1973	Olympiakos
1974	Olympiakos

Cup Winners
1960	Olympiakos
1961	Olympiakos
1962	Olympiakos
1963	Olympiakos
1964	AEK Athens
1965	Olympiakos
1966	AEK Athens
1967	Panathinaikos
1968	Olympiakos
1969	Panathinaikos
1970	Aris Salonika
1971	Olympiakos
1972	PAOK Salonika
1973	Olympiakos
1974	PAOK Salonika

HUNGARY
Association founded: 1901
Colours: red shirts; white shorts
Honours: World Cup, runners-up 1938, 1954; European Championship, 3rd 1964; Olympic Games, winners 1952, 1964, 1968, runners-up 1972, 3rd 1960

League Champions
1960	Ujpest Dozsa
1961	Vasas Budapest
1962	Vasas Budapest
1963	Ferencvaros
*1963	Vasas Györ
1964	Ferencvaros
1965	Vasas Budapest
1966	Vasas Budapest
1967	Ferencvaros
1968	Ferencvaros
1969	Ujpest Dozsa
1970	Ujpest Dozsa
1971	Ujpest Dozsa
1972	Ujpest Dozsa
1973	Ujpest Dozsa
1974	Ujpest Dozsa

*Short season.

Above: Uwe Seeler, leading goalscorer in the West German League in 1956, 1959, 1960, 1961, and 1964, adds another to his tally.

153

Cup Winners

1964	Honved
1965	Vasas Györ
1966	Vasas Györ
1967	Vasas Györ
1968	MTK Budapest
1969	Ujpest Dozsa
1970	Ujpest Dozsa
1971	Ujpest Dozsa
1972	Ferencvaros
1973	Vasas Budapest
1974	Ferencvaros

IRELAND, REPUBLIC OF

Association founded: 1921
Colours: green shirts; white shorts

League Champions

1960	Limerick
1961	Drumcondra
1962	Shelbourne
1963	Dundalk
1964	Shamrock Rovers
1965	Drumcondra
1966	Waterford
1967	Dundalk
1968	Waterford
1969	Waterford
1970	Waterford
1971	Cork Hibernians
1972	Waterford
1973	Waterford
1974	Cork Celtic

Cup Winners

1960	Shelbourne
1961	St Patrick's Athletic
1962	Shamrock Rovers
1963	Shelbourne
1964	Shamrock Rovers
1965	Shamrock Rovers
1966	Shamrock Rovers
1967	Shamrock Rovers
1968	Shamrock Rovers
1969	Shamrock Rovers
1970	Bohemians
1971	Limerick
1972	Cork Hibernians
1973	Cork Hibernians
1974	Cork Hibernians

ITALY

Association founded: 1898
Colours: blue shirts; white shorts
Honours: World Cup, winners 1934, 1938, runners-up 1970; European Championship, winners 1968; Olympic Games, winners 1936, 3rd 1928

League Champions

1960	Juventus
1961	Juventus
1962	AC Milan
1963	Inter-Milan
1964	Bologna
1965	Inter-Milan
1966	Inter-Milan
1967	Juventus
1968	AC Milan
1969	Fiorentina
1970	Cagliari
1971	Inter-Milan
1972	Juventus
1973	Juventus
1974	Lazio

Cup Winners

1960	Juventus
1961	Fiorentina
1962	Napoli
1963	Atalanta
1964	AS Roma
1965	Juventus
1966	Fiorentina
1967	AC Milan
1968	Torino
1969	AS Roma
1970	Bologna
1971	Torino
1972	AC Milan
1973	AC Milan
1974	Bologna

LUXEMBOURG

Association founded: 1908
Colours: red shirts; white shorts

League Champions

1960	Jeunesse Esch
1961	Spora Luxembourg
1962	US Luxembourg
1963	Jeunesse Esch
1964	Aris Bonnevoie
1965	Stade Dudelange
1966	Aris Bonnevoie
1967	Jeunesse Esch
1968	Jeunesse Esch
1969	Avenir Beggen
1970	Jeunesse Esch
1971	US Luxembourg
1972	Aris Bonnevoie
1973	Jeunesse Esch
1974	Jeunesse Esch

Cup Winners

1960	National Schifflge
1961	Alliance Dudelange
1962	Alliance Dudelange
1963	US Luxembourg
1964	US Luxembourg
1965	Spora Luxembourg
1966	Spora Luxembourg
1967	Aris Bonnevoie
1968	US Rumelange
1969	US Luxembourg
1970	US Luxembourg
1971	Jeunesse Hautcharage
1972	Red Boys Differdange
1973	Jeunesse Esch
1974	Jeunesse Esch

NETHERLANDS

Association founded: 1889
Colours: orange shirts; white shorts
Honours: World Cup, runners-up 1974; Olympic Games, 3rd 1908, 1912, 1920

League Champions

1960	Ajax Amsterdam
1961	Feyenoord
1962	Feyenoord
1963	PSV Eindhoven
1964	DWS Amsterdam
1965	Feyenoord
1966	Ajax Amsterdam
1967	Ajax Amsterdam
1968	Ajax Amsterdam
1969	Feyenoord
1970	Ajax Amsterdam
1971	Feyenoord
1972	Ajax Amsterdam
1973	Ajax Amsterdam
1974	Feyenoord

Cup Winners

1960	*No competition*
1961	Ajax Amsterdam
1962	Sparta Rotterdam
1963	Willem II Tilburg
1964	FC Fortuna Geleen
1965	Feyenoord
1966	Sparta Rotterdam
1967	Ajax Amsterdam
1968	ADO The Hague
1969	Feyenoord
1970	Ajax Amsterdam
1971	Ajax Amsterdam
1972	Ajax Amsterdam
1973	NAC Breda
1974	PSV Eindhoven

NEW ZEALAND

Association founded: 1891
Colours: black shirts; white shorts

League Champions

1970	Blockhouse Bay
1971	Eastern Suburbs
1972	Mt Wellington

Cup Winners

1960	North Shore
1961	Northern
1962	Technical Old Boys
1963	North Shore
1964	Mt Roskill
1965	Eastern Suburbs
1966	Miramar Rangers
1967	North Shore
1968	Eastern Suburbs
1969	Eastern Suburbs
1970	Blockhouse Bay
1971	Western Suburbs
1972	Christchurch United

NORWAY

Association founded: 1902
Colours: red shirts; white shorts
Honours: Olympic Games, 3rd 1936

League Champions

1960	Fredrikstad
1961	Fredrikstad
1962	Brann Bergen
1963	Brann Bergen
1964	Lyn Oslo
1965	Valerengen
1966	Skeid Oslo
1967	Rosenborg Trondheim
1968	Lyn Oslo
1969	Rosenborg Trondheim
1970	Stromsgodset Drammen
1971	Rosenborg Trondheim
1972	Viking Stavanger
1973	Viking Stavanger

Cup Winners

1960	Rosenborg Trondheim
1961	Fredrikstad
1970	Ajax Amsterdam
1971	Feyenoord
1972	Ajax Amsterdam
1973	Ajax Amsterdam
1974	Feyenoord
1962	Gjoevik Lyn
1963	Skeid Oslo
1964	Rosenborg Trondheim
1965	Skeid Oslo
1966	Fredrikstad
1967	Lyn Oslo
1968	Lyn Oslo
1969	Stromsgodset Drammen
1970	Stromsgodset Drammen
1971	Rosenborg Trondheim
1972	Brann Bergen
1973	Stromsgodset Drammen

POLAND

Association founded: 1919
Colours: white shirts; red shorts
Honours: World Cup, 3rd 1974; Olympic Games, winners 1972

League Champions

1960	Ruch Chorzow
1961	Gornik Zabrze
1962	Polonia Bytom
1963	Gornik Zabrze
1964	Gornik Zabrze
1965	Gornik Zabrze
1966	Gornik Zabrze
1967	Gornik Zabrze
1968	Ruch Chorzow
1969	Legia Warsaw
1970	Legia Warsaw
1971	Gornik Zabrze
1972	Gornik Zabrze
1973	Stal Mielec
1974	Ruch Chorzow

Cup Winners

1962	Zaglebie Sosnowiec
1963	Zaglebie Sosnowiec
1964	Legia Warsaw
1965	Gornik Zabrze
1966	Legia Warsaw
1967	Wisla Kracow
1968	Gornik Zabrze
1969	Gornik Zabrze
1970	Gornik Zabrze
1971	Gornik Zabrze
1972	Gornik Zabrze
1973	Legia Warsaw
1974	Gwardia Warsaw

PORTUGAL

Association founded: 1914
Colours: red shirts; white shorts
Honours: World Cup, 3rd 1966

League Champions

1960	Benfica
1961	Benfica
1962	Sporting Lisbon
1963	Benfica
1964	Benfica
1965	Benfica
1966	Sporting Lisbon
1967	Benfica
1968	Benfica
1969	Benfica
1970	Sporting Lisbon
1971	Benfica
1972	Benfica
1973	Benfica
1974	Sporting Lisbon

Cup Winners

1960	Belenenses
1961	Leixoes Porto
1962	Benfica
1963	Sporting Lisbon

1964	Benfica
1965	Vitoria Setubal
1966	Sporting Braga
1967	Vitoria Setubal
1968	FC Porto
1969	Benfica
1970	Benfica
1971	Sporting Lisbon
1972	Benfica
1973	Sporting Lisbon
1974	Sporting Lisbon

ROMANIA
Association founded: 1930
Colours: yellow shirts; blue shorts

League Champions
1960	CCA Bucharest
1961	CCA Bucharest
1962	Dynamo Bucharest
1963	Dynamo Bucharest
1964	Dynamo Bucharest
1965	Dynamo Bucharest
1966	Petrolul Ploesti
1967	Rapid Bucharest
1968	Steaua Bucharest
1969	UT Arad
1970	UT Arad
1971	Dynamo Bucharest
1972	Arges Pitesti
1973	Dynamo Bucharest
1974	Universitatea Craiova

Cup Winners
1960	Progresul
1961	Progresul
1962	Steaua Bucharest
1963	Petrolul Ploesti
1964	Dynamo Bucharest
1965	Stinta Cluj
1966	Steaua Bucharest
1967	Steaua Bucharest
1968	Dynamo Bucharest
1969	Steaua Bucharest
1970	Steaua Bucharest
1971	Steaua Bucharest
1972	Rapid Bucharest
1973	Chimia Vilcea
1974	Jiul Petroseni

SPAIN
Association founded: 1905
Colours: red shirts; blue shorts
Honours: European Championship, winners 1964; Olympic Games, runners-up 1920

League Champions
1960	Barcelona
1961	Real Madrid
1962	Real Madrid
1963	Real Madrid
1964	Real Madrid
1965	Real Madrid
1966	Atlético Madrid
1967	Real Madrid
1968	Real Madrid
1969	Real Madrid
1970	Atlético Madrid
1971	Valencia
1972	Real Madrid
1973	Atlético Madrid
1974	Barcelona

Cup Winners
1960	Atlético Madrid
1961	Atlético Madrid
1962	Real Madrid
1963	Barcelona
1964	Real Zaragoza
1965	Atlético Madrid
1966	Real Zaragoza
1967	Valencia
1968	Barcelona
1969	Atlético Bilbao
1970	Real Madrid
1971	Barcelona
1972	Atlético Madrid
1973	Atlético Bilbao
1974	Real Madrid

SWEDEN
Association founded: 1906
Colours: yellow shirts; blue shorts
Honours: World Cup, runners-up 1958, 3rd 1950; Olympic Games, winners 1948, 3rd 1924, 1952

League Champions (League System)
1960	IFK Norrköping
1961	Boras IF Elfsborg
1962	IFK Norrköping
1963	IFK Norrköping
1964	Djurgaarden Stockholm
1965	Malmö FF
1966	Djurgaarden Stockholm
1967	Malmö FF
1968	Oester Vaexjoe
1969	IFK Gothenburg
1970	Malmö FF
1971	Malmö FF
1972	Atvidaberg
1973	Atvidaberg

Cup Winners
1967	Malmö FF
1968	*No competition*
1969	IFK Norrköping
1970	Atvidaberg
1971	Atvidaberg
1972	Landskrona Boys
1973	Malmö FF
1974	Malmö FF

SWITZERLAND
Association founded: 1895
Colours: red shirts; white shorts
Honours: Olympic Games, runners-up 1924

League Champions
1960	Young Boys Berne
1961	Servette Geneva
1962	Servette Geneva
1963	FC Zurich
1964	La Chaux de Fonds
1965	Lausanne
1966	FC Zurich
1967	FC Basle
1968	FC Zurich
1969	FC Basle
1970	FC Basle
1971	Grasshoppers Zurich
1972	FC Basle
1973	FC Basle
1974	FC Zurich

Cup Winners
1960	Lucerne
1961	La Chaux de Fonds
1962	Lausanne
1963	FC Basle
1964	Lausanne
1965	FC Sion
1966	FC Zurich
1967	FC Basle
1968	FC Lugano
1969	St Gallen
1970	FC Zurich
1971	Servette Geneva
1972	FC Zurich
1973	FC Zurich
1974	FC Sion

URUGUAY
Association founded: 1900
Colours: Light blue shirts; black shorts
Honours: World Cup, winners 1930, 1950; South American Championship, winners 1916, 1917, 1920, 1923, 1924, 1926, 1935, 1942, 1960, 1967, runners-up 1919, 1927, 1939, 1941; Olympic Games, winners 1924, 1928

League Champions
1960	Penarol
1961	Penarol
1962	Penarol
1963	Nacional
1964	Penarol
1965	Penarol
1966	Nacional
1967	Penarol
1968	Penarol
1969	Nacional
1970	Nacional
1971	Nacional
1972	Nacional
1973	Penarol

USSR
Association founded: 1912
Colours: red shirts; white shorts
Honours: European Championship, winners 1960, runners-up 1964, 1972; Olympic Games, winners 1956, 3rd (equal) 1972

League Champions
1960	Moscow Torpedo
1961	Kiev Dynamo
1962	Moscow Spartak
1963	Moscow Dynamo
1964	Dynamo Tbilisi
1965	Moscow Torpedo
1966	Kiev Dynamo
1967	Kiev Dynamo
1968	Kiev Dynamo
1969	Moscow Spartak
1970	CSKA Moscow
1971	Kiev Dynamo
1972	Saria Voroshilovgrad
1973	Ararat Erevan

Cup Winners
1960	Moscow Torpedo
1961	Donets Shaktyor
1962	Donets Shaktyor

1963	Moscow Spartak
1964	Kiev Dynamo
1965	Moscow Spartak
1966	Kiev Dynamo
1967	Moscow Dynamo
1968	Moscow Torpedo
1969	Karpaty Lvov
1970	Moscow Dynamo
1971	Moscow Spartak
1972	Moscow Torpedo
1973	Ararat Erevan

YUGOSLAVIA
Association founded: 1919
Colours: blue shirts; white shorts
Honours: World Cup, 3rd 1930; European Championship, runners-up 1960, 1968; Olympic Games, winners 1960, runners-up 1948, 1952, 1956

League Champions
1960	Red Star Belgrade
1961	Partizan Belgrade
1962	Partizan Belgrade
1963	Partizan Belgrade
1964	Red Star Belgrade
1965	Partizan Belgrade
1966	Vojvodina Novi Sad
1967	Sarajevo
1968	Red Star Belgrade
1969	Red Star Belgrade
1970	Red Star Belgrade
1971	Hajduk Split
1972	Zeljeznicar
1973	Red Star Belgrade
1974	Hajduk Split

Cup Winners
1960	Dynamo Zagreb
1961	Vardar Skoplje
1962	OFK Belgrade
1963	Dynamo Zagreb
1964	Red Star Belgrade
1965	Dynamo Zagreb
1966	OFK Belgrade
1967	Hajduk Split
1968	Red Star Belgrade
1969	Dynamo Zagreb
1970	Red Star Belgrade
1971	Red Star Belgrade
1972	Hajduk Split
1973	Dynamo Zagreb
1974	Hajduk Split

Right: Lev Yachin, Moscow Dynamo's custodian in many Russian League successes.

Footballer of the Year Awards

EUROPEAN

1956	Stanley Matthews (Blackpool & England)
1957	Alfredo Di Stefano (Real Madrid & Spain)
1958	Raymond Kopa (Real Madrid & France)
1959	Alfredo Di Stefano (Real Madrid & Spain)
1960	Luis Suarez (Barcelona & Spain)
1961	Enrique Sivori (Juventus & Italy)
1962	Josef Masopust (Dukla Prague & Czechoslovakia)
1963	Lev Yachin (Moscow Dynamo & USSR)
1964	Denis Law (Manchester Utd. & Scotland)
1965	Eusebio (Benfica & Portugal)
1966	Bobby Charlton (Manchester Utd. & England)
1967	Florian Albert (Ferencvaros & Hungary)
1968	George Best (Manchester Utd. & N. Ireland)
1969	Gianni Rivera (AC Milan & Italy)
1970	Gerd Müller (Bayern Munich & West Germany)
1971	Johan Cruyff (Ajax & Netherlands)
1972	Franz Beckenbauer (Bayern Munich & West Germany)
1973	Johan Cruyff (Ajax, Barcelona & Netherlands)

ENGLISH

1947–48	Stanley Matthews (Blackpool)
1948–49	Johnny Carey (Manchester United)
1949–50	Joe Mercer (Arsenal)
1950–51	Harry Johnston (Blackpool)
1951–52	Billy Wright (Wolverhampton Wanderers)
1952–53	Nat Lofthouse (Bolton Wanderers)
1953–54	Tom Finney (Preston North End)
1954–55	Don Revie (Manchester City)
1955–56	Bert Trautmann (Manchester City)
1956–57	Tom Finney (Preston North End)
1957–58	Danny Blanchflower (Tottenham Hotspur)
1958–59	Sid Owen (Luton Town)
1959–60	Bill Slater (Wolverhampton Wanderers)
1960–61	Danny Blanchflower (Tottenham Hotspur)
1961–62	Jimmy Adamson (Burnley)
1962–63	Stanley Matthews (Stoke City)
1963–64	Bobby Moore (West Ham United)
1964–65	Bobby Collins (Leeds United)
1965–66	Bobby Charlton (Manchester United)
1966–67	Jackie Charlton (Leeds United)
1967–68	George Best (Manchester United)
1968–69	Tony Book (Manchester City) / Dave Mackay (Derby County)
1969–70	Billy Bremner (Leeds United)
1970–71	Frank McLintock (Arsenal)
1971–72	Gordon Banks (Stoke City)
1972–73	Pat Jennings (Tottenham Hotspur)
1973–74	Ian Callaghan (Liverpool)

SCOTTISH

1964–65	Billy McNeill (Celtic)
1965–66	John Greig (Rangers)
1966–67	Ronnie Simpson (Celtic)
1967–68	Gordon Wallace (Raith Rovers)
1968–69	Bobby Murdoch (Celtic)
1969–70	Pat Stanton (Hibernian)
1970–71	Martin Buchan (Aberdeen)
1971–72	David Smith (Rangers)
1972–73	George Connelly (Celtic)

Gordon Banks receives England's Footballer of the Year trophy in 1972.

Major British Records

TEAM PERFORMANCES

HIGHEST SCORES*

First-Class Match:		Arbroath	36	Bon Accord	0	5.9.1885
		(Scottish Cup 1st Round)				
International:		England	13	Ireland	0	18.2.1882
FA Cup Tie:		Preston North End	26	Hyde	0	15.10.1887
		(First Round)				
FA Cup Final:		Bury	6	Derby County	0	1903
Scottish Cup Final:		Renton	6	Cambuslang	1	1888
Football League						
Division I:	(Home)	West Bromwich Al.	12	Darwen	0	4.3.1892
		Nottingham Forest	12	Leicester Fosse	0	21.4.1909
	(Away)	Newcastle United	1	Sunderland	9	5.12.1908
		Cardiff City	1	Wolverhampton W.	9	3.9.1955
Division II:	(Home)	Newcastle United	13	Newport County	0	5.10.1946
	(Away)	Burslem Port Vale	0	Sheffield United	10	10.12.1892
Division III:	(Home)	Tranmere Rovers	9	Accrington St.	0	18.4.1959
		Brentford	9	Wrexham	0	15.10.1963
	(Away)	Halifax Town	0	Fulham	8	16.9.1969
Division III(S):	(Home)	Luton Town	12	Bristol Rovers	0	13.4.1936
	(Away)	Northampton Town	0	Walsall	8	2.2.1947
Division III(N):	(Home)	Stockport County	13	Halifax Town	0	6.1.1934
	(Away)	Accrington St.	0	Barnsley	9	3.2.1934
Division IV:	(Home)	Oldham Athletic	11	Southport	0	26.12.1962
	(Away)	Darlington	0	Southport	7	6.1.1973
Scottish League						
Division I:	(Home)	Celtic	11	Dundee	0	26.10.1895
	(Away)	Airdrieonians	1	Hibernian	11	24.10.1959
Division II:	(Home)	East Fife	13	Edinburgh City	2	11.12.1937
	(Away)	Alloa Athletic	0	Dundee	10	8.3.1947

* There are instances of sides scoring as many goals, but where the winning margin is smaller such scores are not given.

MOST GOALS FOR IN A SEASON

Football League		Goals	Games	Season
Division I:	Aston Villa	128	42	1930–31
Division II:	Middlesbrough	122	42	1926–27
Division III:	Queen's Park Rangers	111	46	1961–62
Division III(S):	Millwall	127	42	1927–28
Division III(N):	Bradford City	128	42	1928–29
Division IV:	Peterborough United	134	46	1960–61
Scottish League				
Division I:	Hearts	132	34	1957–58
Division II:	Raith Rovers	142	34	1937–38

MOST GOALS AGAINST IN A SEASON

Football League		Goals	Games	Season
Division I:	Blackpool	125	42	1930–31
Division II:	Darwen	141	34	1898–99
Division III:	Accrington Stanley	123	46	1959–60
Division III(S):	Merthyr Town	135	42	1929–30
Division III(N):	Nelson	136	42	1927–28
Division IV:	Hartlepools United	109	46	1959–60
Scottish League				
Division I:	Leith Athletic	137	38	1931–32
Division II:	Edinburgh City	146	38	1931–32

FEWEST GOALS AGAINST IN A SEASON

Football League		Goals	Games	Season
Division I:	Liverpool	24	42	1968–69 & 1970–71
Division II:	Manchester United	23	42	1924–25
Division III:	Watford	34	46	1968–69
Division III(S):	Southampton	21	42	1921–22
Division III(N):	Port Vale	21	46	1953–54
Division IV:	Gillingham	30	46	1963–64
Scottish League				
Division I:	Celtic	14	38	1913–14
Division II:	Morton	20	38	1966–67

Top: James Ross featured in Preston's 26–0 thrashing of Hyde in the first round of the FA Cup in October 1887. A year later, he put a record seven past the Stoke goalie in a Football League match.
Above: George Camsell scored 59 of Middlesbrough's 122 goals in the Second Division in 1926–27.

Below: In 1971–72, Aston Villa, here playing Brighton (stripes), set new records for the Third Division with 70 points from 46 games, 32 of which they won.

MOST POINTS IN A SEASON

Football League		Points	Games	Season
Division I:	Leeds United	67	42	1968–69
Division II:	Tottenham Hotspur	70	42	1919–20
Division III:	Aston Villa	70	46	1971–72
Division III(S):	Nottingham Forest	70	46	1950–51
	Bristol City	70	46	1954–55
Division III(N):	Doncaster Rovers	72	42	1946–47
Division IV:	Notts County	69	46	1970–71
Scottish League				
Division I:	Rangers	76	42	1920–21
Division II:	Morton	69	38	1966–67

FEWEST POINTS IN A SEASON

Football League		Points	Games	Season
Division I:	Leeds United	18	42	1946–47
	Queen's Park Rangers	18	42	1968–69
Division II:	Doncaster Rovers	8	34	1904–05
	Loughborough Town	8	34	1899–00
	Tranmere Rovers	17	42	1938–39
Division III:	Newport County	22	46	1961–62
Division III(S):	Merthyr Town	21	42	1924–25
				& 1929–30
	Queen's Park Rangers	21	42	1925–26
Division III(N):	Rochdale	11	40	1931–32
Division IV:	Bradford	20	46	1968–69
Scottish League				
Division I:	Stirling Albion	6	30	1954–55

MOST AWAY POINTS IN A SEASON

Football League		Points	Away Games	Season
Division I:	Arsenal	33	21	1930–31
	Tottenham Hotspur	33	21	1960–61
Division II:	Tottenham Hotspur	30	21	1919–20
	Leeds United	30	21	1963–64
Division III:	Bury	29	23	1960–61
	Portsmouth	29	23	1961–62
	Hull City	29	23	1965–66
Division III(S):	Nottingham Forest	32	23	1950–51
Division III(N):	Doncaster Rovers	37	21	1946–47
Division IV:	Walsall	32	23	1959–60
Scottish League				
Division I:	Rangers	37	21	1920–21

FEWEST AWAY POINTS IN A SEASON

The following clubs went through a season without winning a point away from home. All were in Division II of the Football League.

Northwich Victoria	14 away games in			1893–94
Crewe Alexandra	15	,,	,,	,, 1894–95
Loughborough Town	17	,,	,,	,, 1899–1900
Doncaster Rovers	17	,,	,,	,, 1904–05

MOST WINS IN A SEASON

Football League		Wins	Games	Season
Division I:	Tottenham Hotspur	31	42	1960–61
Division II:	Tottenham Hotspur	32	42	1919–20
Division III:	Aston Villa	32	46	1971–72
Division III(S):	Millwall	30	42	1927–28
	Plymouth Argyle	30	42	1929–30
	Cardiff City	30	42	1946–47
	Nottingham Forest	30	46	1950–51
	Bristol City	30	46	1954–55
Division III(N):	Doncaster Rovers	33	42	1946–47
Division IV:	Notts County	30	46	1970–71
Scottish League				
Division I:	Rangers	35	42	1920–21
Division II:	Morton	33	38	1966–67

RECORD HOME WINS IN A SEASON

Brentford won all 21 games in Division III(S), 1929–30

RECORD AWAY WINS IN A SEASON

Doncaster Rovers won 18 of 21 games in Division III(N), 1946–47

MOST DEFEATS IN A SEASON

Football League		Defeats	Games	Season
Division I:	Leeds United	30	42	1946–47
	Blackburn Rovers	30	42	1965–66
Division II:	Tranmere Rovers	31	42	1938–39
Division III:	Newport County	31	46	1961–62
Division III(S):	Merthyr Town	29	42	1924–25
Division III(N):	Rochdale	33	40	1931–32
Division IV:	Bradford	31	46	1968–69
	Barrow	31	46	1970–71
Scottish League				
Division I:	St Mirren	31	42	1920–21
Division II:	Lochgelly United	30	38	1923–24
	Brechin City	30	36	1962–63

Above: Jimmy Greaves, scoring here for England, totalled 357 Football League goals in his prolific career.

FEWEST DEFEATS IN A SEASON

Football League		Defeats	Games	Season
Division I:	Preston North End	0	22	1888–89
	Leeds United	2	42	1968–69
Division II:	Liverpool	0	28	1893–94
	Burnley	2	30	1897–98
	Bristol City	2	38	1905–06
	Leeds United	3	42	1963–64
Division III:	Queen's Park Rangers	5	46	1966–67
Division III(S):	Southampton	4	42	1921–22
	Plymouth Argyle	4	42	1929–30
Division III(N):	Port Vale	3	46	1953–54
	Wolverhampton W.	3	42	1923–24
	Doncaster Rovers	3	42	1946–47
Division IV:	Millwall	7	46	1964–65
	Luton Town	7	46	1967–68
	Swansea City	7	46	1969–70
	Port Vale	7	46	1969–70
	Notts County	7	46	1969–70
Scottish League				
Division I:	Rangers	0	18	1898–99
	Rangers	1	42	1920–21
	Hearts	1	34	1957–58
	Celtic	1	34	1967–68
	Rangers	1	34	1968–69
Division II:	Clyde	1	36	1956–57
	Morton	1	36	1963–64

Below: Bobby Charlton, who won a record 106 caps for England.

LONGEST UNDEFEATED RUNS
Football League
33 First Division games by Leeds United: 18 won and 15 drawn from 26 October, 1968 to 30 August, 1969.

31 games by Liverpool: 22 won and 6 drawn in Division II, 1893–94; the test match to win promotion; 2 drawn in Division I, 1894–95.

30 First Division games by Burnley: 21 won and 9 drawn from 6 September, 1920 to 25 March, 1921.

Away Run: 18 First Division games by Huddersfield Town: 12 won and 6 drawn from 15 November, 1924 to 14 November, 1925.

Home Run: 59 games by Millwall: 43 won and 16 drawn from 24 August, 1964 to 14 January, 1967, during which time they climbed from Division IV to Division II.

Best Start to the Season (42-match season): 19 games undefeated, by Liverpool, Division I, 1949–50. (In 1888–89 Preston North End won the first Championship [22 matches] without a defeat, winning 18 and drawing 4.)

Scottish League
63 First Division games by Celtic from 13 November, 1915 to 21 April, 1917.

LONGEST RUN WITHOUT A WIN
30 games by Crewe Alexandra in Division III(N), 1956–57.

LONGEST FA CUP TIE
9 hours 22 minutes, Stoke City v Bury, 3rd round, January 1955. At Bury, 1–1 after 90 min; at Stoke, 1–1 after 112 min. (abandoned); at Goodison Park, 3–3 after 120 min; at Anfield, 2–2 after 120 min; at Old Trafford, Stoke 3 Bury 2 after 120 min.
FA Qualifying Round
11 hours, Alvechurch v Oxford City, 4th qualifying round, 1971. Alvechurch won 1–0 at Villa Park in the fifth replay.

LONGEST MATCH
203 minutes, Stockport County v Doncaster Rovers, Division III (North) Cup 2nd leg, 30 March, 1946. Because of bad light, play was stopped and there had to be a replay.

INDIVIDUAL PERFORMANCES

MOST INTERNATIONAL APPEARANCES
England
Bobby Moore	108
Bobby Charlton	106
Billy Wright	105

Scotland
Denis Law	55
George Young	53

Wales
Ivor Allchurch	68
Cliff Jones	59

Northern Ireland
Terry Neill	59
Danny Blanchflower	56
Billy Bingham	56

LEADING INTERNATIONAL GOALSCORERS
England
	Goals	Games
Bobby Charlton	49	106
Jimmy Greaves	44	57

Scotland
Denis Law	30	55
Hughie Gallacher	24	19

Wales
Trevor Ford	23	38
Ivor Allchurch	22	68

Northern Ireland
Billy Gillespie	13	25
Joe Bambrick	11	11

Below: In 1927–28, Dixie Dean netted 60 goals for Everton and established a new goalscoring record for the Football League.

MOST LEAGUE GOALS (CAREER)
Arthur Rowley (WBA, Fulham, Leicester, Shrewsbury)	434
Jimmy McGrory (Celtic, Clydebank)	410
Hughie Gallacher (Airdrie, Newcastle, Chelsea, Derby, Notts County, Grimsby, Gateshead)	387
Dixie Dean (Tranmere, Everton, Notts County)	379
Hugh Ferguson (Motherwell, Cardiff, Dundee)	363
Jimmy Greaves (Chelsea, Spurs, West Ham)	357
Steve Bloomer (Derby, Middlesbrough)	352
George Camsell (Durham, Middlesbrough)	346
David Halliday (Dundee, Sunderland, Arsenal, Manchester City, Clapton Orient)	336
Vic Watson (West Ham, Southampton)	317
John Atyeo (Bristol City)	315
Joe Smith (Bolton, Stockport)	314
Harry Johnson (Sheffield United, Mansfield)	309
Harry Bedford (Nottingham Forest, Blackpool, Derby, Newcastle, Sunderland, Bradford, Chesterfield)	309
Bob McPhail (Airdrie, Rangers)	307

MOST LEAGUE GOALS (SEASON)
Football League
		Goals	Games	Season
Division I:	Dixie Dean (Everton)	60	42 (39)	1927–28
Division II:	George Camsell (Middlesbrough)	59	42 (37)	1926–27
Division III:	Derek Reeves (Southampton)	39	46 (39)	1959–60
Division III(S):	Joe Payne (Luton Town)	55	42 (41)	1936–37
Division III(N):	Ted Harston (Mansfield Town)	55	42	1936–37
Division IV:	Terry Bly (Peterborough United)	52	46	1960–61

Scottish League
Division I:	William McFadyen (Motherwell)	52	38 (34)	1931–32
Division II:	Jim Smith (Ayr United)	66	38	1927–28

MOST GOALS IN A MATCH
International:	6	Joe Bambrick	Ireland v Wales	1.2.1930
	5	Charles Heggie	Scotland v Ireland	20.3.1886
	5	Steve Bloomer	England v Wales	16.3.1896
	5	G. O. Smith	England v Ireland	18.2.1899
	5	Hughie Gallacher	Scotland v Ireland	23.2.1929
	5	Willie Hall	England v Ireland	16.11.1938
FA Cup Tie:	9	Ted MacDougall	Bournemouth v Margate (First Round)	20.11.1971
FA Cup Final:	3	William Townley	Blackburn R. v Sheffield W.	1890
	3	James Logan	Notts County v Bolton W.	1894
	3	Stan Mortensen	Blackpool v Bolton W.	1953
Scottish Cup Tie:	13	John Petrie	Arbroath v Bon Accord	5.9.1885

Football League
Division I:	7	Ted Drake	Arsenal v Aston Villa	14.12.1935
	7	James Ross	Preston v Stoke	6.10.1888
Division II:	7	Neville Coleman	Stoke v Lincoln	23.2.1957
	7	Tommy Briggs	Blackburn v Bristol Rovers	5.2.1955
Division III:	5	Barrie Thomas	Scunthorpe v Luton	24.4.1965
	5	Keith East	Swindon v Mansfield	20.11.1965
	5	Steve Earle	Fulham v Halifax	16.9.1969
	5	Alf Wood	Shrewsbury v Blackburn	20.10.1971
Division III(S):	10	Joe Payne	Luton v Bristol Rovers	13.4.1936
Division III(N):	9	Bunny Bell	Tranmere v Oldham	26.12.1935
Division IV:	6	Bert Lister	Oldham v Southport	26.12.1962

Scottish League
Division I:	8	Jimmy McGrory	Celtic v Dunfermline	14.1.1928
Division II:	8	J. Calder	Morton v Raith Rovers	18.4.1936
	8	O. McNally	Arthurlie v Armadale	1.10.1927
	8	J. Dyet	King's Park v Forfar Athletic	2.1.1930

YOUNGEST PLAYERS
International Championship
Northern Ireland:	Norman Kernoghan (17 years 80 days) v Wales	11.3.1936
Wales:	John Charles (18 years 71 days) v N. Ireland	8.3.1950
England:	Duncan Edwards (18 years 183 days) v Scotland	2.4.1955
Scotland:	Denis Law (18 years 236 days) v Wales	18.10.1958

Football League
Albert Geldard (15 years 156 days)	Bradford v Millwall, Div. II	16.9.1929

Youngest in Division I
Derek Forster (15 years 185 days)	Sunderland v Leicester	22.8.1964

Scottish League (Div. I)
Alex Edwards (16 years 5 days)	Dunfermline Ath. v Hibernian	19.3.1962

FA Cup (proper)
Alick Jeffrey (16th birthday)	Doncaster R. v Aston Villa	29.1.1955

FA Cup Final
Howard Kendall (17 years 346 days)	Preston N.E. v West Ham Utd.	2.5.1964

OLDEST PLAYERS
International Championship
Billy Meredith (almost 46) — Wales v England — 15.3.1920
FA Cup (proper)
Billy Meredith (49 years 8 months) — Manchester C. v Newcastle Utd. — 29.3.1924
Football League
Neil McBain (51 years 4 months) — New Brighton v Hartlepools Utd. — 15.3.1947
Oldest in Division I
Sir Stanley Matthews (50 years 5 days) — Stoke City v Fulham — 6.2.1965

LONG SERVICE RECORDS
England
  Jimmy Dickinson: 764 League games for Portsmouth (1946 to 1964)
  Roy Sproson: 756 League games for Port Vale (1950 to 1970–71)
  Terry Paine: 713 League games for Southampton (1957–1974)
  Sir Stanley Matthews: *698 League games for Stoke City and Blackpool (1932 to 1965). He played 886 games altogether including 86 FA Cup ties and 65 internationals.
  Harold Bell: 401 consecutive League games for Tranmere Rovers (1946 to 1955). Including other matches he made 459 successive appearances.
  Ted Sagar: 24 years 1 month with Everton (1929 to 1953).
Scotland
  Bob Ferrier: 626 League games for Motherwell (1919 to 1937)
  Alex Smith: 21 seasons for Rangers from 1894.

* Some record books credit Matthews with 701 League appearances. These include three games played at the start of the abandoned 1939–40 season.

William Townley of Blackburn Rovers.

Jimmy Logan of Notts County.

ATTENDANCE RECORDS

Home international:	149,547	Scotland v England	Hampden Park	17.4.1937
FA Cup Final:	126,047	Bolton v West Ham	Wembley	28.4.1923
FA Cup Tie:	84,569	Manchester City v Stoke	Maine Road	3.3.1934
Scottish Cup Final:	146,433	Celtic v Aberdeen	Hampden Park	24.4.1937
Scottish Cup Tie:	143,570	Rangers v Hibernian (Semi-Final)	Hampden Park	27.3.1948
British Floodlit Record:	107,580	Scotland v Poland	Hampden Park	13.10.1965

Football League

Division I:	83,260	Manchester U. v Arsenal	Maine Road	17.1.1948
Division II:	68,029	Aston Villa v Coventry	Villa Park	30.10.1937
Division III:	48,110	Aston Villa v Bournemouth	Villa Park	12.2.1972
Division III(S):	46,000	Notts County v Nottingham F.	Meadow Lane	22.4.1950
Division III(N):	49,655	Hull City v Rotherham Utd.	Boothferry Park	25.12.1948
Division IV:	37,774	Crystal Palace v Millwall	Selhurst Park	31.3.1961

Scottish League

Division I:	118,567	Rangers v Celtic	Ibrox Stadium	2.1.1939

Records for Other Major Competitions

World Cup:	199,850	Brazil v Uruguay (World record attendance)	Maracana Stadium	16.7.1950
European Cup Final:	127,621	Real Madrid v Eintracht Frankfurt	Hampden Park	18.5.1960
European Cup Tie:	135,826	Celtic v Leeds United	Hampden Park	15.4.1970
European Cup-Winners Cup:	100,000	West Ham Utd. v Munich 1860	Wembley	19.5.1965

Bolton's David Jack.

Goalmouth excitement for the record Third Division gate of 48,110 that saw Aston Villa beat promotion challengers Bournemouth 2–1 at Villa Park in February 1972.

Soccer Chronology

1846 The first rules of soccer drawn up, at Cambridge University.
1857 Sheffield, the oldest soccer club still in existence, founded.
1862 Notts County, the oldest Football League club, founded.
1863 Football Association formed in London on 26 October.
1867 Queen's Park, the oldest Scottish club, founded.
1871 FA Cup proposed and initiated.
1872 First official international, between Scotland and England at Glasgow.
The Wanderers win the first FA Cup final.
1873 Scottish FA formed and Scottish Cup started.
1875 The cross-bar replaces tape on the goal-posts.
1876 FA of Wales formed. The first international between Scotland and Wales.
1878 Referees use whistle for the first time.
1879 First England-Wales international.
Cliftonville, the oldest Irish club, founded.
1880 Irish FA formed and Irish Cup inaugurated
1882 Ireland's first internationals with Wales and England.
International Football Association Board set up.
1883 First Scotland-Ireland International.
The first Home International Championship.
1885 Professionalism legalized in England.
1886 International caps first awarded.
1888 Football League formed.
1889 Preston North End win both the League and the FA Cup.
First FA tour abroad, to Germany.
1890 Irish League formed.
First hat-trick in the FA Cup final, by Blackburn's William Townley.
1891 Scottish League formed.
Referees and linesmen replace umpires.
The penalty-kick introduced.
1892 Goal nets used in FA Cup final for the first time.
Division II of the Football League begins.
1893 Scotland adopts professionalism.
1894 First FA Amateur Cup final.
Division II of Scottish League starts.
1895 FA Cup stolen from a Birmingham shop window. It was never recovered.
1896 Aston Villa win both the League and the FA Cup.
The Corinthians tour South America.
1898 Players Union (now the PFA) set up.
1899 Promotion and relegation first used in the Football League.
1901 Tottenham Hotspur win the FA Cup while a non-League club.
1902 Terracing collapses during the Scotland-England match at Ibrox Park, killing 25.
1904 FIFA formed in Paris, on May 21.
1905 First £1,000 transfer in Britain: Alf Common goes from Sunderland to Middlesbrough.
First international in South America, between Argentina and Uruguay.
1906 England join FIFA.
1907 Amateur FA formed.
1908 England beat Austria 6-1 in Vienna, their first international against a foreign side.
The first Olympic soccer tournament, in London, won by the United Kingdom.

1910 Scotland, Wales, and Ireland join FIFA.
1912 Use of hands by goalkeeper restricted to the penalty area.
1916 The South American Championship first held.
1920 Division III(S) of the Football League started.
1921 Division III(N) first contested.
1922 Promotion and relegation introduced in the Scottish League.
1923 First FA Cup final at Wembley: Bolton beat West Ham before a record crowd.
1925 Offside law changed to require two instead of three defenders between attacker and goal.
1926 Huddersfield Town achieve the first-ever hat-trick of League Championships.

1936 Luton centre-forward Joe Payne scores 10 against Bristol Rovers, a Football League record.
Dixie Dean passes Steve Bloomer's 352 goals in the Football League.
1937 A record 149,547 watch the Scotland-England match at Hampden Park.
1938 Italy retain the World Cup, in France.
Laws of the Game rewritten.
England beat the Rest of Europe 3-0, at Highbury.
Scotland's Jimmy McGrory retires, having scored 550 goals in first-class football, a British record.
1946 British associations rejoin FIFA.
The Burnden Park tragedy: 33 killed and over 400 injured during an FA Cup tie between Bolton and Stoke.
1947 Great Britain beat the Rest of Europe 6-1, at Hampden Park.
1949 Aircraft carrying Italian champions Torino crashes near Turin, killing all on board.

Scenes at the Aztec Stadium, Mexico City, during the opening ceremony in 1970 of the ninth World Cup.

1927 Cardiff City take the FA Cup out of England for the first time.
Mitropa Cup begins.
J. C. Clegg, president of the FA, knighted.
1928 British associations leave FIFA over broken-time payments to amateurs.
First £10,000 transfer: David Jack goes from Bolton to Arsenal.
Dixie Dean scores 60 goals for Everton in Division I, a Football League record.
1929 England lose 4-3 to Spain in Madrid, their first defeat on foreign soil.
1930 Uruguay win the first World Cup, in Uruguay.
F. J. Wall, secretary of the FA, knighted.
1931 Scotland lose 5-0 to Austria in Vienna, their first defeat on foreign soil.
1933 Numbers worn for the first time in the FA Cup final.
1934 Italy win the second World Cup, in Italy.
1935 Arsenal complete a hat-trick of League Championships.
Arsenal centre-forward Ted Drake scores seven goals against Aston Villa at Villa Park, a Division I record.

England beaten 2-0 by Republic of Ireland at Goodison Park, so losing their unbeaten home record against foreign sides.
Rangers win the first 'treble'—Scottish League, Cup, and League Cup.
S. F. Rous, secretary of the FA, knighted.
1950 Uruguay win the fourth World Cup, in Brazil. England, entering for the first time, lose 1-0 to USA. Scotland's unbeaten home record against foreign sides goes in a 1-0 defeat by Austria at Hampden Park.
1952 Billy Wright passes Bob Crompton's record of 42 caps.
Newcastle United retain the FA Cup, the first club to do so in the 20th century.
1953 England draw 4-4 with the Rest of the World, at Wembley.
England lose their unbeaten record at Wembley against foreign opposition, going down 6-3 to Hungary.
1954 West Germany win the fifth World Cup, in Switzerland.
England suffer their heaviest international defeat, 7-1 by Hungary.
The European Union of Football Associations (UEFA) formed.

(Continued on p. 168)

EAF

Colours

Many British clubs have adopted new colours in recent years, partly influenced by the colours of leading Continental clubs. The colours illustrated in this section are the first-choice colours of the clubs at the time of going to press.

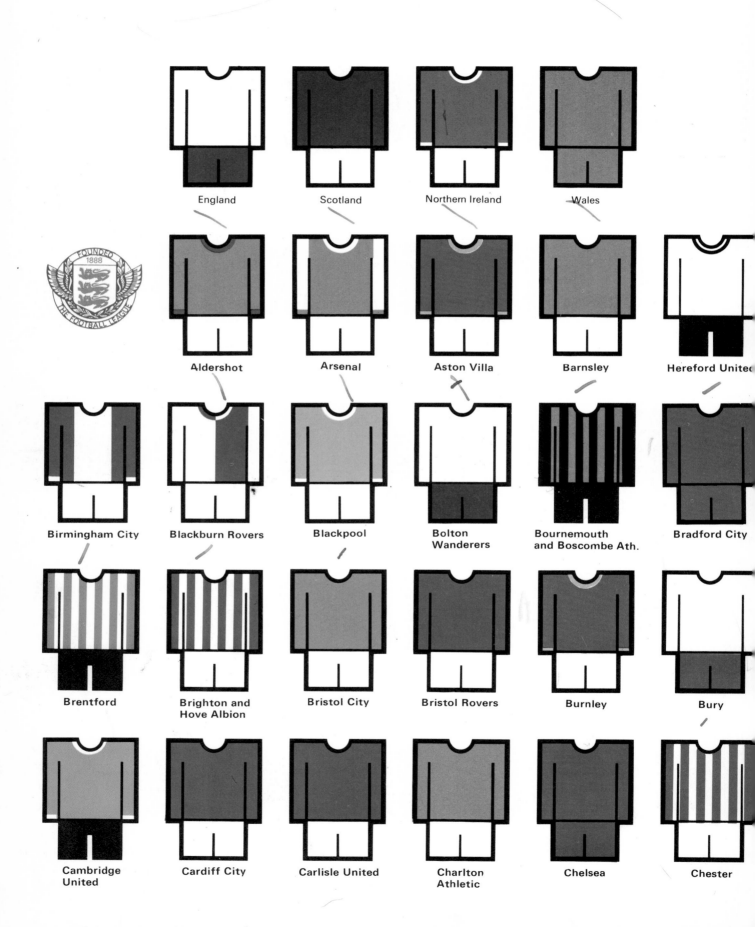

England

Scotland

Northern Ireland

Wales

Aldershot

Arsenal

Aston Villa

Barnsley

Hereford United

Birmingham City

Blackburn Rovers

Blackpool

Bolton Wanderers

Bournemouth and Boscombe Ath.

Bradford City

Brentford

Brighton and Hove Albion

Bristol City

Bristol Rovers

Burnley

Bury

Cambridge United

Cardiff City

Carlisle United

Charlton Athletic

Chelsea

Chester

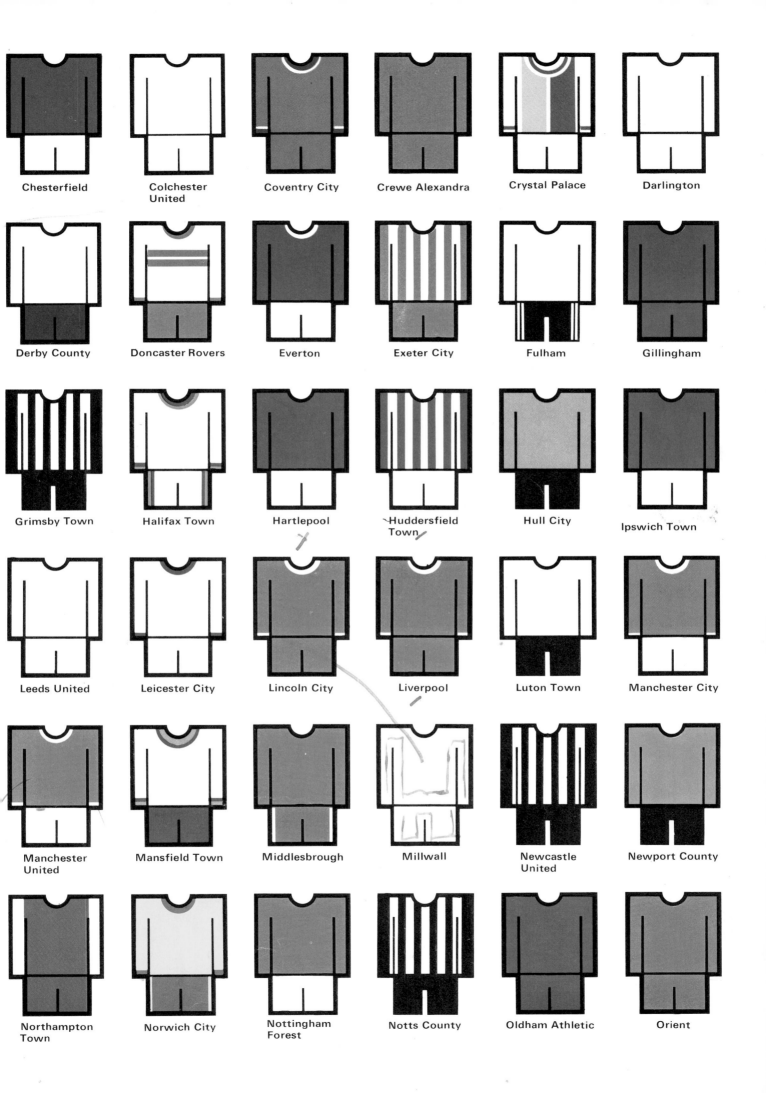

Chesterfield

Colchester United

Coventry City

Crewe Alexandra

Crystal Palace

Darlington

Derby County

Doncaster Rovers

Everton

Exeter City

Fulham

Gillingham

Grimsby Town

Halifax Town

Hartlepool

Huddersfield Town

Hull City

Ipswich Town

Leeds United

Leicester City

Lincoln City

Liverpool

Luton Town

Manchester City

Manchester United

Mansfield Town

Middlesbrough

Millwall

Newcastle United

Newport County

Northampton Town

Norwich City

Nottingham Forest

Notts County

Oldham Athletic

Orient

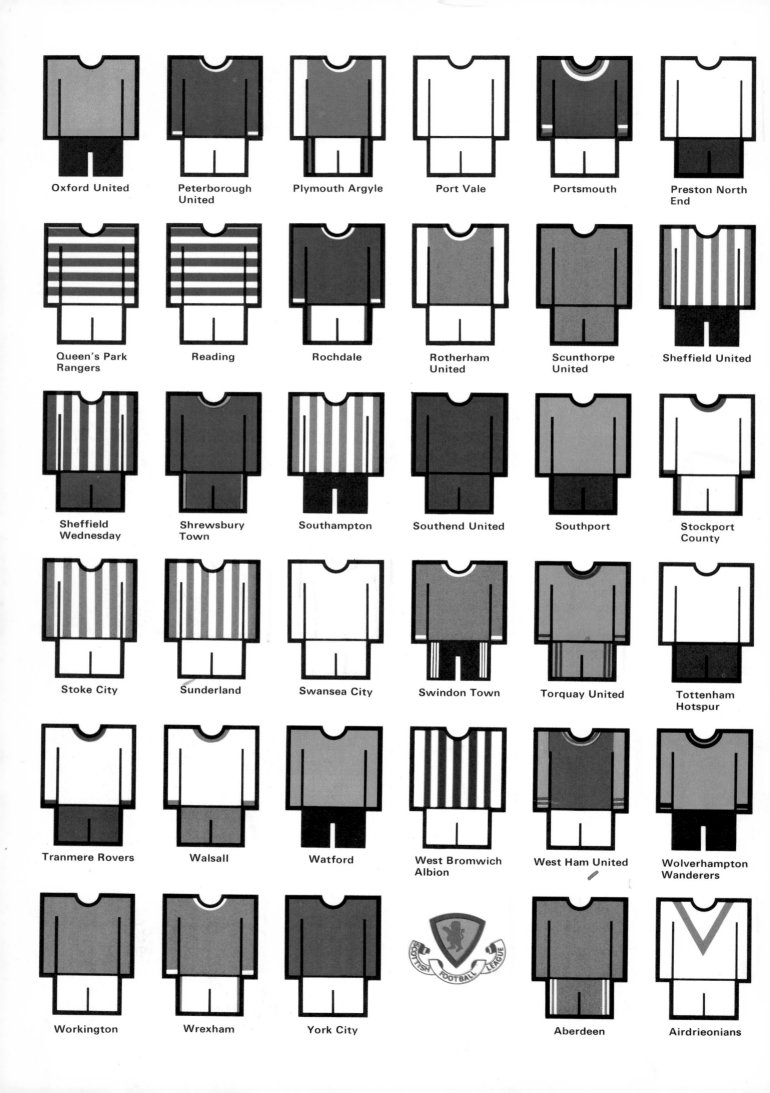

Oxford United	Peterborough United	Plymouth Argyle	Port Vale	Portsmouth	Preston North End
Queen's Park Rangers	Reading	Rochdale	Rotherham United	Scunthorpe United	Sheffield United
Sheffield Wednesday	Shrewsbury Town	Southampton	Southend United	Southport	Stockport County
Stoke City	Sunderland	Swansea City	Swindon Town	Torquay United	Tottenham Hotspur
Tranmere Rovers	Walsall	Watford	West Bromwich Albion	West Ham United	Wolverhampton Wanderers
Workington	Wrexham	York City		Aberdeen	Airdrieonians

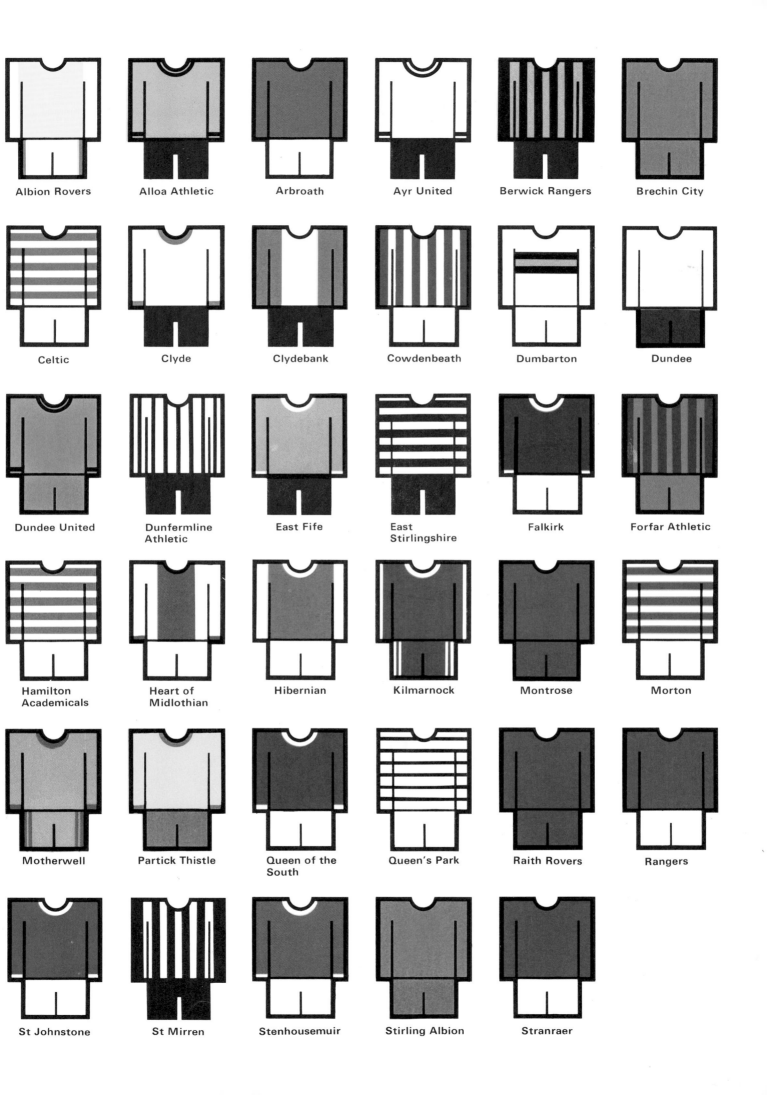

Albion Rovers

Alloa Athletic

Arbroath

Ayr United

Berwick Rangers

Brechin City

Celtic

Clyde

Clydebank

Cowdenbeath

Dumbarton

Dundee

Dundee United

Dunfermline
Athletic

East Fife

East
Stirlingshire

Falkirk

Forfar Athletic

Hamilton
Academicals

Heart of
Midlothian

Hibernian

Kilmarnock

Montrose

Morton

Motherwell

Partick Thistle

Queen of the
South

Queen's Park

Raith Rovers

Rangers

St Johnstone

St Mirren

Stenhousemuir

Stirling Albion

Stranraer

Soccer Postage Stamps

1 A stamp commemorating Hungary's famous 6–3 victory over England at Wembley in 1953, England's first defeat at home by a Continental side.

2 Hungarian World Cup stamps. The top one honours Jules Rimet, the founder of the competition. The Jules Rimet Trophy is on the right.

3 The World Cup is an ideal event for the many small states that issue pictorial postage stamps as a source of revenue. Pelé has appeared on the stamps of numerous countries.

4 For the 1970 World Cup in Mexico, Nicaragua issued a set of stamps depicting 11 of the world's greatest players: Pelé (Brazil), Ferenc Puskas (Hungary), Stanley Matthews (England), Djalma Santos (Brazil), Alfredo di Stefano (Argentina and Spain), Billy Wright (England), Giacinto Facchetti (Italy), Lev Yachin (USSR), Josef Bozsik (Hungary), Bobby Charlton (England), Franz Beckenbauer (West Germany). The 1 cordoba stamp illustrates the flags of the 16 nations competing in Mexico. Although football fans from all over the world might put forward other candidates, no one can deny that the 11 players honoured have made a great contribution to world football and would make a formidable team.

1

2

3

4

5 Politics figures all too often in sport, as is well illustrated in a stamp issued by the Yemen Arab Republic for the 1970 World Cup. All the names of countries competing in the finals are given, except one—Israel, which has been blacked out. Politically incompatible countries are kept well apart by the organizers. Israel and Morocco were seeded in different groups in Mexico and neither reached the quarter-finals.

6 More Hungarian stamps illustrating action from World Cup finals.

7 For 1966, Poland issued a set depicting World Cup finals and the qualifying match in which they beat Scotland 2–1.

But despite this victory they failed to reach the finals.

8 England issued only three stamps to commemorate the World Cup held there in 1966. The stamps were symbolic, but this did not justify a goalkeeper (in the 6d stamp) with shorts and socks of a different colour from those of either team.

9 The Poles, ever eager to record their soccer progress on stamps, were unlucky again in 1970, when Manchester City spoilt the effect of their first-day cover by beating Gornik 2–0 in the final of the European Cup-Winners Cup.

10 It was left to Monaco to commemorate the FA Centenary in 1963.

5

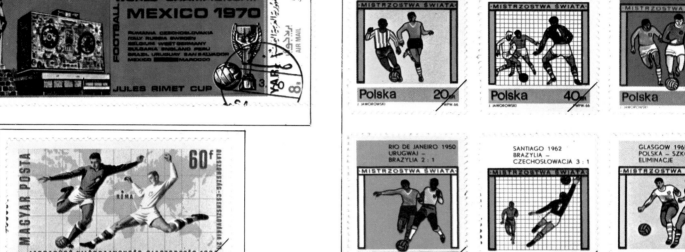

7

6

8

9

10

1955 European Champions Cup and Inter-Cities Fairs Cup begin.
Rest of the World beat Great Britain 4–1, in Belfast.

1956 Real Madrid win the first European Cup. First floodlit match in the Football League: Portsmouth v Newcastle United on 22 February.

1957 George Young retires with a record 53 Scottish caps to his credit.
John Charles of Leeds becomes the first British player to transfer to a foreign club.

1958 Manchester United lose eight players in the Munich air disaster on 6 February.
Brazil win the sixth World Cup, in Sweden.
Sunderland, previously always in Division I, relegated.
Division III and Division IV replace the old Division III North and South.

1959 Billy Wright plays his 100th game for England, against Scotland, and retires at the end of the season with a world record 105 caps.

1960 USSR win the first European Nations' Cup, in Paris.
Real Madrid win the European Cup for the fifth consecutive time.

1961 Sir Stanley Rous becomes president of FIFA.
Spurs win the League and Cup, the first 'double' of the 20th century.
The Professional Footballers' Association (PFA) succeed in abolishing the maximum wage.
Fiorentina win the first European Cup-Winners Cup.

1962 Brazil retain the World Cup, in Chile. Denis Law transfers from Torino to Manchester United, the first transfer over £100,000 paid by a British club.

1963 The centenary of the FA. England beat the Rest of the World 2–1, at Wembley
The Football League's 'retain and transfer' system declared illegal.

Above: In the pageant before the Centenary FA Cup final in 1972, all the teams that had won the Cup were represented. The Wanderers won the first Cup, in 1872.

The 1970 World Cup saw Brazil, with the incomparable Pelé (right), take permanent possession of the Jules Rimet Trophy.

Below: The goal that clinched West Germany's place in the 1974 World Cup final. Gerd Müller (all white) sends Poland's goalkeeper the wrong way for the only goal of the deciding game in Group B.

Spurs win the European Cup-Winners Cup, the first British success in Europe.

1964 Spain win the European Nations' Cup, in Madrid.
More than 300 killed and 500 injured in rioting during an Olympic qualifying game between Peru and Argentina at Lima.
Jimmy Dickinson becomes the first player to make 700 Football League appearances.

1965 Stanley Matthews becomes the first footballer to be knighted.
Arthur Rowley retires, having scored a record 434 Football League goals.
The Football League agree to the substitution of one injured player.

1966 England win the eighth World Cup, in England.
The Football League allow one substitution for any reason.

1967 Alf Ramsey, England's manager, knighted.
Celtic become the first British club to win the European Cup.

1968 Italy win the European Football Championship, in Rome.
A world record transfer: Pietro Anastasi moves from Varese to Juventus for £440,000.
Manchester United win the European Cup: Matt Busby knighted.
Leeds United become the first British club to win the Fairs Cup.

1969 Pelé scores his 1,000th goal.
Leeds win the Football League Championship with a record 67 points.

1970 Brazil win the ninth World Cup, in Mexico, and take permanent possession of the Jules Rimet trophy. Bobby Charlton wins his 106th England cap in the quarter-finals to beat Billy Wright's record.

1971 Britain's worst ever crowd disaster: 66 killed at an Ibrox Park match between Rangers and Celtic.
Arsenal win the League-Cup double.

1972 First UEFA Cup (replacing Fairs Cup): Tottenham beat Wolverhampton in first all-British European final.
West Germany win the European Football Championship, in Brussels.

1973 Ajax win the European Cup for the third consecutive time.
Bobby Moore wins his 108th England cap, a new record.
Johan Cruyff moves from Ajax to Barcelona for £922,300, more than double the previous record.

1974 Joao Havelange of Brazil replaces Sir Stanley Rous as president of FIFA.
West Germany win the 10th World Cup, in West Germany.
Denis Law wins his 55th cap, a Scottish record.

British Club Directory

ENGLAND

Aldershot: *Founded:* 1927. *Colours:* red shirts with blue facings, white shorts. *Ground:* Recreation Ground. *Nickname:* The Shots. *Ground record:* 19,138 v Carlisle United, FA Cup 4th round replay, 28.1.1970.

Arsenal: *Founded:* 1886. *Colours:* red shirts with white collars and sleeves. *Ground:* Arsenal Stadium. *Nickname:* The Gunners. *Ground record:* 73,295 v Sunderland, Division I, 9.3.1935. **Honours:** Fairs Cup: *winners* 1969–70. League Championship: *winners* 1930–31, 1932–33, 1933–34, 1934–35, 1937–38, 1947–48, 1952–53, 1970–71; *runners-up* 1925–26, 1931–32, 1972–73. FA Cup: *winners* 1930, 1936, 1950, 1971; *runners-up* 1927, 1932, 1952, 1972. League Cup: *runners-up* 1967–68, 1968–69.

Aston Villa: *Founded:* 1874. *Colours:* claret shirts with light blue facings, white shorts. *Ground:* Villa Park. *Nickname:* The Villans. *Ground record:* 76,588 v Derby County, FA Cup 6th round, 2.3.1946. **Honours:** League Championship: *winners* 1893–94, 1895–96, 1896–97, 1898–99, 1899–1900, 1909–1910; *runners-up* 1888–89, 1902–03, 1907–08, 1910–11, 1912–13, 1913–14, 1930–31, 1932–33. FA Cup: *winners* 1887, 1895, 1897, 1905, 1913, 1920, 1957; *runners-up* 1892, 1924. League Cup: *winners* 1961; *runners-up* 1963, 1971.

Barnsley: *Founded:* 1887. *Colours:* red shirts, white shorts. *Ground:* Oakwell Ground. *Nickname:* The Tykes. *Ground record:* 40,255 v Stoke City, FA Cup 5th round, 15.2.1936. **Honours:** FA Cup: winners 1912; *runners-up* 1910.

Birmingham City: *Founded:* 1875. *Colours:* royal blue shirts with white vertical stripe, collars, and cuffs, white shorts. *Ground:* St Andrews. *Nickname:* The Blues. *Ground record:* 68,844 v Everton, FA Cup 5th round, 11.2.1939. **Honours:** Fairs Cup: *runners-up* 1958–60, 1960–61. FA Cup: *runners-up* 1931, 1956. League Cup: *winners* 1963.

Blackburn Rovers: *Founded:* 1874. *Colours:* blue and white halved shirts, white shorts. *Ground:* Ewood Park. *Nickname:* The Blue and Whites. *Ground record:* 61,783 v Bolton Wanderers, FA Cup 6th round, 2.3.1929. **Honours:** League Championship: *winners* 1911–12, 1913–14. FA Cup: *winners* 1884, 1885, 1886, 1890, 1891, 1928; *runners-up* 1882, 1960.

Blackpool: *Founded:* 1887. *Colours:* tangerine shirts with white facings, white shorts. *Ground:* Bloomfield Road. *Nickname:* The Tangerines. *Ground record:* 39,118 v Manchester United, Division I, 19.4.1952. **Honours:** League Championship: *runners-up* 1955–56. FA Cup: *winners* 1953; *runners-up* 1948, 1951.

Bolton Wanderers: *Founded:* 1874. *Colours:* white shirts, dark blue shorts. *Ground:* Burnden Park. *Nickname:* The Trotters. *Ground record:* 69,912 v Manchester City, FA Cup 5th round, 18.2.1933. **Honours:** FA Cup: *winners* 1923, 1926, 1929, 1958; *runners-up* 1894, 1904, 1953.

Bournemouth and Boscombe Athletic: *Founded:* 1899. *Colours:* red and black striped shirts, black shorts. *Ground:* Dean Court. *Nickname:* The Cherries. *Ground record:* 28,799 v Manchester United, FA Cup 6th round, 2.3.1957.

Bradford City: *Founded:* 1903. *Colours:* claret shirts and shorts. *Ground:* Valley Parade. *Nickname:* The Valley Paraders. *Ground record:* 39,146 v Burnley, FA Cup 4th round, 11.3.1911. **Honours:** FA Cup: *winners* 1911.

Brentford: *Founded:* 1888. *Colours:* red and white striped shirts, black shorts. *Ground:* Griffin Park. *Nickname:* The Bees. *Ground record:* 39,626 v Preston North End, FA Cup 6th round, 5.3.1938.

Brighton and Hove Albion: *Founded:* 1900. *Colours:* blue and white striped shirts, white shorts. *Ground:* Goldstone Ground. *Nickname:* The Shrimps. *Ground record:* 36,747 v Fulham, Division II, 27.12.1958.

Bristol City: *Founded:* 1894. *Colours:* red shirts, white shorts. *Ground:* Ashton Gate. *Nickname:* The Robins. *Ground record:* 43,335 v Preston North End, FA Cup 5th round, 16.2.1935. **Honours:** FA Cup: *runners-up* 1909.

Bristol Rovers: *Founded:* 1883. *Colours:* blue shirts, white shorts. *Ground:* Eastville Stadium. *Nickname:* The Pirates. *Ground record:* 38,472 v Preston North End, FA Cup 4th round, 30.1.1960.

Burnley: *Founded:* 1881. *Colours:* claret shirts with blue facings, white shorts. *Ground:* Turf Moor. *Nickname:* The Turfites. *Ground*

Top: Bolton Wanderers skipper Joe Smith (left) shakes hands with Jimmy McMullan of Manchester City before the start of the 1926 FA Cup final; The Trotters won 1–0 with a goal by David Jack.
Above: Prince Henry meets the Aston Villa players before the 1920 FA Cup final that saw Villa win the Cup for the sixth time.

Below left: Stanley Matthews, who turned the 1953 Cup final Blackpool's way, in action for the club on his 43rd birthday.
Below: Charlie George, precocious and controversial star of Arsenal's 1970–71 team that completed the League–FA Cup double.

Above: David Webb heads home Chelsea's winner in the 1970 FA Cup final replay.

Below: Colchester manager Dick Graham pours the champagne as his team celebrate their shock 3–2 defeat of Leeds in the fifth round of the 1971 FA Cup.

record: 54,775 v Huddersfield Town, FA Cup 3rd round, 23.2.1924. **Honours:** League Championship: *winners* 1920–21, 1959–60; *runners-up* 1919–20, 1961–62. FA Cup: *winners* 1914; *runners-up* 1947, 1962.

Bury: *Founded:* 1885. *Colours:* white shirts, royal blue shorts. *Ground:* Gigg Lane. *Nickname:* The Shakers. *Ground record:* 35,000 v Bolton Wanderers, FA Cup 3rd round, 9.1.1960. **Honours:** FA Cup: *winners* 1900, 1903.

Cambridge United: *Founded:* 1919. *Colours:* amber shirts with black facings, black shorts. *Ground:* Abbey Stadium. *Nickname:* The United. *Ground record:* 14,000 v Chelsea, friendly, 1.5.1970.

Cardiff City: *Founded:* 1899. *Colours:* blue shirts, white shorts. *Ground:* Ninian Park. *Nickname:* The Bluebirds. *Ground record:* (club) 57, 800 v Arsenal, Division I, 22.4.1953. **Honours:** League Championship: *runners-up* 1923–24. FA Cup: *winners* 1927; *runners-up* 1925.

Carlisle United: *Founded:* 1903. *Colours:* blue shirts, white shorts. *Ground:* Brunton Park. *Nickname:* The Cumbrians. *Ground record:* 27,500 v Birmingham City, FA Cup 3rd round, 5.1.1957.

Charlton Athletic: *Founded:* 1905. *Colours:* red shirts, white shorts. *Ground:* The Valley. *Nickname:* The Haddicks or The Robins. *Ground record:* 75,031 v Aston Villa, FA Cup 5th round, 12.2.1938. *Honours:* League Championship: *runners-up* 1936–37. FA Cup: *winners* 1947; *runners-up* 1946.

Chelsea: *Founded:* 1905. *Colours:* royal blue shirts and shorts. *Ground:* Stamford Bridge. *Nickname:* The Blues. *Ground record:* 82,905 v Arsenal, Division I, 12.10.1935. **Honours:** European Cup-Winners Cup: *winners* 1970–71. League Championship: *winners* 1954–55. FA Cup: *winners* 1970; *runners-up* 1914–15, 1966–67. League Cup: *winners* 1964–65; *runners-up* 1971–72.

Chester: *Founded:* 1884. *Colours:* blue and white striped shirts, white shorts. *Ground:* Sealand Road Stadium. *Nickname:* The Cestrians. *Ground record:* 20,500 v Chelsea, FA Cup 3rd round replay, 16.1.1952.

Chesterfield: *Founded:* 1866. *Colours:* blue shirts, white shorts. *Ground:* Recreation Ground. *Nickname:* The Blues or The Spirites. *Ground record:* 30,968 v Newcastle United, Division II, 7.4.1939.

Colchester United: *Founded:* 1937. *Colours:* white shirts and shorts. *Ground:* Layer Road. *Nickname:* The U's. *Ground record:* 19,072 v Reading, FA Cup 1st round, 27.11.1948.

Coventry City: *Founded:* 1883. *Colours:* sky blue shirts with navy and white facings, sky blue shorts. *Ground:* Highfield Road. *Nickname:* The Sky Blues. *Ground records:* 51,455 v Wolverhampton Wanderers, Division II, 29.4.1967.

Crewe Alexandra: *Founded:* 1876. *Colours:* scarlet shirts and shorts. *Ground:* Gresty Road. *Nickname:* The Railwaymen. *Ground record:* 20,000 v Tottenham Hotspur, FA Cup 4th round, 30.1.1960.

Crystal Palace: *Founded:* 1905. *Colours:* white shirts with claret and blue vertical bands, white shorts. *Ground:* Selhurst Park. *Nickname:* The Glaziers. *Ground record:* 49,498 v Chelsea, Division I, 27.12.1969.

Darlington: *Founded:* 1883. *Colours:* white shirts and shorts. *Ground:* Feethams Ground. *Nickname:* The Quakers. *Ground record:* 21,864 v Bolton Wanderers, League Cup 3rd round, 14.11.1960.

Derby County: *Founded:* 1884. *Colours:* white shirts, blue shorts. *Ground:* Baseball Ground. *Nickname:* The Rams. *Ground record:* 41,826 V Tottenham Hotspur, Division I,

20.9.1969. **Honours:** League Championship: *winners* 1971–72; *runners-up* 1895–96, 1929–30, 1935–36. FA Cup: *winners* 1946; *runners-up* 1898, 1899, 1903.

Doncaster Rovers: *Founded:* 1879. *Colours:* white shirts with red facings and two red hoops, red shorts. *Ground:* Belle Vue. *Nickname:* The Rovers. *Ground record:* 37,149 v Hull City, Division III (North), 2.10.1948.

Everton: *Founded:* 1878. *Colours:* royal blue shirts with white collars, white shorts. *Ground:* Goodison Park. *Nickname:* The Toffees or The Blues. *Ground record:* 78,299 v Liverpool, Division I, 18.9.1948. **Honours:** League Championship: *winners* 1890–91, 1914–15, 1927–28, 1931–32, 1938–39, 1962–63, 1969–70; *runners-up* 1889–90, 1894–95, 1901–02, 1904–05, 1908–09, 1911–12. FA Cup: *winners* 1906, 1933, 1966; *runners-up* 1893, 1897, 1907, 1968.

Exeter City: *Founded:* 1904. *Colours:* red and white striped shirts, red shorts. *Ground:* St James' Park. *Nickname:* The Grecians. *Ground record:* 20,984 v Sunderland, FA Cup 6th round replay, 4.3.1931.

Fulham: *Founded:* 1880. *Colours:* white shirts, black shorts with two white stripes. *Ground:* Craven Cottage. *Nickname:* The Cottagers. *Ground record:* 49,335 v Millwall, Division II, 8.10.1938.

Gillingham: *Founded:* 1893. *Colours:* blue shirts and shorts. *Ground:* Priestfield Stadium. *Nickname:* The Gills. *Ground record:* 23,002 v Queen's Park Rangers, FA Cup 3rd round, 10.1.1948.

Grimsby Town: *Founded:* 1878. *Colours:* black and white striped shirts, black shorts. *Ground:* Blundell Park. *Nickname:* The Mariners or Fishermen. *Ground record:* 31,651 v Wolverhampton Wanderers, FA Cup 5th round, 20.2.1937.

Halifax Town: *Founded:* 1911. *Colours:* white shirts and shorts with tangerine and blue facings. *Ground:* Shay Ground. *Nickname:* The Town. *Ground record:* 36,885 v Tottenham Hotspur, FA Cup 5th round, 14.2.1953.

Hartlepool: *Founded:* 1908. *Colours:* blue shirts, white shorts. *Ground:* Victoria Ground. *Nickname:* The Pool. *Ground record:* 17,426 v

Manchester United, FA Cup 3rd round, 5.1.57.

Hereford United: *Founded:* 1939. *Colours:* white shirts with black collars, black shorts. *Ground:* Edgar Street. *Ground record:* 18,114 v Sheffield Wednesday, FA Cup 3rd round, 4.1.1958.

Huddersfield Town: *Founded:* 1908. *Colours:* blue and white striped shirts, white shorts. *Ground:* Leeds Road. *Nickname:* The Terriers. *Ground record:* 67,037 v Arsenal, FA Cup 6th round, 27.2.1932. **Honours:** League Championship: *winners* 1923–24, 1924–25, 1925–26; *runners-up* 1926–27, 1927–28, 1933–34. FA Cup: *winners* 1922; *runners-up* 1920, 1928, 1930, 1938.

Hull City: *Founded:* 1904. *Colours:* amber shirts, black shorts. *Ground:* Boothferry Park. *Nickname:* The Tigers. *Ground record:* 55,019 v Manchester United, FA Cup 6th round, 26.2.1949.

Ipswich Town: *Founded:* 1880. *Colours:* blue shirts, white shorts. *Ground:* Portman Road. *Nickname:* The Town or Blues. *Ground record:* 33,525 v Arsenal, Div. I, 10.3.1973. **Honours:** League Championship: *winners* 1961–62.

Leeds United: *Founded:* 1920. *Colours:* white shirts and shorts. *Ground:* Elland Road. *Nickname:* The Peacocks. *Ground record:* 57,892 v Sunderland, FA Cup 5th round replay, 15.3.1967. **Honours:** European Cup-Winners Cup: *runners-up* 1972–73. Fairs Cup: *winners* 1967–68, 1970–71; *runners-up* 1966–67. League Championship: *winners* 1968–69, 1973–74; *runners-up* 1964–65, 1965–66, 1969–70, 1970–71, 1971–72. FA Cup: *winners* 1972; *runners-up* 1965, 1970, 1973. League Cup: *winners* 1967–68.

Leicester City: *Founded:* 1884. *Colours:* white shirts with blue facings, white shorts. *Ground:* Filbert Street. *Nickname:* The Filberts. *Ground record:* 47,298 v Tottenham Hotspur, FA Cup 5th round, 18.2.1928. **Honours:** League Championship: *runners-up* 1928–29. FA Cup: *runners-up* 1949, 1961, 1963, 1969. League Cup: *winners* 1964; *runners-up* 1965.

Lincoln City: *Founded:* 1883. *Colours:* red shirts and shorts with white facings. *Ground:* Sincil Bank. *Nickname:* The Imps. *Ground record:* 23,196 v Derby County, League Cup 4th round replay, 15.11.1967.

Liverpool: *Founded:* 1892. *Colours:* red shirts and shorts with white facings. *Ground:* Anfield Road. *Nickname:* The Reds or Pool. *Ground record:* 61,905 v Wolverhampton Wanderers, FA Cup 4th round, 2.2.1952. **Honours:** European Cup-Winners Cup: *runners-up* 1965–66. UEFA Cup: *winners* 1972–73. League Championship: *winners* 1900–01, 1905–06, 1921–22, 1922–23, 1946–47, 1963–64, 1965–66, 1972–73; *runners-up* 1898–99, 1909–1910, 1968–69, 1973–74. FA Cup: *winners* 1965, 1974; *runners-up* 1914, 1950, 1971.

Luton Town: *Founded:* 1885. *Colours:* white shirts, black shorts. *Ground:* Kenilworth Road. *Nickname:* The Hatters. *Ground record:* 30,069 v Blackpool, FA Cup 6th round replay, 4.3. 1959. **Honours:** FA Cup: *runners-up* 1959.

Manchester City: *Founded:* 1894. *Colours:* sky blue shirts with white facings, white

Above: Roy McFarland captained Derby County to the First Division title in 1971–72. Below: Hereford United (white shirts), newcomers to the Football League in 1972.

Above: Huddersfield Town, FA Cup winners in 1922.

Below: Ipswich Town, Football League champions in 1961–62.

shorts. *Ground:* Maine Road. *Nickname:* The Sky Blues or Citizens. *Ground record:* 84,569 v Stoke City, FA Cup 6th round, 3.3.1934. **Honours:** European Cup-Winners Cup: *winners* 1969–70. League Championship: *winners* 1936–37, 1967–68; *runners-up* 1903–04, 1920–21. FA Cup: *winners* 1904, 1934, 1956, 1969; *runners-up* 1926, 1933, 1955. League Cup: *winners* 1970; *runners-up* 1974.

Manchester United: *Founded:* 1878 (reformed 1902). *Colours:* red shirts with white facings, white shorts. *Ground:* Old Trafford. *Nickname:* The Red Devils. *Ground record:* (club) 70,504 v Aston Villa, Division I, 27.12.1920. **Honours:** European Cup: *winners* 1967–68. League Championship: *winners* 1907–08, 1910–11, 1951–52, 1955–56, 1956–57, 1964–65, 1966–67; *runners-up* 1946–47, 1947–48, 1948–49, 1950–51, 1958–59, 1963–64, 1967–68. FA Cup: *winners* 1909, 1948, 1963; *runners-up* 1957, 1958.

Mansfield Town: *Founded:* 1905. *Colours:* white shirts with blue and amber facings, blue shorts. *Ground:* Field Mill. *Nickname:* The Stags. *Ground record:* 24,467 v Nottingham Forest, FA Cup 3rd round, 10.1.1953.

Middlesbrough: *Founded:* 1876. *Colours:* red shirts and red shorts with white stripe. *Ground:* Ayresome Park. *Nickname:* The Borough or Ironsides. *Ground record:* 53,596 v Newcastle United, Division I, 27.12.1949. **Honours:** Amateur Cup: *winners* 1895, 1898.

Millwall: *Founded:* 1885. *Colours:* white

Above: Manchester City skipper Roy Paul on Don Revie's shoulders after the 1956 FA Cup victory over Birmingham City.
Far left: Gordon Banks, whose brilliant goalkeeping helped Stoke City win the Football League Cup in 1971–72.
Left: Sit Matt Busby's Manchester United with the European Cup won in 1968.

Below left: Iam McFaul, hero of St James's Park when Newcastle United won the Fairs Cup in 1968–69.

shirts and shorts. *Ground:* The Den. *Nickname:* The Lions. *Ground record:* 48,672 v Derby County, FA Cup 5th round, 20.2.1937.

Newcastle United: *Founded:* 1882. *Colours:* black and white striped shirts, black shorts. *Ground:* St James's Park. *Nickname:* The Magpies. *Ground record:* 68,386 v Chelsea, Division I, 3.9.1930. **Honours:** European Fairs Cup: *winners* 1968–69. League Championship: *winners* 1904–05, 1906–07, 1908–09, 1926–27. FA Cup: *winners* 1910, 1924, 1932, 1951, 1952, 1955; *runners-up* 1905, 1906, 1908, 1911, 1974.

Newport County: *Founded:* 1911. *Colours:* tangerine shirts, black shorts. *Ground:* Somerton Park. *Nickname:* The Ironsides. *Ground record:* 24,268 v Cardiff City, Division III (South), 16.10.1937.

Northampton Town: *Founded:* 1897. *Colours:* claret shirts with white sleeves, claret shorts. *Ground:* County Ground. *Nickname:* The Cobblers. *Ground record:* 24,523 v Fulham, Division I, 23.4.1966.

Norwich City: *Founded:* 1905. *Colours:* yellow shirts with green facings, green shorts with yellow stripe. *Ground:* Carrow Road. *Nickname:* The Canaries. *Ground record:* 43,984 v Leicester City, FA Cup 6th round, 30.3.1963. **Honours:** League Cup: *winners* 1961–62; *runners-up* 1972–73.

Nottingham Forest: *Founded:* 1865. *Colours:* red shirts, white shorts. *Ground:* City Ground. *Nickname:* The Foresters or Reds. *Ground*

Tom Finney, the pride of Preston.

record: 49,945 v Manchester United, Division I, 28.10.1967. **Honours:** League Championship: *runners-up* 1966–67. FA Cup: *winners* 1898, 1959.

Notts County: *Founded:* 1862. *Colours:* black and white striped shirts, black shorts. *Ground:* County Ground. *Nickname:* The Magpies. *Ground record:* 47,301 v York City, FA Cup 6th round, 12.3.1955. **Honours:** FA Cup: *winners* 1894, *runners-up* 1891.

Oldham Athletic: *Founded:* 1894. *Colours:* blue shirts and shorts. *Ground:* Boundary Park. *Nickname:* The Latics. *Ground record:* 47,671 v Sheffield Wednesday, FA Cup 4th round, 25.1.1930. **Honours:** League Championship: *runners-up* 1914–15.

Orient: *Founded:* 1881. *Colours:* red shirts and shorts. *Ground:* Leyton Stadium. *Nickname:* The O's. *Ground record:* 34,345 v West Ham United, FA Cup 4th round, 25.1.1964.

Oxford United: *Founded:* 1896. *Colours:* gold shirts, black shorts. *Ground:* Manor Ground. *Nickname:* The United. *Ground record:* 22,730 v Preston North End, FA Cup 6th round, 29.2.1964.

Peterborough United: *Founded:* 1934. *Colours:* royal blue shirts with white facings, white shorts. *Ground:* London Road. *Nickname:* The Posh. *Ground record:* 30,096 v Swansea Town, FA Cup 5th round, 20.2.1965.

Plymouth Argyle: *Founded:* 1886. *Colours:* green shirts with white collars and sleeves, white shorts. *Ground:* Home Park. *Nickname:* The Pilgrims. *Ground record:* 43,596 v Aston Villa, Division II, 10.10.1936.

Port Vale: *Founded:* 1876. *Colours:* white shirts and shorts. *Ground:* Vale Park. *Nickname:* The Valiants. *Ground record:* 50,000 v Aston Villa, FA Cup 5th round, 20.2.1960.

Portsmouth: *Founded:* 1898. *Colours:* royal blue shirts with red, white, and blue facings, white shorts. *Ground:* Fratton Park. *Nickname:* The Pompey. *Ground record:* 51,385 v Derby County, FA Cup 6th round, 26.2.1949. **Honours:** League Championship: *winners* 1948–49, 1949–50. FA Cup: *winners* 1939; *runners-up* 1929, 1934.

Preston North End: *Founded:* 1881. *Colours:* white shirts, navy blue shorts. *Ground:* Deep-

dale. *Nickname:* The Lily Whites. *Ground record:* 42,684 v Arsenal, Division 1, 23.4.1938. **Honours:** League Championship: *winners* 1888–89, . 1889–90; *runners-up* 1890–91, 1891–92, 1892–93, 1905–06, 1952–53, 1957–1958. FA Cup: *winners* 1889, 1938; *runners-up* 1888, 1922, 1937, 1954, 1964.

Queen's Park Rangers: *Founded:* 1885. *Colours:* blue and white hooped shirts, white shorts. *Ground:* Ellerslie Road. *Nickname:* The R's. *Ground record:* 33,572 v Chelsea, FA Cup 6th round, 21.2.1970. **Honours:** League Cup: *winners* 1966–67.

Reading: *Founded:* 1871. *Colours:* blue and white hooped shirts, white shorts. *Ground:* Elm Park. *Nickname:* The Biscuitmen. *Ground record:* 33,042 v Brentford, FA Cup 5th round, 19.2.1927.

Rochdale: *Founded:* 1907. *Colours:* royal blue shirts with white facings, white shorts with blue stripe. *Ground:* Spotland. *Nickname:* The Vallians. *Ground record:* 24,231 v Notts County, FA Cup 2nd round, 10.12.1949. **Honours:** League Cup: *runners-up* 1961–62.

Rotherham United: *Founded:* 1884. *Colours:* red shirts with white collar and sleeves, white shorts. *Ground:* Millmoor. *Nickname:* The Merry Millers. *Ground record:* 25,000 v Sheffield Wednesday, Division II, 26.1.52 and v Sheffield United, Division II, 13.12.1952. **Honours:** League Cup: *runners-up* 1960–61.

Scunthorpe United: *Founded:* 1904. *Colours:* red shirts and shorts. *Ground:* Old Show Ground. *Nickname:* The Irons. *Ground record:* 23,935 v Portsmouth, FA Cup 4th round, 30.1.1954.

Sheffield United: *Founded:* 1889. *Colours:* red and white striped shirts, black shorts. *Ground:* Bramall Lane. *Nickname:* The Blades. *Ground record:* 68,287 v Leeds United, FA Cup 5th round, 15.2.1936. **Honours:** League Championship: *winners* 1897–98; *runners-up* 1896–97, 1899–1900. FA Cup: *winners* 1899, 1902, 1915, 1925; *runners-up* 1901, 1936.

Sheffield Wednesday: *Founded:* 1867. *Colours:* blue and white striped shirts with blue collar, blue shorts. *Ground:* Hillsborough. *Nickname:* The Owls. *Ground record:* 72,841 v Manchester City, FA Cup 5th round, 17.2.1934. **Honours:** League Championship: *winners*

1902–03, 1903–04, 1928–29, 1929–30; *runners-up* 1960–61. FA Cup: *winners* 1896, 1907, 1935; *runners-up* 1890, 1966.

Shrewsbury Town: *Founded:* 1886. *Colours:* blue shirts and shorts with amber facings. *Ground:* Gay Meadow. *Nickname:* Town or The Blues. *Ground record:* 18,917 v Walsall, Division III, 26.4.1961.

Southampton: *Founded:* 1885. *Colours:* red and white striped shirts, black shorts. *Ground:* The Dell. *Nickname:* The Saints. *Ground record:* 31,044 v Manchester United, Division 1, 8.10.1969. **Honours:** FA Cup: *runners-up* 1900, 1902.

Southend United: *Founded:* 1906. *Colours:* blue shirts and shorts. *Ground:* Roots Hall. *Nickname:* The Shrimpers. *Ground record:* 28,059 v Birmingham City, FA Cup 4th round, 26.1.1957.

Southport: *Founded:* 1881. *Colours:* old gold shirts, blue shorts. *Ground:* Haig Avenue. *Nickname:* The Sandgrounders. *Ground record:* 20,010 v Newcastle United, FA Cup 4th round replay, 26.1.1932.

Stockport County: *Founded:* 1883. *Colours:* white shirts and shorts with blue facings. *Ground:* Edgeley Park. *Nickname:* The Hatters. *Ground record:* 27,833 v Liverpool, FA Cup 5th round, 11.2.1950.

Stoke City: *Founded:* 1863. *Colours:* red and white striped shirts, white shorts. *Ground:* Victoria Ground. *Nickname:* The Potters. *Ground record:* 51,380 v Arsenal, Division I, 29.3.1937. **Honours:** League Cup: *winners* 1971–72; *runners-up* 1963–64.

Sunderland: *Founded:* 1879. *Colours:* red and white striped shirts, white shorts. *Ground:* Roker Park. *Nickname:* The Rokerites. *Ground record:* 75,118 v Derby County, FA Cup 6th round replay, 8.3.1933. **Honours:** League Championship: *winners* 1891–92, 1892–93, 1894–95, 1901–02, 1912–13, 1935–36; *runners-up* 1893–94, 1897–98, 1900–01, 1922–23, 1934–35. FA Cup: *winners* 1937, 1973; *runners-up* 1913.

Swansea City: *Founded:* about 1900. *Colours:* white shirts and shorts. *Ground:* Vetch Field. *Nickname:* The Swans. *Ground record:* 32,700 v Arsenal, FA Cup 4th round, 17.2.1968.

Sheffield United put pressure on the Cardiff City goal in the 1925 FA Cup final.

Above: West Bromwich Albion, FA Cup winners as a Second Division club in 1931. They won promotion to Division I in the same season.

Below: The 'push and run' Spurs, League Champions in 1950–51. The previous season they had been runaway leaders of Division II.

Swindon Town: *Founded:* 1881. *Colours:* red shirts, black shorts. *Ground:* County Ground. *Nickname:* The Robins. *Ground record:* 28,898 v Watford, Division III, 29.3.1969. **Honours:** League Cup: *winners* 1968–69.

Torquay United: *Founded:* 1898. *Colours:* gold shirts with royal blue facings, gold shorts with royal blue stripes. *Ground:* Plainmoor. *Nickname:* The Gulls. *Ground record:* 21,736 v Huddersfield Town, FA Cup 4th round, 29.1.1955.

Tottenham Hotspur: *Founded:* 1882. *Colours:* white shirts, blue shorts. *Ground:* White Hart Lane. *Nickname:* The Spurs. *Ground record:* 75,038 v Sunderland, FA Cup 6th round, 5.3.1938. **Honours:** European Cup-Winners Cup: *winners* 1962–63. UEFA Cup: *winners* 1971–72; *runners-up* 1973–74. League Championship: *winners* 1950–51, 1960 –61; *runners-up* 1921–22, 1951–52; 1956–57, 1962–63. FA Cup: *winners* 1901, 1921, 1961, 1962, 1967. League Cup: *winners* 1970–71, 1972–73.

Tranmere Rovers: *Founded:* 1883. *Colours:* white shirts with blue facings, royal blue shorts. *Ground:* Prenton Park. *Nickname:* The Rovers. *Ground record:* 22,217 v Barnsley, FA Cup 4th round, 25.1.1936.

Walsall: *Founded:* 1888. *Colours:* white shirts with red facings, red shorts. *Ground:* Fellows Park. *Nickname:* The Saddlers. *Ground record:* 25,453 v Newcastle United, Division II, 29.8.1961.

Watford: *Founded:* 1889. *Colours:* gold

Above: Derek Dougan, bought by Wolverhampton Wanderers in 1967 to help them return to the First Division.

shirts, black shorts. *Ground:* Vicarage Road. *Nickname:* The Hornets. *Ground record:* 34,099 v Manchester United, FA Cup 4th round replay, 3.2.1969.

West Bromwich Albion: *Founded:* 1879. *Colours:* navy blue and white striped shirts with white sleeves, white shorts. *Ground:* The Hawthorns. *Nickname:* The Baggies, Throstles, or Albion. *Ground record:* 64,815 v Arsenal, FA Cup 6th round, 6.3.1937. **Honours:** League Championship: *winners* 1919–20; *runners-up* 1924–25, 1953–54. FA Cup: *winners* 1888, 1892, 1931, 1954, 1968; *runners-up* 1886, 1887, 1895, 1912, 1935. League Cup: *winners* 1965–66; *runners-up* 1966–67, 1969–70.

West Ham United: *Founded:* 1900. *Colours:* claret shirts with blue sleeves, white shorts. *Ground:* Boleyn Ground, Upton Park. *Nickname:* The Hammers. *Ground record:* 44,810 v Birmingham City, FA Cup, 4.3.1933. **Honours:** European Cup-Winners Cup: *winners* 1964–65. FA Cup: *winners* 1964; *runners-up* 1923. League Cup: *runners-up* 1966.

Wolverhampton Wanderers: *Founded:* 1877. *Colours:* old gold shirts with black facings, black shorts. *Ground:* Molineux. *Nickname:* The Wolves. *Ground record:* 61,315 v Liverpool, FA Cup 5th round, 11.2.1939. **Honours:** UEFA Cup: *runners-up* 1971–72. League Championship: 1953–54, 1957–58, 1958–59; *runners-up* 1937–38, 1938–39, 1949–50, 1954–55, 1959–60. FA Cup: *winners* 1893, 1908, 1949, 1960; *runners-up* 1889, 1896, 1921, 1939. League Cup: *winners* 1974.

Workington: *Founded:* 1884. *Colours:* red shirts, white shorts. *Ground:* Borough Park. *Nickname:* The Reds. *Ground record:* 21,000 v Manchester United, FA Cup 3rd round, 4.1.1958.

Wrexham: *Founded:* 1873. *Colours:* red shirts with white facings, white shorts with red stripe. *Ground:* Racecourse Ground. *Nickname:* The Robins. *Ground record:* 34,445 v Manchester United, FA Cup 4th round, 26.1.1957.

York City: *Founded:* 1903. *Colours:* maroon shirts, white shorts. *Ground:* Bootham Crescent. *Nickname:* The City. *Ground record:* 28,123 v Huddersfield Town, FA Cup 5th round, 5.3.1938.

Left: Trevor Brooking, West Ham's skilful midfield operator.

SCOTLAND

Aberdeen: *Founded:* 1903. *Colours:* scarlet shirts, scarlet shorts with double white stripes. *Ground:* Pittodrie Park. *Nickname:* The Dons. *Ground record:* 45,061 v Hearts, Scottish Cup 4th round, 13.3.1954. **Honours:** League Championship: *winners* 1954–55; *runners-up* 1910–11, 1936–37, 1955–56. Scottish Cup: *winners* 1947, 1970; *runners-up* 1937, 1953, 1954, 1959, 1967. League Cup: *winners* 1945–46, 1955–56; *runners-up* 1946 47.

Airdrieonians: *Founded:* 1878. *Colours:* white shirts with red diamond, white shorts. *Ground:* Broomfield Park. *Nickname:* The Diamonds. *Ground record:* 26,000 v Hearts, Scottish Cup 4th round, 8.3.1952. **Honours:** League Championship: *runners-up* 1922–23, 1923–24, 1924–25, 1925–26. Scottish Cup: *winners* 1924.

Albion Rovers: *Founded:* 1881. *Colours:* primrose shirts with white sleeves, white shorts with red stripe. *Ground:* Cliftonhill Park. *Ground record:* 27,381 v Rangers, Scottish Cup 2nd round, 8.2.1936. **Honours:** Scottish Cup: *runners-up* 1920.

Alloa Athletic: *Founded:* 1878. *Colours:* gold shirts with black facings, black shorts. *Ground:* Recreation Ground. *Ground record:* 13,000 v Dunfermline Athletic.

Arbroath: *Founded:* 1878. *Colours:* maroon shirts, white shorts. *Ground:* Gayfield Park.

Ground record: 13,510 v Rangers, Scottish Cup 3rd round, 23.2.1952.

Ayr United: *Founded:* 1910. *Colours:* white shirts with black facings, black shorts. *Ground:* Somerset Park. *Nickname:* The Honest Men. *Ground record:* 25,500 v Rangers, Division I, 17.1.1970.

Berwick Rangers: *Founded:* 1881. *Colours:* black and gold striped shirts, black shorts. *Ground:* Shielfield Park. *Ground record:* 15,000 v Rangers, Scottish Cup 1st round, 30.1.1960.

Brechin City: *Founded:* 1906. *Colours:* red shirts and shorts. *Ground:* Glebe Park. *Nickname:* The City. *Ground record:* 8,022 v Dundee, Scottish Cup.

Celtic: *Founded:* 1888. *Colours:* green and white hooped shirts, white shorts. *Ground:* Celtic Park. *Nickname:* The Tims. *Ground record:* 92,000 v Rangers, Division I, 1.1.1938. **Honours:** European Cup: *winners* 1966–67; *runners-up* 1969–70. League Championship: *winners* 1892–93, 1893–94, 1895–96, 1897–98, 1904–05, 1905–06, 1906–07, 1907–08, 1908–09, 1909–10, 1913–14, 1914–15, 1915–16, 1916–17, 1918–19, 1921–22, 1925–26, 1935–36, 1937–38, 1953–54, 1965–66, 1966–67, 1967–68, 1968–69, 1969–70, 1970–71, 1971–72, 1972–73, 1973–74; *runners-up* 1899–00, 1900–01, 1901–02, 1911–12, 1912–13, 1917–18, 1919–20, 1920–21, 1927–28, 1928–29, 1930–31, 1934–35, 1938–39, 1954–55. Scottish Cup: *winners* 1892, 1899, 1900, 1904, 1907, 1908, 1911, 1912, 1914, 1923, 1925, 1927, 1931, 1933, 1937, 1951, 1954, 1965, 1967, 1969, 1971, 1972, 1974; *runners-up* 1889, 1893, 1894, 1901, 1902, 1926, 1928, 1955, 1956, 1961, 1963, 1966, 1970, 1973. League Cup: *winners* 1956–57, 1957–58, 1965–66, 1966–67, 1967–68, 1968–69, 1969–70; *runners-up* 1964–65, 1970–71, 1971–72, 1972–73, 1973–74.

Clyde: *Founded:* 1877. *Colours:* white shirts with red facings, black shorts. *Ground:* Shawfield Park. *Ground record:* 52,000 v Rangers, Division I, 21.11.1908. **Honours:** Scottish Cup: *winners* 1939, 1955, 1958; *runners-up* 1910, 1912, 1949.

Clydebank: *Founded:* 1965. *Colours:* red shirts with broad white stripes, black shorts. *Ground:* New Kilbowie Park. *Ground record:* 14,900 v Hibernian, Scottish Cup 1st round, 10.2.1965.

Cowdenbeath: *Founded:* 1881. *Colours:* royal blue and white striped shirts, white shorts. *Ground:* Central Park. *Nickname:* The Beath. *Ground record:* 25,586 v Rangers, League Cup quarter-final 2nd leg, 1949–50.

Dumbarton: *Founded:* 1872. *Colours:* white shirts with black and gold bands, white shorts. *Ground:* Boghead Park. *Ground record:* 18,000 v Raith Rovers, Scottish Cup quarter-final, 2.3.1957. **Honours:** League Championship: *winners* 1890–91, 1891–92 (joint). Scottish Cup: *winners* 1883; *runners-up* 1881, 1882, 1887, 1891, 1897.

Dundee: *Founded:* 1893. *Colours:* white shirts, dark blue shorts. *Ground:* Dens Park.

Celtic's Billy McNeill and Tommy Gemmell see 38-year-old Ronnie Simpson frustrate Rangers winger Orjan Persson.

Nickname: The Blues or Dens Parkers. *Ground record:* 43,024 v Rangers, Scottish Cup 2nd round, 7.2.1953. **Honours:** League Championship: *winners* 1961–62; *runners-up* 1902–03, 1906–07, 1908–09, 1948–49. Scottish Cup: *winners* 1910; *runners-up* 1925, 1952, 1964. League Cup: *winners* 1951–52, 1952–53, 1973–74; *runners-up* 1967–68.

Dundee United: *Founded:* 1910. *Colours:* tangerine shirts with black facings, tangerine shorts. *Ground:* Tannadice Park. *Nickname:* The Tangerines. *Ground record:* 28,000 v Barcelona, Fairs Cup 2nd round (2nd leg), 16.11.1966. **Honours:** Scottish Cup: *runners-up* 1974.

Dunfermline Athletic: *Founded:* 1907. *Colours:* black and white striped shirts, black shorts. *Ground:* East End Park. *Nickname:* The Fifers. *Ground record:* 27,816 v Celtic, Division 1, 1968–69. **Honours:** Scottish Cup: *winners* 1961, 1968; *runners-up* 1965. League Cup: *runners-up* 1949–50.

East Fife: *Founded:* 1903. *Colours:* gold shirts with black facings, black shorts. *Ground:* Bayview Park. *Ground record:* 21,515 v Raith Rovers, Division I, 2.1.1950. **Honours:** Scottish Cup: *winners* 1938; *runners-up* 1927, 1950. League Cup: *winners* 1947–48, 1949–50, 1953–54.

Dundee, Scottish League Champions in 1962.

East Stirlingshire: *Founded:* 1894. *Colours:* black and white hooped shirts, black shorts. *Ground:* Firs Park. *Ground record:* 10,000 v St Mirren, Division II, 16.11.1935.

Falkirk: *Founded:* 1876. *Colours:* navy blue shirts, white shorts. *Ground:* Brockville Park. *Nickname:* The Bairns. *Ground record:* 23,100 v Celtic, Scottish Cup 3rd round, 21.2.1953. **Honours:** League Championship: *runners-up* 1907–08, 1909–10. Scottish Cup: *winners* 1913, 1957. League Cup: *runners-up* 1947–48.

Forfar Athletic: *Founded:* 1885. *Colours:* navy and sky blue striped shirts, sky blue shorts. *Ground:* Station Park. *Ground record:* 9,813 v Rangers, Scottish Cup 1st round, 31.1.1959.

Hamilton Academicals: *Founded:* 1870. *Colours:* red and white hooped shirts, white shorts. *Ground:* Douglas Park. *Ground record:* 28,281 v Hearts, Scottish Cup 3rd round, 3.3.1937. **Honours:** Scottish Cup: *runners-up* 1911, 1935.

Heart of Midlothian: *Founded:* 1873. *Colours:* white shirts with maroon panel and facings, white shorts. *Ground:* Tynecastle Park. *Nickname:* The Hearts. *Ground record:* 53,496 v Rangers, Scottish Cup 3rd round, 13.2.1932. **Honours:** League Championship: *winners* 1894–95, 1896–97, 1957–58, 1959–60; *runners-up* 1893–94, 1898–99, 1903–04, 1905–06, 1914–15, 1937–38, 1953–54, 1956–57, 1957–58, 1964–65. Scottish Cup: *winners* 1891, 1896, 1901, 1906, 1956; *runners-up* 1903, 1907, 1968. League Cup: *winners* 1954–55, 1958–59, 1959–60, 1962–63; *runners-up* 1961–62.

Hibernian: *Founded:* 1875. *Colours:* green shirts with white sleeves, white shorts. *Ground:* Easter Road Park. *Nickname:* The Hibs. *Ground record:* 65,850 v Hearts, Division I, 2.1.1950. **Honours:** League Championship: *winners* 1902–03, 1947–48, 1950–51, 1951–52; *runners-up* 1896–97, 1946–47, 1949–50, 1952–53, 1973–74. Scottish Cup: *winners* 1887, 1902; *runners-up* 1896, 1914, 1923, 1924, 1947, 1958, 1972. League Cup: *winners* 1972–73; *runners-up* 1950–51, 1968–69.

Kilmarnock: *Founded:* 1869. *Colours:* blue shirts and shorts, with white facings. *Ground:* Rugby Park. *Nickname:* The Killies. *Ground record:* 34,246 v Rangers, League Cup August 1963. **Honours:** League Championship: *winners* 1964–65; *runners-up* 1959–60, 1960–61, 1962–63, 1963–64. Scottish Cup: *winners* 1920, 1929; *runners-up* 1898, 1932, 1938, 1957, 1960. League Cup: *runners-up* 1952–53, 1960–61, 1962–63.

Montrose: *Founded:* 1879. *Colours:* royal blue shirts and shorts. *Ground:* Links Park. *Ground record:* 6,700 v Celtic, 1938–39.

Morton: *Founded:* 1896. *Colours:* blue and white hooped shirts, white shorts. *Ground:* Cappielow Park. *Nickname:* The Ton. *Ground record:* 23,500 v Celtic, Division I, 1921. **Honours:** League Championship: *runners-up* 1916–17. Scottish Cup: *winners* 1922; *runners-up* 1948. League Cup: *runners-up* 1963–1964.

Motherwell: *Founded:* 1885. *Colours:* amber shirts and shorts with claret facings. *Ground:* Fir Park. *Nickname:* The Well. *Ground record:* 36,750 v Rangers, Scottish Cup 4th round replay, 12.3.1952. **Honours:** League Championship: *winners* 1931–32; *runners-up* 1926–1927, 1929–30, 1932–33, 1933–34. Scottish Cup: *winners* 1952; *runners-up* 1931, 1933, 1939, 1951. League Cup: *winners* 1950–51; *runners-up* 1954–55.

Partick Thistle: *Founded:* 1876. *Colours:* yellow shirts with red facings, red shorts. *Ground:* Firhill Park. *Nickname:* The Jags. *Ground record:* 49,838 v Rangers, Division I, 18.2.1922. **Honours:** Scottish Cup: *winners* 1921; *runners-up* 1930. League Cup: *winners* 1971–72; *runners-up* 1953–54, 1956–57, 1958–59.

Queen of the South: *Founded:* 1919. *Colours:* royal blue shirts with white facings, white shorts. *Ground:* Palmerston Park. *Ground record:* 25,000 v Hearts, Scottish Cup 3rd round, 23.2.1952.

Queen's Park: *Founded:* 1867. *Colours:* thin black and white hooped shirts, white shorts. *Ground:* Hampden Park. *Nickname:* The Spiders. *Ground record:* (club) 97,000 v Rangers, Scottish Cup 2nd round replay, 18.2.1933. **Honours:** Scottish Cup: *winners* 1874, 1875, 1876, 1880, 1881, 1882, 1884, 1886, 1890, 1893; *runners-up* 1892, 1900. FA Cup: *runners-up* 1884, 1885.

Rangers captain John Greig in goalscoring mood against Dunfirmline in March 1971.

Bob McColl was a Queen's Park stalwart before going to Newcastle United in 1901.

Raith Rovers: *Founded:* 1883. *Colours:* royal blue shirts and shorts. *Ground:* Stark's Park. *Ground record:* 32,000 v Hearts, Scottish Cup 2nd round, 7.2.1953.

Rangers: *Founded:* 1873. *Colours:* royal blue shirts, white shorts. *Ground:* Ibrox Stadium. *Nickname:* The Blues or Gers. *Ground record:* 118,567 v Celtic, Division I, 2.1.1939. **Honours:** European Cup-Winners Cup: *winners* 1971–72; *runners-up* 1960–61, 1966–67. League Championship: *winners* 1890–91, 1898–99, 1899–1900, 1900–01, 1901–02, 1910–11, 1911–12, 1917–18, 1919–20, 1920–21, 1922–23, 1923–24, 1924–25, 1926–27, 1927–28, 1928–29, 1929–30, 1930–31, 1932–33, 1933–34, 1934–35, 1936–37, 1938–39, 1946–47, 1948–49, 1949–50, 1952–53, 1955–56, 1956–57, 1958–59, 1960–61, 1962–63, 1963–64; *runners-up* 1897–98, 1904–05, 1913–14, 1915–16, 1918–19, 1921–22, 1931–32, 1935–36, 1947–48, 1950–51, 1951–52, 1957–58, 1961–62, 1965–66, 1966–67, 1967–68, 1968–69, 1969–70, 1972–73. Cup: *winners* 1894, 1897, 1898, 1903, 1928, 1930, 1932, 1934, 1935, 1936, 1948, 1949, 1950, 1953, 1960, 1962, 1963, 1964, 1966, 1973; *runners-up* 1877, 1879, 1899, 1904, 1905, 1921, 1922, 1929, 1969. League Cup: *winners* 1946–47, 1948–49, 1960–61, 1961–62, 1963–64, 1964–65, 1970–71; *runners-up* 1951–52, 1957–58, 1965–66, 1966–67.

St Johnstone: *Founded:* 1884. *Colours:* royal blue shirts with white facings, white shorts. *Ground:* Muirton Park. *Nickname:* The Saints. *Ground record:* 29,972 v Dundee, Scottish Cup 2nd round, 10.2.1952. **Honours:** League Cup: *runners-up* 1969–70.

St Mirren: *Founded:* 1876. *Colours:* black and white stripes, black shorts. *Ground:* St Mirren Park. *Nickname:* The Saints. *Ground record:* 47,428 v Celtic, Scottish Cup 4th round, 7.3.1925. **Honours:** Scottish Cup: *winners* 1926, 1959; *runners-up* 1908, 1934, 1962. League Cup: *runners-up* 1955–56.

Stenhousemuir: *Founded:* 1884. *Colours:* maroon shirts with white facings, white shorts. *Ground:* Ochilview Park. *Ground record:* 13,000 v East Fife, Scottish Cup 4th round, 11.3.1950.

Stirling Albion: *Founded* 1945. *Colours:* red shirts and shorts. *Ground:* Annfield Park. *Ground record:* 26,400 v Celtic, Scottish Cup 4th round, 14.3.1959.

Stranraer: *Founded:* 1870. *Colours:* royal blue shirts, white shorts. *Ground:* Stair Park. *Ground record:* 6,500 v Rangers.

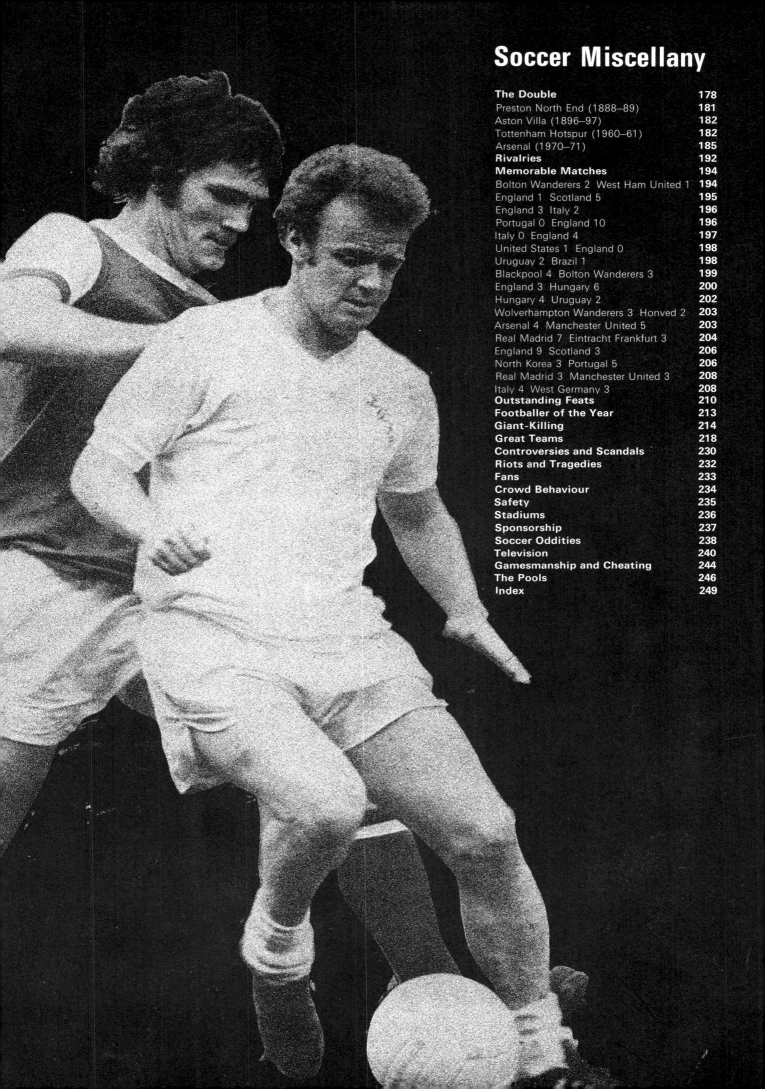

Soccer Miscellany

The Double

Every manager's dream: Arsenal's Bertie Mee gazes proudly at the mementoes of his club's great double in the 1970–71 season — the Football League Championship trophy and the FA Cup.

When Celtic won the Scottish League and Cup in the 1973–74 season, it was the ninth time that they had accomplished 'the double', and they had at last caught up with the record established by their great rivals, Rangers. The feat was first accomplished in Scotland by Celtic in 1907, and with the almost complete dominance of Scottish football by the two Glasgow teams, it is not surprising that they have chalked up 18 'doubles' between them over the years.

Rangers went one further in the 1948–49 season, when they won the four-year-old League Cup as well, a 'treble' they repeated in 1963–64. But Celtic surpassed this in the 1966–67 season by winning all four competitions they entered, the three domestic competitions and the European Cup. And two years later they achieved another domestic treble.

In England, on the other hand, the double has been such a rare feat that at one time it was thought impossible in modern football. Yet it was accomplished in the very first season of the Football League, by Preston North End, in 1889. Aston Villa also did it, only eight years later. But then the fun started. Both League and Cup became increasingly difficult to win, and competition among English League clubs became the most intense in the world.

Many clubs came near. In 1905 Newcastle won the League but were beaten by Aston Villa in the Cup final. And exactly the same fate befell Sunderland in 1913. Between the wars, a number of near misses were recorded and, as time passed, the feat seemed to get more and more out of reach. In 1928 Huddersfield were runners-up in both competitions, as were Arsenal in 1932, in a period when they were dominating English football. And in 1939 it was Wolves' turn to finish 'double runners-up'.

After the war, more near misses were chalked up. In 1948, impressive Cup winners Manchester United had been unable to catch

Left: Celtic open the scoring in the 1967 Scottish Cup final against Aberdeen. Celtic won all three domestic competitions and the European Cup that season, and seven years later chalked up their ninth double.

Right: Manchester United see their chances of the double evaporate as goalkeeper Ray Wood is carried off in the 1957 Cup final against Aston Villa.

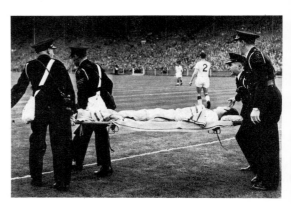

Right: Manchester United, seen notching one of their 28 League wins in the 1956–57 season (Whelan puts one past the Manchester City goalkeeper at Old Trafford), topped the table by eight points. They were perhaps the unluckiest side not to achieve the double until Leeds were frustrated 15 years later.

Arsenal in the League and finished second, seven points adrift. Four seasons later Arsenal were within three games of the double, but a crop of injuries put paid to their chances and they finished in third place, four points behind Manchester United, and narrowly lost the Cup final after playing with 10 men for most of the match.

Indeed, there seemed to be a jinx on double aspirants. West Bromwich's League chances were seriously hampered by a spate of injuries in 1954, and they finished second, four points behind Wolves, but won the Cup. Then, in 1957, came the unluckiest of all double attempts. The brilliant Manchester United 'Busby Babes' sewed up the Championship by eight points and were strong favourites for the Cup. But in the final their goalkeeper was hurt and off the field for most of the game, and they went down 2–1. The team that beat them? . . . Aston Villa, yet again defiantly defending their proud record as the last club to have achieved the double.

Wolves, in 1960, missed the Championship by a single point in a thrilling race, and then won the Cup. They had won the previous two Championships, so once again the dominant English club had been narrowly foiled. But this was not so the following season, when another club took over Wolves' mantle —Tottenham Hotspur. Running away with the Championship from the very start, and relatively free from injuries all season, they made no mistake in the Cup, beating Leicester 2–0 in the final, although it was their opponents who had bad luck with injury.

And so, after a gap of 64 years, the 'impossible double' had been achieved—by a great team who steered clear of misfortune. In League and Cup they played a total of 49 matches, as opposed to the 27 of Preston and the 37 of Aston Villa. And as if this was not enough, they nearly did it again the next season, falling out of the Championship race only at the last (they finished third, four points behind Ipswich), but winning the Cup again.

In the 1960s the pressures on the leading clubs began to build up even more, with

Leeds captain Billy Bremner rides a tackle by Cyril Knowles of Spurs in the 6th round of the 1971–72 FA Cup. Leeds went on to win the Cup, but the magic double still eluded them, when they lost their last League match two days after the Cup final.

League Cup and European fixtures adding to the strain. The pundits were soon declaring the double feat impossible again. Manchester United continued to find it elusive. From 1962 to 1966 they reached the Cup semi-final every year. Only once did they reach the final though, in 1963, when they beat Leicester at Wembley, but they had a disastrous League campaign, finishing fourth from the bottom. They won the Championship in 1965, but lost to Leeds in the Cup.

It was Leeds, in fact, who became the new contenders. Just promoted from the Second Division, they had lost the League race on goal average (with 61 points), and went down at Wembley 2–1 to Liverpool after extra time. Before Leeds' next effort, Manchester United came near to an even greater double, when they won the 1968 European Cup and came within two points of League winners Manchester City.

Then, in 1970, came the magnificent Leeds attempt to win the treble of League, Cup, and European Cup. Beset by injuries to key players, they lost a good lead to Everton in the League and finally finished second. They succumbed to Celtic in the semi-final of the European Cup, and had the FA Cup snatched from their grasp by Chelsea after extra time in the replay. It was perhaps the greatest season experienced by an English club, yet they finished up with nothing, except worldwide admiration and the title of 'champion-runners-up'. One double was achieved that season, however, because Manchester City

Above: The Preston North End side that won the first League title, and with it the first double, in 1888–89. It earned them the nickname of the 'Invincibles'.
Below: John Goodall, Preston's centre-forward and captain.

won the League Cup and the European Cup-Winners Cup.

After Leeds' experience, it was felt that modern conditions really were against a side after the double or better, because the leading clubs were now playing some 60 matches a season. But they were also building up 'squads' of players, 16 or 17 men capable of fitting into first team football, interchangeable, versatile, and experienced. Leeds had developed such a squad, perhaps the best in the world, and Chelsea were not far behind. Everton and Manchester City had fine footballing sides, capable of beating the best. If any team were to do the double in 1970–71, it must surely come from these four. But that season produced new challengers, and the fourth double champions—Arsenal.

Having come out of the wilderness the previous season with a Fairs Cup triumph, Arsenal played 64 matches over the season. They, too, had built up a strong squad, which proved all-important because of early season injuries. Overcoming a seven-point deficit, they overhauled Leeds to win the League in their last match, and then, only five days later, won the Cup after being a goal down in extra time. After that, said the pundits, anything was possible!

And the very next season the double was in danger of becoming commonplace—for Leeds came within a whisker of achieving it. Like Arsenal, they had to win a League match only five days before the final, and at

Wembley they beat Arsenal 1–0 in a colourless Centenary final. But although their run-in had not been quite as strenuous as Arsenal's the previous year, they had to play their last League match only two days after the Cup final. Needing a draw at Molineux, they surprisingly lost 2–1. To do the double, it seemed, a club had not only to master the rest of the teams in League and Cup, they had also to overcome the pile-up of fixtures that had now become a regular end-of-season feature. The quality of the football was suffering, and the Football League could not be held blameless in allowing the congestion to occur.

Preston North End (1888–89)

If any club could claim to have reigned supreme throughout an English season, that club surely must be 'Proud Preston'. The 'Invincibles', as they were called, won the first ever League Championship without losing a game—they won 18 of their 22 matches—and won the Cup without conceding a goal.

This performance in the early days of organized football might well be belittled by those used to the intensity of modern competition, but Preston's deeds are not easily brushed aside. More than forty years later, they were still spoken of in awe, and regarded by many experts as the greatest side of all time.

In goal for the Invincibles was Welsh international James Trainer or Dr R. H. Mills-Roberts, who 'kept' in the Cup final.

Bottom: The second double champions, Aston Villa (1896–97), were also captained by a forward, John Devey (below).

And one of the chief architects of their triumphs was Nick Ross, a stylish full-back at a time when most backs had destructive roles. Preston conceded only 15 goals in their 22 League games. But it was their goalscoring power that marked them as the great side they undoubtedly were. Backed by a powerful half-back line, the forwards ran rings round opposing defences in match after match. Led by the legendary John Goodall, the acknowledged pioneer of scientific football in England, Preston scored 74 League goals. Spare of frame but possessing marvellous ball skills and an inventive football brain, Goodall was the finest centre-forward of his day. He was ably supported by skilful inside-right James Ross, and inside-left Fred Dewhurst who played for Corinthians. Early in the season, Ross scored 7 against Stoke, a division record equalled (by Arsenal's Ted Drake in 1935) but still unsurpassed more than 80 years later. The whole forward line dazzled with brilliant combinations.

Preston finished 11 points clear of runners-up Aston Villa in the League, and beat Wolves 3–0 in the FA Cup final at the Oval. The man who built up this famous side was president and manager Major William Sudell, who was responsible, in the process, for the legalization of professionalism.

Preston's double has since been emulated in much more difficult circumstances, but one record must surely stand for all time—that of going through an English season without a single defeat.

Aston Villa (1896–97)

In the 1890s Aston Villa established themselves as one of the greatest sides in the history of English football. It was during this period that they won five of their six Championships. And although their honours after 1920 were limited to a solitary Cup win in 1957, their tradition as a great club remained with them even when they were struggling to get out of the Third Division in the 1970s.

The highpoint of Villa's period of ascendancy was their 'double' season. They had won the League in 1894, the Cup in 1895, and the League again in 1896. In 1896–97, like double champions Preston before them and Spurs after them, Villa waltzed away with the League Championship, increasing their lead until at the end they had a margin of 11 points to spare over Sheffield United and Derby. They won 21 of their 30 matches, and lost only 4, with a goal record of 73 against 38.

But it is the great Cup final they played in that is remembered more than anything else. They had narrowly beaten Preston in the quarter-finals in a second replay, and had convincingly seen Liverpool off 3–0 in the semi-finals. Their opponents at Crystal Palace in the final were the other half of the Merseyside duo, Everton. A record 66,000 crowd witnessed a thrilling see-saw game which was won and lost in the first half. Centre-forward Campbell opened the scoring for Villa, but they soon found themselves a goal down. Inside-left Wheldon equalized, however, and on the stroke of half-time Jimmy Crabtree scored what proved to be the winner.

There were eight internationals in Villa's double side. Right-back Howard Spencer, in the classic mould of Preston's Nick Ross, was a stylist and the quiet inspiration of the side. Left-half Crabtree played in every defensive outfield position for England. Their captain, inside- or centre-forward John Devey, later became a director of the club. The hub of the side was Scottish international James Cowan, an attacking centre-half who nowadays would be called the 'midfield general'.

The general off the field was also a Scot, George Ramsay, the club's secretary, or manager. Captain of the side from 1876, he became secretary eight years later and served the club in one capacity or another for nearly 60 years. Money was no object in building up the side, and Villa paid transfer fees for such players as right-half John Reynolds, Crabtree, and Wheldon.

The side won further championships in 1899 and 1900, but another double eluded them. It also proved elusive for all the other great clubs for another 64 years.

Tottenham Hotspur (1960–61)

Tottenham's feat in winning both League and Cup in 1960–61 was widely applauded at the time, and deservedly so: the first double for 64 years, after so many clubs had tried and failed, was a remarkable performance.

In retrospect, it was not quite as brilliant an achievement as it appeared then, and was achieved under much less exacting circumstances than those confronting Arsenal ten years later. Spurs did not have the distraction of European competition, nor did they face the additional fixtures created by the League Cup, then in its first season, for they and four other clubs decided against competing. As a result, they played only 49 competitive games, plus one friendly, during the season, compared with the marathon 64-match programme undertaken by their North London neighbours a decade later.

Another point in Tottenham's favour was that the opposition at that time was moderate, taken overall. Although several clubs were capable of fine performances, none had the methodical consistency that was to distinguish teams such as Leeds, Liverpool —and Arsenal—in a later era.

The age of robot defence had not yet come into operation, and Spurs were ideally suited to the situation. They scored 115 goals in their 42 League matches, a total exceeded only four times in First Division history. And no fewer than 13 other clubs that season scored more than 72, the figure

Above: Tottenham Hotspur's captain Danny Blanchflower holds the FA Cup high in a victory salute after the 1960–61 final. That season Spurs became the first side to achieve the double for 64 years.
Below: John White, the brilliant schemer of the Spurs double side.

Above: Spurs battle through the last stages of the League programme in their double season. Against Cardiff at Ninian Park, Maurice Norman, with MacKay in support, heads clear to thwart a Welsh attack.
Centre: In the 5th round of the FA Cup, Spurs beat Aston Villa 2–0 at Villa Park. Spurs centre-forward Bobby Smith lies flat on his back in ecstasy as Cliff Jones's shot beats goalkeeper Geoff Sidebottom.
Below: Spurs return to Villa Park for the semi-final against Burnley, winning 3–0. Maurice Norman (5) and Peter Baker (2) cover as goalkeeper Bill Brown collects under pressure.

top scorers Leeds recorded when finishing second to Arsenal in 1970–71.

But if Tottenham look, at this distance in time, to have had a lot in their favour, there can be no denying—now or ever—the brilliance and attractiveness of their football. Their combination of skill and method, of pace and power, of teamwork and individual artistry, made them perhaps the finest British team of all time. Perhaps only the pre-Munich Manchester United could match

them for entertainment value.

Much of the credit goes to the manager, Bill Nicholson, a taciturn Yorkshireman whose buying of players, particularly in his early years, has rarely been bettered. Nicholson took over in 1958, after a long career as a player, and spent more money than any other British manager in history. The 1960–61 side, expensive enough by prevailing standards, cost very little in comparison with later expenditure. But the art in buying, then as now, is in buying well, and Nicholson certainly did.

Goalkeeper Bill Brown from Dundee, wing-half Dave Mackay from Hearts, and inside-forward John White from Falkirk cost around £80,000 between them. All three started hesitantly, but went on to give the club tremendous service. Nicholson also exchanged the gifted but inconsistent Johnny Brooks for the more direct Les Allen, of Chelsea—an unheralded move that paid tremendous dividends. Danny Blanchflower, Bobby Smith, Maurice Norman, and Cliff Jones had all been signed before Nicholson took control (although as assistant manager to Jimmy Anderson and coach under Arthur Rowe he had had a say in all four moves). These eight provided the nucleus of the double-winning side, yet Nicholson had one of his greatest collective triumphs with the other three members of the team, full-back Peter Baker and Ron Henry and winger Terry Dyson.

All three had spent some years at White Hart Lane, sometimes in the senior side, more often in the reserves. Nicholson's encouragement and perseverance in eradicating their weaknesses helped all three to become immeasurably better players. Baker quickened up and lost the tendency to wildness that had marred his earlier displays. Henry's heading improved until it matched his neat reading of play. And Dyson added previously unknown ball skill to the boundless enthusiasm he had always possessed.

All three, of course, gained confidence through playing in such a fine side, a side in which the sum was considerably greater than the parts, impressive though those parts were. With an ideal contrast between sheer skill, as personified by White and Blanchflower, great pace (Jones), and belligerent strength (Mackay, Smith, and Allen), the Spurs machine ran with near-perfect smoothness, whether the surface was grass, mud, or ice.

Like all great sides, they had some luck, with the run of the ball and particularly in the absence of injuries. White and Blanchflower, for instance, played in every match. So did Allen and Henry. Baker, Brown, and

Norman missed only one each, Dyson two, Mackay five, and Smith six. Only Jones was absent for any length of time, and Spurs had an excellent replacement in another Welsh international, Terry Medwin.

The fact that the team played virtually undisturbed throughout the season was a tremendous help to combination and team-work. In particular, the continual presence of Blanchflower and White was a blessing: had injury put either one out of the side for more than a few fixtures, Spurs might well have missed either or both honours. For these were the two key figures, the pair who dictated play, the couple whose insistence on pure football at all times kept the machine running.

In three of the FA Cup ties, Spurs were sorely troubled by their opponents—Charlton in the third round, Sunderland in the sixth, and Burnley in the semi-finals. The spirit of the first two and the excellent skills of the third all had even the mighty Tottenham in great difficulty. Significantly, it was Blanchflower and White who slowed the first two matches down, who raised their already high level of performance against Burnley, with the result that Spurs recovered.

Equally significantly, in the home semi-final of the European Cup a season later, Spurs beat Benfica (but lost on aggregate) after Mackay had assumed the dominant role. Mackay's part in his club's success was a tremendous one, but his role was entirely different from Blanchflower's. Mackay was the swashbuckler, his colleague was the artist. In the fire and fury of the Benfica match, Blanchflower was subdued, while Mackay ranged the pitch, a living personification of fighting determination. It was magnificent : . . but it was not Tottenham.

Not, at least, the double-winning Tottenham.

In 1960–61, while Mackay had rather less influence on his colleagues and on the crowd, the coolness of Blanchflower—aided with subtle distinction by White's matching talent—had so very, very much to do with the team's greatness.

Eleven straight wins from the start of the season announced that Spurs would be virtually unstoppable. In the end, they set records for the First Division in number of victories (31) and away wins (16), and equalled Arsenal's records of 66 points and 33 away points, and would almost certainly have passed them but for easing off when the title was won, with eight to spare over Sheffield Wednesday.

The second leg of the double, at Wembley, was an anticlimax, for the result was quickly settled by Leicester's losing full-back Chalmers with a leg injury. Spurs had feared that they would be deprived of their trophy by one of the long succession of Wembley troubles: ironically, the blow fell to their opponents, whose brave display against the odds ensured that they took the honours if not the silver. Curiously, the best of their many excellent players was Frank McLintock, who was to lead Arsenal to their emulation of Tottenham's feats a decade later.

But if the Cup Final was a downbeat ending to the season, much of what had gone before will not fade from the memory. During this remarkable season, Spurs drew over $2\frac{1}{2}$ million spectators to their 50 games, and in the vast majority of them they left an indelible impression of a wonderful team riding their luck, doing the simple things quickly and well, and, on many occasions, achieving the seemingly impossible.

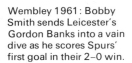

Wembley 1961: Bobby Smith sends Leicester's Gordon Banks into a vain dive as he scores Spurs' first goal in their 2–0 win.

Below: The victorious 1960–61 Spurs side. Standing (l. to r.): Brown, Baker, Henry, Blanchflower, Norman, MacKay. Seated (l. to r.): Jones, White, Smith, Allen, Dyson.

Arsenal (1970–71)

Arsenal's 'double' triumph of the 1970–71 season had all the ingredients of a first-class thriller—excitement, drama, and sheer cliff-hanging suspense. In a remarkable 64-match campaign, for the last 10 weeks of which they played two matches a week, they won both trophies in the last six days of the season. After an epic struggle with Leeds, they took the championship in their last match—against their arch-rivals Tottenham Hotspur at White Hart Lane. And at Wembley they overcame a goal deficit in extra time against Liverpool to snatch victory in the last few minutes.

At the beginning of the season Arsenal were no more than promising challengers for honours, having finished only twelfth in the League in 1969–70. But they had won the European Fairs Cup, their first major trophy for 17 years. Captained by the veteran Scot Frank McLintock, now in the back four, and built round a solid defence, with Bob Wilson outstanding in goal, Arsenal were still at an early stage of development. Any suggestion that this young side could bring off the

Top: Bob Wilson handles safely to relieve Chelsea pressure on the Arsenal goal in August 1970. By May 1971, Arsenal had won the League and the FA Cup, and their captain Frank McLintock (above) had been voted Footballer of the Year.

double would have been dismissed as a flight of fancy.

Before the season started, defender Peter Simpson and midfield schemer Jon Sammels sustained serious injuries. And rising star Charlie George broke an ankle in the first match. So three of their first-choice players were out of the game for weeks or months. These setbacks necessitated a number of changes, two of which were to prove of the utmost significance. The burly, raw 19-year-old Ray Kennedy took over George's striking role and full-back Peter Storey moved into midfield. Kennedy had played but twice in Arsenal's league side and had come on as substitute in the last few minutes of the Fairs Cup final, first leg, heading a vital goal. Slow at first, he soon struck up a fine under-standing with John Radford and was to finish up as Arsenal's top scorer. Storey, Arsenal's so-called 'iron man', was known for his tenacity in the tackle rather than his footballing skills. A great competitor, though, he relished his new role, and was later to be capped for England.

Perhaps the most significant early match

was the home game with Leeds. Champions with a record 67 points two seasons previously, Leeds had bravely chased League, Cup, and European Cup in 1969–70 and narrowly failed in each. This season they were beginning to look invincible, and had won all five of their matches. But despite losing Eddie Kelly, sent off after 22 minutes, Arsenal not only held Leeds to a goalless draw but won an equal share of the play.

Of the next 18 League games, Arsenal won 14 and drew 3. Their sole defeat, an extraordinary 5–0 thrashing at Stoke at the end of September, served as a warning against overconfidence, and no team put more than two goals past them again.

By the time Arsenal's league run was brought to an end in mid-January, the First Division title chase had developed into a two-horse race. Arsenal, with 38 points from 24 games, had narrowed the gap to one point and had a game in hand over Leeds. The next side, Spurs, were eight points adrift. But two successive defeats allowed Leeds, with wins at West Ham and Manchester City, to open up a five-point lead. The critics began to write Arsenal off. But they had reckoned without two factors—Arsenal's refusal to give up . . . and Charlie George.

Manager Bertie Mee put George in for Graham in the 4th round Cup replay with Portsmouth. Arsenal were a goal down and struggling when George scored after a 50-yard run. Long-haired, flamboyant, with a deadly shot and almost telepathic passing ability, George stole most of the limelight.

Above left: Ray Kennedy, who came into the Arsenal side after the first match of the season and retained his place throughout, gets close attention from Ron Harris. Kennedy's partnership with John Radford gave the Gunners a potent front line of attack.

Above right: Peter Storey took over from the injured Peter Simpson in midfield and won England honours in his new role.

Right: Saturday, May 1, and Eddie Kelly's shot beats Gordon Banks to keep Arsenal in the running for the League title . . . and the double.

In Arsenal's 5th round victory in the Maine Road mud he scored both goals—one a mighty free-kick through the Manchester City 'wall', the other after another 50-yard run.

Now every match was a virtual cup final. But when Arsenal lost at Derby, Leeds, winning with disheartening consistency, opened up a seven-point lead (Arsenal had two games in hand). The League position looked bleak, but the turning point came on a Tuesday evening at the beginning of March. Arsenal went to Molineux and gave a glorious display of football in their 3–0 win over a Wolves side placed fourth in the table. It was the first of nine straight wins in the League, a run that took Arsenal to the top of the table, as every Leeds slip was punished by this remorseless Arsenal pressure.

Meanwhile Arsenal had reached the semi-final of the Cup, but found themselves two down at half-time to unfancied Stoke. Now

it was Storey's turn to steal the headlines. He cracked in a volley soon after the interval and then converted a penalty two minutes from time after a Stoke defender had palmed a goalbound McLintock header off the line. Arsenal swept through the replay in brilliant style for a 2–0 win.

The run-in to the last stupendous week was full of drama. Arsenal went to the top on April 17, when Leeds lost at home to West Bromwich in a controversial match, and Charlie George, having a poor game against Newcastle, suddenly flashed in a brilliant winner. Leeds went back on top, however, when they beat Arsenal at Elland Road with a hotly disputed last-minute goal. Arsenal kept in the running by beating Stoke, with a goal by substitute Kelly.

So the scene was set for the last week of the season. Arsenal had to win or draw 0–0 at Spurs on the Monday night to take the title. White Hart Lane had a capacity crowd of 52,000 inside, with the same amount locked out. And Kennedy crowned a remarkable first season with a deserved winner two minutes from the end.

There was no time to dwell upon this triumph, however. There was still a Cup final to play—against a rapidly improving Liverpool side with perhaps the best defence in the country.

Again Arsenal did it the hard way. They made enough chances to have won comfortably, but with no score after 90 minutes the game went into extra time. And when Heighway broke away on the left and scored for Liverpool after two minutes, it looked all up for Arsenal. But they refused to panic, and ten minutes later, Kelly, who had come on in the second half for Storey, took advantage of a rare defensive slip and netted the equalizer.

But it was Charlie George who stole the headlines once more. With eight minutes to go he picked up a Radford pass and slashed a 20-yard drive past the flailing Clemence into the net.

Arsenal had won the Cup and done the 'double'. Frank McLintock, who had been voted Footballer of the Year, collected the trophy—his first after four unsuccessful visits to Wembley. George Graham, who found Wembley a perfect setting for his classy skills, was voted Man of the Match, a personal triumph all the more welcome because he had twice lost his place in the side during the season. Goalkeeper Wilson and all-purpose winger George Armstrong had played in all 64 matches. McLintock, Kennedy, and young Irish right-back Pat Rice, in his first full season, missed only one match. And England internationals Radford, Storey, and left-back Bob McNab missed only two.

Just what had Arsenal accomplished? The quality of their play had come in for some criticism over the season, but the magnitude of their deeds could not be denied. They had won the Championship with 65 points. They had begun with three key members of their side injured for long spells, but had triumphed against mighty Leeds, who finished with a record number of points for the runners-up. They had survived away draws in every round of the Cup and had come back from behind in the semi-final and final. With Fairs Cup and League Cup matches, they had played a total of 64 games. Sometimes they played brilliant, powerful football; frequently they had to rely on teamwork and sheer professionalism for survival. Most important of all for the club, they finally laid the bogey of playing in the shadow of the great Arsenal sides of the past.

Right: Stage one of the double. Ray Kennedy's header beats Pat Jennings of Spurs to ensure the League title goes to Highbury.

Right: The tireless George Armstrong (left) comes back to help full-back Bob McNab as Liverpool attack in the 1971 FA Cup final.

Right: Stage two of the double. Charlie George hits home Arsenal's second goal of the Cup final and the Gunners enter the record books.

Rivalries

Rivalry is a leading ingredient in the recipe that makes up football as a whole: rivalry between clubs, between players, between supporters. There is a particular sense of keenness, an extra-special desire to do well, when the opposition is provided by a long-standing rival. The atmosphere takes on an extraordinary dimension, building up the tension that is always evident before the kick-off, however mundane the fixture may appear to be. And this rivalry is never more keen than in those matches known as 'local derbies', in which two neighbouring sides are in opposition.

At club level in England, the closeness of competition between adjoining teams is particularly emphasized in two cities only 30 miles apart—Liverpool and Manchester. On Merseyside, the twice-yearly meetings between Everton and Liverpool are highlights

Right: Tommy Walker's penalty beats Ted Sagar, enabling the Scots to draw 1–1 with England in 1936. The rivalry between Scotland and 'the auld enemy' is football's oldest. Below: A confrontation between Scotland's striker Peter Lorimer and England's 'keeper Gordon Banks.

of the season, despite the growth of European competition. The same applies to Manchester, with United and City the most implacable of opponents.

Although the players of the opposing teams frequently mingle off the field, at social events, and in internationals, there is little sign of friendliness once they are in action against each other. Not surprisingly, the long history of these derby clashes has contained some unsavoury incidents— George Best of Manchester United was the particular target for abuse after a clash in which City's Glyn Pardoe broke a leg—but in general the games are contested in a sporting fashion.

Liverpool and Everton did much to avoid bitterness between the wars when, after several unseemly incidents, they adopted a suggestion made by a local journalist. From

then on, every meeting has begun with the teams taking the field side by side, as in a Cup final—an indication that friendliness is present, however frenzied the ensuing action. This method produced a memorable scene in August 1966, when the Merseyside pair met in the FA Charity Shield at Goodison Park. Liverpool's Roger Hunt and Everton's Ray Wilson, who had played in England's World Cup side a few weeks earlier, led the teams out, each with a hand on the Jules Rimet trophy. They were followed by Everton captain Brian Labone, holding the FA Cup, and Liverpool skipper Ron Yeats with the

League Championship shield. Never before had these three trophies been paraded at the same time.

Bill 'Dixie' Dean, the great Everton centre-forward, who played in 19 matches against Liverpool during his career, maintained that they were a thing apart from normal fixtures, and his view is shared by many others who have contributed, in however small a way, to this long series that stretches back through more than a century of meetings. Dean, a man with a love of practical jokes, often sent a bottle of aspirins to Liverpool goalkeeper Elisha Scott before a derby game, with a note saying: 'Sleep well—I'll keep you awake tomorrow.' 'Dixie' also played in the greatest clash of them all, in 1933, when Liverpool won 7–4 against the 11 Everton men who won the FA Cup four months later.

But perhaps the most remarkable game of the series was in 1955, when the clubs met in the fourth round of the Cup. Liverpool, then in Division II, had not won an away match all season, but they triumphed 4–0 at Goodison Park, despite being reduced to 10 men by an injury. Their next Cup meeting, in 1966, was played by special arrangement on a Saturday evening, with the overflow crowd watching at Anfield on closed-circuit television. If the pair ever meet in a Cup final (they did not do so in the first 100 years of the Cup although there were three semi-finals between them), Wembley will see the biggest throng of ticketless 'hopefuls' outside the ground in its long history.

The Manchester rivals, likewise, have not met in a final, although their two meetings in the League Cup semi-final in 1969–70 attracted nearly 140,000 spectators. As with Everton and Liverpool, the players like nothing more than to 'put one over' their neighbours, and the history of the Mancunian matches has perhaps more than its fair share of epic games.

One manifestation of local pride is that a club very rarely sells a player to the rival 'across the park', although Sir Matt Busby, who served United as manager for a quarter of a century, used to play for City. The teams concerned prefer to let unwanted men go virtually anywhere else, while the fans steadfastly maintain that 'the other lot' have no player who could possibly be any good!

Several other sets of clubs have similar rivalries, notably in North London, where Arsenal and Spurs provide another clear instance of competition taking on extra meaning twice a season. Arsenal's move to Highbury from their old home in Woolwich was a source of considerable ill-feeling, with Spurs claiming that supporters were being poached. But the celebrated 'vote-catching affair' of 1919 upset Tottenham considerably more—and rightly so.

Spurs finished bottom of the First Division in 1914–15, the last season before soccer was suspended because of World War I, while Arsenal were sixth in Division II. After the war, both sections were increased from 20 clubs to 22, with Chelsea, who had finished one above Tottenham, retaining their place, and Derby and Preston (champions and runners-up of the Second) going up. This left one senior vacancy to fill, and after much lobbying among other clubs at the annual meeting, that vacancy was filled by the election of Arsenal (sixth, remember), while Spurs had to go down. 'Norris should hang' said a notice on a wall near the Arsenal ground after that, a reference to Sir Henry Norris, the Arsenal chairman, who had used his persuasive powers to such good effect. Fortunately, Spurs were promoted immediately, when they topped Division II with a record 70 points.

Not until World War II, however, was the breach between the two clubs healed. Then, with Highbury requisitioned for defence purposes, Spurs allowed Arsenal to use White Hart Lane. And since then, off the pitch at least, the two have been good friends, for all their determination to do better than the other. This was never better illustrated than at the end of 1970–71, when Arsenal needed a win or a 0–0 draw from their last match to take the Championship. By a remarkable stroke of fate, they had to visit Spurs, who could not have tried harder had the title been theirs to contest. A last-minute goal gave the

Gunners victory on a night remarkable as much for the passion of the rival supporters as for that of the players.

Historical grievances play their part, too, in the great Italian rivalry between that formidable Milanese pair, AC Milan and Internazionale. Relations between these two are always potentially explosive, Milan having the reputation as being the more composed, aristocratic club, Internazionale as being the more volatile, impulsive club. Paradoxically, they share the same stadium, San Siro, as they battle for domestic and European honours.

The rivalry dates from March 9, 1908, when a group of dissatisfied Milan members got together in a Milanese restaurant to form 'Inter'. Milan soon had good reason to rue the dissension in their ranks. Founded largely by Englishmen in December 1899 and guaranteed security by a member of the wealthy Pirelli rubber manufacturing firm, they had won the Italian League in 1901, 1906, and 1907. But the 'breakaway' of Inter,

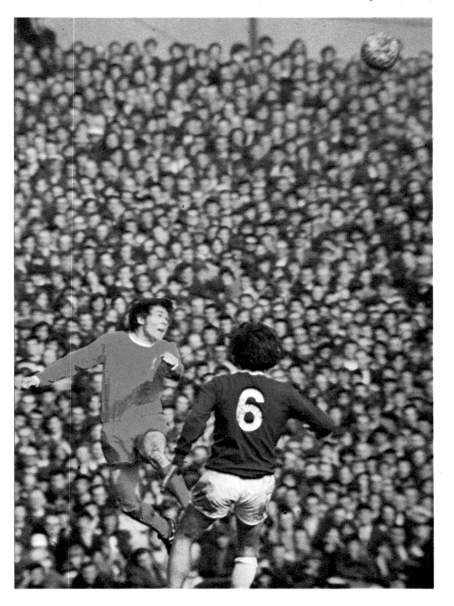

Below: Liverpool v Everton, a local derby with the atmosphere of a major battle.

playing in black and blue stripes to Milan's red and black, was such a setback that not another title was won until 1951.

It took Inter only two seasons to win their first Championship, and between the wars they and Bologna were the chief opposition to the mighty Juventus. AC Milan languished in the wings. With the splendid Peppino Meazza in attack, Inter won four titles between 1920 and 1940, though from 1928 they were known as Ambrosiana-Inter, having been forced by the Fascist regime to amalgamate with US Milanese. AC Milan at this time became Milano.

After World War II, and reverting to their original names, Milan and Inter strove for dominance, only Juventus keeping with them, and the rivalry intensified. Milan, building around the all-Swedish inside-forward trio of Gren, Nordahl, and Liedholm, won three League titles in the 1950s and reached great heights in the 1960s with two more Championships, the European Cup in 1963 and 1969, the Cup-Winners Cup in 1968,

and the World Club Championship in 1969. Inter's record was no less impressive. Beginning with cautious *catenaccio* methods in the 1950s and seeking invincibility under the guidance of the flamboyant Helenio Herrera in the 1960s, they capped domestic successes with the European Cup in 1964 and 1965, trumping this on each occasion with the world title. It was not surprising that local derbies drew crowds of 80,000. Here, in one city, were two of the finest club sides in the world.

Also in Northern Italy is a rather intriguing rivalry between the two Turin clubs, Torino and Juventus. Though perhaps lacking the intensity of that between AC Milan and Inter, their rivalry has a certain unique quality. Though Juventus are by far the more popular club in the country, nicknamed 'The Fiancée of Italy', Torino are the more popular in Turin. The reason for this is that Juventus are controlled by the Agnelli family, who also control the giant Fiat motor works that employs so many Torinese. Their

Above: Tempers boil over in a Manchester derby between City and United. Right: Contrasting reactions of jubilation and dejection in a Liverpool-Everton derby after Cormack has scored the winning goal.

Opposite page: Arsenal and Spurs. This intense North London rivalry, stemming from an injustice after World War I, was tempered by an act of goodwill during World War II.

Left: When Spurs and Arsenal met at White Hart Lane in May 1971, the rivalry between the two clubs took on an extra dimension. If Spurs could beat Arsenal, they would prevent them emulating their own double of 1960–61.

support for Torino is in some sense a gesture of defiance.

In other countries, national dominance is often the reason for the better known rivalries: Anderlecht of Brussels and Standard Liège in Belgium, Ajax Amsterdam and Feyenoord in the Netherlands, FC Austria and Rapid Vienna in Austria. But this is not always so, and in some areas of Britain there can be rivalries between clubs that now rarely meet in regular competition. The Birmingham area, where there is considerable rivalry between clubs, is a good example of this. Aston Villa, Birmingham City, and West Bromwich Albion all draw fervent support, no matter what their League status.

But when these clubs do meet, their contests do not grip the imagination of the public at large in the manner of a Merseyside or Manchester duel, no matter how vital the outcome might be on a more parochial basis.

The same goes for the clubs in Sheffield, Nottingham, and Bristol, where meetings between teams are now few and far between. But there is still a considerable atmosphere of contention in the North-East, where Newcastle and Sunderland were two of the country's most powerful clubs at the turn of the century. Although those days of glory have long since passed, Tyne and Wear still figure prominently in any list of inter-district competition.

The most deadly rivalry of all, however, is that in Scotland, between Celtic and Rangers. The word deadly is not too emotive, for the division between the two Glasgow giants has indeed resulted in death for several people, from religious gang warfare to the appalling disaster of January 1971 when 66 people were crushed to death on an exit stairway as they tried to leave the Ibrox ground. As long ago as 1909, the Scottish Cup was withheld after supporters of the two clubs had rioted, and time after time since then, police and hospital staff have been severely stretched to cope with the aftermath of violence that seems inseparable from any meeting between these two.

The differences are basically religious, Catholic Celtic against Protestant Rangers, while the Scot's traditional love for both a battle and a bottle are other causes of disorder. It is indeed sad that two clubs with such an honour-filled history, who have virtually monopolized soccer in Scotland for over 70 years, should always be associated with the mindless hooliganism of some supporters.

Elsewhere, too, domestic rivalries produce violence off the field to accompany the taut, hard-fought matches on it. In Greece, rival fans of the country's top sides, Olympiakos of Piraeus and Panathinaikos of Athens, have needed little encouragement to wreck the ground if their side looked like losing. In fact the situation in Greece was becoming so unruly that the authorities introduced a new system whereby a point was awarded for any game completed in addition to the usual points for a win or draw. It is a system that might have appealed to Australia's football authorities at one time. The game's large immigrant following found the football field an ideal place to continue their European ethnic feuds—much to the detriment of soccer's development.

In Brazil's Rio League, however, the size of the crowd, more than its behaviour, is

Above: Few rivalries are as bitter on and off the field as that between the two Glasgow clubs, Celtic and Rangers. For local police, trying to control fans, their matches must seem like a nightmare.

what makes the news when rivals Fluminense and Flamengo meet. Two of the largest ever attendances recorded were at 'Flu-Flam' contests in the Maracana Stadium—177,656 in 1963 and 171,599 in 1969. And six-figure attendances are the rule rather than the exception.

In Uruguay, the Penarol–Nacional clashes arouse partisan support throughout Montevideo, the rivalry being increased by the fact that these two clubs dominate the game in that country. Only a mere handful of league titles have escaped one or the other of them, and in the 1950s and 1960s no other club had a look in. But the Uruguayans can cupboard their differences for the time being when the national team play Argentina. This rivalry between the national sides is one that goes back to the 1920s when the two countries contested the 1928 Olympic title and then the 1930 World Cup final—each time with Uruguay emerging victorious. The World Cup final produced several incidents that show just how seriously the Uruguayans and the Argentinians take their football rivalry. The boatloads of Argentinian supporters who crossed the River Plate to Montevideo were searched for arms, and two balls were used in the match—one made in Uruguay, the other in Argentina.

There are no searches for weapons on the England–Scotland border, but Scottish supporters always travel south to Wembley well armed in other respects for the match between the oldest international rivals of all. For England fans, the game against Scotland may be just another match, but in Scotland it is awaited with keen anticipation. It is the focus of an upsurge of militant nationalism. The fierce patriotism of the Scots is never keener than when the 'auld enemy' provide the opposition. The awesome roar of the crowd at Hampden Park and the invasion of London by Scots every other year are notable features of the British football scene.

Political differences have played their part in two other bitter rivalries. In the matches between Austria and Hungary, the political divisions and the inborn distrust of the past can easily find expression on the football field. And the memory of the Spanish Civil War can be only too vivid when Barcelona meet Real Madrid. Never was the rivalry between these two teams as evident as in 1960, when Real were in the running for their fifth consecutive European Cup and Barcelona stood between them and the final. The matches themselves almost pale in comparison with the prelude to them. Real's managerial problems, their search and purchase of new players virtually within weeks of the tie ... Barcelona's determination to equal their rivals by building a 1¾ million pound stadium and assembling a galaxy of stars managed by the incomparable Herrera: such was the background to a clash in which the pride of two cities was at stake. There were 125,000 at Chamartin, 100,000 at Barcelona's Gran Estadio. Both crowds saw Madrid victorious. Herrera, who had dropped his brightest star, Kubala, from the tie, was attacked by angry Catalans as he left after the second defeat, and his resignation was inevitable. There had been so much at stake in this match that someone had to pay. Herrera, soon to find success with Inter-Milan, had discovered the hard way that when rivalry is a manifestation of area pride, victory can be the only result.

Top: A great moment for the Scots as Denis Law puts them on the road to a 3–2 victory over World Cup holders England in 1967. Above: Argentina score through Stabile in the 1930 World Cup against neighbours and bitter rivals Uruguay.

Left: Willie Henderson of Rangers takes on the Celtic defence in the 1969 Scottish Cup final, often an outlet for the emotions of Glasgow's rival factions.

193

F–P

Memorable Matches

Bolton Wanderers (1) **2**   **West Ham United** (0) **0**
Jack, Smith (J.R.)

28.4.23, Wembley; FA Cup final

Miraculously, nobody was killed. Only the good sense of the huge crowd, plus the efforts of the police—notably George Scorey, the man on the white horse—prevented a tragedy at the first Wembley Cup final. The stadium had been completed only four days before the game, and the FA, not realizing the amount of interest generated by both the match and the new venue, did not insist on all-ticket entry. A crowd estimated at a quarter of a million turned up, for although the official attendance was 126,047, many thousands more gained entry by climbing over the walls. Hundreds of people who had reserved seats did not see the match, which was delayed for 40 minutes while the playing area was closed.

When David Jack scored Bolton's first goal, after only two minutes, a West Ham player was struggling to get back onto the pitch, after falling among the crowd. Corners had to be taken from a standing start because there was no room for a run-up. The second goal, a thunderbolt shot from Jack Smith, rebounded into play from the wall of bodies pressed against the netting: 'It almost hit me on the way out', said the scorer.

Although the West Ham skipper, George Kay, always maintained that his side were unlucky, Bolton were generally thought to have deserved their victory. Certainly both sides did well to play any sort of football in such conditions. Afterwards questions were asked in the House of Commons, mainly about safety precautions. The match arrangements were handled by the British Empire Exhibition authorities, but subsequent games at Wembley were staged by the FA, who wisely insisted on ticket-only admission

Opposite page: PC Scorey and his white horse Billy became part of FA Cup history as a result of their efforts to control the crowd at the 1923 FA Cup final between Bolton and West Ham.
Below: Bolton players wait while the police move part of Wembley's record crowd back to the touch-line.

... having refunded almost half their £6,000 share of the gate to unlucky ticket-holders.

Bolton: Pym; Haworth, Finney; Nuttall, Seddon, Jennings; Butler, Jack, Smith (J.R.), Smith (J.), Vizard.
West Ham: Hufton; Henderson, Young; Bishop, Kay, Tresadern; Richards, Brown, Watson, Moore, Ruffell.

England (0) **1**   **Scotland** (2) **5**
Kelly   Jackson 3, James 2

31.3.28, Wembley; Home International Championship

Scotland's most famous victory was achieved by the team known as 'The Wembley Wizards'—the team who humbled England to such an extent that Alex James, the most magical wizard of them all, proclaimed 'We could have had ten'.

The tiny Scottish attack, with Alec Jackson easily the tallest at 5 ft 7 in, swept England aside by playing the pure style of Scottish football: ground passes alternating with individual dribbles. It was a day on which all the front five hit peak form together, the sort of day that comes once in a lifetime, if at all.

Doyen critic Ivan Sharpe summed it up like this: 'England were not merely beaten.

They were bewildered—run to a standstill, made to appear utterly inferior by a team whose play was as cultured and beautiful as I ever expect to see.' And 30 years later Sharpe was still insisting that he had not seen a display to match it.

Scotland were lucky on two counts. First, heavy rain made the Wembley turf, unused for almost a year, markedly different from the mud of the normal March pitch. It was ideal for their style of play. Second, England winger Smith hit a post in the second minute. A dry day, or an early goal against them, could have resulted in an entirely different match.

But football is full of such theories, whereas the record books are concerned only with the facts. The facts of this celebrated match are that Scotland streaked to a sensational success, with Jackson scoring three times (four Huddersfield team-mates were in the England side) and James (then a goalscorer with Preston before he became a goalmaker with Arsenal) hitting two beauties past the overworked Hufton. Kelly scored England's goal direct from a free-kick—one of only six shots his team managed throughout the game.

England: Hufton; Goodall, Jones; Edwards, Wilson, Healless; Hulme, Kelly, Dean, Bradford, Smith.
Scotland: Harkness; Nelson, Law; Gibson, Bradshaw, McMullan; Jackson, Dunn, Gallacher, James, Morton.

The goalscorers of the Wembley Wizards: Alex James (below) and Alec Jackson (bottom).

England (3) 3   Italy (0) 2
Brook 2, Drake   Meazza 2
14.11.34, Highbury

Notable for the excesses of the Italian team, the rugged tackling of Wilf Copping, and the ferocious shooting of Eric Brook, this ill-starred international has gone down in English football history as the Battle of Highbury. But it was also memorable for the goalkeeping of Ceresoli, who saved a penalty from Brook's deadly left foot; for the fact that no fewer than seven Arsenal men played in the England team; and for the elegant play of Peppino Meazza, Italy's centre-forward, when the Italians belatedly decided that the kicking had to stop.

Italy had just won the World Cup, for which England had not entered, so there was particular 'needle' in the game. The large Arsenal contingent came about because several of the original England side dropped out with injuries, and some hours before the kick-off their captain, Eddie Hapgood, was given the leadership of his country. The great day was spoilt when he had his nose broken by a deliberate blow from an Italian's elbow.

After less than two minutes, Luisito Monti, Italy's ruthless Argentinian centre-half, clashed with Arsenal's rugged centre-forward Ted Drake and broke a bone in his foot. He tried to play on, but eventually was persuaded to leave. Italy, reduced to 10 men, spent most of the game, as they believed, 'retaliating'. When they did decide to play football, it was too late.

Above: All is amicable as Luisito Monti and Eddie Hapgood shake hands before the 1934 England-Italy international. The match itself was less than friendly and earned the title Battle of Highbury.

England's attack was splendid in the first half, and though Brook missed his penalty he soon made amends, heading England's first goal and then lashing in a fierce free-kick when Ceresoli foolishly waved his wall away. Before half-time, Drake, pivoting sharply, made it three. In the second half, the Italians suddenly began to concentrate on football. Meazza scored two delightful goals, and only the goalkeeping of Frank Moss saved the day for England. It was most unfortunate that what should have been a classic match in fact degenerated into mayhem.

England: Moss; Male, Hapgood; Britton, Barker, Copping; Matthews, Bowden, Drake, Bastin, Brook.
Italy: Ceresoli; Monzeglio, Allemandi; Ferraris, Monti, Bertolini; Guaita, Serantoni, Meazza, Ferrari, Orsi.

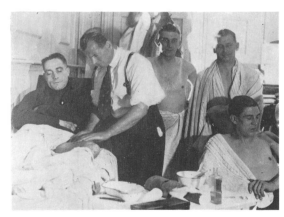

Busiest man after the notorious battle was England trainer Tom Whittaker.
Above: Whittaker works on Wilf Copping with Frank Moss, Cliff Bastin, and Ted Drake in attendance.
Left: Hapgood's broken nose was a painful memento of his first England captaincy.

Portugal (0) 0   England (5) 10
Mortensen 4, Lawton 4, Finney, Matthews

25.5.47, National Stadium, Lisbon

How best to utilize two world-class right-wingers? That was the problem England solved in Lisbon in 1947, to the agony of the Portuguese. Both Tom Finney and Stanley Matthews were superb ball players with magical swerves, but since 1946 the less charismatic Finney had had the edge over his rival. Now, profiting from the fact that Finney was naturally left-footed, England chose him on the left, Matthews on the right. With the rest of the forward line comprising Stan Mortensen, Tommy Lawton, and Wilf

Above: Stan Mortensen, scorer of four goals in England's 10–0 rout of Portugal in 1947.

Mannion, there was little the Portuguese could do.

Within the first two minutes, both Mortensen and Lawton had banged the ball past the Portuguese goalkeeper—and the ball had been changed. Before the match, it was agreed to use the customary full-size ball, but somehow the smaller, lighter Portuguese ball was introduced. Later the rules were bent even further when the 'keeper and then the right-back were substituted.

The change of the ball, however, made little difference. Lawton got England's third goal and then Finney scored a remarkable fourth. Getting the ball near the half-way line, he beat one man, then another, before reaching the goal-line. As he turned for goal a third opponent came at him, only to be beaten as well. Finney then shot past the goalkeeper from the narrowest of angles.

At half-time, a delighted Wilf Copping, once England's uncompromising left-half and now their trainer, told the team: 'I want to see that net so full they can't get a sorbo rubber ball into it.' The forwards obliged him. Lawton increased his tally to four, having completed his hat-trick before the interval; Mortensen got another three; and finally Matthews scored one of his rare goals to help the total to double figures. It was little wonder that the unhappy, bewildered Portuguese team missed the official banquet that night.

Portugal: Azevedo (Capela); Cardoso (Vasco), Feleciano; Amaro, Moreira, Ferreira; Correia, Arajuo, Peyroteo, Travassos, Rogerio.
England: Swift; Scott, Hardwick; Wright, Franklin, Lowe; Matthews, Mortensen, Lawton, Mannion, Finney.

Left: Tom Finney capped a splendid game against Italy at Turin in 1948 with two well taken goals.

Italy (0) 0   England (2) 4
Mortensen, Lawton, Finney 2

16.5.48, Municipal Stadium, Turin

In complete contrast to the 1934 Battle of Highbury, Italy behaved impeccably in defeat at Turin, even though it was a match they might have won, and one they certainly never deserved to lose so heavily.

This was the era in which Italy based their side on the great Torino team. Seven played that day, and there should have been eight. Maroso, the polished left-back, was injured. The inside-forwards, Loik and Mazzola, were particularly impressive.

England gained the upper hand with a magnificent early goal by Mortensen. Matthews sent the ball through to his Blackpool colleague, who set off on a prodigious run to the goal-line. Because the angle to goal was so acute, everyone thought the inside-right would cross to Lawton, but instead he pivoted and sent an astonishing shot past Bacigalupo into the near top corner. It was a goal that Italy has never forgotten.

The Italians then put England under a great deal of pressure, and only superb goal-keeping by the giant Frank Swift, splendidly abetted by Laurie Scott and Neil Franklin, kept them at bay. But it was England who scored again, after 24 minutes, and again it was Matthews who sent Mortensen away past Grezar and Parola to the goal-line. This time Mortensen did pull the ball back, and Lawton's drive put England two up at half-time.

Early in the second half, Swift made yet another remarkable save from a bewildered Gabetto, and finally England got on top. Matthews mesmerized Eliani, Mannion moved the ball sweetly, and Tom Finney capped two sweeping movements with fine goals. Yet despite the score, it was a game in which Italy played just as well as England and which, were it not for Mortensen and Swift, could so easily have gone the other way.

Italy: Bacigalupo; Ballarin, Eliani; Annovazzi, Parola, Grezar; Menti, Loik, Gabetto, Mazzola, Carapallese.
England: Swift; Scott, Howe; Wright, Franklin, Cockburn; Matthews, Mortensen, Lawton, Mannion, Finney.

Above: Frank Swift, whose brilliant performance in the England goal in Turin paved the way for their fine victory over Italy.

United States (1) 1   England (0) 0
Gaetjens

29.6.50, Belo Horizonte; World Cup

'We ain't got a chance', said Bill Jeffrey, manager of the cosmopolitan American team, before the match with England in the 1950 World Cup. England, joint favourites with Brazil, had won 22 and drawn 2 of their 28 previous internationals since soccer restarted after the war. Despite the absence of Stanley Matthews, the presence of Mortensen, Finney, Mannion, and Wright was enough almost to guarantee a flood of goals against the American part-timers. Their captain, Eddie McIlvenny—a Scot like Jeffrey—had gone to the United States after being given a free transfer by Third Division Wrexham . . . and he was thought to be their outstanding player.

Plainly, the Americans had no rightful place in a world tournament, even though the first post-war World Cup, played in Brazil, attracted only a fraction of the later publicity.

But the Americans won. The game that should have provided shooting practice for England only emphasized how inaccurate that shooting was, if a shot was made at all. Too often an extra pass was used instead. The woodwork was struck twice, a Mullen header was cleared from a position seemingly a yard behind the goal-line, the Americans defended valiantly. Whatever the reasons, England could not score once. The Americans did, with a Gaetjens header from their only real chance—in contrast to the many that England wasted.

True, the bumpy pitch, with the spectators crowded in close, was against good football. True, the England players were tired from the domestic season. True, they were ill-prepared, perhaps even scornful of their austere manager, Walter Winterbottom. The days of the Ramsey-style professionalism were still a long way off. And even the jubilant Jeffrey admitted that England would win a return 19 times out of 20. But there was no return. England had lost, in the most surprising turn-up of the nation's history . . . and the name of Belo Horizonte, the little mining town where a soccer disaster took place, became an unhappy joke.

USA: Borghi; Keough, Maca; McIlvenny, Colombo, Bahr; Wallace, Pariani, Gaetjens, Souza (J.), Souza (E.).
England: Williams; Ramsey, Aston; Wright, Hughes, Dickinson; Finney, Mortensen, Bentley, Mannion, Mullen.

Uruguay (0) 2   Brazil (0) 1
Schiaffino, Ghiggia   Friaça

16.7.50, Maracana Stadium, Rio de Janeiro; World Cup Final Pool

The match between Uruguay and Brazil, played before 200,000 impassioned spectators, effectively decided the World Cup of 1950. But it was not the final. There was none, the surviving four teams playing off in a final pool. Brazil, who had been playing superbly, scored 13 goals in their games against Sweden and Spain, and thus had four points. Uruguay had three, having drawn with Spain and beaten Sweden. All Brazil needed was a

Below: Uruguay's Maspoli, the hero of the day, saves bravely in the final pool match of the 1950 World Cup against Brazil.

draw, and with their inside-forward trio of Zizinho, Ademir, and Jair performing miracles of ball control and opportunism, their defeat looked improbable.

Uruguay stuck to the old attacking centre-half game, pivoting around the massive Varela. In attack, Ghiggia, the hunched right-winger, and the inside-forwards Perez and Schiaffino had all played in 1949 as amateurs in a Uruguayan side carpentered together for the South American Championship during a professional players' strike. These young men proved decisive on the day.

The first half was all Brazil, attacking endlessly. But the Uruguayan defence was magnificent: Maspoli a superb 'keeper, Varela a rock in the middle, the little, black Andrade superb at left-half. At half-time Brazil still had not scored, and even though Friaça did so at last just after the interval, Uruguay were getting into the game.

Varela began to forge upfield and Brazil began to look less sure. Twenty minutes into the half, Varela sent Ghiggia up the right wing and Schiaffino, quite unmarked, met his cross, took four strides, and equalized. Brazil's 'diagonal' defence was leaving their left-half Bigode exposed, and 11 minutes from time Ghiggia found Perez, then roared onto the return pass to score the winner. A trick of the sun fittingly bathed Maspoli's goal in fire.

Uruguay: Maspoli; Gonzales (M.), Tejera; Gambetta, Varela, Andrade; Ghiggia, Perez, Miguez, Schiaffino, Moran.
Brazil: Barbosa; Augusto, Juvenal; Bauer, Danilo, Bigode; Friaça, Zizinho, Ademir, Jair, Chico.

Blackpool (1) 4 **Bolton Wanderers** (2) 3
Mortensen 3, Perry   Lofthouse, Moir, Bell
2.5.53, Wembley; FA Cup Final

The 1953 Cup final is arguably the most famous club match of all time, at least as far as British followers are concerned. It will always be known as 'the Matthews match' because of the display given in the last half-hour by the legendary Blackpool winger. By the sheer force of his personality, and by his remarkable skill, he inspired his team to victory after they had been 3–1 down with 20 minutes left.

The game also contained one other noteworthy individual performance—Stan Mortensen's hat-trick, only the third in Cup final history. The fact that this feat is remembered second, not first, is proof of the indelible impression made by Matthews.

Modern theorists, who may have seen the match only on its frequent television reruns, may decry the many errors. Bolton's tactics, when reduced to nine fit men because of

injuries to Bell and Banks, seem particularly inept at this distance in history. But to anyone who was at Wembley on that sunlit day, and saw the 38-year-old Matthews gain a winner's medal at the third attempt, the memory of the thrills, the drama, and the atmosphere will never fade.

Bolton took a quick lead with a goal by Nat Lofthouse, completing his record of at least one in each round. Farm admitted that he should have saved it, and he was similarly at fault with Moir's goal after Mortensen, with a shot deflected by Hassall, had equalized. When Bell defied a pulled muscle to leap and head a third, Bolton seemed certain to win. But Matthews, impeccably served by Fenton and Taylor, then took charge with a single-handed display of all his brilliance. He feinted, swayed, and spurted

Below: Bell defies a pulled muscle to score Bolton's third goal of the 1953 FA Cup final.
Bottom: Hanson punches clear from Mortensen, who scored a great hat-trick for Blackpool.

through time and again, and it was his cross —fumbled by Hanson—that Mortensen poked in for Blackpool's second. Bolton's heroic defence held out until two minutes from time. Then Mortensen drilled a tremendous shot through the 'wall' at a free-kick for the equalizer. And with seconds left, Matthews ghosted down the right flank yet again, an unforgettable figure in orange jersey and baggy white shorts, to give Perry a chance to atone for several previous misses.

Matthews had his medal at last, and football had a new yardstick for measuring great matches.

Blackpool: Farm; Shimwell, Garrett; Fenton, Johnston, Robinson; Matthews, Taylor, Mortensen, Mudie, Perry.
Bolton: Hanson; Ball, Banks; Wheeler, Barrass, Bell; Holden, Moir, Lofthouse, Hassall, Langton.

England (2) 3   **Hungary** (4) 6
Sewell, Mortensen,   Hidegkuti 3, Puskas 2,
Ramsey (pen.)   Bozsik

25.11.53, Wembley

England's first home defeat by foreign opposition—apart from little Eire's largely forgotten 2–0 win at Everton four years earlier—was achieved by perhaps the finest team the world has yet seen. The speedy, fluent, confident Hungarians gave a display that would have shattered any side. England, ill-prepared, possibly over-confident after so many invincible years, were not in the same class. Not that England played badly. Their first two goals were brilliantly taken, but the Hungarians were so good that their margin must have been greater had they not slackened off in the last half-hour, after building a 6–2 lead.

'No European nation has beaten us here, and none ever will.' That was the average insular Englishman's feeling before the match. The Hungarians were unknown in England (the equally insular press had largely ignored their remarkable record of success over the preceding few years), and England were thought to be heading for yet another victory ... simply because they were England. But from the first minute, when Hidegkuti slashed a 20-yard rising shot beyond Merrick, the Hungarians delivered a lesson: a lesson in ball control, in accuracy, in moving into position, in finishing.

The use of a deep centre-forward, with the inside men acting as spearheads, confused the English defence. Likewise they had no answer to the sudden onslaughts by Bozsik, nominally right-half, whose thunderbolts from outside the penalty area produced two goals, one a deflection by Puskas from a free-kick.

As Geoffrey Green wrote in *The Times*, the Hungarians were a side 'of progressive, dangerous artists who seemed able to adjust themselves at will to any demand'. He also wrote: 'English football can be proud of its past. But it must awake to a new future.'

Above: Sandor Kocsis, the 'Golden Head', towers well above England's left-half Jimmy Dickinson at Wembley in 1953.

Although the demand for change resulted in the ending of six international careers that day—Taylor and Robb made only this one appearance in their country's colours—the necessary evolution was a long time coming.

England: Merrick; Ramsey, Eckersley; Wright, Johnston, Dickinson; Matthews, Taylor, Mortensen, Sewell, Robb.

Hungary: Grosics; Buzansky, Lantos; Bozsik, Lorant, Zakarias; Budai, Kocsis, Hidegkuti, Puskas, Czibor.

Right: Puskas (far right) scores Hungary's third goal.

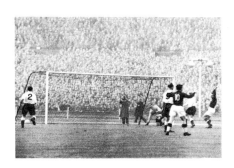

Below: The cat-like Grosics saves a shot from Matthews.

Hungary (1) (2) 4   Uruguay (0) (2) 2
Czibor, Hidegkuti,   Hohberg 2
Kocsis 2

30.6.54, Lausanne; World Cup Semi-Final

Unfavourable conditions often provide an unexpected backdrop to memorable matches, and such was the case with the 1954 World Cup semi-final between Hungary and Uruguay. The Hungarians had come to Lausanne battered and bruised from the vicious 'Battle of Berne' against Brazil three days earlier, and it was thought that the Uruguayans might seek South American revenge. Moreover, torrential rain made conditions seemingly impossible for a classic encounter.

Yet it was. In spite of the miserable conditions, the early exchanges were fast and precise, with the Hungarians gaining the ascendancy. The absence of Puskas was hardly felt as they stretched the makeshift Uruguayans with accurate thrusts and clever possessional play. As the probing Bozsik and the tireless Hidegkuti frequently sparked their wingers into dangerous moves, the Uruguayans found it more and more difficult to turn on the slippery surface.

Czibor opened the scoring for Hungary after 15 minutes, and just after the interval Hidegkuti headed home with a spectacular dive. But in spite of worsening conditions, Uruguay staged a courageous come-back, controlling the game to their own pace and making ground with individual forays. With just a quarter of an hour remaining, they pulled one back when Schiaffino put Juan Hohberg through. Five minutes before time Hohberg had the ball in the net again. He had to be treated on the sideline as a result of his team-mates' congratulatory hugs.

Uruguay carried their momentum into extra time and Schiaffino hit a post as he was tackled by two defenders. He limped back into action, but Hungary gradually asserted themselves again. Finally Kocsis headed in two right-wing crosses. Possibly a more agile goalkeeper than the roly-poly Maspoli might have stopped them, but he would have had to produce above-average saves. When the final whistle blew, Uruguay, the holders, had lost their first World Cup match.

Hungary: Grosics; Buzansky, Lantos; Bozsik, Lorant, Zakarias; Budai, Kocsis, Palotas, Hidegkuti, Czibor.
Uruguay: Maspoli; Santamaria, Martinez; Andrade, Carballo, Cruz; Souto, Ambrois, Hohberg, Schiaffino, Borges.

Left. Grosics punches clear from Souto.
Above: Czibor's shot gives Maspoli no chance, and Hungary lead 1–0.
Right: Hidegkuti's spectacular dive puts the Hungarians two ahead.

Wolverhampton Wanderers (0) 3   Honved (2) 2

Hancocks (pen.),
Swinbourne 2

Kocsis, Machos

13.12.54, Molineux

Though unquestionably played up by a press disquieted by Hungary's double thrashing of England (in November 1953 and May 1954), Wolves' victory over the Hungarian champions Honved was still a fine achievement. Honved, the Army team, had for years been drawing on the talent of Hungarian football at large, and of the great team that beat England, only Nandor Hidegkuti was not from the club.

Wolves, the English champions, challenged them at Molineux. It was a muddy pitch, a bitter night; ideal conditions for the Wolves, who revelled in the long-ball game. Their attacks were built on sweeping passes to flying wingers and brave forwards going in to head home fast crosses.

Honved, admittedly, were not at their best. They were playing out of season, and most of the side had played the previous week against Scotland in Glasgow. Yet by half-time they were two goals in front. The first was a characteristic one by Kocsis. Leaping up to head in a free-kick by Puskas, the 'Golden Head' gave ample evidence of the aerial skills that had recently made him top scorer in the World Cup. Then Machos, the young centre-forward, darted through alone to make it 2–0, and Honved seemed well on the way to victory.

Wolves, however, were famous for their second-half rallies. The brave running of tiny Johnny Hancocks on the wing worried Honved as it worried so many European defences, and they began to give away free-kicks with desperate fouls. At length a foul on Hancocks brought a rather contentious penalty, which Hancocks himself converted. Wolves grew, Honved waned. Another sweeping attack brought the equalizer when Denis Wilshaw crossed for centre-forward Roy Swinbourne to head in. Then Smith and Shorthouse put the powerful Swinbourne through for the winner. It was a fine game, but scarcely one to make Wolves world champions, as one newspaper claimed.

Wolverhampton: Williams; Stuart, Shorthouse; Slater, Wright, Flowers; Hancocks, Broadbent, Swinbourne, Wilshaw, Smith.
Honved: Farago; Rakoczi, Kovacs; Bozsik. Lorant, Banyai; Budai, Kocsis, Machos, Puskas, Czibor.

Right: Billy Wright and Ferenc Puskas lead Wolves and Honved out for their classic encounter.

Arsenal (0) 4   Manchester United (3) 5

Herd, Bloomfield 2,
Tapscott

Edwards, Charlton
Taylor 2, Viollet

1.2.58, Highbury; Football League, Div. I

It takes two sides to make a great match. A trouncing—however well one side may play—is usually attributed to the weakness of the opposition. The Arsenal team that faced Manchester United at Highbury on February 1, 1958 was a middle-of-the-table side that had accomplished nothing. But they raised their performance that afternoon to provide worthy opposition for the famous 'Busby Babes', a side composed mainly of young footballers welded together by manager Matt Busby into the most exciting team of the age.

A capacity 64,000 crowd saw United swing into a 3–0 first-half lead. The giant Duncan Edwards and the mercurial Eddie Colman dominated the middle of the field, and wingers Morgans and Scanlon turned Arsenal inside-out on the flanks. The goals were magically conceived and executed. Edwards began the show as he powered majestically to the edge of the penalty area and hit the ball low and unstoppably into the corner of Arsenal's goal. Bobby Charlton and Tommy Taylor swept in two more, and the spectators, resigned to the result, looked forward to a second-half feast.

It came; but not quite in the way they anticipated. Shortly after the interval Arsenal scored—three times in less than three minutes! Suddenly it was a new game. Inspired by the quality of the opposition and urged on by their captain, Dave Bowen, Arsenal looked like taking charge. But not for long—like the great side they were, United brushed aside this challenge almost contemptuously. Denis Viollet and Tommy Taylor made the score 5–3. But Arsenal were still not finished, and their Welsh international Derek Tapscott pulled one back. Vic Groves almost equalized, but United held out and reasserted their superiority.

It was an unforgettable game, full of all the skills and drama of soccer. And it was, tragically, the last occasion on which the 'Busby Babes' played on British soil. Five days later they lay shattered on a snow-covered airfield in Munich.

Arsenal: Kelsey; Charlton, Evans; Ward, Fotheringham, Bowen; Groves, Tapscott, Herd, Bloomfield, Nutt.
Manchester United: Gregg; Foulkes, Byrne; Colman, Jones, Edwards; Morgans, Charlton, Taylor, Viollet, Scanlon.

Above: Denis Viollet and Tommy Taylor challenge the Arsenal defence as the 'Busby Babes' play their last game in England before the Munich air disaster. Below: Arsenal 'keeper Kelsey and right-back Charlton join forces to save.

Real Madrid (3) 7	Eintracht Frankfurt (1) 3
Di Stefano 3, Puskas 4	Kress, Stein 2

18.5.60, Hampden Park; European Cup Final

At the end of the 1960 European Cup final at Hampden Park, the immense Scottish crowd of more than 127,000 remained to give Real Madrid a deafening ovation. It showed to what extent one of the most critical and chauvinistic audiences in the world had been impressed by the brilliance of the Spanish team, which calmly rode the shock of an early goal to destroy a far from inept Eintracht side.

As it transpired, this match, the fifth of Real's European Cup triumphs, was almost their swan-song. At the same time, it was surely the zenith of the marvellous partnership between Alfredo Di Stefano, the balding Argentinian centre-forward of all work, and Ferenc Puskas, the tubby little Hungarian with the killing left foot.

Eintracht, who had hit six goals in both semi-final legs against Rangers, had a remarkable pair of veterans in the 33-year-old scheming inside-forward Pfaff and the 35-year-old right-winger Kress. It was Kress who put Eintracht ahead after 18 minutes

Above: Di Stefano puts Real Madrid on level terms with Eintracht Frankfurt in the 1960 European Cup final.

Left: Puskas scores Real's fourth from the penalty spot. He and Di Stefano shared Real Madrid's seven goals.

Right: Alfredo Di Stefano, orchestrator of the champions of Europe.

from a pass by Stein, the big, strong centre-forward. That lead lasted just eight minutes. Canario, the Brazilian right-winger—one position Real never seemed to fill satisfactorily—crossed and Di Stefano lashed the ball home. Three minutes later an error by Loy allowed Di Stefano to score another, and later Puskas left-footed a third from the narrowest of angles—eight yards from the near post and a yard from the goal-line. When, just after half-time, the Hungarian scored from a rather harsh penalty, that seemed to be that. It was not.

Real's combination, the variety of their moves, were superb. Often they played possession football with a web of short, neat passes before suddenly accelerating for goal. Puskas scored twice more, Stein made it 2–6, Di Stefano raced through alone for his hat-trick, and finally Stein got a consolatory third. There remained no more but the epithets . . . and memories for those who had seen what many still regard as the finest game ever.

Real: Dominguez; Marquitos, Pachin; Vidal, Santamaria, Zarraga; Canario, Del Sol, Di Stefano, Puskas, Gento.
Eintracht: Loy; Lutz, Hoefer; Weilbacher, Eigenbrodt, Stinka; Kress, Lindner, Stein, Pfaff, Meier.

England (3) 9

Robson, Greaves 3,
Smith 2, Douglas,
Haynes 2

Scotland (1) 3

Mackay, Wilson, Quinn

15.4.61, Wembley; Home International Championship

Frank Haffey, Scotland's goalkeeper, left the field in tears after his country's record defeat. It was not surprising, for the Celtic player—called in because of injuries to two others—had had a nightmare match. At least four of England's goals were directly attributable to his errors. Yet England's display, for all Haffey's generosity, was a remarkable one, full of pace and skill and a continuing hunger for goals. Walter Winterbottom, the often-criticized manager, had welded a fine side out of several good-class players and two outstanding forwards of varying techniques, Jimmy Greaves and Johnny Haynes.

Winterbottom's policy of making as few changes as possible had resulted in a fine season for England: this was their fifth successive victory, with 32 goals scored. Greaves, shortly to leave for Italy, was without a rival as a finisher; Haynes was equally matchless with his imaginative passing. With the tricky Douglas, the robust Smith, and the all-round skill of Charlton, backed up by an astute wing-half in Robson, England's forward line was indeed formidable.

Scotland's tactics were inept, their usual spirit rarely seen. Even allowing for the inroads into their confidence made by Haffey's display, this was still a shamefully spineless performance by a team who, on paper, had looked to have every hope of a draw.

Five goals came in an 11-minute spell during the second half, as the Scottish defensive castle crumbled. Their one consolation was Wilson's goal, a flying header good enough to win any match. What a pity, for him and all his mourning countrymen among the crowd, that it was wasted.

England: Springett; Armfield, McNeil; Robson, Swan, Flowers; Douglas, Greaves, Smith, Haynes, Charlton.
Scotland: Haffey; Shearer, Caldow; Mackay, McNeill, McCann; MacLeod, Law, St John, Quinn, Wilson.

Above: A disconsolate Frank Haffey walks off Wembley in April 1961. Below: The seventh of the nine England goals that passed Haffey into the Scottish net.

North Korea (3) 3

Pak Seung Jin,
Yang Sung Kook,
Li Dong Woon

Portugal (2) 5

Eusebio 4 (2 pens.),
Augusto

23.7.66, Goodison Park; World Cup Quarter-Final

The Koreans, with their curious names and lack of size (their entire World Cup squad averaged 5 ft 5 in), provided surprise after surprise in the 1966 tournament. On arrival, they lost to Russia, but drew with Chile and then beat Italy 1–0, giving their highly paid opponents a lesson in the application of sheer spirit. This meant a quarter-final against Portugal, who had already eliminated holders Brazil with a superb display of attacking football, plus some brutal tackles.

The Koreans, humorously dubbed 'Diddy Men' by Merseysiders, after comedian Ken Dodd's knockabout assistants, promptly took a first-minute lead, and after half an hour were three up. Their relentless chasing, allied to much clever individual work, tore huge holes in the always suspect Portuguese back four.

Then Eusebio, the lithe inside-forward, took control. With considerable assistance from his captain, Coluña, and winger Simoes, the 'Black Panther' cut Korea's lead with a typical goal, then reduced it further from a penalty. In the second half, as the mood of inspiration passed from the little men, he equalized. Now the game was plainly Portugal's for the taking, and Eusebio's tremendous surging run past four men only ended with a foul. Eusebio himself scored from the spot, and Korea's gallant battle was over. A final goal, by Augusto, after the towering Torres had outheaded the defence, was irrelevant.

So the Koreans returned home, after figuring in one of the most remarkable of all

World Cup matches. Sadly, political pressures led to their withdrawal from the 1970 World Cup in the qualifying competition (they refused to visit Israel, a state they did not recognize), and so few Westerners know whether 1966 was a watershed in their football history, or merely a stage in their continuing development.

Portugal: Pereira; Morais, Hilario; Graça, Baptista, Vicente; Augusto, Eusebio, Torres, Coluña, Simoes.
North Korea: Li Chan Myung; Rim Yung Sum, Shin Yung Kyoo; Ha Jung Wong, O Yook Kyung, Pak Seung Jin; Jon Seung Hwi, Han Bong Jin, Pak Doo Ik, Li Dong Woon, Yang Sung Kook.

Above: Li Dong Woon slots North Korea's second goal past the shaky Pereira. Right: Eusebio's penalty restores some sanity to the scoreline and puts Portugal nearer victory.

Below: The Portuguese defence is breached a third time, and scorer Yang Sung Kook crumbles from the effects of a late tackle.

Real Madrid (3) 3

Pirri, Gento, Amancio

Manchester United (1) 3

Zoco (o.g.), Sadler, Foulkes

15.5.68, Santiago Bernabeu Stadium, Madrid; European Cup Semi-Final (2nd leg)

Seldom have Manchester United fought back with such spirit and success as they did in their European Cup semi-final second leg in Madrid in 1968. They had won a tight first leg 1–0 at Old Trafford, thanks to a typically rasping shot by Best. But at half-time in Madrid they found themselves 1–3 behind.

After 32 minutes, the excellent Pirri, a superb midfield right-half always ready to strike for goal, headed in a free-kick to make the aggregate score level. And so it stayed until just before half-time, when an extraordinary burst of activity produced three goals and sent United into the dressing room one behind on aggregate.

First Paco Gento, the indestructible Real outside-left, veteran of every European final the team had played, showed some of his old speed when snapping up a mis-kick by Brennan and racing through to make the score 2–0. Manchester immediately fought back, and were given the encouragement of an own goal by Zoco, the tall second stopper. No doubt that would have satisfied United as a half-time score, but Real ended this three-minute spell by scoring again. Amancio, stocky and alert, banged in a loose ball to make it 3–1.

It was a poor prospect for United, but they did not give up, and 18 minutes from the end

they were rewarded. Pat Crerand took a free-kick, George Best leapt characteristically to head the ball on, and David Sadler, now committing himself to attack rather than defence, squeezed the ball home. Best now had the wind in his sails, and five minutes later, with United throwing everything into attack, he beat his man and turned the ball across the goal for centre-half Bill Foulkes, of all people, to score. The tie was saved. United had made the European Cup final at last.

Real: Betancort; Gonzales, Zunzunegui, Zoco, Sanchis; Pirri, Grosso; Perez, Amancio, Velazquez, Gento.
Manchester United: Stepney; Brennan, Dunne; Crerand, Foulkes, Stiles; Best, Kidd, Charlton, Sadler, Aston.

Italy (1) (1) 4

Boninsegna, Burgnich, Riva, Rivera

West Germany (0) (1) 3

Schnellinger, Müller 2

17.6.70, Aztec Stadium, Mexico City; World Cup Semi-Final

In a game that ended in a strange spate of goals, Italy reached their third World Cup final, after seeming to be at one time on the ropes. Extra time brought a bewildering welter of goals as both teams uncharacteristically threw defence to the winds and went for victory. Yet perhaps the decisive moment was a savage foul by Cera on Beckenbauer as the elegant German half-back flowed through Italy's defence. Beckenbauer had to have his arm strapped to his side, and as Helmut Schoen, the German manager, had used both substitutes, there was no replacing him.

Italy took the lead after only seven and a half minutes when Boninsegna, their centre-forward, got a rather lucky rebound from two German defenders and struck the ball home with his left foot from the edge of the box. In the second half, Italy substituted Gianni Rivera for Sandro Mazzola (son of the famous Torino inside-forward) as they had in the quarter-finals, but they now played cautiously and gave the Germans the initiative.

In the last minute of normal time, the Germans, with Beckenbauer limping, abandoned their *catenaccio*, brought on striker Sigi Held for Patzke, and nearly equalized when his terrific shot was kicked off the line. It was in the third minute of injury time that Grabowski crossed from the left and Schnellinger, the former sweeper, equalized.

Below: David Saddler is congratulated by team-mates after scoring Manchester United's second goal against Real Madrid in the second leg of their 1968 European Cup semi-final.

Five minutes into extra time, a blunder by Italy's substitute Poletti gave Müller an easy goal, only for Burgnich, another scoring defender, to equalize after Rivera's free-kick. Next Gigi Riva pivoted to beat Schnellinger and then score with a long, splendid cross-shot. In the second period, the irrepressible Uwe Seeler nearly scored with a header, then nodded across to Müller, who equalized. But straight from the kick-off, and nine minutes from the end, Boninsegna broke down the left and pulled the ball back for Rivera to hit the winner.

Sceptical Italian journalists dismissed the last phases with one word, 'Basketball', and came out with the headline, 'Danke, Schoen!' Nevertheless, it had been breathlessly exciting.

Italy: Albertosi; Burgnich, Cera, Rosato (Poletti), Facchetti; Bertini, Domenghini, Mazzola (Rivera); De Sisti; Boninsegna, Riva.
West Germany: Maier; Patzke (Held), Schnellinger, Schulz, Vogts; Beckenbauer, Overath, Seeler; Grabowski, Müller, Lohr (Libuda).

Right: Schnellinger equalizes for West Germany in injury time and sends the 1970 World Cup semi-final with Italy into a fantastic period of extra time.

Below: Gianni Rivera beats Sepp Maier to win the Italians a place in the final. Bottom: Gerd Müller scores his last goal of the 1970 World Cup.

Outstanding Feats

Soccer's outstanding feats are usually associated with the scoring of goals, for this, as the television commentators never tire of telling us, is what the game is all about. It is the goalscorers who usually steal the limelight, and whose deeds are recorded for posterity in the record books. Defenders who have a brilliant game, an outstanding season, or a long, consistently good career have few statistics to commemorate their feats, whereas names such as Joe Payne, Dixie Dean, and Arthur Rowley are never forgotten.

Of these, Dixie Dean would have found a place in any list of all-time great centre-forwards whether or not he had established a Football League goalscoring record of 60 goals in the 1927–28 season. This came two seasons after the change in the offside law, to which defenders had not yet fully adjusted. It beat by one goal the League record set by George Camsell the previous season for Middlesborough in the Second Division. Dean needed three goals when Everton played their last League game of the season at home to Arsenal, and he duly obliged with all his side's goals in a 3–3 draw. In all games that season he scored 82. The same season, in less exciting company, Jim Smith of Ayr scored 66 Scottish Division II goals in 38 games, and 84 goals in all.

Dean's record is, perhaps, an unfair yardstick by which to measure today's League goalscoring feats. No one else has ever attained 50 goals in Division I, and when that prolific goal-getter Jimmy Greaves hit 41 for Chelsea in 1960–61 it was the highest for 26 years.

Individual match goalscoring feats have also endured well. Joe Payne notched 10 for Luton on April 13, 1936 in a Division III (South) game. It was his first match as centre-forward. The laurels for the most remarkable debut in first-class football, however, must go to J. Dyet, who scored eight for King's Park in a Scottish Division II match in 1930. The record in British first-class soccer also belongs to a Scotsman—13 goals by John Petrie the Arbroath outside-right in their British record thrashing 36–0 of Bon Accord in the Scottish Cup on September 5, 1885. The very same day, in the same competition, there was a 35–0 result, Dundee Harp beating Aberdeen Rovers.

Team goalscoring records do not have the drama of individual ones, as they are usually associated with the humiliation of one side. The outstanding performances in this respect are the Cup defeats of strong clubs by lowly or non-League teams (see the section on *Giant-Killing*).

Some away victories might be classified as outstanding feats, none more so than Sunderland's 9–1 defeat of Newcastle in December 1908, eight of their goals coming in a 28-minute spell. This was a record away win for Division I, and the losers went on to win the Championship that season, nine points ahead of third-place Sunderland! Arsenal's 7–1 win at Villa Park in

Left: Pelé (right) beats Vasco da Gama 'keeper Norberto Andrada from the penalty spot to score his 1,000th goal, at the Maracana Stadium in November 1969.

December 1935 was remarkable not so much for the score—Arsenal were riding high and Villa were set for relegation—but for the fact that centre-forward Ted Drake scored all seven goals in only eight shots. His other attempt hit the cross-bar.

Perhaps the most dramatic individual goalscoring feat was performed by Charlton's Johnny Summers on December 21, 1957. With only 28 minutes remaining, Charlton were 1–5 down to Huddersfield and had only 10 men, but five goals from Summers helped them to a 7–6 victory.

Soccer 'Houdini' performances such as these are always exciting, and Fulham's life in Division I during the 1960s was full of great escapes. Always floundering near the bottom of the table as the end of the season approached, they seemed to delight in producing winning runs and just escaping relegation. It is perhaps cynical to suggest that Fulham's survival was in itself an outstanding feat, but they performed a number of near miracles to do so. Eventually, however, they ran out of luck, finished bottom, and the very next season plummeted straight through to Division III.

It is a common end-of-the-season phenomenon for a club that has produced consistently poor performances to suddenly find a new lease of life when stared in the face by relegation. One such situation arose in the 1957–58 season, when, at Easter, Lincoln City were propping up the Second Division, five points adrift of the next club, having won only 5 of their 36 matches. They then proceeded to win their last 6 matches, to escape relegation by a single point. They climaxed their 'great escape' with a 3–1 win in their last match after trailing 0–1 with 20 minutes to go.

Another Lincolnshire club, Grimsby Town, produced an equally dramatic finish in the 1931–32 season, but were desperately unlucky to go down from Division I. Bottom with two games left, they faced fifth-placed West Bromwich Albion at the Hawthorns. They found themselves 5–3 down in the second half, with their goalkeeper off the field injured—yet they won 6–5! They went on to beat third-placed Sheffield Wednesday 3–1 in their last game, but one of their rivals, Blackpool, won away, and the valiant 'Mariners' were relegated.

Less dramatic but more substantial feats revealed by the record books are the outstanding career performances of individuals and the long unbeaten runs of teams. It is difficult to compare goalscoring exploits in different parts of the world because seasons and competitions differ widely, but one man stands out. There can hardly be a football fan anywhere who has not heard of Pelé, the acknowledged king of them all, who scored his 1,000th goal in 1969, and continued to bang them in after that. His total includes goals scored in the many friendlies played by his club, Santos, as well as those scored in regular competitions and internationals. But few people outside central Europe know the name of the only other man to have scored 1,000 goals—Franz 'Bimbo Binder', who played for Rapid Vienna, Austria, and 'Greater Germany' in the 1930s and 1940s.

In Britain, goalscorers may be judged on

The first Englishmen to win 100 caps lead their country out on the occasion of their century.
Left: Bobby Charlton, who went on to win 106 caps.
Right: Billy Wright, who won 105 caps altogether.

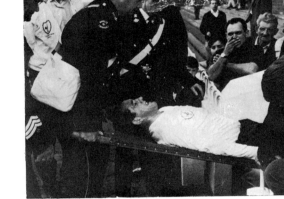

Right: Dave Mackay is carried off after breaking his leg for the second time in nine months. Yet he returned to lead Spurs to Wembley in 1967 and take Derby to the First Division in 1969.

their League records, and Arthur Rowley leads the pack with 434 goals in a post-war career spanning 20 years, 4 clubs, and all 4 divisions. Next comes Scotland's Jimmy McGrory (1922–38) with 410, including a record 397 for one club, Celtic.

Jimmy Dickinson (1946–65) of Portsmouth set the record for League appearances with 764, all for the same club. Roy Sproson was approaching this mark when his career with Port Vale tailed off in the 1970–71 season. The only other man to reach 700 appearances was Stanley Matthews, who became the oldest First Division player of all time when he turned out for Stoke City five days after his 50th birthday. His total of 886 matches included 701 League games, 86 FA Cup ties, and 54 internationals, an even more remarkable record considering the loss of the war years. And in a game where injury is not uncommon, centre-half Harold Bell's 401 consecutive League appearances for Tranmere Rovers in Division III (North) between 1946 and 1955 stands out. The record for successive appearances on the scoresheet was set by Arthur Chandler in 1924–25, when he netted in 16 consecutive League matches for Leicester City.

All club achievements pale before Queen's Park's unbeaten run against Scottish opposition, which lasted from their formation in 1867 until January 1875. Preston North End were unbeaten throughout the 1888–89 season, playing a total of 27 matches in achieving 'the double' (see the section on *The Double*). And Celtic had an unbeaten run of 63 matches from November 1915 to April 1917. The longest recorded undefeated run at home was achieved by the Real Madrid side from February 1957 to March 1965, with 114 wins and 8 draws. At international level, Hungary went 29 matches undefeated between 1950 and 1954.

With the increasing number of international matches played since World War II, seven players had by the early 1970s won a hundred or more caps: Billy Wright and Bobby Charlton of England, Josef Bozsik of Hungary, Thorbjorn Svenssen of Norway, and Djalma Santos, Pelé, and Gylmar of Brazil.

In sharp contrast to these career achievements are the quick-scoring records. As there is no provision for setting a watch to time the first goal of a match, all such records are unofficial. But various claims have been made for Football League matches, capped by a 4-second goal by Bradford's Jim Fryatt against Tranmere Rovers in April 1965, a time confirmed by the referee. Also in the Football and Scottish Leagues are a number of claims for individual hat-tricks scored in three-minutes and for four goals in five minutes.

The record number of hat-tricks in the Football League is credited to Dixie Dean, with 37. Goalscoring in modern football is not what it used to be, and this is another Dean record that is never likely to be beaten —unless there is a drastic change in style, tactics, or the Laws. The outstanding feats of today must be judged by different standards.

Footballer of the Year

Every season, in England, Scotland, and other countries throughout the footballing world, a player is nominated as that country's Footballer of the Year. It could be said that awards to individual footballers are somewhat inappropriate, football being a team sport. Nevertheless, such awards are generally regarded as great honours, and, although not sought after, are usually accepted with pride.

The principal award in Europe, that of European Footballer of the Year, is decided each December by an invited group of football writers from the leading footballing countries in Europe. They nominate five players in order of preference, and the players receive points according to their rating. The award began in 1956 at the instigation of the French weekly *France Football*, and the first winner was Stanley Matthews. By 1971 three other British players had been voted European Footballer of the Year, and all came from Manchester United—Denis Law, Bobby Charlton, and George Best.

Curiously, Stanley Matthews had been the first winner of the English Footballer of the Year award, in 1947–48. This is decided, at the end of the season, on a single vote by members of the English Football Writers' Association, just as the Scottish Footballer of the Year, first awarded in 1965, is chosen by the Scottish Football Writers' Association.

Left: Stanley Matthews and Alfredo di Stefano. Matthews was England's Footballer of the Year in 1948 and 1963, Europe's in 1956. Di Stefano was European Footballer of the Year in 1957 and 1959.

Below: Johan Cruyff, European Footballer of the Year in 1971.

Left: Danny Blanchflower, England's Footballer of the Year in 1958 and 1961.

Below: George Best won both the English and European awards in 1968.

Giant-Killing

Giant-killing—victory for David over Goliath—has a special place in soccer lore. The British, particularly, support the underdog, and the history of British soccer is strewn with the bodies of great club sides conquered by the unfancied, unheralded, and sometimes unknown.

Yet perhaps the most improbable defeat in the annals of the game was suffered by the England international side in the 1950 World Cup at the hands of the United States (see *Memorable Matches*). This 1–0 catastrophe for England must go down as the all-time freak result of international soccer, and it would take a similar reverse for the Americans in baseball or their own code of football to erase the embarrassing memory of it.

Feats of giant-killing occur in cup matches every year, particularly in the FA Cup. This tournament has the reputation of being a great 'leveller', meaning that it inspires the lowly clubs to play above themselves and brings the top clubs down to their opponents' level. 'Cup football' is a term often used to describe the exciting, epic clashes encountered in knockout tournaments, although often it is used as a euphemism for the irresponsible rough play and disregard for the rules exhibited by some clubs in the Cup. Referees have been criticized for turning a blind eye in cup matches to the transgressions of the underdogs, allowing them to compensate for the difference in skill. This 'licence' for rough play is more evident in the earlier rounds of the cup, although the Chelsea–Leeds Cup final replay in 1970 is considered by many critics to be an example of such lax refereeing at a higher level.

Perhaps the most famous of all giant-killing acts, at least in England, was the defeat of the great Arsenal side of the 1930s by Third Division Walsall in 1933. Two seasons previously Arsenal had won the League Championship with a record 66 points. In 1931–32 they had narrowly missed both League and Cup, and that season they were again comfortably leading Division I. It did not seem possible that a team from the Third Division North would give them any trouble even on their own ground. But the impossible happened. There were, of course, excuses. Three of Arsenal's regulars had succumbed to a flu epidemic, and three inexperienced players were drafted into the side. One of these had his name taken and never played for Arsenal again. Another was so nervous that he put his boots on over his socks and suspenders. The tiny Walsall ground was unfamiliar, and if Walsall's game was too vigorous, who could blame them for taking advantage of a lenient referee? Arsenal missed chance after chance and Walsall made the most of their few opportunities. Whatever excuses there were, the scoreline at the end of the game read 'Walsall 2 Arsenal 0', and that is how the rest of the football world saw it. The fact that Arsenal went on that season to chalk up the first of their hat-trick of League Championships underlined Walsall's achievement.

Before that time and since, the Cup has provided a regular quota of giant-killings every year. For a Second Division side to win at home against a First Division team is not unusual, and throughout the years Division II sides have their fair share of victories on senior clubs' grounds. But Crystal Palace's 6–0 defeat of Everton at Goodison in 1922 must rank as one of the

Left: How the papers saw Arsenal's demise at the hands of lowly Walsall in the third round of the 1933 FA Cup.

most extraordinary results of them all. This feat was equalled by non-League Boston United in 1956 when they beat Derby County 6–1 at the Baseball Ground. Admittedly Derby were in the Third Division North at the time, but they finished runners-up that season and champions the next—their only two seasons outside of the top two divisions. It could be said they were concentrating on promotion.

In Scotland non-League clubs regularly surprise teams from the Second Division. Defeats of First Division clubs are more rare, but one notable example was Highland League club Fraserburgh's 1–0 victory over Dundee in 1959. Almost any defeat over the years of the 'big two', Celtic and Rangers, could be deemed a giant-killing act. Rangers have been surprised more than once, but never more so than when they went down to Berwick Rangers 1–0 in 1967. Celtic, however, managed to avoid such embarrassment, at least until the 1971 League Cup final. A First Division club that reaches a cup final can hardly be described as a giant-killer, but Partick Thistle were such outsiders when they met the mighty Celtic that their 4–1 victory was the most unexpected result in Scottish football for many years.

The English League Cup final has also produced its shocks, with Division I sides twice going down to teams from the Third Division—Queen's Park Rangers beat West Bromwich Albion 3–2 in 1967 after being two goals down, and Swindon Town beat Arsenal 3–1 two years later. And there was no question of rough play from the 'minnows'. Like Partick, QPR and Swindon played inspired football—and both clubs went on to promotion to Division II.

Post-war Arsenal became almost a traditional chopping-block for lower clubs, and their defeat by Swindon was the culmination of years of Cup embarrassment. In 1948 they lost at home to Second Division Bradford—and won the Championship—in 1954 it was Norwich (Div. III) at home, in 1958 Northampton (Div. III) away, 1960 Rotherham (Div. II) in the second replay, 1965 Peterborough (Div. III) away, followed by three defeats in five seasons by Second Division clubs. And in 1956 they had narrowly escaped defeat in a replay with non-League Bedford Town after being held 2–2 at home.

Other non-League sides also won Cup fame, not least Yeovil, whose sloping ground first earned notoriety in 1949 when they beat Sunderland 2–1. Ten years later another non-League side, Worcester, shocked Liverpool by the same score. And in 1964 it was Bedford again, beating Newcastle on their own

In the Football League Cup, Third Division sides have twice beaten Division I clubs in the final at Wembley.
Right: Roger Morgan scores and Queen's Park Rangers are on the way to turning a 0–2 deficit into a 3–2 triumph over West Bromwich Albion in 1967.
Below: Peter Downsborough's fine goalkeeping helped inspire Swindon to victory over Arsenal in 1969.

Right: Joyful team-mates congratulate Berwick's Sammy Reid after the goal that knocked Rangers out of the Scottish Cup in 1967. Incidents of giant-killing in the Scottish Cup are rare, which makes Second Division Berwick's feat all the more memorable . . . except for Rangers and their fans.

Right: The North Koreans' shock defeat of Italy in the 1966 World Cup resounded around the world.

Top: Non-League Hereford (white shirts) had left a trail of League clubs, including Division I Newcastle, behind them by the time West Ham beat them in a 1972 fourth round replay.
Above: Third Division Bournemouth, giant-killers of the 1957 FA Cup, meet Manchester United.
Below: Ray Crawford heads Colchester to a shock lead over Leeds in 1971.

ground. Although Newcastle were then in Division II, they have always had a great reputation as cup-fighters. Yet in 1958, as a First Division side, they had been humiliated 3–1 at home by Third Division Scunthorpe United, who gained promotion that year. And their greatest humiliation came in 1972, when they became the first Division I side to lose to non-Leaguers since Sunderland in 1949. They were first held 2–2 on their own ground by Hereford and then lost a much-postponed replay 2–1.

Another great club to suffer more than one indignity in the Cup is Manchester United. In 1967 they lost at home to Second Division Norwich City, who in 1959, as a Third Division club, had beaten them 3–0 and also knocked out Spurs before losing in a semi-final replay with Luton. York City were another Third Division side to reach the semi-finals, in 1955, beating Blackpool and Spurs on the way. Spurs suffered again in 1957 at the hands of Third Division Bournemouth, whose run to the Sixth Round also included a win at Molineux over Wolves. What is even more remarkable about all these results is that Manchester United and Wolves dominated English football in the 1950s, and Spurs were never very far behind.

What is it, then, that makes such results possible? Firstly, football is a team game. If a number of players on one side have an off-day and the ball does not run for them, and if their opponents play above themselves, all striking their best form at the same time and

bringing off remarkable moves, giant-killing becomes possible. In fact, it becomes probable that fairly regularly an upset will occur —because there are additional factors in favour of the underdogs, leaving aside the occasional lax refereeing. It is difficult for a top team to get keyed up against lowly opponents. No matter how much they are aware of it and guard against it, complacency and overconfidence are likely to creep in. And the prospective giant-killers have nothing to lose—they can take risks. The psychological factor is also important. An early goal will inspire them, and if they can manage to keep their opponents out for a spell their confidence will grow. At the same time, their opponents begin to get worried, they hurry their moves and forget to play their normal game. Their anxiety multiplies as the prospect of defeat—and humiliation—begins to loom large, and they go to pieces.

There have been few great sides about which one could say: 'They are professionals through and through; this couldn't happen

to them.' One such side was Leeds United of the late 1960s and early 1970s—which makes their defeat by Colchester United in 1971 even more incredible.

Like Arsenal in 1933, Leeds had won the Championship two years previously with a record number of points (67), had narrowly missed both League and Cup the previous season, and were currently leading Division I. Colchester were struggling for promotion in the Fourth Division with a team built round rejects in their thirties. No one gave them the slightest chance of avoiding a crushing defeat. Leeds were without their captain, Billy Bremner, but in the days of squad football there was no question of drafting in a raw reserve to upset the smooth running of this superb footballing machine.

Colchester began in the only way possible —they ran and ran and tried to unsettle their opponents. They succeeded in doing so, and 34-year-old ex-England centre-forward Ray Crawford headed a goal after 18 minutes. Leeds were rattled, and before they could regain their composure, they were split

wide open again. Crawford, lying on the ground, managed to hook the ball in for his second goal. Leeds came out in the second half fully aware of the task ahead of them and determined to take control. But Colchester, encouraged by their lead, played inspired football, building up incisive, flowing moves. The Leeds defence blundered again, inside-right Dave Simmons swept through and headed the 'no-hopers' into a 3–0 lead, a score that shook the country as it was flashed up on television screens. At last, Leeds rediscovered themselves and, playing coolly, efficiently, and at times brilliantly, pulled two goals back. But they were thwarted by some remarkable goalkeeping by Graham Smith, one of whose saves was as sensational as anything else in the match.

Yet again, the 'impossible' had happened, the 'incredible' just had to be believed. Colchester had performed what many regarded as the greatest giant-killing feat in the history of the FA Cup . . . yet fans still talk about what Walsall did to Arsenal way back in '33.

Above: Crawford, a former England centre-forward, hooks Colchester's second past Sprake. Fourth Division Colchester's 3–2 win over Leeds must rank as one of the shock results of all time.

Great Teams

It is comparatively simple, with the advantage of hindsight, to reflect back through football history and say: 'That was a great team.' It is not always so easy to say why it was great. A team that wins a major competition must be great to some extent to achieve its success. But will its greatness be remembered? Has it, in achieving success, displayed a magnificence, a splendour that people will remember? And has it known success over a period, or was success short-lived and so eventually forgotten?

One criterion of greatness is that the team is associated with certain qualities that immediately spring to mind: a magic, a style, an individuality. Results, though important, are not always the prime consideration. For example, in the period between the wars, England fielded a number of fine sides, but how many are remembered, as, say, the Austrian *Wunderteam* or Vittorio Pozzo's Italians, both of which England beat? England, so endowed with talent, could and did select ever-changing sides. But the Austrians and the Italians relied more on a group of players, and so the teams and their players are remembered when the teams that beat them are sometimes forgotten.

The Austrian *Wunderteam*, defeated 4–3 by England at Stamford Bridge in 1932 but 2–1 victors at Vienna in 1936, were the creation of Hugo Meisl and a little English

coach from Lancashire named Jimmy Hogan. They flourished in the late 1920s and the first half of the 1930s. They were born in the mid-1920s when Meisl and his men, following a heavy defeat by South Germany, decided to persevere with the Vienna School of football —itself a derivative of the old classic Scottish game built on control, short passes, and positioning.

The *Wunderteam* knew many triumphs. In May 1931, they defeated Scotland 5–0 and went on to beat Germany 6–0 and 5–0, Switzerland 8–1, Hungary 8–2, and remain unbeaten for 10 matches until the Stamford Bridge defeat. The team always had an attacking centre-half, of whom Smistik was the best, but the spirit of the Vienna School was best embodied in Mathias Sindelar. A slight centre-forward nicknamed 'The Man of Paper', Sindelar was a marvellous ball artist, the scorer of remarkable individual goals.

The team that ended the *Wunderteam*'s reign was the *Azzurri*, the Italian side of

Below: The Austrian *Wunderteam*, as they were known, coming onto the field to meet England at Stamford Bridge in 1932. Their 4–3 defeat by England ended a brilliant 10-match unbeaten run. Right: The side that assumed Austria's mantle in the 1930s was the *Azzurri*, Italy's national side (seen meeting Prince Arthur of Connaught).

Vittorio Pozzo. Pozzo, Italy's team chief at the 1912 Olympics, drew on the euphoria of the Fascist era of the 1930s to build a splendid side of high morale. It won the World Cup of 1934 in Italy, though it may not have done so without the home advantage, needing a freakish equalizer from Argentinian left-winger Orsi and extra time to beat Czechoslovakia 2–1 in the final. But in 1938, with Silvio Piola a deadly centre-forward, the Italians proved great champions, easily beating Hungary in the Parisian final.

Pozzo, a severe disciplinarian and nicknamed 'The Poor Captain of a Company of Millionaires', based his team's tactics on what he had seen in England before World War I. A particular influence were Manchester United, with their famous attacking centre-half Charlie Roberts. Pozzo's teams were a blend of muscularity and skill, with such ruthless players as the South American centre-halves Monti and Andreolo and such artists as Peppino Meazza. Meazza and

One ... two ... three ... four ... five ... six ... seven goals that underlined Hungary's devastating superiority in their 7–1 thrashing of England at Budapest in 1954.

Gioanin Ferrari were the only two to play in both World Cup-winning sides. One black mark against this great side, however, was their display in the so-called Battle of Highbury of 1934, which they lost 3–2 to England.

Though World Cup success evaded the Hungarians of the 1950s, their right to greatness cannot be denied. In retrospect, however, that marvellous side seems less the product of a superior school of football, as was thought at the time, than the coming together of some outstanding individuals. Despite Gustav Sebes being a fine 'overlord' and Gyula Mandi an efficient coach, and despite the training methods being advanced and sophisticated, the emigration of stars after the 1956 Hungarian Revolution left behind an ordinary team.

The stars of this team, which had only the 1952 Olympic title to show as inadequate reflection of its greatness, were Puskas, Kocsis, Bozsik, and Hidegkuti. Nandor Hidegkuti was the tireless, deep-lying centre-forward, capable of foraging splendidly or scoring a hat-trick, as he did against England at Wembley in November 1953. Ferenc Puskas and Sandor Kocsis both played well upfield: Puskas, the captain, famous for a tremendous left-foot shot and his tactical skill; inside-right Kocsis celebrated for his neat ball play and splendid heading. Behind them, Josef Bozsik was the attacking right-half, forever making skilful forays, while at the back was a line of four defenders, with left-half Zakarias always beside his centre-half Lorant.

For several years, the Hungarians steered clear of international football outside the Iron Curtain. But in 1952 they ventured out at last and won the Olympic title, though hard-pressed by Yugoslavia in the final. The following year they beat Italy 3–0, and in November came their glorious 6–3 victory at Wembley. It was the first time England had lost at home to Continental opposition. In May 1954, they increased the margin, thrashing Billy Wright's men 7–1 in Budapest. The World Cup seemed as good as theirs, but injury to Puskas, who returned to the side too soon, robbed them of the prize. They were beaten 3–2 in the final by West Germany, having already beaten Brazil, in the infamous Battle of Berne, and Uruguay.

That bad-tempered World Cup quarter-final at Berne is one of the few blemishes on the illustrious history of the finest footballing nation—Brazil. Their World Cup record alone speaks for their greatness: third in 1938, runners-up in 1950, quarter-finalists in 1954, winners in 1958 and 1962, and then, after a surprising failure in 1966, winners once more in 1970. But there is more to soccer than trophies and medals. And even if the Brazilians had been beaten in every Jules Rimet competition, they would still have captivated the world by their skill, grace, and exuberance.

Successive Brazilian teams, largely composed of Negroes, have been blessed with an agility beyond the reach of all but a few Europeans. This natural elasticity—part endowed at birth, part induced by a helpful climate—gives them a natural sense of balance and rhythm. There is also the backing of meticulous off-field organization, from coaches and masseurs down to travelling chefs. Team after team has been assiduously prepared, and the results have been spectacular.

Perhaps the key to Brazil's success is their enjoyment of the game for its own sake. Above all, they love to score goals. And

The unstoppable 1958 Brazilian World Cup team. That year they routed Sweden 5–2 in the final at Stockholm.

Above: Carlos Alberto holds the Jules Rimet Trophy aloft after leading Brazil to their third win, a victory that entitled them to permanent possession of the trophy.

Below: The youthful Pelé scores Brazil's fifth goal in the 1958 final against Sweden.

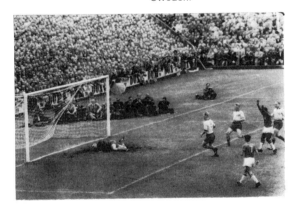

because football, despite the growth of defensive tactics, is still decided by goals, so the attack-accentuated Brazilians maintain their position as world leaders. The incomparable Pelé, Jairzinho, Tostão, Rivelino, Didi, Garrincha, Vavá, Zito, Zagalo; from an earlier era, Zizinho, Ademir, Jair, and Julinho; and of pre-World War II days, Domingas Da Guia and Leonidas—all these and more have had tremendous influence on global football. Even more important they have given incalculable entertainment to millions of their own adoring supporters and millions more around the world.

There lies their greatness. They have entertained and captured the imagination even of non-followers of soccer. It is an honour not many teams could claim, despite fine records. England may have won the World Cup in 1966 and maintained an impressive record afterwards. Italy won the 1968 European Football Championship and were runners-up in the 1970 World Cup. But were they great sides? Did they entertain

millions around the world?

At club level, trophies can be used more often to assess a team's greatness. But they are not the very essence of greatness. The amateur Corinthians, who refused to enter the FA Cup for 40 years, and Leeds United, who dominated so much of the 1960s yet were often pipped at the post, bear witness to that.

The Corinthians, who live on today as the Corinthian Casuals, were founded by N. Lane 'Pa' Jackson in 1882 to provide a basis for a stronger England team to end the domination of the Scots. All public school and university men, they were so successful that on two occasions they provided the entire England side to play Wales.

Although their methods were often robust, in the public school spirit, their sportsmanship was a byword. On the few occasions when they gave away a penalty, the goalkeeper would stand aside to allow a goal. The original team had such stars as W. N. Cobbold, 'The Prince of Dribblers', and the two full-back brothers, A. M. and P. M. Walters, to whom C. B. Fry was a splendid successor. Perhaps the Corinthians' greatest-ever player was their England international centre-forward G. O. Smith.

Though they did not enter the FA Cup until the 1920s, they did sometimes play and beat the holders. They scored nine times against 1903 winners Bury, who themselves had beaten Derby by a record 6–0 in the Cup final. And when the Corinthians did finally enter the competition, though past their days of glory, they had great tussles with Newcastle United and Millwall.

But the great amateur age of such teams as the Wanderers and the Corinthians was by then long past. The coming of professionalism had seen to that. Blackburn Rovers had been the first professional team to challenge the amateur superiority, winning the FA Cup three times in a row from 1884, and again in 1890 and 1891. In 1888–89, the first season of the Football League, another Lancashire club, Preston North End, gained the title of 'The Invincibles' when they won the Championship without losing any of their 22 matches and also took the Cup without conceding a goal. North End, inspired by two of the early soccer legends, James Ross and John Goodall, retained the League title a year later and were second in each of the following three seasons—twice behind Sunderland.

Sunderland were champions 4 times in their first 11 seasons, despite the extra effort involved in fulfilling a long series of friendly matches—necessary in order to meet a wage bill of £3 per player per week, plus five

G. O. Smith (above) and C. B. Fry (below) starred for the Corinthians, the great English amateur side of the 1800s and early 1900s.

Of all the professional sides to emerge in the late 1800s, Blackburn Rovers made sure of a niche in sporting history by winning the FA Cup three times in succession, from 1884 to 1886.

shillings win bonus. In one season they played more friendlies (35) than League games (30), 15 of them in the space of 25 days.

Another great side to emerge at the end of the 19th century were Aston Villa, who emulated Preston's double feat of League and Cup in 1896–97. In the seven years from 1894 they finished 1st, 3rd, 1st, 1st, 6th, 1st, and 1st. Not surprisingly they also contributed a string of players to the rapidly growing international competition.

In the years immediately before World War I, however, one club was undoubtedly Number One—Newcastle United. After being overshadowed at first by neighbouring Sunderland's 'Team of All the Talents', the Tyneside club had a remarkable spell of dominance. They were champions three times in five years from 1904–05, and between then and 1911 they also reached the Cup final five times. Yet they won only once. With such players as Peter McWilliam, Billy McCracken, and Colin Veitch, United enjoyed a hey-day that is still talked about with longing in the North-East of England.

After the war, there was a levelling off among clubs, with the honours being more evenly distributed. But in the 1920s Huddersfield emerged under the inspired management of Herbert Chapman to create a record by winning the Championship three times in a row. The full-back partnership of Roy Goodall and Sam Wadsworth has had few equals, and the same goes for the left-wing pair, Clem Stephenson and Billy Smith. The latter won the Cup for his club in 1922, with a penalty.

Despite Chapman's departure in 1925, Huddersfield were still good enough to complete their hat-trick and finish second in the following two seasons. But Chapman was now creating an even better side from the unpromising material he inherited on going to Arsenal. His evolution of the 'third back' game after the change in the offside law was the first major tactical revolution of the century, and it was the basis of the London club's rise to greatness in the 1930s.

As individuals, Chapman's Arsenal had excellent skill. As a team, they were much, much more than the sum of the parts. The way they combined and worked for each other, allied to their personal talents, brought about the most successful decade any English club had achieved.

Arsenal won the Cup for the first time in 1930—Chapman had rebuilt so widely that only four of the beaten 1927 finalists played in the 2–0 win over Huddersfield—and then the following season became the first London club to win the League Championship. They did it in glorious style as well, with a record

66 points. Perhaps their finest season was 1931–32, although they won nothing. They were second in the League and they lost the Cup final to Newcastle after a disputed goal. In the next season's Cup, they crashed 2–0 to Third Division Walsall, but won the League again. And despite Chapman's sudden death, they held the title in 1933–34 and 1934–35 to equal the Huddersfield treble. They won the Cup again in 1936 and were champions once more in 1937–38.

So, in the space of nine seasons, the Gunners had won the Championship five times, finished second and third once each, and had won twice and been runners-up once at Wembley. In addition, they had 15 players capped for their countries, at a time when internationals were far less numerous than they are today. A record seven of them, plus trainer Tom Whittaker (later manager), were in the England side against Italy in 1934.

Although they became known as the team everyone loves to beat, and the taunt of 'lucky' was frequently levelled at them, Arsenal were not a defensive side. Certainly they organized themselves well in and around their own penalty area, but they revelled even more in attack, particularly when breaking away after a spell of opposition pressure. The long passing of Alex James was ideally suited to the speed of Cliff Bastin and Joe Hulme on the wings and the lion-hearted finishing of centre-forward Ted Drake. During those nine years of greatness, the team so often accused of defensive play scored more goals than any other club in the League.

North of the border, in Scotland, football had been dominated at first by Queen's Park, the great amateur club, who won the Scottish Cup 9 times in its first 18 seasons. But once the League competition was instituted in 1890 and professionalism took a hold, the Glasgow pair of Rangers and Celtic quickly established a dominance that has continued ever since.

The period between the wars belonged to Rangers, at least in League affairs. They won 15 Championships to 4 by their rivals and 1 by an outsider, Motherwell. And in those five seasons when Rangers did not win, they were second three times and third once.

Curiously enough, Rangers were afflicted by a hoodoo in the Cup, for having taken it for the fourth time in 1903 they had to wait 25 years before recapturing it. Then they won five more finals in the next eight seasons! In 1927–28, 1929–30, 1933–34, and 1934–35 they took both trophies.

Much of their inspiration came from

Three famous internationals who played a leading role in Newcastle's successes in the early 1900s:
Top: Peter McWilliam of Scotland.
Above: Colin Veitch of England.
Below: Billy McCracken of Ireland.

manager Willie Struth, who was in office for 34 years from 1920. Struth's forceful personality and excellent judgement ('I know ye can play, laddie, but can you play for US?') enabled his beloved Light Blues to attain remarkable heights of consistency. During that great era, a seemingly endless succession of Ibrox products went on to play for Scotland. Perhaps the three most outstanding were winger Alan Morton, the original 'wee Blue devil', with 31 caps, halfback Davie Meiklejohn, an outstanding captain, and inside-forward Bob McPhail, who scored over 300 goals. Meiklejohn was with the club for 17 years, Morton 13, and McPhail 12, and between them they won 30 Championship medals and 13 Cup medals.

Rangers were in the news again immediately after World War II, when they held Moscow Dynamo to a 2–2 draw at the end of the brilliant Russians' tour of Britain. This team, made up largely of footballers who played ice hockey, has a special place in Russian football. Despite the vicissitudes of war, it was the most spectacular and artistic side the country has ever produced. They played splendid attacking football, with the hard-shooting inside-right Kartsev and the inside-left Bobrov staying well upfield while centre-forward Beskov sometimes dropped back.

Arriving in England in October 1945, Moscow Dynamo started with a 3–3 draw against Chelsea. Two days later they thrashed Cardiff City 10–1, and Britain eagerly awaited the clash with Arsenal. The Gunners desperately reinforced their scratch transitional side with star guests such as

Above: The Newcastle United side that dominated English football between 1904 and 1911, winning 3 League titles and reaching the Cup final 5 times.

Right: Huddersfield Town became the first club to achieve a hat-trick of League Championships, from 1923–24 to 1925–26. They finished runners-up the next two seasons.

Alex James (above) and Ted Drake (right) were just two stars of the Arsenal sides that reigned supreme in the 1930s, with five League titles (including a hat-trick) and two Cup wins.

Stanley Matthews and Stan Mortensen. In spite of this, Dynamo won 4–3 in the fog at Tottenham in a game dubiously refereed by their own Nicolai Latychev.

Following the Rangers match, they went home via Sweden, where they beat Norrköping 5–0, and then Russia withdrew into splendid isolation for another seven years. Post-war Britain was left to muse over the footballing genius that had come and gone so soon.

Two years later, another great side disappeared from the footballing scene, but in the most tragic way. On March 14, 1949, the mighty Torino team, which included the bulk of the Italian international side, were wiped out *en masse* when their aircraft crashed. They had won the Italian League for the past four seasons and were chasing their fifth successive title at the time of the disaster.

The strength of the side, one of the first in Italy to master the third-back game, lay to a great extent in its inside-forward pair, Ezio Loik and Valentino Mazzola. Beside them was the rejuvenated veteran centre-forward from Juventus, Guglielmo Gabetto. Among other outstanding players were the calm and elegant left-back Maroso, goal-keeper Valentino Bacigalupo, and outside-right Menti.

Winners of the 1946–47 Championship by 10 points and the 1947–48 Championship by 16 points, Torino admirably blended power and skill. In defence, right-back Ballarin and centre-half Rigamonti balanced Maroso's skills with their force, and the marking of Grezar at wing-half contrasted with the artistry of the skilful Castigliano. As for Mazzola, the star of stars, he in himself combined both strength and sophisticated technique.

Torino were virtually awarded the 1948–49 Championship, but the days of glory were over. They were never forgotten though, and there was a grim reminder of the disaster in February 1958, when eight of the Manchester United 'Busby Babes' died at Munich. This young side, already League Champions in 1955–56 and 1956–57 and Cup runners-up in 1957, could have gone on to formidable heights. The deaths of Edwards, Byrne, Bent, Colman, Jones, Pegg, Taylor, and Whelan, and the premature retirement of Johnny Berry and Jackie Blanchflower, prevented further greatness.

The 'Busby Babes' were the fruition of Matt Busby's youth policy and United's ruthlessly efficient scouting system. Duncan Edwards, the huge, forceful left-half and an international at 18, came from Dudley in Worcestershire; Bobby Charlton from Ashington, Northumberland; and Liam Whelan, the scheming inside-forward, from Ireland. For Tommy Taylor, the strong inside-left or centre-forward, Busby had paid Barnsley the then huge fee of £29,999 in 1953. The 'Busby Babes' believed in attacking, and in Jackie Blanchflower they had one of the most polished all-round centre-halves of the day. Roger Byrne skippered the team from left-back—and played for England 33 times in succession. Like the clever little right-half Eddie Colman, he was a local discovery.

They won their first title by 11 points from

Right (above): Manchester United, the famous 'Busby Babes', line up for their last game, against Red Star in Belgrade, before the air crash that broke up what was arguably England's greatest post-war club side. (Left to right) Duncan Edwards, Eddie Colman, Mark Jones, Ken Morgans, Bobby Charlton, Dennis Viollet, Tommy Taylor, Billy Foulkes, Harry Gregg, Albert Scanlon, Roger Byrne (capt.).
Right (below): Manchester United raid the Red Star goal during the match at Belgrade.

Manchester United would almost certainly have sealed their greatness in 1957 by adding the Cup to their League title, but fate took a hand and their centre-half Jackie Blanchflower (top) found himself substituting in goal for the injured Ray Wood in the final. United just failed to overcome the handicap of playing with only 10 men for most of the match and lost 2–1 to Aston Villa. Matt Busby (above) built three great Manchester United sides after World War II. He survived the Munich air crash and rebuilt United to such good effect that in 1968 they became the first English club to win the European Cup. Busby was knighted later that year.

Blackpool, their second by 8 points from Spurs. And in 1956 they defied the League by entering the European Cup, giving the great Real Madrid a run for their money in the semi-finals. It was on their way home from a 3–3 draw in Belgrade the following season that their plane crashed on take-off. A bravely rebuilt side reached the final of the FA Cup, and, unlike Torino, Manchester United were to field another great team, in the 1960s.

The achievements and the tragedy of the 'Busby Babes' have, however, tended to obscure the triumphs of United's immediate post-war team, impressive winners of the FA Cup in 1948 and runners-up in the League four times in the first five post-war seasons before at last winning in 1951–52.

Matt Busby was the architect of this side also. But though without a ground—Old Trafford had been bombed and so Maine Road was used—he took over a wealth of talent from the pre-war team: Jack Rowley and Stan Pearson in attack, and Johnny Carey, versatility itself, to captain the side in midfield or at right-back. Then there were John Aston, a stalwart left-back, and tiny left-half Henry Cockburn, destined for England honours. In the beautifully balanced Charlie Mitten and the ebullient Johnny Morris, one of the many local products, United had two splendid forwards, and the purchase of the 'brittle-boned' Jimmy Delaney to play on the right wing was early proof of the Busby genius.

Another manager to produce a great and talented team was the driving authoritarian Stanley Cullis at Molineux. His Wolverhampton Wanderers of the 1950s, criticized but highly successful, scorned elaboration and persisted in a long-ball game, thumping the ball out to the wings, where tiny Johnny Hancocks and long-legged Jimmy Mullen sped away. In the middle, Roy Swinbourne was the ideal do-or-die centre-forward until injury sadly cut short his career.

At wing-half Cullis liked big, strong, forcing players like Eddie Clamp, Ron Flowers, and Bill Slater, the former amateur international who took over the centre-half berth and the captaincy when Billy Wright retired. Wright began as an inside-forward, developed into an England wing-half, and then became a commanding centre-half. Behind them was Bert Williams, one of the finest goalkeepers to play for England.

Wolves won the Championship in 1953–54, 1957–58, and 1958–59, and they almost did the 'double' in 1960, when they beat Blackburn in the Cup but missed the League title by a point. There were also famous home victories over Spartak Moscow and Honved in 1954. But Wolves lacked the versatility required for European Cup success, and a 2–5 thrashing by Barcelona in the thick Molineux mud in the 1959–60 European Cup laid bare the myth of their supremacy.

Yet even Barcelona fell to the greatest team of the 1950s—Real Madrid. It is ironic that Barcelona once waived their rights to Alfredo Di Stefano, the man who inspired Real to victory in the first five European Cup tournaments. The Argentinian's skill, industry, finishing power, and strategy were

225

the motor of the team. But the great man did not suffer rivals gladly. Raymond Kopa, an orchestrator himself for Reims and France, was forced to play on the right wing. Didi and Simonsson hardly kicked a ball. It was only when the Hungarian star Ferenc Puskas arrived to play at inside-left that Di Stefano was willing to brook another 'maestro'. It cannot be disputed, though, that Real's star rose and waned with Di Stefano.

Real's early European Cup-winning teams were blessed with the left-wing partnership of the clever Argentinian inside-forward Hector Rial and the tremendously swift Paco Gento on the wing. Gento played in every one of Real's European finals up to the Cup-winners Cup final in 1971. The defence was strengthened in 1957–58 with the arrival of the ruthless blond Uruguayan centre-half José Santamaria.

Real are best remembered as a team that went for goals. They never much cared about giving them away, because they were always so sure they could get them. The level of technical skill was immensely high, and attacks were built up in the classical manner of a deceptively slow, elaborate approach followed by an explosive finish. They set the seal on their greatness with a magnificent seven-goal display in the 1960 final, after which they won the first World Club Championship.

The European Cup produced a number of fine teams, some of them great, but none could scale the heights attained by Real. Their immediate successors were the enterprising Benfica. They had a fine midfield player in Coluña, excellent wingers in

Augusto and Simoes, and an outstanding centre-half in the strong, mobile Germano. Eusebio and his devastating right foot reinforced them in mid-1961. In England, a refreshingly artistic Spurs had done the 'double' for the first time in the 20th century in 1960–61 (see *The Double*, p. 182), and these two fine footballing sides met in a close, hard tie in the 1961–62 European Cup.

Benfica won that year, but in 1963 they lost to AC Milan, less adventurous but possessing in Gianni Rivera a skilled inside-forward and an incisive leader in the Brazilian José Altafini. Then it was the turn of Milan's rivals, Helenio Herrera's Internazionale. Twice winners of both the European Cup and the World Club Championship, they based their game on the long ball and the quick breakaway. They had many stars: Facchetti, Burgnich, and Picchi in defence, Suarez and Corso in midfield, Mazzola and Jair in attack. But *catenaccio*—their defensive style of play—was king.

This was not so in Brazil, where the Santos team that won the South American Copa de los Libertadores and the World Club Championship in 1962 and 1963 rates among the finest of all. The 1962 team was especially renowned, featuring Pelé at the top of his astonishing form executing brilliant 'one-twos' with the young black centre-forward Coutinho. In goal was the cool, solid Gylmar, and there were other World Cup heroes in the linking right-half Zito and centre-half Mauro. A further weapon in attack was the fierce shooting of outside-left Pepe—especially his left-footed free-kicks.

They were made to work by Penarol in the 1962 South American Cup, winning 2–1 at

Below: Billy Wright, who captained Wolverhampton Wanderers' exciting sides of the 1950s.

Below right: Wolves, shown playing Moscow Spartak at Dynamo Stadium in 1955, helped to pave the way for European club competition with their thrilling floodlit matches at Molineux against Spartak and the Hungarian side Honved.
Below left: Johnny Carey with the FA Cup in 1948, having led the first great Manchester side to one of the finest Cup final victories ever.

home, losing 2–3 in Montevideo, and finally winning the decider 3–0. Benfica, too, gave them a close game in Brazil in the World Club Championship. But in Lisbon Pelé turned on all his magic and scored three goals as Benfica were downed 5–2. Pelé did not play in the second and third matches of the 1963 final against AC Milan, however. The more combative Almir successfully took his place, but the temper of the decider was unworthy of these two fine sides.

Santos were not the only great ball-playing club to be brought to violence in the controversial world championship. Celtic's disgraceful battles with Racing in 1967 were a saddening sight; more so as the brutality lingers in memory longer than the fine performances that led to them. Jock Stein's team deserve better than to be recalled only for their conduct against the Argentinians. At their best they had few equals in British history.

In the ten seasons from 1964–65 to 1973–74 inclusive, Celtic won no fewer than 20 of the 30 domestic trophies at stake—nine consecutive League Championships, six Scottish Cups, and five League Cups. And in 1966–67 they climaxed a domestic treble by becoming the first British club to win the European Cup. Even though they failed somewhat ingloriously in the same contest's final three years later, Stein's achievement in producing such a powerful combination, able to raise their game to the most demanding standards despite the comparatively easy life in domestic football, was truly remarkable.

Like all great managers, he was helped by have many fine players; the effervescent winger Jimmy Johnstone, centre-half Billy McNeill, full-back Tommy Gemmell, and the remarkable veteran goalkeeper Ronnie Simpson. Once given a free transfer by Stein, when with Hibs, Simpson went on to win his first Scottish cap at the age of 38. But the dominant figure during Celtic's triumph was that of Stein himself, an excellent technician and hard taskmaster, but an essentially human and sincere worker for his cause.

In England, the phoenix of Manchester United had risen. Matt Busby, himself severely injured at Munich, had used his talents and authority to rebuild at a fantastic pace. Among those now at Old Trafford were the blond Scottish inside-forward Denis Law, brought from Torino for more than £110,000, Scottish centre-forward David Herd, and the sturdy ex-Celtic right-half Pat Crerand. From Belfast had come a shy 15-year-old named George Best. Bobby Charlton, another Munich survivor, had matured into a superb all-round forward, and Nobby Stiles gave bite to the defence.

Somewhat old fashioned in method (or lack of it) and training, United still had the skill, spirit, and flair to be successful. The Cup was won again in 1963, the Championship in 1964–65 (on goal average after a titanic race with Leeds) and 1966–67. And this time the League title was followed by the European Cup in 1968 and a knighthood for Matt Busby. But as with some other great teams, much of the greatness was in one man, and when Busby relinquished control

Left: Jimmy Greaves challenges the Portuguese 'keeper in the Spurs–Benfica European Cup semi-final clash at White Hart Lane in 1962. Double champions Spurs lost on aggregate to the European champions, who went on to win their second successive title by beating Real Madrid 5–3 in the final.

Top: the forward line of Real Madrid, from left to right: Raymond Kopa (France), Hector Rial (Argentina), Alfredo di Stefano (Argentina and Spain), Ferenc Puskas (Hungary), and 'Paco' Gento (Spain). Perhaps the greatest club side of all time, Real Madrid won the European Cup for the first five seasons of the competition's existence. Above: The Celtic squad in 1970. (Back row, left to right): George Connolly, David Hay, Tommy Gemmell, John Fallon, Billy McNeil (capt.), Evan Williams, Jim Craig, John Hughes, Tommy Callaghan. (Front row, left to right): Jimmy Johnston, Bobby Lennox, Bobby Murdoch, Harry Hood, Willy Wallace, Bertie Auld, Lou Macari, Jim Brogan. Not only did Celtic completely dominate Scottish soccer from 1965 onwards, but they became the first British side to win the European Cup (1967), and again reached the final in 1970, when they surprisingly lost to Dutch champions Feyenoord.

Facing page: Bobby
Charlton with another
member of the United
attack, Denis Law. Law
(1964), Charlton (1966),
and Best (1968) were all
voted European Footballer
of the Year—no other club
in any country could claim
such a record.

On their way to the 1970
European Cup Final, Celtic
beat Benfica (below) and
Leeds.
Centre: Celtic during their
magnificent 1966–67
season, beating Rangers,
their great rivals whom
they consistently over-
shadowed.
Bottom: Bobby Charlton
watches George Best glide
through the Benfica
defence in Manchester
United's victorious 1968
European Cup final.

Manchester United went into a temporary
decline.

The public gaze slowly, almost regret-
fully it seemed, turned on Leeds United.
A mediocre Second Division club when Don
Revie took them over, Leeds had won promotion in 1963–64 and had almost done the
coveted 'double' in 1964–65. As well as being
pipped on goal average by Manchester
United in the League, they lost to Liverpool
in extra time at Wembley.

But outside their immediate area, no one
liked them. They were accused of being a
ruthlessly physical side, despite their skills,
in the image of their tough little captain, the
veteran Scot Bobby Collins. Nevertheless
the criticism had an effect, and Leeds moved
steadily towards a less physical kind of
football to which their skills suited them.
When Collins went, his thigh-bone broken
by a vicious kick in Turin, Johnny Giles, the
Irish right-winger, moved inside to take his
place and to combine admirably with the
small, driving, red-headed half-back Billy
Bremner. The half-back line was completed
by two England men from the North-East,
Jackie Charlton and Norman Hunter. In
Terry Cooper they could boast one of the
finest attacking full-backs in the game.

In 1967–68 the Fairs Cup became Elland
Road's first major trophy, and then the
following season they won the League, with
a record 67 points and with the loss of only
two games. But success had its penalty the
following season: in the running for the
Championship, the FA Cup, and the European Cup, Leeds finished empty-handed,
beaten by Everton, Chelsea, Celtic, and a
ridiculous build-up of fixtures. By now they
had public sympathy and support. Their
greatness was recognized, and even though
Arsenal beat them by a point for the 1970–71
Championship, the Fairs Cup was some
consolation. They finally won the FA Cup
in 1972, beating Arsenal in the final, but
were bitterly disappointed to lose their last
League game two days later, when a draw
would have given them the title and the
'double'.

Arsenal's 'double' that season was a great
achievement, but was it the performance of
a great team? Leeds, consistent and ever-
challenging, had the stuff of greatness.
Arsenal at times promised it. It remained to
be seen, as they continued to do battle in the
1970s in the toughest league competition in
the world, whether posterity would recognize that quality in them.

Leeds United, outstanding
in English and European
football since the late
1960s, earned an
unenviable reputation for
failing at the last hurdle.
Typical was their defeat by
Chelsea (right and below)
in the 1970 Cup final after
they had led three times.

Controversies and Scandals

A game like football, involving so many men, so many matches, cannot be free from controversy for long. The game involves so many events and people that, by its very nature, it is continually the subject of discussion. Not that there is anything wrong with that. Indeed it will be a sad day for soccer if the time ever comes when there is nothing to argue about.

Many of soccer's controversies surround the referee, the sole arbitrator on the field of play. Being human, referees make mistakes: being human, players, officials, and supporters become involved in heated arguments over decisions. As long ago as 1901, Sheffield United were awarded an FA Cup final goal against Spurs, although a film—one of the first made at a soccer match—showed that the ball had not crossed the line. The arguments that followed were a prelude to the 1932 final, when Newcastle equalized against Arsenal after the ball had seemingly gone out of play, and was shown to have done so, again by a film.

Nowadays, of course, television's playback technique puts referees under a nationwide microscope to an unprecedented degree, although what makes for good television is not necessarily good for the game in general. The behaviour of modern players (itself a subject of controversy) is such that officials do not need any further weakening of their authority by outside interference. Much the same applies to many newspaper stories, which can make good reading and help sales while further antagonizing the ruling bodies of the game. It is not altogether surprising that some of the leading bodies seem to have an in-built distrust of the mass media.

Team selection, particularly where national sides are concerned, has always been a subject for debate, as have aspects of the Laws. The difference nowadays is that the disputes are more widely publicized.

Players' wages have always been the subject of controversy, never more so than in 1961, when the FA and Football League finally capitulated to the demands of militant players and agreed to the abolition of the £20-a-week maximum. This ended one controversy but led to another. The resultant free-for-all led to a few clubs cornering more than their fair share of the talent available, and a consequent escalation in transfer fees.

Ground facilities, crowd control, the share-out of the huge amounts of money involved in football pools: these are three more recurring themes of controversy that involve clubs and, indirectly, everyone involved in the game.

But if controversy is continual and, by and large, good for the game, scandal is something different. The word implies some infringement, not only of football rules but also of the law of the land. Fortunately, soccer has had only a few such instances throughout its history, and those that have

Left: Controversial incidents such as those surrounding the transfer of England winger Ian Moore do little to improve the image of English football. Derby claimed they had secured Moore, and paraded their prize at the Baseball Ground. Yet the player eventually went to Old Trafford.

England internationals Tony Kay (right) and Peter Swan (below, in striped shirt) were suspended from playing for life in 1965 for 'throwing' a game to further a betting coup.

taken place nearly all have one common denominator—money. Rumours of 'under the counter' payments to players were rife for years before the 1961 revolution, which roughly coincided with jail sentences and life suspensions on 10 players found guilty of 'rigging' the results of certain matches for betting purposes. The 10 included two England internationals, Peter Swan—capped 19 times—and Tony Kay, and the court action followed disclosures by a Sunday newspaper, *The People*. In 1971 the same paper unearthed two further unsavoury aspects of money's part in soccer affairs, and revealed plots to 'fiddle' turnstile takings and sweepstakes, now run by virtually every club to raise extra funds.

As far back as 1913, a man had been jailed for trying to bribe the West Bromwich and England full-back Jesse Pennington to ensure that his club lost a match. And two years after that, eight players were banned for life after arranging a 2–0 result in a Manchester United–Liverpool game, again because of wagers on the score.

The abolition of the maximum wage may have resulted in a better deal for players, whose niggardly rewards in earlier years had been a scandal of their own, but one side effect was the increasing desperation of the chase after honours. In 1967–68 Peterborough were relegated from the Third Division to the Fourth, by order, for contra-

vening regulations regarding payments, and Port Vale were expelled from the League, but later re-elected, for a similar offence.

The next year Manchester United were fined £7,000 for mishandling financial affairs, and in 1970 Derby had to pay £10,000 on the same charges. Both clubs in reality paid more, for they were also barred from matches against European clubs for 12 months, with consequent effects on gate receipts.

Therefore, in the space of four years, four clubs were convicted of 'bending' the rules. This compared unfavourably with the largely incident-free earlier decades, and football lovers everywhere could only hope that the severity of the sentences would deter others. How many had acted in similar fashion, without being found out, could only remain a subject for conjecture.

Below: Nat Lofthouse's controversial goal in the 1958 FA Cup final. Though the powerful Bolton centre-forward had both feet off the ground when he bundled Harry Gregg and the ball into the net, his goal was allowed.

Top: The television camera catches Tony Brown racing away to make West Bromwich's second goal against Leeds in 1971. Leeds, in strong contention with Arsenal for the League title, complained bitterly that Suggett (right) was offside, but the referee decided he was not interfering with play. The controversy raged for days.

Above: Astle and Brown celebrate their goal while Leeds question referee Tinkler. It was not long before the Elland Road crowd were on the pitch to make their feelings known.

Riots and Tragedies

Though a minority do their best to create havoc, football fans in Britain are generally well behaved. The same cannot be said of those in some countries, however. In the Latin countries especially, the moats and netting that surround the pitches are an indictment of spectator violence. When passions are roused and local or national pride is at stake, it needs only a referee's decision to send hot-blooded fans on the rampage. Too often the rioting ends in tragedy.

Unfortunately, it is usually the innocent who suffer from the irresponsibility and fanaticism of a few. In Buenos Aires in 1968, for example, 73 fans died in the stampedes that resulted when youths threw burning paper into the crowd. Yet even that figure pales in comparison with the fatalities when hundreds of fans rioted at Lima following a disallowed goal in Peru's match against Argentina on May 25, 1964. As windows were smashed and buildings set on fire, the police used tear gas to repel the mob from the pitch. Others in the crowd rushed to get out, only to find the gates locked. In the ensuing panic more than 300 people died and hundreds more were injured. It was the blackest day in football history.

Not all footballing tragedies result from rioting, though. At Ibrox Park in 1902, 25 people were killed when part of the West Stand collapsed shortly after the start of the Scotland–England international. And the same ground was to witness an even worse tragedy in 1971. As happens at most grounds, a number of fans were leaving shortly before the final whistle. But when Rangers equalized against rivals Celtic, some fans going down one of the steep-terraced exits tried to go back into the ground, only to be swamped by those behind them. That day, January 2, 66 died in Britain's worst football disaster.

Prior to that, the worst British crowd disaster had been at Bolton's Burnden Park in 1946. There were already more than 60,000 packed into the ground for the FA Cup quarter-final between Bolton and Stoke, yet still more came over the fences. The massed weight of the pushing and swaying fans was too great. A brick dividing-wall collapsed, sending a section of the crowd surging forward, breaking down the crush

Left, above: The staircase at Ibrox Park where 66 people were killed in January 1971.
Left: Rescue workers lay the casualties out on the pitch where, earlier, Rangers and Celtic had been in conflict.
Right: It was Colin Stein's equalizer that inadvertently led to the disaster. Fans leaving the ground at the time tried to return, only to be swept back by those behind them.

Left: A section of the crowd try to escape police tear gas at Lima, Peru, where more than 300 died in roiting sparked off by a disallowed Peruvian goal.

barriers. More than 500 people were injured; 33 died.

But if these tragic incidents may not always be so well remembered, the tragedy of Munich will have a permanent place in the memory of British football. For at Munich on February 6, 1958, eight of Manchester United's famous 'Busby Babes' died when their aircraft failed to take off. Three were England internationals. Others to lose their life that day were eight journalists, among them former England goalkeeper Frank Swift, and the Manchester United secretary, trainer and coach. It was a tragedy that brought back memories of a May day in 1949 when the aircraft taking Italian League champions Torino home from Lisbon crashed into the Basilica of Superga on the outskirts of Turin. There were no survivors. One of the great teams of modern football, one that included eight Italian internationals, was mourned throughout Europe.

Below: The kind of fanatical support enjoyed by Rangers in Europe. But the behaviour of many Rangers fans at and after the 1972 European Cup-Winners Cup final in Barcelona cost the club one season of European football.

Fans

With their scarves, their hats, their rosettes, and their songs, fans give football the colour and the atmosphere that can transform a Saturday league match into a great sporting occasion. They can also disrupt it by unruly behaviour on the terraces. But the majority of fans go to matches to enjoy the game and to cheer their team to victory. Without them, football would be much the poorer.

The fan is rarely a passive spectator, appreciating the skills of both sides. He is an involved supporter, more concerned with the good and bad play of his own side than with any qualities of the opposition, unless, of course, they resort to foul play. True, there are those fans whose appreciation of the finer points of football will bring them to applaud all good play. But when there is a lot at stake, they are just like all other fans— fiercely partisan with their judgement biased in favour of their team.

Aggressively loyal fans may, however, be a dubious advantage. For one thing, they want success, and as paying customers they feel they have a right to it. They can become very impatient when it does not come. What they may not realize is that the players suffer from their impatience, especially when the slow handclapping starts or a player is 'given the bird' every time he gets the ball, simply because the fans have taken a dislike to him. Footballers are only human, and they must have confidence in themselves to display their skills. The fan who jeers the skilful ball-player the moment he touches the ball and advises him to 'get rid of it' is not supporting his club. He is doing it a disservice, especially if the hounded player requests a transfer and his talents flower elsewhere.

Fans differ from ground to ground, but any player who has opposed Liverpool at Anfield Road will testify to the experience of playing before the Kop. The Kop end of the ground accommodates approximately 28,000 of the most knowledgeable and vociferous football fans in Britain. The internationally famous 'choir' has inspired numerous Liverpool victories and comebacks; their humour has relieved many tense moments. But what players remember most about the Kop is their fairness and appreciation of good football. Other fans trying to imitate the Kop would do well to remember this. Too often the scarf-waving, song-singing section at other grounds is better remembered for its poor behaviour.

233

Crowd Behaviour

At the beginning of the 1971–72 season, two of England's leading clubs were banned from using their grounds—Leeds United for three weeks, Manchester United for two. The clubs themselves had done nothing wrong. The sentences were enforced because of the behaviour the previous season of a small group of their fans. At Elland Road they invaded the pitch to protest a goal; at Old Trafford a knife landed near a Newcastle United player.

These sentences displayed just how seriously the authorities were taking misbehaviour on the terraces. The unfortunate thing was that the well-behaved majority of fans had to suffer too because of the unruly. More unfortunate for British soccer is that these were not isolated instances but part of a growing trend towards violence at football grounds. Not that the violence is confined just to the grounds. Public transport is particularly open to abuse from the hordes of vandals going to games.

What is the answer? The obvious solution would be to keep the rough element out of the grounds. But that is by no means easy. Clubs have tried to ban the known troublemakers from the grounds, only for others to take their place. And the netting enclosures and moats advocated to protect the players and officials, as in some countries, do not protect the innocent fans who go to a match for enjoyment and not for the riot the troublemakers chant for every week. Some so-called fans certainly go prepared for one. The police haul from a 1969 Southampton–Chelsea match included crash helmets, spanners, knives, long nails, and bottles. In 1970, police searching coaches taking Middlesbrough supporters to Bristol found hatchets, meat hooks, chains, and coshes. Inside many grounds, police, armed with 'walky-talky' radios, help to keep the crowds in order.

But could the clubs be doing more? A working party on crowd behaviour at football matches, set up in 1967 by the British minister for sport, recommended that keeping rival fans apart and controlling movement as much as possible by 'penning' would reduce inflammatory situations. How many clubs have acted on this recommendation? Another recommendation was to increase the amount of seating. Seated spectators are less likely to start fighting and throwing missiles, because seating removes the anonymity of the terraces that many of the troublemakers hide behind.

It has been said that the violence on the terraces is a reflection of the violence on the field. If so, the more stringent attitude being taken to foul play may bring a corresponding peace on the terraces. In the meantime, however, many fans, especially women and children, are being frightened away from the game. The problem is too real to be allowed to solve itself, and those who run and profit from football should find the solution.

Enraged fans pelt a policeman and his dog at Lima, Peru, in 1964. The referee had disallowed Peru's equalizer in the match against Argentina. There were scores of deaths in the ensuing stampede.

Left: It takes five policemen to carry out one unruly teenage fan at Highbury.

The changing face of Britain's soccer fans: the unbridled enthusiasm of today's Liverpool fans at Anfield (above, right) contrasts strongly with the decorous behaviour of a crowd at Spurs in 1912.

Safety

Following the tragic death of 66 people at Glasgow's Ibrox Park in January 1971, press and television were full of facts and opinions on safety measures. Opinions differed, but one fact was only too obvious. Britain lacked legislation to make football grounds safer.

Perhaps more disturbing was the fact that, 25 years earlier, an inquiry on the 1946 Burnden Park disaster had recommended the passing of laws to make football grounds comply with the highest standards of safety. It also recommended that grounds should be licensed to hold only a certain number of spectators. The licence would not be issued if the construction and facilities of the ground did not satisfy the licensing authority. Yet nothing was done, despite warnings that packing large crowds into confined areas was asking for trouble—especially when the majority of grounds had been built in the 19th century and had approaches and exits almost designed for disaster.

Licensing, however, has a number of powerful opponents, and their argument that licensing could not have prevented accidents such as that at Ibrox can be strongly supported. But why oppose any measure that can only improve safety precautions at grounds? Surely the lives of the fans are the most important consideration?

Obviously a standard is needed for safety measures. The working party that studied crowd behaviour at football matches in the late 1960s recommended that grounds should be inspected by a neutral person whose report would be included by the clubs with their own annual report to their association. But there was no law to enforce this. It was up to the authorities such as the Leagues and the Football Associations to make sure clubs maintained a high standard and did not delay carrying out necessary repairs.

The best answer to the problem would be a massive rebuilding and renovation of Britain's football grounds. It would cost millions of pounds, but the expense need not necessarily be met by the clubs. The Chester Report on Football suggested a statutory levy on football pools, although it would be a long time being passed if earlier recommendations are anything to go by. Nevertheless, the idea of the pools companies supplying much needed funds to improve grounds is a good one, and it could be implemented if the Football League and Scottish League were to increase the tariff on their fixtures. At present, perhaps too much responsibility is placed on the clubs. And as they cannot write off ground improvements against tax (whereas players are not taxable assets), there is little incentive for some clubs to make major improvements. The time has come for those at the top of the game to ensure the safety of the paying spectator. Even one life lost is too great a price to be paid to remind people that all is not well in the football grounds of Britain.

Left: High wire fencing topped by barbed wire strands surrounding the pitch is a necessary precaution at Toluca, Mexico.
Below: Dozens of small bonfires menace the fleeing fans on the terraces during the match between El Salvador and the USSR in the 1970 World Cup in Mexico.

Stadiums

Since British teams have become involved in European club competitions, the names of the great Continental stadiums have become almost as well known as Britain's own. But no matter how vivid the memories of glorious performances at Madrid's Santiago Bernabeu Stadium or at Milan's San Siro, no ground, for an Englishman or Scotsman, can compare with Wembley or Hampden Park. These grounds are his Mecca, the scenes of international glory and cup final heroism.

Wembley in North London has a capacity of 100,000 all under cover. Yet this fine stadium, so full of atmosphere and football history, is used only a mere handful of times every year. It is the venue for England's full home internationals and occasional internationals at other levels. Matches played there annually are the FA Cup, League Cup, Amateur Cup, and FA Challenge Trophy finals and the University Match. Wembley has also hosted the finals of European tournaments, providing a virtual home advantage for West Ham in the 1965 Cup-Winners Cup and Manchester United in the 1968 European Cup.

But if Wembley is unusual in that it is rarely used, Britain's largest ground, Hampden Park, is equally unusual in that it caters for a crowd of approximately a thousand when owners Queen's Park are at home—and yet can take 134,000 to produce the famous 'Hampden roar' at cup finals and internationals. Naturally enough, the ground holds a number of British records, among them the most at a cup tie (146,433 at the 1937 Scottish Cup final) and the most at an international (149,547 at the 1937 Scotland–England match). The 127,621 who saw Real Madrid demolish Eintracht Frankfurt in 1960 set a record for a European Cup final, and the capacity crowd that watched Celtic beat Leeds in the 1970 European Cup semi-final was the highest attendance at any European club competition fixture.

Such figures, however, pale in comparison with those from Rio de Janeiro's Maracana Stadium. In 1963 a crowd of 177,656 watched a local derby between Fluminense and Flamengo, and the ground boasts the world's largest attendance at a football match— 199,854 at the Uruguay–Brazil decider of the 1950 World Cup. The Maracana Stadium, with its supposed 200,000 capacity, is the world's largest stadium, and others with a capacity of 100,000 or more are Barcelona's Nova Campa (150,000), the Santiago Berna-

beu Stadium (135,000), Hampden Park (134,000), Glasgow's Ibrox Park (118,000), Mexico City's Aztec Stadium (112,000), Central Stadium, Leipzig (110,000), Budapest's Nep Stadium (105,000), Wembley, the Olympic Stadium (Berlin), the Huracan Stadium in Buenos Aires, the Maceio Stadium in Alagôas, Leningrad's Kirov Stadium, Moscow's Lenin Stadium, and the Army Stadium in Bucharest (all 100,000).

Left: The Nep People's Stadium in Budapest.
Below: Hampden Park, Glasgow.
Bottom: The Santiago Bernabeu Stadium, home of Real Madrid.

Sponsorship

At the beginning of the 1970s, British football entered a new era by admitting sponsorship. Certainly, with costs increasing and attendances dropping, the game could do with all the financial help it could get. Wisely, the British administrators did not go to the extreme of allowing commercial interests to sponsor teams and use players as billboard men, advertising products on their shirts. Instead, permission was given to firms to sponsor competitions and awards.

In England, the Football League acted promptly in evolving a strict code of practice to ensure that none of the interested parties were abused. Their four principles stated that the sponsor should get a fair return for his money, that the League and the game should benefit from the sponsorship to the fullest extent, that the competition must be attractive to the spectator, and that the standards of dignity and administrative competence in the competition be upheld.

With sponsors offering large sums of money, more games were added to an already crowded season. Indeed, the Watney's Invitation Cup threw two clubs from each division of the Football League into the competitive arena before the season officially opened. Perhaps the more enterprising of the initial sponsored competitions was the Texaco

International League Board. Better known as the Texaco Cup, it involved clubs from the Football Leagues of England, Scotland, Northern Ireland, and the Republic of Ireland. The sponsors put up £100,000, of which £22,500 went to the Football League, £17,500 to the Scottish League, and £5,000 each to the Irish leagues. All 16 teams in the first round received £1,000 each, with the first-round winners getting an additional £1,500, the second round winners £2,000 each, and the winners of the semi-finals £2,500. From the remaining £9,000 came the administrative expenses, and any surplus was distributed among the participants.

But if sponsorship was providing English soccer with a much-needed financial boost, it was also providing a possible cause of dissension in the British game. At the end of 1971 there were murmurings that the Football League wanted to see the end of the Home International Championship, an important source of revenue for the four Football Associations. The reason, it seemed, was the overcrowded season. Yet the League, through the League Cup, itself ripe for sponsorship, and the new competitions, was the chief culprit as regards overcrowding. It could easily be asked if robbing the international scene of Britain's leading players so that they could promote, say, petrol or beer, was benefiting the game to the fullest extent —one of the League's dictums on sponsorship.

Above: Derby County players receive their tankards from Sir Stanley Rous in the Watney Cup.

Below: Derby, one of the English clubs to benefit greatly from sponsorship, battle it out with Wolves at the Baseball Ground.

Soccer Oddities

FOULKE — THE SHEFFIELD GOAL KEEPER TAKING A KICK

On March 15, 1947, New Brighton manager Neil McBain was pressed into service in an emergency—and became the oldest player to appear in a Football League match. When his team arrived two men short at Hartlepools United, he played in goal. He was 52 years 4 months old at the time.

* * *

On Christmas Day 1940, Tommy Lawton and Len Shackleton played for two Football League clubs on the same day. Lawton played for his own club Everton against Liverpool in the morning and guested for Tranmere Rovers against Crewe Alexandra in the afternoon. Shackleton appeared for the two Bradford clubs: his own Park Avenue and as a guest for City.

* * *

Blackpool's England forward Stan Mortensen made his international debut in a wartime match at Wembley on September 25, 1943—for Wales. Although he was England's reserve, he went on as second-half substitute for the injured Welsh half-back Ivor Powell.

* * *

Jim Milburn and Jack Froggatt were credited with the same own goal in the First Division match between Leicester City and Chelsea on December 18, 1954. Both connected with the ball simultaneously to give Chelsea one of their goals.

* * *

Dixie Dean and Jimmy Greaves were exactly the same age when they scored their 200th League goal—23 years 290 days.

* * *

In a 4th Round FA Cup tie on January 22, 1938, Barnsley's Frank Bokas 'scored' against Manchester United from a throw-in. The ball, thrown from near the corner flag, went into the goalmouth where United 'keeper Tommy Breen deflected it into the net.

* * *

Frank Dudley's first three Football League goals in the 1953–54 season were scored for as many different clubs in as many different divisions: Southend United (Third, South), Cardiff City (First), and Brentford (Second).

* * *

A superior goal average of 0·005, or a two-hundredth, won Portsmouth promotion to the First Division in 1926–27. On the last day of the season, they were level on points with Manchester City for second place, and had a fractionally superior goal average.

Like a row of statues behind the crowd, these keen fans standing on posts got a high-level view of the 1914 Cup final.

All depended on the last matches. Manchester City beat Bradford City 8–0, Portsmouth beat Preston 5–1, and when the final goal averages were determined, Portsmouth were still in front. The actual averages, to five places, were Portsmouth 1·77551, Manchester City 1·77049. Had 'goal difference' determined the places, as it did for the 1970 World Cup groups, City would have romped home. Their 108 goals for to 61 against was much better than Portsmouth's 87 for to 49 against. However, justice was done the following year when City won the Second Division.

* * *

Seventy-one goals were scored in one day in two first round Scottish Cup ties on September 5, 1885. Arbroath beat Bon Accord 36–0 and Dundee Harp beat Aberdeen Rovers 35–0.

* * *

In the 1920s, Plymouth Argyle finished second in the Third Division (South) for six consecutive seasons. It was the most remarkable succession of promotion near misses ever recorded in the Football League.

* * *

It was odd enough when the ball burst during the 1946 FA Cup final between Derby County and Charlton Athletic: it was the first time this had ever happened in a Cup final. But it was even stranger when the ball burst five days later in a League match between the same teams, and the coincidence was extended even farther when the ball burst during the 1947 FA Cup final between

Burnley and . . . Charlton Athletic.

* * *

The Scottish brothers Frank and Hugh O'Donnell played together for 10 teams: St Agatha School, Leven, Fifeshire, Denbeath Violet, Wellesley Juniors, Celtic, Preston North End, Blackpool, Heart of Midlothian, and Liverpool.

* * *

From the end of World War II to 1961, outside-left Alan Daley played for the following clubs: Derby County, Mansfield Town, Hull City, Bangor City, Worksop Town, Doncaster Rovers, Boston United, Scunthorpe United, Corby Town, Mansfield (again), Stockport County, Crewe Alexandra, Coventry City, Cambridge City, and Burton Albion.

* * *

Norman Young spent 10 years with Aston Villa before making his Football League debut against Preston North End at fullback in September 1935.

* * *

Between the wars, West Bromwich Albion had a half-back named Arthur Griffith Stanley Sackville Redvers Trevor Boscowen Trevis—the longest name credited to a Football League player. The shortest name is Ian Ure.

* * *

In the late 1950s, Lincoln City had a centre-half named Ray Long, who was 6 ft tall, and an outside-left named David Short, who was only 5ft 4 in tall.

* * *

The highest and lowest Football League attendances were recorded in the same city —Manchester. The record attendance is the 83,260 for the First Division match between Manchester United and Arsenal at Maine Road on January 17, 1948. The lowest is 13 at Old Trafford on May 7, 1921 for the Second Division game between Stockport County and Leicester City. None of the teams were playing on their own ground. Manchester United were using Maine Road while Old Trafford was being repaired, and Stockport used Old Trafford because their own ground was under suspension.

* * *

The first ground Blackburn Rovers used, in 1874, had a pond in the middle, which was covered with planks and turf before each game.

* * *

Rochdale's Spotland ground had an unlucky spot for the club's centre-forward Frank Lord. On two occasions, in August 1954 and three years later, he broke his leg at exactly the same spot on the ground.

Left: Artist's impression of 'Fatty' Foulke, the Sheffield goalkeeper, taking a goal kick.
Above: During the 1930 Cup final between Arsenal and Huddersfield, the *Graf Zeppelin* airship flew so low over the stadium that the roar of its engines disturbed players and spectators.

Television

The televising of soccer is a constant source of controversy. The big question, of course, is: Is it good for the game? The answer is: Yes, up to a point. And the determination of that point is one of the biggest bones of contention. Not only is there concern about how much soccer, live or otherwise, should be shown, but there is also argument regarding the in-depth examination and criticism of the game and those connected with it by means of TV.

In Britain, at least, the question of how much soccer is shown on TV has been resolved. As a rule, during the season only one match is televised live, the FA Cup final, and on that day there are no other fixtures. Out of season there are a few internationals and European club matches. And every four years even the largest of soccer appetites is satisfied by the saturation coverage of the World Cup.

During the season, highlights of matches may be shown, with 45 minutes each on Saturday night and Sunday afternoon, and usually mid-week. On Saturdays, live radio broadcasts are restricted to the second half only, and there are occasional mid-week broadcasts of important matches. The television companies are not allowed to announce what games they will be showing until after the matches have started, and a similar restriction applies to Saturday radio.

It would appear at first sight that the footballing authorities have been too severe in their attitude towards television. But a study of how the overexposure of baseball on American TV in the 1950s affected attendances is sufficient to demonstrate the dangers of too much broadcasting.

Nevertheless it is a pity that the rules have to be so inflexible. The 1971 FA Cup final between Arsenal and Liverpool was televised live throughout Great Britain and Europe, and was seen by about 400 million viewers in all. Yet, five days earlier, Arsenal's vital last League game of the season against Spurs went uncovered by radio or TV because a Fourth Division match was being played the same night. No highlights were allowed to be shown later that evening; the only concession to the massive footballing public, agog to see the completion of the first leg of Arsenal's 'double', was a two-minute spot on the news bulletins.

The live televising of a cup final requires planning weeks in advance and an Outside Broadcast team of nearly 200—commentators, cameramen, production team, technicians, engineers, and their various assistants. The equipment used includes perhaps 10 cameras, 40 microphones, nearly 30 monitor sets, and more than 20 miles of cable. And this is for just one of the TV companies—both BBC and ITV cover the cup final simultaneously.

Despite the vast amount of technical knowhow and skill that goes towards producing pictures on the screen, television coverage of soccer still receives criticism from sources far and wide—the viewer, the player, the manager, the referee, the administrator, and the press.

The viewer complains when he does not get the picture he wants to see. It is irritating —sometimes infuriating—for the armchair football fan to have thrust at him a close-up of a single player with the ball, when he wants also to see where the opposing players are, whether team-mates are in dangerous positions, and quite often where

'He doesn't miss chances like that', said one TV commentator about Pelé's brilliant goal against Czechoslovakia in the 1970 World Cup . . . The remark was edited out of repeat showings of the game.

the ball carrier is in relation to the goal. The BBC say they like to show 'the clash of drama and wills' in close-up, attempting to attract the non-specialist audience, rather than show 'chessboard tactics'. This reason would seem, however, to be no more than an excuse for increasing the viewing ratings at the expense of the true football follower, who is hooked anyway. And if any viewer wonders what drama or clash of wills there is in the inevitable close-up of the goalkeeper punting upfield or a player taking a corner, he must realize that these are ideal places for cutting when highlights are shown. What happens, in effect, is that a player is shown in close-up taking a corner, and at the moment of impact the producer switches to a camera showing the goalmouth situation. It is then possible, if another corner is later taken from the same side, to use the close-up from the first corner and the goalmouth scene from the later corner. This device is used most frequently when the goalkeeper is punting upfield, and makes for much smoother highlights, even if it is somewhat dishonest.

Perhaps one of the most criticized aspects of television is the commentary. If anything, TV commentary is more difficult than radio, for any mistakes are there for the viewer to see. And the commentator not only has to keep his eyes on the game but also on the monitor sets showing what pictures are being put out. Through his headphones he receives instructions from the producer and information from a 'feed'. He must be able to identify every player instantly, interpret the referee's decisions, convey the atmosphere and excitement to viewers, and to a certain extent interpret the play and confirm what is happening. It is such a difficult job that few men are capable of mastering the technical aspects of it. This is probably why

Above: Special platforms are built on most grounds to accommodate TV cameras.

Below: Technicians put the final touches to one of the cameras covering a match. Such outside broadcasts call for a small army of people to make sure of success.

there are so few commentators who have very much more than a superficial knowledge of the game. And this lack of knowledge is often shown up in remarks about the laws or the referee's handling of the game.

Another often criticized fault is that commentators attempt to be too clever or try to make the game more exciting than it is, using superlative after superlative. (After all, it is not good for the channel's image to be seen to be showing a dull game.) The danger here is that the commentator might run out of superlatives, and when something really superlative does occur on the field he is lost for words or uses the wrong ones. This happened in the 1970 World Cup, when Pelé ran 20 yards under pressure to kill a high 50-yard pass on his chest, drop the ball at his feet, and volley it past the goalkeeper. 'He doesn't miss chances like that', said one commentator, who was saved from further embarrassment when his remark was erased from repeat viewings. But this experience apparently so unnerved him that later 'super'

Above: Inside the TV vans, operators are faced with a mass of controls and an array of monitor sets.

Above: With one eye on their audience viewing figures, TV companies tend to devote most of their coverage to the 'big guns', the First Division clubs. Time given to those in the lower echelons—such as Fulham and Preston, seen here in a Division III struggle— is usually brief and selective.

Below: A mobile TV unit is linked with the stadium where the match to be televised will take place.

goals were greeted with stony silence. This, unfortunately, is not enough for most viewers, who need some sort of confirmation, such as 'It's a goal!', 'It's there!', or 'He's scored!'. But sometimes such remarks seem so trite that the commentator is accused of banality. He just cannot win.

Criticism of the quality of the production, however, becomes insignificant when compared with the argument that rages over the showing of certain types of incidents. The faults and mistakes of both referees and players are analysed and discussed as the incidents are played back, often in slow motion.

The slow-motion replay has become a regular feature of televised sport, and is used in football principally to show the build-up and scoring of goals. This is a great boon to the armchair viewer, who has come to expect it as a right—so much so that spectators at a match often sit back when a goal has been scored and find themselves waiting for the slow-motion replay. But when this technique is used to demonstrate mistakes, the controversy begins.

The biggest sufferer of the slow-motion replay and all that goes with it—'trial by television'—is the referee. A football referee often has to make a snap decision on an incident that lasts a fraction of a second, with thousands of excited fans screaming in his ears and players from both sides claiming the point. It is not easy, and referees are bound to make mistakes. Nevertheless, it is only human nature to want to examine controversial incidents in a game. Was it really hand-ball? Wasn't that player offside before he scored? Surely that was a foul and should have been a penalty? Was the ball over the line? Television provides the means of settling such questions. Quite often the referee is proved right, or the result is inconclusive—it is, for example, particularly difficult to demonstrate the validity or otherwise of offside decisions on TV. But when the referee is shown to be at fault, he might feel that he is being victimized and that his mistakes are being magnified out of all proportion. There is a great danger of this happening, and while it would be absurd to ban the showing of controversial incidents, as has been suggested, the television authorities have a duty to ensure that analyses of this kind are conducted in a responsible and impartial manner.

This is just as important when the subject under the microscope is a player. As a means of recording for posterity the skills of a George Best or a Pelé, the television camera has no equal. Its use, however, to expose individual players guilty of foul play is open to question. The slow-motion replay is an ideal means for spotting such serious misdemeanours as 'foot over the ball', and 'followed through' tackles, but as such should be used by the football authorities in conjunction with referees to detect the habitual culprits and stamp out foul play. It is perhaps unfair that certain players should be pilloried in public just because they play for teams seen frequently on television, and that players should be able to take liberties if there are no TV cameras at the match.

The question of overexposure on television has also worried some managers, who feel

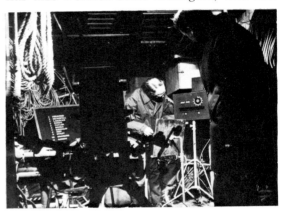

Right: Another view of the interior of the TV van shows caption boards, clock, and half-time score.

Jimmy Hill, former Fulham player and Coventry City manager, later turned his formidable talent to the TV screen to become one of the shrewdest analysts in the game.

that their tactics are being laid bare for all to see week after week. Although the TV screen is hardly the best medium for studying a team's tactics, it can expose the special moves employed at set-pieces such as free-kicks and corners. But that is the price of fame, and as these set-pieces usually involve a certain amount of bluff, a team can turn such overexposure to its own advantage by varying a well-known manoeuvre.

Constant replaying of players' mistakes, however, is another matter, and it must be soul-destroying for, say, a goalkeeper to have repeated reminders of an error that cost his side an important match. It is also perhaps irresponsible to show week after week, as one television programme has, a shot of one player throwing the ball in a fit of temper at an opposing player's head.

The television companies realize that soccer is great entertainment. Apart from the rare live television broadcast and the regular highlights, there are interviews, previews, panels, 'goal of the month competitions', penalty-taking competitions, and even competitions to find the best terrace 'choir'. With careful handling, from both the television and the footballing authorities, TV can only help to create more interest in what is already a hugely popular sport. It is to be hoped that the correct amount of control and responsibility will be exercised so that the vast audience can continue to enjoy the game both on and off the screen.

Gamesmanship and Cheating

The scene was Wembley Stadium, July 30,. 1966, and after 90 minutes play in the World Cup final between England and West Germany the score was 2–2. The Germans had equalized in the dying seconds, and the English team lay demoralized on the ground. Manager Alf Ramsey walked out calmly towards his team and talked quietly to the players, boosting their confidence. After 90 minutes of cut-and-thrust on Wembley's strength-sapping turf, both teams were tired. But when England got up to start the first period of extra time, they showed no signs of flagging. And this was a major factor—perhaps the decisive one—in their famous victory by four goals to two.

The act of gamesmanship—an ostentatious demonstration that they were not as tired as their opponents—was simple psychology. And this is what gamesmanship is all about. It is the art of winning by using methods not directly connected with the skills of the game, but keeping within the laws of the game.

England were on the wrong end of a piece of gamesmanship at Wembley when they were beaten 6–3 by Hungary in 1953. Whether it was intentional or not, the Hungarians confused England by the numbering of their shirts. Playing the revolutionary deep-lying centre-forward game, Hidegkuti was wearing the No. 9 shirt. This created havoc in the England defence, because he was playing more as a traditional wing-half, and centre-half Harry Johnston was drawn all over the field.

Examples of gamesmanship are common during the taking of a penalty. The defending side try to disturb the concentration of the taker with comments, the goalkeeper might lean slightly to one side in an effort to persuade the taker to put the ball on the other side, and the taker himself might try to kid the goalkeeper that he is going to put the ball to a particular side, perhaps by a glance in one direction. Jack Brownsword of Scunthorpe United was a penalty taker who always used to put the ball to the goalkeeper's right, and he rarely missed. Fulham goalkeeper Tony Macedo, well aware of Brownsword's reputation and habits, and knowing that penalty-takers who change their minds often miss, stationed himself next to his right-hand post when the Scunthorpe left-back approached for a spot-kick. But Brownsword did not change his mind, and slotted the ball into the place vacated by the goalkeeper as he dived to his left—a fine example of 'outgaming the gamesman'.

Players have been known to cultivate a ferocious appearance—from the blue-chinned Wilf Copping in the 1930s to the Viking-like Trevor Hockey of the 1970s. And a trick sometimes used before the days of substitutes was for a player who had received attention from the trainer to hobble out to the wing and limp up and down until he got the ball. Then, shaking off his 'injury' like magic, he would hare off towards goal like a greyhound. This, perhaps, was one of the less sporting ploys.

Latterly the term 'gamesmanship' has taken on a more sinister—and entirely erroneous—meaning. Many people refer to the practice of pinching yards at throw-ins and free-kicks or preventing the opposing side from taking a quick free-kick as gamesmanship. It is not gamesmanship, however, it is cheating. 'Diving' in the area to get a penalty and feigning injury to get an opponent booked can also be classified as cheating, or at best as ungentlemanly (and, thus, illegal) conduct. Under the pressures of top professional soccer, it is always tempting to take an unfair advantage, and if one side is allowed to get away with it, others will also resort to these practices.

How can cheating be curtailed? It is not enough for the authorities to tighten up on discipline—these purges never last long, and quite often, with indiscriminate decisions, the innocent suffer along with the guilty. Certainly the Laws need tightening up and even revising. At present the referee has only the caution for punishing such offences as not retreating the mandatory 10 yards at

This kind of trip is a so-called 'professional foul', used to gain advantage by breaking the laws of the game.

Below: A Spurs 'wall' is persuaded to retreat by the referee. Players often manage deliberately to delay free-kicks against them by standing too near the ball, thus giving their defence time to get organized.

a free-kick. One suggestion is to award additional yardage to the team taking the kick, as in rugby. In a tight situation, a player will go as far as he thinks safe in delaying an opposition free-kick. And the referee is reluctant to take a player's name for all but the most blatant tactics. Such decisions, moreover, are bound to vary from referee to referee. Whereas a referee would not find it difficult to award, say, an extra 10 yards on the free-kick for the slightest delaying ploy of the defending side. And defenders would be far less inclined to risk greater danger by employing such tactics, particularly near their penalty area, where a free-kick could be turned into a penalty.

This is just one simple way to curb cheating in soccer. It has been said, particularly by the game's administrators, that the players do not know the Laws. This may be true for the majority of professionals, but until the Laws have been made clear, just, and easy to understand and apply, this state of affairs will probably continue.

Right: Did he fall or was he pushed? Acrobatic dives in the penalty area during goalmouth scrimmages can sometimes fool the best of referees.

Right: The referee takes a long hard look at a tricky situation. Whatever his decision, he'll get a mixed reaction from the spectators.

Below: An out-thrust knee can sometimes be used as a convenient hurdle.

The Pools

'BIG POOLS BONANZA' shriek the headlines, 'East Cheam charlady wins £300,000'. £400,000, £500,000 . . . £1,000,000. . . . Is there no end to it? Many consider it a sad comment on society today that this sort of gross avarice should be encouraged—by the pools promoters, the press, and the public themselves. What was once an enjoyable pastime in which a small flutter could win a fortune has become, many people think, an obscene lottery.

Defensively minded soccer in the 1960s tended to produce more draws on the Saturday fixture lists. So the pools companies came up with the idea of artificially boosting the dividends on the treble chance pool by restricting the maximum three points to 'score draws'; goalless draws became worth only two points. The aim of this ruse is that one person might win £400,000 instead of 40 people winning £10,000 or eight people winning £50,000.

Is this really desirable? It must be for the pools firms, for so great is the competition in this field that such publicity is invaluable. Similarly, it provides copy for the newspapers, who play up the 'human angle'. But are their readers really interested? The stories are nearly all the same, whether the sum won is £50,000 or £500,000. But the bigger the cheque, the larger the headline. The popular press consider it good copy. 'This won't make any difference to my way of life', says the Merioneth miner fingering his cheque for half a million pounds. There would probably be more chance of his achieving this claim and leading a happy and carefree life had he won £50,000, and perhaps another nine people would share his good fortune.

There was once a limit on first dividends, with any balance going to the minor dividends. But in the late 1950s Littlewoods Pools dropped the idea. Although their

In the dying seconds of a semi-final Cup-tie, Denis Law misses a cross by inches. With that miss go Manchester United's chances . . . and perhaps those of a pools punter who had them down for a draw.

decision appeared to go against public opinion, it certainly did Littlewoods no harm, and their business boomed more than ever. Yet the question still remains: Do the people really want these enormous dividends or are they brainwashed into believing they do?

To the Churches' Committee on Gambling, however, any argument about the size of the prizes is purely academic, for they have come out strongly against the pools, regarding it as a menace to young people because it is a form of gambling that enters the home. This was once a strong argument, but with the tie-up of racing and betting on television and the advent of the 'permissive society', pools gambling became a less important target for the Churches.

The first football pools came into existence in the mid-1930s, although 'fixed odds' betting had existed in one form or another since before the turn of the century. (In fixed odds betting, the bookmaker agrees to pay a definite, predetermined sum for successful wagers on the results of matches.) In pools betting, the company collects all the wagers, which are put into a pool; after the deduction of expenses and commission, winnings are paid to successful punters in the form of dividends. The size of the dividends, of course, depends on the number of successful punters.

The pools soon developed into a huge industry, dominated by a few large firms. The newspapers began to include feature articles on the pools, and experts gave advice on systems and on forecasting.

Pools can be divided into two basic types: (1) forecasting the results of a given list of matches (points and results pools, usually from 6 to 14 matches) and (2) forecasting a certain number of matches from a comprehensive or a restricted list. This latter type includes results (home, away, or draw), aways, and draws. As a rule, home wins are the most common results and the easiest to forecast. Draws are the most difficult. And it is this fact that has led to the dominance of the treble chance pool, a post-war phenomenon that has produced all the mammoth pools dividends. The name 'treble chance' derives from the fact that whatever the result—home, away, or draw—each selection scores points. For a long period it was three points for a draw, two for an away (or a void match), and one for a home win. With the advent of the 'score draws' in the late 1960s, a scoreless draw was reduced to two points with an away worth only one and a half.

One of the features of football pools is the 'permutation'. This is a conventional way of writing a large number of entries, or 'lines', without setting them out in full. Some permutations, or 'perms' as they have become known, involve thousands of lines and huge entry fees. The simplest perms are the 'full perms'. For example, in the Four Aways pool, you can make five selections and 'Perm any 4 from 5'. This makes five lines, and it is easy to see that five matches can be combined four at a time in five different ways: ABCD, ABCE, ABDE, ACDE, and BCDE.

All permutations give some sort of guarantee, even if it is not as all-embracing as a full perm. Say, for example, you select nine matches in the Four Aways pool. A full perm of 4 from 9 would run to 126 lines. But the selections can be set out in such a way that 30 lines would guarantee one correct line (of four selections) if five of the nine selections resulted in aways. As there are a number of ways in which these 30 lines can be written, the entry instructions on the pools coupon must refer to an accepted permutation. Pools firms distribute books of such perms to their customers, and newspapers often publish their own plans and perms, which are

Right: Pools clerks hard at work marking coupons. Below: A clerk checks coupons with the help of a computer and TV screen.

Below right: Automatic checking of entries is carried out by optical reading equipment. But in spite of such streamlining of checking techniques, pools firms still employ thousands of workers to check coupons.

accepted by the pools companies. Certain perms, such as full perms, do not require a chart with the perm set out in full for checking purposes. But with the conditional guarantee perms such a chart is essential, so that the entry may be checked when the results are known and there is only one way of writing the entries.

The large pools firms have teams of specially trained personnel for checking the more difficult permutations, and whole armies of staff dealing with the incoming coupons. Elaborate precautions are taken to prevent cheating, and routine procedures range from the numerous code stampings of coupons received to the secret checking of the security men themselves by other security men. In addition, a free advisory service is provided for big winners who may not be used to handling and investing large sums of money. As a result, expenses are considerable, and these, together with the government tax ($33\frac{1}{3}\%$) and the pools company's commission are deducted from the total pool before a dividend can be declared. The only money that goes back to the game itself is the fee—comparatively small (1% after tax)—

now paid to the Football League and Scottish League for use of their copyright fixture lists. It has been suggested that the government plough back some of its revenue from the pools into the game, perhaps to help with ground improvements.

It is clear that the game gets very little out of this huge industry which could not exist without it. But what about the punter, the ordinary man in the street who lays out his twenty or thirty pence every week or the large syndicate that spends twenty or thirty pounds on multi-thousand line entries? Are they getting their money's worth?

It is difficult to assess the true odds of pools dividends, and the size of the big prizes tends to obscure the real probabilities of winning. It is interesting, though, that when the government slapped a similar levy on fixed odds football, it virtually destroyed that form of betting. The reason for this was that the bookmakers had to reduce their odds. The punter could see what he was getting, and he did not like it. Such is the glamour of the pools, however, that it is doubtful whether it would have much effect on the punter if he knew what his chances really were.

Above: Mr Cyril Grimes of Liss, Hants., receives a cheque for £512,683 from Littlewoods managing director Mr Nigel Moores. Mr Grimes was the first person to win half a million pounds on the pools.
Right: Mr Robert Gray and his 17 friends receive their world record £536,313 pools cheque from 'Mr Pastry'

Pools firms have contrived to boost dividends by introducing the 'score draw' Treble Chance. In the 1971–72 season two prizes of more than half a million pounds were won. Instead of discouraging pools punters, this system of giving fewer people more money made the pools even more popular.

Index
(Italic numbers refer to pictures)

Acknowledgements

We gratefully acknowledge the assistance of the following organizations in assembling photographic material for this encyclopedia: The Associated Press Ltd., Australian News and Information Bureau, Colorsport, Paul Gardner, Ray Green, S. W. Hancock Ltd., Impact Press Features, Japan Information Service, Littlewoods Pools, London Express News and Feature Services, The Mansell Collection, High Commissioner for New Zealand, P & L Photo Service, Radio Times Hulton Picture Library, Slazengers Ltd., Syndication International, United Press International (U.K.) Ltd., Vernons Pools, Western Mail & Echo Ltd., Keystone Press

AF–T

Liverpool 25, 28, *28*, 34, *35*, 124, *132*, *134*, *138*, 171, 187, 188, *189*, 215, 233
Lloyd, Larry *134*
Lofthouse, Nat 37, 92, *144*, 199, *231*
Logan, Jimmy *160*
Loik, Ezio 197, 224
Lorimer, Peter *36*, *188*
Lubanski, Wlodzimierz 92
Luton Town 171
Luxembourg 20, 154

M

McBain, Neil 238
McColl, Bob *176*
McColl, Ian 92
McCracken, Bill 67, 92, 222, *222*
McFadyen, Bill 40
McFarland, Roy *171*
McFaul, Iam *131*, *172*
McGrath, Chris *135*
McGregor, William 32
McGrory, Jimmy 40, 92, *147*, 210
McIlroy, Jimmy 92
Mackay, Dave 92, 183, *183*, 184, *212*
McLintock, Frank, *59*, *92*, *184*, 185, *185*, 187
McMenemy, Jimmy 41
McMullan, Jimmy 92, *169*
McNab, Bob 187, *187*
McNeill, Billy *41*, 92, *118*
McParland, Peter 92
McPhail, Bob 41, 92, 223
McWilliam, Peter 92, 222, *222*
Madeley, Paul *112*
Magdeburg 26, 127
Maier, Sepp *15*, *21*
Male, George 67, 92
Maley, Bill 40
Manchester City 25, 26, *26*, 37, 68, *125*, 126, 171–172, 180, 189, *190*, 238
Manchester United 16, *17*, *23*, 24, *33*, 34, 37, *117*, 118, *144*, 172, 178, *178*, 179, 180, 189, *190*, 203–204, 208, 216, 224–225, 227–228, *228*, *229*, 231, 233, 239
Mannion, Wilf 92, 196, 197
Mansfield Town 172
Maracana Stadium 192, 236
Marché, Roger 92
Martin, Con 92
Martin, Norrie *124*, *149*, 215
Masopust, Josef 14, 92
Matthews, Sir Stanley 37, *79*, 92,

92, *169*, 196, 197, 199–200, *200*, 210, 213, *213*, 224
Mazurkiewicz, Ladislao 92–93
Mazzola, Sandrino 17, 23, 93, *93*
Mazzola, Valentino 93, 197, 224
Meadows, Jimmy 37
Meazza, Giuseppe 93, 190, 196, 218
Medwin, Terry 184
Mee, Bertie, 37, *178*
Meiklejohn, David 93, 223
Meisl, Hugo 19, 93, 218
Mercer, Joe *74*, 93
Meredith, Billy 93, *93*, *211*
Merrick, Gil *19*
Mexico 14, 46
Michas, Christos *127*
Middlesbrough 172
Milburn, Jackie 93
Milburn, Jim 238
Mills-Roberts, R. H. 181
Millwall 172
Mitropa Cup 22, 25
Moncur, Bobby *130*
Montgomery, Jim 36
Monti, Luisito 93, 196, *196*
Montrose 176
Moore, Bobby 25, *56*, *93*, 93–94, *123*
Moore, Ian *230*
Morgan, Willie *108*
Morris, Johnny 225
Mortensen, Stan 37, 94, *196*, 197, 199–200, 224, 238
Morton 176
Morton, Alan 94, 223

Moscow Dynamo 22, 26, *126*, 127, 223–224, *224*
Motherwell 39, 40, 176
Moyola Park 42
MTK Budapest 123
Mullen, Jimmy 68, 94, 225
Müller, Gerd 15, *15*, 20, *21*, 94, *94*, *121*, *168*, 209, *209*
Mullery, Alan 20, 28
Munich 1860 25, *25*, *123*, 124

N

Nacional 192
Napoli 25
Nations Cup, *See* European Football Championship
Neeskens, Johan 15, *15*, 94
Nep Stadium, Budapest *236*
Netherlands 15, *15*, 19, 154
Netto, Igor 20, 94
Netzer, Gunter 20, *21*, 94
New Zealand 48, 154
Newcastle United 27, *27*, 28, 37, *131*, 132, *142*, 172, 178, 212, 215–216, 222, *223*, 230
Newport County 172
Nicholson, Bill 94, 183
Non-League football 44
Nordahl, Gunnar 94
Norman, Maurice 183, *183*, 184
North American Soccer League 47
North Korea 14, 50, *106*, 206–207, *215*
Northampton Town 172
Northern Premier League 44
Norway 154
Norwich City *34*, 172, 216
Nottingham Forest 32, 37, 172–173
Notts County *11*, 32, 173

O

Oblak, Branko *108*
Ocwirk, Ernst 94
Odermatt, Karl 94
Oldham Athletic 173
Olympiakos 192
Olympic Games 18, *18*, 109
Orient 173
Orsi, Raimondo 94, 218
Osgood, Peter *56*
Overath, Wolfgang 94
Oxford United 44, 173

P

Pachame 17, *110*
Panathinaikos 24, *24*, 119, 192
Paraguay 46
Partick Thistle 41, 42, *42*, 176, 215
Partizan Belgrade 22, 23, 117
Paul, Roy 94
Payne, Joe *211*, 212
Peacock, Bertie 94
Pelé 13, 14, *14*, 17, *94*, 94–95, *107*, *168*, 210, *210*, 211, *221*, 226, 227, *240*
Penarol *45*, 46, *46*, 192
Pennington, Jesse 95, *95*
Pepe 226
Pereira, Luis *108*
Peru 14, 46
Peterborough United 44, 173, 231
Peters, Martin 14, 25, 95, *123*
Petrie, John 212
Picchi, Armando 95
Piola, Silvio 95, 218
Planicka, Frantisek 95
Plymouth Argyle 173, 238
Poland 15, 18, *18*, *109*, 154, *168*
Popluhar, Jan 95
Port Vale 173, 231
Portsmouth 238

Portugal 14, 154–155, 196–197, 206–207
Pozzo, Vittorio 19, 95, 218
Preston North End 32 173, *180*, 181, 221
Puddefoot, Syd 95